Lecture Notes in Computer Science　　　10272

Commenced Publication in 1973
Founding and Former Series Editors:
Gerhard Goos, Juris Hartmanis, and Jan van Leeuwen

More information about this series at http://www.springer.com/series/7409

Masaaki Kurosu (Ed.)

Human–Computer Interaction

Interaction Contexts

19th International Conference, HCI International 2017
Vancouver, BC, Canada, July 9–14, 2017
Proceedings, Part II

 Springer

Editor
Masaaki Kurosu
The Open University of Japan
Chiba
Japan

ISSN 0302-9743   ISSN 1611-3349   (electronic)
Lecture Notes in Computer Science
ISBN 978-3-319-58076-0   ISBN 978-3-319-58077-7   (eBook)
DOI 10.1007/978-3-319-58077-7

Library of Congress Control Number: 2017939340

LNCS Sublibrary: SL3 – Information Systems and Applications, incl. Internet/Web, and HCI

Printed on acid-free paper

This Springer imprint is published by Springer Nature
The registered company is Springer International Publishing AG
The registered company address is: Gewerbestrasse 11, 6330 Cham, Switzerland

Foreword

The 19th International Conference on Human–Computer Interaction, HCI International 2017, was held in Vancouver, Canada, during July 9–14, 2017. The event incorporated the 15 conferences/thematic areas listed on the following page.

A total of 4,340 individuals from academia, research institutes, industry, and governmental agencies from 70 countries submitted contributions, and 1,228 papers have been included in the proceedings. These papers address the latest research and development efforts and highlight the human aspects of design and use of computing systems. The papers thoroughly cover the entire field of human–computer interaction, addressing major advances in knowledge and effective use of computers in a variety of application areas. The volumes constituting the full set of the conference proceedings are listed on the following pages.

I would like to thank the program board chairs and the members of the program boards of all thematic areas and affiliated conferences for their contribution to the highest scientific quality and the overall success of the HCI International 2017 conference.

This conference would not have been possible without the continuous and unwavering support and advice of the founder, Conference General Chair Emeritus and Conference Scientific Advisor Prof. Gavriel Salvendy. For his outstanding efforts, I would like to express my appreciation to the communications chair and editor of *HCI International News*, Dr. Abbas Moallem.

April 2017   Constantine Stephanidis

HCI International 2017 Thematic Areas
and Affiliated Conferences

Thematic areas:

- Human–Computer Interaction (HCI 2017)
- Human Interface and the Management of Information (HIMI 2017)

Affiliated conferences:

- 17th International Conference on Engineering Psychology and Cognitive Ergonomics (EPCE 2017)
- 11th International Conference on Universal Access in Human–Computer Interaction (UAHCI 2017)
- 9th International Conference on Virtual, Augmented and Mixed Reality (VAMR 2017)
- 9th International Conference on Cross-Cultural Design (CCD 2017)
- 9th International Conference on Social Computing and Social Media (SCSM 2017)
- 11th International Conference on Augmented Cognition (AC 2017)
- 8th International Conference on Digital Human Modeling and Applications in Health, Safety, Ergonomics and Risk Management (DHM 2017)
- 6th International Conference on Design, User Experience and Usability (DUXU 2017)
- 5th International Conference on Distributed, Ambient and Pervasive Interactions (DAPI 2017)
- 5th International Conference on Human Aspects of Information Security, Privacy and Trust (HAS 2017)
- 4th International Conference on HCI in Business, Government and Organizations (HCIBGO 2017)
- 4th International Conference on Learning and Collaboration Technologies (LCT 2017)
- Third International Conference on Human Aspects of IT for the Aged Population (ITAP 2017)

Conference Proceedings Volumes Full List

Human–Computer Interaction

Program Board Chair(s): **Masaaki Kurosu, Japan**

- Jose Abdelnour-Nocera, UK
- Sebastiano Bagnara, Italy
- Simone D.J. Barbosa, Brazil
- Kaveh Bazargan, Iran
- Jose Coronado, USA
- Michael Craven, UK
- Henry Been-Lirn Duh, Australia
- Achim Ebert, Germany
- Xiaowen Fang, USA
- Stefano Federici, Italy
- Ayako Hashizume, Japan
- Wonil Hwang, Korea
- Mitsuhiko Karashima, Japan
- Hiroshi Kato, Japan
- Heidi Krömker, Germany
- Seongil Lee, Korea
- Cristiano Maciel, Brazil
- Naoko Okuizumi, Japan
- Philippe Palanque, France
- Cecile Paris, Australia
- Alberto Raposo, Brazil
- Milene Selbach Silveira, Brazil
- Guangfeng Song, USA
- Hiroshi Ujita, Japan
- Fan Zhao, USA

The full list with the Program Board Chairs and the members of the Program Boards of all thematic areas and affiliated conferences is available online at:

http://www.hci.international/board-members-2017.php

HCI International 2018

The 20th International Conference on Human–Computer Interaction, HCI International 2018, will be held jointly with the affiliated conferences in Las Vegas, NV, USA, at Caesars Palace, July 15–20, 2018. It will cover a broad spectrum of themes related to human–computer interaction, including theoretical issues, methods, tools, processes, and case studies in HCI design, as well as novel interaction techniques, interfaces, and applications. The proceedings will be published by Springer. More information is available on the conference website: http://2018.hci.international/.

General Chair
Prof. Constantine Stephanidis
University of Crete and ICS-FORTH
Heraklion, Crete, Greece
E-mail: general_chair@hcii2018.org

http://2018.hci.international/

Contents – Part II

HCI, Children and Learning

HCI in Complex Human Environments

HCI Case Studies

Contents – Part I

Interaction Design and Evaluation Methods

User Interface Development: Methods, Tools and Architectures

Multimodal Interaction

Emotions in HCI

Games in HCI

Bringing Game Design Models to Life

Sandeep Athavale[✉] and Vasundhara Agrawal

Tata Consultancy Services, Pune, India
{athavale.sandeep,vasundhara.a}@tcs.com

Abstract. Game Design research, in the past few years, has spawned multiple models and frameworks for understanding of games as systems. These models and frameworks predominantly function as pedagogic tools rather than something designers can readily use. The availability of multiple frameworks with varying detail as well as the lack of interactive layers on these frameworks makes it difficult for practicing designers to use them effectively.

In an attempt to overcome this limitation we propose a Unified Game Design (UGD) framework which assimilates components and elements from multiple existing models, frameworks and ontologies. The UGD framework features a superset of the existing elements and creates categories and relationships that makes it more usable.

We explored several applications of the UGD framework in analysis, completion and synthesis of games. However this paper elaborates the interactive implementation of the UGD framework in the generation of game ideas. The game of 'Lets Game it' with the framework's components and elements at its core was designed for the same purpose. The game provokes the designers to create new combinations of components and elements to generate game ideas. We conducted play tests for this game and found that game practitioners found it useful in generating game ideas.

Keywords: Game design · Game components · Game elements · Game research · Unified model · Usable model · Game idea generation

1 Introduction

Game design is the act of deciding what a game system should be and a designer must make hundreds of decisions about the components and elements therein to make a working game [1]. While the availability of several frameworks makes the field of game design rich in knowledge, game designers may lose necessary features when they choose one over the other. This issue of having to choose between frameworks or refer to multiple frameworks led us to a systematic study of 10 popular game design models. A comparative study of the models helped us assimilate their weaknesses and strengths and thus synthesize the Unified Game Design (UGD) framework.

The process of synthesizing the UGD framework involved the categorization of the models into structural, elemental and ontological frameworks and studying their features, elements and components in detail. While the elements for the UGD framework were extracted from the existing models and classified using heuristic principles, techniques such as card sorting were used to define the components of the framework

© Springer International Publishing AG 2017
M. Kurosu (Ed.): HCI 2017, Part II, LNCS 10272, pp. 3–20, 2017.
DOI: 10.1007/978-3-319-58077-7_1

[2]. Section 2 of the paper explains the analysis of existing frameworks and Sect. 3 explains the synthesis of the UGD framework.

Once the UGD framework was synthesized we wanted to make the framework accessible, interactive and 'playable' for experienced as well as novice game designers. We deliberated on various applications of the framework such as providing a choice based interface, rating elements for game analysis or providing a tool to select a combination of elements for game synthesis. The idea of using a game to synthesize game ideas offered us the interactive freedom as well as fun that we were searching for. We therefore chose to design the game 'Let's game it' using the UGD framework for synthesis of game ideas.

The UGD framework defines the flow of the game 'Let's game it'. The game is based on the interrelationships between the different components and elements as supplied by the framework. 'Let's game it', through its gameplay, encourages players to think of game ideas utilizing the structure supplied by the framework. The game gives its players an organized approach to generate game ideas without consciously implementing the game model.

The Sects. 5 and 6 of this paper explain in detail the conception of 'Lets game it', its design process as well as the data collection and discussion assimilated from the playtest sessions. The game was tested with several players consisting of a mix of both experienced as well as novice game designers. The game proved to be a successful implementation of the framework and satisfied its core intention of helping in game idea generation.

2   Analysis of Frameworks

We began our study for establishing a usable framework by searching the game design literature, published since the year 2000. We searched using keywords such as game design models, frameworks, ontologies, classification, components and elements as well as game analysis, evaluation, synthesis, and generation. The study led to the shortlisting of 10 game design frameworks. These were further grouped according to their core focus aspects into structural, elemental and ontological framework. The next sections explain in detail the theoretical analysis of the frameworks based on the classification.

2.1   Structural Frameworks

The MDA model [3] with its simplistic structure of only three primary components mechanics, dynamics and aesthetics provide an easy to understand representation of a game system. The Browne and Maire's [4] model on means, play and ends also follows a structure comparable to the MDA. In this model the rules and equipment replace mechanics and play replaces dynamic. Further, the Takatalo et al.'s [5] model concentrates on establishing the influence of components on one another its approach is also similar to the structure of MDA model by dividing the game design system into game system, play and psychology.

All the three models the MDA [3], the Means, Play and Ends [4] and Takatalo's model [5] differ intrinsically in their details and information but structurally they all represent the same three part flow of a game system.

Although the models discussed above provide us with a strong structural base they do not provide sufficient information on elements of a game system. To achieve a detailed understanding of the same we analyzed and studied the elemental frameworks.

2.2   Elemental Frameworks

The elemental frameworks describe and define the elements that compose a game system. Elias et al.'s [6] work offer an understanding of games through characteristics such as Infrastructure, Game systems, player effort and more. Similarly the work of Schreiber and Loucks [7] often used in teaching game design concentrates majorly on atoms (elements) such as Player Configuration, Objectives, and Elements related to the player. Fullerton's work [8] also offers components similar to Schreiber's model along with conflict, boundaries, outcomes and procedures.

Holopainen [9] proposed a framework for classification of elements based on structural, temporal, holistic and bounding categories. The theory of game elements by Järvinen [10] introduces nine types of game elements under three broader class of systematic, behavioral and compound game elements. He states that any game in the universe can be deconstructed into a unified set of theoretical concepts which can be used to construct new games. This exhibits the importance of elements in a game but it overlooks the need for a structural approach for representing them as proposed by MDA. The last model under study for elemental frameworks was the multidimensional typology of games by Aarseth et al. [11]. The dimensions and variables in their typology include space, time, player structure and control.

However to complete our study of the existing literature which could be successfully implemented in building a framework we needed to understand the game ontology.

2.3   The Ontological Framework

The Game Ontology Project by Zagal et al. [12] helps us understand the hierarchy of the elements in games as well as the relationships between them. The top level of the ontology consists of five elements: interface, rules, goals, entities and entity manipulation. It is based on a hierarchy of concepts which are abstracted from analysis of specific games.

2.4   Comparative Study of Frameworks

In order to understand the commonalities and differences between various frameworks we prepared a comparison Table 1. The columns headings are the top categories that emerge from the frameworks we analyzed.

We have added SGDA framework by Mitgutsch and Alvarado [13] which was not mentioned earlier. This framework gives us an additional dimension of designer intentions or purpose.

The study lead us to a few important conclusions regarding the existing frameworks

- Each model provides its individual unique characteristics rather than being an assimilation or an enhancement of a previously established model.
- The models are either biased to the structural or the elemental aspect of the system.
- The existing frameworks focus more on game mechanics and hence resources and dynamics which are functions of mechanics are underrepresented.
- The elements that designers work on upfront (intention elements) have been underrepresented in the existing models.
- The study of the relationship between the elements and components of a game is as important as the elements and components themselves.
- Table 1 shows a concise view of how each of the frameworks individually do not provide a unified view of the game system.
- The synthesis of the unified model would help designers to refrain from choosing one model over another and thus losing out on important features.

Table 1. Comparison of game frameworks

Source	Game mechanics	Resources/ equipment	Game play/dynamics	Player interaction	Player/experience (aesthetics)
MDA [3]	Mechanics		Dynamics		Aesthetics Player Motivations
Browne and Maire [4]	Rules	Equipment	Play		Player outcomes
Takatalo et al. [5]	Mechanics Narrative Interface		Dynamics	Interactions	Cognition Emotion Motivation
Elias et al. [6]	Basic characteristics	Infrastructure	Randomness Progression	Player effort	
Schreiber and Loucks [7]	Player rules Objectives Rules sequencing	Resources information	Game state	Interaction Player Control	
Fullerton [8]	Player rules Objectives Procedures Boundaries Outcomes	Resources	Conflict/ emergence		
Järvinen [10]	Systemic Goals Rules Interface				Behavioral context
Holopainen [9]	Holistic Bounding		Temporal	Structural (interface)	
Zagal et al. [12]	Interface Goals Rules	Entities		Entity manipulation	
Mitgutsch and Alvarado [13]	Mechanics Narrative				Aesthetics

2.5   Case for Unified Framework

The above comparison suggests that the existing frameworks, though highly acknowledged, are individualistic and not consistent in their representation of game system. They have differences in dimensions, granularity and categorization. Also, some frameworks are represented as structures while others are not and some frameworks describe relationships while others don't.

However, the literature survey provides us with a sufficient list of elements to synthesize a unified model and we attempt to bridge the gaps that the existing framework hold. We therefore propose a Unified Game Design Framework.

3   Synthesis of the Unified Framework

3.1   Scope

Salen and Zimmerman [14], define games as "a system in which players engage in an artificial conflict, defined by rules, that results in quantifiable outcome". The scope of the Unified Game Design Framework would be analysis and design of games which satisfy this definition.

3.2   Structural Classification

The structural classification of the framework is inspired from the various structural frameworks discussed above. The linear flow and the three level categorization of the model is defined by the MDA [3] model and thus the structure of the UGD framework has been classified into structure, dynamics and interaction. The structural diagram as seen in Fig. 1 also represents the role of the designer and the player prominently.

Fig. 1. Structure of the system inspired from MDA

3.3   Elemental Classification

The elemental classification of the framework is an amalgamation of the existing models and class heads therein. According to Jacob [15], classification is systemic arrangement of entities or elements based on analysis of necessary and sufficient characteristics. In order to bring out key relationship between groups of elements which are useful for study, we needed to classify the elements using a consistent approach. Our classification criteria is based on heuristic principles such as below:

- A component will be created when there is clear separation of concern or when elements cannot find a place in any other component.
- Every element should find a place in at least one component (no element will be orphaned).

- Every element should find a place in only one component (no redundancy).
- The classification may reach its final state after few iterations and field use.

The process of classification of components included

1. Enlisting all elements extracted from the literature
2. Removing any duplications, resolving synonyms, breaking up ambiguous elements
3. Conducting bottom-up analysis using card sorting
4. Conducting top down analysis using mind maps
5. Finalizing classification and trees.

This method of classification helped us arrive at the six components of the UGD framework as shown in Fig. 2.

Fig. 2. The six selected components for the UGD framework

An example of classification of the components is shown in Fig. 3. Here the root elements are classified into types of rules, which are further classified into subcomponents of the component 'game structure'.

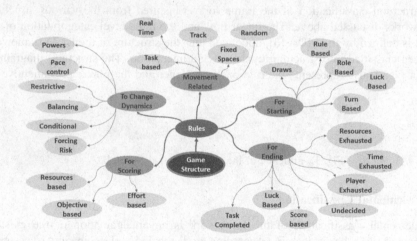

Fig. 3. Expanded view of 'rules' sub component

3.4 Components of the Unified Game Design Framework

The six components of the UGD framework needed to be explained in details in order to understand its implementation as proposed in the sections to come. Therefore, we define each component in detail.

Game Structure. Game Structure is 'the collection, arrangement and integration of elements that the designer directly controls to form the basis for meaningful game play'. The subcomponent of the same is composed of Objectives, Rules, Interface, Layers and Fun aspect. Game levels and difficulty are also a part of this component.

Game Resource. "Resource" is a broad class, used to mean everything that is under control of a single player i.e., Territory, Moves, Objects, Time, and Information, etc. We further classify 'Resource' into two types: Infrastructure Resources which are fixed like field, equipment, layout, fixtures and Transactional Resources which can be traded/consumed/spent by a player such as cards, tokens, information, available turns etc.

Game Dynamics. Dynamics is defined as change in states of game structure during play [3]. The dynamics of a game could lead to predictable paths if the game structure is rigid, and unexpected, nonlinear or complex paths if it is less rigid. The game dynamics is a result of player interaction with structure through the use of resources. Game dynamics includes Events, Actions, State Change, Emergence and Game Setup.

Player Interaction. "Playing a game is making choices within the game system to support actions and outcomes in a meaningful way" [14]. Players interact with each other or with the game structure and resources to make the required choices. Also, players put effort (cognitive/physical) to achieve desired outcomes. This is achieved through the interface provided by the game. The player interface, choices, actions, effort and feedback mechanism forms the player interaction component.

Player Experience. Player experience is the process of seeking desired emotional outcomes from the game play as indicated in the MDA framework [3]. The player experience comprises of aspects that player brings to the game such as ability, goals, prior knowledge of the game and those that the player takes back such as satisfaction, engrossment, learning, new experiences or even frustration.

Designer Intentions. The designer decides the core idea of a game. Mitgutsch and Alvarado [13] suggest that "every game has certain goals and designers follow their explicit or implicit intentions when designing it". The designer also decides the intended audience and what they are expected to experience. The players may derive experiences in addition to the designed experiences but this is an individual player's experience to the game. This component contains elements that help designers make these Sub-components: Context, Purpose, Core concept and Player profiles.

3.5   The Interrelationship Between the Components

In order to establish the interrelationships between the components, we made an analysis of the influence of the six components on each other by creating a matrix as shown in Table 2. In the table, we have referred to Designer Intentions as DI, Game Structure as GS, Game Resources as GR, Game Dynamics as GD, Player Interaction as PI and Player Experience as PE.

Table 2 helps us arrive at interconnects between components as shown in Fig. 4. It shows the influence of the Designer's intentions on the game structure and how the game structure helps to guide and define the game dynamics and resources. Further a player through his/her interaction manipulates the game resources and also creates the dynamics of the game session. The interaction thus created affects the player experience which ensures his return to the game or the gameplay if he/she is a returning player.

Table 2. Interrelationships between components

Components	Designer intentions	Game structure	Game resources	Game dynamics	Player interaction	Player experience
Designer intensions		DI influences and forms GS		Guided by the GS the DI doesn't directly influence the GD	The PI is a result of the GS	The designer imagines the PE
Game structure			GS of a game defines the GR	The GS defines the rules and objectives of the game hence guides the GD	The GS informs and defines the range of PI	PE is influenced by GS
Game resources		GR satisfied GS			GR provides artefacts to interact with	PE is influenced by GR
Game dynamics			Alters the state of the resources		The GD affects the next interactions	The GD creates most of the PE
Player interaction			Player manipulates the resources of a game	The PI generates the GD		The PI creates most of the PE
Player experience	Provides feedback to the designer			PI influences the GD only after the 1st play experience	The PE after the 1st play affects the PI in the consecutive plays	

3.6 The Unified Framework

Once the interrelationship between the components of the framework was established, we needed to establish the space in which the components exists. One would assume that all the components established above are inside the boundary of the game system but when we apply Salen and Zimmerman's [14] magic circle to test the boundary, we understand that a game designer is always outside the system creating it. Also, the player is partly inside and partly outside the circle. This is because a player continues to carry experiences outside the game (for example enmity with other players or the joy of winning). Similarly, the resources are also partly inside and partly outside in cases

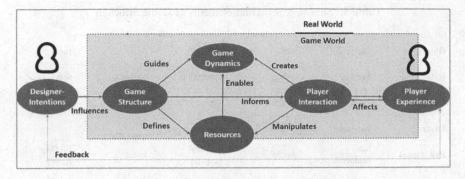

Fig. 4. Proposed unified game design framework

where the games share the resource with activities outside the game. This distinction of the real and the game world is thus represented in Fig. 4.

Figure 4 also brings us to the final representation of the Unified Game Design Framework. Thus, we see that the UGD framework borrows from the strengths of various frameworks as well as interconnects the missing connections to make a complete representation of a game system.

However, the aim of the research was to make a game design model that can be applied to real game situations in an interactive manner. This brings us to the application of the UGD framework as discussed in the next section.

4 Applications of Unified Framework

The UGD framework finds application in the form of analysis, completion and synthesis of games. It can be used to analyze existing games by checking for the structural flow and the existence of the essential components and elements as provided by the framework. The framework can be similarly applied to complete an incomplete game and synthesize a new game. In this paper, we explain the synthesis of a game in detail through an example.

The subcomponents and elements of the component Game Structure have been tabulated in Table 3. To synthesize a new game, we had to choose at least one element under each subcomponent. The elements of capture, movement, control, levels and story/fantasy were randomly picked to define the structure of the game as highlighted in the table.

Please note that for the purpose of idea generation in our example, singular elements have been picked at different level of granularity.

We now define the structure of a game based on the chosen elements.

- The objective of the game is to capture. Let us consider a scene of chase between a thief and a sheriff. While sheriff 'X' is the player controlled character, the thief 'Y' is the AI simulated character.
- The rules are to run through a crowded market space without colliding with the present public.

Table 3. Subcomponents and elements of Game Structure

Objectives	Capture	Race	Collect	Solve	Build
Rules	Starting	Ending	Controlling	Movement	Scoring
Interface	Control	Feedback	Types		
Layers	Facilitator	Modes and Levels	Tournament	Player Configuration	
Fun Aspect	Story/ Fantasy	Aesthetics	Mystery/ Surprise	Luck	Bluffing/ Hiding

- The playable interface is a desktop and the player uses keyboard to play the game.
- The successful capture of the thief in one level takes the player to the next level.
- As the level progresses one has to capture more number of thieves, the fun aspect will be contributed by the change in the scenario or the setting in which the crime takes place.

Each level also reveals a different story or narrative of the theft. This high-level definition of a game was enabled by the component set offered by the UGD framework. Thus, enabling us to successfully define a game without missing any essential factors or features.

However, we can see that this method of choosing from an existing set of elements is cumbersome and not interactive. It would be an exhaustive exercise for a designer to analyze each component and search for the suitable elements. This forces us to find a more interactive and fun implementation of the UGD framework in the form of a game-idea-generation-game.

5   Bringing Game Design Models to Life

As mentioned by Kultima et al. in their paper "while designers are required to be creative on demand, a successful creative process requires a relaxed and playful atmosphere" [16]. In order to create this atmosphere and enable the designers to use the UGD framework effectively we decided to present the framework as an interactive game.

In this context, we searched for existing games used to generate game ideas and found Järvinen and Kultima et al.'s work [10, 17]. We found their work exciting and relevant. We could get an estimate of the effectiveness of using games to ideate on games from their work. We studied their work and tried to overcome the shortcomings of their games. The scorekeeping in the game of 'GameBoard' was designed to make the ideation process feel more like a game [17] and the point-scoring system of the idea generation game 'Gamegame' was too complex to follow [10]. Such learnings helped us deliberate on the gameplay of our game and incorporate innovative solutions to handle the winning and the losing criteria of the game.

The book Game Storming puts forward the idea that "a game can be carefully designed in advance or put together in an instant, with found materials" [18]. This idea compelled us to think that given the right probes in the form of game components and elements, game ideas could be generated over a game session. The rudimentary implementation of this idea has been explained earlier in the form of the thief and the sheriff game.

However, the method of choosing elements from a set provided by the UGD framework was found to be very restrictive and cumbersome. We wanted to make the method more interactive and flexible. The need for randomization and the ease of having multiple combinations instigated us to use tokens instead of static combinations on paper. We segregated the components and elements into different tokens and picked them at random. This method worked well for some time as one could discard a token and pick another one. However, after the players made the first pick the process didn't allow feasible exchange of elements between the players. Thus we prototyped the game with a set of cards. Using cards provided us with the required degree of randomness as they could be easily shuffled, re-sorted, and rearranged to generate new patterns and ideas [18]. Thus, the idea of 'Lets Game It' game was generated based on the components, elements and the structure provided by the UGD framework.

Once the medium of the game was decided, the gameplay of the game was designed on that of matching cards. A player needs to acquire a group of matching cards or collect a set of cards before an opponent player. This particular method of playing cards accentuated the necessity of gathering all the six essential components of the UGD framework to formulate a game.

As creativity can be seen as a combination of insight and special thinking skills [19]. The gameplay has been designed such that it prevents players from getting attached to the very first idea they formulate. The mechanism and the time required for matching or gathering the correct cards gives the players enough time to think of their game idea and the game play.

5.1   Let's Game It - The Game-Idea-Generation-Game

The aim of the game is to collect a set of six cards and form a game idea. The player who does the same fastest wins the game. The printed prototype set of the game has been shown in Fig. 5. The game and its cards, rules etc. have been explained in detail in the next few paragraphs.

The game primarily consists of three kinds of cards, namely the Game Genre, the Game Components and the Game Changer cards.

The Game Genre cards define the genre of the game. The game starts with each player picking a genre card at random. Besides the genre card each player gets a

Fig. 5. 'Let's game it' game prototype

designer intentions card (type: component card). It is mandatory to distribute the designer intentions card in the beginning of the game as it contributes to the theme of the game. The remaining designer intentions cards are then shuffled with the rest of the component and the game changer cards. A set of three cards is then distributed to each player.

The players then pick cards from the deck of remaining cards for the first two rounds. After the first two rounds, most of the players will be left with six cards in hand excluding the genre card. Therefore, third round onwards the players can pick a card from the deck or from the discarded pile of cards (by other players) on the table. In case of a card being picked up from the table only the top most card is available for picking.

As the players keep collecting the six essential component cards each component card enables the players to decide on a particular aspect of their game. Like the 'game resource' card defines the resource in the game and the 'player interaction' card defines the interaction the player (as designer) wants to bring in his game. As the game progresses the players need to collect six different component cards namely: Game Structure, Designer Intentions, Game Resources, Game Dynamics, Player Interaction and Player Experience.

Once a player is in possession of all the six required component cards and is ready with the game idea he/she can declare a 'share session'. In this session he shares his/her game idea with the players on the table. Other players can declare the idea valid or invalid depending on the components used. If the player uses all the components as per the collected cards, he/she wins if not he/she has to take back his/her card and continue playing. In case a player declares and wins, the other players might also choose to share their game ideas or continue playing till the game has only one player left.

5.2   Playtests and Challenges

The initial playtesting was done with some selected elements from each of the component category. The idea of the first prototype was to check if the cards enabled people to think of game ideas. Although the players found the data set of elements very limited they definitely agreed to the method for ideating on games through a game.

In the second prototype we included more elements for each of the components. We also introduced some bonus or 'game changer' cards like Drop Genre card, Claim Back card, Swap Deck card or a Swap Voluntarily card. This proved advantageous in providing the fun and increased the interaction between players. The new cards also slowed down the pace of the game such that the players had more time to study and deliberate on their cards and thus their ideas. Further the game changer cards ensured that there was challenge posed to the players by compelling them to exchange their deck or drop their genre. Such actions helped the player to ideate quicker without getting stuck to their initial ideas.

The play test sessions with the second set proved significant in deciding the final gameplay of the game and also understanding the process of game generation. Along with this, a study of the existing game idea generation models provided us with the understanding that in the process of game design, the genre and theme are the base or the building blocks of a game. Thus, the Designer Intentions card which contributes to the theme of the game are now distributed in the beginning of the game along with the game genre card.

Since the game revolves around gathering the six essential component cards which define the game idea of the player the winning condition also had to be designed accordingly. Thus, the winning condition is a validation or a check for the presence of the six components as mentioned in the cards collected by the players when he/she is narrating his/her game idea. This method of closing the game through the validation of game components by the other players proved quite successful as compared to point or voting systems in games like Gamegame, VNA and Game-seekers [10, 17].

The number of ideas generated per game session varied somewhere between 2–5 ideas depending upon the number of participants. However the main focus of this game is not to count the number of ideas generated but to build an interactive environment that enables participants to discuss their ideas in an informal setting with a systematic approach. 'Let's game it' as a game enables player to suggest or improve upon each other's ideas. The game provides the scope for a dialogue between the participants which proves to be much more productive as compared to the limitations of brainstorming.

The process of data collection and results obtained from the game have been discussed in the next section.

6 Data Collection and Discussion

In order to test and analyze the reception of the game we conducted a three stage qualitative data collection in the form of pre, during and post-game sessions.

6.1 Pre Session

We tested 'Let's game it' with participants having varied background and not necessarily game designers. The game was tested with 17 participants. There were 5 playtesting sessions with a minimum of 2 players and a maximum of 5 players in a game session.

The user group tested were a mix of engineers, researchers, designers, artists and psychologist. Based on the background of the players they were classified into three groups:

- Experienced game designers
- Novice game designers
- Non game designers

For convenience we later merged novice and non-game designers into a single group. We also observed the player interest and their association with the field of games. In order to analyze the results of the playtest sessions in context to the participant's performance we gathered some quick details of their background in terms of how often they played games and if they have designed games previously. We asked them if they loved games and if they thought of games often. These kind of questions helped us in associating the player actions to the outcome of the game in the form of the game ideas.

6.2 During Session

During the session, we made observations and notes of the players based on the following questions:

- How easily was the game understood?
- Which parts of the game were exciting?
- Which aspects of the game helped more in idea generation?
- How does the different components (cards) help in idea generation?
- How was the interaction between the players?

The observations made during the session were noted down in the form of player reactions and responses and were classified under the question heads as shown in Table 4.

The player responses helped us getting the key words or the thematic codes that are frequently used and gives us the idea of how players ideate using components.

Table 4. Classification of responses in thematic codes and memos.

Ease of understanding the game	Exciting parts of the game	Aspects of the game that help in idea generation	Components in the game that help in idea generation	Interaction between the players
What kind of a game does it have to be	I need *just one more component* to complete the idea	I can't freeze my game idea unless I get my *Game structure card*	I need just *one more component to complete the idea*	I *claim* you substitute card
Can I *drop my genre*	I *claim your substitute card*	Oh I didn't know *Designer Intention was so important*	I should have got this card earlier now I am *too far into my game idea* I'll need to redo the whole set	*I know which component you need* and I will make sure you don't get it
Can we claim again *I want that card*	This is *better than brainstorming* for ideas	If I change my Genre I might have to *change my whole game*	I have all the cards *but I am not getting a game idea*	Oh *I give off the card that I don't want...* this is fun
How many cards do I need to collect?	I want to *drop my genre*	I should have got the *Designer Intention card earlier it decides the theme of the game*	I believe it is important to collect the *game structure card*	Can I use his *claim token*
Why do I need to have all the components in my game	I know which component you need and *I will make sure you don't get it*			I like my *genre* and don't want to *exchange* it

6.3   Post Session

Post the playtest sessions we analyzed the results based on the following questions

- What were the number of players per session?
- What were the number of ideas generated?
- What was the background of the winner of a particular session?

The Table 5 shows a quantitative detail of the number of players, their backgrounds, number of game sessions, number of ideas generated and the winner details.

As seen in Table 5 about 13 game ideas were generated during the playtest sessions by 17 different participants. The ideas had to be based on the elements provided by the component cards.

Table 5. Participant and idea details

Players	Skill	No. of players in the game-session	Number of ideas generated	Winner
P1	Novice	3	3 ideas	P2
P2	Novice			
P3	Experienced			
P4	Novice	4	3 ideas	P6
P5	Novice			
P6	Experienced			
P7	Experienced			
P8	Experienced	3	1 idea	P9
P9	Experienced			
P10	Experienced			
P11	Novice	5	2 ideas	P12
P12	Experienced			
P13	Novice			
P14	Experienced			
P15	Experienced			
P16	Experienced	2	1 idea	P17
P17	Experienced			

6.4 Discussion

We discuss the observations from the play testing sessions under three main headers.

Differences Observed in Novice Versus Experienced Designers. The playtesting groups consisted of a mix of novice and experienced game designers and it was observed that both of them performed equally well in terms of using the game components appropriately and generating game ideas. It was mostly observed that the ideas generated by the novice designers were quite unconventional. Their ideas stood out in terms of the theme, the story and the mechanics used by them. On the other hand, the ideas generated by the experienced game designers always had the finesse and covered all the aspects of a game. We can observe from the Table 5 that the winners were mix of both experienced as well as novice game designers.

Aspects that Helped Players Complete Their Game Ideas. One of the major aim of the 'Let's game it' game was also to help practitioners arrive at complete game ideas. In Table 4, we captured the reactions of players where they expressed their need for a particular component card. Reactions like "I can't freeze my game idea unless I get my Game structure card" OR "Oh I didn't know Designer Intention was so important". These reactions show that components like Game Structure, Designer Intentions and Game genre are very important and form the essential element to arrive at a complete idea. In fact in the initial game sessions the Designer Intentions card had to be collected by the player over the game session. However, we observed that since the Designer Intentions card contributed to the theme of the game a lot of players were unable to complete their idea if they got the card really late in the game. This changed the gameplay and the Designer Intention card is now distributed in the beginning of the game.

Obstacles in Game Idea Generation. As seen in Table 5 the number of ideas generated in a session were not equal to the number of participants. This is a result of the incomplete component sets that the players had to collect. This emphasizes on the importance of collecting all the component cards.

The players had to understand that just collecting one card of each of the six components would not suffice in the game. The intelligent implementation of the cards such that they could flow as a game idea was the main challenge that they had to overcome.

7 Conclusion and Future Work

In our proposed work, we sought to identify a framework that is complete in its representation of the structure, elements, and relationships and generic enough to cater to various viewpoints. The Unified Game Design Framework was a result of this vision.

We experimented with several applications of the UGD framework including completion of incomplete games, analysis of existing games and generation of new game ideas. We focused more on idea generation using this framework and conceived 'Lets game it' – a game based on the components and elements provided by the UGD framework. 'Let's game it' drives designers to think of game ideas guided by the structure of the UGD framework. This ancillary implementation of the UGD framework through a game helps us retain the fun and interaction and thus bring the model to life.

However we acknowledge that our framework and its proposed application needs further empirical validation through field studies with a sample set of designers and comparison with other existing methods. We intend to pursue that further. The framework has other potential use cases such as automatic game idea generation which needs to be explored. A library of values for each element of the framework can be created along with a set of rules allowing the generator to spawn multiple but valid elemental combinations or at the aggregate level - new games.

References

1. Schell, J.: The Art of Game Design: A Book of Lenses. CRC Press, Boca Raton (2015)
2. Cairns, P., Cox, A.L.: Research Methods for Human-Computer Interaction. Cambridge University Press, Cambridge (2008)
3. Hunicke, R., LeBlanc, M., Zubek, R.: MDA: a formal approach to game design and game research. In: Proceedings of the AAAI Workshop on Challenges in Game AI, vol. 4 (2004)
4. Browne, C., Maire, F.: Evolutionary game design. IEEE Trans. Comput. Intell. AI Games **2**, 1–16 (2010)

5. Takatalo, J., Häkkinen, J., Kaistinen, J., Nyman, G.: Presence, involvement, and flow in digital games. In: Bernhaupt, R. (ed.) Evaluating User Experience in Games Human-Computer Interaction Series, pp. 23–46. Springer, London (2009)
6. Elias, G.S., Garfield, R., Gutschera, K.R.: Characteristics of Games. MIT Press, Cambridge (2012)
7. Schreiber, I., Loucks, B.: Game design concepts. An experiment in game design and teaching. http://gamedesignconcepts.pbworks.com/f/Game+Design+Concepts+-+An+experiment+in +game+design+and+teaching.pdf
8. Fullerton, T.: Game Design Workshop: A Playcentric Approach to Creating Innovative Games. CRC Press, Boca Raton (2014)
9. Holopainen, J.: Foundations of gameplay. Blekinge Institute of Technology, Karlskrona (2011)
10. Järvinen, A.: Games Without Frontiers: Methods for Game Studies and Design. VDM, Verlag Dr. Müller, Saarbrücken (2009)
11. Aarseth, E., Smedstad, S.M., Sunnanå, L.: A multidimensional typology of games. In: DIGRA Conference (2003)
12. Zagal, J.P., Mateas, M., Fernández-Vara, C., Hochhalter, B., Lichti, N.: Towards an ontological language for game analysis. In: Worlds in Play: International Perspectives on Digital Games Research, p. 21 (2007)
13. Mitgutsch, K., Alvarado, N.: Purposeful by design? In: Proceedings of the International Conference on the Foundations of Digital Games - FDG 2012 (2012)
14. Salen, K., Zimmerman, E.: Rules of Play: Game Design Fundamentals. MIT Press, Cambridge (2004)
15. Jacob, E.K.: Classification and categorization: a difference that makes a difference. Libr. Trends **52**, 515 (2004)
16. Mumford, M.D., Gustafson, S.B.: Creativity syndrome: integration, application, and innovation. Psychol. Bull. **103**, 27–43 (1988)
17. Kultima, A., Niemelä, J., Paavilainen, J., Saarenpää, H.: Designing game idea generation games. In: Proceedings of the 2008 Conference on Future Play Research, Play, Share - Future Play 2008 (2008)
18. Gray, D., Brown, S., Macanufo, J.: Gamestorming: A Playbook for Innovators, Rulebreakers, and Changemakers. O'Reilly, Sebastopol (2010)
19. Bono, E.D.: Lateral Thinking: A Textbook of Creativity. Ward Lock Educational, London (1970)

Bus Runner: Using Contextual Cues for Procedural Generation of Game Content on Public Transport

Alexander Baldwin[1(✉)], Jeanette Eriksson[1,2],
and Carl Magnus Olsson[1,2]

[1] Department of Computer Science and Media Technology,
Malmö University, Malmö, Sweden
{alexander.baldwin, jeanette.eriksson,
carl.magnus.olsson}@mah.se
[2] Internet of Things and People Research Center,
Malmö University, Malmö, Sweden

Abstract. With the support of the regional public transport operator, this paper explores the potential for mobile games to make journeys on public transport more enjoyable. To this end we have developed a game called Bus Runner which is a context-aware endless runner, based on open and shared data. By blending features of the physical world, such as recognisable landmarks, with the game's virtual world, we situate and enhance passengers' experience of travelling on public transport. We identify a set of challenges and opportunities based on the development and evaluation of Bus Runner. These are of relevance not only for game development purposes, but also impact context-driven content generation of infotainment services as a whole.

Keywords: Procedural Content Generation · Context-aware games

1 Introduction

Human impact on the environment and climate change are, and likely will remain, important societal issues. Increasing the attractiveness of using public transport is not only about increasing the effectiveness and timeliness of the transport network, but also about offering travellers a rewarding journey. As has been shown previously [1], context-aware games based on cues from the real-world can be effective in this regard. With the advent of large sets of open data, and the increasing willingness to share data, new opportunities arise for using contextual cues for both utility and more playful purposes.

In this paper, we report on the development of Bus Runner – a context-aware endless runner-style platform game for smartphones – which uses open and shared data. Bus Runner is playable while riding on one of the bus lines in Malmö, Sweden. To promote a changing gameplay experience for each gaming session, thereby increasing replayability, we use Procedural Content Generation (PCG) [2] to create the game's levels. It has been suggested that PCG is particularly suitable for mobile games

M. Kurosu (Ed.): HCI 2017, Part II, LNCS 10272, pp. 21–34, 2017.
DOI: 10.1007/978-3-319-58077-7_2

due to the need to adapt game content to their broad player bases with varying skill levels [3]. Since they are played in many different settings, mobile games also present an opportunity to use location and other physical context factors in the PCG process. Using actual contextual cues from the physical world to feed the procedural content generator is novel to our implementation compared with traditional endless runner games.

The main objective of this study is to explore challenges and opportunities of using contextual data as an input to the procedural generation of levels for mobile games in a public transport setting. To do this, we will share the initial cycles of our design research [4] driven study, where we lean upon development reflections and prototype testing, together with the results of observations and interviews with playtesters.

Furthermore, it is an indirect but purposeful choice to take on a more playful approach to the use of contextual data than what is typically done today, meaning we also hope to promote further exploration of the opportunities this affords. Rather than strive to use context as a way to inform technology to take better (typically from a utility perspective) action, we instead fully embrace the meaning of 'cue' as real-life contextual cues are relied upon to play loosely coupled relationship roles with dynamically generated game objects that first and foremost serve the purpose of increasing the gameplay value.

2 Related Work

2.1 Context-Aware Games

Context-aware games use aspects of the environment in which they are played to adapt their behaviour or content to a particular setting. Despite Schmidt et al.'s [5] assertion that "There is more to context than location", location remains the most common form of context in context-aware games [6–10]. Other forms of context are however also seen, such as air pollution data [11] or driving-related data [1].

Motivations for the use of context-awareness in games vary significantly. Some games aim to affect the behaviour of their users. UKKO [11] is described as a persuasive game for children walking to and from school that makes use of an air-pollution sensor and location data to update the health of a digital pet in order to encourage users to walk through areas that are less polluted and to raise awareness about the issue of air pollution. CABdriver [1] uses driving-related data from a car to make passengers aware of the driver's behaviour, possibly resulting in them challenging this behaviour (such as speeding). Further use of context is to provide appropriate information to users based on their location. Garay-Cortes and Uribe-Quevedo [9] developed a location-based game to help new students get to know their surroundings by providing them with information about landmarks.

Other games use context to inspire curiosity and investigation in their players. For example, GEMS [7] allows users to record stories attached to specific locations and encourages family members and friends to discover these stories as part of a larger science-fiction plot. Free All Monsters! [6] encourages players to visit physical locations to discover monsters designed by other users. Commercially successful games like Pokémon Go [10] also employ a similar strategy, encouraging players to explore the physical world to make in-game discoveries or complete objectives.

With the recent increase in popularity of augmented-, virtual- and mixed-reality systems, many context-aware games, both in the scientific and the commercial domain are making use of these technologies to increase immersion or build a connection between virtual and physical worlds [8–10]. In these cases, the act of exploring physical locations is a key component of the gameplay.

2.2 Procedural Content Generation

Procedural Content Generation (PCG) refers to the algorithmic generation of game content, such as maps, levels or items. Among the possible motivations for the use of PCG in game development is the potential for tailoring game content to the needs and desires of specific players in order to create more engaging and entertaining games [2]. PCG is also useful for increasing the longevity or replayability of a game by continuously generating new and diverse content – something that has been advertised as a selling point in recent games.

Lopes et al. [3] argue that PCG is particularly suitable for mobile games, since their broader audience of more casual players demands support for a wider range of abilities. They also point out that the wide variety of different settings mobile games are played in presents an opportunity for adapting the content of those games to the context in which they are played and suggest that this could produce more meaningful content.

2.3 Context-Aware PCG

Lopes et al. [3] introduce the term Context-Driven PCG as one of their modalities of adaptive PCG. They use it to refer to content that is generated under the influence of players' implicit or explicit demands, such as a player-defined time-constraint. The other modality presented is Experience-Driven PCG, originally coined by Yannakakis and Togelius [12], where content generation relies on player-generated data, such as measured skill level.

While Lopes et al. investigate player-defined time constraints as a form of Context-Driven PCG and player skill level as a form of Experience-Driven PCG, these could both be considered examples of context-awareness according to Schmidt et al.'s [5] model for context-aware mobile computing. More specifically, player-defined time constraints and player skill level both fall into Schmidt et al.'s human factors. In the PCG literature, these human factors have mainly been explored through the use of player modelling for dynamic difficulty adjustment, where a game's difficulty is adjusted according to the player's actions [3, 13] but also by investigating how player modelling can be used to make games more engaging or fun [14]. While not framed as PCG, Olsson [1] takes a similar approach by using the actions of a car's driver to influence the generation of levels for a game played by a passenger, with the goal of influencing the driver's behaviour.

Despite the interest in human contextual factors in Experience-Driven PCG, there has been little investigation of how Schmidt et al.'s [5] second category of contextual factors – the physical environment – can be used as input for PCG systems. As mentioned above, previous research on context-aware games has often used physical context, such as location, but this data is more typically used to modify the behaviour of the system or to decide what type of information to display, rather than as an input to the generation of new content. We thus intend to investigate how the use of contextual data from the physical environment can be combined with human factors to generate content appropriate for a specific setting. Our research approach and results are presented in the following sections.

3   Research Approach

The research reported here relies upon a design research approach [4, 15] to guide the iterative stages of design, development and assessment. Design research was deemed appropriate given the exploratory nature of the work, and the emphasis design research places on practical contributions being considered as scientifically relevant [15].

While two main research cycles (the alpha cycle for the first version of the game, and the beta cycle for the second version) have been used in this research, considerable internal iteration between design and development has been used within each cycle, using self-testing and playtesting with participants familiar with the intentions of the game. This is common in game design [16] and has been motivated as relevant as such testers are more adept at focussing on the particular aspects that are being tested rather than aspects that may not be completed yet. These rapid internal iterations are in line with emergent design [17], and embrace the emergence of agile as well as continuous development principles to a higher degree than seminal approaches of design research (e.g. as outlined by Peffers et al. [4]). The overall research process still remains within the principles and motivations of design research.

For the alpha cycle, we recruited four external testers with two main goals: (1) to assess the difficulty level of the game, and (2) to determine if contextual cues were perceived by the players. For the beta cycle, we used six testers split into groups of three. One of the groups was asked to play the game in practice mode (which allows the game to be played without riding the bus) during a period of one week prior to the formal assessment session. The other group played the game for the first time during the assessment session, thus affording us an insight into differences between early adopters and those with some experience from the gameplay in addition to our overarching exploratory interest in the impact of using context cues to influence procedurally generated content in a game designed for public transport. The formal assessments were made up of two approximately 25 min sessions (depending on traffic and how well the busses kept to their schedule) per group. Researchers acted as observers during testing, taking field notes of game-related events, challenges the players appeared to have, and conditions on the bus. Interviews were recorded and transcribed after each gameplay session, which allowed the field notes to be complemented with more in-depth elaboration from the testers. The results of these sessions are presented in Sect. 5.

At the time of writing this paper, Bus Runner remains in open beta on Google Play and is available for anyone to download and play – either directly on the bus it is intended to be played on, or in practice mode and from anywhere. As long as the APIs and data sources which Bus Runner relies upon for contextual cues do not change, the game will be left available with periodical follow-up through the (fully anonymous) background data we collect. While we have access to such data from the additional players – who found the game on their own through Google Play, or through the advertising campaign that our collaborating public transport operator has done – this paper focusses on the formal alpha and beta playtest session observations and interview sessions. A particular emphasis is given in this paper to the beta cycle as that represents the current state of Bus Runner.

4 Bus Runner

The principal artefact of our design research process is Bus Runner, a context-aware game for bus users in Malmö, Sweden (see Fig. 1). Based on a combination of a number of forms of implicit and explicit contextual data, the game generates levels intended to engage players by reflecting recognisable aspects of their physical location in game. Inspired by the way augmented reality has been used in games to combine novel interactions with familiar environments [10], Bus Runner combines casual gameplay with a simplified representation of the physical world that players can easily recognise (Fig. 2). Context-awareness also provides us with opportunities to tailor the game to the requirements imposed by the intended gameplay setting – a bus – by, for example, choosing an appropriate game duration.

Fig. 1. Screenshot from a game session, showing the player character jumping on a bus shelter.

Bus Runner is a side-scrolling 2D endless runner-style platform game developed in Unity [18] for touchscreen Android devices. The player controls a character running automatically through the hectic streets of Malmö, which are filled with vehicles, stationary obstacles and other pedestrians. In order to avoid colliding with these obstacles, the player can jump by tapping the device's screen or glide slowly back to the ground with an umbrella by pressing and holding the screen. This gliding ability is limited by a finite 'energy' resource, seen in the bar in upper right corner of Fig. 1, which regenerates slowly over time or more quickly by picking up cups of coffee and cinnamon buns. The game's difficulty is adjusted dynamically according to how well the player is performing. If the player makes few mistakes, more difficult objects are likely to appear and energy boosts are harder to come by. As a reward for surviving the harder difficulty levels, the player earns points more quickly.

Fig. 2. Top: a landmark that can appear in the game. Bottom: its real-world counterpart

Context is used in a number of ways in Bus Runner. Before starting a game session, the player chooses a route by selecting it on the screen shown in Fig. 3. Then, rather than using GPS to directly determine the player's location, this location is inferred from the time and data from two providers offering open access to their services. The first of these providers offers an API for retrieving bus schedule data updated several times a minute, allowing us to sufficiently accurately estimate approximately how far a bus is along its route. The second provider is the Data Innovation Platform (DIP), which was developed as part of the same project as Bus Runner and collects data from many open and shared sources and presents this data through a single interface. Through DIP we are able to obtain diverse data including the GPS coordinates of bus stops, lists of landmarks within a specified radius of a location and the name of the city district a given GPS coordinate lies in. Being able to access these data sources through a single API is valuable for a developer since it reduces the number of external dependencies and allows data to be accessed in a more consistent way. Using these combined data sources allows us to predict where the player will be several minutes from now and plan level generation in advance. For example, if the bus is running slowly due to heavy traffic, a section of the game between two stops will be extended. Another use of contextual data is seen in the dynamic adjustment of the game's difficulty based on the player's performance, though this is largely reactive, rather than based on player-modelling.

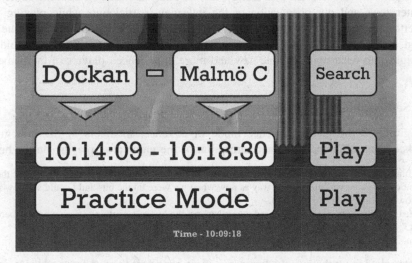

Fig. 3. Before playing, the user selects a start and a destination and can see when the next bus will depart from the start stop. Practice mode starts a game using static or simulated placeholder data instead of real data.

The location and real-time bus timetable data allow the level generator to select suitable components and also allow the duration of the game to be adapted to the length of the bus journey. In this way we hope to create the impression that each play session is custom-made for the player's journey, while also taking into account practical concerns like reminding the player that they have reached their destination by ending the game shortly beforehand.

The version of Bus Runner available at the time of writing is limited to just one of Malmö's bus lines, due to the effort needed to create graphics for more obstacles, landmarks and districts if it were to be expanded to cover more bus lines or the whole city. This means that the potential to examine the game's effects as a driver to motivate exploration within the city is limited. Since the chosen bus line passes through areas with many recognisable landmarks, it may also be difficult to generalise our results to other lines that pass through more residential areas where fewer noteworthy buildings tend to be found.

5   Results of External Playtesting

We have divided the data gathered from interviews with six beta test participants into three categories: (1) sensemaking – the players' processes of understanding the game and drawing connections between context and game content, (2) engagement – the role of context in producing a more entertaining and useful user experience, and (3) awareness – the extent to which players were aware of the connections between the game content and the physical world. These categories were chosen based upon trends in the discussion during the interviews and their relevance to our research goals. Here, we present the most relevant data along with our analysis based on both the content of the interviews and our observation of the interview participants while playing Bus Runner on buses in Malmö. Group 1 had played in practice mode in advance of the test session, while group 2 played for the first time during the session so that we could get an insight into what may separate new and more experienced players of the game.

5.1   Sensemaking

Having played the game's practice mode in advance, members of the first group remarked upon differences in their perception of the game after playing on the bus.

"I think more happened now. When I was playing practice mode I didn't really get what the point of the game was in the same way as now when we were on the bus and I could see how it followed along." (Andy, group 1)
"I just thought that you were supposed to race against the bus or something to see who got there first." (Andy, group 1)
"That's what I thought too, at first." (Simon, group 1)

After playing on the bus, the first group were confident they understood the point of the game:

"You run alongside the bus. You follow it, outside." (Ludwig, group 1)

They also remarked on the differences between the content they had seen in practice mode and on the bus, making a connection between the appearance of landmarks and the route taken by the bus.

"I didn't see Turning Torso this time, but I think I saw it in practice mode." (Simon, group 1)
"Do you have any idea why?" (Researcher)
"We didn't go past it, right?" (Simon, group 1)

When asked about the connections between the physical world and the game, the second group deduced that data from the local public transport provider were used.

"It felt like GPS, but you said it's not." (Casper, group 2)
"I guess it's [local public transport operator]'s timetable." (Jesper, group 2)
"Yeah, they have some digital thing where it has when every bus passes a stop." (Sebastian, group 2)

In some cases the participants assigned more meaning to in-game events than there actually was. For example, the appearance of particularly tricky soft drink can-throwing pedestrians prompted one player to say:

"It feels like [the cola cans] were there to slow you down in case you were progressing too quickly, or something like that" (Ludwig, group 1)

When actually their appearance is a product of dynamic difficulty adjustment intended to increase the challenge for more skilled players. Participants also made indirect connections. One remarked:

"It's affected by how the bus drives too. If there's a lot of traffic it takes longer to arrive at the next bus stop." (Ludwig, group 1)

The game isn't making use of traffic data directly, but heavy traffic is reflected by delays in the real-time bus timetables we use, suggesting that this data may be enough to create the impression of a more complex data than we directly use.

5.2   Engagement

A frequent point of discussion throughout the interviews was how the representation of location in the game allowed the players to engage more fully with the game without the distraction of worrying about when it was time to get off the bus.

"You don't have to look up, so you can use the game for that too: you can see where you are and you know, so you don't miss your stop." (Simon, group 1)
"You don't need to pay attention to two things anymore." (Andy, group 1)
"Exactly." (Simon, group 1)
"You can just look down at the game and you sort of know where you are without even thinking about it." (Andy, group 1)

Beyond the practical benefits of the use of contextual data, the participants valued that the content of the game reflected the physical world outside the bus.

"Is it meaningful that you're sitting on the same green bus that you see and jump on in the game?" (Researcher)
"Yes, I think so. It adds to the engagement or whatever you call it, because it feels more real." (Jesper, group 2)
"It feels like Malmö. You're playing a game that's in Malmö." (Casper, group 2)
"It's always fun to see things that you know really well in games." (Simon, group 1)

Members of the first group commented on the differences between playing on the bus and in practice mode.

"I think it's more appealing to play on the bus… partly because it's a pretty nice way of killing time and also you really keep track of where you are so you can be totally calm about missing your stop." (Ludwig, group 1)

When asked whether they would enjoy the game as much if it were to use the same kinds of contextual data in a different setting, such as in space, there was a general agreement in the second group that the game would still be interesting, but that by losing the concrete connection to the city of Malmö it would not be as entertaining to play.

"It wouldn't be the same thing because you wouldn't recognise the areas in the same way […] I think this fits much better, you get that recognition of the city." (Jesper, group 2)
"I think I would rather play the game as it is now too, simply because you recognise places you've been […] if it was set in space you'd just have asteroids and it wouldn't make the same impression on me at all." (Sebastian, group 2)
"I think that the backgrounds are the most charming bit. If you got rid of those I don't think it would be anywhere near as rewarding." (Casper, group 2)

Furthermore, if the game content was not connected to its physical setting:

"Without the bus information it's just another regular platform game, so it wouldn't be much different from other platform games." (Simon, group 1)

5.3   Awareness

The impact of Bus Runner relies on players being actively aware of the connection between the physical world and the content of the game.

"I saw from the background that it was Malmö central station. I wasn't looking out of the window because I was focussed on the game, but it felt like we should be there so I thought to myself: I'm here now." (Casper, group 2)
"The first thing I thought of in the beginning was probably that bridge over there – you go over it [in the game]. It was immediately recognisable and then the central station and then… there are some, I mean, I recognise the area even though I don't know exactly where I am." (Jesper, group 2)

Most of the participants remarked upon their relative unfamiliarity with the city, particularly the second group.

"I don't live here so it was just the central station [that I recognised]." (Casper, group 2)
"Same here, my sense of direction in Malmö is hopeless." (Sebastian, group 2)
"I haven't lived here that long either and I think it affected my recognition of where we were." (Jesper, group 2)

Despite this, between them, the three participants in group 2 identified at least three of the five landmarks that could appear during their play session.

When asked about the relative importance of the game's background images, which are specific to particular areas of the city, and the moving buses, which are found throughout the whole game a player responded:

"They serve different purposes. The backgrounds give you a bit of an idea of which area you're in. The buses didn't really do that - they felt more like a way of making progress." (Andy, group 1)

5.4   Differences Between Groups

Comparing the two beta test groups, it was clear that the first group had more quickly developed a deeper understanding of the use of contextual cues in the game. Having had the chance to learn and practice the basic mechanics in advance allowed them to focus on understanding the relationship between context and content in the game and to compare the experience of playing the game both inside and outside of its intended setting. In contrast, the second group's interview was centred much more on discussions of the game mechanics and how to play the game most effectively, suggesting that the group needed to get past the initial hurdle of getting used to the gameplay before being able to fully consider why the game is the way it is and how it relates to the physical world. This presents a challenge for developers of games using contextual data to influence content generation since, while any game must consider how best to introduce players to its content, requiring that players understand the connections between the game content and context at the same time as learning the basic mechanics adds an addition element of complexity. A potential solution for this is a more gradual introduction to the game mechanics in order to not overwhelm new players.

6   Discussion

Previous research such as Olsson's CABdriver [1] has shown that it is not necessary for context-aware games to portray realistic settings for their connection to the context factors to be understood, but a very explicit connection like that of location in Bus Runner may be helpful in facilitating this understanding. While augmented reality games like Pokémon Go [10] place game content directly within the real world to make the use of context explicitly, it can be technically challenging to implement well and particularly challenging in settings involving high-velocity motion, such as in a vehicle [19]. Bus Runner presents an alternative through the technically less expensive means of a simplified representation of the physical world and we have seen that this is enough to make players aware of their approximate location. Different systems will clearly require different levels of precision, but our results indicate that the representation of context in Bus Runner is sufficient to allow players to remain aware of what is going on around them without losing engagement with the game.

Something surprising to us was the importance the players associated with the practical use of the game as a tool for updating them about their location while playing so they wouldn't miss their bus stop. Several players remarked that the game required too much attention to simultaneously consider what was going on around them while playing. Without the built-in information to keep them well informed of the physical location of the bus and the guarantee that the game will end before they need to get off it might be difficult for players to balance the need to focus on the game with remaining aware of their surroundings.

For players to be able to trust the information presented to them by the game, this information needs to be reliable. One of the largest problems facing developers of a context aware application is how and where to get access to reliable and accurate data. Bus Runner uses two external data providers and the design research process has occasionally been affected by service outages, bugs or data inaccuracies. Despite this, DIP allowed us to access many different kinds of data through one API, simplifying the process of integrating these data sources into the game, since all data was presented in a common format. It is our view that if useful context aware games are to be developed for use on public transport, it is important that the public transport operator makes an active effort to provide useful, accurate and reliable data to developers.

Of course, a game also needs to be fun to play and one of our goals was to investigate how to use contextual data in a playful way to create fun and appealing interactions and gameplay. Examples of using context-aware games to encourage curiosity and exploration like Free All Monsters! [6] rely on location as a source of contextual data, but the game content does not necessarily have any semantic connection to these locations. In Bus Runner, we rely instead on value added by the connection between locations seen in the game and the physical world. Beta playtesters found the experience of playing a game set in a familiar location enjoyable and valued the familiarity of the surroundings both for their utility and the feeling of recognition they produce.

The extent to which players are aware of how the game content relates to contextual cues may depend on how familiar they are with the game's setting – in this case Malmö. All of our players were at least familiar enough with Malmö to recognise a few landmarks and locations, but a tourist who has never set foot in Malmö before might have a very different experience with the game, due to the loss of an obvious connection between the game content and the physical world. On the other hand, the game could be seen as a way of exploring the city and being introduced to unfamiliar landmarks, thus serving a similar purpose to Garay-Cortes and Uribo-Quevedo's [9] study of using a context-aware game to encourage students to explore locations on a university campus.

While our main focus was on the use of environmental contextual factors – since these have not been extensively explored as inputs to PCG – our results suggest that human context factors remain important. One such factor, player skill level, has consistently been a challenge throughout the research process. During and before alpha testing, the game's difficulty level was significantly higher and was not dynamically adjusted according to player performance. Consequently, several of the players involved at this stage had trouble progressing far enough to see even a single landmark. This severely limited their exposure to some of the context-based features of the game and it was clear that players had no real awareness of their location while playing, recognising only objects such as buses as being from Malmö, rather than perceiving parts of the game as characteristic of a particular area. In contrast, during the beta tests players described a more precise understanding of their location. This points to a need for this kind of game to adapt to player ability in order to preserve a consistent flow in the gameplay whereby the use of contextual data can be seen and understood. This agrees with Lopes et al.'s [3] argument that adaptive PCG should be used to balance games for a wide range of skill levels in mobile games. Yannakakis and Togelius [12] however present a much fuller framework for Experience-Driven PCG than examples based purely on dynamic difficulty adjustment, arguing for player models that capture not just player skill but much more diverse aspects of playing style and how players are emotionally affected by game content. As such, it would be interesting to examine how player modelling could be combined with the kind of context-aware PCG we have presented here to make games that are better adapted to a broad range of players.

7 Conclusions

In this paper, we have presented the results of a design research process intended to explore the use of context cues in the procedural generation of levels for a mobile game. Given the sparsity of studies that combine context-awareness with procedural generation of content, the positive impact in terms of sensemaking, engagement and awareness which players expressed from real-life testing indicates promise for further development and use of such mixed approaches.

Specifically, our results from external beta testers indicate that players are able to remain aware of relevant aspects of their surroundings while focussing fully on the game and without having to divide their attention. This also raises questions for future research about how detailed context representations need to be to still promote awareness, where we are seeing indications that it is appropriate and advantageous to use context cues that represent the general physical area. However, in games (and possibly in other areas as well) it may be desirable to take a less literal approach where creativity and engaging interactions are highlighted. Additionally, when relying on open or shared data rather than internal sensors for contextual data, it is important to have reliable access to accurate data in a consistent format. This can be supported by active efforts from data providers (in our case the local public transport operator) to provide high quality data to developers. Finally, our results indicate that there is a need to adapt content to human factors that may extend beyond simple skill-level-based dynamic difficulty adjustment so that the learning curve or frustration do not distract from players perception of contextual cues. An approach to this is to investigate the role of player modelling in context-aware PCG as an extension to Experience-Driven PCG.

Acknowledgements. This work partially financed by the Knowledge Foundation through the Internet of Things and People research profile, and the Challenge Driven Innovation programme at VINNOVA.

References

1. Olsson, C.M.: Exploring the impact of a context-aware application for in-car use. In: 25th International Conference on Information Systems, Seattle, USA, pp. 11–21 (2004)
2. Togelius, J., Shaker, N., Nelson, M.J.: Introduction. In: Togelius, J., Shaker, N., Nelson, M. J. (eds.) Procedural Content Generation in Games: A Textbook and an Overview of Current Research, pp. 1–15. Springer, Cham (2016)
3. Lopes, R., Hilf, K., Jayapalan, L., Bidarra, R.: Mobile adaptive procedural content generation. In: Proceedings of PCG 2013 - Workshop on Procedural Content Generation for Games, Co-Located with the 8th International Conference on the Foundations of Digital Games (2013)

4. Peffers, K., Tuunanen, T., Rothenberger, M.A., Chatterjee, S.: A design science research methodology for information systems research. J. Manag. Inf. Syst. **24**(3), 45–77 (2007–2008)
5. Schmidt, A., Beigl, M., Gellersen, H.-W.: There is more to context than location. Comput. Graph. **23**, 893–901 (1998)
6. Lund, K., Coulton, P., Wilson, A.: Free All Monsters!: a context-aware location based game. In: Proceedings of 13th International Conference on Human Computer Interaction with Mobile Devices and Services (MobileHCI 2011), pp. 675–678. ACM, New York (2011)
7. Procyk, J., Neustaedter, C.: GEMS: the design and evaluation of a location-based storytelling game. In: Proceedings of 17th ACM Conference on Computer Supported Cooperative Work and Social Computing (CSCW 2014), pp. 1156–1166, ACM, New York (2014)
8. Nolêto, C., Lima, M., Maia, L. F., Viana, W., Trinta, F.: An authoring tool for location-based mobile games with augmented reality features. In: 14th Brazilian Symposium on Computer Games and Digital Entertainment (SBGames), Piaui, pp. 99–108 (2015)
9. Garay-Cortes, J., Uribe-Quevedo, A.: Location-based augmented reality game to engage students in discovering institutional landmarks. In: 7th International Conference on Information, Intelligence, Systems and Applications (IISA), Chalkidiki, pp. 1–4 (2016)
10. Pokémon Go (2016). http://www.pokemongo.com/
11. Dickinson, A., Lochrie, M., Egglestone, P.: UKKO: enriching persuasive location based games with environmental sensor data. In: Proceedings of 2015 Annual Symposium on Computer-Human Interaction in Play (CHI PLAY 2015), pp. 493–498. ACM, New York (2015)
12. Yannakakis, G.N., Togelius, J.: Experience-driven procedural content generation. IEEE Trans. Affect. Comput. **2**(3), 147–161 (2011)
13. Jennings-Teats, M., Smith, G., Wardrip-Fruin, N.: Polymorph: dynamic difficulty adjustment through level generation. In: Proceedings of 2010 Workshop on Procedural Content Generation in Games (PCGames 2010). ACM, New York (2010)
14. Shaker, N., Yannakakis, G.N., Togelius, J.: Towards player-driven procedural content generation. In: Proceedings of 9th Conference on Computing Frontiers (CF 2012), pp. 237–240. ACM, New York (2012)
15. Hevner, A.R., March, S.T., Park, J., Ram, S.: Design science in information systems research. MIS Q. **28**(1), 75–105 (2004)
16. Fullerton, T.: Game Design Workshop: A Playcentric Approach to Creating Innovative Games, 3rd edn. CRC Press, Boca Raton (2014)
17. Olsson, C.M., Eriksson, J.: Methodological capabilities for emergent design. In: HCI International Conference 2014, Heraklion (Crete), Greece (2014)
18. Unity. https://unity3d.com/
19. Brunnberg, L., Juhlin, O., Gustafsson, A.: Games for passengers: accounting for motion in location-based applications. In: Proceedings of 4th International Conference on Foundations of Digital Games (FDG 2009), pp. 26–33. ACM, New York (2009)

Towards the Use of a Serious Game to Learn to Identify the Location of a 3D Sound in the Virtual Environment

Sabrine Boukhris and Bob-Antoine J. Menelas[✉]

Department of Mathematics and Computer Science,
Université du Quebec à Chicoutimi (UQAC),
555 boul. Universite, Saguenay, QC G7H 2B1, Canada
{Sabrine.Boukhris1,Bob-Antoine-Jerry_Menelas}@uqac.ca

Abstract. Since the childhood, one learned to detect, more or less precisely, where a sound is coming from in space. In multiple situations, auditory feedbacks can be used to supplement or to reinforce the visual channel, as the auditory channel helps at monitoring the surrounding beyond the limited field of view: over 360°. In past studies, we have observed that the ability to properly assess the direction of a 3D sound varies greatly from one person to another. In particular, we found that training plays a major role in this task. To allow people to improve their abilities in perceiving the direction of a 3D virtual sound, we described here a serious that targets this learning. The designed game has been implemented in Unreal engine 4. An experiment aimed at assessing the value of that serious game is also presented. We observed that all participants of that study have, for the two level of the game, improved their score after practicing the game for a 10 min period.

Keywords: Serious games · 3D sound

1 Introduction

Living organisms are in a constant interaction with their environment. These interactions allow to perceive through senses and eventually to operate the surrounding world. We, as human being, experiment our own environment as well as our own body only through our sensory organs. As a result, many life situations involve the exploitation of more than one sensory channel. For example, mobility often requires visual and auditory stimuli. More generally, in multiple situations, auditory feedbacks can be used to supplement or to reinforce the visual channel [7, 16], as the auditory channel helps at monitoring the surrounding beyond the limited field of view: over 360°. This probably explains why, since the childhood, one learned to detect, more or less precisely, where a sound is coming from in space. These considerations may probably explain the reason why we observed in recent years a growing popularity for the use of 3D sounds in virtual environments (VE). With this integration, when interacting with virtual objects, the sound feedback comes to reinforce, to complement the visual information [17]. This situation is named as a multi-sensory interaction since more than one

© Springer International Publishing AG 2017
M. Kurosu (Ed.): HCI 2017, Part II, LNCS 10272, pp. 35–44, 2017.
DOI: 10.1007/978-3-319-58077-7_3

sensory-channels (audio-vision) are associated for the benefice of the interaction. It appears that having a multi-sensory rendering can greatly contribute to increase the authenticity and plausibility of the VE, namely its overall coherence. Other studies are questioning whether the use of a multimodal interaction allows users to be more efficient or not in performing a given task [23]. In our study, we want to address an issue that seems to be ahead of such problems. Indeed, we have in some past studies observed that the ability to properly assess the direction of a sound vary greatly from one person to another [18]. In particular, we found that training plays a great positive and significant role in this [17]. Therefore, we want to allow people to improve their abilities to perceive the direction of a 3D sound simulated on a computer.

For this, we focus on the question how to allow people to improve the perception of the direction of a 3D sound simulated on a computer. Our goal is to provide a tool to help people developing their capabilities to detect the direction of a 3D virtual sound. Knowing that serious games are an effective tool for training and learning [2, 21] we hypothesize that running a serious game should lead people to improve their ability to perceive the direction of a 3D sound. This paper describes the design of that serious game. An experiment aiming at assessing the value of that serious game is also presented. We observed that all participants of that study have, for the two level of the game, improved their score after practicing the game for a ten minute period.

The paper is organized as follows: related works are presented at Sect. 2. Section 3 describes the proposed serious game. The realized experiment is presented at Sect. 4 before the conclusion in Sect. 5.

2 Related Work

Sight and hearing are the most exploited human senses. They are involved in multiple ways in the perception of the environment. In this section, we briefly report the use of 3D sounds. We first analyze cues that help at identifying where a sound is coming from in space. Second, we review the use of 3D sounds in VE. However, we do not cover techniques that can be used to simulate a 3D sound in a digital world. Among the most popular, one counts the ambisonic [9], the wave field synthesis and binaural [6].

2.1 Perception of 3D Sounds

In the physics point of view, one defines sound as a mechanical vibration of a fluid, which propagates in the form of longitudinal waves because of the elastic deformation of this fluid. The perception of a sound refers the reception and interpretation of such waves [26]. Six elements are involved in perception of sounds, namely pitch, duration, loudness, timbre, sonic texture and spatial location [5]. Here, we focus on spatial location. To detect the spatial location of a sound source in space, one has to estimate its azimuth, elevation and depth. For this, three cues are mainly used:

- Two binaural cues:
  - Inter-aural Time Difference (ITD): defines the difference in arrival time of a sound between two the ears. ITD informs about the direction or angle of the sound source from the head.
  - Inter-aural Level Difference (ILD): is the difference in loudness and frequency distribution between the two ears.
- Spectral cues linked to the HRTF (Head Related Transfer Function)
  - They correspond to changes in the intensities of frequencies. They are due to several phenomena (diffractions, reflections and attenuations caused by the shoulders, head and ears) that modify the sound waves received at each ear.

For more information regarding the estimation of the distance of a sound source as well as the influence of the visual channel, one can refer to [4].

2.2   Use of 3D Sound in VE

In a real world study, Murray et al. have noticed that when deprived of every sound feedback, people feel being like they were observers not actors of their actions [20]. In a more general way, it appears that having a sound feedback in a VE may make it be more immersive than without. Here, we briefly review the use of sounds in VE.

On of the first use of 3D audio in VE is in improving the quality of life of visually impaired people. Over the last two decades several works have been carried out in this direction. One counts the use of an interactive story telling performed in 3D acoustic virtual environment for blind children [14]. Recently, Balan et al. have investigated whether haptic-auditory feedbacks based training can enhance or not sound localization performance, front-back discrimination and the navigational skills of the visually impaired people [1]. They reported that subjects succeeded to improve their sound localization performance, reduced the incidence of angular precision and reversal errors. Moreover, participants became able to build an effective spatial representation map of the acoustic environment. Picinalli et al. [22] assessed VR for assisting the blind in learning architectural environments throughout an acoustic VR platform. They compared two types of learning through purely auditory exploration. They observed that Navigation in VR acoustic models provided comparable results to real navigation.

The second and main use of 3D sounds in VE is in helping people at locating virtual objects. This usage represents the most straightforward application of 3D sounds in a VE, as it targets the exact same advantage as in a real life situation. Recently, we have used 3D in order to help users at locating virtual vehicles in truck driving simulator [8, 11, 12]. In the same way, Barreau et al. have used 3D sound to enhance the immersive capabilities of a reconstructed sugar plantation [3]. In [10], Gunther et al. study how adding spatialized sound to a VE can help people navigate through it. They observed that adding 3D sounds may reduce time taken to locate objects in a complex environment, but do not increase the acquisition of spatial knowledge. However, the study of Turner et al. [24] suggests that 3D sound could be exploited to extend the apparent depth in a stereoscopic image. Also, Larsson et al. have studied the impact of the reverberation of sound sources moving in space [13]. According to this study, the authors concluded that the reverberation might enhance the sense of presence in the virtual environment.

Another use of 3D sound is in replacing visual feedbacks with sonification. This approach is widespread when analyzing large datasets. Sonification conveys spatial and temporal information of raw data into meaningful auditory signals [25], as Menelas et al. did with haptics [19]. 3D sounds may also serve to complement or to reinforce a visual feedback. In [17, 18], we have study how to exploit audio-haptic interactions for the identification, localization and selection of targets in a 3D VE. We noticed that haptics enable a rapid and precise selection. On the other hand, it appears that the auditory feedback was particularly important in complex situations since it allows perceiving multiple targets at the same time. We have also noticed that the ability to properly assess the direction of a particular sound varies greatly from one user to another. In particular, the results suggested that training plays an important role in this task. Therefore, we want to allow people to improve their abilities to perceive the direction of a 3D sound simulated on a computer. These results were a driving force for the design of the current research.

3 Design of the Game

Given that the goal of the proposed game is to help people developing their capabilities to detect the direction of a 3D virtual sound, we rely on a framework centered on learning for the design of this game. To this end, the framework that caught our attention is proposed by [15]. It is entitled *Motivation and Learning through the facets of a serious game*. In what follows, we describe how these facets led us to design a game that, a priori, should ensure the achievement of targeted educational goals. Thus, the design of the game is centered on six facets. The following presents how these facets are implemented in the game.

- **Pedagogical objective.** The educational objectives of the game are the first step of this design approach. In our case, this facet concerns the identification of knowledge that can be transmitted throughout the game. Here, the goal is to allow the user to be able to identify the direction of an incoming 3D sound.
- **Domain simulation.** This facet is to materialize the environment of the game. As stated previously, the objective is to locate the source of a 3D sound; such a task can be found in various situations of everyday life. For this, to represent the context of the game, we choose a scene that matches an everyday situation. Knowing that youth people are the primary audience of this game, we have retained a possibly familiar environment: a virtual bar (Fig. 1).
- **Interaction with the simulation.** This facet represents the level of playability. It determines the relationship between the actions of the player and the feedbacks of the system; this allows determining the type of the game. Considering our objective, we want the player to experiment the game in a first person view.
- **Problems and progression.** This facet concerns the progression in the game. It defines how to gradually increase the difficulty of each level. The goal is to balance the difficulty level so that it will be neither too low nor too high. Too much facility

Fig. 1. Representation of the visual off the game.

may create a sense of confidence that may cause a lack of practice. Similarly, too much difficulty may discourage a user. For this, we want to create several level of the game that will have an increasing difficulty scale. This will advance the player while keeping his motivation.

The current version of our game has two levels. At the first one, one throws glasses to the player. Glasses can only come from two directions: right or left. At the second level, the player is put in the shoe of a waiter; he is placed in the middle of a bar where he receives orders. Here, the sounds can come from any directions within 360° around the head.

Two more levels (3 and 4) are currently under development. At level 3, multiple sounds will be rendered at the same time in the same conditions of level 2. At this step, there will be no restriction regarding the number of sounds that will be played. This amount will increase from n to $n + 1$ each time the player comes to 80% of good identifications of the appropriate source among n possible sources. At level 4, the complexity will increase a little more as sources will also be place at various elevations.

- **Decorum.** Decorum balances motivation and learning. It consists of many elements that will bring fun to the game in order to push the leaner to achieve the desired objective. To ensure the distractive side, graphics and animations are exploited. As an example, at the first level, an identification of the position of the sound source, the success, is rewarded by a glass of beer. A failure results in the sound of breaking glass.
- **Condition of use.** This facet is intended to define how to exploit the serious game while maintaining its educational and recreational qualities. Given that this game is designed for training, we estimate that users can operate it within different real life conditions. Because of that, we made a casual game that is very simple and easy to use.

4 Implementation and Evaluation

Based on the facets described at previous section, we developed the game using Unreal Engine 4. Here we report, the experiment that aimed at evaluating the proposed game. A total of 15 people (3 women) took part in our experience. Participants are mainly undergraduates and graduated-students in various fields including literature, education and computer science.

4.1 Hardware

The serious game is tested on a 15.6 inch HD LED laptop with optimum resolution of 1366 × 768 pixels. This computer is equipped with an Intel Core i5-2450M processor 2.5 GHz, an NVIDIA GEFORCE GT 525M graphic card and 8 GB of RAM. Windows 8 (×64) Professional is the installed operating system. A professional binaural headphone is used. Subsequently, we present the experimental protocol.

4.2 Experimental Protocol

The purpose of our experiment is to evaluate whether playing the developed game affects or not the capabilities of a person to adequately identify the source of a sound. For this, we want to record two different scores (before and after using the game) for each level of the game. This test aims to verify if there is a variation of the player's score after the use of the game. So the test involves four stages supervised by an appraiser.

1. During the first stage, one explains the experimental protocol to the participant and he is asked to read and sign the consent form. A pre-test form is used to collect certain information: age, gender, current occupation, and level of contact with video games. The test then moves to the second stage.
2. At the second stage, the participant seats in front of the computer. He receives information about the controls of the game. Namely, at each trial, he has to click to trigger the 3D sound. The participant is then invited to familiarize with the game. Thereafter, the learner will be asked to make 10 attempts for each level. These data are stored as initial results.
3. At the third stage, the learner is invited to train with the game for a period of ten minutes. After this time, he moves to step four.
4. In the final stage of the test, participants are once again invited to make ten attempts for each level. As in the second step, the successes are counted. These are the final results.

4.3 Results and Analysis

All the participants have enjoyed the test. Observed scores are reported at Figs. 2 and 3 for the pre-training and post-training.

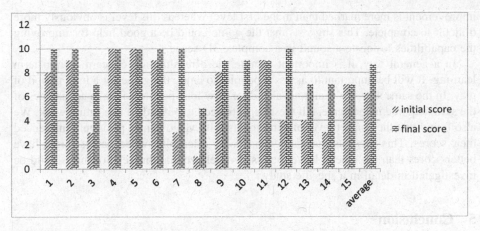

Fig. 2. Scores realized at the first level

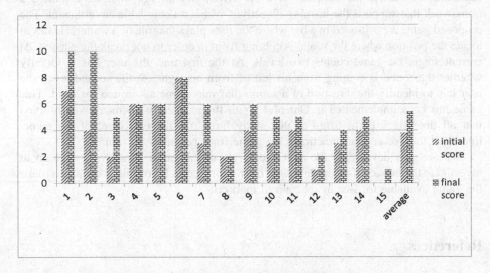

Fig. 3. Scores realized at the second level.

For the first level, we find that all players are at least as good as before using the game. We can observe that the score increases by an average of (38%) from 6.26 to 8.67 after the training session. Although these results show a clear improvement, at this stage we cannot conclude that this game allows improving capabilities for identifying the direction of a 3D sound. In fact, given the high rates of proper identification at this level, it seems that this scenario is fairly easy to complete. Such an observation reinforces other studies that have often mentioned that the identification of the left and right directions is easier for a human.

At the second level, we find that the score increases by an average of (42%) from 3.8 to 5.4 after the training session. With these results, we observe that the improvement is more marked than in the first level whereas this level is obviously more difficult to complete. This suggests that the game could be a good help for improving the capabilities to locate a sound in a complex 3D scene.

In a general way, it is important to note these results only concern a short-term learning. It will be important to assess if people do enjoy the game for a long period of play. In the same way, we want to evaluate for how long people will take advantages of the skill acquired in the game. All these aspects need to be studied in a future work. We also found that the contact level of participants with video games positively influenced their scores. This suggests that participants who often play video games might have better scores than the others. Nevertheless, we believe that this relationship should be investigated in detail in a specific study.

5   Conclusion

In this paper we described the design of a serious for helping people at developing their capabilities to detect the direction of a 3D virtual sound. For this, we exploited a framework that supports the learning objectives within an enjoyable environment. The proposed game is positioned in a bar where the user plays the role of a waiter. He has to locate the position where the sound is coming from in order to not break the glasses. At current stage, the game counts two levels. At the first one, the user has to identify whether the sound is coming from his left or from his right. At the second level, the user has to identify the direction of a sound that may come all around his head. This game has been implemented in Unreal 4. With the realized experiment, we observed that all the fifteen participants of that study have, for the two level of the game, improved their score after practicing the game for a period of 10 min.

We are now developing the next two levels of the game. Moreover, we want to investigate the impact of using this game over a long period. For this, we want to make the game available for free in specialized markets.

References

1. Bălan, O., Moldoveanu, A., Nagy, H., Wersényi, G., Botezatu, N., Stan, A., Lupu, R.G.: Haptic-auditory perceptual feedback based training for improving the spatial acoustic resolution of the visually impaired people. In: 21st International Conference on Auditory Display (ICAD) (2015)
2. Baranowski, T., Baranowski, J., Cullen, K.W., Marsh, T., Islam, N., Zakeri, I., de Moor, C.: Squire's quest! Dietary outcome evaluation of a multimedia game. Am. J. Prev. Med. 24(1), 52–61 (2003). doi:10.1016/S0749-3797(02)00570-6
3. Barreau, J.-B., Petit, Q., Bernard, Y., Auger, R., Le Roux, Y., Gaugne, R., Gouranton, V.: 3D reconstitution of the loyola sugar plantation and virtual reality applications. In: Proceedings of Computer Applications and Quantitative Methods in Archaeology, CAA, Sienna, Italy (2015)
4. Batteau, D.: The role of the pinna in human localization. Proc. Roy. Soc. B168, 158–180 (1967)

5. Burton, R.L.: The elements of music: what are they, and who cares? In: Rosevear, J., Harding, S. (eds.) ASME XXth National Conference Proceedings, Paper presented at: Music: Educating for Life: ASME XXth National Conference, pp. 22–28, The Australian Society for Music Education Inc., Parkville (2015)

6. Berkhout, A.J., de Vries, D., Vogel, P.: Acoustic control by wave field synthesis. J. Acoust. Soc. Am. **93**(5), 2764–2778 (1993)

7. Souza Veriscimo, E., Bernardes, J.L.: 3D interaction accessible to visually impaired users: a systematic review. In: Antona, M., Stephanidis, C. (eds.) UAHCI 2016. LNCS, vol. 9738, pp. 251–260. Springer, Cham (2016). doi:10.1007/978-3-319-40244-4_24

8. Ecrepont, A., Haidon, C., Girard, B., Menelas, B.A.J.: A fully customizable truck-driving simulator for the care of people suffering from post-traumatic stress disorder. In: 2016 IEEE International Conference on Serious Games and Applications for Health (SeGAH), pp. 1–8, May 2016

9. Gerzon, M.A.: Ambisonics in multichannel broadcasting and video. J. Audio Eng. Soc. **33**(1), 859–871 (1985)

10. Gunther, R., Kazman, R., MacGregor, C.: Using 3D sound as a navigational aid in virtual environments. Behav. Inf. Technol. **23**(6), 435–446 (2004)

11. Haidon, C., Ecrepont, A., Girard, B., Menelas, Bob-Antoine J.: Gamification of a truck-driving simulator for the care of people suffering from post-traumatic stress disorder. In: De Gloria, A., Veltkamp, R. (eds.) GALA 2015. LNCS, vol. 9599, pp. 312–322. Springer, Cham (2016). doi:10.1007/978-3-319-40216-1_33

12. Haidon, C., Ecrepont, A., Girard, B., Menelas, B.-A.J.: A driving simulator designed for the care of trucker suffering from post-traumatic stress disorder. In: Ma, M., Oikonomou, A. (eds.) Serious Games and Edutainment Applications, 2nd edn. Springer, Heidelberg (2017)

13. Larsson, P., Vastfjall, D., Kleiner, M.: Effects of auditory information consistency and room acoustic cues on presence in virtual environments. Acoust. Sci. Technol. **29**(2), 191–194 (2008)

14. Lumbreras, M., Sanchez, J.: 3D aural interactive hyperstories for blind children. In: Proceedings of 2nd European Conference Disability, Virtual Reality and Associated Technologies, Skovde, Sweden, pp. 119–128 (1998)

15. Marne, B., Labat, J.M.: Model and authoring tool to help teachers adapt serious games to their educational contexts. Int. J. Learn. Technol. **9**(2), 161–180 (2014)

16. Menelas, B.A.J., Picinali, L., Bourdot, P., Katz, B.F.: Non-visual identification, localization, and selection of entities of interest in a 3D environment. J. Multimodal User Interfaces **8**(3), 243–256 (2014)

17. Menelas, B., Picinali, L., Katz, B.F.G., Bourdot, P.: Audio haptic feedbacks for an acquisition task in a multitarget context. In: 3DUI 2010: Proceedings of IEEE Symposium on 3D User Interface, pp. 51–54 (2010)

18. Menelas, B., Picinali, L., Katz, B.F.G., Bourdot, P., Ammi, M.: Haptic audio guidance for target selection in a virtual environment. In: HAID 2009: Proceedings of 4th International Haptic and Auditory Interaction Design Workshop, vol. 2, pp. 1–2 (2009)

19. Menelas, B., Ammi, M., Pastur, L., Bourdot, P.: Haptical exploration of an unsteady flow. In: EuroHaptics Conference, 2009 and 3rd Joint Symposium on Haptic Interfaces for Virtual Environment and Teleoperator Systems, World Haptics 2009, pp. 232–237. IEEE, March 2009

20. Murray, C.D., Arnold, P., Thornton, B.: Presence accompanying induced hearing loss: implications for immersive virtual environments. Presence: Teleoperators and Virtual Environments, vol. 9, no. 2, pp. 137–148 (2000)

21. Plantevin, V., Menelas, B.A.J.: Use of ecological gestures in soccer games running on mobile devices. Int. J. Serious Games **1**(4), 49–60 (2014)

22. Picinali, L., Afonso, A., Denis, M., Katz, B.F.G.: Corrigendum to "exploration of architectural spaces by blind people using auditory virtual reality for the construction of spatial knowledge". Int. J. Hum. Comput. Stud. **72**(4), 393–407 (2014)
23. Roverud, E., Best, V., Mason, C.R., Streeter, T., Kidd, G.: Evaluating performance of hearing-impaired listeners with a visually-guided hearing aid in an audio-visual word congruence task. J. Acoust. Soc. Am. **139**(4), 2210 (2016)
24. Turner, A., Berry, J. Holliman, N.: Can the perception of depth in stereoscopic images be influenced by 3D sound? In: Proceedings of SPIE 7863, Stereoscopic Displays and Applications vol. XXII, p. 786307, 14 February 2011. doi:10.1117/12.871960
25. Vézien, J.M., Ménélas, B., Nelson, J., Picinali, L., Bourdot, P., Ammi, M., Lusseyran, F.: Multisensory VR exploration for computer fluid dynamics in the CoRSAIRe project. Virtual Reality **13**(4), 257 (2009)
26. Walters, E.G.: Chapter 2: Station equipment. In: Fundamentals of Telephone Communication Systems. Western Electrical Company (1969)

Can Online Games Survive Longer?

Yuchen Gui[1], Eugene Hoyt[2(✉)], and Fan Zhao[2]

[1] School of Digital Media, Savannah College of Art and Design,
Savannah, GA, USA
yucgui20@student.scad.edu
[2] Department of ISOM, Florida Gulf Coast University, Fort Myers, FL, USA
{ehoyt, fzhao}@fgcu.edu

Abstract. The area of Online gaming has been widely researched with one glaring omission, the role of national culture in explaining online game playing differences across countries. The purpose of this study is to exam how and why national culture affects online game playing and how to extend online game playing time from a culture perspective. The findings would be beneficial in the theoretical understanding of the online game playing behavior.

Keywords: Gaming · Online games · National culture · Acceptance

1 Introduction

Along with the development of the Internet, the consumption of online games has become a significant economic, social, entertainment, and cultural phenomenon worldwide [1]. In recent years, online games have gained popularity around the world. According to the Entertainment Software Association [2], computer and video game industry has made at least $15 billion every year. Online games are computer controlled games, including both PC games and video games, played by consumers over network technology, especially through the Internet. Online games can be categorized into multiplayer and single-player games. At present, multiplayer games, especially massively multiplayer online games (MMOGs) are most successful among all online games. According to trade estimates, only massively multiplayer online role playing games (MMORPGs), one type of MMOGs, encompass a subscription of more than 50 million players with annual expenses of $12 billion in 2012 [3]. Since MMOGs are the most acceptable and popular online games, the term "online games" in this paper refers to MMOGs.

The rapid growth of online games has caught the attention of the gaming industry especially with respect to revenue potential. The growth of digital streaming capability of games has provided a faster and more robust vehicle to get gaming to the masses quicker than ever before. That is why understanding the individual player dynamics has become important in this industry before designing any game for a vendor or developer. One wrong move and it could spell disaster on future earnings or the credibility of the company if a new game fails. That is why the it is critical to completely investigate consumers' online behavior.

M. Kurosu (Ed.): HCI 2017, Part II, LNCS 10272, pp. 45–53, 2017.
DOI: 10.1007/978-3-319-58077-7_4

Per Lo and Chen [4], the profitable life cycle of an online game goes down to 8 months to a year from 18 months to 3 years in average in the past. This means much of online game players switch their games every 8–18 months. Game developers try to prolong the life span of a game to increase the overall profit. However, they are facing two serious issues: market competitiveness and customers expecting higher quality. Every year, there are more than several hundred new online games available in the market from various game developers. Typical customers only focus on one or two online games at a certain time whereas some are demanding with all aspects, including game stories, game graphics, game services, and so on [5]. The quality of the game construction goes a long way in player buy in and retention. Therefore, it is increasingly important to study the reasons for retaining customers in the game.

As suggested by Semeijin et al. [6], maintaining customer loyalty not only lowers the cost of acquiring new customers, but also brings in substantial revenues in the long run. Typically, the longer time players play the online games, the more money they will spend on the game, and this will bring more revenue to the game vendors or developers through added content after purchase to further the longevity of the game. Many studies have been working on critical factors influencing customers' acceptances of online games and customers' intensions of continually playing online games. However, only a few studies focus on the national culture impact in respect to players' attitudes toward on online game playing. According to NewZoo analysis [7], in 2016, the top two countries with the highest total revenues in gaming industry are China and USA (see Fig. 1).

TOP 20 COUNTRIES
BY GAME REVENUES | 2016

CHANGE	RANK	COUNTRY	POPULATION (M)	ONLINE POPULATION (M)	TOTAL REVENUES (M$)
▲ 1	1	CHINA	1,382.3	788.8	24,368.8
▼ 1	2	USA	324.1	293.6	23,598.4

Fig. 1. Game revenues in 2016

Every year in China, there are over 100 new online games developed by different vendors. However, less than 5% of games last more than two years as a MMOG before a significant decline in user base. By contrast, in United States, less than 30 new online games are available each year and over half of them last more than three years. A quick comparison of the discrepancy in the amount of new games created each year between the two countries indicates an issue with the amount of time players invest in their current game before moving onto a brand-new game. Therefore, we believe there may be some culture impact involved in online game playing. Empirical research conducted to date focused on how to extend current customers' playing time and how to increase online game players' loyalty from a national culture perspective. The purpose of this study is to examine how and why national culture affects online game playing and how to extend online game playing time from culture perspectives. The literature review considers previous research to date and expands on it with the culture perspective to offer better insight on the impact culture has on paying habits across countries.

2 Literature Review

For years, researchers focus online game acceptance and continuous game playing [8–10]. However, limited studies paid attention to the role of national culture in explaining online game playing differences across countries. Per Waarts and Van Evaerdingen [11], national culture is one of the key factors influencing Information Systems innovation adoptions. Therefore, this paper tries to explain the relationship between online game playing and national culture. United States and China are two countries that rank in the top two with highest revenue in 2016. Therefore, in this study, we are focusing the online game players in these two countries.

Per Davis [12], culture is a set of values, ideas, meanings and symbols that help individuals communicate, interpret, and build relationships among members of a society and gives a sense of identity and understanding of acceptable beliefs and behaviors in the society. There are three well-known theories on national culture studies. Hall [13] classified national cultures based on the level of context and monochromic and polychromic perspectives. The level of context distinction of culture is determined between rule-based and relationship-based cultures. In low context cultures (e.g., Germany and North Americans), people most likely use explicit words to communicate and store information while, in high context cultures (e.g., China and Japan), interpretation is adopted to pass the information across the country. The second distinction in Hall's theory is measured by a culture's attitude toward time [13]. People in monochromic cultures more likely work on one thing at a time while people in polychromic cultures tend to work on multiple things at a time.

Trompenaars [14] identifies seven national culture dimensions based on people's attitude toward problem solving. To increase the efficiency of problem solving, people in different countries tend to have different set of implicit logical assumptions in their solutions. Trompenaars [14] argues that these solutions differentiate each culture from others regarding to the problems. Table 1 shows the summary of the dimensions.

Table 1. Dimensions in Trompenaars' national culture model

Dimensions	Characteristics
Universalism versus particularism	People follow the rules or rely more on relationships
Individualism versus communitarianism	People emphasize group benefits or individual freedom
Specific versus diffuse	People believe in overlap of work and personal life or not
Neutral versus emotional	People express emotions explicitly or not
Achievement versus ascription	People value a person as what you do or who you are
Sequential time versus synchronous time	People prefer work in sequence or complete them simultaneously
Internal direction versus outer direction	People control the nature or be controlled by nature

Hofstede [15] introduced a five-dimension classification of cultures based on a survey of employees in IBM subsidiaries located in fifty countries: power distance, individualism/collectivism, masculine/feminine, uncertainty/avoidance, and long versus short-term orientation. He argues that national cultures can be differentiated in values. Therefore, we can identify and describe national cultures quantitively in different categories. Since Trompenaars' model is similar to those of Hofstede [16], and Hofstede's model is more quantitative oriented, in this study, we adopted Hofstede's model to study the national culture issues of online game playing.

There are five dimensions in Hofstede's model. **Power distance index (PDI)** is more about social structure rather than personalities. It identifies how societies under different cultures regulate the behavior of their members. In large power distance countries, the less powerful members expect and accept the inequality of power distribution. Lower power members are required to be obedient and respectful to higher power members. For example, employees are rarely encouraged to challenge their superiors. In countries with lower distance power, children are allowed to contradict their parents or challenge their teachers. In online game playing, game players must face different virtual scenarios and solve the problems in the game to gain more experiences and higher level for the role in the game. According to Hofstede [15], people in countries with high power distance often try to find rules and follow the rules whereas people in countries with low power distance more like explore and be flexible. Therefore, when playing online games, players with high power distance tend to find more rules to obey. However, most of the current online games are designed to offer more of a flexible virtual world to encourage unpredictably. Thereby, encouraging players to explore more in their games. Therefore, people in high power distance countries are more likely to drop their current online games even though formatted with various events and agile virtual environments. Hence, we suggest the following hypothesis:

H1: The higher the country's PDI score, the more likely online game players in that country are to drop the online games quickly.

According to Hofstede [15], uncertainty creates anxiety and people feel threatened by uncertain or unknown situations, for example, knowledge of a life after death. Uncertainty Avoidance Index (UAI) describes how people adapt or cope with these uncertain or unknown situations. In high UAI cultures, people tend to adopt technology, law, rules, and religion to decrease the ambiguity of situations by making events clearly interpretable and predictable. People in high UAI cultures will not take unnecessary risks and only plan and complete those actions with enough value that they can explicitly approve based their past experiences.

Since online game players are quite familiar with the current game they are playing, from UAI perspective, they have enough knowledge about this game without too much ambiguity. However, switching to another game may cause more uncertainty because of the player's inexperience with playing the new game before. Therefore, to avoid uncertain issues of game playing, players in high UAI cultures are inclined to stay in the same game they are playing now. Hence, we suggest the following hypothesis:

H2: The higher the country's UAI score, the more likely online game players in that country are NOT to drop the online games quickly.

Individualism and collectivism index (IDV) represents the relationship between the individual and collectivity or the group in a certain society. Individualism and collectivism impact the decision making of a person in the society. Individualism culture is more toward personal decision making with less influence from the surrounding collectivity or group. For example, converting oneself from believing one religion to another is a highly individual activity in the countries with high individualism score while, in high collectivism countries, it is more reasonable that people tend to change their views together with their surrounding groups. Even playing online games is an individual decision. Players tend to play the game with friends or someone they know in real life. Therefore, the decision of playing the game or switching to a new game can easily be impacted by anyone around with similar interests, who most of the time are other players in the same game. Hence, we suggest the following hypothesis:

H3: The higher the country's IDV score, the more likely online game players in that country are NOT to drop the online games quickly.

The fourth dimension in Hofstede's model is Masculinity (MAS) and Femininity. Basically, Hofstede [15] argues that gender differences come from the natural differences between men and women. Culture could be more Masculinity or more Femininity according to how the societies define and follow norms in different ways. From his survey, Hofstede found two basic facts. First, historically, masculine cultures tend to be more militaristic; second, masculine cultures tend to be more competitive while feminine cultures try more to encourage cooperation. Masculine cultures focus more on ambition, competition, and material values. Most all current online games are based on adventure or violent games. Therefore, players with high masculinity culture tend to play the online games. However, to gain more competency, this type of player may try to play newer games with more different and various militaristic experiences. Hence, we hypothesize the following:

H4: The higher the country's MAS score, the more likely online game players in that country are to drop the online games quickly.

In his second edition of Culture's Consequences, Hofstede [15] defines a new dimension of national cultures: Long- Versus Short-Term Orientation. This Long-Term Orientation Index (LTO) score is based on a Chinese Value Survey (CVS) conducted in 1985 from students in 23 different countries. Cultures with high LTO scores tend to persist for a longer time with higher perseverance. The key words in LTO connotations summary are persistence, perseverance, personal adaptability to different circumstances, and believe of the happening of the most important events in life in future. On the contrary, people in Low LTO cultures expect quick results, prefer personal steadiness and stability, and believe that the most important events in life occurred in past or occur in present instead of future. Therefore, we expect that people in high LTO cultures are more likely to focus on future results with long strategy and operations planning, and more receptive to changes which may offer better results in the future, while as people in low LTO cultures tend to emphasize short term benefits and are resistant to change. Obviously, players, after they played same game long enough, i.e. over a year or two, will have a formative understanding of the role they played in the game and a clear vision of future in the game. Players in High LTO cultures will expect better entertainment in the future new games and do not care too much for current game playing. Therefore, player in high LTO cultures will prefer player more new games rather than staying in the same game long enough.

H5: The higher the country's LTO score, the more likely online game players in that country are to drop the online games quickly.

3   Research Method

To exam the research model, a preliminary survey was conducted. The survey was sent to two classes in a Chinese University with 154 students and two classes in a US University with 84 students. All students are sophomore from college of Business. A total of 187 surveys were completed and 86 (36 from US and 50 from China) were used in the analysis. Students who do not play online games or played less than 3 h per week were dropped. Tables 2 and 3 show the demographics of the players in both countries.

Table 2. Demographics of online game players in both countries

Demographics	US	China
Average age	21.7	21.1
Average years playing online games	9.5	10.3
Hours/week playing online games	8.1	14.4
How many online games playing now	1.2	2.5

Table 3. Demographics with gender

	US		China	
Gender	Male	Female	Male	Female
Number of participants	30	6	39	11
Average age	21.67	21.9	21.1	21.2
Average years playing online games	10.12	6.4	10.9	8.1
Hours/week playing online games	8.58	5.7	15	12.2
How many online games playing now	1.2	1	2.6	2

The items used in this survey were adapted from Hofstede's IBM and China survey questionnaires [15]. The reliability of the items was evaluated using Cronbach's alpha [17]. The coefficient alphas for the PDI, UAI, IDV, MAS, and LTO were 0.78, 0.80, 0.85, 0.81, and 0.77, respectively. Pearson's correlation coefficients were also determined to assess the convergence validity. Since all the attribute coefficients were somewhere from high to moderate ranges, they were all retained for future analysis. Additionally, there were no concerns about multi-collinearity because none of the coefficients was extremely high.

4 Discussion

The data were analyzed using multiple linear regression analysis. The purpose of a regression analysis is to relate a dependent variable to a set of independent variables. Regression analysis, therefore, was the most appropriate analytical technique in this study to determine the relationship between customer commitment and innovation characteristics, between customer attitude and innovation characteristics, and between customer commitment and customer attitude. Table 4 shows the hypothesis testing results along with the conclusions whether the hypothesis is supported by the statistical analysis at a < .05.

Table 4. Summary of regression analysis results

Hypothesis	Independent variable	t-value	Significance	Support
H1	PDI	3.816	<0.001	Yes
H2	UAI	−3.176	0.012	Yes
H3	IDV	−2.941	0.017	Yes
H4	MAS	1.998	0.046	Yes
H5	LTO	5.231	<0.001	Yes

As demonstrated by the data analysis above, this preliminary study supports all the hypothesis we proposed. Consequently, we can answer the research question in our study. First, national cultural variables, such as PDI, UAI, IDV, MAS, and LTO are related to continuous online game playing; Secondly, national culture should be added to the acceptance and continuous usage framework in online game studies. Table 5 shows the summary of hypotheses testing of this study.

Table 5. Summary of testing the hypotheses 1 to 5

Culture variable	Hypothesized influence on cloud computing adoption	Results
Power distance index (PDI)	Positive	Confirmed
Uncertainty avoidance index (UAI)	Negative	Confirmed
Individualism index (IDV)	Negative	Confirmed
Masculinity index (MAS)	Positive	Confirmed
Long-term orientation index (LTO)	Positive	Confirmed

Our study provides substantive conclusions about the effects of national culture dimensions on continuous online game playing behaviors. We formulated a number of hypotheses regarding the influences of various national culture dimensions, such as

PDI, UAI, DVI, MAS, and LTO. According to our data analysis, we found evidence to support all of our hypotheses. We can preliminarily conclude that national culture does influence the continuous online game playing behaviors. Hofstede dimensions appeared to be a good theoretical background for online game playing behavior studies. Higher levels of the Power Distance, Masculinity, and Long-Term Orientation positively influence the continuous online game playing behaviors, while higher level of the Uncertainty Avoidance, and individualism has a significant negatively influence on continuous online game playing behaviors.

5   Conclusions

This research is the first study distinguishing continuous online game playing behaviors differences between different national cultures by adopting Hofstede's cultural dimension model. Our findings suggest that attention should be paid to differences between different areas, such as China and US. Per different culture and regulations, Chinese and US online game players have different player behaviors and decision-making habits. Additionally, the results from this study can help game vendors and developers to adjust their design strategies and marketing campaigns regarding to different online game players per each country's cultural traits.

This empirical study would also provide theoretical background to researchers who are working on online game research. This is the very first paper discussing online game playing behaviors under cultural circumstances. This research not only provides substantive conclusions about the effects of national culture dimensions influencing online game playing behaviors, but also emphasizes the importance of culture differences in online game study. Culture issues could be an additional dimension in many other online game acceptance or continuous playing studies. Researchers therefore can further expend their research models to more generalized applications.

The empirical findings would be beneficial in the theoretical understanding of the online game playing behavior. It may also help in driving the development and execution of a better acceptance and continuous use framework in online game playing research.

National culture played an important role in this research study even though it was limited to only focusing on two different cultural areas in the online game playing behavior research. In the future, we are planning to expend to other nations, such as European countries to further test the relationship between the cultural differences and online game playing. Additionally, we notice that in our preliminary study, in both countries, female players played much less than male players did. In social science studies, gender is one of the key factors influencing the study results. If we put gender as a control variable in our study, we may get some new information about online game playing in different countries. Thereby, providing more research for developers to capture new customers not already playing or provide better information on current players not included in our current research. Another variable to consider when researching the role of females from other countries is that they may be playing silently. Based on culture norms discussed per Hofstede, it is very likely that gender could have played a role in underestimating the number of females that are currently playing to avoid detection from their male counterparts.

References

1. Marchand, A., Hennig-Thurau, T.: Value creation in the video game industry: industry economics, consumer benefits, and research opportunities. J. Interact. Mark. **27**(3), 141–157 (2013)
2. Entertainment Software Association: Essential facts about the computer and video game industry (2014). http://www.theesa.com/facts/pdfs/esa_ef_2014.pdf
3. PC Gamer: Infographic shows $13 billion spent worldwide on MMOs in 2012 (2013). http://www.pcgamer.com/2012/12/15/mmo-infographic/
4. Lo, N., Chen, S.: A study of anti-robot agent mechanisms and process on online games. In: IEEE International Conference on Intelligence and Security Informatics, pp. 203–205 (2008)
5. Wu, J., Li, P., Rao, S.: Why they enjoy virtual game words? An empirical investigation. J. Electr. Commer. Res. **9**(3), 219–230 (2008)
6. Semeijn, J., Riel, A., Birgelen, M., Steukens, S.: E-services and offline fulfillment: how e-loyalty is crated. Manag. Serv. Qual. **15**(2), 182–194 (2005)
7. NewZoo: 2016 Global Games Market Report (2017). https://newzoo.com/insights/articles/global-games-market-reaches-99-6-billion-2016-mobile-generating-37/
8. Sweetser, P., Wyeth, P.: GameFlow: a model for evaluating player enjoyment in games. ACM Comput. Entertain. **3**(3), 3–24 (2005)
9. Hsu, C., Lu, H.: Consumer behavior in online game communities: a motivational factor perspective. Comput. Hum. Behav. **23**, 1642–1659 (2004)
10. Choi, D., Kim, J.: Why people continue to play online games: in search of critical design factors to increase customer loyalty to online contents. Cyberpsychol. Behav. **7**(1), 11–24 (2004)
11. Waarts, E., van Everdingen, Y.M.: The influence of national culture on the adoption status of innovations. Eur. Manag. J. **23**(6), 601–610 (2005)
12. Davis, S.: Managing Corporate Culture. Ballinger Publishing Co., Cambridge (1984)
13. Hall, E.: Beyond Culture. Anchor Press, Garden City (1976)
14. Trompenaars, F.: Riding the Waves of Culture: Understanding Cultural Diversity in Business. Nicholas Brealey Publishing, London (1994)
15. Hofstede, G.: Culture's Consequences. Sage Publications, Thousand Oaks (2000)
16. Krumbholz, M., Maiden, N.: The implementation of enterprise resource planning packages in different organizational and national cultures. Inf. Syst. **26**, 185–204 (2001)
17. Cronbach, L.: Essentials of Psychology Testing. Harper and Row, New York (1970)

A Case Study for Enhancing Mobile Games' Immersion in Terms of User Interface Design

Xiaoneng Jin[1][(✉)] and Jing Guan[2]

[1] College of Design and Innovation, Tongji University, Shanghai, China
Xiaoneng_jin@163.com
[2] School of Design, The Hong Kong Polytechnic University, Hong Kong, China
Guanjing99@gmail.com

Abstract. The mobile games have a huge potential market and the total revenue is predicted to increase at more than 10% per year through 2020. Therefore, it will make mobile games as the largest segment of the global video games industry by a wide margin at that time. In addition, it is widely accepted by gamers, developers, and game researchers that immersion is one of the most important parts of game play experience. This paper will report a case study about researching how to enhance mobile gamer's immersion in terms of a third person shooter games' user interface design. We begin by reviewing existing notions of engagement and immersion in gaming experience, and then survey related practical and theoretical work about methods increasing gamers' immersion, in the context of user interface design. Then, we proposed four key methods, which can enhance the games' immersion in terms of user interface design. By using these methods, designer can design the game UIs efficiently, no matter design new UIs or iterate old UI versions.

Keywords: Mobile game · Immersion · User interface design · Third person shooter game

1 Introduction

This paper reports a case study about researching how to enhance mobile gamers' immersion in terms of a third person shooter game's user interface design. It is widely accepted by gamers, developers, and game researchers that immersion is one of the most important parts of game play experience [1]. In the general context of gaming, the term immersion can be described as an experience involved and engaged in the imagination space in which the game is played [2].

Since the small-size screen is a mainly influence factor of the immersion experience of mobile games, we conducted a practical mobile game demo to research how to enhance mobile game players' immersion in terms of user interface design, by developing a game demo named *"The Legend of Demon Hunter"*, which is a third-person shooter (TPS) and role-playing game (RPG). The primary goal of this study was to test our assumptions about factors, which could increase the sense of engagement and immersion gameplay. We began by reviewing existing notions of engagement and immersion in gaming experience, and then surveyed related practical and theoretical

© Springer International Publishing AG 2017
M. Kurosu (Ed.): HCI 2017, Part II, LNCS 10272, pp. 54–62, 2017.
DOI: 10.1007/978-3-319-58077-7_5

work concentrated on methods increasing gamers' immersion, in the context of user interface design. Then, we proposed some key factors to enhance the game's immersion in terms of user interface design.

2 Background

According to Lewis's report [3], The mobile games have a huge potential market and the total revenue is predicted to increase at more than 10% per year through 2020. Therefore, it will make mobile games as the largest segment of the global video games industry by a wide margin at that time. Extensive previous research about immersion in PC and Console gaming has been conducted (e.g. [4, 5]) since the 1990s [6], however, it still remains unclear whether mobile games have the possibility and potential to be immersive [7].

Several studies support the contention that screen size is an important variable for game immersion. Lombard and Ditton [6] stated that a 52" color television screen with surround sound could bring participants a better sense of participation and involvement than a 5" black and white television with mono sound. Besides, Hou et al. [8] research also supports the greater presence that players could have greater enjoyment and engagement on larger screens than on small portable screens. However, most of these studies only concentrated on passive viewing and for video games. There are also some other factors, such as tasks, internal consistency and fantasy, contributing to games' immersive experience [7].

From our own experience, the game designers, game artists, and software developers play a relevant important roles during the PC games' developing. On the contrary, the user experience department is to some extent ignored. Mobile games are different from PC games. Since mobile games' market owns a variety of games and software packages are relatively small, the players become lacking of patience. If mobile games can't attract players in a short time, the players will quit the game immediately, and no longer open it. What's more, players will uninstall the game for releasing the store space. Therefor, except for the game playability, the UI plays an important role in the era of mobile game. In fact, a better quality of game UI can reduce the learning times greatly and give users game immersion deeply. The relation between Game designer, Game artist, Software developer during the era of mobile game and PC game are shown respectively in Fig. 1.

To sum up, UX plays an important role in the era of mobile game, and researchers and designers pay attention to improve the user experience of mobile devices. For instance, they focus on how to use the mobile Apps efficiently, easy to learn and decrease the misunderstanding, and etc. But most of them are the tools Apps of mobile and seldom focus on the immersion. However, Mobile games as one special kind of mobile Apps, which have difference between game and normal tools Apps dramatically, especially in the immersion area. Hence, our study will focus on the innovation design of UI for improving the game immersion and enhancing the game players' immersion. In addition, in this paper, we summarize some design methods for readers to learn.

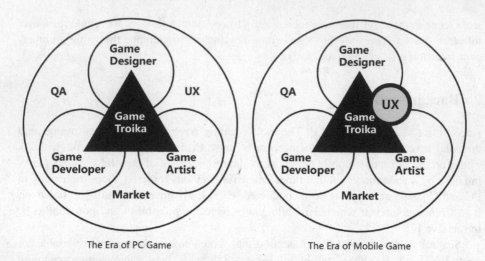

The Era of PC Game   The Era of Mobile Game

Fig. 1. The relation between game designer, game artist and game developer

3   Case Studies

Based on the problems mentioned above, we summarize some design methods (or guidelines), which can help designers to improve the immersion of games: 1. Hidden and Highlight Widgets Properly. 2. Combining Widgets Together. 3. Strong Corresponding & Instant Feedback & Motion Design. 4. Operational Consistency (Fig. 2).

In this case study, we conducted a practical mobile game demo to research how to enhance mobile game players' immersion in terms of user interface design. We designed some game demo's UIs through four design methods mentioned above. This game demo is named *"The Legend of Demon Hunter"*, which is a third- person shooter (TPS) and role-playing game (RPG).

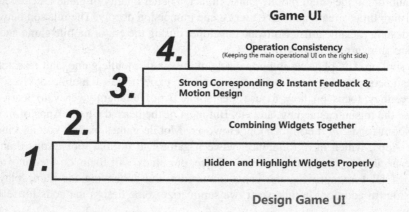

Fig. 2. Four methods to enhance the immersion of game

3.1 Hidden and Highlight Widgets Properly

Hidden and highlight widgets properly: hiding the widgets when a specific function has not been activated, so that players could pay more attention to the game flow instead of the widgets.

In this game, we improve the game immersion by refining the buff bar. We didn't consider much about the colour and shape of the buff bar from the very beginning. The buff bar was designed in the normal style, which is filled the same colour from the head to bottom. We can see the new UI design of the buff bar below (Fig. 3). As players don't need to pay attention to the buff bar in the early time, the buff bar uses the low bright colour that is similar with the game's background. The players can focus on the core experience of the game- "Charge Shooting". When the buff's process bar approaches the terminal point, the shape of the buff bar becomes stronger and the colour becomes brighter, which attracts players' attention and encourages them to get a buff. Table below (Table 1) shows that the different status of buff bar.

Fig. 3. New UI design of the buff bar (Color figure online)

Table 1. The different status of buff bar

3 Status	Examples	Interpretations
A		From the beginning, the buff bar uses the dark colour that is similar with the game's background
B		The buff bar's shape becomes stronger and the colour becoms brighter
C		The change of colour and shape attracts players' attention and encourage them to get a buff

3.2 Combining Widgets Together

Combining widgets together: combining the widgets with similar function together to be an independent widget, which enable them to be browsed and used easily. Especially for some widgets that have important effect on players' experience, make sure that they are designed tidily enough, so that making more space for the game graphics.

The figure below illustrates the difference "Charge Shooting" widgets between before and after. Before, the progress bar of charge shooting and sight are divided as two parts respectively. Because their distance is not near, player's eyes must pay attention to both the progress bar and the sight. Hence, player's eyes must up and down to see whether the process bar is finished. Obviously, the player's flow is interrupted easily. For improving this design, we iterate the UI design and design a new one, which makes progress bar and the sight as a combined widget, so that players can more focus on the target and enhance the game immersion dramatically. Besides, the game will have more space for showing the graphics instead of UIs (Fig. 4).

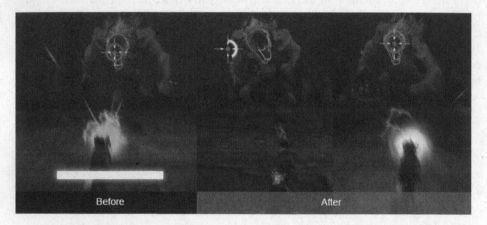

Fig. 4. The different "Charge Shooting" widgets between before and after

3.3   Strong Corresponding and Instant Feedback and Motion Design

Strong corresponding: the color of the ammunition is the same with the shot. When players touch the fire ammunition button (B), the color of the shot button (C) is orange too; when players change the fire ammunition to the ice ammunition, the shoot button's color will switch to purple, which enhances the relationship and correspondence between them (Fig. 5).

Instant feedback & motion design: When gun is loading ammunition, the decoration of the small angle behind the button will walk around. On the one hand, the motion of instant feedback tells the user that the current button has been clicked. On the other hand, it makes the game more interesting and more like real shooting game, especially when the ammunition filled the charger one by one and action synchronized with the role, which seems very authentic. Besides, it will reduce the user's boring feelings as the loading lasts 2 s during which time player can't do anything. Hence, focusing on motion of UI will transfer user's attention and enhance the games' immersion dramatically.

In addition, instant feedback also includes the special status' feedback, which can enhance the games' immersion as well. In this case, we design three special status UIs, such as lacking of blood, shooting tip and damage texts. There are three special status

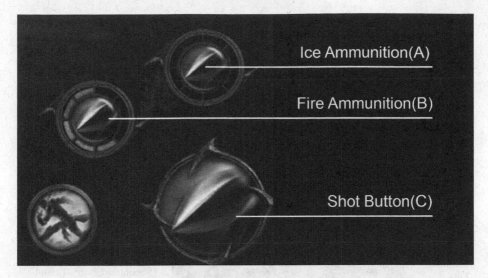

Fig. 5. The explanation of operational buttons of game (Color figure online)

UI examples shown in Table 2. (1) Lacking of blood: When player is lacking of blood, the screen corners will shows red. It is directly to tell the player that the role is lacking of blood. It makes the players feel more tension. But when the players kill the monster finally, it will build up toward a climax. (2) Warning tips: Warning tip is a good way to remind the players to do some important actions. On the one hand, it makes the player feel nervous. On the other hand, when the tips come out with the special game sound together, it contributes to enhance the immersion. In this case, the monster makes the roaring sound, and the left of screen shows a shooting tip (Shoot head, hurry!) simultaneously so that remind the players to have a "charge shooting" to interrupt the boss's roaring. Otherwise, the players will get critical damage from the monster. (3) Damage Texts: The normal damage is a small text with white color. On the contrary, the critical damage will show a big text with red color. Because of the contrast, the players get a great sense of accomplishment and enhance the sense of immersion.

3.4   Operation Consistency

Operation consistency is a way to reduce user's learning time and promote user's flow. When we design the UIs of the case game - *"The Legend of Demon Hunter"*, we think that most people use right hand. As a result, in the early design phase, we determine the right hand as the main operating hand. At the same time, the main operating buttons are placed in the right side of the thumb's fan-shape hot area so that users can touch the button through the right thumb efficiently. In addition, the information layers are displayed on the left. When we design the game's UIs, this principle is executed from beginning to the end. There are three game UI examples shown in Table 3: Main operating UI, Chapter choosing UI, game results UI, which are the most familiar UIs in the TPS mobile game. It illustrates that the main operating buttons of game users' interfaces are placed on the right and the information contents are placed on the left.

Table 2. The UI examples of special feedback status

Special Status UIs	Examples	Interpretations
Lacking of Blood		When player is lacking of blood, the screen corners will shows red. It is directly to tell the player that the role is lacking of blood
Shooting Tips		The monster is roaring and coming out the roaring sound, and the left of screen shows a shooting tip (Shoot head, hurry!) simultaneously so that remind the players to have a "charge shooting" to interrupt the boss's roaring
Damage Texts		The normal damage is a small text with white color. On the contrary, the critical damage will shows that a big text with red color

4 Discussion and Future Work

In this study we developed a TPS mobile game and concluded four important methods for enhancing the immersion in terms of game user interface. According to these methods, people can not only design the immersive game UIs quickly but also examine the game UIs efficiently.

However, designing game UI is a complex process, especially when designer want to attain a good immersion of game. These four aspects mentioned above are just a small part that can enhance the immersion of game. In the future research, on the one hand, we will explore more design methods of game UI. On the other hand, we will evaluate our game demo by conducting a qualitative evaluation study. During the evaluation study, we will involve 30 participants who have different degrees of prior experience of playing mobile games. We measured participants' immersion by letting them complete Jennett's 31-item Immersion Questionnaire [9] after playing the game.

Table 3. The UI examples of right-hand operation

Game UI Category	Examples	Interpretations
Main Operation UI		The main operating buttons is placed on the right so that users can touch the button through the right thumb efficiently
Chapter Choosing UI		The chapter choosing buttons and the game start button are placed on the right side so that users can touch the button through right hand efficiently. Besides, the content of the chapters is placed on the left
Game Results UI		The two buttons of "Retry" and "Next" are both placed in the fan-shaped hot area of the right hand so that users can touch the button through the right thumb efficiently

5   Conclusion

This paper reports an case study about researching how to enhance mobile gamers' immersion in terms of a third person shooter game's user interface design. We explored some new methods for improving the immersion in designing UI of hardcore mobile game area. Four methods for strengthening the immersion of mobile games below:

- Hidden and Highlight Widgets Properly.
- Combining Widgets Together.
- Strong Corresponding & Instant Feedback & Motion Design.
- Operation Consistency.

By using these methods, designer can design the game UIs efficiently, no matter design new UIs or iterate old UI versions. Most importantly, the game will obtain better sense of immersion, especially when these methods guide the designers to design game UIs.

Acknowledgments. The game UI studies in this paper involve *"The Legend of Demon Hunter"* which is a game demo from Mini4 Team in Netease Games. Thanks to game designers and developers involved: Yang Fang, Wei Haomin, Tang Zhangpeng, Wang Qiang, Xu Chunwei, Lin Yujie, etc. At the same time, thanks to the academy of Netease Games, we have a chance to study the UI immersion of game through taking part in the practical mobile game development. We also appreciate the senior game interaction designer: Zhai Nan who provides some key advices to us.

References

1. Brown, E., Cairns, P.: A grounded investigation of game immersion. In: Proceedings of CHI 2004, pp. 1279–1300. ACM Press (2004)
2. Adams, E., Rollings, A.: Fundamentals of Game Design. Prentice Hall, Upper Saddle River (2006)
3. Ward, L.: Worldwide Mobile and Handheld Gaming Forecast, 2016–2020. IDC
4. Qin, H., Patrick Rau, P.-L., Salvendy, G.: Measuring player immersion in the computer game narrative. Int. J. Hum. Comput. Interact. **25**(2), 107–133 (2009)
5. Nacke, L., Lindley, C.A.: Flow and immersion in first-person shooters: measuring the player's gameplay experience. In: Proceedings of the 2008 Conference on Future Play: Research, Play, Share. ACM (2008)
6. Lombard, M., Ditton, T.: At the heart of it all: the concept of presence. J. Comput.-Med. Commun. **3**(2), 107–133 (1997)
7. Lavender, T., Gromala, D.: Portable presence: can mobile games be immersive games. In: International Conference on Entertainment Computing, vol. 2012 (2012)
8. Hou, J., et al.: Effects of screen size, viewing angle, and players' immersion tendencies on game experience. Comput. Hum. Behav. **28**(2), 617–623 (2012)
9. Jennett, C., et al.: Measuring and defining the experience of immersion in games. Int. J. Hum. Comput. Stud. **66**(9), 641–661 (2008)

Who is with You? Integrating a Play Experience into Online Video Watching via Danmaku Technology

Lili Liu[1,2(✉)], Ayoung Suh[2], and Christian Wagner[2]

[1] College of Economics and Management, Nanjing University of Aeronautics and Astronautics, Nanjing, China
llili2@cityu.edu.hk
[2] School of Creative Media and Department of Information Systems, City University of Hong Kong, Kowloon Tong, Hong Kong SAR
{ahysuh, c.wagner}@cityu.edu.hk

Abstract. Online video watching coupled with audience interaction through comments overlaid on the video screen is becoming increasingly popular in China. By incorporating features of social media into the design, the underlying Danmaku technology enables users to post comments while viewing videos. The comments are then projected as scrolling titles onto the video screen, invoking a lively and playful viewing experience. Little is yet known about the unique nature of the technology and its attraction, despite growing scholarly and practical interest in Danmaku technology. In this paper, we investigate user experiences to understand the nature and impact of Danmaku technology. We report on a focus group discussion with experienced users of Danmaku video sites. Our findings suggest that the Danmaku functions (interface design, control, augmented display, anonymity) and Danmaku comments (density, relevance, timeliness, subdivision) play essential roles in creating a play experience (company, fun, emotional release, sense of belonging, attentiveness). Design principles and possible applications of Danmaku technology are discussed.

Keywords: Danmaku video · Danmaku function · Danmaku content · Play experience · Distractive experience

1 Introduction

Watching videos online is becoming increasingly popular in China. According to a recent report from China Internet Network Information Center (CNNIC), online video viewership reached 513 million in June 2016. On the internet, video sites, such as YouTube, exemplify a social environment in which rich levels of computer-mediated interaction between audiences are facilitated [8]. Viewers can share opinions related to videos through comments and rating systems. Instead of watching videos passively and alone, audiences continuously demonstrate their desire for interaction with others and a technologically advanced viewing experience [2, 14]. For instance, some viewers watch videos online while simultaneously chatting with others using a text chat feature [18], thus creating a more compelling social experience [14]. Doughty et al. [5, 6] note

© Springer International Publishing AG 2017
M. Kurosu (Ed.): HCI 2017, Part II, LNCS 10272, pp. 63–73, 2017.
DOI: 10.1007/978-3-319-58077-7_6

that social media services (e.g., Twitter) are also changing the way people consume online videos, with audiences watching videos while using social media to broadcast their thoughts and emotions.

The introduction of Danmaku technology on video sites has provided new opportunities for richer viewing experiences [9]. Incorporating social media features, Danmaku technology enables audiences to post comments while watching videos. The comments are overlaid as synchronous, written text on the videos, visible to the author and other viewers [15]. Danmaku technology broadcasts a user's expressed thoughts, sentiments, opinions, and emotions related to what he or she is watching as short on-screen comments. The comments are delivered as a "stream of consciousness" and appear overlaid on the video, synchronized to the video timeline but unevenly distributed. At key moments, numerous scrolling comments are projected on the video screen. The comments somewhat resemble the visual impact of a barrage of bullets in early 2D shooter games, which led to the name Danmaku (Japanese for "bullet curtain"). Figure 1 presents a screenshot of a video with Danmaku comments enabled on Bilibili.com.

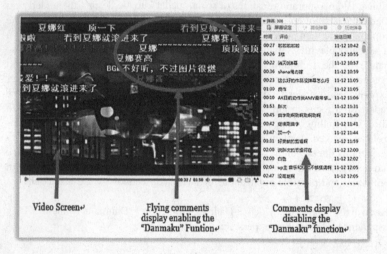

Fig. 1. A screenshot of a video on Bilibili.com (source: http://www.bilibili.com/video/av715040/)

The first Danmaku video site, NicoNico Douga, originated in Japan in December 2006. Since then, Danmaku technology has been enthusiastically adopted in China. The most popular Chinese Danmaku site is Bilibili.com. The site was originally marketed to a subcultural user base through a focus on anime, comics, and games. Later, site managers tried reach a larger, more mainstream audience by expanding the brand to include diverse videos, such as movies, dramas, and variety shows. Danmaku use appears to have greatly affected Bilibili, which has maintained a top 10 ranking among Chinese video sites despite being launched only recently (2009) and having no major financial backing. Alexa.com ranked Bilibili at 231 among the world's most successful sites (January 23, 2017). Other mainstream video sites in Mainland China, including LETV, IQIYI, and Tudou, have since been providing Danmaku functionality as well. Table 1 summarizes the key differences between Danmaku and traditional video sites.

Table 1. Danmaku video sites vs. conventional video sites

	Danmaku video sites	Conventional video sites
Location of comments	Displayed as flying subtitles overlaid on the video screen, moving from right to left	Displayed in the comment area, separate from the video screen
Timeline of comments	Broadcasted to audiences in real-time, synchronized to the video timeline	Broadcasted to audiences as a thread ordered according to the historical time when the comments were made
Examples	Bilibili.com	YouTube.com

As a result, many people are changing how they consume videos. However, research interest has been lagging behind popular interest. For instance, prior research investigated either the correlation between comments and video popularity [19] or how Chinese tags for foreign movies are accepted among viewers [13]. Thus, motivations and outcomes of watching videos with overlaid comments remain under-investigated. Contradicting popular interest, scholars in human computer interaction (HCI) have contended that reading text would distract the user from watching the video, thus disrupting the viewing experience [18]. In fact, empirical evidence shows that audiences are enthusiastic about watching videos with Danmaku [3]. Thus, we conducted an exploratory study of the nature of Danmaku video watching, with the aim of identifying why audiences favor Danmaku video sites.

2 The Play Theory of Mass Communication

We draw on the play theory of mass communication to understand users' motivations and the consequences of watching Danmaku videos. The theory is based on a primary assumption: media users are extremely active and engaged in the media consumption process [11]. The play theory of mass communication contends that the masses use media to fulfill their own desires for play instead of as a serious source of information or education [16]. The author [16] introduced his belief in audience participation as follows: "I don't think of media consumption as merely entertainment in a non-ego-involving sense, but at its best as a highly developed form of subjective play." This absorption and the decreasing self-consciousness that it inspires are vital to achieving the individual development that characterizes communications play.

Modern mass media, coupled with the globalization of information dissemination exchange, has created an information-driven and knowledge-based society; it has also led to the play theory of mass communication being criticized for its narrow focus. After all, people use mass and interactive media not just for play, but also for education and information [1]. The maturing of the Internet era, bringing about a new interactivity within media, is again profoundly changing the theoretical and practical context of communication theory. For instance, it appears that the Danmaku phenomenon is, as the author described, emphasizing communication and providing subjective play experiences for audiences via instant and highly synchronized information [20, 21]. Therefore, rediscovering the play theory of communication may provide theoretical support for identifying characteristics of the play experience in watching Danmaku videos.

3 Methodology

We employed the focus group discussion method for this exploratory study to carry out in-depth group interviews. In focus group research, participants are selected because they are a purposive, although not necessarily representative, sampling of a specific population. The group is "focused" on a given topic [17], leading to the development of a theoretical understanding of cognitive, behavioral, situational, and environmental factors [10]. Following Gwinner et al. [7], we recruited thirteen postgraduate students as participants. Three or four focus groups are usually recommended unless the research needs to address many research questions [11]. The thirteen participants were thus assigned to three groups (five in group 1, five in group 2, and three in group 3). All participants had self-reported experiences in watching Danmaku videos, of varied length and intensity.

All groups met the focus group moderator in the same room. Before the discussion, all participants were asked to provide demographic information (see Table 2).

Table 2. Participant demographics

Group	Participant ID	Gender	Age	Frequency of usage	Average duration of usage	Favorite video type
Group 1	1-A	F	23	Everyday	1 h	Animation, music videos
	1-B	F	22	4–6 times per week	1–2 h	Drama
	1-C	F	24	Once a week	2 h	Movie, drama
	1-D	F	21	Once per 3 months	3–5 h	Drama
	1-E	F	22	Twice per month	6 h	Variety show, animation
Group 2	2-A	M	24	Once a week	2–3 h	Drama
	2-B	F	22	2–3 times per week	3–4 h	Animation, drama, music videos
	2-C	F	22	Once a week	2–3 h	Drama
	2-D	F	21	Once a month	1–2 h	Documentary, drama, variety show
	2-E	F	21	Once per 2 months	3 h	Variety show, drama
Group 3	3-A	M	21	Once a month	1–2 h	Documentary
	3-B	F	22	1–2 times per month	1–2 h	Variety show
	3-C	F	23	Everyday	2–4 h	Animation, game videos

Participants were then seated in a circle to discuss their experiences. All groups met with the same moderator. Each focus group discussion lasted for 1 h. The moderator recorded the discussion, which was held in Chinese. Afterwards, two bilingual PhD students separately translated the discussion into English. The PhD students then compared translations and provided a final English version of the discussion.

4   Results

4.1   Danmaku Function

We extracted four components of Danmaku functionality: interface design, control, augmented display, and anonymity.

Interface Design. Interface design refers to the design of video sites. Participant 1-A said, "The ease of use of the interface is the key factor that determines whether I continuously use a particular video site or not." Participant 2-B added, "I like to use Bilibili because the videos are clearly classified into different categories. Thus, it is very easy to find videos I am interested in according to the classification." Participant 3-B observed, "The most popular videos on Bilibili.com are updated on the homepage frequently and in a timely manner. Users are always aware of what is popular."

Control. Control is the degree to which a person believes that using a particular system is effortless [4]. Participants emphasized the importance of control in generating a play experience. For example, Participant 1-C said, "I am able to customize my comments, such as text color, text size, and text location." Participant 2-D said, "I am able to filter the Danmaku comments. For example, I can set up some keywords in the Danmaku system, and then insults, quarrels, and different perspectives containing these keywords are blocked and not shown when I watch the video. By doing this, I may selectively read the comments I like." Participant 3-A remarked, "There is a peer-moderation system on Danmaku video sites. If there are any inappropriate comments, I am able to report them to administrators. The administrators delete inappropriate comments very quickly, which makes the Danmaku atmosphere friendlier."

Augmented Display. Part of the appeal of Danmaku video sites is that, compared with comments posted in an area separate from the videos, audiences are able to add comments while watching videos and the comments are shown as moving subtitles overlaid on the video screen. Furthermore, during playback, the comments appear at the particular point in the video timeline when they were posted originally. The resulting augmented display is composed of two sub-dimensions: (1) comments are augmented with the video screen, and (2) comments are augmented through the video timeline. Participant 1-E said, "The comments are projected directly on the video as part of a scrolling information feed that moves from right to left." Participant 2-A added, "The comments are projected into the comment feed based on the point in time during viewing that they were input by the user."

Anonymity. All of the Danmaku comments are shown without attribution, so the mode of communication is completely anonymous. Anonymity encourages viewers to add comments. Participant 1-D highlighted this: "Anonymity makes me more willing to post comments and express my real feelings". Participant 2-A added, "In an anonymous context, I don't feel the pressure that I have to post something right or something that others like."

4.2 Danmaku Content

We extracted four aspects of Danmaku comments: density, relevance, timeliness, and specificity.

Comment Density. Comment density refers to information introduced per time unit [12]. Low comment density indicates that little communication is triggered by the video, while high comment density indicates the opposite. Participant 3-C expressed, "I don't like to watch videos with low density because it feels like that there are not many other viewers, which is boring. I also don't like to watch videos with high density because there are too many comments that cover the videos, preventing me from watching videos." Participant 1-B added, "Moderate comment density is preferred. In that case, I can watch the video and the comments at the same time, which for me is great fun."

Comment Relevance. Comment relevance refers to whether the comment is relevant to the video content. Participant 2-E said, "I like comments that are relevant to the video content. For example, when there is a sad atmosphere, comments such as 'so sad' and 'cry me a river' resonate with me." Participant 1-C said, "When I was watching *House M.D.*, I did not understand the meaning of a medical term. Then viewers left comments that explained the term precisely, which made me feel very good." Participant 3-C said, "I hate jokes when a sad scene is playing, which ruin the aesthetics."

Comment Timeliness. Comment timeliness refers to comments related to a specific scenario are shown at the appropriate playback time. Participant 2-B said, "For example, if I was watching a 10-minute video, the comments about the content at the fifth minute should be posted and displayed at that time. If you posted a comment at the 6th minute, the video may be presenting a totally different subject, so your comment would turn out to be irrelevant."

Comment Specificity. Comment specificity refers to whether the comments are allocated to and specified for a specific playback time. Participant 1-B observed, "Most of the comments on conventional video sites are general feedback about the entire video; there are rarely comments on a particular scene. Actually, when I was watching a video, I had strong feelings about particular emotional scenes rather than the whole video. Thus, I prefer to read the comments targeted to specific scenes."

4.3 Play Experiences

We identified five elements contributing to play experience: company, fun, emotional release, sense of belonging, and attentiveness.

Company. All of the participants reported a feeling of being with company while watching videos with Danmaku comments. Participant 1-C said, "Comments overlaid on videos make me feel that there are people somewhere who are watching the videos together with me." Participant 2-E added, "The anonymous comments help to break the restriction of time and location, which makes me feel that at this moment, someone else is watching the same video with me, and is trying to communicate with me by adding Danmaku comments." Participant 2-C stated, "On conventional online video sites, prior audiences' comments are listed as a thread. It is easy to tell when they posted the comments and who the commenters are. If I find that the latest comments on a video were posted a long time ago, for example, two years ago, this makes me feel that the video is out-of-date and that nobody is watching it anymore. I will not leave a comment on the video as I feel that it is a waste of time since nobody will watch this video and read my comments. However, on the Danmaku video sites, users are unaware of the time the comments were posted. Once I play a video, every comment is perceived as having been posted at the time I am watching it. Thus, I leave comments, and I believe that my comments will be read and replied to by the next viewers."

Fun. Viewers watch Danmaku videos for fun. Participant 1-A, 1-E, 2-B, 2-C, 3-B and 3-C all agreed. 3-C voiced, "I feel very entertained when I watch videos with overlaid comments, because I can always find novel, amusing, and inspiring comments."

Emotional Release. Audiences watch Danmaku videos to express their feelings with others. Participant 2-C, for instance, remarked, "When I have some feeling in my mind while watching a video, I am eager to express it. The Danmaku system helps me accomplish this." Participant 1-D added, "When I have strong feelings about a scene, I can immediately express it at the specific playback time, which makes me feel an emotional release."

Sense of Belonging. Users watch Danmaku videos because they favor collective forms of membership and participation, and because they enjoy belonging to a group that shares the same interest [3]. Participant 3-B affirmed, "Compared with the element of strong relationships, which involves attachment or intimacy, I am satisfied with superficial relationships, such as the sense of belonging elicited by finding a group of people who have similar perspectives. I am not seeking to build one-to-one relationships with other viewers in the way that I do on social network sites." Participant 3-C stated, "There is no need to know who posted the Danmaku comments. What I really care about is whether other viewers share similar opinions or emotions about the videos." Participant 1-E noted, "When I think some part of a video is hilarious, I am very happy to see that others have the same feelings as I do. I am not the only one who finds it funny."

Attentiveness. Watching Danmaku videos helps maintain user focus on this behavior. Participant 1-D mentioned, "There are some videos that I find less enjoyable, and thus, I cannot watch them for more than 10 min. However, when the videos are combined with Danmaku comments, I can watch full videos that last for one hour. Interesting Danmaku comments make my viewing experience more enjoyable and help maintain my attention."

4.4   Distracting Experiences

We summarized distracting experiences as perceived intrusiveness and cognition overload. Concerning perceived intrusiveness, Participant 2-A explained, "The type of videos I am going to watch determines whether I will watch Danmaku comments or not. For example, I like Danmaku comments when I am watching entertaining contents, such as variety shows, music videos, or dramas. However, when I am going to watch movies or serious dramas, Danmaku comments are distracting" As for cognition overload, Participant 3-C mentioned, "I can't watch videos and Danmaku comments together for a long time, since processing the information from both sides makes me feel stressed. I turn off the Danmaku function if I feel tired."

We summarized the nomination frequency of above mentioned sub-dimensions in Table 3. In particular, each sub-dimension has been nominated by more than half of the group discussion participants. For example, ten out of thirteen participants nominated interface design, which provides additional justification for the sub-dimensions we have identified.

Table 3.   Number of sub-dimension nominations

Construct	Sub-dimensions	Number of nominations
Danmaku function	Interface design	10/13
	Control	11/13
	Augmented display	13/13
	Anonymity	9/13
Danmaku content	Comment density	9/13
	Comment relevance	8/13
	Comment timeliness	7/13
	Comment specificity	9/13
Play experience	Company	13/13
	Fun	13/13
	Emotional release	10/13
	Sense of belonging	11/13
	Attentiveness	8/13
Distractive experience	Perceived intrusiveness	10/13
	Cognition overload	9/13

5   Discussion

People's online video watching habits are being subjected to forces of change as technology advances. Evidence from Danmaku video sites shows that media technologies are evolving from traditional mass media (e.g., YouTube) to those that can address modern audience demands for direct and instant communication, thus offering an enhanced user experience. Understanding the nature of Danmaku video watching is the focus of our study. The results of focus group discussions show that despite the obvious shortcomings (perceived intrusiveness and cognition overload), watching

Danmaku videos appears to be intriguing and attractive [3]. We attribute the attractiveness of Danmaku video sites to the facilitation of the play experience among users. Play experience is composed of five key components: company, fun, emotional release, sense of belonging, and attentiveness. Furthermore, our findings suggest that Danmaku functions (interface design, control, augmented display, anonymity) and Danmaku comments (density, relevance, timeliness, subdivision) are essential in creating the play experience. We then propose a conceptual framework based on the group discussion findings as shown in Fig. 2.

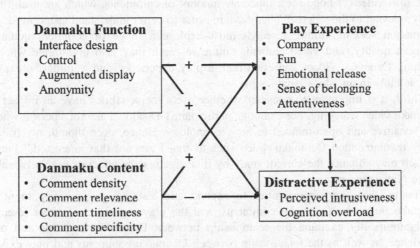

Fig. 2. Conceptual framework

The present study, though exploratory, can extend our understanding of the play theory of mass communication. By adopting the theory, we introduced the concept of play experience and found it supported by the evidence. This, in turn, implied that users consider whether they can have fun, feel that they are among company, release their emotions, and experience belonging to a group of people with similar interests. Our study also has the potential to extend the research on user participation in Danmaku video sites by examining the indicators of play experience. Thus this study adds useful knowledge about the design of Danmaku functionality and the moderation of Danmaku content to affect users' play experience, which in turn predicts users' intention to participate. In order to improve video site performance, practitioners may wish to focus on advancing Danmaku functions and regulating Danmaku comments.

Our study leaves many questions unanswered, which may trigger additional research. First, the type of video shown may determine whether audiences will display overlay comments. As participant 1-A said, "I never watch serious videos together with Danmaku comments. Most of the Danmaku comments are funny, hence not appropriate to be shown on solemn occasions. For example, during a military parade, when the presidents of different countries are gathered, it is impolite to make fun." By contrast, participant 3-C said, "I hope there are lots of Danmaku comments when I am watching a variety show. More comments will create a better play experience. Sometimes I'll wait until there are large amounts of comments before I watch the video." Further research could explore the impact of video genre or mood, and investigate how people perceive Danmaku comments.

Second, users may watch comments to obtain a utilitarian experience (e.g., information seeking). Participant 1-A, for instance, said, "I can always get useful information from the Danmaku comments. Other viewers may provide information about the background music, the actors, historical events, which I will miss if I only watch videos." In addition, participant 2-B stated, "I care more about the comment usefulness for serious videos. I hope for a moderate amount of comments, which are useful and highly relevant to the videos." Therefore, in order to better understand users' needs for information seeking, future research must explore a range of comment quantity, comment quality, and video content. Future research may also investigate whether watching Danmaku videos can elicit both a play experience and a utilitarian experience, notably in an educational setting.

Third, it is important to consider whether users' personalities have an impact on Danmaku video watching. For example, participant 1-D said, "I am not a person who is very sensitive and open-minded to new technology. Hence, even though my friends highly recommended Danmaku video sites to me, I am not that interested." Future research may enhance the current study by investigating the effect of user personality on the play experience.

Finally, there are opportunities to expand and test our propositions, to refine Danmaku functions, Danmaku comments, and the play experience. Further research could empirically examine the relationship between Danmaku functions and play experience, as well as the relationship between Danmaku comments and play experience. Given various types of video, user personalities have the potential to influence play experience in diverse ways, so it would be beneficial to conduct research incorporating these factors. Likewise, additional research is needed to examine other experiences obtained from watching Danmaku videos, notably utilitarian experiences.

Acknowledgements. This research was supported in part by grants No. CityU 11531016 from the Research Grants Council of the Hong Kong SAR awarded to the second author and CityU 11507815 awarded to the third author.

References

1. Akinjogbin, S.A., Kayode, O.O.: The play theory: a critique from the communitarian context. J. Commun. Cult. **2**(3), 111–119 (2011)
2. Cesar, P., Bulterman, D.C.A., Jansen, A.J.: Usages of the secondary screen in an interactive television environment: control, enrich, share, and transfer television content. In: Tscheligi, M., Obrist, M., Lugmayr, A. (eds.) EuroITV 2008. LNCS, vol. 5066, pp. 168–177. Springer, Heidelberg (2008). doi:10.1007/978-3-540-69478-6_22
3. Chen, Y., Gao, Q., Rau, P.L.P.: Understanding gratifications of watching danmaku videos – videos with overlaid comments. In: Rau, P.L.P. (ed.) CCD 2015. LNCS, vol. 9180, pp. 153–163. Springer, Cham (2015). doi:10.1007/978-3-319-20907-4_14

4. Davis, F.D.: Perceived usefulness, perceived ease of use, and user acceptance of information technology. MIS Q. **13**(3), 319–340 (1989)
5. Doughty, M., Rowland, D., Lawson, S.: Co-viewing live TV with digital backchannel streams. In: Proceedings of the 9th International Interactive Conference on Interactive Television, pp. 141–144. ACM (2011)
6. Doughty, M., Rowland, D., Lawson, S.: Who is on your sofa? TV audience communities and second screening social networks. In: Proceedings of the 10th European Conference on Interactive TV and Video, pp. 79–86. ACM (2012)
7. Gwinner, K.P., Gremler, D.D., Bitner, M.J.: Relational benefits in services industries: the customer's perspective. J. Acad. Mark. Sci. **26**(2), 101–114 (1998)
8. Haridakis, P., Hanson, G.: Social interaction and co-viewing with YouTube: blending mass communication reception and social connection. J. Broadcast. Electron. Media **53**(2), 317–335 (2009)
9. Johnson, D.: Polyphonic/pseudo-synchronic: animated writing in the comment feed of Nicovideo. Japan. Stud. **33**(3), 297–313 (2013)
10. Kidd, P.S., Parshall, M.B.: Getting the focus and the group: enhancing analytical rigor in focus group research. Qual. Health Res. **10**(3), 293–308 (2000)
11. Krueger, R.A., Casey, M.A.: Focus Groups: A Practical Guide for Applied Research. Sage Publications, Thousand Oaks (2014)
12. Lang, A., Park, B., Sanders-Jackson, A.N., Wilson, B.D., Wang, Z.: Cognition and emotion in TV message processing: how valence, arousing content, structural complexity, and information density affect the availability of cognitive resources. Media Psychol. **10**(3), 317–338 (2007)
13. Lin, X., Ito, E., Hirokawa, S.: Chinese tag analysis for foreign movie contents. In: Proceedings of the 13th IEEE/ ACIS International Conference on Computer and Information Science, pp. 163–166 (2014)
14. Mantzari, E., Lekakos, G., Vrechopoulos, A.: Social TV: introducing virtual socialization in the TV experience. In: Proceedings of the 1st International Conference on Designing Interactive User Experiences for TV and Video, pp. 81–84. ACM (2008)
15. Shen, Y., Chan, H., Hung, I.: Let the comments fly: the effects of flying commentary presentation on consumer judgment. In: Proceedings of the 35th International Conference of Information Systems (2014)
16. Stephenson, W.: The Play Theory of Mass Communication. Transaction Publishers, Piscataway (1964)
17. Thomas, L., Macmilian, J., Mccoll, E., Hale, C., Bond, S.: Comparison of focus group and individual interview methodology in examining patient satisfaction with nursing care. Soc. Sci. Health **1**(4), 206–220 (1995)
18. Weisz, J.D., Kiesler, S., Zhang, H., Ren, Y., Kraut, R.E., Konstan, J.A.: Watching together: integrating text chat with video. In: Proceedings of the SIGCHI Conference on Human Factors in Computing Systems, pp. 877–886. ACM (2007)
19. Wu, Z., Ito, E.: Correlation analysis between user's emotional comments and popularity measures. In: Proceedings of the IIAI 3rd International Conference on IEEE Advanced Applied Informatics (IIAIAAI), pp. 280–283 (2014)
20. Liu, H.L.: 传播游戏理论再思考. 新闻学论集 **20**, 192–196 (2008)
21. Xie, M., He, J., Feng, Z.L.: 大众传播游戏理论视角下的弹幕视频研究. 新闻界 **2**, 37–40 (2014)

Multi-screen and Multi-device Game Development

Paulo S. Mendez[1], J.C. Silva[2], and José Luís Silva[3,4,5(✉)]

[1] Universidade da Madeira, Funchal, Portugal
2054013@student.uma.pt
[2] EST/DIGARC, Instituto Politécnico do Cávado e do Ave, Barcelos, Portugal
jcsilva@ipca.pt
[3] Madeira-ITI, Funchal, Portugal
jose.luis.silva@iscte.pt
[4] Instituto Universitário de Lisboa (ISCTE-IUL), Lisbon, Portugal
[5] ISTAR-IUL, Lisbon, Portugal

Abstract. Users are interacting with an increasing number of devices and screens. However, these screens are usually used independently without collaboration between them. Although there have been several advances in multi-screen applications the game community does not seem to have fully explored this opportunity as yet. This paper presents an approach for the development of mobile multi-screen and multi-device games. The approach aims to enable and foster the creation of multi-device games sharing information via a centralized screen and is demonstrated by means of an example, the well-known Casino Roulette game. The results of a preliminary evaluation of the game are also presented.

Keywords: Multi-screen · Multi-device · Game development

1 Introduction

Nowadays users have become accustomed to carrying several devices (e.g. smartphone, tablet) in addition to being able to use devices available in the environment (e.g. screens). This might be beneficial as users have several screens available to interact with at any one time, but it might also pose some drawbacks such as how the user divides their attention between devices. The multitude of devices that can be interacted with simultaneously has triggered opportunities such as multi-screen and multi-device applications development and has enabled the emergence of improvements both in terms of user experience and methods of interaction offered. In fact, new applications are being developed, from apps with distributed interfaces through to games using several devices simultaneously (e.g. a smartphone and a smart TV).

Despite all advancements that have been made in this field and surprisingly, for us, there is no game available in the IOS and Android app stores which explores this concept. Indeed, several applications use inter-device communication technologies but most of them focus on chat and data transfer. These facts together with the desire to provide a different user experience has motivated the development of this work. This

© Springer International Publishing AG 2017
M. Kurosu (Ed.): HCI 2017, Part II, LNCS 10272, pp. 74–83, 2017.
DOI: 10.1007/978-3-319-58077-7_7

work presents the development of an approach for the creation of games based on several screens and devices.

The paper presents an analysis of the state of the art in Sect. 2. Based on this analysis, the added value of the proposed approach and its architecture are presented in Sect. 3. In Sects. 4 and 5 a case study to illustrate the approach and the results of a preliminary user study are respectively presented. Finally, conclusions and future work are outlined in Sect. 6.

2 State of the Art

Nowadays, some users frequently use several devices "simultaneously". For instance, watching TV while interacting with their laptop or checking text messages on their smartphone. In several situations, sharing information between devices is valuable. Motivated by this situation multi-screen and multi-device solutions have been developed.

Some solutions like Allshare [1] or Chromecast [2] enable sharing of content across connected devices. Other solutions focus on facilitating the creation of multi-screen applications. Chmielewski and Walczak [3] present a uniform way of building smart multi-device applications. Bassboss et al. [4] present an approach for developing multi-screen applications and enabling traditional web applications to use multi-screen capabilities with minimal effort. Along the same lines, Sarkis et al. [5] present a refactoring system that splits a web application into parts ready for distribution across devices. This means that existing web applications based on a single-screen can be transformed into multi-screen applications. Other works focused on the development of second screen approaches (e.g. [6]).

In the game community, some approaches have explored this aspect. For instance, Nintendo 3DS [7] possesses two screens and the associated games use both but without any centralized device. Wu et al. [8] developed a multi-screen cyber-physical video game. The developed game uses inertial sensors and 4 screens without using any centralized device. Some physical casinos have a Casino Roulette video game instead of a physical version. This video game is like the one illustrated in this paper but was developed with the sole purpose of being based in a casino and it is not mobile like ours. This means that players are not able to play it with their own devices.

Instant Places [9] enables users to interact with public displays using their own devices. This approach is similar to ours but is not a game. Improvements are being made in the game community in several areas, developments [10, 11], applications [12, 13], interaction among others however, we are unaware of any mobile multi-screen and multi-device game that makes use of a centralized screen working as a game board shared by all players.

3 Approach

This section describes the proposed approach both at architectural and implementation levels.

3.1 Architecture

In Fig. 1, the architecture of the system is presented. The element A represents the host (e.g. the iPad) and elements B and C the clients (e.g. the iPhones). The communication between the elements was made thanks to the Multipeer Connectivity framework [14] that supports both Wi-Fi and Bluetooth technologies.

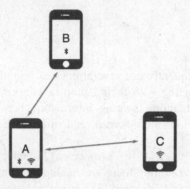

Fig. 1. Architecture using the Multipeer Connectivity framework

3.2 Implementation

The approach was developed using the Apple Xcode IDE (version 7.3) and using the Swift language. The Operating System used was the iOS9 but compatibility with more recent version is supported.

The implementation is supported by the stated communication channel (Multipeer Connectivity framework) that supports peer-to-peer connectivity and the discovery of nearby devices. In addition, the channel is used to synchronize the devices and share information between them. It is also customizable for different purposes. This initial implementation was made only for IOS devices but implementations for Android devices and inter Operating Systems are planned as future work.

The implementation was divided into 2 parts: (i) Server - usually running on iPads (to improve the User Experience due to the presence of larger screens) (ii) Clients - usually running on iPhones and, follows the typical client-server architecture. The server waits for clients to establish an individual connection with it. Each client possesses the same Graphical User Interface (GUI) which is different from the GUI of the server. All interfaces developed are responsive and were tested with devices of different screen sizes.

Once all clients are connected the game can start. On one hand, each time the server reaches a different state all clients are automatically notified. On the other hand, clients must explicitly send information to the server. In addition, a synchronization mechanism was used to guarantee that all devices are synchronized.

During development, the guarantee that new multi-screen and multi-device mobile games can be easily developed based on this approach was given particular attention.

4 The Example

The example used corresponds to the development of a casino gambling game, i.e., the Roulette game. The game was developed for IOS devices and typically works with a tablet (i.e. an iPad) in the center of the space, working as the board of the game. In addition, several smartphones (i.e. iPhones), one for each player, are used to interact with the game and to complement the information provided by the tablet. The game can be played simultaneously with up to 7 players.

Some modifications to the original version of the game were made to increase interest in the game as it is played without real money transactions. Furthermore, particular attention was given to the user experience and usability of the game, for instance, interactions such as drag and drop and ambient music are supported. Interfaces running on clients and server are presented in Figs. 2 and 3 respectively.

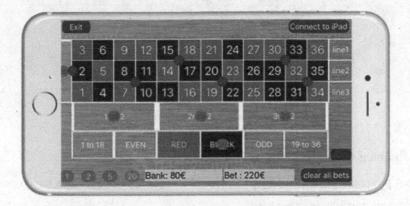

Fig. 2. Client play menu (Color figure online)

4.1 Rules of the Game

The rules of the game typically consist of choosing to place bets on either a single number or a range of numbers, colors – red or black, whether the number is even or odd, or in different groups. To determine the winning number and color, both wheel and ball spin and then the ball falls into one of the 37 colored and numbered pockets of the wheel. In the case of success the player wins a percentage of the bet otherwise the bet is lost. Several players can play simultaneously and can bet at any time before the wheel starts spinning.

Aimed at enhancing the user experience provided and since no real money is used, modifications to the original Roulette game were introduced. The goal of the game is to end the game with the most winnings. The game consists of 5 rounds with 5 spins each. The player ending the game with the highest number of winnings has won. Players do not have to bet on every spin. In addition, the option to use winnings to buy enhanced elements of the game (e.g. different board styles) was introduced.

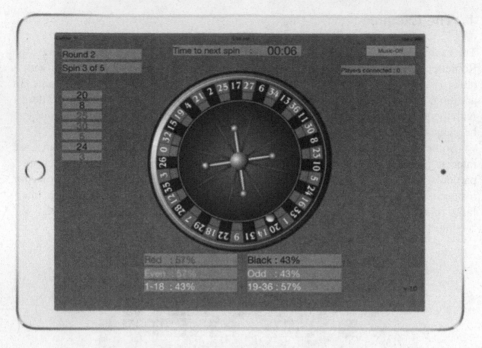

Fig. 3. Server play menu (Color figure online)

4.2   Running the Game

Figure 4 presents the initial client GUI presented to the user. It provides three options:

- Play – to start playing the game;
- Shop – to buy enhanced elements (e.g. backgrounds);
- Help – to obtain help.

Fig. 4. Initial menu of the client GUI – Roulette game

In case the user selects the play option a GUI like the one presented in Fig. 2 is presented. The user should first connect to the iPad (clicking on the top right button).

Once a successful connection is made, bets can start, varying between the value of 1 and 20 per betting chip. Drag and drop, long press and click are examples of different types of interactions supported by the game.

The shop option enables the user to access a virtual shop. Since no real money transactions are made, this shop is intended to make use of the money won.

Figure 3 presents the GUI of the iPad. It indicates the players connected, time left to the next spin, the history of winning numbers, statistics and the ability to control the ambient music.

5 Evaluation

A user study was performed with end users who played the game. At the end they were asked to complete a questionnaire that addressed four aspects (as defined in the standard USE questionnaire [15]): participant characterization; usefulness; ease of use; and user satisfaction. Subjects were asked to answer on a 7 point Likert scale with values from −3 (strongly disagree) to +3 (strongly agree). The questionnaire included open questions on the strengths and weaknesses of the game, and enabled the participants to make any further comments if they wished.

5.1 Participants

Ten people voluntarily participated in the experiment. They were not compensated for their participation. Participants were aged between 18–24 (9 males, 1 female), where 2 had completed high-school, and 8 had bachelor's degrees. With regard to current videogame playing frequency, 7 participants stated they frequently play games, 2 play irregularly and 1 occasionally. Only eight participants had already played the original Roulette game. Eight participants had never played any videogame using more than one screen prior to the experiment.

5.2 Apparatus

The developed solution was deployed with the following devices:

- iPad 2 with 9, 7 inches – working as the board of the game;
- iPhone 5 with 4 inches – working as client;
- iPhone 6 with 4, 7 inches – working as client;
- iPhone 6S Plus with 5, 5 inches – working as client;

5.3 Procedure

Groups of participants (varying between 2 and 4 members) met the experimenter and were escorted to the experiment room. The experimental procedures were discussed orally with each group and participants were encouraged to ask questions. Each participant of the group was then given an iPhone (different models were used) with the game previously installed. Participants were then asked to launch the game and connect to the board of the game (i.e. to the iPad). Afterwards the group of participants played the game until the end. Each game lasted 500 s and is composed of 5 rounds with 5 spins each. The game was played with 3 groups, 2 of them with 3 participants and one with 4. During the evaluation, the experimenter took notes of the reactions and comments made by the users. After ending the game participants were asked to answer the post-experiment questionnaire (see Appendix A) handed to them and to indicate basic demographics (gender, age, academic background) as well as relevant previous experience.

5.4   Measures

The measures used in this study were the post-experiment questionnaire and reaction while playing the game. The post-experiment questionnaire was composed of 32 questions and was divided into six sections: Subject characterization, Usefulness, Ease of Use, Ease of Learning, Satisfaction, and Open questions.

5.5   Results

Overall, the participants' reactions to the game were quite positive. According to the data collected through the 10 questionnaires all criteria but one obtained a mode of 3. The usefulness criteria which was the weakest aspect received a mode of 2.

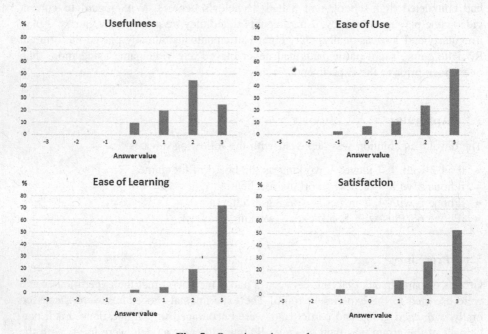

Fig. 5. Questionnaire results

Participants found it easy to learn and to use and were satisfied with it. None answered any questions negatively in Usefulness and Ease of Learning criteria and very few in Ease of Use and Satisfaction criteria (see Fig. 5).

In the open questions participants made several comments such as a re-bet option should be provided as well as an option to undo the last bet. The remaining comments were positive. Participants enjoyed playing and liked the concept of the game. Some examples of comments made are: "The game is fun to play with friends", "I liked a lot the experience", "Amazing game".

Overall the results of this preliminary user study indicated a positive reaction to the concept of the game and to the game itself. These results should be interpreted carefully due to the lower number of participants but they provide us with some insight.

6 Conclusions and Future Work

This paper presents an approach for the development of mobile games based on several screen and devices. The creation of multi-device games sharing information via a centralized screen is the type of game the approach aims to foster. We believe this approach constitutes a step towards the development of mobile multi-device and multi-screen games and an improvement for the entertainment community.

The approach was demonstrated by means of an example, the well-known Casino Roulette game. An evaluation of the game developed was accomplished with ten . participants. The results of this preliminary user study has provided us with insights that have led us to believe that games following this approach might be well accepted.

As future work, further evaluations are needed both with end users and developers. The latter is important to demonstrate that the approach can be reused in the development of new games using this concept. Furthermore, the expansion of the approach to support devices using different operating systems (e.g. Android OS) and, its exploration in different contexts (e.g. in a car) is also intended. The possibility of making these multi-screen/device games available in on-line App Stores is being considered.

Acknowledgments. José Luís Silva acknowledges support from Fundação para a Ciência e a Tecnologia (FCT, Portugal), through project UID/EEA/50009/2013.

A Appendix

I - Post-experiment questionnaire

Subject characterization	Strongly disagree			...	Strongly agree		
	-3	-2	-1	0	1	2	3
1. Age:							
2. Gender:							
3. Academic background:							
4. Do you often play computer games?							
5. Have you ever played the Original Roulette game?							
6. Have you ever played a game using more than one screen?							
Usefulness							
7. It meets my needs							
8. It does everything I would expect it to do							
Ease of Use							
9. It is easy to use.							
10. It is simple to use.							
11. It is user friendly.							
12. It requires the fewest steps possible to accomplish what I want to do with it.							
13. It is flexible.							
14. Using it is effortless.							
15. I can use it without written instructions.							
16. I don't notice any inconsistencies as I use it.							
17. Both occasional and regular users would like it.							
18. I can recover from mistakes quickly and easily.							
19. I can use it successfully every time.							
Ease of Learning							
20. I learned to use it quickly.							
21. I easily remember how to use it.							
22. It is easy to learn to use it.							
23. I quickly became skillful with it.							
Satisfaction							
24. I am satisfied with it.							
25. I would recommend it to a friend.							
26. It is fun to use.							
27. It works the way I want it to work.							
28. It is wonderful.							
29. I feel I need to have it.							
30. It is pleasant to use.							
Open Questions:							
31. Indicate what you consider the strong and weak points of the game.							
32. Other comments.							

References

1. Samsung. AllShare Play. http://www.samsung.com/us/2012-allshare-play/. Accessed 7 Feb 2017
2. Google. Chromecast. https://www.google.com/intl/pt_pt/chromecast/. Accessed 7 Feb 2017

3. Chmielewski, J., Walczak, K.: Application architectures for smart multi-device applications. In: Proceedings of the Workshop on Multi-device App Middleware, Multi-Device 2012, pp. 5:1–5:5. ACM, New York (2012). http://doi.acm.org/10.1145/2405172.2405177
4. Bassbouss, L., Tritschler, M., Steglich, S., Tanaka, K., Miyazaki, Y.: Towards a multi-screen application model for the web. In: Proceedings of the 2013 IEEE 37th Annual Computer Software and Applications Conference Workshops (COMPSACW 2013), pp. 528–533. IEEE Computer Society, Washington, D.C. (2013). http://dx.doi.org/10.1109/COMPSACW. 2013.96
5. Sarkis, M., Concolato, C., Dufourd, J.-C.: The virtual splitter: refactoring web applications for themultiscreen environment. In: Proceedings of the 2014 ACM Symposium on Document Engineering (DocEng 2014), pp. 139–142. ACM, New York (2014). http://dx. doi.org/10.1145/2644866.2644893
6. Cruickshank, L., Tsekleves, E., Whitham, R., Hill, A., Kondo, K.: Making interactive TV easier to use: interface design for a second screen approach. Des. J. **10**(3), 41–53 (2007)
7. Nintendo 3DS. http://www.nintendo.com/3ds. Accessed 20 Oct 2016
8. Wu, C.-H., Chang, Y.-T., Tseng, Y.-C.: Multi-screen cyber-physical video game: an integration with body-area inertial sensor networks. In: PerCom Workshops (2010)
9. José, R., Otero, N., Izadi, S., Harper, R.: Instant places: using Bluetooth for situated interaction in public displays. IEEE Pervasive Comput. **7**(4), 52–57 (2008)
10. Gomes, T.E.O., Abade, T., Harrison, M.D., Silva, J.L., Campos, J.C.: Developing serious games with the APEX framework. Workshop on Ubiquitous Games and Gamification for Promoting Behavior Change and Wellbeing, pp. 37–40 (2013)
11. Gomes, T.E.O., Abade, T., Campos, J.C., Harrison, M.D., Silva, J.L.: A virtual environment based serious game to support health education. ICST Trans. Ambient Syst. **1**(3), 1–6 (2014). EAI (European Alliance for Innovation)
12. McClarty, K.L., Orr, A., Frey, P.M., Dolan, R., Vassileva, V., McVa, A.: A literature review of gaming in education. Research report. Pearson Education (2012)
13. Connolly, T.M., Boyle, E.A., MacArthur, E., Hainey, T., Boyle, J.M.: A systematic literature review of empirical evidence on computer games and serious games. Comput. Educ. **59**(2), 661–686 (2012). Elsevier
14. Multipeer Connectivity Framework. https://developer.apple.com/reference/ multipeerconnectivity. Accessed 20 Oct 2016
15. Lund, A.M.: Measuring usability with the USE questionnaire. STC Usability SIG Newslett. **8**(2), 3–6 (2001)

Examining Enjoyment in Gamifying Physical Exercise and a Healthy Diet

Khasfariyati Razikin[1,2(✉)], Dion Hoe-Lian Goh[1], and Chei Sian Lee[1]

[1] Wee Kim Wee School of Communication and Information,
Nanyang Technological University, Singapore, Singapore
{khas0003,ashlgoh,leecs}@ntu.edu.sg
[2] SAP Innovation Center Network Singapore,
SAP Asia Pte Ltd., Singapore, Singapore

Abstract. This paper examines the role of gamification for enjoyment in physical exercise and a healthy diet. The lack of motivation for these health-related behaviors is associated with the rising incidence of cardiovascular diseases, diabetes, hypertension, and obesity. Gamification involves leveraging on enjoyment derived from game mechanics that could galvanize individuals to exercise and consume healthier meals. Literature has also noted that enjoyment is associated with competing activities, personal investments, valuable opportunities, social constraints, and social support. This work introduces Zest!, a gamified application designed to enhance enjoyment to exercise and diet. Zest! aims to enhance enjoyment by entwining exercising and dieting activities with game mechanics. An evaluation was conducted to understand users' perception of enjoyment associated with exercising and dieting as a result of using Zest!. It validates the game mechanics in enhancing the enjoyment to the activities. A total of 70 participants took part in the study and used it for two days. During the study, the participants were given tasks to utilize the available features. A questionnaire was administered at the end of the study to elicit their perceptions. Regression analyses were performed on the data collected. The results indicate that gamified applications has to potential to enhance enjoyment for physical exercise and a healthy diet. The implications from this study are presented.

Keywords: Gamification · Physical exercise · Healthy diet · Game mechanics · Enjoyment

1 Introduction

The rising incidence of cardiovascular diseases, diabetes, hypertension, and obesity calls for an examination of the lack of motivation to exercise and maintain a healthy diet. Regular exercise combined with consuming healthy food has been noted to be more beneficial than doing the individual activities alone [1] and long term engagement have resulted in sustained and maintenance of body weight [2]. Gamifying exercising and dieting has been proposed to galvanize individuals to take appropriate action [3]. Employing game mechanics, which are features found in games, with health-related activities is argued to invoke enjoyment that could motivate people to continue

© Springer International Publishing AG 2017
M. Kurosu (Ed.): HCI 2017, Part II, LNCS 10272, pp. 84–98, 2017.
DOI: 10.1007/978-3-319-58077-7_8

exercising [4] and consume healthier meals [5] despite experiencing setbacks [6]. Even though enjoyment is perceived to be important for health-related behaviors [7], it has not been extensively investigated in previous studies [8].

Enjoyment is associated with competing activities, restraining barriers, and social support [9, 10]. Competing activities that are perceived to be less attractive than exercising and dieting have a negative relationship with enjoyment. In contrast, restraining factors that reduces the individual's intent to terminate engaging in these activities have a positive association with enjoyment. Three types of restraining barriers have been identified. First, personal investments are time, effort, and financial resources put into the activity. Second, social constraints are the expectations and norms that create feelings of obligation to continue with the activity. Third, valuable opportunities are the prized prospects that only available through participation. Additionally, social support is also expected to have a positive relationship with enjoyment [10]. Although antecedents to the enjoyment of health activities have been identified, there is a lack of examination of the related game mechanics [8].

Given the research gap, this study aims to examine: *What are the game mechanics that could enhance enjoyment of physical exercise and a healthy diet?* The contribution of this work is two-fold. First, it introduces Zest!, a gamified application designed to enhance enjoyment of exercising and dieting. Second, it presents the implications from a user study that elicited users' perception of enjoyment from game mechanics.

The following section delves deeper into the discussion on the gamification and enjoyment of physical exercise and a healthy diet. It also provides an overview of the studies of gamified applications. The section that follows introduces Zest!, a gamified application that enhances the enjoyment of physical exercise and a healthy diet. The methodology section describes the process to answer the research question through a user evaluation. The results section presents the outcome of the evaluation while the discussion section reflects on the findings. The concluding section provides the implications together with the limitations of this work.

2   Related Work

2.1   Gamification

The increasing interest surrounding gamification the academia and industry signals the need to examine it in greater depth. Gamification entwines daily activities with game-like mechanics to motivate and sustain users' interest [3]. The mechanics found in video games are utilized in non-game situations to provide an enjoyable environment for users [3]. The commonly adopted mechanics are points, levels, and leaderboards [11]. Game mechanics are used in various domains that include health [12, 13], language learning [14], and personal tasks and habits [15].

Gamification differs from other genres in the following ways. These applications are set apart from video games through their purpose. The latter are played for purely hedonic reasons, while the former are used for hedonic and utilitarian purposes [16]. With respect to serious games, these are full-fledged games that are typically used for simulations in training and education. These games rely on the graphical and interactive nature of games to bring the full experience of the simulation to the user. In contrast, gamified applications adopts the relevant game mechanics to motivate users regardless of the context of use [17].

Game mechanics are utilized in gamified applications for physical exercise and healthy diet to bring enjoyment. Previous studies have underscored the relevance of these mechanics to motivate individuals in health-related behaviors [18]. These mechanics are intertwined with physical exercise activities and have yielded positive results [19, 20]. Similarly, game mechanics are used in encouraging healthy dieting and studies have highlighted the association with enjoyment [5, 21]. Furthermore, studies have examined the effects of gamifying both exercising and dieting [22–24].

To date, only three studies have utilized game mechanics with physical exercise and dieting. Vivospace [24] combines gamification for physical exercise and healthy diet. This application enables users to log the exercise they did and meals they had. Users could make their goals such as to run 5 km in 25 min or lose 5 kg in 2 weeks. Furthermore, they could share their logs with other users and provide encouragement to these individuals. Meanwhile, in SpaPlay [23], users are given the mission to maintain the condition of a health spa by exercising and consuming healthy food. Upon completion, users are awarded points and currency that could be used to maintain the upkeep of the spa. These studies showed that gamification could increase exercise activities and improve diet but the duration of exercise and healthy food consumed remained below the recommended amount [22]. Furthermore, the studies did not measure the participants' perception of enjoyment [8].

2.2   Enjoyment

The extent of work surrounding gamified applications for health-related activities indicates the importance of enjoyable experiences. Enjoyment is the positive affective state in reaction to a stimulus that galvanizes individuals into action [25]. As enjoyment is a powerful emotion that could drive an individual to overcome adversity [6], it has been adopted as a psychological construct to understand the factors that galvanize individuals to take action. Due to this, it has been adopted for activities involving health-related behavior change [26].

The importance of enjoyment for physical exercise has been noted in population and empirical studies. Respondents in population surveys shared that enjoyment was relevant for them to exercise [27]. Among the correlates to physical exercise, enjoyment was found to be a strong predictor [28]. Although enjoyment is noted to be important, it seems to be elusive to individuals as highlighted by the lack of motivation to engage in physical exercise [7].

Enjoyment of a healthy diet refers to the preference for healthy food [29], which is consumed to meet the recommended daily amount of energy and nutrition [30]. Empirical studies have noted enjoyment to be a strong predictor of a healthy diet when compared with other correlates [31]. It is also associated with meeting the recommended amount of fruit and vegetable intake [32]. Despite the relevance of enjoyment to improve individuals' diet, many do not hold it in high regard as healthy food is perceived to be unappetizing [33] and the portion size would not satiate hunger [34].

From the perspective of gamification, enjoyment is a fundamental aspect as it motivates individuals to engage in the task [35]. It is defined as the sense of fun experienced by the individual while using the gamified application [36]. As features from games are adopted, it is expected that gamified applications would be able to bring an enjoyable experience for the user, leading them to use the application and engage in health-related activities [35]. However, related studies on gamification have used concepts like intrinsic motivation [37] and flow [38] interchangeably with enjoyment, making it difficult to pinpoint the precise nature of enjoyment [8].

2.3   Antecedents to Enjoyment

Literature has identified five antecedents to enjoyment, namely competing activities, personal investments, social constraints, valuable opportunities, and social support. Competing activities describe the appeal of other activities that might derail engagement [9]. These alternative activities are those that are more appealing than health-related activities and would make them less enjoyable. Studies have indicated that physical exercise to be enjoyable when other activities are not appealing [39]. Similarly, when individuals are presented with healthy and less healthy food, they would be more likely to enjoy the healthier option [40]. Related studies on gamified applications have argued for the importance of applications to increase the appeal of engaging these activities [21].

Personal investments refer to the time, effort, and financial means needed for the activity and cannot be recovered [9]. When an individual engages in physical exercise, they might need to purchase equipment and/or club memberships, set aside time, and put in an effort. Similarly, healthy dieting would involve putting in time for shopping, preparation, and cooking [34]. Investing into health-related activities has been found to be associated with enjoyment of physical activities [41] and dieting [42].

Social constraints reflect the expectations and social norms that bring the feelings of obligation for the individual to continue with the activity [9]. It is the perceived sense of obligation from others that pressures the individual to persist. For physical exercise, social constraints improve the individual's sense of enjoyment [10]. Similarly, a healthy diet is related to the norms and expectations of their family and friends [43].

Valuable opportunities are the prized prospects only available through continued involvement in the activity [9]. These anticipated opportunities are related to the physical, psychological or sociological benefits of health-related activities [41]. Exercising provides the opportunity to improve one's competency and the chance to be with friends [44]. For a healthy diet, this is characterized by the perceived competence in preparing healthy food [34].

Social support refers to the support available from other individuals that could help in the engagement of health-related activities [45]. It describes how the support provided by others who are considered significant leads to persistence in the individual. It has been noted that individuals engaging in physical exercise could receive support from others [46]. Social support is also found to be associated with fruit and vegetable consumption [47]. The relationship between social support and enjoyment has been empirically validated in related studies [39, 48].

In sum, previous studies have established that game mechanics could help users to engage in physical exercise and a healthy diet. The outcome from the studies also noted that the duration exercised and amount of healthy food consumed were below the recommended amount. Although the adoption of gamification mechanics hints that enjoyment is relevant, the concept of enjoyment has yet to be examined. Furthermore, the antecedents introduced have not been applied in the context of gamification.

3 Zest!

Zest! is a gamified application that aims to motivate users by making exercising and dieting activities enjoyable through gamification. Users' are challenged to balance the calories burned through exercising with the calories consumed from meals [49]. The definition of the antecedents to enjoyment were used to guide the choice of features available in Zest!. In total, there are six functions in Zest!. The main screen provides an overview and navigation links to other functionalities in the application. The remaining five functions, namely 'Move,' 'Eat,' 'Learn,' 'Connect,' and 'Ranking,' have separate screens. Zest! was implemented on the Android platform as part of a multi-tier architecture that is comprised of the mobile client, Web service, and database. It was developed for Android 2.3.5. The Web service was developed using PHP. The database which stores the data is a MySQL database.

The main navigation screen (Fig. 1) is presented to the user after logging into Zest!. It provides an overview of relevant information related to health behavior to the user, and access to the different features in Zest!. The tailored message, which is the greeting on top of the screen, embody the concept of competing activities. It is system-generated addressed to individuals [50]. The messages increase the appeal of engaging in these health-related activities by highlight the importance of these behaviors [51] and is personalized with the user's name to make it relevant for him/her. At the same time, the messages are tailored to either galvanize them when they had not earned any points in the current day or to praise them when they had logged exercises and meals.

Fig. 1. Zest! main navigation screen

Figure 2 presents the main screen for 'Move' and 'Eat.' In 'Move,' the user logs a physical exercise that had been undertaken. The workouts that have been done on a particular day are listed with the details of the activity, calories burned and points earned. In 'Eat,' the user logs the meals consumed for breakfast, lunch, dinner, and snacks. The meals consumed are listed with the caloric intake from the food and the points earned. The points earned, which are associated with personal investments, are awarded to reflect the effort put in by the user [11].

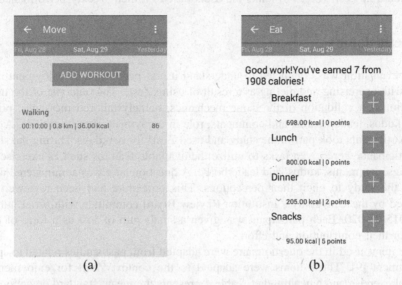

(a)   (b)

Fig. 2. (a) 'Move' screen, and (b) 'Eat' screen

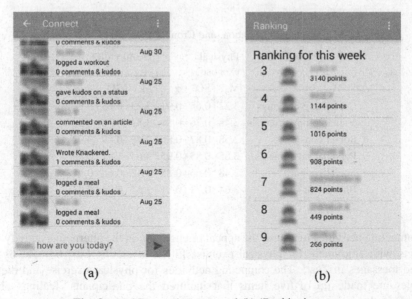

(a)   (b)

Fig. 3. (a) 'Connect' screen, and (b) 'Ranking' screen

Figure 3a presents the 'Connect' screen with a list of feeds showing the users' activities. It also presents the users' statuses and kudos (appraisals from others). The appraisals reflect the community expectations to restraint the individual in continuing to exercise and dieting [52]. Social support is provided through the comments feature, and this enables users to interact with others [53].

Linked with valuable opportunities is the leaderboard that ranks the users by the points earned. It is an indicator of their effort with others in the community [11]. The leaderboard in Zest! (Fig. 3b) ranks the users based on their weekly performance.

4 Methodology

A user evaluation was conducted to understand users' perception of enjoyment associated with exercising and dieting as a result of using Zest!. The outcome of the users' perception is a validation of the game mechanics, namely tailored messages, points, levels, kudos, leaderboards, and comments, role in enjoyment of the activities. A total of 70 participants took part in the study and used Zest! for two days. During the study, the participants were given tasks to utilize the available features such as exercise and meal logs, comments, kudos, and leaderboard. A questionnaire was administered at the end of the study to elicit their perceptions. This procedure had been reviewed and approved by the University's Institution Review Board committee with serial number IRB-2015-03-020. Each participant was given a small sum of $10 as a form of gratitude for their contribution and effort.

The items used in the questionnaire were adapted from past studies related to sports commitment [9]. These items were adapted to the context Zest! for enjoyment of physical exercise and a healthy diet. Table 1 presents the mean, standard deviation and Cronbach's alpha for each variable.

Table 1. Mean, standard deviation, and Cronbach's alpha of the variables

Variables	Physical exercise			Healthy diet		
	M	SD	α	M	SD	α
Competing activities	3.22	0.65	0.91	3.23	0.65	0.91
Valuable opportunities	3.48	0.76	0.86	3.52	0.76	0.88
Social constraints	2.58	0.82	0.85	2.40	0.89	0.92
Personal investments	3.85	0.85	0.95	3.64	0.81	0.89
Social support	3.48	0.66	0.85	3.42	0.66	0.91
Enjoyment	3.64	0.73	0.91	3.64	0.75	0.91

Competing activities measures the appeal of engaging in the alternative activity that conflicts with enjoyment for physical exercise [39] and dieting [40] brought by the tailored messages in Zest!. The competing activities for physical exercise and dieting variables are made up of five items that inquired the participants' feelings about engaging in the activities each. Personal investments measures the user's perception of the resources that have been invested into physical exercise [10, 39] and a healthy diet [54] through the game mechanics of points and levels available in Zest!. The variables that measured personal investments for exercising and dieting were made up of three items each. Social constraints measures the feeling of obligation to continue exercising [10] and dieting [43] from the community in Zest! through kudos. Each of the variables for social constraints in physical exercise and a healthy diet were measured by four items. Valuable opportunities measures the participants' perception of the possibilities that are only available through using Zest! to engage in physical exercise [39] and a healthy diet that is embodied in the leaderboard. Four items made up the variables for valuable opportunities in exercising and dieting respectively. Social support measures the participants' feelings of encouragement and support that others provide through the comments for engaging in physical exercise [10] and dieting [47]. Three items queried the social support they received in Zest! to motivate exercising and dieting each.

There are two dependent variables. One dependent variable is participants' perception of enjoyment in physical exercise and is made up of four items. Another dependent variable was the participants' perception of enjoyment of a healthy diet and it was made up of three items.

The 70 participants were between 21 years old and 49 years old (M $= 27.22$, SD $= 7.06$). Male participants made up the majority (62.86%). In terms of education background, the majority of the participants were from Computer Science/IT (48.57%, N $= 34$), Engineering (22.86%, N $= 16$), and Arts, Humanities, and Social Sciences (20.00%, N $= 14$) disciplines. A small segment of the participants used mobile fitness applications. They used these applications to log their exercise (27.14%, N $= 19$) and meals (10%, N $= 7$) at least once a month. They also used these applications to search for health-related information on a monthly basis (17.14%, N $= 12$). Additionally, they also indicated that they play games on social networking applications on their mobile phones (37.14%, N $= 26$).

5 Results

From the data collected, regression analyses were conducted to examine the relationships of competing activities, personal investments, social constraints, valuable opportunities, and social support with enjoyment.

5.1 Regression Analyses Results for Physical Exercise

Table 2 presents the outcome of regression analysis for physical exercise. The model was found to be statistically significant (Adjusted $R^2 = 0.48$, $F(64, 5) = 13.79$, $p < 0.001$) and accounted for 48% of the variance. The results showed that the competing activities variable has a negative association with enjoyment to physical exercise ($\beta = -0.27, p < 0.01$). This outcome indicates that the tailored messages in Zest! were able to reduce the attractiveness of other activities and in turn making exercising more enjoyable.

Table 2. Linear regression analysis for enjoyment of physical exercise (N = 70)

Independent variables	Standardized beta	t-values
Competing activities	−0.27	−2.70**
Personal investments	0.13	1.19
Social constraints	0.02	0.22
Valuable opportunities	0.49	4.33***
Social support	−0.07	−0.63
Adjusted R^2	0.48***	

Note: a. dependent variable is "Enjoyment of physical exercise"

b. **p < 0.01, ***p < 0.001

Additionally, the results indicated that the valuable opportunities variable is positively associated with enjoyment of physical exercise ($\beta = 0.49, p < 0.001$). The results highlight that the gamification features in Zest!, which were able to show the opportunities that were only available in the application, made physical exercise enjoyable for the participants. The leaderboard embodies opportunities for physical exercise.

However, there were no significant associations between the variables of personal investments ($\beta = 0.13, p = 0.24$), social constraints ($\beta = 0.02, p = 0.83$), and social support ($\beta = -0.07, p = 0.53$) with enjoyment of physical exercise. The outcome suggests that the points, levels, kudos, and comments might not be able to make exercising enjoyable.

5.2   Regression Analyses Results for a Healthy Diet

The results for the regression analysis for a healthy diet is presented in Table 3. The model was found to be statistically significant (Adjusted $R^2 = 0.44$, $F(64, 5) = 11.78$, $p < 0.001$) and it contributed to 44% of the variance. The results showed competing activities have a negative relationship with the enjoyment of a healthy diet ($\beta = -0.29$, $p < 0.01$). It suggests that the tailored messages in Zest!, which reduces the likelihood of the participant in engaging in alternative activities and enhance the feeling of enjoyment towards a healthy diet.

Table 3. Linear regression analysis for a healthy diet (N = 70)

Independent variables	Standardized beta	t-values
Competing activities	−0.29	−2.70**
Personal investments	0.32	3.16**
Social constraints	−0.11	−1.08
Valuable opportunities	0.26	2.35*
Social support	0.19	1.89
Adjusted R^2	0.44 ***	

Note: a. dependent variable is "Enjoyment of a healthy diet"

b. *p < 0.05, **p < 0.01, ***p < 0.001

As expected, the results demonstrated a significant positive association between personal investments and the enjoyment of a healthy diet ($\beta = 0.32, p < 0.01$). This highlighted that points and levels in Zest! reflected the resources put in for dieting and in turn made it more enjoyable.

The result indicated that valuable opportunities have a significant positive association with the enjoyment of a healthy dieting ($\beta = 0.26, p < 0.05$). The outcome indicates that the leaderboard could enhance the feeling of enjoyment for a healthy diet.

However, there were no significant associations between social constraints ($\beta = -0.11, p = 0.28$) and social support ($\beta = 0.19, p = 0.06$) with enjoyment. Compared to other features, the related features, namely kudos and comments, need users to interact with one another.

6 Discussion

The results of our work yielded the following findings. First, there are significant relationship for competing activities and valuable opportunities with enjoyment of physical exercise. The findings suggests that reducing the appeal of competing activities is associated with enjoyment. Presenting personally relevant messages that highlight the value of engaging physical exercise reduces the users' focus on other activities as individuals are more likely to be receptive to messages that are personally relevant to them [50]. For instance, addressing the users by their name captures their attention and offering suggestions is a call to action. Additionally, providing valuable opportunities are associated with enjoyment. The anticipation of such opportunities helps to enhance the users' enjoyment of physical exercise [28]. One such opportunity in Zest! is the recognition of user's abilities through leaderboards [55]. The leaderboard compares the user's effort with respect to others.

Second, there were non-significant relationships for personal investments, social constraints, and social support on enjoyment of physical exercise. For personal investments, the finding may contradict prior studies that argued for the importance of personal investments [11]. The outcome could be attributed to the lack of clarity highlighting the users' effort to their physical exercise. The features that embody personal investments in gamified applications has to reflect the users' effort in a meaningful way that could be understood easily [55]. The lack of significant association for social constraints suggests that the participants did not feel part of the community as they used the application for two days. They were not familiar with the expectations and norms in the community. For such behavior to be established, both time and a substantial community size are required [56]. Third, there is no significant association with social support. For such support to be formed, a substantial size is required and attaining this would require time. Like before, the participants used Zest! for two days indicating that they might not be familiar with other users and this may have limited the support available [53].

Third, there are significant relationship for competing activities, personal investments, and valuable opportunities with enjoyment of a healthy diet. It is found that competing activities have a negative association with the enjoyment of a healthy diet. It corroborates with prior studies that have examined using messages in gamified applications to stress the value of healthy diet to the user [21] The messages that were tailored to the user were able to encourage users to consume healthier meals. Additionally, personal investments are related to enjoyment. The features, points, and levels, translate the effort put in by the user through the awarding of points [28] and attainment of levels [55]. Put together, indicating the effort put in by users through these features led them to a more enjoyable experience in healthy dieting. Also, valuable opportunities have a positive relationship with enjoyment. The outcome highlights the importance of providing novel opportunities for the individual to maintain their diet as advocated in previous studies [22]. The leaderboard in Zest that highlights the effort put in by the user for dieting is a recognition of their effort.

Fourth, there was no significant relationships for social constraints and social support with enjoyment of a healthy diet. The nascent user community might not have been established long enough to form social norms. The two days that the participants took part in the study could be considered too short for them to be acquainted with one another and they were more focused on their activity [57]. For social support, the participants might not be familiar with others to give the necessary encouragement that they might need to make dieting more enjoyable. This finding could also be attributed to the duration of the study as the participants might need time to be familiar with others [58].

7 Conclusion

Three design implications could be derived from the findings. First, game mechanics that are representation of personal investments into these activities is essential to enjoyment. Gamification designers could consider integrating game mechanics that emphasize effort put in by the user for improving their health. This could be done by tying the desired behaviors to the relevant mechanics. For instance, points are linked to the calories expended during exercising and the consumption of healthy food. Similarly, levels reflects users' progress and raises awareness of their status.

The second implication is associated with the valuable opportunities that are only found in gamified applications. It is envisaged that game mechanics could endorse users health-related behaviors only by using the application. Leaderboards could provide the much needed recognition of users' competence. However, there are users who might be deterred by the competitive aspect of leaderboard as they have different abilities and focus from other users [37]. Instead of integrating a global leaderboard that ranks all users, leaderboards could be used to compare groups of users who shares similar abilities or interest.

Finally, the appeal of competing activities could be reduced by enhancing the value of using the gamified applications. As a recommendation, gamified applications with tailored messages could appeal to the user's value in maintaining a healthy lifestyle. Based on the context, the application provides appropriate messages to galvanize the users to nudge users into action.

This study has also examined the concept of enjoyment for gamification of health-related activities. It has presented the antecedents to enjoyment. The study has provided empirical evidence that game mechanics could enhance enjoyment of physical exercise and a healthy diet. It is further substantiated in Zest!, where the game mechanics associated with the antecedents are put together. Thus, gamified applications is a promising intervention for motivating users to engage in physical exercise and a healthy diet.

There are caveats to this study. First, the variables measured were psychological variables and there were no measures of actual behavior. Although enjoyment is argued to be an important aspect for motivation, empirical studies have indicated the mediating role of enjoyment to actual behavior [10, 44]. Second, the user evaluation of Zest! was conducted over two days. However, previous studies have examined the long-term usage of applications with to understand the behavioral outcome [22, 23]. Therefore, it is pertinent to conduct a longitudinal study to affirm the relevance of the game mechanics. Third, the small sample size of the participants who took part in this study is another limitation. The number of participant might limit the generalizability of this study.

References

1. Fleig, L., Kerschreiter, R., Schwarzer, R., Pomp, S., Lippke, S.: 'Sticking to a healthy diet is easier for me when I exercise regularly': cognitive transfer between physical exercise and healthy nutrition. Psychol. Health **29**, 1361–1372 (2014)
2. Foster-Schubert, K.E., Alfano, C.M., Duggan, C.R., Xiao, L., Campbell, K.L., Kong, A., Bain, C.E., Wang, C.Y., Blackburn, G.L., McTiernan, A.: Effect of diet and exercise, alone or combined, on weight and body composition in overweight-to-obese postmenopausal women. Obesity **20**, 1628–1638 (2012)
3. Deterding, S., Sicart, M., Nacke, L., O'Hara, K., Dixon, D.: Gamification: using game-design elements in non-gaming contexts. In: 2011 Annual Conference Extended Abstracts on Human Factors in Computing Systems, pp. 2425–2428. ACM, New York (2011)
4. Goh, D.H.-L., Razikin, K.: Is gamification effective in motivating exercise? In: Kurosu, M. (ed.) HCI 2015. LNCS, vol. 9170, pp. 608–617. Springer, Cham (2015). doi:10.1007/978-3-319-20916-6_56
5. Jones, B.A., Madden, G.J., Wengreen, H.J., Aguilar, S.S., Desjardins, E.A.: Gamification of dietary decision-making in an elementary-school cafeteria. PLOS One **9** (2014)
6. Ryan, R.M., Deci, E.L.: Self-determination theory and the facilitation of intrinsic motivation, social development, and well-being. Am. Psychol. **55**, 68–78 (2000)
7. Hagberg, L.A., Lindahl, B., Nyberg, L., Hellénius, M.-L.: Importance of enjoyment when promoting physical exercise. Scand. J. Med. Sci. Sports **19**, 740–747 (2009)
8. Crutzen, R., van't Riet, J., Short, C.E.: Enjoyment: a conceptual exploration and overview of experimental evidence in the context of games for health. Games Health J. **5**, 15–20 (2016)
9. Scanlan, T.K., Carpenter, P.J., Schmidt, G.W., Simons, J.P., Keeler, B.: An introduction to the sport commitment model. J. Sport Exerc. Psychol. **15**, 1–15 (1993)
10. Weiss, M.R., Kimmel, L.A., Smith, A.L.: Determinants of sport commitment among junior tennis players: enjoyment as a mediating variable. Pediatr. Exerc. Sci. **13**, 131–144 (2001)
11. Richter, G., Raban, D.R., Rafaeli, S.: Studying gamification: the effect of rewards and incentives on motivation. In: Reiners, T., Wood, L.C. (eds.) Gamification in Education and Business, pp. 21–46. Springer, Cham (2015)

12. http://www.sparkpeople.com/
13. http://www.fitocracy.com/
14. https://www.duolingo.com/
15. https://www.superbetter.com/
16. Werbach, K.: (Re)defining gamification: a process approach. In: Spagnolli, A., Chittaro, L., Gamberini, L. (eds.) PERSUASIVE 2014. LNCS, vol. 8462, pp. 266–272. Springer, Cham (2014). doi:10.1007/978-3-319-07127-5_23
17. Seaborn, K., Fels, D.I.: Gamification in theory and action: a survey. Int. J. Hum.-Comput. Stud. **74**, 14–31 (2015)
18. Kamal, N., Fels, S., Blackstock, M., Ho, K.: The ABCs of designing social networks for health behaviour change: the VivoSpace social network. In: Kranakis, E. (ed.) Advances in Network Analysis and its Applications, pp. 323–348. Springer, Heidelberg (2013)
19. Ahtinen, A., Huuskonen, P., Häkkilä, J.: Let's all get up and walk to the North Pole: design and evaluation of a mobile wellness application. In: Proceedings of the 6th Nordic Conference on Human-Computer Interaction: Extending Boundaries, pp. 3–12. ACM, New York (2010)
20. Lin, J.J., Mamykina, L., Lindtner, S., Delajoux, G., Strub, H.B.: Fish'n'Steps: encouraging physical activity with an interactive computer game. In: Dourish, P., Friday, A. (eds.) UbiComp 2006. LNCS, vol. 4206, pp. 261–278. Springer, Heidelberg (2006). doi:10.1007/11853565_16
21. Peng, W.: Design and evaluation of a computer game to promote a healthy diet for young adults. Health Commun. **24**, 115–127 (2009)
22. Baranowski, T., Baranowski, J., Thompson, D., Buday, R., Jago, R., Griffith, M.J., Islam, N., Nguyen, N., Watson, K.B.: Video game play, child diet, and physical activity behavior change: a randomized clinical trial. Am. J. Prev. Med. **40**, 33–38 (2011)
23. Durga, S., Seif El-Nasr, M., Shiyko, M., Sceppa, C., Naab, P., Andres, L.: Leveraging play to promote health behavior change: a player acceptance study of a health game. In: Ma, L., Jain, L.C., Anderson, P. (eds.) Virtual, Augmented Reality and Serious Games for Healthcare 1, pp. 209–230. Springer, Berlin (2013)
24. Kamal, N., Fels, S., Blackstock, M., Ho, K.: VivoSpace: towards health behavior change using social gaming. In: Anacleto, J.C., Fels, S., Graham, N., Kapralos, B., Saif El-Nasr, M., Stanley, K. (eds.) ICEC 2011. LNCS, vol. 6972, pp. 319–330. Springer, Heidelberg (2011). doi:10.1007/978-3-642-24500-8_35
25. Ryan, R.M., Patrick, H., Deci, E.L., Williams, G.C.: Facilitating health behaviour change and its maintenance: interventions based on self-determination theory. Eur. Health Psychol. **10**, 2–5 (2008)
26. Lawton, R., Conner, M., McEachan, R.: Desire or reason: predicting health behaviors from affective and cognitive attitudes. Health Psychol. **28**, 56 (2009)
27. Nielsen, G., Wikman, J.M., Jensen, C.J., Schmidt, J.F., Gliemann, L., Andersen, T.R.: Health promotion: the impact of beliefs of health benefits, social relations and enjoyment on exercise continuation. Scand. J. Med. Sci. Sports **24**, 66–75 (2014)
28. Lewis, B.A., Williams, D.M., Frayeh, A., Marcus, B.H.: Self-efficacy versus perceived enjoyment as predictors of physical activity behaviour. Psychol. Health **31**, 1–14 (2015)
29. Cornil, Y., Chandon, P.: Pleasure as an ally of healthy eating? Contrasting visceral and Epicurean eating pleasure and their association with portion size preferences and wellbeing. Appetite **104**, 52–59 (2016)
30. Appleton, K.: Visualising healthy eating. A role for enjoyment in the use of visualisation for increasing fruit consumption. Appetite **83**, 356 (2014)

31. Williams, L.K., Thornton, L., Crawford, D.: Optimising women's diets. An examination of factors that promote healthy eating and reduce the likelihood of unhealthy eating. Appetite **59**, 41–46 (2012)
32. Shaikh, A.R., Yaroch, A.L., Nebeling, L., Yeh, M.-C., Resnicow, K.: Psychosocial predictors of fruit and vegetable consumption in adults: a review of the literature. Am. J. Prev. Med. **34**, 535–543 (2008). e511
33. Raghunathan, R., Naylor, R.W., Hoyer, W.D.: The unhealthy = tasty intuition and its effects on taste inferences, enjoyment, and choice of food products. J. Mark. **70**, 170–184 (2006)
34. Macdiarmid, J.I., Loe, J., Kyle, J., McNeill, G.: "It was an education in portion size". Experience of eating a healthy diet and barriers to long term dietary change. Appetite **71**, 411–419 (2013)
35. Rigby, C.S.: Gamification and motivation. In: Walz, S.P., Deterding, S. (eds.) The Gameful World: Approaches, Issues, Applications, pp. 113–138. The MIT Press, Cambridge (2015)
36. Suh, A., Wagner, C., Liu, L.: The effects of game dynamics on user engagement in gamified systems. In: 2015 48th Hawaii International Conference on System Sciences (HICSS), pp. 672–681. IEEE, California (2015)
37. Song, H., Kim, J., Tenzek, K.E., Lee, K.M.: The effects of competition and competitiveness upon intrinsic motivation in exergames. Comput. Hum. Behav. **29**, 1702–1708 (2013)
38. Mellecker, R., Lyons, E.J., Baranowski, T.: Disentangling fun and enjoyment in exergames using expanded design, play, experience framework: a narrative review. Games Health J.: Res. Dev. Clin. Appl. **2**, 142–159 (2014)
39. Casper, J.M., Gray, D.P., Stellino, M.B.: A sport commitment model perspective on adult tennis players' participation frequency and purchase intention. Sport Manag. Rev. **10**, 253–278 (2007)
40. McCann, M.T., Wallace, J.M., Robson, P.J., Rennie, K.L., McCaffrey, T.A., Welch, R.W., Livingstone, M.B.E.: Influence of nutrition labelling on food portion size consumption. Appetite **65**, 153–158 (2013)
41. Alexandris, K., Zahariadis, P., Tsorbatzoudis, C., Grouious, G.: Testing the sport commitment model in the context of exercise and fitness participation. J. Sport Behav. **25**, 217–230 (2002)
42. Beals, K.P., Godoy, J.M.: Commitment to change: an examination of the maintenance of health-behavior changes. In: Martin, L.R., DiMatteo, M.R. (eds.) The Oxford Handbook of Health Communication, Behavior Change, and Treatment Adherence, pp. 286–301. Oxford University Press, Oxford (2013)
43. Yun, D., Silk, K.J.: Social norms, self-identity, and attention to social comparison information in the context of exercise and healthy diet behavior. Health Commun. **26**, 275–285 (2011)
44. Wankel, L.M.: The importance of enjoyment to adherence and psychological benefits from physical activity. Int. J. Sports Psychol. **24**, 151–169 (1993)
45. Uchino, B.N., Cacioppo, J.T., Kiecolt-Glaser, J.K.: The relationship between social support and physiological processes: a review with emphasis on underlying mechanisms and implications for health. Psychol. Bull. **119**, 488 (1996)
46. Eyler, A.A., Brownson, R.C., Donatelle, R.J., King, A.C., Brown, D., Sallis, J.F.: Physical activity social support and middle-and older-aged minority women: results from a US survey. Soc. Sci. Med. **49**, 781–789 (1999)
47. McSpadden, K.E., Patrick, H., Oh, A.Y., Yaroch, A.L., Dwyer, L.A., Nebeling, L.C.: The association between motivation and fruit and vegetable intake: the moderating role of social support. Appetite **96**, 87–94 (2016)
48. Motl, R.W., Dishman, R.K., Saunders, R., Dowda, M., Felton, G., Pate, R.: Measuring enjoyment of physical activity in adolescent girls. Am. J. Prev. Med. **21**, 110–117 (2001)

49. Haskell, W.L., Lee, I.-M., Pate, R., Powell, K.E., Blair, S.N., Franklin, B.A., Macera, C.A., Heath, G.W., Thompson, P.D., Bauman, A.: Physical activity and public health: updated recommendation for adults from the American College of Sports Medicine and the American Heart Association. Circulation **116**, 1081–1093 (2007)
50. Petty, R.E., Cacioppo, J.T.: The Elaboration Likelihood Model of Persuasion. Springer, New York (1986)
51. Bull, F.C., Kreuter, M.W., Scharff, D.P.: Effects of tailored, personalized and general health messages on physical activity. Patient Educ. Couns. **36**, 181–192 (1999)
52. Hamari, J., Koivisto, J.: "Working out for likes": an empirical study on social influence in exercise gamification. Comput. Hum. Behav. **50**, 333–347 (2015)
53. Cavallo, D.N., Tate, D.F., Ries, A.V., Brown, J.D., DeVellis, R.F., Ammerman, A.S.: A social media–based physical activity intervention: a randomized controlled trial. Am. J. Prev. Med. **43**, 527–532 (2012)
54. Hollywood, L.E., Cuskelly, G.J., O'Brien, M., McConnon, A., Barnett, J., Raats, M.M., Dean, M.: Healthful grocery shopping. Perceptions and barriers. Appetite **70**, 119–126 (2013)
55. Mekler, E.D., Brühlmann, F., Tuch, A.N., Opwis, K.: Towards understanding the effects of individual gamification elements on intrinsic motivation and performance. Comput. Hum. Behav. **71**, 525–534 (2016)
56. Tsai, H.-T., Bagozzi, R.P.: Contribution behavior in virtual communities: cognitive, emotional, and social influences. MIS Q. **38**, 143–163 (2014)
57. Kim, H.-S., Sundar, S.S.: Can online buddies and bandwagon cues enhance user participation in online health communities? Comput. Hum. Behav. **37**, 319–333 (2014)
58. Centola, D., van de Rijt, A.: Choosing your network: social preferences in an online health community. Soc. Sci. Med. **125**, 19–31 (2015)

Sources of Computer Game Enjoyment: Card Sorting to Develop a New Model

Owen Schaffer[✉] and Xiaowen Fang

College of Computing and Digital Media, DePaul University,
243 South Wabash Avenue, Chicago, IL 60604, USA
Owen.Schaffer@gmail.com, XFang@cdm.depaul.edu

Abstract. Understanding what makes computer games enjoyable is important not only for game design, but for the design of any interactive experience where it is important that users will want to use the design. We define enjoyment broadly as the positive evaluation of your experience. Existing models of game enjoyment are either not comprehensive enough, were not generated by empirical research, or both. We aim to fill this gap in the literature with a card sorting study exploring participants' experience and mental models around what leads to computer game enjoyment. A broad literature review identified 167 sources of enjoyment. Our research group conducted an open card sort with these items to identify 24 initial categories of enjoyment sources. Sixty participants will sort the 167 sources of enjoyment into the 24 categories, plus a "not a source of enjoyment" category. After every ten participants, we will calculate inter-rater agreement with Randolph's free-marginal multi-rater kappa. We hope this research will lead to a new, more comprehensive and content valid model of the sources of computer game enjoyment.

Keywords: Computer games · Enjoyment · Games user experience · Positive psychology · Positive emotions · Affect · Valence · Card sorting · Affinity diagram · Human-Computer interaction

1 Introduction

Game Designers and Human-Computer Interaction practitioners need to know what makes games enjoyable if they are going to engineer enjoyable designs. We define computer game enjoyment as the extent to which players positively evaluate their experience playing games on computerized devices (PCs, consoles, smart phones, etc.). Computer games are played for the enjoyment they provide, but there is not a consensus about what makes games enjoyable, or the sources of computer game enjoyment.

Understanding the sources of computer game enjoyment is important not only to improve the design of games to make them more enjoyable, but to improve any design where we want users to want to use the system, or we want users to keep coming back. In other words, whenever user engagement and retention are design goals, designers will benefit from designing for user enjoyment.

© Springer International Publishing AG 2017
M. Kurosu (Ed.): HCI 2017, Part II, LNCS 10272, pp. 99–108, 2017.
DOI: 10.1007/978-3-319-58077-7_9

Designing for enjoyment is important when creating games with a purpose beyond enjoyment, serious games or educational games. Enjoyment is important when we are trying to make business systems or other non-game systems more game-like, a process known as gamification or gameful design. So, understanding what makes computer games enjoyable is an important research question with broad applications for the design of systems and interactive experiences.

Existing models of what makes computer games enjoyable are not comprehensive enough to capture the full breadth of possible sources of enjoyment, and most were not generated by empirical research. This research aims to fill that gap. Our aim is to generate a new, more comprehensive model of computer game enjoyment. Using existing models as inspiration for possible sources of enjoyment, we plan to explore people's mental models of what makes games enjoyable using a card sorting approach.

2   Previous Research

2.1   Specific Theories: Flow and Self-Determination

Several theories have suggested specific sources of game enjoyment. Flow theory suggests that tackling a series of optimal challenges that stretch the skills of the player without overwhelming them is one source of enjoyment (Nakamura and Csikszent-mihalyi 2002). There are three flow conditions that lead to flow, which in turn leads to enjoyment: optimal challenges, clear goals, and immediate feedback.

Self-Determination Theory proposes that fulfilling psychological needs for competence, relatedness, and autonomy (Ryan and Deci 2000). Competence is the perception that you are good at what you are doing, relatedness is a sense of social connectedness and belonging, and autonomy is the sense that you have chosen to do what you are doing. Self-Determination Theory says that an environment that meets these needs facilitates intrinsic motivation, which leads to enjoyment.

Ryan et al. (2006) applied Self-Determination Theory (SDT) specifically to games to develop the Player Experience of Need Satisfaction (PENS) model. The PENS model expanded the SDT model to include Presence, feeling like you are there in the game or like you are one of the characters, and Intuitive Controls, which is how much the game controls make sense, are easily mastered, and do not distract from your sense of being in the game.

Flow Theory and Self-Determination Theory are frequently cited sources of game enjoyment, but they do not provide a comprehensive picture of what makes games enjoyable. Instead, they dig deeply into specific sources of enjoyment. Similarly, Koster (2013) proposed that the main thing that makes games fun is learning. These are all inspiring theories, but do not give us a comprehensive picture of what makes computer games enjoyable.

2.2   Theories of Games and Play

Sutton-Smith (2009, p. 215, p. 219–220) presented several sources of enjoyment in his rhetorical analysis of play: progress, fate (which I would call looking forward to uncertain outcomes), power over others, identity, imagination, peak experiences (i.e. flow), and frivolity. Caillois (1961) proposed a classification of games into competition, chance, simulation, and vertigo, or a combination of these elements.

These theories of games and play are based on rhetorical analysis and philosophical contemplation respectively. So, they were not generated by or supported by empirical evidence.

2.3 Player Types and Motivations to Play Games

Bartle (1996) created a model of four motivations to play online games based on the idea that players can act or interact with the world and other players: Achiever, Socializer, Killer, and Explorer. Bartle's model was theoretical and not based on empirical evidence.

Yee (2006) created a model of motivations to play online games with three components: achievement, social, and immersion. The construct validity of this model was assessed with a large-sample survey and factor analysis. However, because the items used to generate Yee's survey were based on Bartle's model, it may not be comprehensive enough. Bartle's model was not generated by any empirical research, and so his model and the models built off of it appear to be limited, incomplete, and lacking in content validity.

Brown and Vaughan (2010) proposed eight play personalities: The Joker, The Kinesthete, The Explorer, The Competitor, The Director, The Collector, The Artist/Creator, and The Storyteller. These play personalities were then expanded and popularized by Fullerton (2014) as player types, and included The Achiever and The Performer. As Brown and Vaughan pointed out, there was no scientific basis for these play personalities. However, they do suggest possible sources of computer game enjoyment.

2.4 Taxonomies of Game Enjoyment

Quick et al. (2012) created a six-factor taxonomy of game enjoyment supported by factor analysis of survey data: Fantasy, Exploration, Fidelity, Companionship, Challenge, and Competition. Their survey asked participants to rate how important each of 18 game design features were to their enjoyment of video games. However, they did not discuss how they came up with those 18 game design features. So, it appears the content of the taxonomy developed by Quick, et al. was not generated by any research, and may be lacking in comprehensiveness and content validity as a result.

Lazzaro (2004, 2009) suggested that there are four pathways to emotion that drive play that she called the Four Keys to Fun: Easy Fun (Novelty & Curiosity), Hard Fun (Challenge & Fiero), People Fun (Friendship & Amusement), and Serious Fun (Altered States & Relaxation). Lazzaro (2004) generated these four keys with interviews and observations of 60 people playing their favorite games, but the four keys are only part of the results of that research. Lazzaro sorted qualitative data into affinity groups that resulted in twelve models of what facilitated enjoyment. However, Lazzaro only presented the four keys, which she called the most important pathways to emotion in games, rather than also presenting the groupings or the twelve models that led to the four keys. This suggests that the Four Keys to Fun may be only part of the bigger picture of what makes games enjoyable.

Lazzaro (2004) also identified and defined several positive emotions people experience while playing their favorite games, such as Fear, Surprise, *Naches* (Yiddish for enjoying the accomplishments of mentees), *Fiero* (Italian for triumph and pride), and *Schadenfreude* (German for enjoying the pain of others).

Garneu (2001) listed 14 forms of fun, including Beauty, Problem Solving, Thrill of Danger, Physical Activity, and Creation. This list was not generated or supported by empirical research.

Korhonen et al.(2009) drew on previous models, especially building on Costello and Edmonds's (2007) pleasure framework, to create 20 categories of playful experiences they called the playful experiences or PLEX framework, including Completion, Discovery, Relaxation, Sensation, Expression, Subversion, and Fellowship. Lucero and Arrasvuori (2010) developed a set of PLEX cards with one playful experience on each card, and used these cards to inspire the design of playful experiences for three design projects. Korhonen et al. (2009) only assessed the PLEX framework by interviewing thirteen game players and finding that they mentioned each of the PLEX categories during the interviews.

These theoretical frameworks and taxonomies can inspire questions to ask participants, but are not comprehensive models of what makes computer games enjoyable.

2.5 Positive Psychology

Positive Psychology is the empirical science of positive traits, experiences, relationships, and institutions (Seligman and Csikszentmihalyi 2000). None of the existing theories of what makes games enjoyable we have found have included a review of the positive psychology research literature.

Park et al. (2004) and Peterson and Seligman (2004) created a classification of 24 Character Strengths and Virtues (CSV) as Positive Psychology's response to Clinical Psychology's *Diagnostic and Statistical Manual of Mental Disorders* (DSM). While the CSV focuses on the traits or qualities of people, one of the criteria used to develop the CSV was that each strength or virtue needs to be fulfilling. So, the experience of using each character strength or virtue provides a different fulfilling, positive experience. Each of these positive experiences may be potential sources of computer game enjoyment.

Peterson et al. (2005) suggested three sources of happiness: flow, pleasure, and meaning. We have discussed flow already (see Sect. 2 above). A life of pleasure or hedonism is about maximizing sensory pleasure and minimizing pain. A life of meaning or eudemonia is about feeling that your life serves a greater purpose beyond yourself, typically by serving other people or humanity, making the world a better place, or feeling that your life will have a lasting positive impact that will continue after you die. Peterson, Park, and Seligman found that these three sources of happiness were empirically distinguishable and that an orientation towards flow, pleasure, and meaning each individually predicted life satisfaction and combined as a three-way interaction to predict life satisfaction. These three sources of happiness are most likely sources of positive experiences or enjoyment as well, but they are far from a comprehensive model of enjoyment sources.

Positive psychology research has also explored positive emotions. Fredrickson (2009) discussed ten positive emotions such as serenity, interest, hope, pride, and inspiration. Shiota (2014) explored how different positive emotions serve different adaptive functions, presenting a taxonomy of functionally discrete positive emotions that shows the evolutionary basis and benefit of eight emotions (see also Shiota et al. 2014). Shiota's taxonomy includes positive emotions such as enthusiasm, contentment, nurturant love, amusement, and awe. This taxonomy also lists the adaptive function of each emotion, such as contentment encouraging people to rest in safety to digest and encode routes to success, amusement leading people to develop flexible, complex cognitive-behavioral repertoires through play, and awe serving the adaptive function of accommodating new information from one's environment.

Condon et al. (2014) suggested that there may be atypical positive instances of emotions that are typically considered negative. They called atypically positive instances of fear, anger, and sadness pleasant fear, pleasant anger, and pleasant sadness. So, the thrill of a rollercoaster ride may be an example of pleasant fear, and the anger we feel towards villains in a story could be an example of pleasant anger.

The existing models of what makes games enjoyable are not comprehensive enough. Other than the concept of optimal challenge from flow theory, we have yet to see research on game enjoyment take full advantage of positive psychology research and theories.

3   Method

3.1   Preparation of Materials

To develop a more comprehensive model of the sources of game enjoyment, we conducted a broad literature review and generated a list of 167 potential sources of enjoyment and their definitions. We drew on all of the sources described in the literature review above, as well as a wide range of psychology, games, play, and human-computer interaction research, and we developed some original items as well. We listed each source of enjoyment with its definition and references in a spreadsheet.

Our research team then conducted three open card sorting sessions to categorize these sources of enjoyment. The 167 sources of enjoyment and their definitions were each printed on cards. Then, in separate sessions, we individually sorted the items into groups and labeled the groups. Synthesizing these results gave us 24 initial categories of enjoyment sources (see Table 1).

3.2   Procedure

We plan to conduct six rounds of card sorting to iteratively refine and improve these categories, similar to the method used by Moore and Benbasat (1991), to ensure the

Table 1. Initial categories of enjoyment sources with descriptions

Category of enjoyment sources	Description (Shortened)	Possibly related potential sources of enjoyment
Control & choice	Feeling able to direct, determine, or influence desired outcomes, including how those outcomes are achieved	Autonomy, customization, collecting
Pride for achievement	Triumph experienced when you feel responsible for reaching desirable outcomes through great effort	Pride, Fiero (Italian), completion
Perceived ability	Feeling confident that you have the skills and abilities needed to achieve desired outcomes	Self-efficacy, competence, performance feedback
Progress	Movement or advancement towards desired outcomes	Progress, immediate progress feedback
Optimal challenge	Doing an activity that is difficult enough to stretch your skills to their limits without being so difficult that it overwhelms you	Optimal challenge, optimal pacing
Step-by-step guidance & clear goals	Feeling that your actions are being supported or facilitated so that you know what to do next throughout an activity	Guidance, clear proximal goals
Open-minded strategizing	Thinking through the best way to do an activity with an open mind	Strategy, open-mindedness
Creating & improvising	Creating and creative expression, whether spontaneously improvised or carefully crafted	Improvised play; simulation, role-playing, performing
Body movement & exercise	The experience of moving your body	Kinesthetic movement, cardiovascular exercise
Life goals, meaning, or purpose	The sense that your actions are helping fulfill your life's purpose, giving your life meaning, or contributing to how you want to be remembered after you die	Meaning or purpose, task significance, legacy
Learning & skill improvement	Fulfilling a desire to improve your knowledge, skills, and abilities	Kaizen (Japanese), practice, constructive feedback or opportunities for learning, awe or wonder
Suspense & surprise of uncertain outcomes	The suspenseful anticipation of surprise and the surprise itself	Anticipation of uncertain outcomes, hope, surprise
Variety & novelty	The degree of variation and newness among the actions you are taking or in your ongoing experience	Novelty, skill variety, variety of experiences

(*continued*)

Table 1. (*continued*)

Category of enjoyment sources	Description (Shortened)	Possibly related potential sources of enjoyment
Social bonding & belonging	Forming and maintaining strong, stable interpersonal relationships and friendships with others	Belonging or relatedness, collaboration or cooperation, helping others, compassion
Social superiority & controlling others	Feeling superior to others or higher in the social hierarchy than others. Directing the actions of others to achieve your desired outcomes	Competition, directing others, power over others, schadenfreude (german), leadership
Identity & maintaining a positive self-image	Feeling that your actions are consistent with your identity.	Distinctiveness of identity, continuity of identity, self-esteem
Perceived danger	A perceived threat of harm that makes you feel tense and makes you want to either run away or fight	Pleasant fear, pleasant anger, thrill of danger
Excitement & vitality	Vigorous, high-spirited, alert attention focused on your actions or your ongoing experience	Vitality, optimal level of physiological arousal
Safety & non-seriousness	Fulfilling a desire to be free from harm. Reducing or avoiding harm	Protecting others, familiarity, non-seriousness or lack of real-world consequences
Relaxation & serenity	A calm state free from physical or mental tension or concern. Conserving or regenerating your energy	Relaxation, serenity or contentment, escape from real-life problems, relief, catharsis
Humor, laughter, & amusement	Laughter and playful joy resulting from humor, or unexpected incongruity in a safe social context	Laughter, humor, amusement or non-serious social incongruity
Elevation & inspiration	Appreciating and being inspired by unexpected acts of kindness or compassion	Inspiration, elevation, appreciation of moral beauty, appreciation of excellence
Savoring & gratitude	Paying attention to and appreciating the joys, pleasures, and other positive experiences in your life	Savoring, gratitude, reminiscing or nostalgia
Sensory pleasure	Positively experienced sensory perceptions, including sight, sound, smell, taste, and touch	Sensory pleasure, altered states of consciousness, sexual desire or eroticism, vertigo, altered perception of time, appreciation of beauty
Not a source of enjoyment	These cards are not potential sources of computer game enjoyment	

content validity of our new model. Each of the six rounds will have ten participants who will each complete the study one-on-one with the researcher, giving us a total of sixty participants.

Participants will individually sort 167 cards, each with a potential source of enjoyment and its definition printed on it, into the 24 initial categories, plus a "Not a Source of Enjoyment" category (see Table 1 above). Each category and description of that category will be printed on cards as well. We will ask participants to create new categories if any of the sources of enjoyment do not fit in the categories presented. Participants will also be asked if they feel any sources of computer game enjoyment are missing, and in which category they would place those additional sources.

Next, participants will fill out a questionnaire to collect demographic information and computer gaming habits. Demographic questions include native language, age, and gender. Gaming habits questions include the number of years they have been playing video or computer games, frequency of playing games, and the genres of games they typically play.

3.3 Planned Analysis

After each round of ten participants, we will calculate the Randolph's (2005) free-marginal multi-rater kappa values of inter-rater agreement between participants. This free-marginal kappa is appropriate because participants are free to assign any number of items to each category. If the multi-rater kappa values are below our target of 0.7, we will revise the categories, their descriptions, and any confusing sources of enjoyment. We will continue until either our target multi-rater kappa value is met or we have run six rounds of card sorting.

This iterative card sorting method is intended to develop a more robust and comprehensive model of the sources of game enjoyment, grounded in the mental models and experience of our participants, with more content validity than existing models. We hope this new model will lead to design guidelines for Human-Computer Interaction practitioners, games user researchers, and game designers that will help make their games and other designs more enjoyable.

3.4 Limitations

The model we are hoping to develop is a general model of computer game enjoyment. We plan for this model to be a beginning and not an end, a springboard for further research. We plan to use the final categories of enjoyment sources from this study as factors to develop a questionnaire measure. The relative importance of these factors to players' enjoyment of computer games is likely to vary across game genres, across individual games, across user groups, and over time. These differences are definitely worthy of future research. However, we view this basic research to develop a general model of the sources of computer game enjoyment as a critical first step that must be taken before digging deeper into how to optimize enjoyment for different games and different groups of users.

The categories of enjoyment sources that come out of this research are not intended to be a formula for making cookie-cutter computer games or paint-by-numbers gamification, but a classification framework to help designers think in a more clear and intentional way about how to make designs more enjoyable to use. Rather than a recipe dictating to designers how to design, the categories are meant to be a way to think about and work with the different flavors of enjoyment. Suspense and surprise, humor and danger, excitement and relaxation, optimal challenge and pride for achievement, and so on – these flavors of positive experience give designers a framework or a toolkit to design for enjoyment. We hope the categories of enjoyment sources that come out of this study will also lead to further research to validate this new model and to investigate the effectiveness of each category in more detail.

4   Current Progress and Next Steps

We have IRB approval and we are in the process of recruiting participants and conducting the study. We plan to present the results from this study at the conference.

We hope this research will lead to a new, more comprehensive model of what makes games enjoyable. We would like to see this new model applied as broadly as possible, to make designs people will want to use, to engineer enjoyable experiences, and to make life a little bit more fun for everyone.

References

Bartle, R.: Hearts, clubs, diamonds, spades: players who suit MUDs. J. Virtual Environ. (1996). http://mud.co.uk/richard/hcds.htm

Brown, S., Vaughan, C.: Play. How it Shapes the Brain, Opens the Imagination, and Invigorates the Soul. Avery, New York (2010)

Caillois, R.: Man, Play, and Games. University of Illinois Press, Champaign (1961)

Costello, B., Edmonds, E.: A study in play, pleasure and interaction design. In Proceedings of the 2007 Conference on Designing Pleasurable Products and Interfaces, pp. 76–91. ACM (2007)

Condon, P., Wilson-Mendenhall, C.D., Barrett, L.F.: What is a positive emotion? The psychological construction of pleasant fear and unpleasant happiness. In: Tugade, M.M., Shiota, M.N., Kirby, L.D. (eds.) Handbook of positive emotions, pp. 60–81 (2014)

Fredrickson, B.: Positivity. Harmony, New York (2009)

Fullerton, T.: Game Design Workshop: A Playcentric Approach to Creating Innovative Games, 3rd edn. AK Peters/CRC Press, Boca Raton (2014)

Garneu, P.A.: Fourteen forms of fun (2001). http://www.gamasutra.com/view/feature/227531/fourteen_forms_of_fun

Korhonen, H., Montola, M., & Arrasvuori, J.: Understanding playful user experience through digital games. In: International Conference on Designing Pleasurable Products and Interfaces (Vol. 2009) (2009)

Koster, R.: Theory of Fun for Game Design, 2nd edn. O'Reilly Media, Sebastopol (2013)

Lazzaro, N.: Why We Play Games: Four Keys to More Emotion Without Story (2004). http://xeodesign.com/xeodesign_whyweplaygames.pdf

Lazzaro, N.: Why we play: affect and the fun of games. In: Sears, A., Jacko, J.A. (eds.) Human-Computer Interaction: Designing for Diverse Users and Domains, pp. 155–176 (2009)

Lucero, A., Arrasvuori, J.:. PLEX cards: a source of inspiration when designing for playfulness. In: Proceedings of the 3rd International Conference on Fun and Games, pp. 28–37. ACM, New York (2010)

Moore, G.C., Benbasat, I.: Development of an instrument to measure the perceptions of adopting an information technology innovation. Inf. Syst. Res. **2**(3), 192–222 (1991)

Nakamura, J., Csikszentmihalyi, M.: The concept of flow. In: Snyder, C.R., Lopez, S.J. (eds.) Handbook of Positive Psychology, pp. 89–105. Oxford University Press, New York (2002)

Park, N., Peterson, C., Seligman, M.E.: Strengths of character and well-being. J. Soc. Clin. Psychol. **23**(5), 603–619 (2004)

Peterson, C., Park, N., Seligman, M.E.: Orientations to happiness and life satisfaction: The full life versus the empty life. J. Happiness Stud. **6**(1), 25–41 (2005)

Peterson, C., Seligman, M.E.: Character Strengths and Virtues: A Handbook and Classification. Oxford University Press, Oxford (2004)

Quick, J.M., Atkinson, R.K., Lin, L.: Empirical taxonomies of gameplay enjoyment: personality and video game preference. Int. J. Game-Based Learn. (IJGBL) **2**(3), 11–31 (2012)

Randolph, J.J.: Free-marginal multi-rater kappa: an alternative to Fleiss' fixed-marginal multi-rater kappa. In: Joensuu University Learning and Instruction Symposium 2005, Joensuu, Finland, 14–15 October 2005 (2005)

Ryan, R.M., Deci, E.L.: Self-determination theory and the facilitation of intrinsic motivation, social development, and well-being. Am. Psychol. **55**(1), 68 (2000)

Ryan, R.M., Rigby, C.S., Przybylski, A.: The motivational pull of video games: a self-determination theory approach. Motiv. Emot. **30**(4), 344–360 (2006)

Seligman, M.E.P., Csikszentmihalyi, M.: Positive psychology: an introduction. Am. Psychol. **55**, 5–14 (2000)

Shiota, M.N.: The evolutionary perspective in positive emotion research. In: Tugade, M.M., Shiota, M.N., Kirby, L.D. (eds.) Handbook of positive emotions (pp. 44–59) (2014)

Shiota, M.N., Neufeld, S.L., Danvers, A.F., Osborne, E.A., Sng, O., Yee, C.I.: Positive emotion differentiation: a functional approach. Soc. Pers. Psychol. Compass **8**(3), 104–117 (2014)

Sutton-Smith, B.: The Ambiguity of Play. Harvard University Press, Massachusetts (2009)

Yee, N.: Motivations for play in online games. CyberPsychol. Behav. **9**(6), 772–775 (2006)

Mobile and Wearable Interaction

When Technology Supports Urban Mobility: Improvements for Mobile Applications Based on a UX Evaluation

Rodrigo L.A. Almeida$^{(\boxtimes)}$, Lana B. Mesquita, Rainara M. Carvalho, and Rossana M.C. Andrade

Group of Computer Networks, Software Engineering and Systems (GREat) Department of Computer Science, Federal University of Ceará, Fortaleza, Brazil {rodrigoalmeida,lanamesquita,rainaracarvalho,rossana}@great.ufc.br

Abstract. The development of applications that helps urban mobility has been pushed by the increase of processing capacity and miniaturization of the mobile device as well as the improvement of speed and availability of Internet. Such applications can support users in several activities such as tracing routes and searching for addresses. In this scenario, this work aims to: *(i)* understand how users use urban mobility applications; *(ii)* evaluate the quality of interaction and interface into real applications called "Waze" and "Meu Ônibus"; and *(iii)* improve the applications based on the results of the evaluations. Moreover, this study also suggests a set of recommendations for urban mobility applications in developing countries like Brazil.

Keywords: Urban mobility · Mobile applications · Usability · User experience · Evaluation methods

1 Introduction

Urban Mobility represents a major problem in medium and large cities of Brazil [14,18]. The main reason is the amount of people living in urban areas. For instance, according to the latest census of the Brazilian Institute of Geography and Statistics (IBGE)[1], the number of people living in urban spaces continues to grow and represents 84% of the population [6].

Moreover, the infrastructure capacity and quality of the city do not correspond the growth of the population, what consequently creates many problems, for example, traffic jam, roads in bad conditions, low number of public transports, excess capacity of people in public transports, among others.

The evolution of the information technologies, especially mobile technology, enables the development of solutions to minimize the problems mentioned

R.L.A. Almeida—Scholarship (MDCC/DC/UFC) sponsored by FCPC.

L.B. Mesquita—Scholarship (MDCC/DC/UFC) sponsored by FUNCAP.

R.M.C. Andrade—Researcher scholarship - DT Level 2, sponsored by CNPq.

[1] http://goo.gl/ckJf7k.

© Springer International Publishing AG 2017
M. Kurosu (Ed.): HCI 2017, Part II, LNCS 10272, pp. 111–130, 2017.
DOI: 10.1007/978-3-319-58077-7_10

before [3]. For example, we can cite the use of sensors to collect user information [5,7,8,16,27], the improvements in processing power of mobile devices, and the increased speed and availability of Internet [17].

Examples of these solutions are mobile applications for several means of transport (*e.g.,* car, bus, taxi, and bicycle). These solutions are changing the way people move. Currently, there are applications to trace routes, check traffic flow, monitor transports in real-time, and so on. Thus, the user experience of such technologies is an important factor to ensure their use and adoption.

There is previous research about user experience with urban mobility applications [4,9,28]. Nevertheless, more investigation is necessary to understand and to improve the user experience with such technologies in a large city in a developing country like Brazil. In this context, the XV Brazilian Symposium on Human Factors in Computational Systems launched an evaluation competition with the following theme "User Experience in Urban Mobility Applications"[2]. In this competition, researchers should use HCI evaluation methods to discover UX problems. In this scenario, our team, who are the authors of this paper, participated in this contest with two goals: *(i)* understand how people use urban mobility apps in Brazil; and *(ii)* evaluate the most used urban mobility applications.

To understand how people use mobile applications and what are their opinion about them, we used a *Survey*, in which we identified two most used applications: Waze[3], the Brazilian version, and "Meu Ônibus"[4], that means My Bus in English.

To evaluate the identified applications, we used a Heuristic Evaluation [21] and a Usability Testing [20]. The first one gives the necessary input to decide how to apply the next one. For example, we chose the problematics activities to explore in the usability evaluation by users.

Therefore, this paper presents not only an overview of the results from the competition [1], but also an evolution of this work by *(i)* performing a *Sentiment Analysis* in the Google Play reviews and *(ii)* proposing improvements for the identified problems. The purpose of the Sentiment Analysis is to identify the level of user satisfaction through the opinionated content and categorize it as positive, negative or neutral, as well as many other studies [10,23,24,29]. To suggest the improvements of the interfaces, first, we performed a brainstorming based on the previous results [1] with HCI experts to plan the improvements. After that, we applied a *Survey* with users to evaluated the suggestions of the interface. As a consequence of this research, this study also suggests a set of recommendations for urban mobility applications in developing countries like Brazil.

This paper is organized as follows: Sect. 2 presents the adopted methodology, which is composed of three phases and each one has a description of the used methods and instruments. Section 3 shows the primary results of all used

---

[2] http://ihc2016.mybluemix.net/br/cfp.jsp.

[3] Waze - https://play.google.com/store/apps/details?id=com.waze\&hl=pt.

[4] Meu Ônibus - https://play.google.com/store/apps/details?id=br.com.m2m.meuon ibus&hl=pt.

methods. Section 4 presents a discussion of the results, along with a set of recommendations for urban mobility applications in Brazil. Finally, Sect. 5 presents the conclusions of this work.

2 Methodology

The adopted methodology of this work is composed of three phases (See Fig. 1). The first two phases are from the evaluation competition, except the sentiment analysis, which we performed for this paper. The third phase is an evolution of the work from the contest, which is the main contribution of this paper. We present each one in the next subsections.

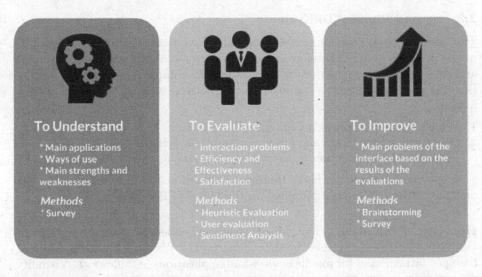

Fig. 1. Adopted methodology

2.1 First Phase - To Understand

This first phase aims to *understand* how users are using urban mobility applications. We defined the following three questions to achieve this goal:

1. What are the most popular applications used to support user locomotion?
2. How users use these applications?
3. What are its main strengths and weaknesses in the users' opinion?

The technique used to collect the data was a *Survey* since this is a good way to get answers to specific questions from a large number of people [25]. We use the *Google Forms*[5] platform to craft the online survey. It has four sections of fifteen questions. The first section concerns user consent to participate in the survey and confirm if he/she uses urban mobility applications. The second section concerns to user demographics. The third section deals with questions about the use of transport in daily activities. The fourth and final section is related to the use of technology for urban mobility.

Through the analysis of survey responses, it was possible to trace two profiles of users and to identify two most used applications ("Waze" and "Meu Ônibus"). Additionally, we could identify the most used features, the suggestions for improvement, several kinds of urban mobility, and technology issues. All this information was useful for the second phase of this work. The answer for the first-phase question is present in the results section.

2.2   Second Phase - To Evaluate

This phase aims to *evaluate* the user experience with two applications identified in the previous phase. Therefore, we collect data about efficiency, effectiveness, and satisfaction, as well as problems and interface improvement opportunities. Like the previous phase, we define three questions to support the evaluation, as follows:

1. Which interaction problems did users have to face?
2. How much effectiveness and efficiency users can achieve their goals?
3. What are the satisfaction the user about of these applications?

Then, we use three methods: Heuristic Evaluation [21], User Evaluation [20] and the *Sentiment Analysis*, applied on the Google Play reviews.

Heuristic Evaluation. The set of heuristics called SMASH (Smartphone Usability Heuristics) was used by three experts [11]. We chose this set because it has specific heuristics for mobile devices and applications, as follows: *1-* Visibility of system status; *2-* Match between system and the real world; *3-* User control and freedom; *4-* Consistency and standards; *5-* Error prevention; *6-* Minimize the user's memory load; *7-* Customization and shortcuts; *8-* Efficiency of use and performance; *9-* Aesthetic and minimalist design; *10-* Help users recognize, diagnose, and recover from errors; *11-* Help and documentation; and *12-* physical interaction and ergonomics. Three experts, who have at least two years of experience in researching human-computer interaction, performed the evaluation.

The activities for evaluators performing in each application were based on the most used features by users who answered the survey of phase 1. The following activities have been defined for "Meu Ônibus": *(1)* to view transport schedules; *(2)* to verify which lines pass through a particular place; *(3)* to find bus stops; and *(4)* to find an itinerary/route of a bus. For "Waze": *(1)* to verify traffic real-time; *(2)* to search by address; *(3)* to verify travel time between two locations; *(4)* to create a route; and *(5)* to follow the route real-time.

---

[5] The following link provides a copy of our survey: https://github.com/GREatPesquisa/2017-Research-Urban-Mobility-Applications.

User Evaluation. Ten users (seven men and three women) were recruited to use "Meu Ônibus" and "Waze". We selected users by taking into account the two profiles identified in the survey results (see Fig. 2). Five members represent the profile A, so they used "Meu Ônibus". The other five represents the profile B and then used "Waze". The results section contains the profiles explanation.

The activities performed by the users were the same as those carried out by the experts in the heuristic evaluation. The device used for both "Meu Ônibus" and "Waze" was the LG Nexus 5 model with 2GB of RAM and 2.3 GHz Quad Core processor. The versions used for "Meu Ônibus" and "Waze" applications were: 1.0 and 4.3.0.2, respectively. We delivered this device to the user with the application already configured for use. Finally, we performed two pilot tests, one for "Meu Ônibus" and another for "Waze", with different users from those recruited for the evaluations.

The data collection consisted of observing the users performing the activities. In "Meu Ônibus", all activities were performed in the laboratory. In "Waze", only one of the activities was carried out in the field due to its nature: *(v)* track the path in real-time. For that, the places of origin and destination were predetermined by the evaluators and previously said to the users. Thus, the execution of this activity required the user's car. Therefore, the "Waze" assessment was performed only by users who had a driver's license, own car and availability to use it during the evaluation.

During the observation sessions, we planned to obtain the following data: completeness of the activity, number of interactions and number of problems. The following instruments were used to collect them: think-aloud technique [22], audio recordings and videos of the screens, both performed by the Az Screen Recorder application[6], and also notes taken by the observers.

Finally, the interpretation and consolidation of results were performed. For the interpretation of the data, we analyzed the user interaction videos, *think-aloud* audio transcripts, and notes from the observer. Three HCI evaluators performed the analysis of the data which resulted in a list of problems and improvements opportunities.

Sentiment Analysis. With the purpose of understanding better the user perception about the select applications, we analyzed their Google Play[7] reviews, which can provide a general opinion from the users about them [13]. The perceived value of reviews on the Web is uncontested and constitute an attractive area for exploration [10]. Sentiment analysis systems are being applied in almost every business and social domain because opinions are central to nearly all human activities and are key influencers of our behaviors [15]. For example, consumer surveys show people cite product reviews as a top influencer in purchase decisions [19].

---

[6] http://az-screen-recorder.br.uptodown.com/android.

[7] The official app store for the Android operating system - https://play.google.com/store.

Unfortunately, reading through the massive amounts of product reviews available online from many e-communities, forums, and newsgroups is not only a tedious task but also an impractical one [31]. So, to analyze by classifying sentiment polarity of reviews at the document level is a consolidated solution to solve this problem and it has been used in some research, such as [13,23,29].

Sentiment analysis is a language processing task that uses a computational approach to identify opinionated content and categorize it as positive or negative. Also, it tries to define the expressions of opinion and mood of writers [10], and it can analyze evaluations, attitudes, and emotions from written language [15].

There are many tools, application programming interfaces (API's) and services that provide sentiment analysis, as SentiWordNet [2], AlchemyAPI [30], PowerReviews[8], or BuzzMetrics[9]. Saif et al. [26] evaluated popular tools for entity extraction and concept identification, and, based on this information, we chose the AlchemyAPI to apply.

AlchemyLanguage is a collection of natural language processing APIs that help you understand the sentiment, keywords, entities, high-level concepts and more [30]. Natural language processing APIs available through AlchemyLanguage add a high-level semantic information, and it is capable of performing: Entity Extraction, Sentiment Analysis, Emotion Analysis, Keyword Extraction, Concept Tagging, Relation Extraction, Taxonomy Classification, among others.

We developed a system to automatized the Sentiment Analysis by using the AlchemyAPI: SANGRIa (Sentimental ANalysis Googleplay RevIews)[10]. Data collected by SANGRIa help us understand better the user satisfaction.

2.3 Third Phase - To Improve

The goal of this phase is to propose improvements that can be adopted by the applications to enhance the user experience. Like the previous phases, we have defined questions to help guide this step:

1. What kind of improvements can be incorporated to enhance the user experience?
2. What is the opinion of users about the improvements?

To help answer these questions, we performed a brainstorming [12] session with the same team of experts who participated in the heuristic and user evaluations. The researchers conducted each of two sessions for approximately two hours. Sessions began with a recap of the biggest problems of each application, followed by discussions and sketching proposals for solutions to each problem. As a result, the meetings provided a set of improvements for each application. Then, we apply modifications in the application interfaces.

---

[8] PowerReviews - http://www.powerreviews.com/.

[9] BuzzMetrics - http://buzzmetrics.com/.

[10] The code of SANDRIa is available in https://github.com/GREatPesquisa/SANGRIa.

In order to validate the modifications, we developed an online questionnaire[11] showing them for the same users who participated in the evaluation. "Waze" questionnaire had seven questions and "Meu Ônibus" had nine questions. Questions were about the found issues and the improvements suggested. Therefore, for each issue was pointed out a solution. In this way, the user had to score on a five-point Likert Scale if that solution was meaningful to the user experience or not. According to the users' answers, it was possible to map which solutions best suited the users' needs.

3   Results

The following subsections describe the primary results from each method used.

3.1   First Phase - To Understand

The survey reached 17 Brazilian states, and Ceará was the state with the most replies counted (81%). The survey obtained 345 respondents, 59% male respondents and 41% female respondents. The main results achieved by this method was the definition of the user profiles, as shown in Fig. 2, and the identification of two most used applications.

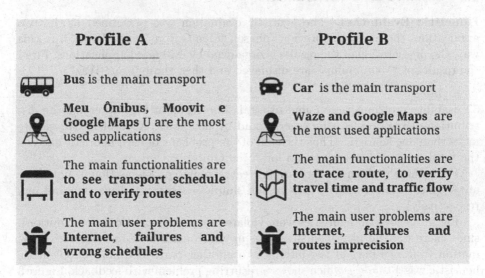

Fig. 2. Profiles A and B

The two profiles have the following characteristics in common: the user is in the 21–30 age group, does not feel safe using his means of transport, lives in a large city that has a vast network of public transportation and heavy traffic.

---

[11] The following link provides a copy of surveys used in the third phase: https://github.com/GREatPesquisa/2017-Research-Urban-Mobility-Applications.

The main difference between the profiles is in the means of transportation used in everyday life. Profile A uses car and profile B uses bus.

The user profiles and the ranking of the applications in the questionnaire guided the selection of the applications. The most chosen application to help bus mobility was "Meu Ônibus" (15%), selected to Profile A. To a particular transport, the most chosen was "Waze" (52%), selected to Profile B.

In "Meu Ônibus", the main features used are: see transport schedules; verify the route of public transport; check which transport lines pass through a certain place; and check stops of transport. The main features used in "Waze" application are to trace a route; search by address; check travel time between places, and check the flow of real-time traffic. Thus, these features guided the activities of heuristics and user evaluation in both applications of each profile.

Additionally, the questionnaire identified the main problems faced by each user profile. The main problems encountered by profile A are the Internet connection, application crashes and wrong schedules. The main problems faced by Profile B are route updating and accuracy, Internet connection, in safe routes and application crashes. Thus, this information was useful for evaluators to gain an understanding about the difficulties people face during interaction with the selected applications.

3.2   Second Phase - To Evaluate

Heuristic Evaluation. The heuristic evaluation was performed in the two applications chosen by the previous phase ("Meu Ônibus" and "Waze"). In this way, the presentation of the results is organized by evaluated applications. First, the results of "Meu Ônibus" are displayed and then those from "Waze".

Meu Ônibus
33 usability problems were found in total. The graph of Fig. 3 presents the distribution of the problems by severity and by heuristics. A problem can violate more than one heuristic. Thus the sum of the problems of each heuristic exceeds the total value of problems found for "Meu Ônibus".

From these problems, there are few catastrophic problems (four), but there are a considerable number of severe and simple severity problems (ten and ten, respectively).

Figure 3 shows all heuristics were violated, except Heuristic 6 (Recognition), since there were no identified situations in which users have to memorize information from one part of the interface to another part. The most problematic heuristic was *Visibility*, which shows a recurring problem with feedback. Figure 3 illustrates one of the problems encountered about this. This problem happens because map feedback messages to inform point locations are very fast, if the user is walking or distracted, he/she will not see the message.

Waze
In the evaluation of the "Waze" application, we consolidated fifteen usability problems. The graph of Fig. 4 shows the distribution of these problems by severity and by heuristic. From these problems, 2 are catastrophic, 7 are major, 6 are minor, and only 1 is cosmetic.

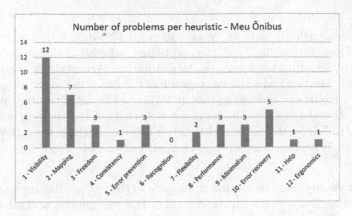

Fig. 3. Number of Problems per Heuristic - "Meu Ônibus"

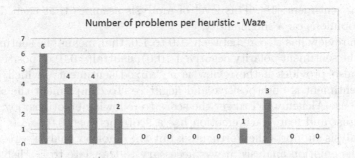

Fig. 4. Amount of problems per Heurístic - "Waze"

The heuristics Correspondence and Real World presented the most problems. For example, when the user adds a stop location between the beginning and the destination, displaying next to the final destination the expression "ETA". This expression is not clear, since it is not commonly used by to Brazilian users. "ETA" is English acronym for the expression "Estimated Time of Arrival'.

User Evaluation. The presentation of the user evaluation results is organized by applications. In this way, the results of "Meu Ônibus" are first described and then those of "Waze".

Meu Ônibus
The evaluation with all users of "Meu Ônibus" identified 28 interaction and interface problems. After eliminating duplicated problems, we consolidated 13 different problems. From the four activities performed in the evaluation, Activity 3 (to find bus stops) was the most problematic, since no user could perform it because they even could not find the feature. The activity that presented the highest completeness by the users was Activity 1 (to view transport schedules), which deals with the basic feature of the application, which is to check the time of transport. The feature checks how long the bus arrives at the user's current bus stop.

Waze

The evaluation with all users of "Waze" identified 30 interaction and interface problems. After eliminating duplicated problems, it found 11 different problems. From the five activities performed in the evaluation, Activity 3 (to verify travel time between location) was the most problematic since the users have difficult to find and understand how doing this in "Waze". The activities that presented the highest completeness by the users were Activity 4 (to create a route) and Activity 5 (to follow the route real-time). The completeness by activities four and five is good because they are one of main features of "Waze".

Sentiment Analysis. The sentiment analysis in the GooglePlay reviews has the focus on distinguishing between statements of fact vs. opinion, and on detecting the polarity of sentiments being expressed [13]. Sentiment analysis was used at a document level to classify whether a whole opinion document expresses a positive or negative sentiment [15]. This level of analysis assumes that each document expresses opinions on a single entity.

So each review has a score between -1.0 to 1.0, that means the sentiment rate indicates the sentiment polarity negative (<0.0), neutral($=0.0$) or positive(>0.0). The API also provides if the review is a "mixed sentiment", which indicates that the sentiment is both positive and negative. To complement the sentiment results, we use AlchemyAPI to get the score to following emotions: joy, sadness, anger, disgust and fear. Each emotion has a score between 0.0 to 1.0. The sentiment analysis supports the Portuguese, but the emotion analysis does not. So, to apply the emotion analysis, it was necessary to translate to English by using a service GoogleTranslate[12].

Since the GooglePlay Reviews are available only for your owners, all the reviews were getting manually, what limited our data acquisition. GooglePlay platform classifies the reviews to show in three orders: newest, rating and helpfulness.

The sentiment analysis data results are an estimate, and this approach could have errors due to bad translations, the presence of unrecognized characters, like keyboard shortcuts for emoticons, swear words, popular terms not recognized to the dictionaries, even grammatical problems of writing. The last one frequently occurs in the reviews, which hinders a more accurate result. Besides having available services on the Internet that could insert artificial positive reviews to an application achieve a high level of the rank, known as Opinion Spam [15], e.g., ReviewApp4u[13]. So, the results are considering as complementary to others applied in the next phases.

Meu Ônibus

Figure 5 shows the results of "Meu Ônibus" application based on 189 reviews got in a three-month period classified by newest reviews. The sentiment rate found in the results was balanced with 38% negative reviews and 40% positive reviews. Comparing the emotions found in the reviews, sadness (0.28) and joy (0.34)

---

[12] Google Translate - https://translate.google.com.br.
[13] http://www.reviewapp4u.com.

highlighted, also balanced. Given these results, the general sentiment about this application is neutral, in which neither the positive sentiments, and emotions, nor the negative stand out.

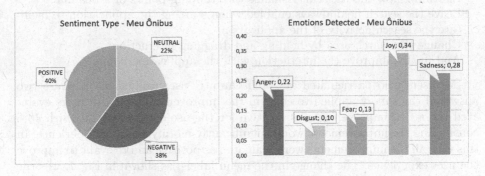

Fig. 5. Sentiment analysis of "Meu Ônibus"

Waze

Figure 6 shows the results of "Waze" application based on 293 reviews got in one-month period classified by helpfulness reviews. We chose these parameters to get the reviews due to a lot of reviews to "Waze" in GooglePlay platform every day. The sentiment rate shows the negative reviews (34%) are substantially over the positive reviews (24%). Comparing the emotions found, anger (0.29) and sadness (0.36) highlighted. As a result, the sentiment and emotions about this application are more negative than positive, different from "Meu Ônibus" application.

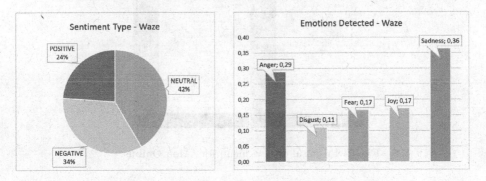

Fig. 6. Sentiment analysis of "Waze"

3.3 Third Phase - To Improve

As a result of brainstorming sessions, we planned improvements in the interface of each application. In the "Meu Ônibus" application, we made the following changes:

– Modifications in the main menu of the application to leave the features clearer, for example, the term "adjustments", which increases or decreases the search area, was modified to "fit in the search radius";

- Allow the user to search the itinerary of a bus or favorite line;
- Display the direction of the bus line clearly in the application to facilitate the user's understanding of this information;
- Informing how the user can visualize the stopping points of a bus line;
- Leave the search field always enabled when starting the application to facilitate the search activity of the application;
- Change the search area by holding and dragging interaction;
- And finally, improve the interaction with the application support.

All users who participated of "Meu Ônibus" user evaluation in phase two answered the survey applied to confirm the improvements. 60% of users evaluated the set of improvements as positive for the use experience, of which 40% considering the improvements would significantly modify the user experience. In this way, all the improvements were evaluated as positive and relevant to improve the user experience. The change in the menu labels, as shown in Fig. 7, was the less friendly item in the user evaluation. About this improvement, 20% thought it would not modify the user experience, 20% found a neutral modification and 60% scored as significant changing the user experience.

Fig. 7. Proposal of new menu for "Meu Ônibus"

The modification most well evaluated by the users was the search field enabled upon entering the application as showed in Fig. 8. Some users in user evaluation, phase two, were not aware of the application's search feature.

Improvements to "Waze" are related to:

- The presence of foreign terms misunderstood by users.
- The search result and the planned route overview in the application (Fig. 9).
- The difficult access of some features such as the conversion list.
- The way the application instructs users on the route.
- The possibility of signaling areas considered unsafe due to the occurrence of robberies.

Fig. 8. Welcome screen proposal of "Meu Ônibus"

In the case of safety-related improvement of suggested routes, by flagging an area as unsafe, the application would avoid suggesting such parts on the route, or it would signal the dangerousness to users' pay attention as they navigate the stretch.

All users in "Waze" user evaluation participated in the evaluation of the improvement proposals. 60% of users evaluated the set of improvements as significant changes from users, 20% rated as good changes to user experience, and the other 20% believe modifications would not change the user experience. The most significant improvement for users was security-related (80%) as showed in Fig. 10. Modifying the search result to see the entire planned route on the map and the reduction of the steps was considered a positive change by 40% of users and a significant change by 40%, of which 20% believes that it would not improve the experience of use.

Users positively evaluated the rest of the improvements. The set of improvements was praised by users and considered relevant if the application implements them. The modifications vary in degrees of complexity, but by the users' willingness the security-related improvement, if implemented, would significantly transform the user experience. Even though the application can not guarantee the user that the suggested routes are safer, the users would feel more secure when using the application. It would slightly alleviate the tension of the users when they move between places in the city, improving their day to day.

4   Discussion

Mobility is a daily reality to great and medium-sized cities. Providing means of transportation that assist users in their most diverse destinations is a social duty of government and society. Technologies of urban mobility have the objective of helping the population to have a better displacement between places. Among

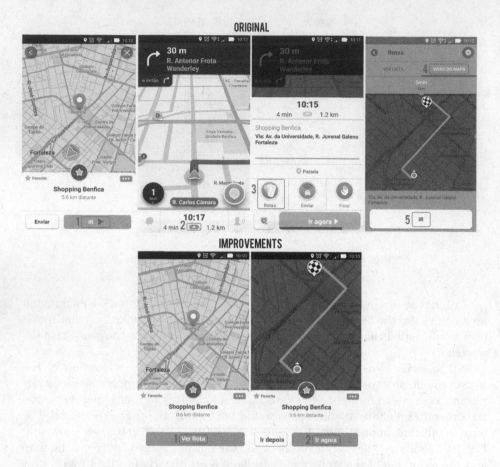

Fig. 9. New way to interact with "Waze" search result

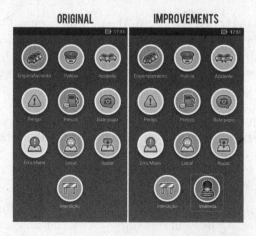

Fig. 10. Security enhancements for "Waze"

these technologies, urban mobility applications have emerged as a resource for improving and optimizing users' lives.

Urban mobility applications need to address a multitude of information to suit to the reality lived by users. Thus, providing accurate, reliable and secure route and address information significantly influences user loyalty. Even though urban mobility applications are suited to the needs of the population, there are factors beyond the scope of applications.

Through the methodology and results of the evaluation, we identified four recommendations for urban mobility applications in the Brazilian context. The recommendation descriptions are in Table 1.

The recommendations are based on recurring principles of usability and human-computer interaction, and also on recurring themes identified in all phases of the methodology. In the third phase of the methodology, it was possible to perceive that some problems faced by the users are solved through the execution of simple ideas. In this way, providing applications that support urban mobility, which perform simple activities and always maintain a clear and objective *feedback* (recommendation 1 in Table 1) is a difficult but possible task. Such difficulty is set up due to the large amount of information that is needed to meet users' needs. The use of maps and detailed information on routes and places supplied the user needs but constitutes an interface overloaded with information. These features typically require interactions that can be cumbersome with elements with a large amount of information, such as zoom interactions and clicks on the map. To maintain a consistent informational level with the objective of the user in the interface is necessary. The improvements proposed mostly had the focus of minimizing the informational burden and transmitting it in a clear manner, do not keeping the information that lead users to unnecessary or incorrect interactions.

Another issue that significantly affected the user experience was the lack of synchronicity between the *information provided by the system with the reality lived by the users* (recommendation 2 in Table 1). Bad routes, wrong schedules, and false information in the context of urban mobility have a profound impact on the user's daily life.

A major problem faced by users of mobile applications is dependence on the Internet connection. Although extremely necessary, the quality of the connection is not always good to offer a good user experience. As a result, applications should *minimize network dependency* (recommendation 3 in Table 1), allowing in a short amount of time with the connection the user receive the most relevant information for the user context. In addition to connection, another essential component for systems that support mobility is GPS, that, attached to the connection, allows the location of addresses and the elaboration of routes. Problems with GPS and connection need to be treated in a proper and distinct way so that user actions are efficient and accurate.

When proposing an application of urban mobility, the social aspects (recommendation 4 in Table 1) related to the context of user use should receive attention. In our research, safety is the most important aspect. In other countries,

Table 1. Recommendations for urban mobility applications in Brazil

Recommendations	Description	Examples
Feedback	Pay attention to provide a clear feedback and keep the user informed about the actions made by the application	When using maps or providing routes to users, make clear the information for the means of transport that the user will use. By car name the streets, an overview of the route. If it is Bus, line name, a route to be traversed, stop points and landmarks if they exist
Reliability	Ensure the reliability of the information provided to users	Do not provide incorrect time and wrong information in real time. If there are unforeseen problems with public transport, prepare a way to notify them about it
Connection	Project well the dependency the connection of app	Provide off-line services to users such as routing and transport schedules. See intelligent ways of providing services in possible connection losses
User context	Consider factors related to the context of use and social aspects suggesting, itineraries and routes safety for users	Try to protect the user from unwanted situations such as dangerous areas or unwanted destinations resulting from the context of use

perhaps other social aspects are more relevant than safety. Applications need to be aware of the social context in which they operate.

Regarding the applications evaluated in phases 2 e 3 of the methodology, "Meu Ônibus" presented serious problems of *feedback* and visibility of the system's features, even that the sentiment analysis showing a neutral sentiment, maybe due to the importance and to the usefulness of the application in your daily activities. The application tends to not leave the user satisfied with their user experience. The problems of "Meu Ônibus" make day to day life of users more difficult. Thus, through phase 3 of the methodology, the simple ideas adoption could solve some problems. Such improvements have had a very positive reception by users. In addition to being mostly simple improvements, they are mostly functions that the application already presents, but difficult access or understanding to users. In this way, if "Meu Ônibus" adopts some of the evaluated solutions the users would better understand the dynamics of use of the application, providing a better user experience and greater loyalty in the utilization of the application by the users.

In the evaluation of "Waze", we encountered that external factors to the application have a profound impact on the user experience, also presented in the sentiment analysis, that showed a negative user perception. The application needs to handle with factors such as the drop in connection, lack of GPS synchronization, and *social factors* in the best way for the users. Security-related improvement was the most highly valued and most significant improvement for users. This result reinforces the users' concern about the issue. Besides security, the other improvements presented an optimization in the activities and features treated in the scope of the realized improvements. Improvements have some variations of complexity, but even the simple ones are essential for the user experience.

5   Conclusions

Urban mobility in Brazil is a big issue that needs a lot of discussion with users to reach a good evaluation. However, the evolution of mobile technologies helps to minimize some of the urban mobility problems. For example, there are several mobile applications to various types of transport (*e.g.,* Google Maps, Waze, Uber, Meu Ônibus, Moovit, Bicicletar, Strava) avaliable.

This work did an investigation into the experience of using urban mobility applications in a large Brazilian city. This work complements the results presented in the evaluation competition of the XV Brazilian Symposium on Human Factors in Computational (IHC 2016) [1]. We added in this paper more methods of evaluation (sentiment analysis and assessment of the improvements proposed by the HCI experts) that makes possible to deepen aspects related to user satisfaction and to visualize some solutions of the problems faced by the users. The adopted methodology provided a real insight into the context of the urban mobility experience by the users, their main problems and what kind of solutions could be adopted to improve the use experience of the applications. Thus, from this methodology, the results of the research allowed tracing two profiles of users that move around using mobile applications like "Waze" and "Meu Ônibus", which are the ones chosen to be evaluated in our work.

In the "Meu Ônibus" application, we found 33 usability problems in the heuristic evaluation, and the user evaluation found 13 problems. The problems encountered by these two methods mainly concern feedback. Failures with the Internet connection or user location were recurring, and these are not reported in an appropriate manner to the user or within a reasonable time. A set of improvements has been proposed by some of the experts in the user experience and also evaluated by the users. These improvements varied in degree of complexity and were well accepted by the users with the productive potential to improve the user experience of "Meu Ônibus".

"Waze" presented 15 usability problems in the heuristic evaluation and the user evaluation presented 11 problems. Results of the assessment with the users were more worrisome, because they identified external factors that have a profound impact on the dynamics of the application's functionalities and the user experience. Problems such as dangerous routes have been detrimental to the safety of the user. This scenario runs against to one of the principles of the national urban mobility policy. "Waze"'s security enhancement has been rated best by users. If "Waze" presented a similar feature, users would feel more confident and safety when moving around the city and using the app.

As a future work, we intend to evaluate more urban mobility applications and identify more issues to be explored. Also, we intend to conduct a new survey and recognize more user profiles for other means of transportation such as subway, taxi and bicycle. Based on that, further enrichment of the recommendations for urban mobility applications is necessary.

Acknowledgments. We would like to thank the CTQS/GREat team for the technical support for this work and also the "CAcTUS - ContextAwareness Testing for Ubiquitous Systems" project, supported by CNPq (MCT/CNPq 14/2013 - Universal) under grant number 484380/2013-3.

References

1. Almeida, R.L.A., Mesquita, L.B.M., Carvalho, R.M., Junior, B.R.A., Andrade, R.M.C.: Quando a tecnologia apoia a mobilidade urbana: Uma avaliação sobre a experiência do usuário com aplicações móveis. In: Proceedings of the XV Brazilian Symposium on Human Factors in Computer Systems (IHC 2016). Sociedade brasileira de Computação - SBC, Porto Alegre, Brazil (2016, in Portuguese)
2. Baccianella, S., Esuli, A., Sebastiani, F.: SentiWordNet 3.0: an enhanced lexical resource for sentiment analysis and opinion mining. In: LREC, vol. 10, pp. 2200–2204 (2010)
3. Behr, A., Corso, K.B., Nascimento, L.F.M.D., Freitas, H.M.R.D.: Mobilidade urbana sustentável e o uso de tecnologias de informação móveis e sem fio: em busca de alternativas para a cidade de porto alegre/rs. Gestão Contemporânea [recurso eletrônico]. Porto Alegre **10**(14), 61–90 (2013)
4. Bollini, L., De Palma, R., Nota, R., Pietra, R.: User experience & usability for mobile geo-referenced apps. A case study applied to cultural heritage field. In: Murgante, B., et al. (eds.) ICCSA 2014. LNCS, vol. 8580, pp. 652–662. Springer, Heidelberg (2014). doi:10.1007/978-3-319-09129-7_47
5. Carvalho, C.M., Rodrigues, C.A., Aguilar, P.A., de Castro, M.F., Andrade, R.M.C., Boudy, J., Istrate, D.: Adaptive tracking model in the framework of medical nursing home using infrared sensors. In: 2015 IEEE Globecom Workshops (GC Wkshps), pp. 1–6. IEEE (2015)
6. Carvalho, C.H.R.D.: Desafios da mobilidade urbana no Brasil. Instituto de Pesquisa Econômica Aplicada (IPEA) (2016)
7. Carvalho, R.M., Santos, I.S., Meira, R.G., Aguilar, P.A., Andrade, R.M.C.: Machine learning and location fingerprinting to improve UX in a ubiquitous application. In: Streitz, N., Markopoulos, P. (eds.) DAPI 2016. LNCS, vol. 9749, pp. 168–179. Springer, Cham (2016). doi:10.1007/978-3-319-39862-4_16
8. Carvalho, R.M., Andrade, R.M.C., Oliveira, K.M., Sousa Santos, I., Bezerra, C.I.M.: Quality characteristics and measures for human-computer interaction evaluation in ubiquitous systems. Softw. Qual. J. **24**, 1–53 (2016)

9. Gabrielli, S., Forbes, P., Jylhä, A., Wells, S., Sirén, M., Hemminki, S., Nurmi, P., Maimone, R., Masthoff, J., Jacucci, G.: Design challenges in motivating change for sustainable urban mobility. Comput. Hum. Behav. **41**, 416–423 (2014). http://www.sciencedirect.com/science/article/pii/S0747563214003045
10. Ghorbel, H., Jacot, D.: Sentiment analysis of french movie reviews. In: Pallotta, V., Soro, A., Vargiu, E. (eds.) Advances in DART. SCI, vol. 361, pp. 97–108. Springer, Heidelberg (2011). doi:10.1007/978-3-642-21384-7_7
11. Inostroza, R., Rusu, C., Roncagliolo, S., Rusu, V., Collazos, C.A.: Developing smash: a set of smartphone's usability heuristics. Comput. Stand. Interfaces **43**, 40–52 (2016)
12. Ivanov, A., Cyr, D.: Satisfaction with outcome and process from web-based meetings for idea generation and selection: the roles of instrumentality, enjoyment, and interface design. Telematics Inform. **31**(4), 543–558 (2014)
13. Kim, S.M., Pantel, P., Chklovski, T., Pennacchiotti, M.: Automatically assessing review helpfulness. In: Proceedings of the 2006 Conference on Empirical Methods in Natural Language Processing, EMNLP 2006, pp. 423–430. Association for Computational Linguistics, Stroudsburg (2006). http://dl.acm.org/citation.cfm?id=1610075.1610135
14. Leite, D.F.B., Rocha, J.H., Batista, C.D.S.: Busão: um sistema de informações móvel para auxílio à mobilidade urbana através do uso de transporte coletivo. IX Simpósio Brasileiro de Sistemas de Informação, pp. 170–181 (2013)
15. Liu, B.: Sentiment analysis and opinion mining. Synth. Lect. Hum. Lang. Technol. **5**(1), 1–167 (2012)
16. Maia, M.E.F., Fonteles, A., Neto, B., Gadelha, R., Viana, W., Andrade, R.M.C.: LOCCAM - loosely coupled context acquisition middleware. In: Proceedings of the 28th Annual ACM Symposium on Applied Computing, SAC 2013, pp. 534–541, ACM, New York (2013). http://doi.acm.org/10.1145/2480362.2480465
17. Maia, M.E., Andrade, R.M., de Queiroz Filho, C.A., Braga, R.B., Aguiar, S., Mateus, B.G., Nogueira, R., Toorn, F.: Usable-a communication framework for ubiquitous systems. In: 2014 IEEE 28th International Conference on Advanced Information Networking and Applications, pp. 81–88. IEEE (2014)
18. Marx, R., de Mello, A.M., Zilbovicius, M., de Lara, F.F.: Spatial contexts and firm strategies: applying the multilevel perspective to sustainable urban mobility transitions in Brazil. J. Cleaner Prod. **108**, 1092–1104 (2015)
19. McGlohon, M., Glance, N.S., Reiter, Z.: Star quality: aggregating reviews to rank products and merchants. In: ICWSM (2010)
20. Nielsen, J.: Usability Engineering. Elsevier, Amsterdam (1994)
21. Nielsen, J., Molich, R.: Heuristic evaluation of user interfaces. In: Proceedings of the SIGCHI Conference on Human Factors in Computing Systems, pp. 249–256. ACM (1990)
22. Nielsen, J., Clemmensen, T., Yssing, C.: Getting access to what goes on in people's heads? Rreflections on the think-aloud technique. In: Proceedings of the Second Nordic Conference on Human-Computer Interaction, pp. 101–110. ACM (2002)
23. Pang, B., Lee, L., Vaithyanathan, S.: Thumbs up? Sentiment classification using machine learning techniques. In: Proceedings of the ACL 2002 Conference on Empirical Methods in Natural Language Processing - Volume 10, EMNLP 2002, pp. 79–86. Association for Computational Linguistics, Stroudsburg (2002). https://doi.org/10.3115/1118693.1118704
24. Pupi, S., Pietro, G., Aliprandi, C.: Ent-it-UP. In: Stephanidis, C. (ed.) HCI 2014. CCIS, vol. 435, pp. 3–8. Springer, Cham (2014). doi:10.1007/978-3-319-07854-0_1

25. Rogers, Y., Sharp, H., Preece, J., Tepper, M.: Interaction design: beyond human-computer interaction. netWorker: Craft Netw. Comput. **11**(4), 34 (2007)
26. Saif, H., He, Y., Alani, H.: Semantic sentiment analysis of Twitter. In: Cudré-Mauroux, P., et al. (eds.) ISWC 2012. LNCS, vol. 7649, pp. 508–524. Springer, Heidelberg (2012). doi:10.1007/978-3-642-35176-1_32
27. Santos, R.M., Oliveira, K.M., Andrade, R.M.C., Santos, I.S., Lima, E.R.: A quality model for human-computer interaction evaluation in ubiquitous systems. In: Collazos, C., Liborio, A., Rusu, C. (eds.) CLIHC 2013. LNCS, vol. 8278, pp. 63–70. Springer, Cham (2013). doi:10.1007/978-3-319-03068-5_13
28. Silva Junior, D.P., Souza, P.C., Maciel, C.: Establishing guidelines for user quality of experience in ubiquitous systems. In: Streitz, N., Markopoulos, P. (eds.) DAPI 2016. LNCS, vol. 9749, pp. 46–57. Springer, Cham (2016). doi:10.1007/978-3-319-39862-4_5
29. Turney, P.D.: Thumbs up or thumbs down? Semantic orientation applied to unsupervised classification of reviews. In: Proceedings of the 40th Annual Meeting on Association for Computational Linguistics, ACL 2002, pp. 417–424. Association for Computational Linguistics, Stroudsburg (2002). http://dx.doi.org/10.3115/1073083.1073153
30. Watson, I.: Alchemyapi. https://www.ibm.com/watson/alchemy-api.html. Accessed 02 Feb 2017
31. Zhang, R., Tran, T.T.: Helping E-commerce consumers make good purchase decisions: a user reviews-based approach. In: Babin, G., Kropf, P., Weiss, M. (eds.) MCETECH 2009. LNBIP, vol. 26, pp. 1–11. Springer, Heidelberg (2009). doi:10.1007/978-3-642-01187-0_1

MAEK: Intuitive Instructional Content Delivered on a Smartphone Platform

Tess Bailie(✉), Kelly A. Sprehn, and Trevor Savage

Draper, Cambridge, MA, USA
{tbailie,ksprehn,tsavage}@draper.com

Abstract. As new and better versions of smartphones come out, users increasingly have their old models of smartphones unused at home. Smartphones have remarkable capabilities, and it seems that these unused phones are a waste of potential. The MAEK project was inspired by the question: what if the computing power of a personal phone wasn't handheld? Where else could this tech exist? If it were imbedded in a more public environment instead of contained to the hand or pocket, does it open up new interaction opportunities? The MAEK project at Draper explored these questions. Using a User-Centered approach, a team of designers at Draper researched, designed, prototyped, and tested a product (MAEK) that proved the new and exciting interactions of personal cellphone tech embedded in the environment. This project included 4 parts: the adhesive case hardware, the gesture recognition computer vision, the automatic video parsing, and the user experience of the application interface. This paper focuses on the user experience.

Keywords: Gesture · Hands-free · Gesture control

1 Introduction

The number of people owning and using smartphones across the globe is high, 68% of adults in advanced economies in 2015 reported owning a smartphone. This number is rising, with even developing countries showing large growth rates of adults owning smartphones [1]. As the proliferation of technology continues, the market of available technology is also getting more powerful. The validity of Moore's Law in which the capabilities of a computer chip will double every two years, was recently shown to still exist [2]. As processing power and connectivity continue to increase, the number of interactions users can have with a smartphone have stagnated. Most design innovations take place "under" the screen, as visual and interaction design for applications. Personal assistants introduce voice-based command, and the IOS 3D touch release added slightly more depth to screen-based interactions [3]. Our goal with this research project was to expand interactions well beyond the screen, to consider a broader environment than can be afforded by phone-in-hand. Our hypothesis was that this expansion could increase the scenarios and environments where the smartphone could play a role in task completion.

M. Kurosu (Ed.): HCI 2017, Part II, LNCS 10272, pp. 131–141, 2017.
DOI: 10.1007/978-3-319-58077-7_11

2 Concept Generation – Phase 1

The scope of this project limited hardware to just the smartphone in our pocket. These devices have impressive computing power and come with built-in sensors: microphone, light, proximity, accelerometer, and at least one camera. Although other devices, sensors, and processing exists, we sought to capture current use cases without complicating the experience beyond the capabilities of users now.

We started with the assumption that smartphones could be placed in a Draper-proprietary case incorporating Zman^{TM} material that could adhere to a vertical surface, creating a hands-free interaction opportunity with the phone. We most wanted to explore two major areas. In the first phase, we explored the tasks and environments where this hands-free phone experience could have the most impact. Once we had determined a good use case, our second phase explored how to optimize the usability of a hands-free phone in this scenario.

As a note, because of the nature of the Zman^{TM} material, and the idea of a gecko climbing walls, we refer to the case or the case and phone as the "Gecko Phone".

2.1 Research Methods

To explore our hypothesis from an HCE perspective, we conducted exploratory user research. We began by framing the solution and user space of interest. We designed a number of research activities to explore that space, and then developed a set of high-level concepts. We then validated these concepts with target users. To explore this space thoroughly, there were a number of dimensions we needed to examine. The first was defining the targeted audience, or the types of users we wanted to focus our efforts with. Once we had a defined user group, we began to explore what unmet needs these users have that relate to cell phones. We also needed to explore the unique capabilities enabled by Zman^{TM} technologies and how that pairs with the native capabilities of cell phones.

Four different techniques helped us assess our user requirements and needs from the capabilities of a surface-mounted phone. First, a diary study clarified the contexts that people were in when they would be using their phones. The second study, brainstorming cards helped generate ideas based on user types, locations, and phone capabilities. The third study used storytelling to gather ideas about edge use cases. Finally, the results were sorted and culminated in an affinity diagram.

Diary Study. The first was a diary study in which we texted surveys to our participants four times a day for two days each (a work day and a weekend day). A diary study provides the opportunity for near-real time feedback about exactly where a person is and what they are doing [4]. A diary study removes recall bias for short-term feedback. We performed this study twice, with a total of 11 participants. Each participant was asked five questions about where they were, what they were doing, how they were using their phone, and any problems with that phone usage. The final question asked the user to brainstorm in place: to use the context around them and the task that they were performing to identify uses of a gecko phone. Each participant also filled out an introductory demographic survey and an exit survey that asked them to reflect on their time in the study and provide additional thoughts and concepts.

Brainstorming Cards. Our second activity was a card matching activity. Card matching allows users to expand on their ideas by pairing sometimes-nonsensical cards together and providing a backstory or context [5]. We created a set of cards that included different user types and locations. We held two sessions of this activity, with three participants in each (plus the researchers). The first session focused on creating pairings of users and locations and then brainstorming problems that could be solved through the use of a surface-mounted phone. For the second session we added a set of cards that captured the capabilities of the phone itself, such as cameras, accelerometers, and WIFI connectivity. In this session we asked users to create sets from all three types of cards. This allowed us to pair "what" and "why" as well as "how" questions that helped form better user context with real-world capabilities.

Physical Story Telling. Our third activity was a physical storytelling activity. Storytelling furthers the creative process, allowing participants to imagine use cases and capabilities beyond their everyday life [6]. For this activity we created physical items that represented technologies in multiple sizes and form factors: anything from small sensors to phones to laptops and televisions. We also included shapes and sizes without particular technologies in mind to prompt creativity. We started the session by telling a story: "I'm going to the park to fly my quadcopter" and then drawing that setting on the whiteboard. From there we had our participants extend that story with their physical props. One would tape a "phone" to the board and say "I stick my phone to the quadcopter so I can take a picture from up above." Another user might extend the story by saying "there's a road next to the park that had an accident. I use my gecko phone as a beacon for the paramedics." We told a single story until it ran out, then started with a new story, repeating this process until the session ended.

Affinity Diagramming. The fourth activity was affinity diagramming, which was a continuous process over the course of the study. The affinity diagramming process comes out of Beyer and Holtzblatt [7], in which sticky notes are used to list findings, which are then clustered naturally by their relatedness to other sticky note findings. As we received results, we began printing them out and sticking them in groups of similarity, but without an overarching organization scheme in mind. This process allows organization to spring organically from the data. With each activity we added more data and named these organic groups. At times we found an intriguing group and decided to develop an activity around it. As we completed this from the diary study, the storytelling grew out of one such grouping. The affinity organizations allowed us to review and reorganize the data multiple times in order to understand what we had really captured. Once we had grouped all of the data, we reviewed it to gain insights of the groups to reach our high level finding categories.

2.2 Major Findings

Phase 1 research resulted in two major findings. The first was that the smartphone as a tool was not a good fit for every environment. Environments are often extremely dynamic, and technology that cannot sense to react to those findings can be a mismatch for a changing setting. The second finding was that phones are capable of more than users are able to do with them. This occurs when the device fails to adapt to the users context (where they are and what they are doing) and when the phone fails to bridge the divide between physical and digital. When a phone is used to accomplish a digital task, such as answering email or reading an article, that divide is very small. It becomes larger when the device is used for a more physical task, such as following a recipe. Our plan was to design an application for the phone that made the phone a better fit for physical environments by bridging that gap.

2.3   Storyboards Through Speed Dating

In order to select a use case from phase 1, the team implemented a research method called speed dating. The team generated 23 concepts for a potential device. These concepts were portrayed as storyboards (see Fig. 1), which were then presented to 29 research participants (14 women). A storyboard provides a visual and verbal example of a problem the user may have, how technology could be implemented to address that problem, and a solution with the technology solution integrated into the task. This speed dating process had participants pick their most and least favorite concepts and discuss which aspects of the concepts elicited strong reactions from them.

Keeping my Phone Findable & Safe

A phone can easily get lost on the clutter of a table or come into harms way in an environment like a kitchen. A gecko phone could let me remove my phone from horizontal clutter, keeping it both easily findable and safe.

| While I'm at work, I stick my gecko phone to the side of your desk so that it doesn't get buried under the clutter on your desk. | While I'm cooking and doing dishes, I keep the gecko phone stuck to the cabinets so that it doesn't get water or food splashed onto it. | I am playing with my kids and want to keep my phone out of their reach. I place it up high on a wall where they can't reach it well enough to use the upward pulling motion required to remove it. | At night I stick my gecko phone to the wall next to the door. When I go to leave in the morning it's right at eye level, which makes it easy to see and remember. |

Fig. 1. Storyboards were used to sum up Phase 1 findings and get feedback from potential users.

These results were quantified (Fig. 2) to determine which ideas were best to pursue. Figure 3 shows the top three storyboards. These ideas included "Monitor This," (Fig. 3a) "Master Chef," (Fig. 3b) and "Selfie Stick" (Fig. 3c).

A competitive market analysis to identify the largest gaps in technology between the three top options. With the analysis of people using gestures while cooking, the integration of gestures provided an opportunity for us to advance the technology best in their area. This analysis revealed MasterChef was the best route to pursue.

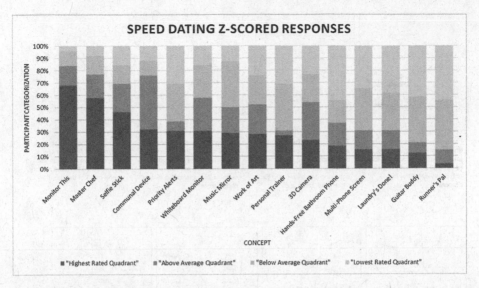

Fig. 2. Speed dating adjusted responses by Highest Rated, Above Average, Below Average, and Lowest Rated Quadrants.

2.4   Concept to Pursue: Masterchef

The team implemented a proof-of-concept prototype of the MasterChef idea. The MasterChef concept was a recipe tutorial that displayed step-by-step instructions for how to make challah bread using photos for each step. This application could be navigated using either voice or gesture commands. Researchers tested this concept using a Wizard-of-Oz prototype, wherein from the users perspective the prototype is fully functional but many parts of the software are "faked" or remote controlled by the experimenter. This prototype was tested with five participants *in situ*, with participants standing in a kitchen. Since cooking is often a partnered task, user pairs were communicating between each other using verbal cues. Beyond verbal cues, and with a cooking partner, participants started resorting to gestures to facilitate the cooking process. This finding helped shape subsequent studies and developments.

3   Phase 2 – Validating Our Solution

In Phase 1 the team determined that hands-free navigation of instructional content was the best use case to explore. At the beginning of Phase 2, the team decided to better understand how users approach and use existing instructional video content. The researchers performed a survey with 26 anonymous participants online. Their free-response quotes are captured here.

The survey revealed interesting findings. The main issue users have with video tutorials is the pacing: *"I find instructional videos do not fit with the speed I prefer to learn at. Mostly they are too slow, except in the few instances where I need to pour over an image, then they move too quickly."*

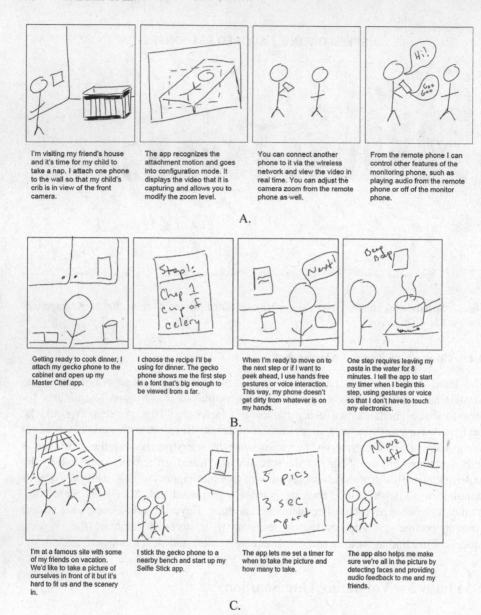

Fig. 3. Storyboards for the top three concepts. (A.) Monitor This, where the gecko phone is used as a portable camera and audio monitor. (B.) Master Chef, where the gecko phone contains the recipe and can be mounted out of the mess of cooking. (C.) Selfie Stick where the gecko phone can assist users in taking a series of selfies.

Users want to be able to skip through content they don't need and slow down or repeat content they're less certain about. Users find video content most helpful for learning a specific part of a task but not necessarily for the entire task: *"[I would use a video to learn] cooking methods or skills...like chopping vegetables faster...–NOT recipe videos."*

Users want to be able to navigate away from irrelevant information quickly or, better yet, not be shown that information at all. When users get stuck, they find it cumbersome to pause and navigate a video to watch step by step. Certain tasks, especially spatial tasks, are best portrayed by video.

We selected an origami video as our test case. Origami projects already have difficulty ratings and plentiful existing online content. We were able to find a task that was easy enough for a non-expert to get started but difficult enough to guarantee that a user would need to go back through and navigate the video to re-watch steps. Each step in an origami project is extremely dependent on the previous step having been executed well. Origami is a highly spatial task, which makes it a good candidate for video instruction over audio-only or written instructions. Finally, this project presented few barriers to collect data as it can be carried out in an unspecialized environment and requires few specialized or potentially dangerous elements, such as a heat or a sharp object.

Wizard of Oz.   In order to validate our video choice and interaction methods, we had an open-ended wizard of Oz testing session with three participants. Users were shown the video and asked to navigate it entirely by voice at first. They were encouraged to be conversational. The researcher involved interpreted the verbal cues from the participants and used a remote control to navigate video playback. Users were then asked to generate some of their own methods of controlling the video. All three users selected to use gesture controls. The major finding from this observation was that users asked specifically to go back to certain steps (*"Show me that again"*) instead of going back by a certain amount of time ("rewind 15 s").

From this perspective, we learned that controlling video playback using relative positioning and more natural interaction techniques was going to be the most usable.

4   Final Deliverable - MAEK

MAEK, an odd combination of letters, stands for Motion Activated Expert Kontroller. From the combination of gestures (Motion Activated), smart video parsing (Expert), we explored the usability of controlling an instructional video (Kontroller).

This project included four components: the Zman^{TM} case hardware, the gesture recognition computer vision, the automatic video parsing, and the user experience of the application interface incorporating video parsing and gesture recognition. This section focuses on using the case, recognition, and video parsing to build the user experience.

4.1 Gestures

Gestures provide a physical control mechanism that is available for the user when their hands are not occupied by holding a phone. Gestures can come naturally as physical expressions to convey more meaning. They can be taught to provide non-intuitive, semantic meaning to movement. Gestures can also be customized to the situation in which the user operates, to maintain semantic relevance.

Gestures have certain advantages and disadvantages from other interaction methods. Humans have a natural tendency to extend their communication methods beyond their words, to include body movements. The concept of gesturing extends from this [8]. In modern technology, designers have taken advantage of gestures as a way to remove an extra control device that can be lost or malfunction. Unfortunately, gestures do have their shortcomings. Developing software both sensitive and robust enough to detect intentional movements is not a trivial task. Despite the challenges, we chose to move ahead with hand-based movements or poses as control and input to our system.

There are a number of pre-existing gesture languages: American Sign Language, hand signals for tactical missions, and even fish market bartering all rely on poses and movements of the hands to create meaning. Karam [9] builds a taxonomy of gesture-based interactions. Based on her research and other sources, "Gesticulation" is the most natural use of hand and body movement to enhance communication. This is also one of the hardest forms to interpret from a technical perspective. The nuances of motioning with your hands are not easily detectable, even by humans. Thus, more formal methods are preferred for set human-computer interactions.

With the understanding that gesticulation needs more development from both a semantic and software perspective, generating a set of known gestures became our goal. These known gestures should be intuitive so as to require little training, simple so as to be repeatable, and distinct so as to be recognized by currently available camera and software equipment. The goal is for this information to help us design rich and innovative touch-free interactions with an instructional video on a phone able to be mounted at eye-level. It is interesting to note that as we design the gestures, recognition software, and video interface, gestures often require attention to determine affirmation or feedback. From the storyboarding activity in Phase 1, we learned of the importance of gestures and semantics when communicating steps in a process. "This one," and "That one," combined with gestures will indicate specifics without touching the object of interest. With the Wizard of Oz origami task in Phase 2, we learned that users like to use gestures to move relative amounts forward or backward from a video.

To develop a set of intuitive gestures that would be able to be recognized by a COTS phone, we took to our human-centered design methodology. In a second round of Wizard of Oz testing, we tested with eight participants. For this round of testing, the researchers defined a set of hand gestures that users were to use to control the video. We captured their hand gestures to train our computer vision model and gathered usability feedback.

Their only control mechanism for the video was to use their hands in repeatable motions, at which time the wizard would interpret the gesture and act accordingly. The final gestures involved three dynamic hand motions. The first, play/pause, was simply holding up a closed fist (Fig. 4a). The second was to skip a sub-step, in which users held up two fingers and moved their hand to the right to skip forward or to the left to skip backwards (Fig. 4b). The third gesture was a version of the second, in which users held up an open hand to skip forwards and backwards by an entire chapter (meaningful and related group of consecutive sub-steps; Fig. 4c). This round of testing validated that the gestures collected were usable and intuitive for the participants to use to navigate a video as well as easily differentiated by computer vision.

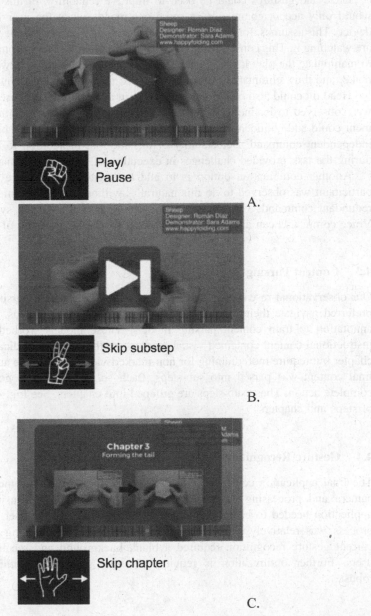

Fig. 4. The final gestures: (A.) Play/pause, (B.) Skip a sub-step, and (C.) A version of the second, skip forwards and backwards by an entire chapter

4.2   Multimodal Interactions

In addition to hand-based, touch-free gestures, we considered some options that combine commands across different modalities (across gestures, voice, gaze, and possibly head tilt) in order to either expand the commands available, or to increase the reliability of the inputs.

Gaze and gestures could be used to improve reliability. In this case, the system would only accept commands or some commands when the user is looking at the device. This assumes, for example, that the user would not rewind the video unless they are watching it. This constrains the user to remove their attention from the origami task to manipulate the play location of the video. This is an assumption we did not want to make, and thus, eliminated the option for gaze and gesture-based interactions.

Head tilt could also be used in place of or in addition to hand-based gestures. Users were observed to instinctively tilt their heads when they were confused. This movement could add confidence that users want to pause or go back or be used as a more independent command. Detectability of this motion, in addition to head movements during the task provided challenges in execution of this as a command.

Another combination option is to add both gesture and voice commands. One participant was observed to do this naturally, without explicit prompting. The use of redundant commands would increase the confidence in what the system recognizes. Voice commands can also change the context or precise meaning of a gesture.

4.3   Content Parsing

Our observational research revealed the importance of content parsing. Users greatly preferred navigate their content by meaningful steps and sub-steps. We used human annotation to train content parsing models. These models worked well when the instructional content contained visual markers on the screen to indicate a new step or chapter but require more training for non-marked videos to be done automatically. Our final content was parsed into sub-steps. Each sub-step contains no more than one complete action. These sub-steps are grouped into chapters. See Fig. 4 for an example of steps and chapters.

4.4   Gesture Recognition

The final application could be controlled via gesture using only the phones built-in camera and processing power. In order to control the phone using gestures, the application needed to be calibrated to the background and the user. This calibration process was relatively simple and included in a user onboarding interaction. The current gesture recognition required a blank background and recalibration between users. Further optimization is required for this gesture recognition to be more robust.

5 Conclusion

Hands-free interaction proved to be a good way to improve the utility of instructional video content. Users who were able to navigate their content with quick hand gestures reported improved usability. An important part of this navigation was parsing content into meaningful steps, an action that results in improved navigation and usability. Further research will be required to make automatic parsing and automatic gesture recognition more robust. Field-testing opportunities would allow the researchers to test these findings in an experimental environment.

Acknowledgments. We would like to thank the internal funding from Draper as it permitted us to pursue bold ideas.

References

1. Poushter, J.: Smartphone ownership and Internet usage continues to climb in emerging economies. Pew Research Center (2016). http://www.pewglobal.org/2016/02/22/smartphone-ownership-and-internct-usage-continues-to-climb-in-emerging-economies/. Accessed 28 Feb 2017
2. Sneed, A.: Moore's law keeps going, defying expectations. Sci. Am. **19**, 5 (2015)
3. Apple: The Advantage of 3D Touch. https://developer.apple.com/ios/3d-touch/. Accessed 28 Feb 2017
4. Flaherty, K.: Diary Studies: Understanding long-term user behavior and experiences. Nielsen Norman Group (2016). https://www.nngroup.com/articles/diary-studies/. Accessed 28 Feb 2017
5. Nielsen, J.: Card Sorting: Pushing users beyond terminology matches. Nielsen-Norman Group (2009). https://www.nngroup.com/articles/card-sorting-terminology-matches/. Accessed 28 Feb 2017
6. Hagan, M.: Storytelling brainstorm. Open Law Lab (2015). http://www.openlawlab.com/2015/03/30/storytelling-brainstorm-technique/. Accessed 28 Feb 2017
7. Beyer, H., Holtzblatt, K.: Contextual Design: Defining Customer-Centered Systems. Elsevier, Amsterdam (1997)
8. Kendon, A.: Gesture: Visible Action as Utterance. Cambridge University Press, Cambridge (2004). ISBN 0-521-83525-9
9. Karam, M.: A framework for research and design of gesture-based human-computer interactions. University of Southampton, ECS, Doctoral thesis (2006)

Predictive Model for Group Selection Performance on Touch Devices

Per Bjerre[1], Allan Christensen[1], Andreas K. Pedersen[1],
Simon A. Pedersen[1], Wolfgang Stuerzlinger[2(✉)], and Rasmus Stenholt[1]

[1] Aalborg University, Aalborg, Denmark
[2] School of Interactive Arts + Technology (SIAT),
Simon Fraser University, Vancouver, Canada
w.s@sfu.ca

Abstract. Users spend hours making selections with ineffective tools, we therefore examine selection methods for efficiency in various touch trials. In a preliminary study three alternative selection methods were identified, we compared these to a smart selection tool. The study showed that a single selection method was the fastest; however, when the amount of targets increased, a multiple selection tool became more efficient. A secondary study with more targets revealed similar results. We therefore examined the single selection method against traditional selection methods in a user study. The results reveal a model of the average action and time cost for all methods within the parameters of mental preparation and target addition. The study revealed that the most favored selection methods were a lasso and brush selection tool. The study provides evidence towards a predictive model of selection performance for multiple target selection trials.

1 Introduction

Selecting multiple objects can be tedious when interacting with systems. These selection operations tend to require high user accuracy and intense visual attention. Users have a large amount of tools available to perform selection tasks, and these tools can have different purposes. Novice users have difficulties identifying the most optimal selection tool for a given scenario. Stenholt showed that users prefer using simple tools several times rather than a more complex one fewer times [1]. This indicates that selection tools are not always used as intended.

We examine Lazy Selection, a stroke based tool designed for efficient target selection, with the ability to select multiple targets with a single stroke action. The stroke crosses the elements of interest and can be of any length. The system interprets the user's stroke and predicts the user's intent, requiring less user accuracy compared to normal selection techniques [2]. One issue with such methods is that they sometimes select the wrong targets in a drawing (denoted prediction errors). Prediction errors occur when there are ambiguities between the user's strokes and the drawing.

© Springer International Publishing AG 2017
M. Kurosu (Ed.): HCI 2017, Part II, LNCS 10272, pp. 142–161, 2017.
DOI: 10.1007/978-3-319-58077-7_12

For the first user study, we examine how to adjust prediction errors on a touch device, by expanding the tools available for handling these errors with user defined gestures. We investigate which of these tools perform best in terms of time usage and amount of errors. In the second user study we increased the amount of targets to examine the effect. For the third user study, we investigate the most efficient tool from the previous studies against traditional selection tools in various scenarios to determine, which of these tools perform best in terms of actions, time usage, and amount of errors when the target amount is increased. The study results in a linear regression model of the most efficient selection methods for multiple selection trials.

2 Related Work

Touch Interaction. Direct touch manipulation involves the user interacting directly with content on a touch-sensitive display. The advantage of direct touch was highlighted by Forlines et al., who found that the interaction felt more natural when interacting through direct touch compared to a mouse [3]. The results showed that it was faster to interact directly. Yet, when target size decreased, the selection time increased. Regarding hand preference with direct touch, previous studies showed that participants prefer unimanual gesture interaction (one handed interaction) and that unimanual gestures used less time than bimanual ones (two handed interaction) [4].

Wills examined different types of selection and identified three criteria that interaction techniques should adhere to: simple, powerful, and forgiving [5]. Users also prefer to use simpler interactions repeatedly over complex ones that require fewer actions to complete a task [1,6].

Traditional Selection Tools for Image Manipulation. Image manipulation tools, such as Gimp [7], provides users with a variety of selection tools for selecting desired content in an image. James et al. mentioned that selection tools are crucial for detailed image manipulation to accurately apply effects to individual parts of an image [8]. Selection tools highlight an area in an image, where the user can then apply effects. In GIMP one of the common tools for region selection is Rectangle Select. With this tool the user draws a rectangle and selects everything in the associated area. This tool is also used in file managers for file and folder selection [5]. Another common selection tool is Lasso. This tool selects all targets inside a freely defined (closed) path that the user is drawing [5,8]. According to James et al., on a touch based device, users find the Lasso tool more precise compared to mouse users on a desktop [5,8]. This is also supported by Kin et al., as their study identified a higher selection performance for one finger touch compared to mouse-based interaction [9]. In a similar study, Stenholt tested the Rectangle, Brush, Lasso, and Magic Wand selection methods in various 3D selection trials. The results showed that Brush was faster than Lasso. In the experimental trials, Rectangle used significantly fewer actions than the other tools, but was also the slowest [1].

Gestalt Principles. To identify the best alternative for multi-touch interaction, we explored the Gestalt principles. These principles were first examined in 1923 [10]. Whenever points (or previously formed groups) have one or several characteristics in common, they get perceptually grouped and form a new, larger visual target, known as a Gestalt, which is often explained as shape or form [11]. The Gestalt principles apply to the visual, auditory, tactile, and haptic modalities [12–14]. Here we focus only on the visual modality.

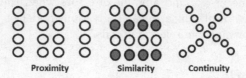

Fig. 1. Illustration of some Gestalt principles. Proximity refers to the distance between targets. Similarity groups targets that are similar in appearance. Continuity refers to groups that appear when targets lie on a line or curve.

There is no definitive list of Gestalt principles, but some of the commonly used ones are proximity, similarity, closure, continuity, and symmetry, e.g., [14, 15]. Some of these can be seen in Fig. 1. The proximity principle assumes that if a number of targets lie close together, they will naturally be considered to be grouped together. If a number of targets lie scattered, but have similar visual features, then they can also form a group [16]. Co-linear targets also form groups. Similarity implies that targets that look similar will be perceived as a group, which can be due to a variety of cues. The similarity principle can be divided into categories, such as form, size, color, brightness, orientation, and texture. All these categories can work towards making targets look similar and therefore enable the targets to form Gestalts [16].

Perceptual Grouping Methods. To further investigate the Gestalt principles, we explore relevant work that applied the principles for selection methods and to design experiments.

Thorisson created an algorithm to find perceptual groupings with the Gestalt principles of proximity and similarity [16]. Desolneux et al. stated that their participants perceived groups, when targets appeared inside a closed curved line or when targets aligned symmetrically across a straight line. Lastly, they identified that the continuity occurs when targets align in a line [11] Dehmeshki and Stuerzlinger created PerSel, which utilizes the Gestalt principles to predict the group of targets to select based on a flick gesture on a single target as input. They found that PerSel outperforms standard selection methods such as the Lasso and Rectangle selection techniques, when users have to select targets that are perceptually grouped [17].

Surveying the work discussed above, we can state that the individual targets to be selected in our experiment should have the same size, to ensure an equal baseline. Several studies used four traditional selection tools: brush, rectangle, lasso, and tap. We decided to use tapping and Lazy Selection as our baseline to compare against. Lastly, we also use stimuli based on the Gestalt principles, also because they help users quickly understand the task.

3   Methods and Materials

A pilot study focused on user interactions and accuracy of Lazy Selection established that the predictions are frequently inaccurate. This was also pointed out by the authors of Lazy Selection [2]. In our pilot study, users colored sketches on a tablet with the original Lazy Selection software. We asked them to indicate when and where a selection error occurred and to correct the selection with the tools available in Lazy Selection. We observed that inaccuracies occurred when targets were positioned in dense clusters or when selections involved many targets. The fat finger problem also increased the chance for errors, as it makes it hard to select specific targets without selecting other surrounding targets [18,19]. The results also showed that users would redo a selection, rather than utilize the provided adjustment tools. If the initial prediction was undesirable, subsequent predictions were typically also not desired.

We then conducted an elicitation pilot by prompting users to use gestures intuitive to them to adjust such predictions. Our observations identified that people preferred direct interaction on the targets, rather than more abstract gestures to perform this task. These results are consistent with the findings of Forlines et al. [3]. A distinct pattern observed throughout the test was that users preferred to swipe and flick on targets as an interaction technique for selecting or de-selecting targets. Other common interaction patterns included using movements similar to how an eraser would be used on paper, as well as using symbols on top of targets such as a line or a cross, typically to remove targets from the selection. However, the described interaction technique of flicking or swiping on a target to "remove" the selection (more precisely the highlighting associated with selection) was predominant.

Based on the findings from our pilots and previous research, we chose three gestures to adjust the predictions of Lazy Selection. These gestures consist of two gestures based on the pin and flick concept and a click (Tap) gesture. Figure 2 illustrates all four gestures investigated in our work. Tap was selected due to being the simplest possible gesture for toggling a selection. The two pin and flick gestures were included because of their similarity to the delete gesture suggested by Wobbrock et al. [4]. Moreover, several users suggested this gesture during the elicitation pilot. With the Lazy Selection tool, users would first mark an area where they wanted to change the selection. When they lifted their finger, the algorithm would then toggle the selection inside the marked area, as determined by the Lazy Selection algorithm. Using Tap, users could then select individual targets by tapping said targets. For the uni- and bimanual pin and flick gestures, users would first pin the target(s) they wanted to act upon and then perform a flick gesture. In the unimanual method, the fingers that initially performed the pin on the undesired target(s) would also perform the flick gesture, which meant that the interaction could be performed with a single hand. For the bimanual method, the algorithm first waits for a pin gesture to occur on one (or more) target(s) and then looks for a flick at a separate location. This will then act on the pinned target(s). This operation can be applied with one or two hands, as desired. However, users were encouraged to use the method with both hands.

The flick serves both as a confirmation of the pin gesture and also simulates that the selection is "flicked away" from the target(s).

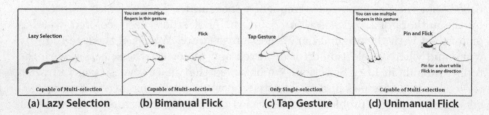

(a) Lazy Selection   (b) Bimanual Flick   (c) Tap Gesture   (d) Unimanual Flick

Fig. 2. Illustration of the gestures used during the study. (a) shows interaction with the original Lazy Selection technique. The user draws a stroke over targets to select them. (b) illustrates interaction with the Bimanual Pin and Flick gesture. The user pins one (or more) targets with one hand, and flicks away with the other hand to indicate the selection of the pinned targets. (c) shows an interaction with a tap gesture. The user taps and releases his/her finger on each target that needs to be selected. (d) illustrates an interaction with the Unimanual Pin and Flick gesture. The user first pins targets with one or more fingers and then toggles the selection by flicking with these fingers.

3.1   First User Study

The first user study compared the four mentioned interaction methods, with the original implementation of Lazy Selection as the control. The purpose of this study was to determine, which touch-based gestures are efficient to correct the predictions made by the Lazy Selection algorithm.

3.1.1   Hypotheses

The study had four hypotheses:

1. The **amount of actions** used is significantly different between the methods.
2. The **completion time** is significantly different between the methods.
3. The **amount of user-generated errors** between the methods is significantly different.
4. The **user preference** between the methods is significantly different.

Within the stated hypotheses we expect Tap to have the lowest completion time and be the most efficient method for small sets of targets, as it is the simplest method [20]. For larger sets, we expect Tap to decrease in efficiency, as it needs one action per target. We expect that users will prefer the unimanual pin and flick gesture, as it seems to be very intuitive to use, and was also suggested by users during initial testing. According to our observations in the pilots, we do not expect a significant difference in completion time between the individual methods, as all methods seem to be equally fast at correcting predictions. Lastly, the bimanual pin and flick gesture is expected to be the least preferred gesture, as research and our initial pilot indicate that users prefer to use one hand when interacting with a tablet [4, 21].

Response Variables. We identified three main response variables for our user study: number of actions, completion time, and number of user-generated errors. We also investigated the participant's preferred interaction technique through questionnaires and an interview. This yielded both qualitative and quantitative measurements. The quantitative measurements consisted of five point Likert scales to rate the methods. The qualitative data provided us with the participant's thoughts on the best interaction technique.

The system tracked the number of actions, by counting the number of times a gesture was completed. Timing began when participant touched the surface and ended when a trial was completed. The last response variable was the user-generated errors. For this we recorded video of the participants during the trials. An error occurred whenever the participants selected something other than the desired targets and had to correct the prediction.

3.1.2 Experimental Procedure and Equipment

We ran the user study on an Android tablet that interacted with a desktop-based implementation of Lazy Selection over Splashtop (www.splashtop.com) via a sufficiently fast wireless network. This kept our test comparable with previous results from Lazy Selection, while also investigating its potential for touch interaction. The setup also makes future comparisons to mouse-based interactions easily accessible.

Thirty participants (6 females) participated in the experiment. Ages were between 20 and 27, with an average of 23.27. All participants were students and were either at least familiar with touch interfaces and painting applications.

The user study was designed as a factorial experiment, with interaction methods and complexity as factors. The interaction method factor had four levels: Lazy Selection, Tap, unimanual pin and flick, and bimanual pin and flick. The complexity factor had three levels: easy, medium, and hard.

For the user study, a prediction scenario was created, where users had to deselect specific targets in the trials. In terms of user actions, the prediction scenario functions exactly the same as a selection scenario and thus all results are comparable with selection tasks. Each interaction method was evaluated with three trials involving drawings of different complexity. Each participant was first introduced to the study. Then a questionnaire with demographic questions was filled, followed by an explanation of how the trials would work. The participant was then placed in front of the tablet. For each interaction method a piece of paper with an illustration of the gesture mechanics was placed in front of the user. The illustrations can be seen in Fig. 2. Subsequently and for each trial, the facilitator presented the participant with a drawing with a predefined set of erroneously selected targets (indicating a prediction error). Such errors were colored in red and needed to be removed from the trial for successful completion. After a trial had been completed, the next one was presented. The three complexity levels used during the experiment are illustrated in Fig. 3. Selection complexity was defined by the proximity of targets, as well as the amount of overlapping targets. This makes it progressively harder to adjust the selection to the correct result. The order of the trials always increased in complexity. After the participant had completed all three trials for an interaction method, a short training session for the next interaction method was used to familiarize subjects. Once they felt comfortable enough, they resumed the trials.

A within subject design was used, where each user went through all combinations of interaction methods and complexity levels. Therefore each participant went through a total of 12 trials (4 input methods times 3 complexity levels). The order of presentation for each interaction method was determined via a Latin Square to reduce potential learning effects.

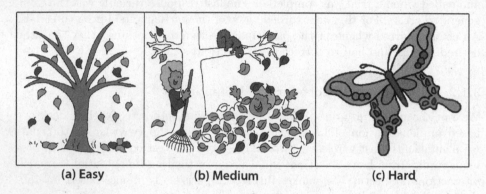

| (a) Easy | (b) Medium | (c) Hard |

Fig. 3. Illustration of the drawings used for experimental trials. In each drawing the participant had to de-select all red targets. The complexity of the drawings increases throughout the experiment. (A) easy task, with nine red-colored targets in the image. (B) medium task, with ten targets. (C) hard task, with seven targets to de-select. (Color figure online)

Results. The analysis of the quantitative data was done with the R statistical software package with $\alpha = 0.05$. The analyzed data is based on the response variables: actions, time, and errors. Repeated measures ANOVA was used for all analysis. In the cases where the normality and homoscedasticity assumptions could not be upheld, the non-parametric Friedman test was used instead. The qualitative measurements gathered through the experiment, i.e., the favored interaction method, and easiest method to use.

Hypothesis 1. The data for number of actions was not normally distributed. A Friedman Ranked Sum test revealed that H1 is supported, because the Lazy Selection method used significantly fewer actions per exercise in relation to the difficulty of the exercises compared to the other designs ($\chi_{11}^2 = 165.87$, p = 0).

Hypothesis 2. The data for time usage was not normally distributed. A Friedman Ranked Sum test revealed that H2 is supported ($\chi_3^2 = 48.4$, p $\ll$ 0.001). The test identified that Tap was significantly faster than the other interaction techniques, with Lazy Selection also being faster than both uni- and bimanual pin and flick. A logarithmic plot of the distribution of time values averaged across all complexity levels can be seen in Fig. 4.

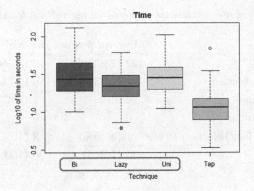

Fig. 4. Logarithm of time in the first user study. The figure indicates that the tap gesture needed significantly less time across all complexity levels. The red rounded rectangle indicates no significant difference between the contained methods. (Color figure online)

Hypothesis 3. This hypothesis deals with the number of errors for each interaction method. Users generally made few selection errors during the experiment. The data was not normally distributed. Yet, the Friedman Ranked Sum test revealed that there is a significant difference between Tap and Lazy Selection with Tap being superior ($\chi^2_{11} = 34.22$, p = 0.0003). Due to the overall low selection error count we could not detect other differences.

Hypothesis 4. For the ratings of the interaction methods, we used a Friedman Ranked Sum test to identify significant differences in the preference between the different interaction methods ($\chi^2_3 = 52.82$, p $\ll$ 0.001). According to this test, Tap was ranked highest, followed by Lazy Selection, then unimanual pin and flick, and finally bimanual pin and flick.

Qualitative Data. Table 1 summarizes the collected qualitative data. The participants who preferred Tap stated intuitiveness and simplicity as the primary reasons for their preference. However, most users mentioned that for more complex images with more targets, they would likely prefer the other techniques due to being able to select multiple targets with one action. The participants who preferred Lazy Selection mentioned the ability to select multiple targets at once as a positive feature. They also highlighted that the method still supported tapping individual targets. A large majority of the participants, 27 (90%), preferred to use one hand during the trials. Participants mentioned that for the bimanual pin and flick gesture one could mark targets with one hand, and then lift the hand before doing the flick with the other, thus being able to see which targets would be affected. This could partially counteract the fat finger problem [18,19].

3.2 Second User Study

The results from the first user study indicated that for small sets of targets (up to 10), Tap performs the best. Consequently, we decided to run a second

Table 1. Table showing user preference and ease of use ratings for the four techniques.

Method	User preference	Ease of use
Tap	22 (73.33%)	20 (66.66%)
Lazy selection	7 (23.33%)	6 (20%)
Bimanual	0	1 (3.33%)
Unimanual	0	0
Both lazy selection & tap	1 (3.33%)	3 (10%)
Total	30 (100%)	30 (100%)

user study to investigate performance in more complex scenarios, to identify if the results change with higher target counts.

The hypotheses and the experimental setup of this study are identical to the first one (Sects. 3.1.1 and 3.1.2). However, the selection trials were based on the visual Gestalt principles [14]. Examples of target arrangements for the second user study can be seen in Fig. 5. The Gestalt groupings were focused primarily on the principles of proximity, similarity, and continuity. Test participants again had to remove all red colored targets.

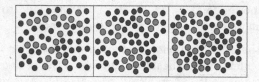

Fig. 5. Examples of drawings used for trials during the second user study. In each drawing the participant had to de-select all the red targets. There was a minimum of 17 and a maximum of 43 targets. (Color figure online)

Twelve participants (3 females) participated in this study, between 23 and 30 years old with an average of 25.16. The purpose of the test was to examine if and how some of the selection methods benefit from Gestalt-based target groups.

Results. For the results of the second user study, we examine the same response variables for trials involving larger target groups. We expect the results to be similar to the first user study, but with the multiple target selection methods having an advantage in terms of all response variables, because more targets had to be selected in the trials. The data from the second user study did not follow a normal distribution.

Hypothesis 1. The Friedman Ranked Sum test revealed that there is a significant difference for the amount of actions used between all interaction methods ($\chi^2_3 = 33.91$, p $\ll 0.001$). The test reveals that Lazy Selection used the fewest actions, followed by Tap, then the unimanual gesture, and the bimanual method with the most actions. The distribution of logarithmic action values averaged across all complexity levels can be seen in Fig. 6. A logarithmic transformation is used to better illustrate the differences between the techniques.

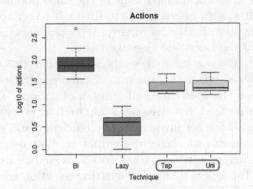

Fig. 6. Logarithm of number of actions in the second study. The figure indicates that Lazy Selection needed on average a significantly lower amount of actions across all trials, whereas the bimanual pin and flick gesture required the most actions. The red rounded rectangle indicates no significant difference between the contained methods. (Color figure online)

Hypothesis 2. For the amount of time used to de-select each group, the test reveals that there is a significant difference between all methods, ($\chi_3^2 = 33.3$, p $\ll 0.001$). The Friedman Ranked Sum test identified that the fastest interaction method was Tap, followed by Lazy Selection, which is faster than unimanual pin and flick. Bimanual pin and flick is the slowest.

Hypothesis 3. The Friedman Ranked Sum test for the amount of user-generated errors during the study shows the same result as the previous one, namely that there is no significant difference between the interaction techniques ($\chi_3^2 = 1.57$, p $= 0.67$). Again, users only made few errors during the test.

Hypothesis 4. Based on a Friedman Ranked Sum test, we identified a significant difference between the user ratings of the gestures during the study ($\chi_3^2 = 27.52$, p $\ll 0.001$). Lazy Selection and Tap were rated highest, with no significant difference between the two, significantly higher than uni- and bimanual pin and flick, with no significant difference between these two.

Qualitative. In the qualitative questions, 3 out of 12 subjects stated that they preferred Tap, whereas 9 out of 12 stated a preference towards Lazy Selection. A Test of Equal Proportions test shows that there is a significant difference between these ratings ($\chi_1^2 = 4.17$, p $= 0.04$). When asked about the easiest design to use, 6 out of 12 participants stated that Tap was the easiest to use, whereas the other 6 stated that Lazy Selection was the easiest one. Further comments on this question shows that the participants who found Lazy Selection to be the best tool, but also stated that Tap was easier to use, clarified that they needed to examine the path they wanted to take before using Lazy Selection, whereas they could use Tap instantly. All participants preferred to interact with a single hand during the trials, and mentioned some of the same potential improvements to some of the gestures, such as being able to lift their hands to see the selection before completing the flick. Furthermore, several participants mentioned a dislike for the predictions of the Lazy Selection algorithm.

The results from the second user study shows that the efficiency of Tap is substantially reduced when the amount of targets increases. In the study Lazy Selection needed the least time and number of actions. Tap is still a good and simple selection method, but does not scale well, as every additional target requires a selection. To further investigate the efficiency and scalability of Tap in a selection environment, we chose to conduct another user study, where we investigate Tap in different selections scenarios. This enables us to identify *when* the effectiveness of Tap is less than other existing selection methods.

The results from the second user study shows that the efficiency of Tap is substantially reduced when the amount of targets increases. In the study Lazy Selection needed the least time and number of actions. Tap is still a good and simple selection method, but does not scale well, as every additional target requires a selection. To further investigate the efficiency and scalability of Tap in a selection environment, we chose to conduct another user study, where we investigate Tap in different selections scenarios. This enables us to identify *when* the effectiveness of Tap is less than other existing selection methods.

3.3   Final User Study

The main purpose of this user study is to create a predictive model, from which we can determine when one selection method is superior to another. The instability caused by the Lazy Selection algorithm led to a general dislike of the prediction choices. Instead of Lazy Selection we decided to investigate a simple brush, as used in several image manipulation software. To generalize the model a bit further, we chose to test lasso and rectangle selection methods. Figure 8 shows the methods used in the study. The goal of the predictive model is to provide us with information as to when one selection method is superior in both time and number of actions compared to the other methods.

Trial Design. To reduce the bias for any individual selection method in the stimuli, the study consists of four sets of trials, where each set is targeted at being most advantageous for a single specific method, while still being possible to achieve with all methods. This ensures that one method does not have an advantage throughout the entire study. For each set, three images with a similar number of targets were created. The amount of targets was set to 10, 20 and 40, to explore the scalability of all the methods. The four sets of trials can be seen in Fig. 7, where the users had to select all the correct targets in the images and avoid selecting the incorrect targets. In trial set 1, 2, and 4 the correct targets

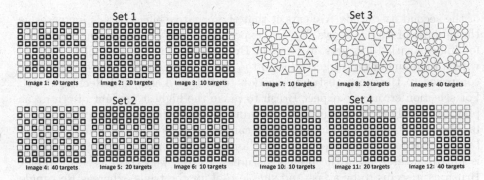

Fig. 7. Illustration of the stimuli used for the final user study trials. The trials consisted of four different images, with three complexity levels in each set (10, 20, and 40 targets). For the images in set 3, the users had to select all the circles. In the rest of the images, the users had to select all the targets with a thin black line and avoid selecting the incorrect targets (targets with a thick black line). Each set was created so that one selection method would have an advantage. Set 1 was targeted towards Brush, Set 2 towards Tap, Set 3 towards Lasso, and Set 4 was targeted towards Rectangle.

are the squares with a thin black line and the incorrect targets are the ones with a thick black line. In set 3, the users had to select all the (groups of) circles and avoid all the other targets. This set was targeted to give an advantage to Lasso selection. The design of the trials is again based on the Gestalt principles of similarity and proximity.

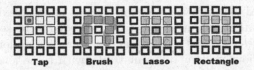

Fig. 8. Illustration of the selection methods used in the final user study. Tap and Brush select the targets that they directly interact with, whereas Rectangle and Lasso select all targets inside the selected region (including the center target). All methods can be utilized as a tap, when selecting single targets.

Hypotheses. For the model, we look at the same response variables as in the earlier studies (Sect. 3.1.1), i.e., actions used, time spent, and user errors (incorrect target selections). These are tracked in the same way as in the previous studies. The user ratings and comments given throughout the study are examined, to see if the qualitative and quantitative results are homogenous.

Within the stated hypotheses we expect Tap to use the highest amount of actions on average, as it is a single target selection method and therefore requires the user to select all targets individually. This is also supported by the results of the second user study. We expect that the negative effect of this increases as the number of targets grows. We also expect that Tap will be among the fastest for images with 10 targets. We expect Brush to be the fastest tool for images with a high amount of targets, due to the direct interaction. This reduces time, compared to the more abstract selection tools (i.e., Lasso and Rectangle) [4]. For selection errors, we expect Brush to make the highest amount of errors, as pilot testing shows that Brush is more prone to errors due to the thickness of the brush and the direct interaction, which can cause users to easily select incorrect targets. We do however expect that the amount of errors during the experiment is low in general, as in the previous studies. Lastly, we expect users to prefer Brush as it seems to be a fast and simple tool for the trials, whereas Rectangle seems to have a disadvantage from being inflexible in most trials.

Response Variables. The response variables used in the final study are the same as those in the two previous ones, namely: number of actions, completion time, and number of user-generated errors. These are also tracked in the same way as in the previous studies.

Experimental Procedure and Equipment. The final user study used the same equipment and software as the previous studies. Sixteen participants (2 female) took part in the study. Ages were between 21 and 27, with an average of 24.19. All participants reported to be students and daily usage of touch devices.

The user study was designed as a factorial experiment, with interaction methods and image complexities as factors. The interaction method had four levels: Tap, Lasso, Rectangle, and Brush.

The images used for the trials had three levels of complexity, which in this case was defined as the amount of targets that needed to be selected. The complexity of the images was set to 10, 20, and 40 target selections, and the users had to make selections on four different trials, with three levels of complexity each, which meant 12 trials in total. A within subjects design was used, where each user would try all interaction methods on all the different complexity levels, for each trial. The order of presentation was determined via Latin Squares to reduce potential learning. Each method was furthermore evaluated through two conditions, where one was a timed condition and the other was a perfect completion condition. In the timed condition users had 25 s to select as many targets as possible and the amount of errors was tracked for later analysis. In the perfect completion condition, users had to select all targets in the image and correct all selection errors. A trial was completed when no selection errors were present, and all the correct targets had been selected. The four sets of three complexity levels used during the experiment are illustrated in Fig. 7.

In the user study, each participant was first introduced to the project. Then a demographic questionnaire was filled, followed by an explanation of how the timed and perfect conditions would work. The participant was placed in front of the tablet and presented with the four selection methods, to ensure that s/he understood the interactions required to complete the trials. This was done through a short training session, where the users could practice the individual interaction methods. After the training session, the user would begin with the timed or perfect condition. This was counter-balanced so that half of the participants started with timed, and the other half with perfect. For each condition, the users would complete all trials, followed by the trials for the second condition. After a participant had completed both conditions with all interaction methods, we administered the final questionnaire and a semi-structured interview.

Results. We performed a two-way ANOVA on both the actions and time data as dependent variables, with the selection methods and the two conditions as independent variables. We then used linear regression to examine the differences between the individual selection methods as a function of the amount of targets in the trials. For each response variable, we further analyzed the two conditions individually, to see the differences in results between the time condition and the perfect completion condition. For each of the hypotheses we modeled the time and number of actions with a linear equation, $y = TA * x + MP$, depending on the number of targets x. The constant term corresponds roughly to the mental preparation (abbreviated as MP) and the linear factor to the time/actions required to add a target (abbreviated as TA). For the qualitative measurements, we asked also how users went about the task.

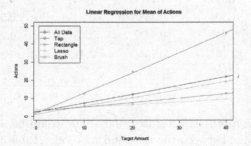

Fig. 9. Figure illustrating the mean distribution of the action data for the timed condition. Each line represents a selection method. The R^2 value for all data is $R^2 = 99.99\%$, for Tap: $R^2 = 99.82\%$, Rectangle: $R^2 = 99.89\%$, Lasso: $R^2 = 91.73\%$, and Brush: $R^2 = 97.21\%$. The graph for time looks similar, except that the conditions are not spread out as much. (Color figure online)

Hypothesis 1. Hypothesis H1 states that there would be a significant difference in the number of actions used between the selection methods. The results for both conditions are shown in Table 2. The actions data did not comply with the assumptions of the ANOVA. Instead ART (Aligned Rank Transform for non-parametric Factorial Analysis) was used [22]. The results show that there was a significant difference in the amount of actions used between the selection methods ($F_{3,45} = 20980.22$, $p \ll 0.001$). The Tukey-Kramer post-hoc test showed that there was a significant difference between all selection methods with Tap requiring the most actions followed by Rectangle, Brush, and Lasso in the given order. There was no significant difference in the actions used between the two conditions. Using linear regression we examine the differences between the selection methods for the individual conditions. For the timed condition, the test revealed that there was a significant difference between the methods for all data ($r^2 = 0.19$, p $\ll$ 0.001). Tap requires the least actions for MP, but the most actions per TA. Conversely, Lasso required the most actions for MP, but the least actions per TA. The distribution of the action data for the time condition can also be seen in Fig. 9, where each colored line represents a selection method. For the perfect condition, the test revealed that there was a significant difference between the methods ($r^2 = 0.23$, p $\ll$ 0.001). The results show that Rectangle requires the fewest actions for MP, and Tap again has the most actions per TA. Lasso again requires the most actions for MP, but has the fewest actions per TA.

Table 2. Table showing the coefficients (y = TA * x + MP) describing the average amount of actions. Both the timed and perfect condition are shown. * indicates significance, p < 0.05.

Methods	MP (timed)	TA (timed)	MP (perfect)	TA (perfect)
All methods	2.44*	0.49*	1.97*	0.55*
Tap	1.84	1.11*	1.63	1.10*
Rectangle	1.30	0.45*	0.34	0.55*
Lasso	3.85*	0.14*	3.48*	0.22*
Brush	2.76*	0.25*	2.41	0.32*

Hypothesis 2. The hypothesis H2 states that there would be a significant difference in the time usage between the selection methods. Table 3 shows the times. A two-way ANOVA was performed between the two conditions and the selection methods, after applying a logarithmic transformation to the data. The results show that there was a significant difference in the amount of time used between the selection methods ($F_{3,1531} = 17.70$, p $\ll$ 0.001 and $1 - \beta \cong 1$, $\eta^2 = 0.28$). A Tukey-Kramer post-hoc test showed that Tap used significantly more time than the other methods. There was also a significant difference in time between the two conditions ($F_{1,1531} = 45.61$, p $\ll$ 0.001 and $1 - \beta \cong 1$, $\eta^2 = 0.25$). A Tukey-Kramer post-hoc test showed that significantly more time was spent on the perfect condition. Using linear regression we examine the differences between the selection methods for the individual conditions. The results from the timed condition revealed that all methods had a significant difference in completion time for the trials ($r^2 = 0.42$, p $\ll$ 0.001). The results showed that Tap had the highest time per TA in a trial. Brush had the lowest MP time. Lasso had lowest time per TA, but it also the highest MP of the methods. For the perfect

condition, the test revealed that there was a significant difference between the methods ($r^2 = 0.34$, $p \ll 0.001$). The results show that Tap had the highest time per TA. Lasso had the lowest time per TA, but also had the highest MP of all the methods. Rectangle had the lowest MP time.

Table 3. Table showing the coefficients ($y = \text{TA} * x + \text{MP}$) describing the average time in seconds. Both the timed and the perfect condition are shown. * indicates significance, $p < 0.05$.

Methods	MP (timed)	TA (timed)	MP (perfect)	TA (perfect)
All methods	3.09*	0.34*	2.15*	0.51*
Tap	3.05*	0.48*	3.00*	0.56*
Rectangle	3.25*	0.34*	1.16	0.55*
Lasso	3.53*	0.26*	3.07*	0.43*
Brush	2.52*	0.28*	1.36	0.49*

Hypothesis 3. Hypothesis H3 deals with the number of selection errors that users made during the study. Users generally made few selection errors, with a few exceptions. To analyze the selection errors for the study we compute the sensitivity and specificity for each method. This was only done for the timed condition, as there were no errors in the perfect condition. Sensitivity is calculated by dividing the amount of correct selections with the amount of possible correct selections. Dividing the number of remaining incorrect targets with the possible incorrect targets yields specificity. We used a Test of Equal Proportions to calculate the sensitivity and specificity. The computed data can be seen in Table 4.

Table 4. Table illustrating the sensitivity and specificity data for the timed condition. The sensitivity and specificity is shown in percent.

Method	Sensitivity (percent)	Specificity (percent)
Tap	97.88%	99.92%
Rectangle	98.73%	95.66%
Lasso	99.89%	95.39%
Brush	99.51%	96.33%

Sensitivity is significant $\chi^2_3 = 107.7297$, $p \ll 0.001$. The data reveals that Tap was the worst and Lasso selection the best method in terms of sensitivity. For specificity the test showed a significantly different amount of selection errors that users made ($\chi^2_3 = 476.4897$, $p \ll 0.001$). Users made the most incorrect target selections with Lasso, and the fewest incorrect target selections with Tap.

Hypothesis 4. Hypothesis H4 states that there would be a significant difference in user preference between the methods. Based on a Friedman Ranked Sum test, we identified a significant difference between the user ratings of the selection methods during the study ($\chi_3^2 = 15.42$, P < 0.001). Brush and Lasso were rated highest, with no significant difference between the two. Rectangle and Tap received the lowest rating, with no significant difference between the two.

Qualitative Data. In the questionnaire, participants were asked as to how they solved the trials. Nine participants (56.25%) stated that their goal was to complete the selections as fast as possible. Five participants (31.25%) had a combination between as fast as possible and with as few errors as possible. The last two participants (12.5%) tried to solve the trials with as few errors as possible without considering the time spent. From observations and comments from the participants we found that most participants wanted to be able to adjust the size of the tools during the completion of the trials. This was especially the case for Brush selection, as the implemented width was, according to several participants, too wide for the selections. Furthermore, some participants stated that Tap was annoying for the trials that required many target selections, but that it was a good selection tool for trials with fewer targets.

4   Discussion

In the first two user studies we initially expected that a lower number of actions would be necessary for the interaction techniques that supported selection of multiple targets with a single action (Lazy Selection and both pin and flick gestures). The results from both user studies confirm that Lazy Selection required fewer actions compared to the other methods.

In both user studies Tap was found to be the fastest interaction method, even when the amount of target selections was increased for the second user study. One potential explanation of this is that the Lazy Selection algorithm requires a bit more computation time than Tap and thus has a slight delay. More importantly, users often had to redo the interaction when selecting multiple targets with one action due to issues with gesture accuracy and/or failures of the Lazy Selection algorithm. These results further motivate the choice of using a simple Brush selection for the final user study. Our implementation of Brush was indistinguishable to Tap in terms of computation time.

In the final study we expected that a higher amount of actions would be necessary for Tap, as the other methods (Brush, Lasso, and Rectangle) were able to select multiple targets at the same time. Most users clearly understood that the tools were able to select more targets at once if applicable. The results from the final study confirm the expectation that for each added target (TA), Tap on average needed at least twice as many actions as the other methods. Yet, the constant, mental preparation (MP), cost of the task was lower for Tap than most of the other methods. These results were conclusive for both the timed and perfect completion conditions. This also corresponds to the comments from the second user study, where some participants mentioned that it required more time to examine the path they wanted to take with the multiple selection tools, compared to Tap.

The results further show that in our creation of a model for the performance of the selection methods, Lasso was the most efficient tool in the amount of actions needed for a higher amount of targets. An example of this is for the timed condition, Rectangle is the most efficient tool in the amount of actions used until about seven targets, then Brush is the best for eight and nine targets, and Lasso is more efficient for trials from ten and above selections. However, given that these values are so close together, we can only state with authority that Lasso and Brush require the fewest actions for the highest number of targets. The Friedman Ranked Sum test for 40 targets confirmed these findings as Tap was ranked lowest, followed by Rectangle, and Lasso, and Brush. There was no significance between the latter ($\chi_3^2 = 33.525$, p $\ll 0.001$).

For the completion time, we initially expected Tap to be the fastest selection method for trials with few targets (as in our other studies), and that Brush would be the fastest for higher amounts of targets. However, these expectations were not met, as Tap was never the fastest selection method for both the timed and perfect conditions. For the timed condition, Brush was the fastest selection tool, which corresponds to the results found by Stenholt [1]. Based on some exploratory extrapolations, we believe that Lasso might eclipse Brush beyond 50 targets, but this is far from conclusive.

For errors, we calculated the sensitivity and specificity of the individual methods for the timed condition. While the amount of incorrect selections is low, there is an overall difference between the methods. The data shows that while users made the most correct selections with Lasso (within the given time frame), they also made the most incorrect selections with this method, more than with Brush. These results contradict the qualitative results, as users stated that the width of Brush was too wide which made it easier to inadvertently select targets compared to Lasso. For Tap the opposite was the case, as users had the fewest correct selections within the given time, and also the fewest incorrect selections. Observations during the user study confirm this, as most users tended to have issues selecting all targets within the given time frame for Tap, but made few selection errors. These results indicate that even though Tap might be a slow selection method (especially for trials with many targets), the direct interaction of the method makes it easier to be precise.

The expectation in terms of user preference was that, due to its simple nature, users would prefer Brush, as it might be the best method for most situations. However, this was only partially true, as Lasso was rated the highest, but with no significant difference between the two. For the final study, Tap was rated lowest, but with no significant difference between it and Rectangle. Inspecting the qualitative data reveals that some users tended to prefer Lasso, as it could be used as a thin version of Brush. Enabling users to adjust the width of Brush might be beneficial, but the error results indicate that this is not the case. The qualitative results also revealed that most users chose to complete the trials as fast as possible without committing too many selection errors at the same time.

The implementation of the selection methods allowed them to be utilized as a tap for selecting single targets. The observations during the user studies showed that most users tended to use all the methods as Tap in the trials where the targets were not clustered (mainly seen in set 2 of the final user study). This further shows that Tap is simply unbeatable for a small amount of targets or where the targets are spread out over the entire image. Some users also stated this during the study.

5   Conclusion and Future Work

This work initially discussed several alternative approaches for adjusting a selection for the smart selection algorithm, Lazy Selection. The main goal was to identify if the adjustment of the set of selected targets could be improved through touch-based interactions. Three interaction techniques were designed for this task; a single touch tap (Tap), and a unimanual and bimanual pin and flick gesture. The results of two user studies showed that only Tap had an advantage compared to Lazy Selection in terms of time, while Lazy Selection required fewer actions on average. The advantage of Tap was especially relevant in trials with a low amount of target selections. This motivated a final user study to examine at which level other techniques become superior in efficiency.

The main purpose of the final user study was to build a predictive model around different existing selection methods. In the study Lazy Selection was replaced with simple brush selection and compared against lasso, rectangle and tapping. We investigated the number of actions and time needed to select targets in a timed, and perfect condition. The contribution of the final user study:

- A predictive model for the amount of targets and time needed to select a set of targets.
- Users preferred the lasso and brush selection methods.
- Tap has poor scalability in regards to the amount of targets.
- The lasso and brush selection methods improves in efficiency as the target amount increases.
- Participants prefer Tap for trials with a low amount of targets.

Acknowledgments. Many thanks to the authors of Lazy Selection for making their implementation available to us. Thanks to all those who participated in the various studies in the project. Some of the work was performed at York University. We acknowledge funding from NSERC.

References

1. Stenholt, R.: Efficient selection of multiple objects on a large scale. In: VRST 2012, pp. 105–112 (2012)

2. Xu, P., Fu, H., Au, O.C., Tai, C.L.: Lazy selection: a scribble-based tool for smart shape elements selection. In: SIGGRAPH 2012, vol. 31, no. 6, pp. 51–60 (2012)
3. Forlines, C., Wigdor, D., Shen, C., Balakrishnan, R.: Direct-touch vs. mouse input for tabletop displays. In: CHI 2007, pp. 647–656 (2007)
4. Wobbrock, J.O., Morris, M.R., Wilson, A.D.: User-defined gestures for surface computing. In: CHI 2009, pp. 1083–1092 (2009)
5. Wills, G.J.: 524.288 ways to say "this is interesting". In: Information Visualization 1996, pp. 54–60 (1996)
6. Stenholt, R., Madsen, C.B.: Poster: brush, lasso, or magic wand? Picking the right tool for large-scale multiple object selection tasks. In: 3DUI 2012, vol. 1, pp. 163–164 (2012)
7. Kimball, S., Mattis, P.: GNU Image Manipulation Program (2014)
8. James, D.: Crafting Digital Media - Audacity, Blender, Drupal, GIMP, Scribus, and Other Open Source Tools. Springer, Heidelberg (2009)
9. Kin, K., Agrawala, M., DeRose, T.: Determining the benefits of direct-touch, bimanual, and multifinger input on a multitouch workstation. In: Proceedings of Graphics Interface, pp. 119–124 (2009)
10. Wertheimer, M.: Untersuchungen zur Lehre von der Gestalt. Psychologishe Forschung 4 (1923)
11. Desolneux, A., Moisan, L., Morel, J.M.: From Gestalt Theory to Image Analysis: A Probabilistic Approach. Springer, Heidelberg (2008)
12. Chang, D., Nesbitt, K.V., Wilkins, K.: The Gestalt principles of similarity and proximity apply to both the haptic and visual grouping elements. In: AUIC 2007, vol. 64, pp. 79–86 (2007)
13. Gallace, A., Spence, C.: To what extent do Gestalt grouping principles influence tactile perception? Psychol. Bull. **137**(4), 538–561 (2011)
14. Todorovic, D.: Gestalt principles. In: Cognitive Science Conference94, vol. 3, no. 12, p. 5345 (2008)
15. Rome, E.: Simulating perceptual clustering by Gestalt principles. In: 25th Workshop of the Austrian Association for Pattern Recognition, OAGM/AAPR, pp. 191–198 (2001)
16. Thórisson, K.R.: Simulated perceptual grouping: an application to human-computer interaction. In: Proceedings of the Sixteenth Annual Conference of the Sognitive Science Society, pp. 876–881 (1994)
17. Dehmeshki, H., Stuerzlinger, W.: Design and evaluating of a perceptual-based object group selection technique. In: BCS 2010, pp. 365–373 (2010)
18. Au, O.K.C., Tai, C.L., Fu, H.: Multitouch gestures for constrained transformation of 3D objects. In: Computer Graphics Forum, vol. 31, no. 2 (2012)
19. Wigdor, D., Wixon, D.: Brave NUI World: Designing Natural User Interfaces for Touch and Gesture. Morgan Kaufmann, Burlington (2011)
20. Mizobuchi, S., Yasumura, M.: Tapping vs. circling selections on pen-based devices: evidence for different performance-shaping factors. In: CHI 2004, pp. 607–614 (2004)
21. Wagner, J., Hout, S., Mackay, W.E.: BiTouch and BiPad: designing bimanual interaction for hand-held tablets. In: CHI 2012, vol. 1, pp. 2317–2326 (2012)
22. Wobbrock, J.O., Findlater, L., Gergle, D., Higgins, J.J.: The aligned rank transform for nonparametric factorial analyses using only ANOVA procedures. In: CHI 2011, pp. 143–146 (2011)

Exploring Predictors of Mobile Device Proficiency Among Older Adults

Kimberly Champagne and Walter R. Boot$^{(\boxtimes)}$

Department of Psychology, Florida State University, Tallahassee, FL, USA
kjc15e@my.fsu.edu, boot@psy.fsu.edu

Abstract. Technology adoption rates of older adults typically lag behind those of their younger counterparts; a digital divide. This is unfortunate because technology has many potential benefits for older people. Among older adults, attitudes and cognitive abilities predict computer and Internet adoption, use, and proficiency. However, an important trend over the past two decades has been the rise of mobile computing (specifically with respect to smartphones and tablet computers). High quality interactions with mobile technology critically depend upon individuals' technology proficiency, making it important to understand how mobile device proficiency might be anticipated. This paper explored predictors of mobile device proficiency among older adults (65+) using a dataset from a cognitive intervention study that included 60 participants. Measures of computer and mobile device proficiency were obtained. Demographic variables and assessments of reasoning ability, processing speed, and executive control were collected and explored as predictors of mobile device proficiency. Even within this older adult sample, mobile device proficiency was related to age, but contrary to predictions, cognition was not significantly related to mobile device proficiency; the strongest predictor of mobile device proficiency was computer proficiency. This implies some transfer of proficiency from one technology platform to another. These results have implications for predicting quality technology interactions given the link between interaction quality and technology proficiency.

Keywords: Technology · Older adults · Individual differences · Cognition · Digital divide

1 Introduction

Although the gap between technology adoption rates of younger and older adults has been shrinking for decades, a substantial digital divide still exits. This can clearly be observed in recent U.S. survey data from the Pew Research Center [1]. In 2016, 36% of older adults (65+) reported not using the Internet over the past year, compared to only 1% of 18–29 year-olds, and 22% of adults overall. With respect to mobile devices an even greater divide is observed. Fifty-eight percent of older adults reported not owning a smartphone in 2016, compared to only 8% of adults 18–29 years of age. This is unfortunate because the use of the Internet and mobile devices have many potential benefits to older adults [2]. For example, an older adult with limited mobility can still shop and bank online even if they have difficulty leaving their home. Smartphone

© Springer International Publishing AG 2017
M. Kurosu (Ed.): HCI 2017, Part II, LNCS 10272, pp. 162–171, 2017.
DOI: 10.1007/978-3-319-58077-7_13

applications (apps) can assist older adults in managing their health, and for older adults with one or more chronic diseases, apps can help them manage their schedule of medications. The Internet has a wealth of resources (global and national resources, as well as resources specific to their community) that may be beneficial to older adults, but up to 36% of older adults in the U.S. may have difficulty accessing these resources. Finally, technology can provide enrichment and social activities, such as games and video conferencing with friends and family members, which has the potential to improve well-being [3]. Older adults who are not computer proficient or do not have access to the Internet are at a disadvantage. The digital divide is even more pronounced for older, lower-income, lower-education, rural, and minority older adults. Even for older adults who are computer proficient, they may still be locked out of the benefits of being able to utilize the same resources on a mobile platform, restricting when and where they have access to important resources. Younger adults are far more likely to own a smartphone compared to a non-smartphone, while this pattern is reversed for older adults.

Why is it that older adults lag in terms of technology use? About one-third of adults who do not use the Internet in the U.S. cite usability issues as the main reason [4]. Non-users report frustration using the Internet, lack of relevant knowledge, and feelings that they are too old to learn how to use the Internet. About one-third of non-users report feelings that the Internet isn't relevant to them as the main reason for non-use. These individuals state that they don't need to use the Internet, aren't interested in using it, and feel as though Internet use is a waste of time. These responses are broadly consistent with popular models of technology acceptance and adoption in which perceived ease of use and perceived usefulness primarily dominate decisions of whether or not to adopt new technology [5, 6].

Technology design may play another important role in influencing the technology adoption rates of older adults. As we age we can expect to experience some degree of perceptual and cognitive decline. These changes are a natural consequence of the aging process. However, if the design of technology does not take these changes into account, and does not recognize the fact that older adults may not have the same mental models related to technology as younger adults, older adults may experience difficulty and frustration, discouraging their adoption and use of technology [7]. Aging specific models of technology use and adoption highlight the important role of cognition [8, 9]. This role is confirmed in studies finding that among older adults, successful use of technology across a variety of technology types appears to be related to working memory, executive control, and reasoning ability [e.g., 10, 11]. The implication is that with proper design and careful consideration, as well as a focus on training to build up relevant mental models, the quality of older adults' interactions with technology might be improved and the digital divide might be greatly reduced.

Technology proficiency also likely plays an important role in technology adoption and the quality of a user's experience. Take, for example, an Internet-based system an older adult might use to track their health and receive information about nutrition and exercise to maintain a healthy lifestyle. If an older adult's basic computer and Internet proficiency is low, it is unlikely that they will have success using this system or that their interaction with this system will be positive. This makes understanding factors related to computer proficiency also broadly important for understanding technology adoption and user experience for a range of systems and software packages. Recently Zhang et al. [12] explored the best predictors of computer proficiency in an older adult sample (ages 60 to 95). To measure computer proficiency, the authors used a validated questionnaire specifically designed for older adults with a wide range of computer experience, the Computer Proficiency Questionnaire (CPQ) [13]. Age and education were significant predictors of proficiency. Cognition (psychomotor speed and inductive reasoning) uniquely predicted computer proficiency such that those with greater cognitive abilities tended to be more computer proficient. Socio-emotional variables were also important, with positive affect and a greater sense of control predicting some aspects of computer proficiency.

The current study aimed to explore similar questions asked by Zhang and colleagues regarding technology proficiency. Rather than explore predictors of computer proficiency, we explored predictors of mobile device proficiency (computing using a tablet or smartphone). We believe that this is important as much of the computing many individuals engage in everyday now takes place on mobile devices. Further, as mentioned previously, there is a substantial age-related digital divide for mobile devices such as smartphones and tablet computers. Understanding predictors of mobile device proficiency is also important as there are inherent advantages to mobile computing compared to desktop computing because apps and resources can be accessed from anywhere, and a lack of mobile device proficiency may "lock out" older adults from these advantages. Finally, the perceptual and cognitive demands of smaller mobile devices, and also differences in complexity between software that may be on desktop computers and mobile devices, may result in the predictors of mobile device proficiency being different compared to computer proficiency.

We explored these issues using the Mobile Device Proficiency Questionnaire (MDPQ) [14]. This measure, based on the Computer Proficiency Questionnaire, has been demonstrated to be a reliable and valid measure of smartphone and tablet computer proficiency. All analyses reported here are exploratory rather than confirmatory, as they constitute the combination and reanalysis of previously reported data [14–16]. These papers provide a full description of all measures and procedures, which will be summarized briefly here. Of primary interest are demographic and individual difference characteristics and how they relate to mobile device proficiency.

2 Methods

The current project reused data from a study in which cognitive abilities were measured before and after a tablet-based brain training intervention [15, 16]. Measures of computer and mobile device proficiency were also collected before training. Analyses are based on a dataset consisting of data from 60 participants who completed the intervention. The average age of participants included in the analyses reported here was 72 years ($SD = 5.2$) and the sample was 57% female. Approximately 67% of the sample had a college degree or higher.

2.1 Surveys

Computer proficiency was assessed with the short form of the Computer Proficiency Questionnaire, the CPQ-12 [13]. This measure has 12 questions, but correlates highly with the full 33-question version of the CPQ. As an example, the CPQ-12 asks participants to rate statements like the following: *I can: Use a computer to watch movies and videos*. Ratings were made on a 5-point scale (1 = Never tried, 2 = Not at all, 3 = Not very easily, 4 = Somewhat easily, 5 = Very easily). Mobile Device Proficiency was assessed using the Mobile Device Proficiency Questionnaire (MDPQ) [14]. This measure, based on the CPQ, specifically asks participants to rate their proficiency performing tasks with mobile devices such as smartphones and tablet computers (a description of these devices and photographs were provided on the first page of the questionnaire). The MDPQ consists of 46 questions, and features the following sub-scales: Mobile Device Basics, Communication, Data and File Storage, Internet, Calendar, Entertainment, Privacy, and Troubleshooting and Software Management. Subscale scores were calculated by averaging the response to each question in that subscale. A total mobile device proficiency score was calculated by summing all subscale scores. Participants also completed a demographics questionnaire that collected information about income, education, and age.

2.2 Cognitive Measures

Before and after the intervention, participants completed a variety of cognitive assessment measures. We used pre-intervention scores in all of the reported analyses since at least one measure suggested the intervention may have influenced outcome measure performance. Detailed descriptions of measures are previously reported [15]. Reasoning ability was measured with Form Boards [17], Letter Sets [17], Paper Folding [17], and Ravens Matrices [18]. Processing speed was measured using Pattern Comparison [19] and a Reaction Time task [20]. Memory was assessed with a version of the Corsi Block Tapping task [21]. Finally, executive control was measured using a Task-Switching task [20] and Trails B (adjusted for Trails A performance) [22].

3   Analyses

First, a principal components analysis (PCA) with varimax rotation was conducted to reduce the cognitive data. Then, bivariate correlations explored the relations among the variables of interest. Finally, linear regression analyses explored the best predictors of total mobile device proficiency, as well as proficiency related to basic, intermediate, and difficult mobile device tasks.

4   Results

Principal Components Analysis. A principal components analysis (PCA) was performed on the cognitive dataset. This analysis revealed three factors that accounted for approximately 60% of the variance in the data (Table 1).

Table 1. PCA components extracted from cognitive dataset.

	Component		
	1	2	3
Ravens	**.510**	**.516**	.036
Letter Sets	.376	**.786**	.086
Form Board	**.513**	.025	.044
Paper Folding	−.154	**.817**	.032
Task-Switch	−.188	.280	**.719**
Corsi Block	**.732**	−.018	−.107
Reaction Time	−.197	.117	**−.785**
Pattern Comparison	**.701**	.000	.385
Trails B (Minus A)	**−.711**	−.331	.070

A diverse set of tasks loaded onto the first component, though in general these tasks all had relatively high visuospatial demands (spatial reasoning, spatial memory, visuospatial judgments). Although this first component appears to be more complex than that, for the sake of simplicity we refer to it as the *Visuospatial* factor. Reasoning and problem-solving tasks most highly loaded onto the second component. We refer to this as the *Reasoning* factor. Finally, the two tasks that required quick responses loaded most highly onto the third component, which we interpret as a *Processing Speed* factor. Note that Reaction Time, Task Switch, and Trails B are all measures for which better performance is associated with lower scores, explaining negative factor loadings.

Bivariate Correlations. Next we explored potential correlations between the variables of primary interest. These variables included age, education, technology proficiency, and cognition (Table 2). Contrary to predictions, neither computer nor mobile device proficiency were predicted by cognitive abilities. However, higher levels of education were associated with greater mobile device proficiency, and higher levels of computer proficiency were associated with higher levels of mobile device proficiency. Education also predicted cognitive performance with respect to the *Reasoning* factor.

Predictors of Mobile Device Proficiency. Finally, we explored the question of primary interest: Which factors best predict mobile device proficiency? A linear regression analysis was conducted with Mobile Device Proficiency (Total Score) as the criterion variable and age, education, computer proficiency (CPQ-12), and the three cognitive factors as predictor variables. This model accounted for 49% of the variance in proficiency ($F(6, 46) = 7.44, p < .001$). The strongest predictor was computer proficiency, followed by age (Table 3). As computer proficiency increased, so did mobile device proficiency. As age increased, mobile device proficiency decreased. Contrary to predictions, cognitive abilities did not significantly predict mobile device proficiency (all p values > .40).

It's possible that important predictors might vary for different domains of mobile device proficiency. We explored predictors of subscale scores of the MDPQ that reflected proficiency with respect to basic, intermediate, and difficult mobile device tasks. The Basics subscale of the MDPQ assessed proficiency with simple tasks such as

Table 2. Correlations among technology proficiency, demographic, and cognitive measures. Note that Ns varies due to missing or incomplete data for some tests.

		Age	Education	CPQ	MDPQ	Visuospatial	Reasoning	Processing speed
Age	Pearson corr.	1	.021	−.120	−.241	−.168	−.159	−.074
	N	60	60	58	59	56	56	56
Education	Pearson corr.	.021	1	.255	**.266***	.154	**.298***	−.141
	N	60	60	58	59	56	56	56
CPQ	Pearson Corr.	−.120	.255	1	**.683****	.119	−.063	.102
	N	58	58	58	57	54	54	54
MDPQ	Pearson corr.	−.241	**.266***	**.683****	1	.077	−.050	.111
	N	59	59	57	59	55	55	55
Visuospatial	Pearson corr.	−.168	.154	.119	.077	1	.000	.000
	N	56	56	54	55	56	56	56
Reasoning	Pearson corr.	−.159	**.298***	−.063	−.050	.000	1	.000
	N	56	56	54	55	56	56	56
Processing speed	Pearson corr.	−.074	−.141	.102	.111	.000	.000	1
	N	56	56	54	55	56	56	56

*Correlation is significant at the 0.05 level (2-tailed).
**Correlation is significant at the 0.01 level (2-tailed).

Table 3. Linear regression analysis predicting Mobile Device Proficiency (Total) from age, education, computer proficiency, and cognition.

Model	Unstandardized coefficients		Standardized coefficients	t	Sig.
	B	Std. error	Beta		
(Constant)	14.162	15.410		.919	.363
Age	**−.400**	**.198**	**−.224**	**−2.027**	**.048**
Education	1.115	.923	.145	1.207	.233
CPQ	**1.135**	**.215**	**.594**	**5.285**	**<.001**
Visuospatial	−.009	.994	−.001	−.009	.993
Reasoning	−.882	1.037	−.098	−.851	.399
Processing speed	.122	.990	.013	.124	.902

turning the device on and typing using a touchscreen (Table 4). The same predictors were entered into the linear regression analysis. This model accounted for 35% of the variance in the Basics subscale score ($F(6, 46) = 4.05$, $p < .01$). The strongest predictor was computer proficiency. However, in this analysis age was not a significant predictor, nor were any of the cognitive ability measures (all p values > .51).

Proficiency with respect to mobile device tasks of intermediate difficulty was explored using the Internet subscale of the MDPQ (Table 5). This subscale measures proficiency with tasks such as using search engines and shopping online. The same predictors were entered into a linear regression analysis. The model accounted for 44% of the variance in Internet subscale scores ($F(6, 46) = 6.05$, $p < .001$). Again, computer proficiency was the strongest predictor, followed by age. Unexpectedly, reasoning ability *negatively* predicted Internet proficiency using mobile devices.

Table 4. Linear regression analysis predicting Mobile Device Basics subscale scores of the MDPQ from age, education, computer proficiency, and cognition.

Model	Unstandardized coefficients		Standardized coefficients	t	Sig.
	B	Std. error	Beta		
(Constant)	−.354	2.774		−.128	.899
Age	−.014	.036	−.049	−.388	.699
Education	.077	.166	.063	.463	.646
CPQ	**.167**	**.039**	**.553**	**4.331**	**<.001**
Visuospatial	.040	.179	.027	.222	.826
Reasoning	−.124	.187	−.087	−.663	.511
Processing speed	−.112	.178	−.077	−.628	.533

Table 5. Linear regression analysis predicting Internet subscale scores of the MDPQ from age, education, computer proficiency, and cognition.

Model	Unstandardized coefficients		Standardized coefficients	t	Sig.
	B	Std. error	Beta		
(Constant)	3.707	2.867		1.293	.203
Age	**−.082**	**.037**	**−.258**	**−2.224**	**.031**
Education	.176	.172	.129	1.024	.311
CPQ	**.165**	**.040**	**.486**	**4.125**	**<.001**
Visuospatial	.106	.185	.065	.573	.569
Reasoning	**−.461**	**.193**	**−.289**	**−2.390**	**.021**
Processing speed	−.041	.184	−.025	−.220	.827

Table 6. Linear regression predicting Troubleshooting and Software Management subscale scores of the MDPQ from age, education, computer proficiency, and cognition.

Model	Unstandardized Coefficients		Standardized Coefficients	t	Sig.
	B	Std. Error	Beta		
(Constant)	2.287	2.526		.905	.370
Age	−.064	.032	−.222	−1.970	.055
Education	.082	.151	.066	.541	.591
CPQ	**.177**	**.035**	**.578**	**5.030**	**<.001**
Visuospatial	.047	.163	.032	.287	.776
Reasoning	−.188	.170	−.130	−1.104	.276
Processing speed	.121	.162	.082	.745	.460

Finally, we examined the Troubleshooting and Software Management subscale as a measure of proficiency with respect to difficult mobile device tasks. This subscale focuses on updating device and application software, recovering from a crash of the device, and deleting unwanted applications. Entering the same predictors into a regression analysis, this model accounted for 47% of the variance in the Trouble Shooting subscale ($F(6, 46) = 6.80$, $p < .001$). Computer proficiency was a strong predictor, though age was a marginally significant predictor as well (Table 6). Cognitive abilities did not predict proficiency with these more challenging mobile device tasks (all p values $> .27$).

5 Discussion

There exists a striking age-related digital divide with respect to mobile device ownership, and many older adults do not have the proficiency to perform tasks using smartphones and tablet computers [14]. This puts them at a disadvantage with respect to benefiting from mobile devices and applications, and inexperience and low levels of proficiency can result in lower quality technology interactions. The purpose of this exploratory set of analyses was to better understand factors that relate to mobile device proficiency.

Interestingly, even within this older adult sample (65+), greater age was associated with less mobile device proficiency. This is likely due to less mobile device experience being associated with increasing age within the older adult cohort. This speaks to the diversity of the older adult cohort; not all individuals over the age of 65 are alike. However, in addition to experience, this may also be partly due to sensory and physical changes that make mobile device use more challenging. Surprisingly, we found little evidence that cognitive abilities were related to mobile device proficiency or even computer proficiency (Table 2). This is in contrast to a recent study using similar measures [12]. Why did we find that cognition did not predict proficiency while this previous study did? Statistical power may be one explanation, with this previous investigation assessing 97 participants, and our dataset containing data from only 60 participants (with even fewer entering analyses due to missing data). Second, at this point, many older adults have some experience using computers. Because many older adults have some computer experience, proficiency may be driven primarily by cognitive factors rather than experience factors. However, since many older adults do not have experience with mobile devices, in this case, differences in proficiency may be largely experience based. Finally, it should be noted that like many laboratory studies, our participants were screened for cognitive impairment. This means the range in cognitive abilities observed was lower compared to the general population, and it is not appropriate to anticipate a lack of a relationship between cognition and mobile device or computer proficiency in the general population.

The most consistent predictor of mobile device proficiency was computer proficiency. This implies some transfer of either knowledge or attitudes toward technology from one form of technology to another, which may be important in encouraging the adoption of technology useful to older adults. Providing experience with an easy-to-use system, or appropriate technology training, may facilitate technology use more broadly through this mechanism. Previous findings suggest that technology use can increase self-efficacy and reduce technology anxiety, which may partly explain the positive relationship between mobile device and computer proficiency. While exploratory, these results provide insight into mobile device proficiency and factors that may shape technology adoption.

Acknowledgments. We gratefully acknowledge support from the National Institute on Aging, NIA 2P01AG017211, Project CREATE IV – Center for Research and Education on Aging and Technology Enhancement (www.create-center.org).

References

1. Internet/Broadband Fact Sheet, 12 January 2017. http://www.pewinternet.org/fact-sheet/internet-broadband/. Accessed 15 Feb 2017
2. Charness, N., Boot, W.R.: Aging and information technology use: potential and barriers. Curr. Dir. Psychol. Sci. **18**(5), 253–258 (2009)
3. Czaja, S.J., Boot, W.R., Charness, N., Rogers, W.A., Sharit, J.: Improving social support for older adults through technology: findings from the PRISM randomized controlled trial. Gerontol. (in press)
4. Zickuhr, K.: Who's Not Online and Why? (2013). http://www.pewinternet.org/2013/09/25/main-report-2/. Accessed 20 Sept 2016
5. Davis, F.D., Bagozzi, R.P., Warshaw, P.R.: User acceptance of computer technology: a comparison of two theoretical models. Manag. Sci. **35**(8), 982–1003 (1989)
6. Venkatesh, V., Morris, M., Davis, G., Davis, F.D.: User acceptance of information technology: toward a unified view. MIS Q. **27**(3), 425–478 (2003)
7. Fisk, A.D., Rogers, W.A., Charness, N., Czaja, S., Sharit, J.: Designing for Older Adults: Principles and Creative Human Factors Approaches, 2nd edn. CRC Press, Boca Raton (2009)
8. Chen, K., Chan, A.H.S.: Gerontechnology acceptance by elderly Hong Kong Chinese: a senior technology acceptance model (STAM). Ergonomics **57**(5), 635–652 (2014)
9. Czaja, S.J., Charness, N., Fisk, A.D., Hertzog, C., Nair, S.N., Rogers, W.A., Sharit, J.: Factors predicting the use of technology: findings from the Center for Research and Education on Aging and Technology Enhancement (CREATE). Psychol. Aging **21**(2), 333–352 (2006)
10. Czaja, S.J., Sharit, J., Hernandez, M.A., Nair, S.N., Loewenstein, D.: Variability among older adults in internet health information-seeking performance. Gerontechnology **9**(1), 46–55 (2010)
11. Taha, J., Czaja, S.J., Sharit, J., Morrow, D.G.: Factors affecting usage of a personal health record (PHR) to manage health. Psychol. Aging **28**(4), 1124–1139 (2013)
12. Zhang, S., Grenhart, W.C., Mclaughlin, A.C., Allaire, J.C.: Predicting computer proficiency in older adults. Comput. Hum. Behav. **67**, 106–112 (2017). doi:10.1016/j.chb.2016.11.006
13. Boot, W.R., Charness, N., Czaja, S.J., Sharit, J., Rogers, W.A., Fisk, A.D., Mitzner, T., Lee, C., Nair, S.: The computer proficiency questionnaire (CPQ): assessing low and high computer proficient seniors. Gerontologist **55**, 404–411 (2015)
14. Roque, N.A., Boot, W.R.: A new tool for assessing mobile device proficiency in older adults: the mobile device proficiency questionnaire. J. Appl. Gerontol. (in press)

15. Souders, D.J., Boot, W.R., Blocker, K., Vitale, T., Roque, N.A., Charness, N.: Evidence for narrow transfer after short-term cognitive training in older adults. Front. Aging Neurosci. **9**, 41 (2017)
16. Boot, W.R., Souders, D., Charness, N., Blocker, K., Roque, N., Vitale, T.: The gamification of cognitive training: older adults' perceptions of and attitudes toward digital game-based interventions. In: Zhou, J., Salvendy, G. (eds.) ITAP 2016. LNCS, vol. 9754, pp. 290–300. Springer, Cham (2016). doi:10.1007/978-3-319-39943-0_28
17. Ekstrom, R.B., French, J.W., Harman, H.H., Derman, D.: Kit of Factor-Referenced Cognitive Tests. Educational Testing Service, Princeton (1976)
18. Ravens, J.: Advanced Progressive Matrices: Set II. H.K. Lewis, London (1962)
19. Salthouse, T.A., Babcock, R.L.: Decomposing adult age differences in working memory. Dev. Psychol. **27**(5), 763–776 (1991)
20. Boot, W.R., Champion, M., Blakely, D.P., Wright, T., Souders, D.J., Charness, N.: Video games as a means to reduce age-related cognitive decline: attitudes, compliance, and effectiveness. Front. Psychol. **4**, 1–9 (2013)
21. Corsi, P.M.: Human memory and the medial temporal region of the brain. Ph.D. thesis, McGill University, Montreal, Quebec, Canada (1972)
22. Reitan, R.M.: The relation of the trail making test to organic brain damage. J. Consult. Psychol. **19**(5), 393–394 (1955)

The Research of Wearable Device User Fatigue Based on Gesture Interaction

Wen-jun Hou[1,2], Chun-jing Wu[1], and Xiao-lin Chen[1(✉)]

[1] School of Digital Media and Design Arts,
Beijing University of Post and Telecommunications, Beijing 100876, China
buptwcj@foxmail.com, cxl95@163.com
[2] Beijing Key Laboratory of Network and Network Culture,
Beijing University of Post and Telecommunications, Beijing 100876, China

Abstract. In this paper, in order to study the user fatigue of gesture interaction of wearable device, we combine Surface electromyography (sEGM) and the subjective fatigue evaluation of users to evaluate the fatigue degree of the basic interactive gestures of the left arm. By analyzing the normalized date of the sEMG in time domain, we featured the EMG discharge. We also find that the operation of information content has lower physical fatigue compared with the operation of physical device and layer structure. And because of the asymmetry of gesture, gesture of different direction has different fatigue even they belong to same type. And we build a model by combining sEMG and the subjective fatigue feeling evaluation of users to mapping the relationship between the objective energy expenditure and subjective fatigue. The result of this experiment provides basis and measures for fatigue detection, mission planning and the design of gesture interaction.

Keywords: Hand gesture · Wearable device · Fatigue evaluation

1 Introduction

With the development of technology and science, wearable devices such as smart watch and smart bracelet become more popular. And the increasing use of wearable devices has promoted interest in gesture input techniques for interaction. Hand gesture as one of the contact-free input techniques allows users interact with systems more naturally compared with other traditional contact input techniques such as keyboard and mouse. However, hand gestures also cause obvious fatigue problem during operating device due to the diversity and large movements range of hand gestures. Therefore, it's very important to evaluate and measure the fatigue of hand gesture interaction, which can provide a reasonable basis for gesture interaction design.

There are mainly five methods to evaluate the fatigue degree [1–5]. The first method is the subjective evaluation method which is using users' sense of self to evaluate the fatigue degree. The second method is that the biomechanical evaluation method which is conducting biomechanical analysis of joints according to the force constrains of operations. The third is the physiological signal evaluation method which is analyzing the fatigue state by measuring ECG, EEG and surface EMG (Surface

© Springer International Publishing AG 2017
M. Kurosu (Ed.): HCI 2017, Part II, LNCS 10272, pp. 172–182, 2017.
DOI: 10.1007/978-3-319-58077-7_14

electromyography, sEMG) and other physiological signals. The forth is the energy metabolism evaluation method which is evaluating the functions of a human body by measuring the oxygen consumption, respiratory rate and other biochemical indexes of the operator. The fifth is the transmitter fatigue evaluation method of muscle tissue which is evaluating human muscle fatigue degree by measuring the density of neurotransmitters.

Surface electromyography (sEMG) is a non-invasive and simple method to record the biological electric signals during neuromuscular activities by electrodes attached to human skeletal muscle surface. Surface electromyography(sEMG) contains a great deal of information of status of neuromuscular contraction function which can quantitatively reflect the degree of fatigue muscle activity. It has high academic value in the field of human engineering. Brog [7] subjective evaluation is generally acknowledged to medical community that can reflect human fatigue condition by reflecting heart rate condition to a large extent. Ge Shuwang et al. [8] conducted the research about right arm in the static posture and found out that sEMG and Borg scores showed a significant correlation. Song Haiyan et al. [9] studied the characteristics of surface electromyography of human upper limb muscles in daily life. Wang Lejun et al. [10] conducted the research about the fatigue of finger extensor caused by clicking mouse quickly by monitoring sEMG. Liu Chang et al. [11] studied the users' fatigue of non-contact human-computer interactive gestures of large screen device. Due to the differences such as hardware equipment, usage, usage scenarios, recognition patterns, the gesture interaction of wearable devices is very different with other products, yet there is no research on the user fatigue of gesture interaction of wearable devices (Fig. 1).

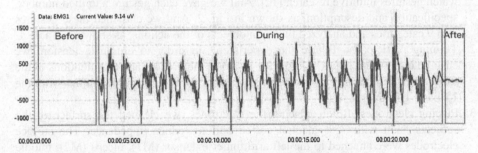

Fig. 1. The SEMG signals before, during and after an action.

By comparing the difference of these five methods, we decided to combine surface electromyography (sEGM) and the subjective fatigue evaluation method (Brog) to reflect the fatigue condition of left arm after performing a basic interactive gesture of wearable devices. Our experiments analyzed the characteristics of gesture interaction of wearable device by combining the subjective and objective data, and established the fatigue evaluation model, which can provide the basis and reference for analyzing and monitoring the operating load of gesture interaction of wearable device, designing interactive gestures and planning tasks.

2 Method

2.1 Experimental Subject

We selected 10 participated (5 males and 5 females, the average age is 23.3) who were in good condition and didn't perform any strenuous physical activities in 24 h before the experiment. They were all at good mental state and they weren't in any kinds of bad conditions like lack of sleep or listlessness. And they all worn watches on left wrest in daily life. Before the experiment, all the subjects were familiar with the experimental procedures and agreed to participate in the experiment voluntarily.

2.2 Experimental Equipment

Ticwatch smart watch was worn by the participants to simulate the use of smart watches.16 guide wireless physiological recorder was used for collecting surface EMG. Notebook computer was used to connect the wireless physiological recorder which can record test data. This experiment was carried out in the usability laboratory of Beijing University of Posts and Telecommunications, and the laboratory temperature was tested under the condition of 20–26.

2.3 Experimental Method

1. Selecting gestures. We selected 15 basic interactive gestures through the smart watch gestures intuitive research [12]. And we gave each gesture a unified number, specification and description, as shown in Fig. 2. And we classified these gestures into 9 categories and analyzed the main objects of the actions, as shown in Table 1.
2. Training participates. Before the experiment, in order to eliminate tension, we ensured every participates to know the purpose, the process and the attentions of the experiment. And every participate was asked to learn and become familiar with the 15 basic gestures.
3. Placing electrodes. Before placing the electrodes, we cleaned the surface of the subjects' skin with 75% alcohol cotton ball to reduce impedance. The surface electrodes were attached to the left arm finger extensor (M1), biceps (M2), middle deltoid (M3). And these three muscles had the most direct correlation and monitored the EMG status of the shoulder and the upper arm, the elbow and the wrist muscles. Two of the three recording electrodes were attached along the longitudinal axis of the muscle fibers, and another reference electrode formed triangle with the two electrodes, and the distance between the electrodes is 2–3 cm.
4. Conducting experiment. During the experiment, participants were asked to choose a comfortable sitting position in a resting for state 3–5 min and we collected the EMG signal of the three muscles in the state of rest for 1–2 min. At the beginning of each test, participates were asked to perform the same gesture 10 times in a normal speed. We recorded the sEMG signals in the implementation process. And the Brog 10 level subjective fatigue table was hanging in the front of participates during the experiment. And participates were asked to report the score of the fatigue after performing a gesture 10 times. The interval between each gesture was 30 s (Table 2).

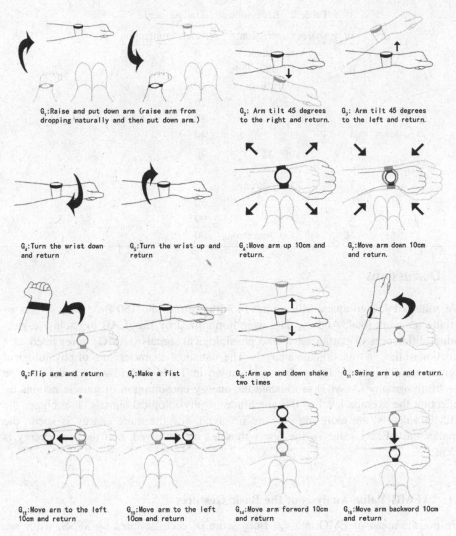

G_1:Raise and put down arm (raise arm from dropping naturally and then put down arm.)

G_2: Arm tilt 45 degrees to the right and return.

G_3: Arm tilt 45 degrees to the left and return.

G_4:Turn the wrist down and return

G_5:Turn the wrist up and return

G_6:Move arm up 10cm and return.

G_7:Move arm down 10cm and return.

G_8:Flip arm and return

G_9:Make a fist

G_{10}:Arm up and down shake two times

G_{11}:Swing arm up and return.

G_{12}:Move arm to the left 10cm and return

G_{13}:Move arm to the left 10cm and return

G_{14}:Move arm forword 10cm and return

G_{15}:Move arm backword 10cm and return

Fig. 2. Basic interactive hand gestures

Table 1. Gesture classification

Types	Gestures	Operation objects
Raising and putting down	G_1	Physical device
Shaking	G_{10}	
Fliting	G_8	Structural level
Making a fist	G_9	
Tilting	G_2, G_3	Contents
Turning	G_6, G_7	
Moving vertically	G_4, G_5	
Swinging	G_{11}	
Moving horizontally	G_{12}, G_{13}, G_{14}, G_{15}	

Table 2. Borg subjective fatigue scale

Borg score	Description	Muscle contraction
0	Insentience	0
0.5	Extreme light	5
1	Very light	10
2	Light	20
3		30
4		40
5	Strong	50
6		60
7	Very strong	70
8		80
9		90
10	Extreme strong	100

3 Discussions

We collected 450 groups sEMG signals (4500 gestures) and 150 Brog user subjective fatigue scores in total. And the data were normalized by ErogLAB to exclusive individual differences of participants. The physiological signals (sEMG) is regarded as a function of time in time domain analysis. The statistical characteristics of physiological signals are obtained by the analysis, as shown in Table 3. And we use the average electromyography (AEMG) to indicate the energy consumption of muscle actions by reflecting the average level of the amplitude of physiological signals. The bigger the AEMG value is, the more muscles are involved, and the more energy is spent; the smaller the AEMG value is, the fewer muscles are involved, and the less energy is spent.

3.1 AEMG Value Analysis of the Basic Gestures

We got the mean of EMG and the Borg score of each gestures by SPSS, while we summed the AEMG value of the three muscles of each gesture up, as shown in Table 4.

The data in Table 4 showed that five of the gestures have the highest figure extensor fatigue degree, which are flipping arm, turning the wrist up, raising and putting down arm, turning the wrist down, and swinging arm up. Five of the gestures have the lowest figure extensor fatigue degree, which are moving arm up 10 cm, moving arm down 10 cm, moving arm to the right, tilting 45 degrees to the left, and moving arm to the left. Five of the gestures have the highest biceps fatigue degree, which are flipping arm, swinging arm up, moving arm forward 10 cm, moving arm down 10 cm, shaking arm up and down two times. Five of the gestures have the lowest biceps fatigue degree, which are moving arm up 10 cm, turning the wrist up, moving arm to the left 10 cm, turning the wrist down, and making a fist. Five of the gestures have the highest middle deltoid fatigue degree, which are raising and putting down arm, swinging arm up, shaking arm up and down two times, moving arm to the right

Table 3. AEMG and Borg score of the 15 gestures

Partici-pants	Index	G_1	G_2	G_3	G_4	G_5	G_6	G_7	G_8	G_9	G_{10}	G_{11}	G_{12}	G_{13}	G_{14}	G_{15}
P_1	M_1	0.25	0.09	0.03	0.29	0.57	0.07	0.07	0.38	0.09	0.07	0.18	0.03	0.07	0.14	0.12
	M_2	0.21	0.15	0.08	0.07	0.10	0.06	0.14	0.26	0.03	0.22	0.22	0.06	0.10	0.18	0.09
	M_3	0.19	0.13	0.10	0.09	0.09	0.14	0.09	0.14	0.08	0.13	0.20	0.14	0.15	0.11	0.09
	Borg	3.00	2.00	2.00	2.00	2.00	1.00	1.00	4.00	2.00	1.00	4.00	1.00	3.00	2.00	2.00
P_2	M_1	0.33	0.18	0.13	0.37	0.36	0.09	0.12	0.30	0.07	0.16	0.11	0.18	0.21	0.18	0.20
	M_2	1.66	1.02	0.88	0.08	0.32	0.78	1.15	1.27	0.05	0.79	1.16	0.27	0.98	1.18	1.05
	M_3	0.21	0.11	0.11	0.03	0.03	0.11	0.06	0.30	0.03	0.44	0.62	0.15	0.54	0.12	0.17
	Borg	0.00	2.00	2.00	1.00	1.00	3.00	4.00	3.00	2.00	2.00	3.00	3.00	2.00	3.00	2.00
P_3	M_1	0.o5	0.06	0.04	0.06	0.08	0.09	0.05	0.12	0.08	0.06	0.07	0.04	0.03	0.04	0.04
	M_2	0.15	0.18	0.21	0.21	0.37	0.19	0.27	0.49	0.06	0.41	0.39	0.16	0.26	0.30	0.31
	M_3	0.03	0.04	0.04	0.02	0.02	0.03	0.03	0.04	0.02	0.09	0.08	0.04	0.04	0.04	0.04
	Borg	2.00	2.00	3.00	1.00	1.00	2.00	3.00	4.00	2.00	3.00	5.00	3.00	4.00	3.00	4.00
P_4	M_1	0.25	0.06	0.10	0.16	0.27	0.13	0.12	0.51	0.09	0.15	0.17	0.05	0.05	0.08	0.15
	M_2	1.16	0.26	0.19	0.05	0.11	0.18	0.85	1.58	0.02	0.14	0.74	0.08	0.14	0.76	0.18
	M_3	0.79	0.11	0.06	0.04	0.04	0.05	0.04	0.10	0.02	0.20	0.08	0.11	0.10	0.06	0.09
	Borg	2.00	2.00	2.00	1.00	1.00	2.00	2.00	3.00	1.00	3.00	2.00	3.00	3.00	2.00	3.00
P_5	M_1	0.10	0.02	0.02	0.09	0.25	0.03	0.03	0.20	0.06	0.05	0.11	0.02	0.02	0.03	0.04
	M_2	0.28	0.08	0.05	0.03	0.04	0.07	0.11	0.21	0.02	0.17	0.22	0.03	0.10	0.10	0.09
	M_3	0.13	0.08	0.10	0.05	0.03	0.05	0.05	0.09	0.05	0.17	0.09	0.12	0.08	0.08	0.05
	Borg	2.00	2.00	1.00	4.00	1.00	3.00	3.00	3.00	2.00	4.00	4.00	2.00	4.00	3.00	4.00
P_6	M_1	0.04	0.05	0.02	0.07	0.06	0.03	0.03	0.11	0.04	0.03	0.03	0.01	0.01	0.03	0.02
	M_2	0.21	0.07	0.05	0.04	0.06	0.09	0.07	0.25	0.02	0.19	0.22	0.03	0.06	0.11	0.07
	M_3	0.08	0.09	0.06	0.06	0.05	0.07	0.06	0.07	0.04	0.17	0.11	0.05	0.04	0.06	0.05
	Borg	3.00	5.00	3.00	4.00	3.00	2.00	1.00	4.00	1.00	3.00	2.00	1.00	1.00	1.00	0.00
P_7	M_1	0.05	0.04	0.03	0.07	0.11	0.02	0.02	0.13	0.03	0.07	0.10	0.05	0.03	0.04	0.03
	M_2	0.14	0.05	0.06	0.04	0.09	0.06	0.06	0.19	0.02	0.21	0.16	0.10	0.12	0.14	0.09
	M_3	0.12	0.04	0.03	0.03	0.03	0.04	0.03	0.06	0.02	0.09	0.13	0.14	0.06	0.05	0.05
	Borg	1.00	3.00	0.50	2.00	1.00	3.00	4.00	5.00	1.00	4.00	5.00	3.00	4.00	5.00	5.00
P_8	M_1	0.02	0.02	0.02	0.03	0.03	0.02	0.02	0.04	0.04	0.03	0.04	0.02	0.02	0.03	0.02
	M_2	0.04	0.02	0.02	0.02	0.03	0.02	0.02	0.06	0.01	0.06	0.09	0.02	0.03	0.03	0.04
	M_3	0.03	0.03	0.04	0.03	0.03	0.04	0.03	0.04	0.03	0.04	0.05	0.04	0.05	0.03	0.04
	Borg	3.00	3.00	2.00	4.00	2.00	5.00	4.00	4.00	1.00	3.00	5.00	2.00	5.00	3.00	3.00
P_9	M_1	0.26	0.05	0.07	0.11	0.31	0.08	0.08	0.33	0.06	0.07	0.17	0.03	0.04	0.04	0.07
	M_2	0.32	0.21	0.40	0.05	0.10	0.13	0.15	0.17	0.03	0.22	0.85	0.06	0.10	0.07	0.11
	M_3	0.13	0.14	0.04	0.03	0.03	0.03	0.03	0.05	0.02	0.04	0.07	0.09	0.06	0.03	0.04
	Borg	0.50	3.00	2.00	3.00	0.50	1.00	3.00	2.00	0.50	6.00	1.00	3.00	4.00	4.00	2.00
P_{10}	M_1	0.05	0.01	0.01	0.03	0.05	0.01	0.02	0.09	0.03	0.02	0.06	0.01	0.01	0.02	0.03
	M_2	0.13	0.06	0.12	0.03	0.04	0.04	0.09	0.23	0.02	0.12	0.32	0.07	0.06	0.08	0.18
	M_3	0.06	0.04	0.03	0.02	0.02	0.03	0.02	0.05	0.02	0.03	0.07	0.04	0.04	0.04	0.04
	Borg	1.00	4.00	4.00	5.00	3.00	3.00	4.00	5.00	3.00	5.00	5.00	3.00	4.00	4.00	3.00

10 cm, and flipping arm. Five of the gestures have the lowest middle deltoid fatigue degree, which are moving arm up 10 cm, moving arm down 10 cm, turning the wrist down, turning the wrist up, and making a fist. So we found that two gestures have the relatively high fatigue degree of all three muscles, which are flipping arm and swinging arm up.

Table 4. Mean of AEMG and mean of Borg score

Gestures	M1	M2	M3	Sum	Brog
G_1	0.14	0.43	0.18	0.75	1.75
G_2	0.06	0.21	0.08	0.35	2.80
G_3	0.05	0.21	0.06	0.32	2.15
G_4	0.13	0.06	0.04	0.23	2.70
G_5	0.21	0.13	0.04	0.37	1.55
G_6	0.06	0.16	0.06	0.28	2.50
G_7	0.05	0.29	0.05	0.39	2.90
G_8	0.22	0.47	0.09	0.79	3.70
G_9	0.06	0.03	0.04	0.12	1.55
G_{10}	0.07	0.25	0.14	0.46	3.40
G_{11}	0.10	0.44	0.15	0.69	3.60
G_{12}	0.04	0.09	0.09	0.23	2.40
G_{13}	0.05	0.19	0.12	0.36	3.40
G_{14}	0.06	0.30	0.06	0.42	3.00
G_{15}	0.07	0.22	0.07	0.36	2.80

The AEMG value of figure extensor, biceps and middle deltoid represent the left forearm, arm and shoulder muscles fatigue status, therefore we sum the AEMG value of three muscles up to evaluate the fatigue situation of human upper limb. And we found that three gestures have significantly higher fatigue degree than other gestures, which are flipping arm, raising and putting up arm, and swinging arm up. So we should avoid the frequent use of these three gestures in interaction design and task planning. And we found that three gestures have relatively lower fatigue degree than other gestures, which are turning the wrist down, moving arm to the left, and making a fist. So these three gestures have a lower fatigue degree and a better experience.

3.2   Gesture Types and Fatigue Analysis

We analyzed the 15 basic gestures according to the types of gestures (Fig. 3). And we found that three types of gestures have high fatigue degree because of the large action range and the number of involved muscle groups, which are flipping army, raising and putting down arm, and swinging arm up. And the shaking gesture has a small action range but have a high frequency. So the fatigue degree of this gesture is also in the upper level. There are four types of gestures have relatively low and very close fatigue degree due to small action range and mainly using the biceps, which are moving horizontally, moving vertically, tilting and turning. Making a fist has significantly lower fatigue degree than others because of the mainly using the figure extensor muscles. Combined with the operation objects of different types of gestures in Table 1, we can see that the gestures the operation objects of which are physical device (raising and putting down, shaking) and structural level (flipping) have higher degree of fatigue. Thus, it should be considered to use a flat information architecture to reduce the operation of the physical device and of the structure level in the process of wearable

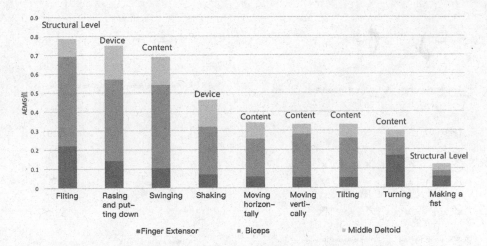

Fig. 3. AEMG value of gesture types in descending order

device task planning and interaction designing. And place more emphasis about the user experience on the operation of contents of the interface information.

3.3 Gesture Direction and Fatigue Analysis

There are 4 kinds of basic gestures which are tilting, turning, moving horizontally, and moving vertically. Subdivision gestures of these types are the gestures moving in the same mode but in the symmetrical direction. From the Table 4, we found that there is a difference in the energy consumption between the same type gestures in different directions because of the asymmetry of body movements. In the Fig. 4, for the human left arm, turning down the wrist is superior to turning up(P = 0.00); tilting to the left is superior to tilting to the right(P = 0.29); moving up is superior to moving down (P = 0.14); moving to the left is superior to moving to the right(P = 0.25); and moving backward is superior to moving forward(P = 0.28). In the design process of gesture interaction, it should be considered that choosing a more appropriate direction can reduce users' fatigue degree. For example, we can select turning the wrist down and tilting to the lift as the gestures which can operate the content lists.

3.4 Gesture Fatigue Model

It can be seen from Table 4 that with the increase of the fatigue degree, the corresponding Borg value of the fatigue degree is also increased, and it can be speculated that there may be a functional relationship between them. The AEMG value and Borg value of G1(lifting and putting down left arm) have a big difference because that this gesture is one of the daily arm actions which might have a influence on the Borg score. So we excluded the data of G1 as singular data. We used fitting method to process data. And the correlation between the AEMG value and the Borg value is mainly dependent

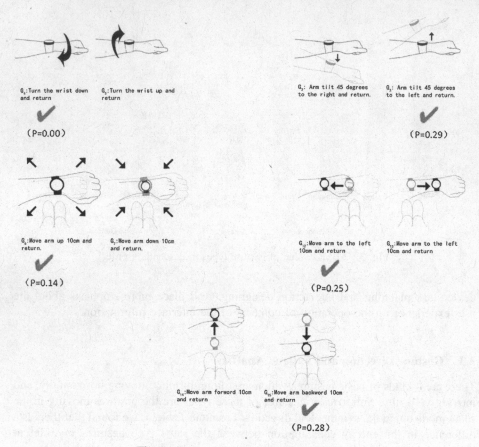

Fig. 4. Gesture direction recommendation

on the correlation coefficient of the results. The Borg score is taken as the independent variable x, and the AEMG summation value of each gesture is taken as the dependent variable y. And we use the quadratic regression model, cubic regression model and exponential regression model to fit the data in the Table 3. And according to the comparison, it is best to use the cubic regression model to fit the data, and the fitting model is Formula 1.

$$y = 0.1693x^3 - 1.162x^2 + 2.6387x - 1.6859. \tag{1}$$

The Correlation coefficient R2 is 0.7945, which are shown in Fig. 5. And it is generally believed that the model can be considered as a fatigue evaluation model when the R is 0.85.

In this model, the subjective fatigue degree and surface EMG are mapped. Through the model, we can know that the relationship between user's subjective fatigue and muscle energy consumption is nonlinear. The user's subjective fatigue degree score ranged from 1.5 to 3.8. With x = 3 as the critical point, when the energy consumption

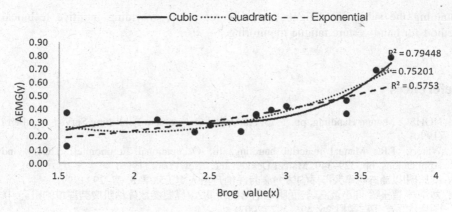

Fig. 5. User fatigue evaluation model of gesture interaction

is less, the user's subjective fatigue sensitivity is higher; when the energy consumption is more, the user's subjective fatigue sensitivity decreases. We can observe the variation of the user's fatigue directly and evaluate the user's fatigue state by this model.

4 Conclusions

This experiment was designed to study the user fatigue of wearable devices what are based on hand gestures interaction such as smart watch. In this study, the sEMG surface electromyography and Borg subjective fatigue assessment were used to measure and evaluate the user's fatigue degree of gestures.

By comparing the AEMG value of basic gestures, we can acknowledge the energy consumption characteristics of different muscle groups and of each gesture. By analyzing the relationship between the gesture types and the objects they operate, it can be known that gestures for operating equipment and information hierarchy consume more energy than gestures for operating contents. Thus, it should be considered to use a flat information architecture to reduce the operation of the physical device and of the structure level in the process of wearable device task planning and interaction designing. And place more emphasis about the user experience on the operation of contents of the interface information. And via the cross analysis of movement direction and fatigue of gestures, we find that there is a difference in the energy consumption between the same type gestures in different directions because of the asymmetry of body movements. Therefore, in order to reduce user fatigue during the usage of device, gesture direction should be taken into consideration when designers select interactive methods for devices. All these analyses provide references for wearable devices task-planning and gesture design.

This study also establishes a user fatigue evaluation model of gesture interaction of wearable devices, which can reflect the relationship between objective energy consumption and subjective fatigue. In the practical application, we can use the fatigue evaluation model to predict the change of surface electromyography (sEMG) by obtaining the subjective fatigue evaluation of users, providing intuitive technical method for hand gesture fatigue monitoring.

References

1. NOHSC: Manual Handling, pp. 1–15. Australian Government Publishing Service, Canberra (1990)
2. Waters, T.R.: Manual material handling. In: Occupational Ergonomics: Theory and Applications, pp. 329–349. Marcel Dekker, Inc., New York (1996)
3. 蔡启明.以动态心率为指标的体力疲劳评价方法.人类工效学 **5**, 27–29 (1999)
4. 刘洪涛,曹玉珍,谢小波,等.表面肌电信号的时变AR模型参数评估肌疲劳程度的研究.中国生物医学工程学报 **26**, 493–497 (2007)
5. Blomstrand, E., Saltin, B.: BCAA intake affects protein metabolism in muscle after but not during exercise in humans. Am. J. Physiol. Endocrinol. Metab. **281**, E365–E374 (2001)
6. 胡晓,王志中,任小梅,等.基于非线性尺度小波变换的表面肌电信号的分类.生物医学工程学杂志 **23**(06), 1232–1235 (2006)
7. Borg, G.: Psychophysical scaling with applications in physical work and the perception of exertion. Scand. J. Work Environ. Health **16**, 55–58 (1990)
8. 葛树旺,陈松林,付圣灵,等.手臂静态姿势负荷的肌电实验研究.工业卫生与职业病 **34**, 220–223 (2008)
9. 宋海燕,等.日常生活活动中人体上肢肌肉表面肌电特性研究.生物医学工程学杂志 **06**, 1177–1180 (2009)
10. 王乐军,等.sEMG指标监测快速点击鼠标致指伸肌疲劳的适用性评价研究.体育科学 **01**, 62–71 (2013)
11. 刘畅.基于手势的非接触式人机交互中用户疲劳的评价与研究.华南理工大学 (2013)
12. 侯文君,吴春京.基于数据分析的智能手表手势直觉化交互研究.包装工程 **22**, 13–16+21 (2015)

Z-Force Cubic Interface

Jung Huh[1(✉)], Hoon Sik Yoo[2], and Da Young Ju[1]

[1] Yonsei Institute of Convergence Technology,
Yonsei University, Incheon, South Korea
jhuh3226@gmail.com, dyju@yonsei.ac.kr
[2] Technology and Design Research Center,
Yonsei University, Incheon, South Korea
yoohs@yonsei.ac.kr

Abstract. Z-force cubic interface is a 3D interface using the cube as a core design element and utilizing z-force touch as the general interaction medium. Unlike previous research conducted to provide the 3-dimensional interface or new ways of controlling interfaces, z-force cubic interface combines effective mediums to provide intuitive and real-life like control of virtual mobile space. A prototype was produced to conduct heuristic research on the concept and several z-force touch gestures with high applicability were chosen as a controlling system. 3D navigation of the cube, zooming in and out, and unconstrained manipulation of application mimics real word interactions, leading to improvements in usability. Utilizing the 3D cube to see 360-degree photos or videos and sending VR emotions pulled down the boundaries between the conventional interface and reality. Interactive feedback of incoming alerts and notifications by rotation or resizing the cube itself works as an intuitive and entertaining factor for operating mobile space. Z-force cubic interface, as a whole, tries to give users a novel opportunity of experiencing the real world in a virtual mobile space without additional equipment, such as VR gadgets.

Keywords: Z-force interaction · 3D touch gesture · Cubic interface

1 Research Background and Purpose

Former 2D interfaces required numerous performances of users to implement certain tasks, such as reaching to see favorite picture takes 3 steps of tapping camera roll icon, back button to see categories of albums, and finally tapping favorite category icon. It also provided a limited span of feedback interactions, whether wobbling or becoming transparent, due to limited 2D space. To complement and solve these usability issues of performing several steps for designated actions and limitations of interactions that mobile space could give as a feedback, 3D interface, especially the cube interface, was chosen as an effective means of interaction for its simple 3D structure able to contain diverse functions. Furthermore, z-force or 3D touch technology, suggesting new ways of control with the possibility of recognizing different pressure given, has been introduced to provide users the experience of a wide scope of interactions and to reduce the depth on using mobile interface, reducing the gap between real and simulated physical objects displayed on screen by utilizing real world metaphor [1]. In an era

© Springer International Publishing AG 2017
M. Kurosu (Ed.): HCI 2017, Part II, LNCS 10272, pp. 183–192, 2017.
DOI: 10.1007/978-3-319-58077-7_15

where different mediums exist to enhance user's experience in operating virtual space, it is necessary to design a new 3D interface with natural control methods mimicking real-world interactions of people also with providing varied feedback that could be conducted only in 3D mobile space (Fig. 1).

Fig. 1. Concept image for research

2   Related Work

Studies are aimed to provide users with a diverse experience in operating mobile space and are divided into research on 3D interface exceeding the limitations of a two-dimensional space and new ways of controlling the interface such as 3D touch.

2.1   Research on 3D Interface

Studies on the 3D interface using the cube has been conducted, which often appeared as an interaction medium in previous research concerned with the 3D interface. A research utilized a virtual cube interface using its rotation for running applications exceeding the limitations of 2D GUI. The work used each side of the cube to map respective functions providing fun and allowing multitasking for users [2]. Another study suggested a cubic-like 3D user interface for multi-dimensional data browsing using an arrangement of 3D space and three axes to allow users to access data in necessary [3]. Also, Visualization technique for presenting heretical information accessible through CRT display was devised [4]. Z-agon, a palmtop sized mobile multi-display browser cube, operates by physical movements of the cube to change channels of the contents assigned to each side of the cube [5]. Wang et al. [6] proposed a representation method of Content-Aware Cube unwrapping to manufacture actual stereo shapes using a panorama cube. Moreover, a study on Cubee, a cubic 3D display for physics-based interaction, suggested an interactive cubic fish tank VR display, bringing a dynamic simulation into the participant's physical space and creating a unique physical experience with computer-generated animation through a 3D display system [7] (Table 1).

Table 1. Different usage of cubic metaphor in previous studies

	Usage of cube metaphor
1	Running different applications or channels
2	Data browsing and visualization
3	(Content-aware) Panorama display
4	VR display

2.2 Research and Application of New Ways of Controlling the Interface

Studies were conducted on novel ways of controlling the interface by recognizing the force pressed onto the z-axis; the nanta, application program shows different movements and splashing of water responding to dissimilar strengths given to the z-axis [8]. Heo et al. [9] suggested a novel force-enhanced touchpad with multi-level user interaction capable of tracking finger hover and measuring normal and shear forces together. This technology was applied and tested in video browsing, substituting the joystick in precisely supporting video control. Multimodal zoomable user interface using 3D touch interaction was studied using a sensor array to measure the distance, responding to the position and distance of the user's finger relative to the screen [10]. Research to prove the usability of MTUIs (multi-touch user interfaces) for manipulating 3D objects on mobile devices was conducted, compared to that of tradition GUI buttons [11]. PUYO-CON enables input based on direct touch, force, and shape transformation on soft material for enhancing entertainment experiences for game players [12]. These studies showed the possibility of using and mimicking physical properties in controlling virtual mobile space (Table 2).

Table 2. Different suggestions of controlling the interface in previous studies

Suggested controlling method	Application
Force pressed onto z-axis	Music operation
	Video control
	Zoom in & out
	Manipulate 3D objects

While various studies giving users the opportunity to experience novel 3D interfaces and interactions have been conducted, there seem points of improvement, allowing users to feel a sense of 3-dimensional space by combining merit of cube metaphor with a new way of input method with spatial awareness. In other words, whether being just a 3-dimension cube interface or providing a new way of controlling the interface individually, an integrated interface following user's needs for experiencing virtual 3D mobile space and using various applications in intuitive and convenient ways is needed. Therefore, z-force cubic interface suggests a cubic interface united with z-force touch interaction, which mimics real-life physical manipulation, providing users an experience of virtual 3-dimensional space.

3 System Design

Z-Force cubic interface focuses on providing a novel experience by using the cube as an interactive medium and applying z-force touch on the overall function of the UI to provide real-life like interaction and differentiated service for using mobile space. 3D cube featured with z-force touch allows users to intuitively experience a 3D interface.

3.1 Prototype Device

For concept development, a prototype was designed and installed in Android tablet and smartphone. The application consists of 15 simple 3D cubes on one phase, able to move along the z-axis for the new set of phase with long pressing, a second, which worked as a substitute of force pressing. Functions of zoom in and out, rotation of each cube, and running application assigned to the sides of cube located at the center were designed for the gesture development appropriate for the system (Fig. 2).

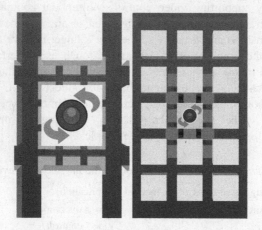

Fig. 2. Design of the application prototype

3.2 Z-Force Touch Gesture

Z-force cubic interface, using z-force touch as an interactive medium, utilizes a highly applicable input method based on research defining z-force touch gestures and user's preferences [13]. Several touch gestures were chosen, considering previous heuristic research with developed prototype, resulting in fixation of the following touch gesture in controlling the interface (Fig. 3 and Table 3).

3.3 Navigation

Z-force cubic interface provides a unique navigation system, giving an experience as if one is controlling an object in real life and offer two types of navigation system, controlling independent or groups of cube and manipulating axis of the interface.

Fig. 3. Heuristic research on the concept and its feasibility

Table 3. Suggestion of touch gestures according to different functions

No.	Function	Touch gesture style
1	Repositioning cube	Z-Force(strong) touch
	Flipping photo/memo	
	Sensing VR icon	
2	Flipping photo/memo in cube	Z-Force(strong) touch & tap
3	Zoom in/out	Z-Force(strong) pinch open/close
4	Implementing cubic application	Tap
5	Rotating cube	Drag

Each cube is rotational along the x, y, and z-axis following the movement of the finger dragging. Users force click on an icon and are able to easily drag over to the desired shortcut of application, which is assigned on each side of the cube.

Fig. 4. Navigation system of z-force cubic interface (alteration of the icon's location, z-axis control, running application)

Applications run by simply tapping on the designated icon. Sets of icons are pushed back and forth moving along the z-axis by force pressing the clear space between the icons as if objects from distance get closer with stretching out one's hand away. Z-force cubic interface provides zoom in/out function, allowing users to adjust the number and the size of the icons seen on the screen from the maximum of 15 cubes to minimum of only one when zoomed (pinched) with force (Figs. 4, 5 and 6).

Fig. 5. Rotation of a single cube

Fig. 6. Zoom in/out function of z-force cubic interface

3.4 Manipulation of Application

Z-force touch gives the experience of controlling virtual space in manipulating applications with natural metaphors. Through swiping the icons along the x, y, and z-axis, users can get a preview of detailed functions of the application. For the message cube, along with the function of providing shortcuts on each side of the cube, such as creating new messages, frequent or favorite contacts, the user can get the simplified preview on the recent message just by rotating the cube. The z-force touch allows users to have additional control on a single cube such as flipping through photos. Cube on YouTube allows users to check the updated, trending, watching videos and allows users to search videos without the inconvenience of running the application.

Swiping with force pressing is applied on seeing lists of album or notes giving the feeling of as if one reaches and pushes farther to bring an object out in real life. Z-force touch interface also uses a 3D cube to see a 360-degree photo or video and allow users to send virtual icons such as a heart via text messaging (Figs. 7, 8 and 9).

Fig. 7. List view on swiping with force pressing

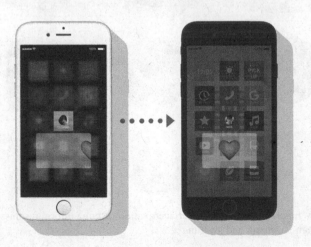

Fig. 8. Sending VR icon to partner

Fig. 9. Previewing video on watch

3.5 Interactive Feedback

One of the unique functions of the z-force cubic interface is its alerts provided by rotating or resizing the icon itself, giving user intuitive feedback and fun. On incoming alerts, the cube automatically rotates to give an instinctive alert for missed calls, SNS alerts, and etc. For notification interaction, the cube notifies the users by shrinking and swelling, moving beyond the static feedback of current interfaces (Fig. 10).

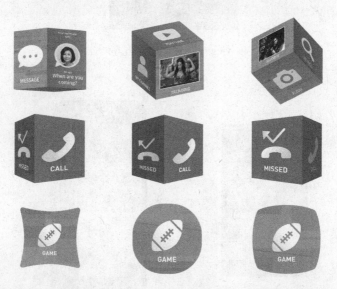

Fig. 10. Preview function of the cube interface/rotation of cube informing missed calls/update notification through shrinking and swelling

4   Discussion & Conclusion

In this paper, a novel means of experiencing mobile space, a z-force cubic interface was introduced. The concept of z-force cubic interface combines virtual 3D cubic interface with z-force touch interaction which takes after real-life natural movements and suggested different applicable functions and interaction on using the system. This research aims to open a new era for users to experience 3D mobile interface without additional equipment such as VR gadgets. With a customizable and dynamic interface, along with the various functions it provides, users will be capable of controlling diverse, intuitive, and virtual 3D mobile space with enhanced usability and fun.

Acknowledgments. This research was supported by the MSIP (Ministry of Science, ICT and Future Planning), Korea, under the "ICT Consilience Creative Program" (IITP-R0346-16-1008) supervised by the IITP (Institute for Information & communications Technology Promotion).

References

1. Minsky, M.R.: Manipulating simulated objects with real-world gestures using a force and position sensitive screen. In: ACM SIGGRAPH Computer Graphics, vol. 3, pp. 195–203. ACM (1984). doi:10.1145/800031.808598
2. Kangseok, C., Hancho, P., Jihwan, P., Soojin, K., Junsoo, P., Byoungil, A.: Crystal cube UI: user interface for mobile device using circular interaction of virtual cubes. In: The HCI Society of Korea, pp. 949–953 (2009). (in Korean)
3. Seokyeol, K., Jinah, P.: Rotatable cubic user interface for multi-dimensional data browsing. In: The HCI Society of Korea, pp. 350–352 (2013). (in Korean)
4. Rekimoto, J., Green, M.: The information cube: using transparency in 3d information visualization. In: Proceedings of the Third Annual Workshop on Information Technologies & Systems (WITS 1993), pp. 125–132 (1993)
5. Matsumoto, T., Horiguchi, D., Nakashima, S., Okude, N.: Z-agon: mobile multi-display browser cube. In: CHI 2006 Extended Abstracts on Human Factors in Computing Systems, pp. 351–356. ACM (2006). doi:10.1145/1125451.1125528
6. Wang, Z., Jin, X., Xue, F., He, X., Li, R., Zha, H.: Panorama to cube: a content-aware representation method. In: SIGGRAPH Asia 2015 Technical Briefs, p. 6. ACM (2015) doi:10.1145/2820903.2820911
7. Stavness, I., Vogt, F., Fels, S.: Cubee: a cubic 3D display for physics-based interaction. In: ACM SIGGRAPH 2006 Sketches, p. 165. ACM (2006). doi:10.1145/1179849.1180055
8. Min-Ji, L., KangRyeol, L., WonHyo, K., Kwang-Bum, P., Younglea, Z., Youngsam, M., Dae-Sik, S., Kunnyun, K: A study on tactile UI and force sensing 3D touch screen for smart phone. In: The HCI Society of Korea, pp. 395–398 (2013). (in Korean)
9. Heo, S., Han, J., Lee, G.: Designing rich touch interaction through proximity and 2.5 D force sensing touchpad. In: Proceedings of the 25th Australian Computer-Human Interaction Conference: Augmentation, Application, Innovation, Collaboration, pp. 401–404 ACM (2013). doi:10.1145/2541016.2541057
10. Laquai, F., Ablassmeier, M., Poitschke, T., Rigoll, G.: Using 3D touch interaction for a multimodal zoomable user interface. In: Smith, Michael J., Salvendy, G. (eds.) Human Interface 2009. LNCS, vol. 5617, pp. 543–552. Springer, Heidelberg (2009). doi:10.1007/978-3-642-02556-3_61

11. Fiorella, D., Sanna, A., Lamberti, F.: Multi-touch user interface evaluation for 3D object manipulation on mobile devices. J. Multimodal User Interfaces **4**(1), 3–10 (2010). doi:10.1007/s12193-009-0034-4
12. Hiramatsu, R.: Puyo-con. In: ACM SIGGRAPH ASIA 2009 Art Gallery & Emerging Technologies: Adaptation, p. 81. ACM (2009). doi:10.1145/1665137.1665200
13. Yoo, H.S., Jeong, S.Y., Kim, K.D., Ju, D.Y.: Defining Z-force touch gestures and user's preference (defining Z-force touch gestures and user's preference). Des. Converg. Study **14**(3), 73–85 (2015). (in Korean)

Meyboard: A QWERTY-Based Soft Keyboard for Touch-Typing on Tablets

Yuki Kuno[✉] and Buntarou Shizuki

University of Tsukuba, Tsukuba, Japan
{kuno,shizuki}@iplab.cs.tsukuba.ac.jp

Abstract. In this paper, we present a soft keyboard, called Meyboard, which enables the user to touch-type. To achieve this, we designed the Meyboard such that the bottom row of the QWERTY layout is omitted, and the positions and sizes of the keys are automatically adjusted to user's fingers while the user is typing. Omitted keys are input by performing a flicking action on the remaining keys. This design allows the user to type faster and more accurately than with a conventional soft keyboard, even if the user does not see the keys while typing. We have implemented a Meyboard prototype, and have performed a longitudinal user study involving one participant. The results show that in the final week of the user study, the participant is able to type at a rate of 40.7 words per minute, with an error rate of 4.57%.

Keywords: Touch screen · Text entry · Eyes-free input · Adaptable interface · Gestures · Flick · Reduced keyboard · Longitude user study

1 Introduction

Touch-typing is the typing method in which a user does not need to visually observe the positions of the keys, but rather detects the positions of keys by touching them while typing. This results in a highly effective typing performance, because the user can focus on the text without shifting his/her eye line to detect the positions of keys. In contrast, conventional soft keyboards displayed on the touch screens of tablet computers (referred to hereafter as tablets) are difficult to use for touch-typing. The reason for this is that the user cannot feel the positions of keys by touching them, because the keys are merely images displayed on the flat surface of the touch screen. Thus, the user is forced to adjust the positions of his/her fingers to the keys by seeing both of them while typing.

The aim of our research is to develop a soft keyboard for tablets with a touch screen that facilitates touch-typing. The key idea is to place keys at the positions of each of the user's fingers. To achieve this, we implemented a soft keyboard that identifies the user's fingers. This enables the user to input text more accurately than on an conventional soft keyboard, even if the user cannot feel the keys. We implemented a prototype, called Meyboard (Fig. 1), which adopts a QWERTY-based layout.

© Springer International Publishing AG 2017
M. Kurosu (Ed.): HCI 2017, Part II, LNCS 10272, pp. 193–207, 2017.
DOI: 10.1007/978-3-319-58077-7_16

Fig. 1. Typing with the Meyboard.

2   Related Work

A similar approach to our research, where the shapes and positions of keys are adjusted to the user's hands, has been adopted by LiquidKeyboard [12], CATKey [5], personalized input [3], the study of Gunawardana et al. [7], and the study of Go and Tsurumi [6]. In contrast to the above work, we focus on improving the performance of touch-typing on a soft keyboard by dynamically adjusting the QWERTY-based layout.

Research on input for visually impaired users has achieved nonvisual input on soft keyboards. BrailleType [11], BrailleTouch [13], and Perkinput [1] adopt Braille, where the user inputs a letter by inputting the Braille pattern corresponding to the letter. While these soft keyboards suit users who are familiar with Braille, we posit that a different method is required for users who do not satisfy this assumption. Our approach exploits the user's familiarity with the QWERTY layout.

While the Meyboard adopts flicking actions for typing, the adoption of flicks on a QWERTY-based soft keyboard is not new. Gestyboard 2.0 [2] also uses flicks to type keys and achieve touch-typing using the QWERTY layout. Although Gestyboard uses flicks for typing most of the keys, in order to maintain the stability of the input, we consider flicking to be stable but time-consuming. Therefore, we designed the Meyboard to employ flicks as seldom as possible in typing.

We omitted the bottom row of the QWERTY layout, in order to reduce the number of keys in the Meyboard and achieve touch-typing. The 1Line keyboard [8] adopts a similar approach. This is a QWERTY-based soft keyboard with only one row. Therefore, the input from the user contains ambiguities. The input is determined by selecting a word from a list that is estimated by the system using the dictionary. In contrast, our approach contains neither a phase for word selection nor a dictionary. Instead, we attempt to achieve touch-typing by doubling the number of keys compared with the 1Line keyboard, and adopting additional input actions.

3   Meyboard

The layout of the Meyboard (Fig. 2) is based on the QWERTY layout, with some additional features.

- The position and size of each key is adjusted to fit the user's fingers while the user is typing.
- The bottom row of the QWERTY layout (i.e., that containing Z–M and some punctuation keys) is omitted. We hypothesized that the user could precisely touch keys without seeing them if we limit the number of keys to one or two in each column. We still display the omitted keys in a "collapsed" format, for practice.

In addition, we changed the colors of the R, F, U, and J keys to make it easier for the user to visually locate these keys while practicing with the Meyboard. We also displayed the letter that will be typed when holding the shift key on left side of each key.

Fig. 2. Key layout of the Meyboard.

3.1   Adjusting Keys (Calibration)

When the user places four fingers (index to little fingers) on the touch screen, the Meyboard defines the key layout for one half of the keyboard. For example, if the user places their four left fingers down, then the top and middle rows of the left half of the QWERTY layout (i.e., the positions and sizes of Q–T and A–G) are defined. We refer to this action as *calibration*. To describe the process roughly, the heights of the keys are defined using the coordinates of the touch points of the user's four fingers, and the widths of the keys are defined using the distancing between those coordinates. Note that if the user place eight fingers (index to little fingers of both hands), the Meyboard defines the key layout for both halves of the keyboard.

The details of the calibration are as follows.

- The height of keys in each column in the top row are set as the distance between the top of the Meyboard and the position of the each finger, and the height of keys in each column in the middle row (in the QWERTY layout) are set as the distance between the position of the each finger and the bottom of the Meyboard, if the following process of fixing the height is ignored. Therefore, every height of keys in a row are different with each other (Fig. 3).

Prior to the above process, adjustments are made to these y coordinates to prevent the keys from being too small to touch effectively. Specifically, all of the touch points are moved downwards so that the midpoint of the vertical distance between the highest and the lowest touch points is on the center line of the Meyboard (Fig. 4). As a result, the heights of the keys are made sufficiently large, while keeping them adjusted to the user's fingers.

– The width of a key is set as the horizontal distance between the two midpoints of three adjacent fingers, as shown in Fig. 3. The exceptions to this are the R, F, U, and J keys, where the widths of these are set as twice the horizontal distance between the index finger and the midpoint of the index and middle fingers, to ensure that the T, G, Y, and H keys are reachable for the index fingers. The midpoint between the left and right index fingers is considered as the boundary between the left and right halves of the keyboard. Therefore, the widths of T and G (Y and H) are set as half of the horizontal distance between the edge of R and F and the edge of U and J.

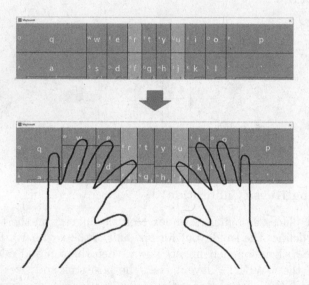

Fig. 3. Calibration of the Meyboard.

3.2   Input Method

To allow the user to input 30 letters (alphabet + punctuations) with 20 keys, we divided keys into several areas, as follows, and assigned a specific input action to each area, as shown in Fig. 5:

Home (A–F, J–L) and UpperHome (Q–R, U–P, A–F, J–L, and quote)
These are the home keys and keys above the home keys. Home keys are those where the user places their fingers in the default position for touch-typing on a hard keyboard.

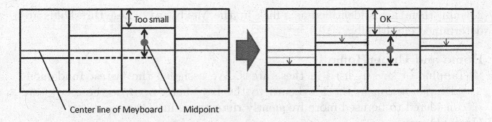

Fig. 4. Height adjustment of keys in the Meyboard.

UnderHome (Z–V, M, comma, period, and question)
These are the keys placed below the home keys.
TopCenter and MiddleCenter (T, Y, G, and H)
These are the keys placed at the center of the top and middle rows of the QWERTY layout.
BottomCenter (B and N)
These are keys placed at the center of the bottom row of the QWERTY layout.

Note that the some punctuation keys in this layout (semi-colon and slash) are replaced with others that have higher rates of use (quote and question), according to the layout of the standard soft keyboard in Windows 10.

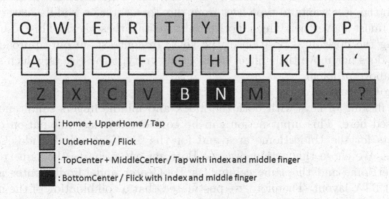

Fig. 5. Areas that divide the keys of the QWERTY layout, and input actions for typing these keys in the Meyboard.

Before describing each input action, we will define the tap and flick actions that are used as the fundamental input actions in the Meyboard. If the user touches down on the touch screen with their finger and removes it within 450 ms without moving the finger more than 2.8 mm, then this is identified as a tap by the Meyboard. On the other hand, if the user touches down on the touch screen with their finger and removes it within 500 ms after moving the finger more than

2.8 mm, then this is identified as a flick by the Meyboard. These thresholds are determined empirically.

Home and UpperHome

Tapping of keys is used in these areas. We assigned the fastest fundamental input action in the Meyboard to the keys here, because these keys are considered to be used more frequently than those in other areas.

UnderHome

The actions of flicking keys down is used here. For example, if the user flicks downwards on either the Q or A key, a Z is entered. Although flicking is slower than tapping, its input action is simple, and can easily be learned by the user. Moreover, the keys in the UnderHome area are considered to be used less frequently than those in the Home and UpperHome area. Therefore, the drawback that flicking is slow is diminished compared to its merits.

From this point on, we simply refer to a downwards flick as a flick, because only downwards flicks are used in the Meyboard.

TopCenter and MiddleCenter

Here, the tapping of keys with both the index and middle fingers simultaneously is used. Typing is distinguished between the TopCenter and MiddleCenter by the row of the key that is tapped by the index finger. If the user taps a key in the top row of the QWERTY layout (R or U) with their index finger, then the key from TopCenter is entered (T or Y). If the user taps a key in the middle row of the QWERTY layout (F or J) with their index finger, then the key from MiddleCenter is entered (G or H). In a conventional soft keyboard, when the user wants to type keys from the TopCenter or MiddleCenter area, they must move their finger horizontally to tap these keys. This results in losing the horizontal position of the keys. In contrast, in our approach the user does not move their finger horizontally to type these keys, which solves the above problem.

BottomCenter

The flicking of keys with both the index and middle fingers simultaneously is used here. This input action can be considered as a combination of the inputs for the UnderHome area and for the TopCenter and MiddleCenter areas. We chose this action because BottomCenter shares the same row as UnderHome and the same column as TopCenter and MiddleCenter in the QWERTY layout. Therefore, we postulated that a combination of the inputs of UnderHome and TopCenter or MiddleCenter could be easily learned by the user. In the same manner as when typing keys from the TopCenter and MiddleCenter area, only the movement of the index finger is used to determine if the input is a flick.

We designed the Meyboard to perform the calibration (i.e., setting the key layout for one half of the keyboard) automatically while the user is typing. To achieve this, Meyboard performs the calibration when the user inputs keys that are frequently used in sentences, namely space, enter, shift, and backspace, where we assigned four or eight finger touch gestures (index to little fingers of one or both hands) to these keys. Specifically, space is entered by tapping the left four fingers; enter is entered by tapping the right four fingers; shift is entered by placing and holding the four fingers of either the left or right hand, and the input continues until the four fingers are removed; and backspace is entered by tapping the four fingers of the right hand while placing and holding the four fingers of the left hand. In particular, the user has to input backspace by using eight fingers. As a result, this design adjusts all of the keys of the Meyboard to the latest position of the user's fingers whenever the user tries to correct an error, thus preventing further error.

4   User Study

We conducted a user study to investigate the touch-typing performance of the Meyboard. Figure 6 illustrates our experimental setup, where we used a Panasonic Let's Note CF-AX2 (11.6 inches, 1366 × 768 pixels) as the tablet. We did not display any keys on the Meyboard in this study, only the area of the board itself (Fig. 7), in order to simulate touch-typing conditions. The input area of the Meyboard is 1366 × 350 pixels, which is approximately 10.4 inches. The participant was one of the authors. This user study was conducted using a customized application whose original was a typing practice application released freely [14].

Fig. 6. Experimental setup.

We chose the task of inputting short English phrases. The phrases are chosen from the phrase set provided by MacKenzie and Soukoreff [9], but the first word of each phrase is capitalized, and a period follows the last word. We capitalized the first letter with the intention of activating the calibration of the Meyboard at least once during the input of a phrase, by forcing the input of a shift, which activates the calibration. In this study, the participant always has to correct any errors they make. If the participant makes any errors, then a corresponding number of cross marks appear. Such a cross mark disappears if the user inputs

Fig. 7. Meyboard in the user study, where no keys are shown.

a backspace to correct the error. Note that inputting a backspace also activates the calibration.

The participant input three sets each day, each consisting of 10 different phrases. The phrases in each set were chosen randomly, without duplicates. Inputting the three sets took approximately 10 to 15 min. The study was conducted for 147 days. Therefore, 441 sets were typed by the participant, which is equivalent to 1,323 phrases or 136,207 letters (not counting errors).

4.1   Results

Figure 8 shows the input rate in words per minute (wpm) [4], with a fitted logarithmic curve. This is calculated as follows:

$$\frac{1}{5} \frac{\text{Incoming keystrokes except mistakes (times/set) - 1}}{\text{Input time (minutes/set)}}$$

The maximum wpm achieved using the Meyboard in the user study was 45.6. The mean and standard deviation of the input rate in the final week of the study were 40.7 wpm and 2.67 wpm, respectively.

Figure 9 shows the error rate. The minimum error rate achieved using the Meyboard in the user study was 0.32%. The mean and standard deviation of the error rate in the final week of the study were 4.57% and 1.80%, respectively.

When a long-term study is conducted, the observed performance tends to follow a power law [10]. As a result, the curve of the performance becomes almost straight in a double logarithmic chart. Figure 10 shows the double logarithmic chart of the time required to input 100 characters. As the curve is nearly straight, the performance observed in this study can be considered reasonable. Moreover, it is predicted that the input rate would reach approximately 47.6 wpm after one year (i.e., after 1095 sets).

We compared the touch-typing input rate achieved using the Meyboard with results from related work. Li et al. [8] showed that the average input rate for a soft keyboard on a 9.7 inch iPad (with the QWERTY layout) and on a 1Line keyboard were 53.9 wpm and 30.7 wpm, respectively. Note that the participants in this evaluation were able to type on a hard keyboard at 82.6 wpm, which is faster than most casual users. Therefore, the performance of the participants also tended to be faster on the iPad soft keyboard. Considering the above, the touch-typing input rate of 40.7 wpm achieved on the Meyboard is noteworthy. Gestyboard [2], which is a the QWERTY-based keyboard employing flicks, has achieved an input rate of 21.6 wpm after typing 11,000 characters. Considering the time that passed until the total number of input characters reached that number in our Meyboard study, the input rate estimated using the fitted line shown in Fig. 10 is 27.2 wpm, which indicates the potential of the Meyboard. The average input rate of the Braille-based soft keyboard Perkinput [1] was 38.0 wpm, which is approximately the same as the Meyboard. Overall, these results suggest that the touch-typing performance achieved using the Meyboard in this study is promising.

5 Discussion

To analyze the content of the participant's errors, we collected logs of all key inputs during the study, and counted the number of letters in each phrase to be typed and the numbers of errors in (Fig. 11).

Figure 11a shows the number of letters to be typed during the user study. This result shows that letters from the bottom row make the fewest appearances. (Capital letters: top 2,544, middle 1,480, and bottom 707. Small letters: top 57,209, middle 33,684, and bottom 20,193) This result is consistent with the design of the Meyboard, where we omitted the bottom row of the QWERTY layout and instead employed a flick action, which is easy to learn but time consuming. Figure 11b shows the numbers of errors for each letter. Figure 11c shows the error ratio for each letter, which is the number of errors (Fig. 11b) divided by the number of appearances (Fig. 11a) multiplied by 100 (to give a percentage). Among the capital letters, which require a shift to type, Z, Q, G, A, B, and R are prone to errors. Among the small letters, z, j, x, w, b, and c are prone to errors. These results indicate that inputs with the left hand are more prone to errors, and this tendency increases with inputs using the shift key. In particular, inputs that use a flick with the left little finger, i.e., z or Z, show the highest error ratios.

To further analyze the types of error the participant had made for these letters, we identified every incorrect or omitted input using the following algorithm:

1. The algorithm compares the phrases in the study and the participant's input in terms of letters. Correct inputs are skipped.
2. If a letter in a phrase differs from the input, then the algorithm focuses on the next letter of the input. If this matches the letter from the phrase, then the input is identified as an omission. Otherwise, it is identified as a mistake.
3. When an error is detected, the algorithm observes the next input letter and then ignores every further input until the correct letter. This is to avoid falsely identifying inputs following an omission with multiple mistakes.

For example, if the text was "force" and the input was "frce", then the algorithm would detect the omission of the 'o'. As another example, if the text was

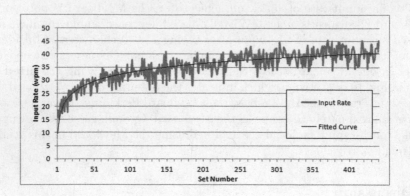

Fig. 8. Input rate (wpm) on the Meyboard.

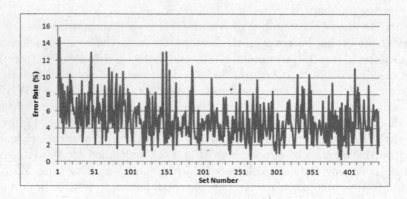

Fig. 9. Error rate on the Meyboard.

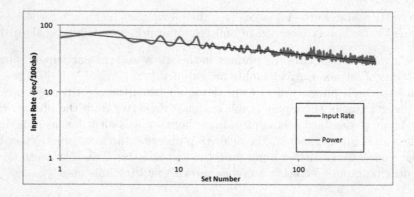

Fig. 10. Input rate (seconds per 100 letters) on the Meyboard.

a: Number of appearance of each letter.

Q	W	E	R	T	Y	U	I	O	P
28	292	126	86	1123	106	28	397	125	233
A	S	D	F	G	H	J	K	L	"
415	287	212	106	121	168	48	30	93	0
Z	X	C	V	B	N	M	;	:	!
10	0	162	71	129	91	244	0	0	0

q	w	e	r	t	y	u	i	o	p
189	1843	13957	7272	8890	2709	3571	7569	9216	2053
a	s	d	f	g	h	j	k	l	'
7971	6888	3501	2154	2441	4832	287	1249	4361	0
z	x	c	v	b	n	m	,	.	?
114	291	3047	1362	1552	6712	2515	0	4600	0

b: Number of error of each letter.

Q	W	E	R	T	Y	U	I	O	P
6	16	7	9	80	0	2	14	6	16
A	S	D	F	G	H	J	K	L	"
55	17	13	3	19	10	4	0	0	0
Z	X	C	V	B	N	M	;	:	!
5	0	4	3	14	5	7	0	0	0

q	w	e	r	t	y	u	i	o	p
7	119	414	301	291	87	147	264	259	87
a	o	d	f	g	h	j	k	l	'
262	114	82	68	58	170	25	37	100	0
z	x	c	v	b	n	m	,	.	?
18	24	130	49	81	237	68	0	78	0

c: Error ratio of each letter. (in percentile)

Q	W	E	R	T	Y	U	I	O	P
21.43	5.48	5.56	10.47	7.12	0.00	7.14	3.53	4.80	6.87
A	S	D	F	G	H	J	K	L	"
13.25	5.92	6.13	2.83	15.70	5.95	8.33	0.00	0.00	—
Z	X	C	V	B	N	M	;	:	!
50.00	—	2.47	4.23	10.85	5.49	2.87	—	—	—

q	w	e	r	t	y	u	i	o	p
3.70	6.46	2.97	4.14	3.27	3.21	4.12	3.49	2.81	4.24
a	s	d	f	g	h	j	k	l	'
3.29	1.66	2.34	3.16	2.38	3.52	8.71	2.96	2.29	—
z	x	c	v	b	n	m	,	.	?
15.79	8.25	4.27	3.60	5.22	3.53	2.70	—	1.70	—

Fig. 11. Results of appearance in the user study. Contrast represents size of the value.

"force" and the input was "firce", then the algorithm would detect the mistake concerning the 'o'.

As a result of this identification process, errors can be categorized into the following patterns:

Pattern 1: Mistype capital letters as small letters (e.g., mistype A as a.)
Pattern 2: Mistype flick as tap (e.g., mistype z as a).
Pattern 3: Mistype tap as flick (e.g., mistype G as B).
Pattern 4: Mistype as the other row (e.g., mistype w as s).
Pattern 5: Mistype as the other column (e.g., mistype p as o).
Pattern 6: Unnecessary input from index or middle finger (e.g., mistype R as T).
Pattern 7: Lack of input from index or middle finger (e.g., mistype b as v).
Pattern 8: Omission.
Pattern 9: Others.

Moreover, error patterns occurring with high rates (over 1.00%, and occurring more than twice) are presented in Tables 1 and 2.

Most often, the participant made a mistakes by performing the wrong actions on the correct key required for the input. Mistakes between the keys (i.e., Patterns 4 and 5) also occurred, but not significantly often. The low error rate for Patterns 4 and 5 indicates that the calibration of the Meyboard works effectively. In particular, the low error rate for Pattern 4 (the highest was mistyping w as s, with an error rate of 3.31%) demonstrates the suitability of our assumption in designing the Meyboard such that the user can precisely locate two keys in each column without seeing them.

However, the results also show that mistakes involving typing keys from different rows still occur, especially for the bottom row, which requires flicks for the input (pattern 2). Pattern 2 shows a high error rate for letters using the left index or middle fingers. It appears that it may be necessary to reconsider the threshold for identifying flicks (moving the finger by more than 2.8 mm) for these fingers.

Mistakes also occur for inputs involving the use of both the index and middle fingers simultaneously, which exist in the TopCenter, MiddleCenter, and BottomCenter areas (Patterns 6 and 7). It appears that the participant struggled to switch between using one or two fingers correctly. It will be a subject of our future work to investigate whether the errors in patterns 6 and 7 decrease as the user adapts to the Meyboard.

It is also clear that the mistyping of capital letters as small letters (Pattern 1) occurred with a high error rate. We examined the logs, and determined that either the participant failed to input the shift (by placing four fingers) or the order of the input was reversed. For example, the participant frequently mistyped A as a by placing their four fingers after tapping the a. We suspect this is because placing four fingers is more difficult than tapping or flicking using one or two fingers. However, we designed the Meyboard to perform calibration frequently by assigning the shift input to the calibration process. Therefore, there is a

Table 1. Error patterns and rates for capital letters.

Error	Correct letter	Error rate	Pattern
A	Z	50.00	2
q	Q	17.86	1
a	A	11.33	1
g	G	9.09	1
T	R	5.81	6
t	T	4.99	1
H	J	4.17	6
s	S	3.83	1
d	D	3.77	1
w	W	3.08	1
(Omission)	P	2.58	8
G	H	2.38	9
G	B	2.33	2
V	B	2.33	7
H	N	2.20	2
n	N	2.20	1
B	G	1.65	3
F	G	1.65	7
Quote	O	1.60	9
W	E	1.59	5
Space	H	1.19	9
O	I	1.01	5

Table 2. Error patterns and rates for small letters.

Error	Correct letter	Error rate	Pattern
a	z	9.65	2
s	x	6.19	2
(Omission)	z	5.26	8
s	w	3.31	4
(Omission)	j	3.14	8
u	j	2.79	4
z	q	2.65	3
d	c	2.49	2
h	j	2.09	6
Quote	p	1.95	4
u	y	1.48	7
y	h	1.35	4
Comma	n	1.31	7
n	m	1.27	6
v	b	1.22	7
g	b	1.16	2
c	b	1.10	7
d	e	1.09	4
(Omission)	q	1.06	8
r	t	1.03	7
e	x	1.03	9
t	r	1.00	6
c	d	1.00	3

possibility that this mistake is a drawback of the Meyboard, which should be further investigated.

Omissions (Pattern 8) mostly occurred in letters that were input using the left little and medicine fingers, especially during continuous inputs by the same hand (e.g., "iza" as "ia" and "two" as "to"). It will be a subject of our future work to investigate the causes of omissions.

State of the art soft keyboards incorporate error-collection functions based on language models. The accuracy of the Meyboard may also be improved if by implementing such functions.

6   Conclusions

In this paper, we have presented the Meyboard. This is a soft keyboard that enables touch-typing, which is difficult to achieve using conventional soft keyboards.

The Meyboard facilitates touch-typing by omitting the bottom row of the QWERTY layout, and adjusting the positions and sizes of the remaining keys to fit the user's fingers. The user employs tapping and flicking actions using one or two fingers to input 30 characters using 20 keys. Adjustment of the positions and sizes of the keys on one side of the Meyboard occurs whenever the user places down four fingers from a single hand. This input action is also employed for inputting the shift, space, enter, and backspace, which are used frequently whilst typing phrases.

A user study found that a participant using the Meyboard was capable of touch-typing at a maximum input rate of 45.6 wpm and the mean input rate in the final week of the study were 40.7 wpm, which is promising in comparison with related work.

The logs of the input from the user study show that the key adjustments of the Meyboard have a positive effect in reducing errors resulting from typing keys from the wrong column. However, it is also seen that particular input actions in the Meyboard, such as the tap, place-and-hold, or flick with two or four fingers, appear to introduce new patterns of errors.

Our future work will involve determining the causes of these new errors and attempting to reduce their occurrences. Moreover, we plan to conduct a further user study involving more participants, in order to compare the performance of the Meyboard with existing soft keyboards.

References

1. Azenkot, S., Wobbrock, J.O., Prasain, S., Ladner, R.E.: Input finger detection for nonvisual touch screen text entry in Perkinput. In: Proceedings of Graphics Interface 2012, GI 2012, pp. 121–129 (2012)
2. Coskun, T., Wiesner, C., Artinger, E., Benzina, A., Maier, P., Huber, M., Grill, C., Schmitt, P., Klinker, G.: Gestyboard 2.0: a gesture-based text entry concept for high performance ten-finger touch-typing and blind typing on touchscreens. In: Holzinger, A., Ziefle, M., Hitz, M., Debevc, M. (eds.) SouthCHI 2013. LNCS, vol. 7946, pp. 680–691. Springer, Heidelberg (2013). doi:10.1007/978-3-642-39062-3_49
3. Findlater, L., Wobbrock, J.: Personalized input: improving ten-finger touchscreen typing through automatic adaptation. In: Proceedings of the 2012 ACM Annual Conference on Human Factors in Computing Systems, CHI 2012, pp. 815–824 (2012)
4. Gentner, D.R.: Keystroke timing in transcription typing. In: Cooper, W.E. (ed.) Cognitive Aspects of Skilled Typewriting, pp. 95–120. Springer, Heidelberg (1983)
5. Go, K., Endo, Y.: CATKey: customizable and adaptable touchscreen keyboard with bubble cursor-like visual feedback. In: Baranauskas, C., Palanque, P., Abascal, J., Barbosa, S.D.J. (eds.) INTERACT 2007. LNCS, vol. 4662, pp. 493–496. Springer, Heidelberg (2007). doi:10.1007/978-3-540-74796-3_47
6. Go, K., Tsurumi, L.: Arranging touch screen software keyboard split-keys based on contact surface. In: CHI 2010 Extended Abstracts on Human Factors in Computing Systems, CHI EA 2010, pp. 3805–3810 (2010)
7. Gunawardana, A., Paek, T., Meek, C.: Usability guided key-target resizing for soft keyboards. In: Proceedings of the 15th International Conference on Intelligent User Interfaces, IUI 2010, pp. 111–118. ACM, New York (2010)

8. Li, F.C.Y., Guy, R.T., Yatani, K., Truong, K.N.: The 1Line keyboard a QWERTY layout in a single line. In: Proceedings of the 24th Annual ACM Symposium on User Interface Software and Technology, UIST 2011, pp. 461–470 (2011)
9. MacKenzie, I.S., Soukoreff, R.W.: Phrase sets for evaluating text entry techniques. In: CHI 2003 Extended Abstracts on Human Factors in Computing Systems, CHI EA 2003, pp. 754–755 (2003)
10. Newell, A.: Mechanisms of Skill Acquisition and the Law of Practice, pp. 1–55. Lawrence Erlbaum Associates, Hillsdale (1981)
11. Oliveira, J., Guerreiro, T., Nicolau, H., Jorge, J., Gonçalves, D.: BrailleType: unleashing braille over touch screen mobile phones. In: Campos, P., Graham, N., Jorge, J., Nunes, N., Palanque, P., Winckler, M. (eds.) INTERACT 2011. LNCS, vol. 6946, pp. 100–107. Springer, Heidelberg (2011). doi:10.1007/978-3-642-23774-4_10
12. Sax, C., Lau, H., Lawrence, E.: LiquidKeyboard: an ergonomic, adaptive QWERTY keyboard for touchscreens and surfaces. In: Proceedings of the Fifth International Conference on Digital Society, ICDS 2011, XPS, pp. 117–122 (2011)
13. Southern, C., Clawson, J., Frey, B., Abowd, G., Romero, M.: An evaluation of BrailleTouch: mobile touchscreen text entry for the visually impaired. In: Proceedings of the 14th International Conference on Human-Computer Interaction with Mobile Devices and Services, MobileHCI 2012, pp. 317–326 (2012)
14. TinqWill: C# Tips (Japanese). http://www.geocities.jp/tinqwill/cs.html

Vouch-T: Multimodal Text Input for Mobile Devices Using Voice and Touch

Minyoung Lee and Gerard J. Kim[(⊠)]

Digital Experience Laboratory, Korea University, Seoul, Korea
{mignonOoOb, gjkim}@korea.ac.kr

Abstract. Entering text on a small mobile device is not easy due to the relatively small screen space and the fat finger problem. We consider a multimodal text input method, called Vouch-T (Voice + tOUCH - Text) combining the touch and voice input in complementary way. With Vouch-T, the user makes an approximate touch among densely distributed alphabetic keys, accompanied with the voice input to effectively disambiguate the target among possible candidates. We have assessed the potential of Vouch-T in terms of the usability and performance compared to the conventional touch-only based method. We considered two types of text input layout, namely, the QWERTY and 3×4 telephone keypad on two sizes of mobile devices, the smart phone and smart watch. The comparative simulation experiment validated that the multimodal approach of Vouch-T improves the input performance and usability for the smaller-sized smart watch, but only marginally for the larger smart phone.

Keywords: Keyboard · Text input · Multimodal input · Voice · Smart watch · Smart phone · Usability · Task performance

1 Introduction

Small multi-purpose mobile devices, such as the smart phone and smart watch, often require text input, albeit mostly simple and comprising of just several words or phrases such as in short text messages, entering phone numbers and contact and making daily schedules. Despite such a need, text entry on small mobile devices remain to be not so easy, e.g. on smart phones. The situation is obviously worse with the even smaller smart watches. While in many cases, smart watches are used in a supplementary way to the smart phone where the text entry is made instead. But it is also true that smart watches are gaining popularity as an independent unit, sometimes over-taking the usual roles (e.g. including those as related to text entry) of the smart phones.

Therefore, while it is not likely smart watches will be replacing smart phones, there are still definite merits to improving the text input capabilities of smart watches so that it can be increasingly used independently from a mother device like the smart phone. In fact, various proposals have been made and techniques developed for facilitating simple text/command input for small screened smart watches, using touch gestures, hand/finger written letter recognition, multi-layer keyboard, distributed icon layout, voice recognition, and etc. [4, 7, 8, 11, 14, 15, 26, 27].

© Springer International Publishing AG 2017
M. Kurosu (Ed.): HCI 2017, Part II, LNCS 10272, pp. 208–224, 2017.
DOI: 10.1007/978-3-319-58077-7_17

In the light of this situation, we consider a multimodal input method as an attractive and classic solution to improving interaction performance and user satisfaction, particularly even more effective under difficult operating conditions [17]. We propose to combine two modalities, namely, touch and voice. Touch input has high familiarity and good ergonomic accessibility, but limited by the fat finger problem (or equivalently, the screen size) [11, 22] and sensitive to user motion [1]. Voice input is mostly immune to user motion, but its reliability may suffer by environment noise. However, such respective characteristics can complement each other very well in coping with the difficult operating condition of smart watch. The pioneering work of "Put-that-there" [3] had illustrated how two lesser reliable modality input methods can complement each other to boost the overall recognition performance.

In our case, the user can attempt to touch among densely distributed small icons or keys and while difficult to pinpoint at a target, the finger position will at least be in the vicinity of the wanted key or icon. The accompanying voice input can be used effectively (despite some environment noise) to disambiguate the target among just a small number of possible candidates, if not recognize the target right out (see Fig. 1). Such a process has the added benefit of relieving the burden of the user having to

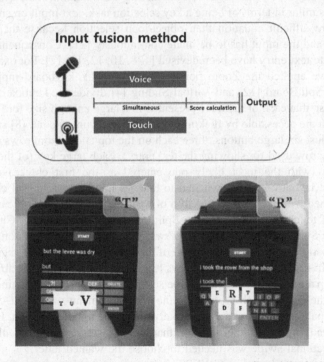

Fig. 1. The interaction model of Vouch-T for text entry on small mobile devices: (1) 3 × 4 keypad: the user touches a particular cell containing the target letter, and a second menu containing three possible letters appears, chosen by a near simultaneous voice input (left), and (2) QWERTY: the user touches a particular target letter on the layout, which is disambiguated by a near simultaneous voice input (right).

consciously pinpoint to the already small icons/keys. We call this approach the "Vouch-T" (Voice + tOUCH for Text input)[1].

We assess the potential of Vouch-T in terms of the usability and performance compared to the conventional touch-only based method through a simulation experiment. In the study, two types of text input layout and device size are considered respectively, namely, the QWERTY and 3 × 4 telephone keypad layout on the smart phone and even smaller smart watch.

2 Related Work

Even before smart watches were commercially available and became popular, several input methods for small media devices have been studied [1, 2, 19]. Albinsson et al. [1] introduced the Zoom-pointing in which the user first enlarges the interaction space (nearby the target) enabling easier selection of small objects. Roudaut et al. [19] developed similar methods called the TapTap and Magstick. Baudisch et al. [2] proposed to use the back of the device (although not applicable for smart watches) in order to avoid the occlusion by the fingers in interacting with small screened devices.

Although similar in terms of being a key selection task, text input on smart watches present a more difficult situation than object/icon selection because there are many possible keys and the input has to be made continuously [21]. Consequently, methods more specific to text entry have been devised [4–8, 10, 12, 14, 17]. For example, Oney et al. [17] have applied the Zoom pointing to QWERTY keyboard input for smart watches. The SplitBoard [12] and Virtual Sliding [4] divide the keyboard layout into several parts (so that each of them are presented in a large enough size for fast selection of keys) which are accessible by flicking through them. Dunlop et al. [8] suggested for a layout with just six large buttons, three each on the top and bottom rows of the watch screen (middle row used for showing the text entry). Each large key (of the six) maped to 3–6 letters (with the most likely one entered as the first choice) covering all alphabets. The layout could be switched to that for numbers or special characters by flicks. Combined with the auto-completion of words, this method significantly reduced the number of touches compared to the Splitboard or Virtual Sliding. Chen et al. [5] developed the SwipeBoard that used two swipes in a continuous fashion, which first enlarged the part (grouped in three letters) of the QWERTY keyboard, then picked the wanted letter from the three. The DragKeys [6] used a circular menu, spatially mapped in the 8 principal directions. The first swipe selected the group that contained the target letter among the eight, which brought up the subgroup menu with the 1–5 letters laid out in 4 principal direction, but the most likely one in the middle position. If the wanted letter was already in the middle position, that letter was entered by default, otherwise one more directional swipe was needed to choose the wanted letter.

For those methods based on QWERTY layout, a minimum of two flicks/swipes is inescapable (and possibly more for special characters or capitalization), while those

---

[1] In a previous work, we have suggested for the same basic idea, combining touch and voice, for digit input on smart watches [27].

with non-QWERTY layout generally require a significant amount of training to get oneself skillful and acquire effectiveness. Moreover, approaches that rely on touch input and thus use multi-step input naturally exhibit a trade-off between the size of the key (and ease of selection) and the number of steps required to complete the input.

Voice input is increasingly being used for small hand-held devices with the improved recognition accuracy and easily accessible cloud based high end services. Voice input performs quite stably for entering single or short composite commands/words, but still limited in terms of their accuracy being sensitive to environmental noise and speaker characteristics [16]. In order to reduce the effects of the environmental noise, it is often the case that the user has to speak inconveniently close to the device (and visually confirm the command is recognized).

Instead, using voice to help type in the individual letter, as proposed here, could be a viable alternative (at least for entering short amount of texts). By relying on letters only, the voice recognition engine could be much lighter (to be even put locally on a smart watch itself) and the accuracy improved (e.g. with the voice recognition itself having less target candidates for a match (i.e. just the alphabets) already filtered by the touch input. In fact, such a multimodal input method is an attractive and effective solution to improving interaction performance, leveraging on different individual characteristics of the fused methods. For instance, the pioneering work of "Put-that-there" [3] had illustrated how two lesser reliable modality input methods can complement each other to boost the overall recognition performance. While multimodal interfaces are increasingly being applied to mobile and hand-held devices (e.g. touch + speech [23], speech + gesture [13, 23, 25], and speech + pen [9]), not many exist for making input to smart phones or watches. Voice input method, by itself or in combination with others, has rarely been applied to alphanumeric entry (by individual letters).

3 Vouch-T

As noted, Vouch-T combines touch and voice for individual letter input on small mobile devices. The touch input is selected because it is the most natural, popular and familiar to most users and has good ergonomic accessibility. The reliability of touch input is much affected by the size of the key, finger size and user motion. The voice input is selected for its ease of use and independence of its reliability to user motion. It is still generally less reliable than touch input due to environment noise, distance to the microphone, accent, intonation and other speaker characteristics. We project that these modality characteristics can complement each other to improve the usability and recognition performance.

The interaction model for entering a letter is simple (Fig. 1): (1) make an approximate touch on a familiar but small keyboard displayed on the smart device (generating possible candidates around the vicinity of the touch position), and (2) accompany a voice input to single out the target letter (and vice versa). The interaction model is expected to be fast (by the simultaneous or one stage sequential one-stage input [20]), easy (by just an approximate touch and using familiar vocabulary with light cognitive load), and accurate (by combining multiple evidences for recognition [18]).

In our study, Vouch-T is tested using two keyboard layouts, namely, the 3×4 keypad and the traditional QWERTY. More detailed explanation follows.

3.1 3×4 Keypad Layout

The telephone keypad is an ad hoc layout originally used for the old rotary and touch tone phones as a quick and dirty way to enter text. It may not be as popular as the QWERTY keyboard, but still somewhat familiar. There are 12 keys laid out in a 3×4 grid, and each cell is mapped to three or four alphabets, ordered from the top to bottom and left to right (see Fig. 1 – lower left). This layout has an advantage over the QWERTY for being compact, thereby making each button larger than those of the QWERTY (given the same screen space area). To enter a letter, two touches would be needed, first to select the group, then to select among the three letters in the group.

With Vouch-T, after the initial input, instead of another touch, the voice input is used to disambiguate among the three possible targets. The computational load for the voice input would be thus low, and relative recognition performance high, because there are only three search targets. Note that the voice input alone may not be sufficient for selecting among "all" letters, e.g. because of the usually relatively far microphone location and the environment noise in a mobile situation. Since, the three letters (assigned to a button) are already known, the voice input can be made simultaneously with the touch.

3.2   QWERTY Layout

The QWERTY layout is arguably the most popular alphanumeric key input layout, adopted for most typewriters and keyboards (including the virtual and touch screen) [30]. Depending on variations, all alphabets (plus special characters) are individually mapped to a single key (about 33 keys). Therefore, while it is the most familiar, it is also error-prone due to the reduced size given a small mobile device screen. A single touch/press is enough to enter a letter.

With Vouch, for each letter, the probability of the simultaneously accompanied voice input match and a score based on the distance from the finger touch input are used to compute a score to determine the finally selected letter. The final score is a weighted sum of the two factors, with the weights (w_1 and w_2) set empirically. As for the distance based score, a small circle is drawn around a given letter whose radius is set by the nearest neighboring letter (see Fig. 2). If a touch is made outside the circle, a full score of 1 is given for that letter. Otherwise, the normalized distance score is actual distance to the target letter divided by the radius of the circle. That is,

$$\text{Score(letter)} = \left\{ w_1 * \left(1 - P_{\text{voice\_recognition}}(\text{letter})\right) + w_2 * D(\text{letter}) \right\}^{-1}, \quad (1)$$

where $P_{\text{voice\_recognition}}(\text{letter})$ is the voice recognition score/probability for given letter and $D(\text{letter})$, the normalized distance score defined as:

Fig. 2. Computing the distance based score for a given letter, "d". The position of the letter "d" is denoted L, the actual touch location, T, and the radius of circle, r. Outside the circle the normalized distance is clamped to 1, otherwise, (T−L)/r.

$$D(letter) = 1, \text{if } |T-L| > r, \text{otherwise} = |T - L|/r, \tag{2}$$

where T is the touch position, L, the letter position, and r is the distance to the closest neighboring letter from L.

4 User Study

4.1 Experimental Design

We experimentally compared Vouch-T to the conventional unimodal touch-only method in terms of the text entry performance and usability. The main purpose of the experiment was to highlight the projected advantage of the multimodal approach for the small layout/key size. Comparison of Vouch-T to other notable "specialized" small screen text entry methods [4, 5, 8, 12, 17], as summarized in the Related Work section, is left as future work.

The experiment was designed as a 3 factor (2 layout types × 2 interface types × 2 screen sizes), but divided into two parts (Experiments 1-1 and 1-2): 2 layout types × 2 interface types on the smart phone and the same on the smart watch (thus two 2 factor, 2 × 2 within-subject repeated measure). Table 1 summarizes the experimental design and the total of eight test conditions.

The user was given a set of short sentences to enter under the respective test condition, and the following dependent variables were measured: (1) task completion time/rate (e.g. words per minute), (2) number of individual key inputs, (3) error rate (e.g. number of backspace/delete keys used), and (4) responses to the usability survey questions (answered in the 7 level Likert scale asking the ease of use, naturalness, ease

Table 1. Experimental design and the eight test conditions

Independent variable	Interaction type	Layout type	Symbol
Experiment 1-1: screen size type = smart phone	Touch-only	QWERTY	P-TQ
	Touch-only	3 × 4 Keypad	P-T34
	Vouch-T	QWERTY	P-VQ
	Vouch-T	3 × 4 Keypad	P-V34
Experiment 1-2: screen size type = smart watch	Touch-only	QWERTY	W-TQ
	Touch-only	3 × 4 Keypad	W-T34
	Vouch-T	QWERTY	W-VQ
	Vouch-T	3 × 4 Keypad	W-V34

of learning, fatigue, general satisfaction/future usage and preference, we omit the actual questionnaires for lack of space). We hypothesized that Vouch-T would be significantly superior to the touch-only interface at least for the case of smart watches for both QWERTY and 3 × 4.

4.2 Experimental Task and Set-up

The user was given a set of short sentences to enter under the respective test condition. For each condition, the subject was given 20 sentences all sampled from the MacKenzie and Soukoreff's test set [28], such that all alphabets would have to be used at least once. All subjects were given the same set of sentences. A different set of 20 sentences were used for each test condition.

As for the experimental set-up, the LG G2 was used as the smart phone and the LG G-Watch for the smart watch (both running the Android operation system) on which the respective key layout was displayed in the lower half and text entry made/shown in the upper. Figure 3 shows the screen display with the respective key layout on the smart phone and smart watch.

Ideally, the experiment should have been carried out with actual voice recognition used and running on the smart phone or smart watch. However, in the case of the smart phone, no voice recognition software API (on the Android) that provides recognition certainty values could be found. Using the cloud based service would present the same problem (plus latency for the fast paced stream of individual letter input vs. word level recognition). Moreover, smart watches (including the one we tested) are not computationally powerful enough to run voice recognition to begin with. Therefore, our experiment simulated the use of the voice by preconfiguring the letter recognition probability values off-line. Our implementation used the Daum Newtone speech recognition API (for the Android) was used with which only the top 10 ranked recognized candidates were made available [29]. We estimated the probabilities of each letter recognition, $Prob_{est}$ (letter), in this way.

$$Prob_{est}(letter) = \frac{\sum_i w_i x_i}{\sum_{allletters} Prob_{est}(l)}, w_i = 1/2^i. \tag{3}$$

where, w_i is the weight given to the rank i, and X_i is the number of occurrences of the letter with rank i. The weight was arbitrarily set to $1/2^i$ (e.g. half decay function) for the

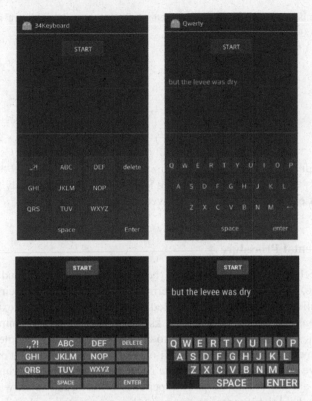

Fig. 3. The 3 × 4 keypad and QWERTY key layout on the smart phone (top) and smart watch (below). The key layout was located in the lower half part of the screen and the input made and shown in the upper part. The start button was used for the testing purpose.

ith ranked data. Thus, for example, if in an attempt to recognize the letter/word, "a" (pronounced "eigh") 10 times, the "a" could be ranked the first, 5 times, ranked the second, 3 times, ranked the third, 0 times, and the fourth, 2 times (see Table 2 as an example), resulting into:

$$Prob_{est}(\text{"a"}) = 0.5 * 5 + 0.25 * 3 + 0.125 * 0 + 0.0625 * 2 = 3.375$$
(unnormalized)

Since voice recognition performance is quite speaker-dependent, the performance table as shown in Table 2 was constructed and probabilities computed for each subject. Even so, such an estimation is not correct. Yet, it was deemed close enough for modelling the gross behaviour of the letter recognition performance and assessing the effect of adding the voice input to the touch. The user was still instructed to speak out the desired letter (assumed to be correct) even though the recognition was simulated according to the preconfigured probabilities internally.

In actual practice, combining the touch and voice brought about the synergistic effect of disambiguation. For instance, in the case of 3 × 4 key layout, when entering for the letter "D" (thus pressing the "DEF" button and speaking out "dee"), the voice

Table 2. Recognition results (10 runs) for the letter "a" (pronounced "eigh") and rankings of the possible matches (top 10)

Run no.	Rankig (w_i)				
	1 (1/2)	2 (1/4)	3 (1/8)	...	10 (1/1024)
1	a	j	h	...	n
2	a	h	j	...	m
...				...	
10	a	k	j	...	l

recognition produces the match candidates in the approximate order of {"b," "p"," "d," "t," "v," "e," "k," "g," "a," "j"}. Despite the letter "d" being ranked only the third, "b" and "p" are not even considered and removed from the match list.

4.3 Experimental Procedure

Ten paid subjects (5 men and 5 women between the ages of 20 and 36, mean = 27.9/SD = 5.36) participated in the experiment. After collecting their basic background information, the subjects were briefed about the purpose of the experiment and given instructions for the experimental tasks. A short training (3–7 min or until the subject felt sufficiently trained) was given to allow the subjects to become familiarized with the experimental process and the touch-only or Vouch-T based text entry methods on the respective devices. All subjects were right handed, used to wearing watches on their left wrist, and never had the prior experience of using the smart watches.

The subjects held the smart phone or wore the smart watch in their left hand/wrist comfortably. The user sat and interact using their upper body naturally with one's arms and fingers (see Fig. 4). There were total of 8 different treatments (or conditions), namely, 2 interfaces × 2 key sizes × 2 devices (total 8 blocks). Each treatment was presented in a balanced fashion using the Latin square methodology. The user carried out the given text entry task (e.g. "I am a boy you are a girl"). In each treatment block,

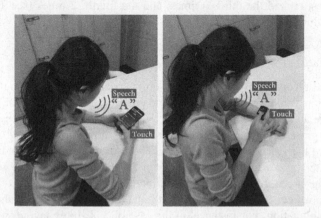

Fig. 4. A subject carrying out the experimental task (entering 20 sentences) using the smart phone (left) and the smart watch (right).

the user entered a series of 20 sentences. The task started by the user pressing the "start" button, then 20 sentences would appear for which the user was to enter. The single block was finished by touching the "enter" button after entering all the sentences. Both the task completion time and the number of delete key usage were recorded. The user was asked to make the entries correctly as fast as possible. If errors were made, the user had to use the backspace/delete key to make corrections. After the session, the subjects filled out a usability questionnaire. The user rested between each treatment and the total experimental session took about 1 h.

5 Results

5.1 Smart Phone

On the smart phone, subjects clearly performed better in terms of the task completion time using the QWERTY (P-TQ and P-VQ) vs. 3×4 (P-T34 and P-V34, Tukey/p-value = 0.05). Subjects reported of the strong preference of the QWERTY and the unfamiliarity and fatigue with the 3×4. While using the voice was helpful for improving the typing performance for the 3×4 (P-V34 < P-T34), it was not so for the QWERTY (no statistically significant difference between P-TQ and P-VQ). On the smart phone, the keys were sufficiently large and touch-only operation too familiar, making the effect of the voice disambiguation only marginal. See Fig. 5.

Figure 6 (top) shows the total number of keys entered for the four test conditions. Only the case of P-T34 showed an excessive (almost two times) key input compared to the others with a statistically significant difference by ANOVA (vs. P-V34, p-value = 0.000). On the other hand, Fig. 6 (bottom) shows the number of delete/backspace keys used for making corrections, and both touch-only cases, P-TQ and P-T34 exhibited much higher rates (but no statistically significant difference). It supports what was observed with the task completion time results in that the while the added voice input helped the text input using the 3×4 key layout, it was the reverse for the QWERTY (more proportion of delete keys over the total key input with P-VQ than with P-TQ).

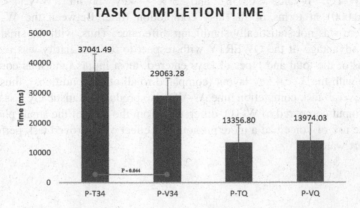

Fig. 5. Task completion time (time taken for entering 20 sentences) on the smart phone.

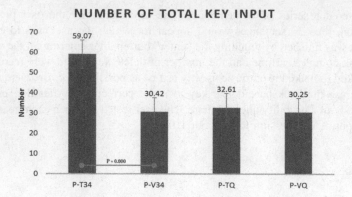

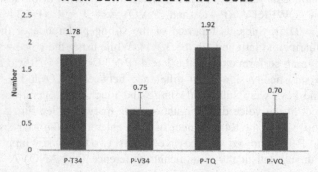

Fig. 6. Total number of key inputs made (top) and total number of delete keys used (bottom) on the smart phone.

5.2 Smart Watch

On the smart watch, Fig. 7 shows that the added voice input helped both the QWERTY (W-VQ < W-TQ, p-value = 0.033) and 3 × 4 key layout (W-V34 < W-T34, p-value = 0.000) in terms of the task completion time. Between the W-VQ and W-V34, there was not statistically significant difference. Thus, with the smaller sized watch, the advantage of the QWERTY with respect to the familiarity was reduced.

In terms of the total and types of keys entered, most inputs (and thus corrections) were made with the 3 × 4 key layout (compared to all other conditions), thus causing the longer overall task completion time. W-VQ also produced statistically less total and delete key input compared to W-TQ, differently from the case of the smart phone (See Fig. 8). The use of voice had a more pronounced effect of improved task performance on the smart watch.

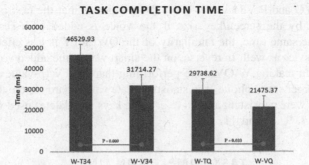

Fig. 7. Task completion time (time taken for entering 20 sentences) on the smart watch.

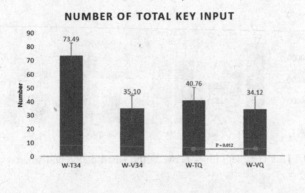

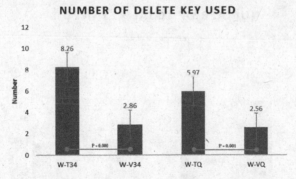

Fig. 8. Total number of key inputs made (top) and total number of delete key inputs made (bottom) on the smart watch.

5.3 Smart Phone Vs. Smart Watch

Between the smart phone and smart watch, as can be expected, the task complete times were generally longer on the smaller sized smart watch (P-VQ vs. W-VQ, P-TQ vs. W-TQ (nearly two times, p-value = 0.000), P-V34 vs. W-V34, and P-T34 vs. W-T34,). However, the difference was not statistically significant when the voice was used

(P-VQ vs. W-VQ and P-V34 vs. W-V34). This indicates that the task performance is less influenced by the screen/key size if the voice is added as a secondary input channel, and the same time, the familiarity of the QWERTY is less effective with the smaller sized device as well. In reverse, on the smart watch, the added voice turned out to be effective in making W-QV more performing than W-TV (p-value = 0.033), and not so on the larger smart phone. The statistical data with regards to the total and types of keys entered were consistent as well (e.g. more keys and deletes used with the smart watch). See Figs. 9, 10 and 11.

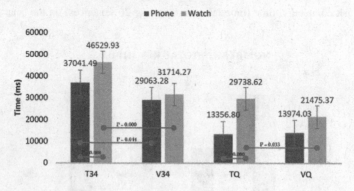

Fig. 9. Task complete times between the smart phone and smart watch.

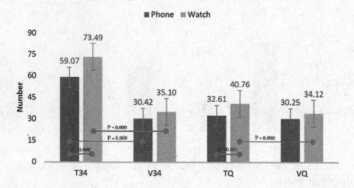

Fig. 10. Total number of keys used between the smart phone and smart watch.

5.4   Usability

The usability survey generally confirmed our general expectation of the familiarity and preference of the QWERTY over the 3 × 4 layout, and higher subjective usability (over most categories) when the larger phone was used to enter the text. Users also

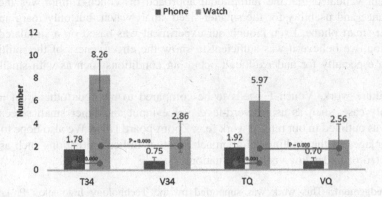

Fig. 11. Total number of delete keys used between the smart phone and smart watch.

generally felt that the added voice modality helped improve the usability for both the QWERTY and 3 × 4 layout and also for both the smart phone and smart watch.

5.5 Summary

The quantitative experiment results can be summarized as follows.

- The input performance was better on the larger smart phone (than on the small smart watch) as easily expected.
- The added voice input modality was helpful on the smaller smart watch for both QWERTY and 3 × 4 key layout, but, on the smart phone, not so on the smart phone, only for the 3 × 4.
- On the smart phone, the best performance was obtained with the QWERTY (P-TQ) where the Vouch-T did not help very much.
- On the smart watch, the best performance was obtained with QWERTY-V (W-VQ) Vouch-T did help in a significant manner.
- QWERTY was preferred over the 3 × 4 on both devices due to its familiarity.

6 Conclusion

In this paper, we presented a prototype implementation of Vouch-T which mixes up the use of touch and voice in a multi-level alphanumeric input for small hand-held or wearable devices. The combination of voice and touch creates a synergy in that it effectively allows for the use of larger sized keys on the screen and near simultaneous input across the input levels, making it a faster method.

We have assessed the potential of Vouch-T in terms of the usability and performance compared to the conventional touch-only based method. We considered two types of text input layout, namely, the QWERTY and 3 × 4 telephone keypad on two sizes of mobile devices, the smart phone and smart watch. The comparative simulation experiment validated that the multimodal approach of Vouch-T improves the input performance and usability for the smaller-sized smart watch, but only marginally for the larger smart phone. Even though our experiment was based on a simulated voice recognition, we believe it was sufficient to show the effectiveness of the multimodal approach especially for under difficult operating conditions such as with small smart watches.

As future work, Vouch-T needs to be compared to methods other than just the touch-only case, such as using word-level voice input and other small screen input methods as outlined in our related work (e.g. Zoom-board [17]). We also hope to assess the advantages of the multimodal approach in other difficult situations such as while moving and or under low visibility situations.

Acknowledgement. This work was supported by the Technology Innovation Program (or Industrial Strategic Technology Development Program (10053638, International technology standardization of 3D data information, and industrialization) funded By the Ministry of Trade, Industry & Energy (MOTIE, Korea) and also by Basic Science Research Program through the National Research Foundation of Korea (NRF) funded by the Ministry of Science, ICT & Future Planning (No. 2011-0030079).

References

1. Albinsson, P.A., Zhai, S.: High precision touch screen interaction. In: Proceedings of the SIGCHI Conference on Human Factors in Computing Systems (CHI 2003), pp. 105–112. ACM (2003)
2. Baudisch, P., Chu, G.: Back-of-device interaction allows creating very small touch devices. In: Proceedings of the SIGCHI Conference on Human Factors in Computing Systems (CHI 2009), pp. 1923–1932. ACM (2009)
3. Bolt, R.A.: "Put-that-there": Voice and Gesture at the Graphics Interface. ACM, New York (1980)
4. Cha, J.M., Choi, E., Lim, J.: Virtual sliding QWERTY: a new text entry method for smartwatches using Tap-N-Drag. Appl. Ergon. **51**, 263–272 (2015)
5. Chen, X.A., Grossman, T., Fitzmaurice, G.: Swipeboard: a text entry technique for ultra-small interfaces that supports novice to expert transitions. In: Proceedings of the 27th Annual ACM Symposium on User Interface Software and Technology (UIST 2014), pp. 615–620. ACM (2014)
6. Cho, H., Kim, M., Seo, K.: A text entry technique for wrist-worn watches with tiny touchscreens. In: Proceedings of the Adjunct Publication of the 27th Annual ACM Symposium on User Interface Software and Technology (UIST 2014), pp. 79–80. ACM (2014)
7. Darbara, R., Senb, P. K., Dasha, P., Samantaa, D.: Using hall effect sensors for 3D space text entry on smartwatches. In: Proceedings of the 7th International Conference on Intelligent Human Computer Interaction (IHCI 2015) (2015)
8. Dunlop, M.D., Komninos, A., Durga, N.: Towards high quality text entry on smartwatches. In: CHI 2014 Extended Abstracts on Human Factors in Computing Systems, pp. 2365–2370. ACM (2014)

9. Dusan, S., Gadbois, G. J., Flanagan, J.L.: Multimodal interaction on PDA's integrating speech and pen inputs. In: INTERSPEECH (2003)
10. Funk, M., Sahami, A., Henze, N., Schmidt, A.: Using a touch-sensitive wristband for text entry on smart watches. In: CHI 2014 Extended Abstracts on Human Factors in Computing Systems, pp. 2305–2310. ACM (2014)
11. Holzinger, A.: Finger instead of mouse: touch screens as a means of enhancing universal access. In: Carbonell, N., Stephanidis, C. (eds.) UI4ALL 2002. LNCS, vol. 2615, pp. 387–397. Springer, Heidelberg (2003). doi:10.1007/3-540-36572-9_30
12. Hong, J., Heo, S., Isokoski, P., Lee, G.: SplitBoard: a simple split soft keyboard for wristwatch-sized touch screens. In: Proceedings of the SIGCHI Conference on Human Factors in Computing Systems (CHI 2015), pp. 1233–1236. ACM (2015)
13. Kurihara, K., Goto, M., Ogata, J., Igarashi, T.: Speech pen: predictive handwriting based on ambient multimodal recognition. In: Proceedings of the SIGCHI Conference on Human Factors in Computing Systems (CHI 2006), pp. 851–860. ACM (2006)
14. Kwon, S., Choi, E., Chung, M.K.: Effect of control-to-display gain and movement direction of information spaces on the usability of navigation on small touch-screen interfaces using Tap-N-Drag. J. Ind. Ergon. **41**(3), 322–330 (2011)
15. Leiva, L.A., Sahami, A., Catalá, A., Henze, N., Schmidt, A.: text entry on tiny QWERTY soft keyboards. In: Proceedings of the SIGCHI Conference on Human Factors in Computing Systems (CHI 2015), pp. 669–678. ACM (2015)
16. Nebeling, M., Guo, A., Murray, K., Tostengard, A., Giannopoulos, A., Mihajlov, M., Bigham, J.P.: WearWrite: orchestrating the crowd to complete complex tasks from wearables. In: Proceedings of the 28th Annual ACM Symposium on User Interface Software and Technology (UIST 2015), pp. 39–40. ACM (2015)
17. Oney, S., Harrison, C., Ogan, A., Wiese, J.: ZoomBoard: a diminutive QWERTY soft keyboard using iterative zooming for ultra-small devices. In: Proceedings of the SIGCHI Conference on Human Factors in Computing Systems (CHI 2013), pp. 2799–2802. ACM (2013)
18. Oviatt, S.: Mutual disambiguation of recognition errors in a multimodel architecture. In: Proceedings of the SIGCHI Conference on Human Factors in Computing Systems (CHI 1999). pp. 576–583. ACM (1999)
19. Paliwal, K., Basu, A.A.: Speech enhancement method based on Kalman filtering. In: Proceedings of the IEEE International Conference on Acoustics, Speech, and Signal Process (ICASSP), pp. 177–180 (1987)
20. Roudaut, A., Huot, S., Lecolinet, E.: TapTap and MagStick: improving one-handed target acquisition on small touch-screens. In: Proceedings of the Working Conference on Advanced Visual Interfaces, pp. 146–153. ACM (2008)
21. Schüssel, F., Honold, F., Schmidt, M., Bubalo, N., Huckauf, A., Weber, M.: Multimodal interaction history and its use in error detection and recovery. In: Proceedings of the 16th International Conference on Multimodal Interaction, pp. 164–171. ACM (2014)
22. Siek, K.A., Rogers, Y., Connelly, K.H.: Fat finger worries: how older and younger users physically interact with PDAs. In: Costabile, M.F., Paternò, F. (eds.) INTERACT 2005. LNCS, vol. 3585, pp. 267–280. Springer, Heidelberg (2005). doi:10.1007/11555261_24
23. Tsourakis, N.: Using hand gestures to control mobile spoken dialogue systems. Univ. Access Inf. Soc. **13**(3), 257–275 (2014)
24. Turunen, M., Hurtig, T., Hakulinen, J., Virtanen, A., Koskinen, S.: Mobile speech-based and multimodal public transport information services. In: Proceedings of MobileHCI 2006 Workshop on Speech in Mobile and Pervasive Environments (2006)
25. CMU Sphinx. http://cmusphinx.sourceforge.net/
26. Watch, L.G.: http://www.lg.com/us/smart-watches/lg-W100-g-watch/

27. Lee, J., Kim, G.J.: Vouch: multimodal input for smart watches under difficult operating conditions using touch and voice. J. Multimodal Interfaces (2016, submitted)
28. MacKenzie, I.S., Soukoreff, R.W.: Phrase sets for evaluating text entry techniques. Ext. Abstracts CHI 2003, pp. 754–755. ACM Press (2003)
29. Newtone, D.: https://developers.daum.net/services/apis/newtone
30. QWERTY. https://en.wikipedia.org/wiki/QWERTY

Model Based Dialogue Control
for Smartwatches

Rainer Lutze[1](✉) and Klemens Waldhör[2]

[1] Dr.-Ing. Rainer Lutze Consulting, Wachtlerhof, Langenzenn, Germany
rainerlutze@lustcon.eu
[2] FOM University of Applied Sciences, Nuremberg, Germany
klemens.waldhoer@fom.de

Abstract. The presented approach solves the problem of organizing a well-structured dialogue between a smartwatch wearer and a *health assistance app* running on the smartwatch. Especially for emergency situations, when the app has concluded the presence of *several* threatening health or security hazards. Such situations require an effective, *joint* handling of all acute health and security hazards in *one* combined dialogue. Otherwise, the *domain specific knowledge* for concluding present hazards has been isolated deliberately into *separate* units for efficient maintenance and comprehensibility. It is represented in a declarative way by finite state machines. A multitude of such finite state machines will be executed simultaneously in the app for monitoring *all* relevant potential health and/or security hazards. Furthermore, *the tactical knowledge for dialogue handling* of concluded hazards is represented independently from the *domain specific knowledge* by "critical dialogue sections", CDSs. A CDS has an internal activity structure for controlling the dialogue with the smartwatch wearer in order the handle the concluded hazard. During the execution of a CDS, the smartwatch I/O and communication devices are exclusively attached to the CDS. Effective handling of such concluded hazards does typically include to establish a speech connection with distant family members or a home emergency call center. This can be achieved via the integrated cellular phone of the smartwatch. The selection of the situationally most appropriate hazard for handling is done via a central scheduler utilizing a blackboard. Our application framework relieves the software developer from dealing with the details and obstacles of effective dialogue implementation and allows to focus on the domain specific knowledge and handling logic of the assistance app.

Keywords: Smartwatch · Assistance app for the elderly · Application framework · Behavioral pattern · Critical dialog section · Model based dialogue control · Blackboard · Priority based scheduling · Ambient assisted living · AAL · ADL · EDL

1 Introduction

Smartwatches are well suited for monitoring health and/or security hazards for elderly people. They can support a self-determined and safe life in the familiar home until the very high age. Software assistance apps running on standard forefront smartwatches

M. Kurosu (Ed.): HCI 2017, Part II, LNCS 10272, pp. 225–239, 2017.
DOI: 10.1007/978-3-319-58077-7_18

(e.g. LG Urbane 2™, LG Sport™, Samsung Gear S3 Frontier™) provide much more functionality far beyond the capabilities of traditional emergency push buttons [1]. The traditional solution typically relies on the wearer of the device to initiate an alert in case of an emergency. The smartwatch assistance app additionally will continuously monitor the activity patterns and vital parameters of the smartwatch wearer. The app will recognize from the smartwatch sensor signals the events of daily living (EDLs, like *tumbles, leaving or returning at home*), the excessive duration of activities of daily living[1] (ADLs like *naps, bedtimes, outdoor walks*), substantial deviations of the usual daily routine (indicating potential *illness, depressions or mental disorder*) and abnormal heart rates (indicating *bradycardia, tachycardia*) [2].

The app will conclude the presence of health and/or security hazards based on recognized EDLs, ADLs and their sequencing in the course of time. The smartwatch app then will autonomously decide when and how to inform about the hazardous situation. Pre-alerting the smartwatch wearer, who is the user of the health assistance app, is always the first step of handling the hazard. Our chosen smartwatch devices include an integrated 3G/LTE cellular phone. The essence of our hazard handling includes transmitting data about the acute hazards to distant family members and/or a home emergency call center (e.g. current geographic location of the user, vital data). If situationally appropriate and agreed with the user, a speech connection will be established additionally via the 3G/LTE phone to clarify the situation on the spot.

By utilizing 3G/LTE communication, the smartwatch assistance app does not depend on any susceptible infrastructure like Bluetooth or Wi-Fi connections. The assistance app can transmit data and establish a speech connection from practically anywhere. Such smartwatch solutions constitute the next generation of home emergency call systems – extending also the reach of their services beyond the boundaries of the familiar home.

But, the plenitude of health hazard monitoring tasks performed by the assistance app and the very small display of the smartwatch (about 1.4" diameter for today's smartwatches) raise substantial challenges on how the interaction between the app and the smartwatch wearer can be designed cognitive efficiently and at eye's level. The basic idea behind the smartwatch assistance app is an **aid** for realizing a self-determined and safe life of the smartwatch wearer. It must not end up as a surveillance **agent** jeopardizing the privacy or dismantling the decision-making ability of the user. In the following we describe a model based dialog control approach and a supporting application framework for achieving this principal task.

---

[1] ADLs have been a central issue in organizing professional nursing practice and for determining the independency status of elderly people. They have been introduced by Sidney Katz more than 60 years ago. In Germany, Liliane Juchli has elaborated these ADLs for a systematic professional care management [3]. In our work, we focus on a small subset of computationally tractable ADLs.

2   Requirements Analysis

The bundle of requirements for dialogue design between the smartwatch assistance app and the smartwatch wearer, user, can be differentiated in human smartwatch interaction as well as software engineering aspects.

2.1   Human Smartwatch Interaction

The interaction with the user is based on the core privacy by design principles [4, 5]: The user should be always kept in control of interaction and data transmission as long as he conscious and remains capable to act. Very tangible privacy relevant data about his location, activity patterns, vital parameters, ... shall only be exchanged based on a prior approval of the user. This requirement will be fulfilled via a "pre-alert", by which the reasons for the intended data transmission will be explained to the user. A conscious user still capable to act shall be empowered to stop the intended data transmission at any time. Otherwise, in a real hazardous situation where those preconditions on the user will not be fulfilled, it is important that the data transmission resp. the alerting really takes place automatically without the necessity of a manual intervention of the user.

The situation is further complicated by the fact that, if the health assistance app has concluded the presence of *several* hazards, these must be jointly handled in *one* combined dialogue. Only **one** speech connection to distant family members or a call center has to handle all pending matters, in order to enable a potential external reaction/intervention as fast as possible.

The interaction between the user, the smartwatch app and potentially distant family members or the call center typically includes the following six consecutive steps (ids for these steps in [...] brackets for later reference):

1. **[Inform]** *informing* the user about the concluded acute hazards ("pre-alerting") and *explaining*, why the assistance app has concluded (and is assuming) the presence of the hazardous situation,
2. **[Propose Decision]** *asking* the user for a (unilateral or bilateral) decision: if for example distant family member resp. the call center shall be called (alerted) or if everything is OK (and no data transmission and speech connection shall take place),
3. **[Wait]** *waiting* for a reaction from the user. Within this period (about 30 s) the user needs to perceive the information presented to him and to make up his mind about the appropriate reaction in the current situation,
4. **[Confirm]** *confirming* the immediate consequences of a decision taken the user resp. indicating the immediate consequences of an omitted decision, if not obvious,
5. **[Transmit]** *transmitting* relevant location and health data to distant family members resp. a call center, if this is situationally appropriate and the user has indicated his consent with this step or does not respond at all in the assumed hazardous situation.
6. **[Clarify]** *placing a clarification call,* if this is situationally appropriate and the user has indicated his consent with this step or does not respond at all in the assumed hazardous situation. The prior transmitted data will be typically presented to the responding person and will help to understand the user's momentary situation on the spot.

The described interaction sequence constitutes a fixed dialogue pattern for our application domain. Patterns are a well-established approach in software engineering (see [6], Sects. 6.3, 6.4) esp. in the creation of reusable and adaptable software, solving a given recurring problem and presenting a solution for it. We name this new pattern "critical dialogue section" (CDS). Based on [6] a CDS can be classified as "behavioral pattern".

A "critical dialogue section" (CDS) must not be interrupted by other activities, dialogues and messages in order not to *mentally overload* the user. For example, incoming phone calls or potentials pre-alerts about additional concluded hazards shortly afterwards need to excluded during the execution of the CDS. In congruence with the well-known operating system concept of a "critical section" (see [7], Sect. 6.2), also the CDS shall be either executed completely or not at all and only by a single process. There are in fact situations when the section should not be executed at all, for example for safety reasons when the user is driving at high speed on a highway. Or, if the smartwatch is not worn at that moment. This situation is also the one exception to the mandatory complete execution of the CDS. If the wearer decides to drop the smartwatch during the execution of the section, which will be signalized by the heart rate sensor, its continuation obviously does not make sense.

The sketched inherent complexity of a smartwatch dialogue design and implementation quests for a systematic model and supporting framework for handling this complexity. Based on our experience, this is one of the most crucial productivity factors for the realization of comprehensive smartwatch apps.

2.2   Software Engineering Factors

The knowledge about an appropriate handling of health and/or security hazards is empirical, volatile and based on best practices. This knowledge will grow and must be optimized daily. Any implementation must take this into account. We are still dealing with the first generation of programmable wearable devices with a complete new spectrum of sensors, interpretation and interaction possibilities. Therefore, a declarative representation of the interaction with the smartwatch user offers decisive advantages with respect to maintainability and changeability of the software [6].

Another software engineering aspect aims at the separation of the health resp. security hazard conclusion and handling knowledge into separate *knowledge chunks*. Although the monitoring of all hazards must be executed by the smartwatch app *simultaneously*, concluding the presence of independent hazards and describing their handling shall be represented *separately in different modules*. This alleviates the comprehensibility and maintainability of the software (»*divide et impera*« principle). Each module shares as a *common secret* [8] the specific knowledge for best practice reasoning about related hazards and their appropriate handling. For example, Fig. 3 describes the combined hazard handling of four related health and security hazards: *leaving_home, reentering_home, a runaway_situation or excessive_absence_from_home*, which might occur during monitoring the absence of a user from his home. Handling these hazards is completely independent from handling the health hazard of *insufficient_drinking* (fluid ingestion) or the health hazard handling for *abnormal_heart_rates* and thus these latter hazard handlings should be represented independently.

2.3 Aspects of Practice

Today, there is no single, universal technology known for the detection of health and/or security hazards. Many sudden EDLs (e.g. *tumbles*) can be recognized from the motion sensors of the smartwatch via *artificial neural networks (ANNs)* with a very high precision [11]. This is also true for short term activities like *drinking, combing or tooth brushing*. Other activities, which have a longer duration (*e.g. falling asleep for a nap*) can best be detected by monitoring the user's behavior via a finite state automaton. The progress in concluding such activities will be modelled by state transitions of the automaton following the different stages of the recognition process. The state transitions of the automaton will be triggered by EDLs, other ADLs or timing constraints. For example, the health hazard of *insufficient_drinking* (fluid ingestion) can be concluded, if no drinking ADLs will be observed over a longer time. Figure 2 describes a simple two state automaton for handling this health hazard. Each drinking ADL recognized by an underlying ANN will reset the timer controlling the state transition of the automaton.

3 System Architecture

The application software architecture [6] of our smartwatch solution is based on a hierarchical, multi-layer structure [9, 10], where – by definition – an upper layer *uses* functionality from the lower layers. The structure is depicted by the UML component diagram in Fig. 1.

The **bottom layer** of our software architecture consists of two four components: the motion analysis, location analysis, the WAN communication control and the local interaction control component. The **motion analysis** component contains an *artificial neural net*work (ANN). It condenses 39 statistical parameters calculated from a sliding time windows of 10 s applied to the sensor signals of the smartwatch (*accelerometer, gyroscopes, barometer, heart rate, ...*) into the set of recognized EDLs, ADLs (cf. [11] for details). The neural network combines a good training capability by samples sets of movement patterns with a good recognition rate for the EDLs, ADLs. (cf. [12, 13] for example for details of the recognition of ADL *drinking, fluid ingestion*). The **location analysis** component recognizes EDLs like *leaving home* or *leaving an agreed vicinity of the home (geofencing)* by analyzing and interpreting the WiFi and GPS sensor information. If the individual rooms of the home have been equipped with bluetooth beacons [14], or the varying home Wi-Fi signal is scrutinized for similarity with reference patterns [15], also an indoor localization will be possible. The **WAN communication control** component will be used for transmitting relevant data in the [transmit] step of CDS execution and for placing a 3G/LTE phone call in the [Clarify] step of CDS execution. Similar, the first four [Inform], [Propose Decision], [Wait] and [Confirm] steps of CDS execution use the **local interaction control** component for displaying their output on the smartwatch screen and getting to know the user's reaction on the presented information.

The **medium layer** consists at its core of two components. First, a multitude of UML *finite state machines,* USMs. Each USM describes the reasoning about a single or

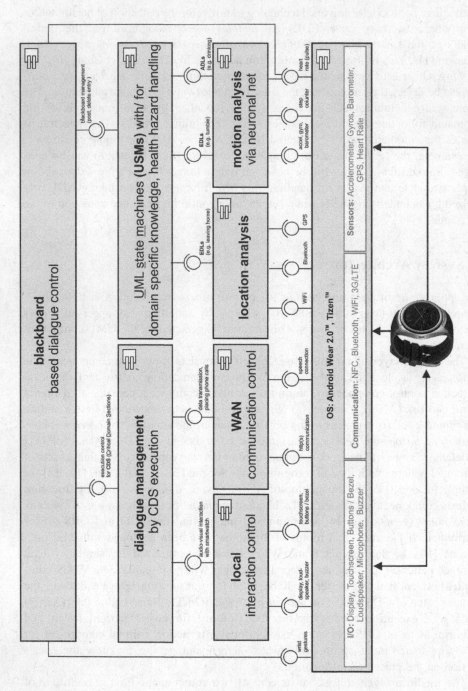

Fig. 1. Hierarchical structure of the smartwatch assistance app as UML component diagram

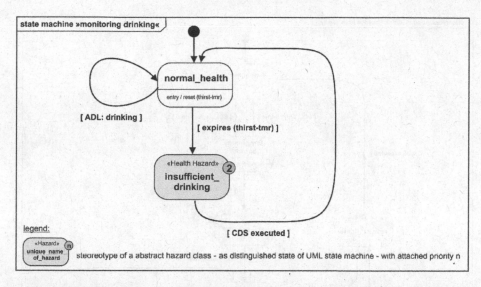

Fig. 2. UML finite state machine for concluding the health hazard *insufficient_drinking*

a group of related health and/or security hazards in a declarative way (see Fig. 3, Sect. 4 for details). Each USM typically contains a least one concluded hazard. These concluded hazards are distinguished states of the USMs which will be written or deleted from the blackboard, as soon as the USMs enters or leaves such states as their current state. All finite state machines are executed simultaneously, and the state transitions of the machines are triggered by the detected ADLs, EDLs and their occurrence, duration or absence in real time. The second component of this medium layer is the dialogue manager, which executes the specific CDSs. A CDS contains the dialogue tactical knowledge for handling a specific (group of) health or security hazard. The dialogue manager is controlled and used by the blackboard based, central scheduler on the top layer.

The **top layer** consists of a *blackboard* [16] as central synchronization mechanism between the different finite state machines and their concluded hazards on the medium layer. The central, *priority based scheduling mechanism* selects one of those hazards currently on the blackboard *for execution*. The execution of the selected health or security hazard is delegated to the dialogue manager containing the specific CDSs. During the execution of the respective [Inform], ... [Clarify] steps of the selected CDS the I/O and communication devices of the smartwatch are exclusively reserved and attached to the section. The scheduler uses the entries on the blackboard as its input data for the scheduling algorithm and passes the set of acute hazards to the dialogue manager for instantiation of the corresponding CDS pattern.

The functionality of the middle and top layer can best be compared to Fowler's »*model, passive view and presenter*« pattern, elaborating from the well-known MVC pattern [17]. This pattern has decisive advantages with respect to testing the health assistance app.

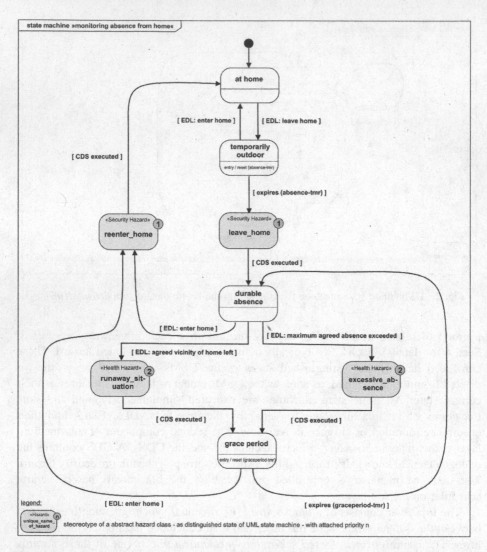

Fig. 3. UML finite state machine for concluding several health and security hazardsin the scope of a user's absence from home

4   Towards a Formal Dialogue Model

4.1   Health Hazard Conclusion and Handling via USMs

For concluding the presence of a health hazard from the sequencing of recognized EDL and ADLs occurring over the course of time, the domain specific knowledge is described by a UML finite state machine (USM) (see also [9]). A single USM models an individual hazard and its associated handling process including the execution of the

CDS. It describes the *domain handling knowledge* in a *declarative* and *maintainable* manner. All defined USMs within the health assistance app will be executed/interpreted simultaneously.

The progress of the reasoning process about the hazard is modelled via different states of an USM, whereby the handling of a finally concluded hazard is represented by a CDS as a distinguished state of the machine. The state transitions of the USM depend (a) on its current state, and, (b) as "input", on:

- elapsed (real) time periods for which the USM is already in the current state,
- the recognized EDLs, ADLs as momentary output of the location analysis or motion analysis component.

4.2   Synchronized Health Hazard Handling via a Blackboard

The synchronization of the different USMs is done via a backboard [16]. In the scope of a state transition from an old state s_{old} to current state s_{new}, a USM posts a new current state s_{new}, which is of class «Hazard» , as a new entry on the blackboard. Posting a CDS on the blackboard, pragmatically represents the request for execution, dialogue handling, of this hazard. If, for any reason, an USM changes its current state s_{new} of class «Hazard» to a different successor state, the specific hazard is erased from the blackboard, denoting a withdrawal of the prior execution request. Pragmatically for a moment in time, the set of all specific hazards on the blackboard at that time denote the set of all concluded and assumed, acute health and security hazards.

The blackboard is organized by different priority levels, so the priority attached to the health or security hazard by the corresponding USM state will determine on which blackboard level the hazard will be posted Table 1.

The decision about the requested execution and their prioritizing and sequencing will be done by the central scheduler of the blackboard.

4.3   Priority Based Scheduling

The **central scheduling algorithm** of the blackboard controls the dialogue with the user by selecting one of the specific hazards on the blackboard with highest priority for execution. The execution of the selected health or security hazard is delegated to the dialogue manager containing the specific CDS for this hazard. The selected CDS will

Table 1. Blackboard priority levels

Priority level	Health hazard or security hazard
5 (high)	*manual_call_request*
4	*abnormal_vital_parameters*
3	*tumble*
2	Deviant Behavior (*insufficient_drinking, excessive_absence, excessive_nap, excessive_bedtime, runaway_situation, ...*)
1 (low)	Smart Home Control (*leave_home, reenter_home*)

be granted exclusive access to the smartwatch I/O and communication devices for the time period of their execution. Because the execution of the CDS typically may include a call, speech connection, to a distant family member or call center, this execution time may be of unforeseeable duration. During this interval, the CDS can present its explanation, confirmation, ... texts on the smartwatch screen, use microphone and loudspeaker for the speech connection and can accept input from the mic, touchscreen, buttons or bezel of the smartwatch. The scheduling, i.e. selection of a posted hazard for execution, will be governed by the following **scheduler rules**:

(a) **Inhibition rule:** only select a CDS when there are no inhibitory facts presents: (1) an ongoing execution on another CDS or (2) a user moving too fast.
(b) **Eligibility rule:** only select a CDS with unique name p for execution, for which in the [Inform], [Confirm] steps for dynamic text configuration, a text is listed and associated with {p} or the *exact set* of all acute health hazards on the blackboard.
(c) **Highest priority rule:** unambiguously select the specific CDS with a blackboard entry of highest priority, if applicable.
(d) **Most comprehensive selection rule**: if there is more than one CDS with highest priority, select the specific CDS which handles (in its action blocks by the corresponding unique names) the *exact set* of all acute health hazards on the blackboard.
(e) **Most recently added rule**: if rule c) still selects more than one CDS, select the most recent added CDS for execution.

4.4   The Execution of CDS for Dialogue Handling of Health and Security Hazards

Controlling the execution of health or security hazard dialogue handling by CDS combines two main advantages:

- It supports a *conceptually complete* and *systematic* user dialogue, in which:

  a. The dialogue is performed on eye's level and the user is always informed about the conclusions of the system. In the [Inform] step the user gets to know all concluded acute health hazards. A dynamic text configuration mechanism can produce different explanation texts tailored to the specific configuration of acute health hazards (see below). In the later [Confirm] steps the user gets to know the immediate consequences of his taken decision.
  b. in the [Propose Decision] step, choices are restricted to (unilateral) affirmation or (bilateral) YES/NO decisions. This restricts the cognitive complexity for the targeted user group of elderly citizens.
  c. all potential reactions of the user to the presented information – including an omitted reaction - will be considered in the [Confirm] step.

- The implemented framework for the CDS behavioral pattern involves many comfort features:

  a. deferring the execution of a CDS – for safety reasons - if the user is moving (*potentially steering a car*) at high speed. This will be automatically determined from analyzing the location information by the scheduler (via GPS). Similar, a CDS execution will not start as long as the smartwatch is not worn.

b. blocking incoming calls during the execution of the section.
c. stopping/fading down a running MP3 player for the execution time of the CDS.
d. blocking the disturbance of the section by overlapping starts of other CDSs or other alternative usage of the smartwatch I/O devices.
e. catching the attention of the user by putting the assistance app in the foreground of the smartwatch display for a presented pre-alert and catching the attention of the user by haptic and acoustic signals.
f. checking for a rising of the arm/wrist rotation in order to detect when the user starts to actively perceive the presented pre-alert information about the health hazard (and thus calculating a fair waiting time for the user's reaction),
g. aborting the CDS resp. cancelling a (scheduled or ongoing) call when the user drops the smartwatch during execution of the section.

The dialogue manager component will typically contain a set of different CDS stereotypes for the specific hazard classes.

In their [Inform] and [Confirm] action blocks these CDS stereotypes have rules for dynamic text configuration based on the set of acute health or security hazards on the blackboard. Those rules mention the set of hazards as preconditions, which must be present, when the specific text will be used for an explanation or confirmation text. Accordingly, different data may be transmitted in the [Transmit] phase of CDS execution, based on the set of acute hazards on the blackboard. This can be actively utilized for controlling privacy. For example, when the security hazard *manual_call_request* will be executed. Heart rate data will only be transmitted to a distant communication end point if a concluded hazard *abnormal_vital_parameters* is also present on the blackboard. The geographic location data of the user will only be transmitted, if an *excessive_absence* or *runaway_situation* is also present on the blackboard at this moment. If none of these hazards is present at the moment when the user requests the manual call, based on the configured rules no data will be transmitted just before the call.

In order to perform this dynamic text configuration resp. configuration of data transmission, the dialogue manager will instantiate the utilized CDS with the set of all present hazards on the blackboard. This set will be passed to the dialogue manager from the central scheduler, when the scheduler delegates the execution of the dialogue management for a selected hazard to the dialogue manager.

The hazards on the blackboard, which will be used in the preconditions of applied dynamic text configuration rules or data transmission rules will be denoted as *"referenced hazards"* by the execution of the CDS. Pragmatically, the execution of the CDS is assumed to jointly handle the dialogue for all "referenced hazards". Therefore, the later completion of the CDS execution will be signaled by the dialogue manager component as well to the specific USM, which has posted the selected and executed hazard on the blackboard and to all the USMs of the *"referenced hazards"*. This is done by sending the event "CDS executed" to the USMs. This event will cause a corresponding state transition of those USMs. In the course of this state transition, the corresponding USMs will erase their handled hazards from the blackboard (Figs. 4 and 5).

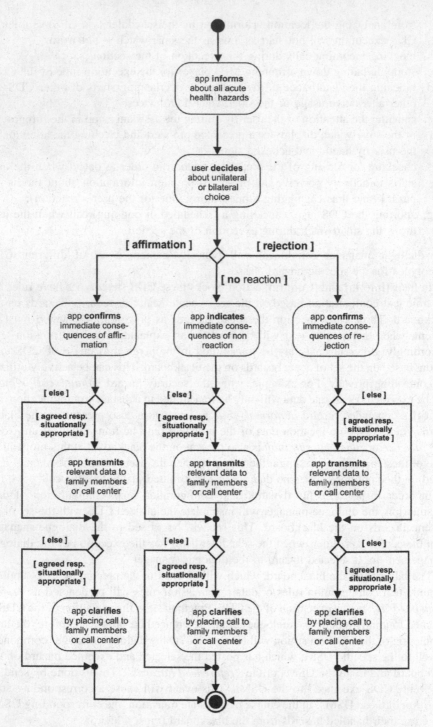

Fig. 4. Behavioral pattern for Critical Dialogue Section (CDs) as UML activity diagram

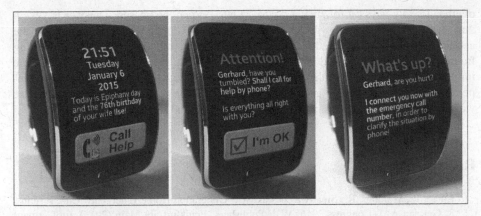

Fig. 5. Health Assistance App for Samsung Gear S™. <u>Left</u>: Default display when no health hazard has been detected. *Middle*: Result of [Inform], [Propose Decision] steps for tumble CDS (pre-alert). *Right*: Result of [Confirm] step for tumble CDS, if no user decision has been taken

5 Discussion

A field test of the developed assistance app for the *Samsung Gear S™* (cf. [18] for detailed results) showed that most flaws appear in the design and implementation of the dialogue with the user, and are not caused by missing or malfunctioning functional features. For example, we originally had not considered that a dialogue sequence should be postponed for safety reasons, when the user is driving at high speed on a highway. Or, that the start or continuation of a CDS does not make sense if the user drops the smartwatch and retires to bed. These aspects now have been integrated in the application framework and will be automatically checked and considered as a comfort feature of dialogue implementation for all future applications based on the framework.

More situational awareness for inhibiting CDS execution would be possible by additionally considering digital maps and mapping the current user position on relevant geographic objects ("map matching"). Thus, it could be identified whether the user is driving on a street or by railroad. Or, if the wearer is moving in a condensed town center or on a rural highway. In practice, the computational effort and the energy consumption for implementing these features must be accounted against the gain in comfort. The described functionality increase remains only of secondary importance as long as the topmost, mandatory goal of running the health assistance app over a full 18 h day with at least a 10% battery reserve for emergency calls is not fully achieved.

6 Conclusions

Battery capacity resp. energy consumption is the most scare and valuable resource for a smartwatch. Therefore, one might ask: Does the use of the model based application framework [16] for a formal dialogue management and the resulting computational overhead really pays off for such a device? Our – experience based – answer is yes, in that the application framework allows to focus on domain specific issues of the application and the application logic. The proposed model and its implementing framework relieves the software developer from most aspects the concise dialogue implementation. Moreover, the presented model ensures a consistency and completeness of the dialogue design and implementation for the application, which otherwise would be difficult to achieve and would bind substantial development resources.

References

1. Lutze, R., Waldhör, K.: Smartwatches as Next Generation Home Emergency Call Systems. 8. German AAL Congress 2015. VDE Publishers, Frankfurt am Main (2015). (in German)
2. Lutze, R., Waldhör, K.: Integration of stationary and wearable support services for an actively assisted life of elderly people: capabilities, achievements, limitations, prospects–a case study. In: Wichert, R., Mand, B. (eds.) Ambient Assisted Living. 9. AAL Congress Frankfurt 2016. Springer, Heidelberg (2017). ISBN 3-319-52321-X
3. Juchli, J.: Krankenpflege - Praxis und Theorie der Gesundheitsförderung und Pflege Kranker. Georg Thieme Publishers, Stuttgart (1987). ISBN 3-135-00005-2
4. Dennedy, M.F., Fox, J., Finneran, T.R.: The Privacy Engineer's Manifesto: Getting from Policy to Code to QA to Value. Apress, Berkeley (2014)
5. Cavoukian, A.: Privacy by Design - The 7 Foundational Principles. Information and Privacy Commissioner of Ontario, Canada, Toronto (2011)
6. Sommerville, I.: Software Engineering, 10th edn. Pearson Publishers, London (2016). ISBN 0-133-94303-8
7. Silberschatz, A., Galvin, P.B., Gagne, G.: Operating System Concepts, 7th edn. Wiley, Hoboken (2005). ISBN 0-471-69466-5
8. Parnas, D.L.: On a Buzzword: Hierarchical Structure, pp. 336–339. North Holland Publishing Company, Amsterdam (1974). Reprinted in: Broy, M., Denert, E. (eds.) Software Pioneers – Contributions to Software Engineering. Springer Publishers, pp. 501–513 (2002). ISBN 3-540-43081-4
9. Lutze, R., Waldhör, K.: A smartwatch software architecture for health hazard handling for elderly people. In: IEEE International Conference on HealthCare Informatics (ICHI 2015), Dallas, pp. 356–361 (2015). doi:10.1109/ICHI.2015.50
10. Lutze, R., Waldhör, K.: The application architecture of smartwatch apps – analysis, principles of design and organization. In: Mayr, H.C., Pinzger, M. (eds.) INFORMATIK 2016. Lecture Notes in Informatics (LNI), vol. P259, pp. 1865–1878. Springer Publishers, Bonn (2016). ISBN 978-3-88579-653-4, ISSN 1617-5468
11. Lutze, R. Waldhör, K.: Smartwatch based tumble recognition – a data mining model comparison study. In: 18. IEEE International Conference on E-Health Networking, Application & Services (HealthCom 2016), Munich, pp. 1–6 (2016). doi:10.1109/HealthCom.2016.7749464
12. Waldhör, K., Baldauf, R.: Recognizing Trinking ADLs in Real Time Using Smartwatches and Data Mining. Rapid Miner Wisdom Conference 2015, Ljubljana, Slovenia (2015)
13. Lutze, R., Baldauf, R., Waldhör, K.: Dehydration prevention and effective support for the elderly by the use of Smartwatches. In: 17. IEEE International Conference on E-Health Networking, Application & Services (HealthCom 2015), Boston, pp. 404–409 (2015). doi:10.1109/HealthCom.2015.7454534

14. De, D., Bharti, P., Das, S.D., Chellappan, S.: Multimodal wearable sensing for fine-grained activity recognition in HealthCare. IEEE Internet Comput. **19**(5), 26–35 (2015)
15. Schindhelm, C.K., MacWilliams, A.: Overview of indoor positioning technologies for context aware AAL applications. In: Wichert, R., Eberhard, B. (eds.) Ambient Assisted Living, pp. 273–291. Springer, Berlin (2011). 3-642-42396-5
16. Engelmore, R.: Blackboard Systems. Addison-Wesley Publishers, Boston (1989). ISBN 0-201-17431-6
17. Fowler, M.: Patterns of Enterprise Application Architecture. Addison-Wesley Publishers, Boston (2003). ISBN 0-321-12742-0
18. Klein, B., Reutzel, S., Roßberg, H., Bienhaus, D., Lutze, R., Hofmann, J., Dallwitz, D., Sütö, S., Heinrich, H., Donath, M.: Connecting Wearables to Smart Home and Personal Alarm Technologies. Acceptance and Usability, Future Living Spaces Congress 2016, pp. 109–115. VDE Publishers, Frankfurt/Main (2016)

Notification System to Encourage a User to Refrain from Using Smartphone Before Going to Bed

Kazuyoshi Murata[1(✉)], Kouhei Shigematsu[2], and Yu Shibuya[2]

[1] Aoyama Gakuin University, Kanagawa, Japan
kmurata@si.aoyama.ac.jp
[2] Kyoto Institute of Technology, Kyoto, Japan
shigematsu@hi.is.kit.ac.jp, shibuya@kit.ac.jp

Abstract. Many people use their smartphone before going to bed. However, using a smartphone before sleeping can cause problems, such as difficulty falling asleep and light sleep. We propose a notification system to encourage a user to refrain from using smartphone before going to bed. The proposed system displays messages about influence of sleep on plans for the next day and health risks of smartphone use. In addition, the proposed system displays the time remaining before going to bed. We conducted an experiment to confirm the effectiveness of the proposed system and discuss the results of this experiment. The target of the proposed system is university students in Japan. From the experimental result, features of the proposed system motivate participants to think about not using their smartphones. However, the participants did not actually refrain from using them.

Keywords: Smartphone · Sleep · Notification system

1 Introduction

Many people often use their smartphone before going to bed. Some even use their own smartphones in bed. In Japan, over three-quarters of smartphone users use their device in bed just before falling asleep [1]. An Internet survey about quality of sleep in Japan [2] indicated that 48.6% of users who use a smartphone over 30 min before going to bed reported that they had difficulty falling asleep. Moreover, the survey indicated that 59.5% of those users reported light sleep.

A physiological study has reported the influence of blue light on the circadian system [3]. Blue light at night can be produced from not only computer screen, but also smartphone screen. The risks associated with blue light from a smartphone screen have increased due to the rapid increase in the duration and frequency of smartphone use [4]. Bauer et al. proposed ShutEye [5], which promotes awareness of activities that contribute to healthy sleep habits. ShutEye displays activities that are known to affect sleep, e.g., consuming caffeine and napping, on the smartphone's wall paper and lock screen. ShutEye could increase awareness of healthy sleep habits. However, using a smartphone before sleeping can cause problems, such as difficulty falling asleep and

© Springer International Publishing AG 2017
M. Kurosu (Ed.): HCI 2017, Part II, LNCS 10272, pp. 240–249, 2017.
DOI: 10.1007/978-3-319-58077-7_19

light sleep. Thus, reducing the use of a smartphone before sleeping is needed to realize healthy sleep habits.

In this study, we propose a notification system that encourages users to refrain from using a smartphone before going to bed. The proposed system displays messages about influence of sleep on plans for the next day and health risks of smartphone use. These messages appear on the screen when the smartphone wakes from sleep mode. In addition, the proposed system displays the time remaining before going to bed. These messages are also shown in the notification bar. We conducted an experiment to confirm the effectiveness of the proposed system and discuss the results of this experiment.

A previous survey reported that 72% of university students in Japan have a smartphone and use it daily [6]. Another survey in Japan reported that approximately 30% of university students in Japan indicated that their amount of sleep decreased after they started using a smartphone [7]. Therefore, target of the proposed system is university students in Japan.

2 Notification System Design

We propose a notification system to encourage smartphone users to refrain from using their smartphones before going to bed. The following three types of messages are displayed on the smartphone.

- A message about the influence of sleep on plans for the next day
- A message about health risks of smartphone use.
- A messages about the time remaining before going to bed.

The first type of message is intended to strengthen the user's motivation to sleep early for the next day's plan. The user who saw this messages is expected to stop using the smartphone. The second type of message is intended to make the user aware of health risks of smartphone itself. The third type of message is intended to remind the user of his/her bed time and prevent the user from long-term use of smartphone unconsciously.

When using the proposed system, the user inputs his/her wake-up time, a plan for the next day, and desired hours of sleep. From this information, the system sets an estimated bedtime automatically. The notifications are displayed on the screen of smartphone each time it wakes from sleep mode from two hours prior to the estimated bedtime until the wake-up time or until the user stops using his/her smartphone, as shown in Fig. 1.

Figure 2(a) shows the screen used to input the wake-up time. When a user inputs their wake-up time and taps the "Next" button, the input screen for the next day's plan is displayed (Fig. 2(b)). This screen presents a list of activities selected with university students in mind, e.g., "playing sports", "going to class," and "taking test." The user can make multiple selections. After the user selects activities and taps the "Next" button, the input screen for hours of sleep is displayed, i.e., 6, 7.5, and 9 h (Fig. 2(c)). The user selects one item to set their hours of sleep. The hours of sleep options were determined from the fact that the average hours of sleep is approximately 7 to 8 h [8]

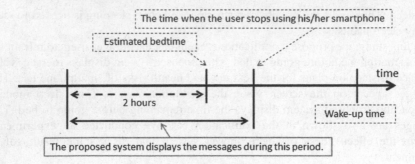

Fig. 1. Timing of notifications

and that the sleep cycle is approximately 90 min. When the user selects the hours of sleep and taps the "Next" button, an input screen to complete the process is displayed (Fig. 2(d)). When the user taps the "Completion" button, the system begins to display notifications.

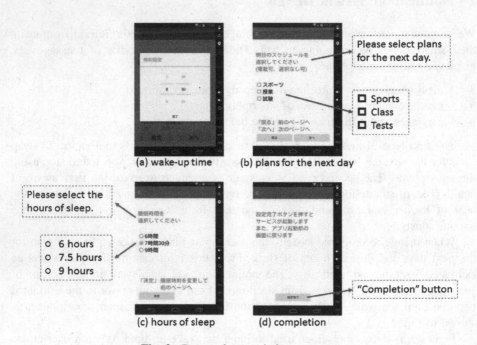

Fig. 2. Proposed system's input screens

2.1 Messages About the Influence of Sleep on Plans for the Next Day

The list of messages about the influence of sleep on plans for the next day is shown below. In this type of message, the topic of messages is changed according to plans for the next day. Therefore, the topic of message that the user sees can change every day.

- The plan for the next day is "playing sports"
  - "Sufficient sleep increased basketball shooting accuracy (9% improvement for free throws and three-point field goals)." [9]
  - "Sufficient sleep increased speed resulting in faster sprint times." [9]
  - "Sufficient sleep remarkably improves physical and mental performance."
  - Approximately 85% of athletes place importance on sleeping for physical condition management." [10]
- The plan for the next day is "going to class"
  - "At this rate, you will be late for class."
  - "At this rate, you will fall asleep in class."
  - "Lack of sleep reduces concentration in class."
  - "Lack of sleep reduces the ability to think in class."
- The plan for the next day is "taking a test"
  - "If you do not go to sleep as soon as you memorize information, you may forget it."
  - "Sacrificing sleep for extra study time is counterproductive." [11]
  - "You will be sleepy during tests."
  - "Your brain will not be working during tests."

2.2 Messages About the Health Risks of Smartphone Use

The list of messages about the health risks of smartphone use is shown below. In this type of message, the topic of messages that the user sees is the same every day.

- "Using a smartphone deteriorates of visual acuity and causes inflammation of the retina."
- "Using a smartphone increases weight gain."
- "Using a smartphone causes poor sleep."
- "Using a smartphone causes lifestyle disease."
- "Using a smartphone causes eye fatigue."
- "Using a smartphone increases stress and risk of depression."

2.3 Messages About the Remaining Time Until the Time of Going to Sleep

The remaining time until going to sleep is notified by the following notification methods.

- Display the remaining time while simultaneously showing messages about the influence of sleep on plans for the next day
- Display the remaining time on the notification bar at the top of the screen

Figure 3 shows an example notification message when the smartphone wakes from sleep mode. There are messages about the health risk and the time remaining until going to sleep.

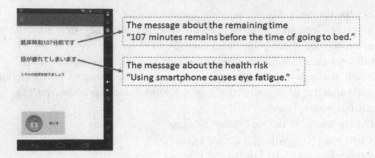

Fig. 3. Example notification message when the smartphone wakes from sleep mode

It is possible that a user may be doing important work on his/her smartphone. Therefore, the notification message for the remaining time is displayed on the notification bar to not interrupt the user's tasks. This type of message is displayed on the notification bar as a blue, yellow, or red icon (Table 1). When the user swipes the notification bar down, details about the remaining time are displayed (Fig. 4).

Table 1. Icon color and timing of notification messages

Color of icon	Start timing of notifying messages	End timing of notifying messages
Blue	2 h prior to estimated bedtime	0.5 h prior to estimated bedtime
Yellow	0.5 h prior to estimated bedtime	Just estimated bedtime
Red	After estimated bedtime	The time when the user stops using his/her smartphone

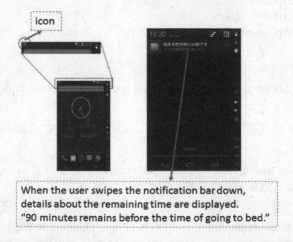

Fig. 4. Example notification message for the remaining time

3 Experiment

We conducted an experiment to confirm that participants refrained from using smartphone when using the proposed notification system. Four volunteers (age 19–23, male) were recruited from Kyoto Institute of Technology. The experimental period was eight days. All participants installed three types of notification system (Table 2) onto their own smartphone. Two of the four participants used each notification system in the following order.

- 1st period (two days): No-notification system
- 2nd period (two days): Proposed system
- 3rd period (two days): Common-notification system
- 4th period (two days): No-notification system

Table 2. Notification systems

	No-notification system	Common-notification system	Proposed system
Influence of sleep on plans for the next day	No	No	Yes
Health risks of smartphone use	No	Yes	Yes
Time remaining before going to bed	No	Yes	Yes

The other two participants used each notification system in a different (the second and the third periods were switched). During the overall experimental period, the participants were not forced to complete any specific tasks without answering the following questionnaire at wake-up time each day.

Q1. How carefully did you read the notification message? (1: Not carefully, 2: Slightly carefully, 3: Moderately carefully, 4: Very carefully)

Q2. Did you think that you should refrain from using the smartphone two hours before the estimated bedtime until the estimated time? (1: Not at all, 2: Slightly yes; 3: Yes, 4: Strongly yes)

Q3. Did you refrain from using the smartphone two hours before the estimated bedtime? (1: Not at all, 2: Slightly yes, 3: yes, 4: Strongly yes)

Q4. Did you think that you should refrain from using the smartphone between the estimated bedtime and the actual bedtime? (1: Not at all, 2: Slightly yes; 3: Yes, 4: Strongly yes)

Q5. Did you refrain from using the smartphone from the estimated bedtime until the actual bedtime? (1: Not at all, 2: Slightly yes, 3: yes, 4: Strongly yes)

Q6. Did you think that you should refrain from using the smartphone after the actual bedtime? (1: Not at all, 2: Slightly yes; 3: Yes, 4: Strongly yes)

Q7. Did you refrain from using smartphone after the actual bedtime? (1: Not at all, 2: Slightly yes, 3: yes, 4: Strongly yes)

Moreover, there were free description forms to provide reasons for the replies to Q2 to Q7. Note that Q1 was omitted when the participant used the no-notification system (first and fourth periods).

After finishing the fourth period, the participants were asked to answer the following final questionnaire. In addition, they were asked to provide reasons for their replies to each question.

Q1. Please arrange the systems you used first, second, and third in order of effectiveness relative to refraining from using the smartphone.
Q2. Please arrange the systems in the order you would prefer for actual use.

The operation time was defined as the time since the smartphone woke from sleep mode until it shifted to sleep mode again. The total operation time was defined as the summation of the operation time. The total operation time before the estimated bedtime was measured. In addition, the total operation time after the estimated bedtime until falling asleep was also measured.

4 Experimental Results

Questionnaire at Wake-up Time

Figure 5 shows the mean scores for Q1 to Q7. A Friedman test revealed significant differences among the mean scores for each notification system for Q4 and Q7 ($p < 0.05$).

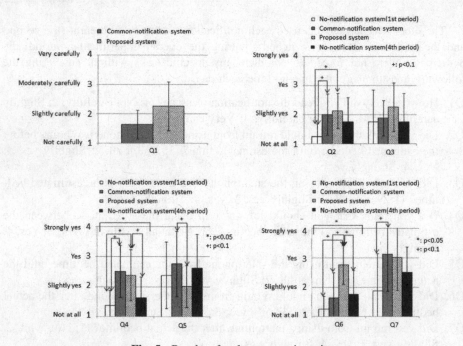

Fig. 5. Results of wake-up questionnaire

Final Questionnaire

Figure 6 shows the ranking results for Q1 and Q2. The proposed system was ranked first for both Q1 and Q2. However, a Friedman test revealed no significant differences.

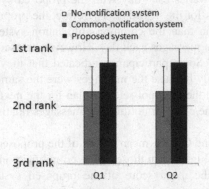

Fig. 6. Results of final questionnaire

Total Operation Time

Figure 7 shows the mean total operation time for each notification system. When the participant used the smartphone before the estimated bedtime, the mean total operation time for the common-notification system was less than that of the other notification systems. In contrast, when the participant used the smartphone after the estimated bedtime, the mean total operation time for the no-notification system in the first period was the shortest among all notification systems. However, a Friedman test revealed no significant difference among the notification systems.

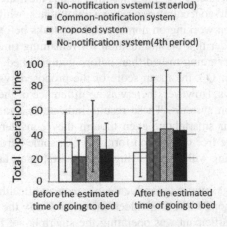

Fig. 7. Total operation time

5   Discussion

The results for Q1 indicate that the participants read the notification messages of the proposed system more carefully than that of the common-notification system. The topic of notification messages varies each day with the proposed system because the messages are related to plans for the next day. Therefore, the proposed system could gain more participant attention than the common-notification system which repeated the same topic of notification messages each day. However, the score was slightly over 2, i.e., "Slightly carefully." Some participants indicated that they did not read the notification messages carefully because the messages were the same as the previous day's messages. In these cases, they did not select a plan for the next day. We consider that these opinions indicate the effect of notification messages relative to plans for the next day.

In the results of Q2 and Q4, the mean scores of the proposed system and common-notification system were higher than those of the no-notification system, and there was no difference between the mean score of the proposed system and the common-notification system. In the free description for these questions, some participants indicated that they considered refraining from using smartphones when they saw the notification messages about health risks. These messages about health risks were notified by both the proposed system and the common-notification system. On the other hand, the participants did not mention messages related to plans for the next day. From these results for Q2 and Q4, we consider that messages about health risks were effective to make participants refrain from using the smartphone. However, it was not clear whether messages about plans for the next day were effective, although these messages were effective to gain the attention of the participants, as mentioned in the discussion related to Q1.

In the free description form for Q6, one participant indicated that he considered refraining from using the smartphone when he noticed a change in the color of the icon. Q6 was about the time after participants went to bed until they fell asleep. There was no description about icon changes in the questions about the time before going to bed because the participant concentrated on the smartphones while they were in bed, whereas they were often working on non-smartphone tasks before going to bed. From these results, we consider that the notification for remaining time until going to sleep was more effective after going to bed than before going to bed.

From the results for Q3, the mean score of the proposed system was greater than that of the other systems. However, there was no difference of the mean total operation time among notification systems. These results indicate that the participants did not refrain from using their smartphone even though they considered doing so with the proposed system. In the free description form for Q3, some participants indicated that they were communicating with friends using their smartphones, talking or chatting with SNS.

Notification messages about the influence of sleep and health risks were displayed only when the smartphone woke from sleep mode, and only the icon notification was performed while the participant was operating the smartphone. In the free description form for Q5, one participant indicated that he did not attempt to refrain from using the smartphone because he saw the icon notification only and did not see other notification messages. Therefore, we consider that a mechanism to notify messages about the influence of sleep and health risks are required even while operating a smartphone.

As mentioned previously, the proposed system made users conscious about refraining from using smartphones. However, whether the participants actually refrain from using the smartphone depended on what the participants were doing at that time. In addition, many of smartphone users may have already recognized the negative effect of smartphone use such as health risks and these users may be feeling unpleasant with these notifications. We need to survey on this point in the future work.

6 Conclusion

Using a smartphone just before sleep can decrease the quality of sleep. We have proposed a notification system to encourage users to refrain from using a smartphone to obtain healthy sleep habits. Experimental results indicated that the features of the proposed system encouraged participants to think about refraining from using their smartphones. However, the participants did not actually refrain from using their smartphones. In future, we plan to implement a method to display messages about the influence of sleep and health risks while using smartphone. In addition, we plan to conduct a long-term experiment with more participants.

References

1. Mobile Marketing Data Lab. https://mmdlabo.jp/investigation/detail_1433.html. (in Japanese)
2. GLAFAS. http://www.glafas.com/news/topics/151201jins_jins_screen_night_use.html. (in Japanese)
3. Cajochen, C., Frey, S., Anders, D., Späti, J., Bues, M., Pross, A., Mager, R., Wirz-Justice, A., Stefani, O.: Evening exposure to a light-emitting diodes (LED)-backlit computer screen affects circadian physiology and cognitive performance. J. Appl. Physiol. **110**(5), 1432–1438 (2011)
4. Oh, J.H., Yoo, H., Park, H.K., Do, Y.R.: Analysis of circadian properties and healthy levels of blue light from smartphones at night. Sci. Rep. **5**, 11325 (2015)
5. Bauer, J.S., Consolvo, S., Greenstein, B., Schooler, J., Wu, E., Watson, N.F., Kientz, J.: ShutEye: encouraging awareness of healthy sleep recommendations with a mobile, peripheral display. In: CHI 2012 Proceedings of the SIGCHI Conference on Human Factors in Computing Systems, pp. 1401–1410 (2012)
6. Cross Marketing. https://www.cross-m.co.jp/report/it/sp20140407/. (in Japanese)
7. Smartphone Riyou to Izonkeikou. http://www.soumu.go.jp/main_content/000209896.pdf. (in Japanese)
8. The NHK Monthly Report on Broadcast Research, April 2011, pp. 2–21 (2011). (in Japanese)
9. Mah, C.D., Mah, K.E., Kezirian, E.J., Dement, W.C.: The effects of sleep extension on the athletic performance of collegiate basketball players. Sleep **34**(7), 943–950 (2011)
10. AJITOREONLINE. http://www.ajinomoto.co.jp/ajitoreonline/rest/. (in Japanese)
11. Mail Online. http://www.dailymail.co.uk/sciencetech/article-2192087/Revision-cramming-Sacrificing-sleep-study-make-worse-exams-homework.html

Features and Quality of a Mobile Application Employed in a Speech-Language Therapy

Tihomir Orehovački[1]([⊠]), Dijana Plantak Vukovac[2], Zlatko Stapić[2],
and Tatjana Novosel-Herceg[3]

[1] Department of Information and Communication Technologies,
Juraj Dobrila University of Pula, Zagrebačka 30, 52100 Pula, Croatia
tihomir.orehovacki@unipu.hr
[2] Faculty of Organization and Informatics, University of Zagreb,
Pavlinska 2, 42000 Varaždin, Croatia
{dijana.plantak,zlatko.stapic}@foi.hr
[3] VaLMod Speech-Language Pathology Centre,
Ante Starčevića 25, 42000 Varaždin, Croatia
tatjana.novoselherceg@gmail.com

Abstract. This paper introduces *mLogoped*, a mobile application for delivering remote speech-language pathology (SLP) therapies. With an aim to examine quality of a *mLogoped* application, an empirical study was carried out. Participants in the study were parents of children diagnosed with SLP disorders. Data was collected with pre- and post-use questionnaire. Items in pre-use questionnaire were related to the participants' computer literacy, their experience in using mobile devices and applications, and their preferences with respect to attending online SLP therapies. After spending a week using the application, the study participants examined its quality by means of user version of Mobile App Rating Scale (uMARS) post-use questionnaire adapted to SLP domain. An analysis of collected data revealed to what extent mLogoped has met one subjective (perceived quality) and four objective (engagement, functionality, aesthetics, and information quality) facets of mobile quality.

Keywords: mLogoped · uMARS · Speech-language therapy · Mobile application · Quality evaluation · Empirical study

1 Introduction

New technologies are significantly reshaping healthcare sector and one of the fastest growing branches in Digital Health is *mHealth*, or mobile health, which denotes the practice of medicine and public health assisted by smartphones [18]. According to [9] the growth rate of use of mHealth smartphone applications is more than 42% in last two years with more than 259.000 applications available on the market in the year 2016. This growth is triggered by enabling mobile technologies, increasing number of smartphone users, and broad categories of applications aimed at healthcare professionals, patients and general public. While some applications are mobile versions of their printed or computer counterparts (e.g. mobile library of medical terms, mobile electronic health records), the other can assist in disease diagnosis, patient monitoring,

© Springer International Publishing AG 2017
M. Kurosu (Ed.): HCI 2017, Part II, LNCS 10272, pp. 250–262, 2017.
DOI: 10.1007/978-3-319-58077-7_20

or provide an interface between sensors attached to the patient's body and a medical device that registers patient's health status.

Despite these encouraging numbers and trends, patients in Croatia with speech-anguage disorders have only a few opportunities to be digitally assisted in performing therapeutic exercises. Thus, in this paper we propose a model and architecture of a platform that enables delivery of a personalized video instructions to this specific target group. An application named *mLogoped* (abbreviation for a "mobile speech-language therapist") is developed for Android and iOS platform and is supported by RESTful [12] backend web service and web application for speech therapists. The main content of the applications are educational video lessons specifically designed in collaboration with speech therapists to help caregivers and children with pediatric speech sound disorder (dyslalia) or undeveloped speech in performing correct pronunciation of a particular sound.

The remainder of the paper is structured as follows. Brief overview of current advances in the field is offered in the next section. Evaluated mobile application is introduced in the third section. Employed research methodology is described in the fourth section. Study findings are presented in the fifth section. Concluding remarks with limitations of conducted study are provided in the last section.

2   Background to the Research

There is a broad range of health-related mobile applications which provide medical and healthcare support for health professional and everyday life: applications for medical providers; applications for medical education and teaching; specialty or disease-specific applications; applications for patients and the general public (including health and fitness applications), as well as other applications [2]. Among mHealth publishers, 56% of them identify chronically ill people as the main target group for developing disease-specific applications, followed by the health and fitness mobile applications (33%) [9]. Mobile health applications for patients and general public include wide range of domains and target groups, e.g. apps for diabetics, apps for asthmatic patients, apps for pregnant women, apps for psychiatric patients, apps for patients with speech disorders, to mention only a few.

Surprisingly, the results of the systematic mobile applications' characteristics review [19], show that tracking, although being a core function of most health applications, does not contribute to the user satisfaction as much as features that save time. Furthermore, Mendiola et al. found that users also value simple and intuitive applications which are aligned with Nielson's findings on usability [20] and applications that provide structured information. Finally, users are keen on sharing their health data with chosen individuals. These characteristics presented the solid ground for the features of application *mLogoped* we describe in this paper.

Mobile applications for speech-language disorders also benefit from today's achievements in technology. According to Furlong [21] these applications can assist in speech therapy, increase practice time, give feedback on the accuracy of users' practice, enhance families' engagement in therapy or strengthen the relationship between the patient and speech therapist. On top of that, children, as a specific and very vulnerable target group [23], especially benefit from often, effective and intensive therapy [22]. Furthermore, Furlong states that the use of mobile applications in an intervention can positively influence some of very important factors that affect therapy effectiveness: the therapy time could increase without the increase of time spent with therapist; practice could be performed in personal and relaxing settings; technology could increase enjoyment and motivation etc.; all of these leading to better and faster therapy results. Although there are studies confirming these hypotheses in other mHealth fields, Furlong states that evidence in using mobile applications in therapies of speech sound disorders is sparse [21].

A broad range of mHealth applications and specific domains they cover set out additional requirements regarding application development and its quality. While quality of mobile applications in general is assessed by star ratings and written feedback from the app users, those criteria are insufficient and uninformative [5]. Many researchers express concerns about the quality of health-related mobile applications, e.g. identifying poor reliability or accuracy of applications [6, 7]. Concern about the quality of mHealth applications is further underpinned by the fact that majority of mHealth publishers (51%) come from non-healthcare industries, e.g. IT and tech companies or app developers, while only 28% of publishers have healthcare background. However, 85% of developers consult to some extent (in-house or externally) with healthcare practitioners while building the mHealth applications [9].

A recent attempt to identify the most important criteria for evaluation of mobile health applications resulted in development of Mobile App Rating Scale (MARS) [8] that was later adapted to user version of Mobile App Rating Scale (uMARS) [1]. Mobile App Rating Scale was confirmed as a simple and reliable tool for assesing the quality of mHealth applications in four objective categories (engagement, functionality, aesthetics, and information quality), and one subjective category (perceived quality) dimensions of mobile quality [8]. It has also been applied to speech-language pathology (SLP) domain, in the quality assessment of the mobile apps for management of childhood speech sound disorders [21].

A mobile SLP application *mLogoped* described in this paper is developed with an aim to provide parents and their children easy, constant and accurate treatment of speech disorders at home. The application is adherent to web application *eLogoped* which was developed to evaluate the quality of video lessons employed in telerehabilitation of pediatric speech disorder (dyslalia) [4]. Video lessons were designed and developed according to the principles of Cognitive Theory of Multimedia Learning (CTML) and were further described in [3, 4, 10, 11]. Videos were implemented in a learning management system and tested with five children and their parents in the pilot study [4]. The perceived quality of video lessons was examined by a questionnaire, indicating that video artefacts were of very high quality and prepared professionally, with some less favorable aspects of the quality like visual appeal, quality of audio, or availability of video. Qualitative assessment and parent/child experience with video artefacts is described in [3].

Feedback received in our initial studies motivated us to design and develop *mLogoped* mobile application and further explore the scope of online remote speech-language treatments.

3 Mobile Application

In this section we will present a brief overview of requirements towards the functionalities of *mLogoped* platform. It will include specification of mobile application, web application and web services which stand for main software components. Software requirements presented in this section are excerpt from detailed specification which is aligned with IEEE's Software Requirements Specification Standard [13].

Purpose of the *mLogoped* platform is to enable speech therapist to deliver video lessons to their patients in a simple and convenient way. The usual procedure involves speech therapist demonstrating and explaining exercises that patients are supposed to repeat at home on a daily basis. However, patients may forget or misinterpret the given instructions and thus perform exercises in non-optimal manner. Thus, *mLogoped* is intended to ensure that instructions and explanations on exercises are delivered in a form of video lessons directly to the patients through the mobile application.

Our *mLogoped* platform is standalone and independent system. The only prerequisite is a stable internet connection necessary for mobile application to communicate with web service to fetch data and stream content. The system architecture is given in Fig. 1.

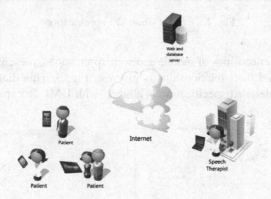

Fig. 1. mLogoped platform architecture

The core component of this platform is a set of web services located on the web server. These services accept and process requests from web and mobile applications, communicate with database and file servers and serve the clients with data and video streams. Web services form a *mLogoped* API (Application Programming Interface) which is based on RESTful architecture [15]. Having in mind different options of formatting the messages containing information exchanged between clients and web services [16, 17], we decided to use JSON (Eng. JavaScript Object Notation) notation as it, in our particular case, has more advantages over other notations and formats. An excerpt from full API specification, specifying a service endpoint responsible for providing clients an information on a specific lesson is given in Fig. 2.

Method	URL
GET	api/1/lesson/{id}*

*Required header attributes
Authorization: Bearer {token}

Response

Status	Response

200	{
	  "status": 200,
	  "data":[{
	    "id":2,
	    "title":"Lesson2",
	    "description":"Lesson desc",
	    "thumbnailPath":"www.url.com/thumbnail.png",
	    "averageRating":3.00,
	    "videoPath":"www.url.com/video.mp4",
	    "createdAt":"2014-11-11",
	    }
	  ]
	}

404	{
	  "status": 404,
	  "data":[{
	    }]
	}

Fig. 2. Excerpt from API specification

The overall functionalities of mobile and web applications, presented in the form of use cases (UCs) and their relationships is given in Fig. 3. This diagram, along with other diagrams in detailed specification is aligned with UML 2.5 specification [14].

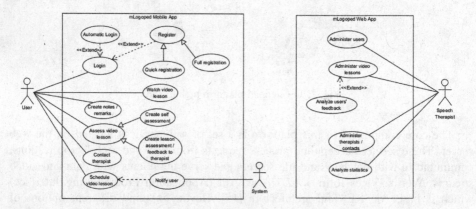

Fig. 3. Applications' use cases

Upon new video instructions or video lessons are published on the platform (UC: Administer video lessons), the users are automatically notified with pushed notifications (UC: Notify user). Through the native Android and iOS design, *mLogoped* provides users with the possibilities of registering and logging into the application (UC: Login + extension), searching, viewing and bookmarking available video content. Special attention is put on a design of functionalities available while the video lesson is being streamed and viewed (UC: Watch video lesson): users can put private remarks on the concepts presented in the lesson (UC: Create notes), can track and note their own progress (UC: Create self-assessment) and can give feedback on the lesson to their speech therapist (UC: Create lesson assessment). Finally, there are options of scheduling the lesson with automatic reminder within the application (UC: Schedule video lesson) and directly contacting the available speech therapists by phone (UC: Contact therapist).

On the other hand, apart from aforementioned UC of administering the video lessons, the speech therapist uses web application and can create, observe or block users (UC: Administer users), obtain detailed report on feedback the users gave to a particular lesson (UC: Analyze users' feedback), create or change a list of available therapists for direct contact (UC: Administer therapists) and get an insight to statistical data on lessons views (UC: Analyze statistics). However, speech therapist does not have the possibility to observe private notes or self-assessments made by users.

The screenshots representing the Android (Fig. 4) and iOS mobile application (Fig. 5) include several functionalities, namely list of available lessons, and options regarding viewing lessons and creating notes and feedbacks.

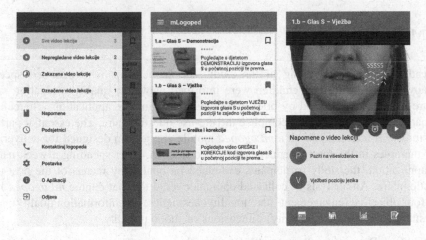

Fig. 4. mLogoped Android screenshots

According to the application classification presented in MARS questionnaire [8], above presented application directly targets and focuses physical health, while indirectly targets several categories: well-being, reducing negative emotions and stress, behavior change and goal setting. In terms of theoretical background, the following

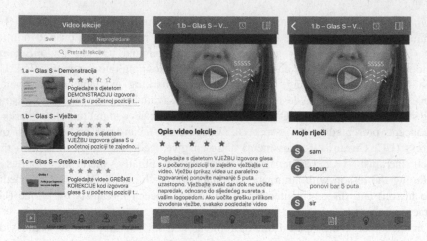

Fig. 5. mLogoped iOS screenshots

categories apply: assessment, feedback, information/education, monitoring/tracking, goal settings, advice and acceptance commitment therapy. Affiliation of the mobile applications is partially University and partially Speech Therapy Center. The platform is suitable to all age groups, although, the children under the age of 12 should be supervised when using the app. Finally, technical aspects of the application that apply include the following: password protection and login, app sends reminders, and app needs access to the Internet to function properly.

4 Methodology

Procedure. At the beginning of the study, the participants who attended speech therapy sessions with their children were informed about the quality evaluation procedure which was followed by brief introduction of a mobile application. Thereafter, the participants were asked to complete the pre-use questionnaire. The essential part of the study was interaction with a *mLogoped* mobile application designed for delivering SLP therapies in the form of educational video lessons. After spending a week using the application, the study participants examined its quality by means of the post-use questionnaire. An analysis of collected data uncovered to what degree *mLogoped* has met four objective (engagement, functionality, aesthetics, and information quality), and one subjective (perceived quality) dimensions of mobile quality.

Apparatus. Data was collected with two questionnaires. The first one was administrated among participants before study took place. It was composed of 28 items related to computer literacy of respondents, their experience in using mobile applications and devices, and needs and preferences of SLP clients with respect to SLP therapies provided online. The second questionnaire was completed by study participants after their children spend one week in interaction with a mobile application. Items in the post-use questionnaire were adopted from uMARS [1] questionnaire and adapted for speech-language application domain. It should be noted that original pool of items introduced in [1] was enhanced with an item related to the assessment of resolution and aesthetics of video artefacts and one item meant for measuring the added value of performing online SLP therapies by means of *mLogoped* mobile application. Responses to the post-use questionnaire items were modulated on a five point Likert scale (1 – strongly disagree, 5 – strongly agree).

5 Results

Participants. A total of nine parents of children diagnosed with at least one speech disorder were involved in the study. Majority (77.78%) of parents were female whereas most (66.67%) of the children were male. Respondents originated from 6 different Croatian counties where 44.44% of them were from Varaždin county. Children ranged in age from 5 to 9 years (M = 6.22, SD = 1.394). Regarding the information and communication technologies they are commonly employing, all of them are using smartphones, 55.56% is using desktop computers, 44.44% is using laptops, 33.33% is using a headset with a microphone and digital camera, 22.22% is using tablets, and 11.11% is using a microphone connected to the computer and a webcam. When frequency of using particular information and communication technologies is considered, majority (77.78%) of parents is employing computers up to one hour a day at home while 44.44% of them is using smartphones up to 2 h per day for both private and business purposes. As much as 88.89% of study participants are owners of Android-based smartphone for at least two years. Regarding the purpose of using their smartphones, 33% of study subjects are continuously sending and receiving messages via free services such as Viber and WhatsApp; 44.44% of them are often sending and receiving e-mails, reading news on various web portals and sites of interest, and taking photos; 44.44% of parents are neither rare nor often taking phone calls and making videos; 55.56% of participants are rarely using their smartphones for performing educational activities; 44.44% of respondents are rarely using short messaging service, watching podcasts on services such as YouTube and Vimeo, and employing applications for enhancing productivity such as calendar, reminders, calculator, navigation, and to-do list; 33.33% of subject is rarely playing games on their smartphones; 55.56% have never used their smartphone for the purpose of interaction on social network sites such as Facebook, Twitter, LinkedIn, and Instagram, online shopping on sites such as eBay and Amazon, internet banking, and listening to music. None of study participants has never used applications for monitoring and planning the diet (calorie counter, menu planning) nor other health-related applications. On the other hand, 44.44% of parents have rarely used applications for improving cognitive functions (brain teasers). In addition, 88.89% of respondents have never employed applications for measuring and monitoring physical conditions (e.g. weight, sleeping rhythm, etc.), applications for measuring and monitoring physical activities (e.g. heart rate, distance traveled on foot or by bicycle, etc.), applications for physical fitness improvement (workout applications), applications for assistance in correcting the health problem, and other applications as a supplement to SLP therapy. Finally, 77.78% of subjects have never used applications for women's health and/or monitoring of pregnancy nor applications for improving the mental state (for relaxing, relieving stress, meditation, etc.).

All children were diagnosed with dyslalia disorder, 55.55% of them were visiting the speech therapist due to stuttering, and one child was diagnosed with delayed speech development disorder. A total of 44.44% of children attended SLP sessions in their hometown and additional 11.11% of patients were visiting a SLP therapist who is resident in another town of their county. Two respondents reported they were visiting two or more SLP therapists, one of whom is outside their hometown or county. Remaining 22.22% of children were attending a SLP therapist who was not resident in their home county. All parents expressed their readiness to include their children in online SLP sessions where 66.67% of them were interested to participate in it from time to time, while 33.33% of parents were interested to participate in it most of the time. Majority (77.78%) of parents were willing to include their children in online SLP sessions during and after completing the therapy. The same number of parents reported they would carry out SLP sessions by themselves and under the supervision of a speech therapist. Regarding the form of online SLP sessions, majority of respondents were interested in video demonstrations of certain speech exercises (88.89%), speech therapy exercises in the form of computer games that are available on the Web (88.89%) or can be installed on the smartphone or tablet (77.78%), and communication with the speech therapist via video link (55.55%). When the monitoring of child's progress in online SLP therapy is taken into account, all parents would like to have insight into assignments their child needs to do until the next appointment with a speech therapist, 44.44% of them would like to have an insight into therapies being carried out while 88.89% of parents would like to help in improving required skills of their child as well as employ computer games that monitor child's performance over a certain period of time.

Findings. According to the results of data analysis, 55.56% of respondents believe that *mLogoped* is moderately interesting mobile application because it was capable to engage children for up to 5 min. Since *mLogoped* has proved that it can entertain SLP patients for up to 5 min, 66.67% of study participants finds it moderately fun. As much as 44.44% of subjects reported that *mLogoped* allows basic customization of its features (e.g. sound, content, notifications, etc.). It was also discovered that 33.33% of parents think that *mLogoped* offers basic interactive features (e.g. reminders, sharing options, etc.) to function adequately. In addition, 77.78% of study subjects stated content of *mLogoped* in terms of visual information, language, and design is perfectly appropriate for targeted audience.

When performance of *mLogoped* is considered, 33.33% of parents reported that its responsiveness it timely and that it does not have technical bugs. Study findings indicate that due to its intuitiveness and simplicity, 88.89% of users was able to employ *mLogoped* immediately. It was also uncovered that 55.56% of respondents perceived *mLogoped* as easy to use and understand mobile application. Moreover, 66.67% of participants believe that gestural design is perfectly consistent and intuitive across all screens of evaluated mobile application.

Outcomes of data analysis indicate that 33.33% of subjects find *mLogoped* professional, simple, clear, orderly, and logically organized mobile application optimized to the device on which its content is displayed. Furthermore, 44.44% of study participants perceived resolution graphics and visual design of *mLogoped* as highly proportionate and stylistically consistent throughout. It was also found that 55.56% of parents believe that resolution and clarity of video artefacts offered by *mLogoped* is very high. Regarding the visual appeal, 55.56% of respondents think that *mLogoped* is, due to its seamless graphics, consistently and professionally designed mobile application.

Taking into account the quality of information, 44.44% of participants stated that *mLogoped* provides highly accurate description of its functionalities. The collected data also imply that 66.67% of parents perceived information offered by *mLogoped* as comprehensive and concise with links to more information and resources. A total of 77.78% of subjects reported that visual explanation of therapies through video artefacts is perfectly clear, logical, and correct. Regarding the credibility of evaluated mobile application, 77.78% of respondents agree that content it provides originates from legitimate and specialized source.

The data gathered from study participants revealed that 66.67% of them would recommend *mLogoped* to everyone who might benefit from its use. The same percentage of parents think that their children would use *mLogoped* at least once a month in the next one year. Study findings also revealed that 66.67% of study subjects mostly agree they would pay for using the *mLogoped*. It was also discovered that 55.56% of respondents reported that *mLogoped* is one of the better applications they have used.

A total of 44.44% of study participants strongly agree that *mLogoped* increases awareness of the importance of conducting online SLP therapies. Results of data analysis revealed that 55.56% of parents think that *mLogoped* increases extent of knowledge with respect to performing online SLP therapies. Similarly, 55.56% of respondents believe that employment of *mLogoped* encourages the creating of positive attitude towards the implementation of online SLP therapies. The same percentage of study subjects reported that using the *mLogoped* increases the level of motivation in addressing SLP disorders. It was also found that 44.44% of parents mostly agree that employment of *mLogoped* encourages users to ask for further assistance (if required) in resolving SLP disorders. In addition, study findings indicate that 66.67% of parents agree that using the *mLogoped* increases the frequency in conducting online SLP therapies. Finally, 55.56% of respondents mostly agree that employment of *mLogoped* enhances efficiency in addressing SLP disorders.

6 Concluding Remarks

The aim of this paper was two-fold: to present functionalities of mobile application *mLogoped* developed to assist in the treatment of pediatric speech disorder and to explore quality of *mLogoped* mobile application as perceived by its users. The application *mLogoped* provides parents and their children easy, constant and accurate treatment of pediatric speech disorders at home. Since the application is available anytime anywhere, it enables quick and easy access to video instructions needed to perform accurate exercise. Furthermore, video content also demonstrates typical mistakes in position of speech apparatus, so the user (parent) can recognize them and learn how to avoid them, which accelerates a progress during treatment. Finally, a parent is more confident in performing the exercises with a child when instructions are always accessible.

By building on a basis of identified valuable characteristics of mHealth applications, along with identified important features of applications targeting speech-language and speech-sound disorders, we designed, developed and presented in this paper the architecture and functionality of *mLogoped* platform. It has three main components, consisting of web service endpoints connected to database and file servers, mobile applications for Android and iOS platform and web application for speech therapists.

Consequently, an empirical study was conducted during which data on users' experience in interacting with mobile devices and applications was collected with pre-use questionnaire whereas data on facets of perceived mobile quality was gathered by means of post-use questionnaire. The analysis of data collected with post-use questionnaire revealed pros and cons of *mLogoped* mobile application. In particular, we found that advantages of *mLogoped* are related to the appropriateness of provided content, easiness of use, clarity of visual information and credibility of offered content. On the other hand, identified disadvantages are mostly associated with some technical issues, customizability of features and lack of functionalities that would further facilitate interaction between user and application which indicated that there is still room for improvement.

As with all empirical studies, some limitations which require further examination have to be noted. The first one deals with the homogeneity of participants. Although children diagnosed with at least one SLP disorder are a representative sample of *mLogoped* users and thus their parents convenient sample of respondents in our study, outcomes of perceived quality assessment might vary if it would be evaluated by more heterogeneous group of users. The second limitation is that the findings cannot be generalized to all types of mobile applications designed for providing remote therapies except to the one involved in the study. Keeping the aforementioned in mind, study results should be interpreted with caution.

Considering there is a lack of studies on implementing SLP therapies in the form of mobile applications in general and the assessment of their quality in particular, we believe that findings presented in this paper significantly add to the extant body of knowledge thus establishing a foundation for further theoretical and empirical advances in the field. However, to draw generalizable sound conclusions and to examine the robustness of reported findings, further studies should be carried out.

References

1. Stoyanov, S.R., Hides, L., Kavanagh, D.J., Wilson, H.: Development and validation of the user version of the mobile application rating scale (uMARS). JMIR Mhealth Uhealth **4**(2), 1–5 (2016). doi:10.2196/mhealth.5849. e72

2. Boulos, M.N.K., Brewer, A.C., Karimkhani, C., Buller, D.B., Dellavalle, R.P.: Mobile medical and health apps: state of the art, concerns, regulatory control and certification. Online J. Public Health Inform. **5**(3), e229 (2014)

3. Vukovac, D.P.: Employing educational video in speech-language telerehabilitation with children: insights from interviews with parents. In: Chova, L.G., Martínez, A.L., Torres, I.C. (eds.) Proceedings of EDULEARN 2016, Valencia: IATED Academy, Spain, pp. 5435–5444 (2016)

4. Plantak Vukovac, D., Orehovački, T., Novosel-Herceg, T.: Inspecting the quality of educational video artefacts employed in speech-language pathology telerehabilitation: a pilot study. In: Antona, M., Stephanidis, C. (eds.) UAHCI 2016. LNCS, vol. 9739, pp. 480–491. Springer, Cham (2016). doi:10.1007/978-3-319-40238-3_46

5. Girardello, A., Michahelles, F.: AppAware: which mobile applications are hot? In: 2010 12th International Conference on Human Computer Interaction with Mobile Devices and Services, pp. 431–434, ACM, New York, September 2010

6. O'Neill, S., Brady, R.R.: Clinical involvement and transparency in medical apps; not all apps are equal. Colorectal Dis. **15**(1), 122 (2013)

7. Visvanathan, A., Hamilton, A., Brady, R.R.: Smartphone apps in microbiology–is better regulation required? Clin. Microbiol. Infect. **18**(7), E218–E220 (2012)

8. Stoyanov, S.R., Hides, L., Kavanagh, D.J., Zelenko, O., Tjondronegoro, D., Mani, M.: Mobile App rating scale: a new tool for assessing the quality of health mobile apps. JMIR Mhealth Uhealth **3**(1), e27 (2015). doi:10.2196/mhealth.3422

9. Research2Guidance: mHealth App Developer Economics 2016 – The current status and trends of the mHealth app market, 6th annual study (2016). research2guidance.com

10. Orehovački, T., Plantak Vukovac, D., Novosel-Herceg, T.: Educational artefacts as a foundation for development of remote speech language therapies. In: Vogel, D., Guo, X., Linger, H., Barry, C., Lang, M., Schneider, C. (eds.) Transforming Healthcare Through Information Systems. LNISO, vol. 17, pp. 95–109. Springer, Cham (2016). doi:10.1007/978-3-319-30133-4_7

11. Vukovac, D.P., Novosel-Herceg, T., Orehovački, T.: Users' needs in telehealth speech-language pathology services. In: Proceedings of the 24th International Conference on Information Systems Development, pp. 1–12. Harbin Institute of Technology, Harbin (2015)

12. Fiedling, R.T.: Architectural Styles and the Design of Network-Based Software Architectures. Doctoral dissertation, University of California, Irvine (2000)

13. IEEE Computer Society, IEEE Recommended Practice for Software Requirements Specification (IEEE Std 830-1998). New York, USA (1998)

14. OMG, Unified Modeling Language 2.5 Specification (formal/2015–03-01), Needham, MA, USA (2015). http://www.omg.org/spec/UML/2.5

15. Hourani, M., Shambour, Q., Al-Zubidy, A., Al-Smadi, A.: Proposed design and implementation for RESTful web server. J. Softw. **9**(5), 1071–1080 (2014)

16. Becker, J., Matzner, M., Müller, O.: Comparing architectural styles for service-oriented architectures–a REST vs. SOAP case study. In: Papadopoulos, G.A., Wojtkowski, W., Wojtkowski, G., Wrycza, S., Zupancic, J. (eds.) Information Systems Development, pp. 207–215. Springer US, Boston (2009)

17. Mulligan, G., Gracanin, D.: A Comparison of SOAP and REST implementation of a service based interaction independence middleware framework. In: Proceedings of the 2009 Winter Simulation Conference (WSC 2009). Austin, Texas, USA, (2009)

18. Adibi, S. (ed.): Mobile Health: A Technology Road Map. Springer, Switzerland (2015). ISBN 978-3-319-12817-7

19. Mendiola, M.F., Kalnicki, M., Lindenauer, S.: Valuable features in mobile health apps for patients and consumers: content analysis of apps and user ratings. JMIR Mhealth and Uhealth. **3**(2), e40 (2015)
20. Nielsen, J., Mack, R.L.: Usability Inspection Methods. Wiley, New York (1994)
21. Furlong, L.M., Morris, M.E., Erickson, S., Serry, T.A.: Quality of mobile phone and tablet mobile apps for speech sound disorders: protocol for an evidence-based appraisal. JMIR Res. Protoc. **5**(4), e233 (2016)
22. Baker, E., McLeod, S.: Evidence-based practice for children with speech sound disorders: part 2 application to clinical practice. Lang. Speech Hear. Serv. Sch. **42**(2), 140 (2011)
23. Lewis, B.A., Freebairn, L.: Residual effects of preschool phonology disorders in grade school, adolescence, and adulthood. J. Speech Lang. Hear. Res. **35**(4), 819 (1992)

Research on Discussion of Gender Difference in Preference for Smart Watches Based on Fuzzy Analytic Hierarchy Process

Tianxiong Wang[✉] and Feng Shan

School of Art, Guizhou Normal University, No. 116, Baoshan North Road, Yunyan District, Guiyang 550001, China
1192913346@qq.com, 80780162@qq.com

Abstract. As wearable devices have been intelligentized in recent years, many high-teach companies launch smart watches successively. These companies constantly upgrade shapes and functions of smart watches. However, market performances of some products are not up to the expected standard, since smart watches are in the leading-in period of product life cycle and the market demand remains unclear. Furthermore, because different consumer groups have different consumer psychologies and behaviors, they show various preferences for functions of smart watches. For instance, male group tends to be more rational and regular in consumer behaviors, while female group is more sensitive with active thinking and strong initiative in consumer behaviors. Moreover, female group prefers to pursue fashion and novelty, purchase some new products and try new life. As a result, how to locate developments of smart watches in light of needs of different users is an important research topic. According to the questionnaire data, this research adopts Fuzzy Analytic Hierarchy Process (FAHP) to explore the differences of consumer psychologies and behaviors of customers in product preferences, concluding the determinant attributes for attracting consumers to buy products. Compared with traditional Analytic Hierarchy Process (AHP), FAHP combines AHP and fuzzy theory. Ambiguous problem assessments must use the concept of fuzzy function in FAHP to calculate fuzzy weights. This research adopts questionnaire survey to handle research questions in hierarchical analyses. Similarity aggregation method is utilized to integrate opinions of research objects. Then, FAHP is used to figure out importance degrees of all hierarchies, analyzing the differences of the two groups in preferences for functions of smart watches. First of all, this research collects opinions of experts and experienced product designers through surveying users of smart watches. In addition, various kinds of evaluation criteria are selected. The representative five criteria and thirteen sub-criteria are arranged through classification. The five criteria are battery time, interaction, communication, security and APP development. The thirteen sub-criteria are voice, touch, physical, auxiliary communication, independent communication, waterproof, theftproof, time management, geographic information, intelligent life, sports health, sociality and battery time. After confirming the hierarchical structure established by five criteria and thirteen sub-criteria, this research adopts paired comparison method to design the questionnaire. Moreover, this research sets up paired matrix table of questionnaire data in accordance with the defined evaluation values of fuzzy linguistic. Besides, this research integrates opinions of research

M. Kurosu (Ed.): HCI 2017, Part II, LNCS 10272, pp. 263–275, 2017.
DOI: 10.1007/978-3-319-58077-7_21

objects through similarity aggregation method, calculating fuzzy weights for obtaining eigenvectors and eigenvalues. Eventually, this research conducts criteria ranking of all data from assessment criteria and sub-criteria. That is how to infer the differences of different gender consumers in preferences for functions of smart watches. According to the methods and results of this research which can be aimed at different target populations, development strategies of smart watches are proposed respectively and recommendation of product function combination is presented in light of different target markets.

Keywords: Fuzzy Analytic Hierarchy Process (FAHP) · User preference · User psychology · User behavior · Product development

1 Introduction

In recent years, wearable intelligent products on the market has been developing rapidly, which mainly refers to the integrated use of various types of identification, sensing, connectivity and cloud services interaction and storage technology, instead of handheld devices or other equipment, to realize the new daily wearable device of user interaction, entertainment, monitoring of the human body and other functions. In the wearable product design, wearable technology is being integrated into wearable devices, to achieve the science and technology of functions, which is a key application of wearable devices, including embedded technology, identification technology (such as voice, gestures, and eye), sensor technology, connection technology, flexible display technology and so on. The data of iiMedia Research shows that a variety of equipment shipments reached 2 million 300 thousand in the Chinese wearable device market in 2012, and the market scale reached 610 million yuan. It is expected that shipments in Chinese wearable device market in 2015 would reach more than 40 million, and the market scale would reach 11 billion 490 million yuan. IiMedia Research believe that Chinese wearable device market will get rapid growth and become the core of the global wearable device market with the gradual rise of the global wearable device market. Different wearable devices with forms will also enter into people's lives from all aspects, so wearable devices will become the market focus.

With the development of wearable smart products, smart watches undoubtedly become the focus. Specifically speaking, the smart watch has a smart watch system, equipped with a smart phone system to be connected to the network. It can achieve multiple functions, and can synchronize the phone's text messages, e-mail, photos, and music, etc. At the same time, with the development of mobile technology, watches are paid attention to increasing the function of mobile. For example, watch can be used to show time only in the past. Today, it also can through intelligent mobile phone and home network connected to the Internet, display the information, Twitter, news, weather information and other content. This smart watch is becoming a new type, such as Samsung Galaxy Gear 2 - smart watch will make voice control, camera, telephone, intelligent perception, the local MP3 player and infrared remote control widely used in this product. In addition, the Gear2 can use a lot of new advanced sensors to track your heart rate when you are exercising, recording the number of steps you take every day, in order to effectively measure your motion state. Voice input is also the highlight of this product, as it allows you to record and answer messages, setting the schedule, open and close, as well as some other basic tasks. Obviously, this smart watch can give users more intelligent user experiences.

With the development of technology, product features have become increasingly complex, which conflict with human's simplicity needs when they use the product. So people become to concern the usability of the product. Availability has become an indispensable part for consumers to buy products (Mack and Sharples 2009). Furthermore, when users use smart watches, there will be obstacles, slow operation and easy mistake-making, which puts forward higher requirements for product availability. Kansei Engineering, a new products design technology concerning about consumer emotional experience or sensory needs, has been widely used in product availability studies in recent years. Such as: Han et al. (2001) is available for different emotional definition and dimension of division based on user satisfaction of consumer electronics products; Huang et al. (2013) proposed the concept of appearance availability, and she thought the appearance of the product is an important attribute characteristics which can bring certain impacts to the availability of product. Camargo et al. (2014) proposed a method that based on the study of semantic attributes of products and the analysis of usability test data after analyzing the relationship of product semantic attributes by integrating user perception. It can be seen that the use of Kansei Engineering for quantitative research on product usability can enable designer more effective to find the availability of the main and objective factors, then the design can be improved.

2   Literature Review

2.1   Outline of Analytic Hierarchy Process

Analytic hierarchy process (AHP), developed by Thomas L. Saaty of the University of Pittsburgh in 1971, is applicable for decision-making problems with uncertainties and multiple evaluation criteria.

AHP is a systematic approach for complex problems, which features in constructing the complicated decision-making problem into a type of hierarchical structure. Thus the complex relationship of the impact factors could be systematically connected and the assessment items are decomposed from the high-level assessment criteria to the lower-level one until the lowest level of the candidate program, and through a comprehensive quantitative assessment to obtain objective decision-making results (Saaty 1980).

In summary, the purpose of AHP is to deal the problem with uncertain factors under multiple evaluation criterion and reduce the burden of thinking through systematic dismantling and pairwise comparison to quantify the results; Then re-integration of quantitative data to obtain weight to help decision-makers determine the merits of the strategy and reduce the risk of strategic errors. According to the Saaty (1980) study, the field of application of the Analytical Hierarchy Process approach includes decision priorities, alternatives plan, selection of best practices, determination of requirements, resource allocation, forecasting result or risk assessment, performance measurement, system design, ensuring system stability, optimization, planning, conflict resolution and other 12 categories of problems.

Cheng and Mon (1994) pointed out that the AHP method has five missing project in the decision-making assessment: 1. AHP method is mainly used in clear (non-fuzzy) decision-making. 2. The AHP method uses an asymmetric scale to measure the problem. 3. The AHP method can not cover the uncertainty of human cognition. 4. The ranking of the AHP method is rather unclear. 5. Decision-makers subjective judgments, choices and preferences which have a great impact to the selection results of AHP method; then, the judge is wrong, the decision-making results are not correct. Although the AHP method is simple, easy to solve and can deal with qualitative and quantitative properties of the advantages simultaneously, but it's assessment scale is the degree of human perception to things, which has been divided into nine scales to be measured. So it can't fully cover subjectivity, fuzzy and uncertain factors of human cognition. For example, when the problem is complex, sensitive, incomplete information, decision-making program is not sufficient to fully reflect the decision-making environment, or expert knowledge of the program is not comprehensive enough to determine the human judgment with a variety of possibilities at this time, unable to point out that a certain value in comparing two important degree of judgment, just only description by language. Fuzzy Hierarchy Analysis (FAHP) can be used to transform fuzzy language expression into fuzzy scale data, which is more suitable for the fuzziness of semantic judgments in real environment (Zheng Jing Vulgar 2003).

2.2   Outline of Fuzzy Analytic Hierarchy Process

The AHP of Saaty is easily operated and widely used in multi-criteria decision-making. However, the human's fuzzy knowledge about scale, which AHP can not express, is the biggest disadvantage. So when the AHP method is put forward, it causes numerous scholars discussion and also appeared a lot of improved methods. Van Laarhoven and Pedrycz (1983) introduced the concept of fuzzy number into the pairwise comparison matrix of AHP in 1983, and developed the Fuzzy Analytic Hierarchy Process (FAHP) to solve the subjective, fuzzy and inaccurate problems in traditional Analytic Hierarchy Process.

Buckley (1985) combines the fuzzy set theory and the hierarchical analysis method to transform the expert opinion to the fuzzy positive and reciprocal value matrix by using the trapezoidal fuzzy number. Then the fuzzy weight is obtained through the geometric mean that the alternatives about the fuzzy weights are calculated by cascade connection. Finally, use the weight of each alternative fuzzy membership function graphics and figure out the priority of the program. Although the method is more stringent, the calculation is very complicated.

Zhang Meijuan (2003) pointed out that the real environment is a fuzzy environment, in view of human's uncertain thinking characteristics, so the Analytic Hierarchy Process is expanded to the fuzzy environment. The fuzzy hierarchy analysis can be constructed on the fuzzy Decision-making problem to deal with effectively and it can make up for the Analytic Hierarchy Process disadvantage of not solving the problem that it lack of fuzziness. Wei et al. (2005) used fuzzy complementary judgment matrix to replace Van Laarhoven and Pedrycz used forward and backward value matrix about FAHP method in the study of supplier selection in enterprise logistics outsourcing which can avoid the asymmetry of measurement scale and has the advantage with being easy to use.

In summary, scholars have pointed out that we must import the concept of fuzzy in the complexity environment when AHP is used to assess the weight because human thinking is so uncertain that subjective cognition or semantic scale asymmetry problem often affect the decision-making results. In the application of FAHP, the decision-making factors of pairwise comparison are set in five groups and six groups, and the fuzzy semantic comparison table proposed is used to reduce the evaluation scale by Chen and Hwang (1992) which is in accordance with the habit of the questionnaire fillers. The selected questionnaire will be converted into triangular fuzzy numbers and substituted into the fuzzy complementary judgment matrix which is different from the general inverted value matrix. This method can solve the problem of AHP (Non-fuzzy) decision to make on the scale of asymmetric measurement of things and human knowledge of uncertainty and other issues. In summary, this study uses Fuzzy Analytic Hierarchy Process to calculate the importance of each level to analyze the different functional preferences degree of men and women in the smart watch. First of all, through the smart watch user research and the views collection of experts and designers, filter out the evaluation criteria and sort out the representative criteria and sub-criteria. After determining the criteria to establish the hierarchical structure by means of the two paired criterion comparison method to design the questionnaire, and then definition evaluation values base on fuzzy semantic. The questionnaire data is built into the matrix table, then the fuzzy weight value is calculated to get the eigenvector and the eigenvalue. Finally, the evaluation criteria and the sub-criterion are used to calculate the questionnaire data which could be sorted. This paper deduces the difference between male and female consumers in the functional preference of smart watches.

3 Use Fuzzy AHP to Extract Customer Preferences Factors on the Core Attributes

3.1 Method of Fuzzy AHP

AHP (Analytic Hierarchy Process) was originally put forward by Saaty in the early 1970s to solve the problem of allocating scarce resources in the military. In order to adapt to the linguistic features of human judgment, the concept of fuzzy is integrated into AHP to measure the core attributes of smart watches and the relative importance of relevant degree (customer preference). In general, fuzzy AHP consists of the following steps:

Firstly, through the research on users of smart watches and opinions collected from experts and experienced product designers, select the criteria of evaluating and sort out 5 representative criteria and 13 sub-criteria by classification. These criteria consist of five criteria including battery time, way of interacting, communications, security, development of APP and 13 sub-criteria including speech, touch, physic, auxiliary communication, independent communication, waterproof, theftproof, time management, geographic information, smart life, sports health, sociality and battery time. After deciding the criteria and sub-criteria, compare 4 criteria with each other, and then compare 12 sub-criteria in pairs.

Secondly, collect judgment opinions from different experts. If the evaluator S evaluates m core attributes, and the expert k makes a pairwise comparison by fuzzy scale, the relative importance between Ci and Cj is shown in the following fuzzy matrix (Table 1):

Table 1. Random index used by fuzzy AHP

The sequence of matrices (standard number)						
n	2	3	4	5	6	7	8
RI	0	0.58	0.90	1.12	1.24	1.32	1.41

$$S_k = \begin{bmatrix} \tilde{b}_{11k} & \tilde{b}_{12k} & \cdots & \tilde{b}_{1mk} \\ \tilde{b}_{21k} & \tilde{b}_{22k} & \cdots & \tilde{b}_{2mk} \\ \vdots & \vdots & \vdots & \vdots \\ \tilde{b}_{m1k} & \tilde{b}_{m2k} & \cdots & \tilde{b}_{mmk} \end{bmatrix} \quad i = 1, 2, \cdots m,$$

$$j = 1, 2 \cdots m, \ k = 1, 2, \cdots S,$$

$\tilde{b}_{ijk}$ represents the fuzzy preference between C_I and C_J. This preference is evaluated by the evaluator K. And then the experts' decision are aggregated by eqs, as shown in the formula.

$$\tilde{b}_{ij} = (L_{ij}, M_{ij}, U_{ij}) \tilde{b}_{ji} = \tilde{b}_{ij}^{-1} = \left(\frac{1}{U_{ij}}, \frac{1}{M_{ij}}, \frac{1}{L_{ij}} \right)$$

$$L_{ij} = \min_k (\tilde{b}_{ijk}), M_{ij} = median_k(\tilde{b}_{ijk}), U_{ij} = \max_k(\tilde{b}_{ijk})$$

$$b_{ij} = \left(\frac{L_{ij} + M_{ij} + U_{ij}}{3} \right)$$

$\tilde{b}_{ij}$ represents an aggregated fuzzy number, but b_{ij} represents the defuzzification fragility of the usage of "Regional Center" scheme.

Thirdly, calculate the largest eigenvalues and their corresponding eigenvectors in order to estimate the weight of the m criterion:

$$A = \begin{bmatrix} b_{11} & b_{12} & \cdots & b_{1m} \\ b_{21} & b_{22} & \cdots & b_{2m} \\ \vdots & \vdots & \vdots & \vdots \\ b_{m1} & b_{m2} & \cdots & b_{mm} \end{bmatrix}$$

$$AW = \lambda_{max} W$$

Among them A is the m × m fragility matrix of m attributes, γ_{max} is the maximum eigenvalue of matrix A, and W is the corresponding eigenvector. In this study, eigenvectors are considered as customer preferences (importance weights).

Finally, check the consistency of the matrix. The transport property means if C1 is better than C2 and C2 is better than C3, then C1 is better than C3. The consistency index (CI) and the consistency ratio (CR) shown below are used to determine the consistency of the quality of decision:

$$CI = \frac{\lambda_{max} - n}{n - 1},$$

$$CR = \frac{CI}{RI},$$

Among them CI represents a index of inconsistency (a value closer to zero represents greater consistency) and RI is a random index. If the value of CR exceeds 0.1, the decision-making process is considered to be inconsistent. Therefore, the evaluators need to revise their evaluation viewpoints. Finally, the weighted value reflects the degree of influence and importance of the perceptual evaluation index on the smart watches, and analyzes the preference characteristics of the smart watches by gender differences.

3.2 Process of Investigation

Taking the smart watches as evaluation object, 10 types of common smart watches on the market are selected. And some users are interviewed. Among them 30 people are asked to answer the questionnaire, including 15 males and 15 females. Those people include experienced smart watch users, researchers and scholars engaged in product design, and people who are familiar with smart watch, such as shopping guides. They have been asked to mark the product equative index after finishing the questionaire. In addition, some design major students are also invited to take the test. There are two main reasons for selecting this group as subjects: First, the group is a fashion group and they use the smart watches in high-frequency so they have the ability to complete the requirement test for all tasks; Second, they are sensitive to appearance availability and perceived usability of smart watches than the average person. So that they are scoring has a certain degree of distinction. The task test includes five criteria, which are battery time, interaction, communication, security and APP development, and 13 sub criterias, which are voice, touch, physical, auxiliary communication, independent communication, waterproof, theftproof, time management, geographic information, intelligent life, sports health, sociality and battery time. The evaluation grades were 1–9 grade, taking the efficiency into consideration of the research, participants can just tick the corresponding number of criteria in the questionnaire while marking, which are easily operated so that this marking process can be widely accepted by the users.

Ask the subjects of the interview to compare the functional indicators of the first layer of products with each other, which are interaction and communication, interaction and security, interaction and development of APP, interaction and battery time, communications and security, communication and development of APP, communication and battery time, security and development of APP, security and battery time, development of APP and battery time, as shown in Table 2. For example, as for interaction and communication, choosing 1 means they are both important, and tick in the corresponding direction of the preferred function. Choosing one of 2, 3 and 4 means slightly important. Choosing one of 4, 5 and 6 means more important. Choosing one of 7, 8 and 9 means very important. And the number 23456789 is the degree of importance. The larger the number, the more important is the function. Then we ask the subjects to fill in the comparison table of the second layer function. The comparison of the second layer function is the detailed classification for indicators of the first layer, so there are four second layer function comparison table in total. For example, way of interacting is divided into three categories including speech, touch and physic. The mutual comparison among these three types is the second layer comparison of the interactive function. The users can select the appropriate level of numbers. Finally, ask the subjects to evaluate the second layer function of smart watches, as is shown in Tables 3, 4, 5 and 6.

Table 2. The first layer function comparison of smart watch

	9	8	7	6	5	4	3	2	1	2	3	4	5	6	7	8	9	
Interaction																		Communication
Interaction																		Security
Interaction																		Development of APP
Interaction																		Battery time
Communication																		Security
Communication																		Development of APP
Communication																		Battery time
Security																		Development of APP
Security																		Battery time
Development of APP																		Battery time

Table 3. The comparison of the second layer security feature index of smart watch

	9	8	7	6	5	4	3	2	1	2	3	4	5	6	7	8	9	
Waterproof																		Theftproof

Table 4. The comparison of the second layer communication feature index of smart watch

	9	8	7	6	5	4	3	2	1	2	3	4	5	6	7	8	9	
Auxiliary communication																		Independent communication

Table 5. The comparison of the second layer interaction feature index of smart watch

	9	8	7	6	5	4	3	2	1	2	3	4	5	6	7	8	9	
Speech																		Touch
Speech																		Physic
Touch																		Physic

Table 6. The comparison of the second layer development of APP feature index of smart watch

	9	8	7	6	5	4	3	2	1	2	3	4	5	6	7	8	9	
Time management																		Geographic information
Time management																		Smart life
Time management																		Sports health
Time management																		Sociality
Geographic information																		Smart life
Geographic information																		Sports health
Geographic information																		Sociality
Smart life																		Sports health
Smart life																		Sociality
Sports health																		Sociality

4 An Analysis of Men and Women's Preference for Smart Watch

4.1 Men's Preference for Smart Watches

According to Table 7, the top five indicators of men's preference for smart watches according to importance from top to bottom are battery time, voice interaction function in interactive mode level, smart life and sports health function in the development of APP level, and waterproof function in the security level. The following is the specific discussion.

As for men's preference for smart watches, battery time is the most prominent feature. In general, due to the diversified development of smart watches and its important role in our daily lives, users rely more on smart watches. Therefore, battery time has also become an important factor to evaluate smart watches. In particular, when users use smart watches in the daytime, they not only watch the clock, but also read the news through the watches connecting to WIFI. Besides, they also make voice calls with friends or family, send and receive text messages and monitor the state of physical movement in real time. These functions are indispensable in use, and they are all based on the power to complete their tasks, which highlights the importance of battery time of the smart watches. If the smart watches lack of electricity, it will bring about a

Table 7. The detailed data of weight distribution about criteria (male)

Criteria	Weight between criteria (%)			Sub criteria	Weight within criteria (%)			Weight among criteria (%)
Interaction	0.1077	0.1822	0.3129	Speech	0.4429	0.596	0.7952	0.1086
	0.1077	0.1822	0.3129	Touch	0.236	0.3107	0.4101	0.0566
	0.1077	0.1822	0.3129	Physic	0.0714	0.0932	0.1277	0.0170
Communication	0.0692	0.1131	0.1975	Auxiliary communication	0.339	0.4995	0.7718	0.0565
	0.0692	0.1131	0.1975	Independent communication	0.3237	0.5005	0.737	0.0566
Security	0.0484	0.0799	0.1324	Waterproof	0.7217	0.8537	1.0073	0.0682
	0.0484	0.0799	0.1324	Theftproof	0.1247	0.1463	0.1741	0.0117
Development of APP	0.1614	0.2867	0.4917	Time management	0.0891	0.1723	0.337	0.0494
	0.1614	0.2867	0.4917	Geographic information	0.045	0.0831	0.1736	0.0238
	0.1614	0.2867	0.4917	Smart life	0.1702	0.3407	0.6686	0.0977
	0.1614	0.2867	0.4917	Sports health	0.1329	0.2662	0.513	0.0763
	0.1614	0.2867	0.4917	Sociality	0.0771	0.1377	0.2521	0.0395
Battery time	0.1564	0.2635	0.4354	Battery time	1	1	1	0.2635

consequence that the products can not be used normally, so that the users can not finish what they originally wanted to do, which makes people feel that it isn't practical, which undoubtedly degrades the user experience. Therefore, battery time has become the most important factor of smart watches. As is pointed out in Apple's promotional literature, the most important feature of Apple Watch is battery time. Other features ranging from health tracking to send and receive text messages are all additional features. According to this, battery time has become the most important factor of smart watches. On the other hand, because of the fast pace of modern life, men are busier in their work and have more compact routines. Therefore, a kind of smart watches which need to recharge repeatedly will increase their trouble in life, which will make them fed up with it. For this reason, smart watches with long battery time catch more attention and recognition of the men.

According to the statistics, users' concern for the voice interaction is second only to the battery time. The specific reasons are mainly divided into three aspects: 1. The natural restriction of the small screens of smart watches requires a higher standard for their human-computer interaction function. This limitation leads to the consequence that it is not suitable for accurate keyboard input and touch gestures, especially in blocking nearly entire screen with a finger. This requires that the users have to click it and input things accurately with their fingertips. This is obviously not suitable for men with large hands. Therefore, voice interaction has become the most reasonable way; 2. Because men attach great importance to efficiency, the natural direct interaction with the machine is particularly important. And language is the most common and direct way of human communication. Male users can wake up the device at any time, "seamlessly" access to information and give instructions without any sense of jerky and acosmia. This is the most direct and convenient way of interacting of the smart watches.

According to Table 7, in the development of APP application, users attach more attention to battery time and voice than smart life and sports health, but smart life and sports health are ranked close to the top. Smart life is a life service mobile software designed for users, which is powerful to provide users with remote control of household appliances, set timing tasks and other human services. So it is easy to build cloud intelligent life. Specific performance: 1. As for the control household appliances remotely, users can control the switches and other functions at any time. An application can control all the household appliances, in order to meet the needs of living leisurely of more men, which makes life more convenient. 2. The flexibility to set the timing task, accurate execution of the program on time. 3. Share your equipment with family and friends with one click, and enjoy smart life easily. At the same time, the APP of sports health catches more attention of men. Nowadays, male office workers often spend time in the office so that they are unable to have long-time outdoor activities and specially spend time on exercise in the gym. Therefore, they try to record their daily steps and running with APP of the smart watches, which makes it easy to understand their own amount of exercise. Besides, this APP also has some additional features, such as recording daily sleep situations, informing you deep sleep time, light sleep time and awake times every day. And it collects statistics of users weekly and monthly, so the historical statistics can be easily read. Therefore, it catches attention of men.

At the same time, the waterproof function in the security level has also caught attention of male consumers. Waterproof function enhances the practicality of the watches. In the case of rain, the watches are likely to be wet. Therefore, waterproof is an indispensable function of smart watches. In addition, based on the habit of watching clock while swimming, a smart watch used to be worn while swimming will undoubtedly appeal to users. In a word, the waterproof function is a more useful additional feature for male users in the design of smart watches.

4.2 Women's Preference for Smart Watches

According to Table 8, the battery time of smart watch is the biggest concern for women, next is intelligent Life, and then followed by sports health. In the wake of developments in science and technology, smart watch increasingly offers added functionality and strong adaptability, which lead to tremendous improvements in smart watches on power consumption. However, women pay more attention on battery time while they use smart watches. This is because in the process of using smart phones, women spend more time on chatting online, looking through news and shopping online. These has made battery time become the most basic factor, at the same time, a long time of battery provide basic security services. Therefore, better battery time of smart watch has become key concerns when women choose and buy watches.

After battery time, intelligent life is the most focused application for female users, there are three main points: First, some applications of smart life installed on smart

Table 8. The detailed data of weight distribution about criteria (Female)

Criteria	Weight between criteria (%)			Sub criteria	Weight within criteria (%)			Weight among criteria (%)
Interaction	0.1614	0.2817	0.4917	Speech	0.1702	0.3107	0.6686	0.0875
	0.1047	0.1912	0.3029	Touch	0.236	0.3217	0.4131	0.0615
	0.1077	0.1841	0.3126	Physic	0.0714	0.0833	0.1243	0.0153
Communication	0.0673	0.1128	0.1975	Auxiliary communication	0.3382	0.4983	0.7724	0.0562
	0.0694	0.1129	0.1975	Independent communication	0.3237	0.521	0.723	0.0588
Security	0.0491	0.0769	0.1322	Waterproof	0.7217	0.8519	1.0113	0.0655
	0.0473	0.0779	0.1326	Theftproof	0.1247	0.1471	0.1742	0.0115
Development of APP	0.1614	0.2872	0.4921	Time management	0.0893	0.1726	0.3272	0.0496
	0.1614	0.2876	0.4917	Geographic information	0.0452	0.0842	0.1746	0.0242
	0.1077	0.1823	0.3129	Smart life	0.4429	0.587	0.7952	0.1070
	0.1614	0.2823	0.4917	Sports health	0.1702	0.3345	0.6686	0.0944
	0.1616	0.2847	0.4918	Sociality	0.0771	0.1396	0.2523	0.0397
Battery time	0.1564	0.2647	0.4354	Battery time	1	1	1	0.2647

watch that has remote control function. These Apps can operate remotely a portion of household appliances. Smart watch is more convenient relative to the mobile phone. Second, in allusion to home intelligent security systems, users can quickly alert when they wear smart watches. Thus, users can deal with the problem immediately. Nevertheless, mobile phone is not portable in some occasion. Third, women just pass out wrist to show their watches and then can be scan payment when they are shopping in the mall, which makes the way of consumption is more convenient, and the application is very popular among female users.

According to statistics, women's concern for the voice interaction is second only to battery time and smart life. There are three reasons: 1. Smart watches can not only calculate steps as their basic function, they can also detect the users' physical condition and acquire more accurate data than mobile phones because they are close to the skin for a long time; 2. Smart watches are more convenient than mobile phones because users can wear watches but not holding mobile phones for the whole day. For example, in the process of exercise or long-distance running, it is not convenient to carry mobile phones due to the larger amplitude of movement. However, smart watches can be worn on the wrists all the time, so the data of sports health are more comprehensive; 3. The smart watches have a unique health detection function. For example, Cling, a kind of smart watch, is equipped with the light sensor and temperature sensor at bottom, which can directly monitor users' heart rate and body surface temperature and other healthy statistics. It has a more comprehensive intelligent detection function, so the sports health application of smart watches has been favored by users. Furthermore, the sports healthy application of the smart watches specifically function to record the user's trajectory in order to show the sports results for users in the process of wearing the watches. In addition, this application can also set the target training volume in order to stimulate the users' desire to exercise, thus promoting them to complete the target volume positively. Therefore, the application of sports health encourages women to take exercises and keep fit effectively, which catches attention of women.

References

Mack, Z., Sharples, S.: The importance of usability in product choice: a mobile phone case study. Ergonomics **52**(12), 1514–1528 (2009)

Han, S.H., Yun, M.H., Kwahk, J.: Usability of consumer electronic products. Int. J. Ind. Ergon. **28**, 143–151 (2001)

Huang, W., Wang, F., Wu, J.: Usability research of personal consumer electronics based on user emotion. Light Ind. Mach. **31**(4), 115–118 (2013)

Camargo, M., Wendling, L., Bonjour, E.: A fuzzy integral based methodology to elicit semantic spaces in usability tests. Int. J. Ind. Ergon. **44**, 11–17 (2014)

Cheng, C.-H., Mon, D.-L.: Evaluating weapon system by analytical hierarchy process based on fuzzy scales. Fuzzy Sets Syst. **63**, 1–10 (1994)

Van Laarhoven, P.J.M., Pedrycz, W.: A fuzzy extension of Saaty's priority theory. Fuzzy Sets Syst. **11**, 199–227 (1983)

Wei, Z., Shen, J.-S., Chen, J.-J.: Applied research on MF suppliers selecting for MF outsourcing decision. J. Beijing Jiaotong Univ. (Soc. Sci. Edn.) **4**, 32–35 (2005)

Three-Finger-Tap Methods for Navigation in 3D Scenes on Tablet

Hongyu Wang[✉], Takeshi Umezawa, and Noritaka Osawa

Graduate School of Advanced Integration Science, Chiba University,
Chiba, Japan
{homyetw,ume}@chiba-u.jp, n.osawa@faculty.chiba-u.jp

Abstract. This paper proposes two three-finger-tap methods designed for navigation in three-dimensional (3D) scenes. The proposed methods can be implemented in 3D applications installed on a tablet. One method integrates rotation, scaling, and translation (RST) into the specification of a triangle as a region of interest. The other is a point-of-interest (POI) method using multi-touch techniques without a virtual widget. Two experiments showed that the proposed methods perform better than a conventional RST method in two kinds of 3D scenes. Moreover, questionnaire results support the conclusion that the two methods not only performed better than a conventional POI method, but also enabled users to interact as freely and precisely as with a conventional RST method.

Keywords: 3D virtual environment · Multi-touch · 3D navigation

1 Introduction

Various three-dimensional (3D) application programs have been implemented on tablets. A 3D virtual environment in an application typically includes a virtual space that is wider than a scene viewed on a tablet display from one viewpoint. Users must change viewpoints to navigate in the virtual environment and want to control the viewpoint camera easily. Although viewpoint movement has been studied extensively in 3D virtual environments, investigating how to use fingertips on a multi-touch screen of a tablet to move the viewpoint on a tablet remains difficult. In this paper, we propose using three-finger-tap navigation methods in 3D virtual environments.

Generally speaking, if there is an area of interest in a scene, we want to navigate efficiently to see that area. In conventional 3D navigation methods, navigation must be decomposed into actions such as rotation, zooming, and translation. Moreover, we must apply these actions in an appropriate order. However, decomposition is unnecessary when changing viewpoints in the real world, and it is difficult for many people who are not skilled to navigate on a tablet using decomposition. User interfaces for 3D navigation without decomposition have not been sufficiently investigated. Therefore, we propose and evaluate methods of navigating by designating a region of interest using multi-touch contact and moving the viewpoint to ensure that the region enters the field of view appropriately.

© Springer International Publishing AG 2017
M. Kurosu (Ed.): HCI 2017, Part II, LNCS 10272, pp. 276–287, 2017.
DOI: 10.1007/978-3-319-58077-7_22

We organize the remainder of this paper as follows. We present some previous work in Sect. 2. Section 3 describes our two methods in detail. We show our experiments and discuss our user study in Sects. 4 and 5, respectively. Finally, in Sect. 6, we draw conclusions and suggest directions for future work.

2   Related Work

In 3D virtual environments, typical interaction tasks [1] include navigation, object selection and manipulation, and system control. Navigation and manipulation in 3D scenes require six degrees of freedom (DOF), but the input of each contact finger on a touch screen provides only two DOF. In addition, Jankowski and Hachet [7] showed that over the past few decades, input devices have mostly included a mouse, a keyboard, and a touch screen, and we expect that this will persist till the next decade. Therefore, researchers have proposed many solutions to the problem of how to use those input devices for more effective interaction.

2.1   Rotation-Scaling-Translation Methods

The rotation, scaling, and translation (RST) method has been used widely for interaction in two-dimensional (2D) contexts, with many 3D applications also using RST on multi-touch tablets. The RST method enables the control of rotation, scaling, and translation using multi-touch gestures. Reisman et al. [12] described a screen-space method that extends 2D RST semantics into 3D environments. Their method captures the semantics of the traditional 2D RST multi-touch method and extends its principles into the 3D environment. The principles define a controllable mapping between points in the environment and on the screen. This RST method can be used not only to manipulate 3D objects, but also to navigate in a 3D virtual environment and can provide solutions for curbing ambiguities and rotational exhaustion. However, the screen-space method has two drawbacks, *bimanual interaction* and *decomposition*. A user can interact with three or more touch points, as he or she can use his or her two hands for navigation or manipulation, perhaps creating a limitation because one hand cannot pass through another. A user must decompose navigation into rotation, scaling, and translation operations.

2.2   Point-of-Interest Methods

Mackinlay et al. [10] proposed a viewpoint movement technique called point-of-interest (POI). Given a user-selected location point on the surface of a target, the POI technique determines a normal vector at the given point and calculates the distance between the point and the new camera and then rotates the virtual camera and face toward the point automatically. This technique suggests the metaphor of "go to" and has several advantages such as ease-of-use and speed. As a typical example, Hachet et al. proposed a method, called Navidget [4], that permits speedy and easy positioning of a camera by a user. A user first selects the POI by a pen or mouse, then a spherical widget is popped up, and it guides the user to specify the orientation of the camera. This method extends the POI technique by enabling additional controls, exercised by circling motion and virtual widget. In other words, this method overcame the drawback of the user's inability to specify the distance between the positions of a viewpoint and a target (POI) and the orientation of the viewpoint. We have noticed that while Navidget [4] works well for navigating in 3D virtual environments, a user must first draw a circle to select the target and then wait for the virtual widget to appear. In other words, navigation is decomposed into two steps.

Mackinlay *et al.* [10] categorized navigation into *general, targeted, specified coordinate*, and *specified trajectory movement*. The POI technique is included in targeted movements, and many researchers have extended this technique using different key points. UniCam [13] is implemented as a click-to-focus method that aims at automatically choosing the endpoint of the camera orbit according to the proximity of the edges of some object. Drag'n Go method [11] combines the POI technique with some features of direct manipulation. Because it is based on a trajectory path between camera and target, the method can fully control its position and distance relative to a target and its traveling speed. Declec *et al.* [3] proposed a method that extends the POI technique using a trackball to control camera movement. Users drag the POI on the surface of the target to keep the area of interest visible. However, this method can be used only to examine models closely using a touch screen or mouse.

2.3   Other Conventional Methods

Not only in navigation, many two- or three-touch 3D manipulation techniques have been proposed (cf. Table 1). One two-finger method [9] is based on the idea of encoding the DOF by the movement of two fingers of one hand. Two tabletop methods, shallow-depth [5] and sticky tools [6], use one-, two-, or three-touch contact to control five or six DOF. Knoedel and Hachet [8] showed that it takes less time for a user to manipulate objects by directly touching the screen where the object is displayed than with indirect touch, i.e., touching a touchpad instead of touching the screen, while indirect interaction improves efficiency and precision, especially in 3D virtual environments.

Table 1. Classification of each method by features

Item \ Method	Navidget	UniCam	Drag'n Go	ScrutiCam	Screen-space	Two-finger	Sticky Tools	DS	Shallow-depth
Contact Points	one	one	one	one	one/two/three or more	two	one/two/three	one/two/three	one/two/three
Manipulation/ Navigation	navigation	navigation	navigation	navigation	manipulation/ navigation	manipulation	manipulation	manipulation	manipulation
Input	mouse/touch/ stylus	mouse/stylus	touch	mouse/touch	touch	touch	touch	touch	touch

2.4 Region-of-Interest

Brinkmann [2] describes use of a user-specified rectangle as a region of interest (ROI) in digital compositing. The ROI is widely used in computer vision, but not in 3D navigation. We use this concept for 3D navigation. When a user specifies an ROI in 3D scenes, the viewpoint is changed to obtain a new position and orientation to enable the ROI to be seen appropriately within a display. We think it is important for a user to be able to move a viewpoint easily to see his or her ROI in 3D navigation. Jankowski and Hachet [7] observed that touch input favors direct and fast interaction. Especially, since the appearance of the iPhone in 2007, multi-touch techniques have been used widely. In light of these considerations, we propose and evaluate three-finger-tap methods.

3 Proposed Methods

We propose two methods for viewpoint movements in 3D virtual environments using a three-finger tap. The principal idea of one method, the ROI method, is to let a user specify a triangle area he or she wants to see as an ROI. The other method, the Tripod method, is a multi-touch extension of Navidget. Both of the proposed methods integrate translation and rotation (moreover the ROI method can also integrate scaling into one operation) rather than decomposing movement into RST, in contrast to Navidget and the screen-space method [12] Both of our methods determine the direction of the viewpoint using three-finger touch in order, and thus it is possible to move the viewpoint to see the rear of an object.

3.1 ROI Method

If a user is interested in an area, he or she can specify the area. The ROI method enables a user to specify an ROI by a triangle with three-finger touch and then move the viewpoint to see the ROI appropriately on the screen in one operation. A user taps three points U, P, W on the screen, causing rays to be cast through the three points from the current viewpoint, hitting the surfaces of target 3D virtual objects on A, B, C, respectively (cf. Fig. 1). Points A, B, C form an ROI ($\triangle ABC$) in a 3D scene. The new viewpoint will face the ROI. The viewpoint V is on the normal $\vec{n}$ of $\triangle ABC$, which is through G, the center of mass of $\triangle ABC$. The distance between V and G is adjusted to m, and the ROI is fully and appropriately displayed on the screen. The distance m is expressed by the formulas

$$m = \frac{\frac{1}{2}h}{tan\frac{\alpha}{2}} = \frac{\frac{1}{2} \times \gamma h_{max}}{tan\frac{\alpha}{2}} \tag{1}$$

$$h_{max} = max\{h_B, h_C\} \tag{2}$$

where $h_B = \frac{\overrightarrow{AB} \cdot \overrightarrow{AG}}{\left|\overrightarrow{AG}\right|}$, $h_C = \frac{\overrightarrow{AC} \cdot \overrightarrow{AG}}{\left|\overrightarrow{AG}\right|}$, α is the angle of the vertical field of view,

$max\{h_B, h_C\}$ is the maximum of h_B and h_C, h is the height of the vertical field of view,

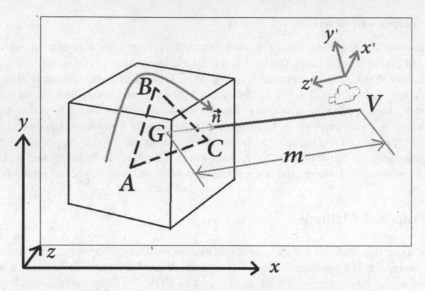

Fig. 1. ROI method

and γ is a size coefficient that we set to $\gamma = \frac{10}{9}$ in our experiment to ensure that the screen displays a scene that includes the complete ROI from the new viewpoint.

3.2   Tripod Method

The Tripod method aims to improve Navidget [4], which uses the metaphor of circling for selection and the mode of rotating the viewpoint orientation using a spherical widget. The principal idea of Tripod method is that we do not need to use widget, but instead can use terrain or objects near the target to complete the navigation. Differently from Navidget, we do not use a widget for changing orientation. The Tripod method uses a three-finger tap to define a center of rotation B (the second touched point) in the scene and the position and direction in a conical space (using the first and third touched points A and C) which is defined by the normal vector of the triangle (cf. Fig. 2). The definitions of symbols in the figures are the same as in the ROI method except that in this method GV is a definable value whose best value depends on the target size (a value of one to five times the target size is appropriate for viewing all of the target).

4   Experiments

We conducted a pilot study to improve our understanding of how our two methods perform in different scenes.

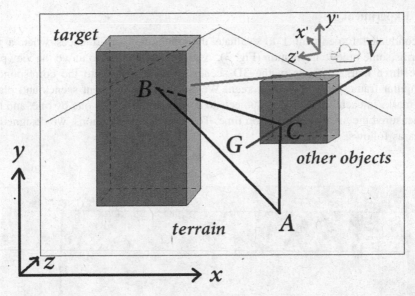

Fig. 2. Tripod method

4.1 Goal

We compared our two methods with two conventional methods: RST and POI. We evaluated the performance of all of the methods against two different kinds of task scenes. After the experiments, we conducted a questionnaire survey. The questionnaire and its results helped us to understand subjects' attitudes and feedback on each method regarding which method is simpler and more effective. In addition, we evaluated how effective each method is for each scene, and how users feel about each method.

4.2 Subjects

Ten subjects (five women and five men) participated in the experiments. They are all right handed, averaging 24 years of age. All of them are university students who had no previous familiarity with our test environment or methods.

4.3 Apparatus

We implemented our proposed methods in a virtual environment using the game development platform Unity (version 5.3.4f1). The experiments used ASUS ZenPad3s 10 (2016), a 9.8-inch tablet with a 2,048 × 1,536 pixel multi-touch screen, with Android OS v6.0 installed. Users placed the tablet on the desk and interacted with our environments using their right hands.

4.4   Experiment 1

We conducted Experiment 1 to evaluate the methods' performances when a user performs some precise navigation (Fig. 3). A subject was asked to move the viewpoint to see three marked points in the 3D scenes and put them into the corresponding rectangular frames drawn on the screen. We selected ten different scenes and placed three marks in each scene, asking subjects to complete the scenes one by one, and then we measured the average completion time. To cover many situations, we designed the scenes as follows:

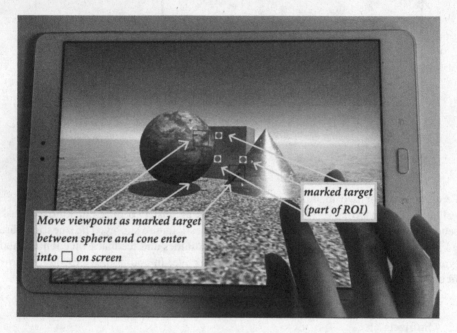

Fig. 3. Experiment 1

(1) Selecting three primitive shapes: sphere, cube, and cone;
(2) Designing ten scenes to show an area of interest: The front, side, top, and back of an object; containing two objects with the gap between the objects visible; containing two objects with one blocked by the other; containing two objects with both objects visible from an aerial view; containing three objects and watching from the side of the object; containing three objects, with all three objects from the gap between two objects visible; and containing three objects with all three objects visible from an aerial view;
(3) Using different conditions in different scenes: width of gap, size of object, and initial position of the viewpoint camera.

4.5   Experiment 2

We conducted Experiment 2 to evaluate the methods when a user navigates in a 3D landscape, such as on the street or plaza, with regard to how he or she navigates to a specified target fast (Fig. 4). Virtual buttons with ordinal numbers were placed in a 3D landscape, and then a subject was asked to press the virtual buttons in ascending order. This task included ten scenes, in each of which a subject was required to enlarge a virtual button sufficiently for it to be seen, but we did not prescribe a strict distance or direction. To cover various situations, we designed the scenes as follows:

(1) Designing a large space, such as a city block, including buildings and a plaza;
(2) Selecting ten different locations for target buttons: on a roof, in a window, and on the ground of a plaza;
(3) A virtual arrow is displayed to mark the position of a virtual button to reduce search time;
(4) When we are sufficiently close to a button, its color is changed to show proximity.

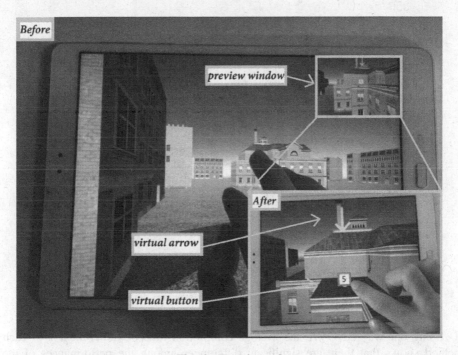

Fig. 4. Experiment 2

4.6   Procedure

Each subject was asked to sit in a chair, and the tablet was placed on a desk. Subjects performed two experiments in the same order, Experiment 1 first and then Experiment 2.

We designed a training session with five scenes. Subjects first practiced each method, and then participated in the experiment. In each experiment, a Latin square was used to counterbalance methods with subjects.

After the experiments, we asked the subjects to fill in a five-point Likert scale questionnaire, including the items "ease-of-use," "ease-of-understanding" "interact-fast," "interact-precisely," and "interact-freely," and also interviewed them. They rated the items between 1 (strongly disagreement) and 5 (strongly agreement), indicating strong disagreement, disagreement, neutrality, agreement, and strong agreement.

4.7 Result

As shown in Fig. 5, Experiment 1 showed that the average completion times of the Tripod and POI methods were shorter than RST and ROI methods, and Experiment 2 showed that the average completion times of the ROI and Tripod methods were shorter than those of Method RST and Method POI.

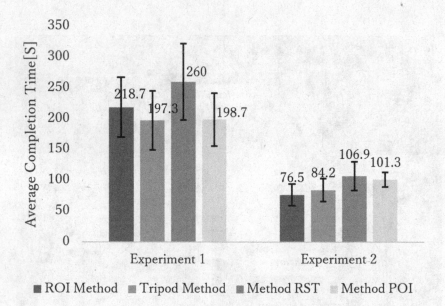

Fig. 5. Average completion time with standard deviation bars

Using one-way ANOVA, the average completion time of Experiment 1 of each method shows that there are significant differences among the performances of the methods Experiment 1 ($F(3,36) = 2.997$, $p < 0.043$). And in Experiment 2, the result also shows that there are significant differences within groups ($F(3,36) = 5.503$, $p < 0.003$).

The Tukey's HSD test shows that the differences are significant ($p < 0.05$) between group pair (1) ROI and POI and (2) ROI and RST, and marginally significance between Tripod and RST in Experiment 2.

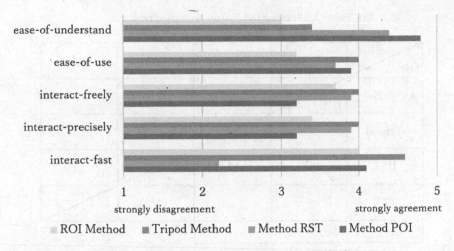

Fig. 6. Subjective evaluation of the four methods

These results suggest that the proposed methods are effective in both Experiment 1 for accurate viewpoint adjustment and Experiment 2 for fast navigation. Differences between our proposed methods are not clearly shown in the experiments.

The questionnaire (cf. Fig. 6) result suggested that the average ratings of "You can use the system quickly" in the POI method is 4.1, in the Tripod method is 4.6, and in the ROI method is 4, better than the 2.2 in the RST method. The Wilcoxon signed rank test (cf. Table 2) showed that compared with the RST method, the ROI, Tripod, and POI methods were significant for "interact-fast." Tripod method was marginally significant for "interact-freely," compared with the POI method. Furthermore, the test also indicates that the Tripod method performed better on "interact-precisely" than the POI and ROI methods. However, the average rating on the item "You can understand the system easily" for the ROI method is 3 and for the Tripod method is 3.4, while the RST method scores 4.4 and the POI method scores 4.8. The Wilcoxon signed rank test also showed that the RST and POI methods were more significant than the ROI and Tripod methods. It seems that the subjects did not fully understand the relationship between the proposed methods and the 3D scenes, because the subjects underwent training in the methods only once, and several of them did not have a sense of 3D environments. We need to do further experiments to clarify the features of the proposed methods.

5 Discussion

Regarding the scenes of Experiment 1, in which all three objects have smooth surfaces, we did not consider including some cases of irregular objects, such as sculptures, when designing the experiment. In Experiment 2, when the button is located in the window or in a very far position, two subjects could not control the camera appropriately and thus moved the viewpoint to within a building or to a very far position through a building or an unexpected location, by using the POI method. Therefore, considering its characteristics, the performance of the POI method in Experiment 1 requires reverification.

Table 2. Summary of Wilcoxon signed rank test

precisely / fast	ROI	Tripod	RST	POI
ROI		*		
Tripod				△
RST	**	**		
POI			**	

**: 0.01   *: 0.05   △: 0.1

use / freely	ROI	Tripod	RST	POI
ROI		△		
Tripod	△			
RST				
POI		△		

**: 0.01   *: 0.05   △: 0.1

understand	ROI	Tripod	RST	POI
ROI		*	**	**
Tripod			*	**
RST				
POI				

**: 0.01   *: 0.05   △: 0.1

The RST method is considered to be not bad, except for "interact-fast." For the items "interact-freely" and "interact-precisely," the POI method is the worst. If the user is trained adequately, our two methods might provide effective user interfaces for navigating precisely, freely, and fast in most 3D scenes.

6 Conclusion

We proposed two 3D camera-positioning methods for 3D navigation and compared them with two conventional methods. Two experiments suggested that the proposed techniques perform better than the conventional RST method without three-touch contact in two different settings, although further investigation is needed. In the future, we will evaluate the proposed methods in further scenes including some that contain difficult shapes and irregular objects.

References

1. Bowman, D.A., Kruijff, E., Laviola, J.J., Poupyrev, I.: An introduction to 3-D user interface design. Presence: Teleoper. Virtual Environ. **10**, 96–108 (2001)
2. Brinkmann, R.: The Art and Science of Digital Compositing, p. 184. Academic Press, San Diego (1999)
3. Declec, F., Hachet, M., Guitton, P.: Tech-note: ScrutiCam: camera manipulation technique for 3D objects inspection. In: IEEE Symposium on 3D User Interfaces 2009, pp. 19–22 (2009)
4. Hachet, M., Decle, F., Knödel, S., Guitton, P.: Navidget for 3D interaction: camera positioning and further uses. Int. J. Hum. Comput. Stud. **67**(3), 225–236 (2009)
5. Hancock, M., Carpendale, S., Cockburn, A.: Shallow-depth 3D interaction: design and evaluation of one-, two- and three-touch techniques. In: Proceedings of SIGCHI Conference on Human Factors in Computing Systems, pp. 1147–1156 (2007)
6. Hancock, M., Ten Cate, T., Carpendale, S.: Sticky tools: full 6DOF force-based interaction for multi-touch tables. In: Proceedings of the ACM International Conference on Interactive Tabletops and Surfaces, pp. 133–140 (2009)
7. Jankowski, J., Hachet, M.: Advances in interaction with 3D environments. Comput. Graph. Forum **34**(1), 152–190 (2015)
8. Knoedel, S., Hachet, M.: Multi-touch RST in 2D and 3D spaces: studying the impact of directness on user performance. In: Proceedings of the 2011 IEEE Symposium on 3D User Interfaces, pp. 75–78 (2011)
9. Liu, J., Au, O.K.C., Fu, H., Tai, C.L.: Two-finger gestures for 6DOF manipulation of 3D objects. Comput. Graph. Forum **31**(7), 2047–2055 (2012)
10. Mackinlay, J.D., Card, S.K., Robertson, G.G.: Rapid controlled movement through a virtual 3D workspace. In: Proceedings of the SIGGRAPH Computer Graphics, vol. 24, pp. 171–176 (1990)
11. Moerman, C., Marchal, D., Grisoni, L.: Drag'n Go: simple and fast navigation in virtual environment. In: IEEE Symposium on 3D User Interfaces, pp. 15–18 (2012)
12. Reisman, J.L., Davidson, P.L., Han, J.Y.: A screen-space formulation for 2D and 3D direct manipulation. In: Proceedings of the 22nd Annual ACM SIGGRAPH Symposium on User Interface Software, pp. 69–78 (2009)
13. Zeleznik, R., Forsberg, A.: UniCam—2D gestural camera controls for 3D environments. In: Proceedings of the 1999 Symposium on Interactive 3D Graphics, pp. 169–173 (1999)

HCI, Children and Learning

The Social Nature of Programming: Children and Fluency

M. Cecilia C. Baranauskas[✉] and Marleny Luque Carbajal

Institute of Computing, NIED – UNICAMP, Campinas, Brazil
cecilia@ic.unicamp.br,
marleny.carbajal@students.ic.unicamp.br

Abstract. Computational thinking has gained a revival as a movement to promote the early teaching of programming concepts in the schools; it has been considered a fundamental skill in the contemporary world, not only for computers scientists but also for anyone in the future. In fact, in the last decades, the digital technology has provoked profound transformations in a world in which computer systems are underlying objects of the physical and social world, mediating our actions in society. This amplified view of the computational technology in our life brings to question the reach of the 'computational thinking' concept and leads us to reflect on what would mean fluency with (digital) information technology. In this work, we argue that a wider understanding for 'computing' should be addressed if we are to construct computer-based applications that enrich human life in the world. In this paper, we revisit the concept of computational thinking from its origins in computer science to the educational use of it, and address programming as designing in different layers of sign system, bringing issues of the social and informal nature (culture, commitments) to the formal and technical levels of programming. A case study with the design and use of a low cost tangible programming learning environment illustrates our proposal. The article ends up with a discussion on how the proposal faces risks of exaggerating the enthusiasm for the subject and concludes highlighting main findings.

Keywords: Computational thinking · Tangible User Interface · Social construction

1 Introduction

The apparent fluency of the young people with digital technologies has been observed by their facility in sending text messages, playing online games, browsing the Web. Nevertheless, these so-called "digital natives" are not necessarily fluent in creating digital technology (their own games, animations, etc.); as highlighted by Resnick et al. [20], "It's as if they can "read" but not "write" (p. 62).

The expression "computational thinking" has gained popularity and interest of academics in the last years, especially after the publication of Wing [24] claiming *"Computational thinking is a fundamental skill for everyone, not just for computer scientists"* (p. 33). Although the concept is still fuzzy, there is some acknowledgement regarding its meaning as the mental processes that take place when solving 'problems'

© Springer International Publishing AG 2017
M. Kurosu (Ed.): HCI 2017, Part II, LNCS 10272, pp. 291–308, 2017.
DOI: 10.1007/978-3-319-58077-7_23

by creating computer programs to solve them. In general, the subject is studied observing and analyzing the way youth are engaged in programming activities during their learning processes.

This subject is definitely not new as Papert [17], already in the sixties, pioneered the Logo language construction and started to study the learning processes of children, engaged in 'powerful ideas' mediated by the Logo programming language constructs and the artefacts designed to reach their possibilities. More recently, the work of Resnick and colleagues with the Scratch language, which has roots in Logo's tradition, has confirmed that programming helps people to learn important problem solving and design strategies such as modularization, iterative design, carrying this knowledge, in some way, to other domains. Moreover, and more important, programming provides opportunities for meta-thinking, as it involves the creation of external representations of someone's problem-solving process [20].

In this work, we argue that programming is not just a move on internal (in the head) and external (in the program) representations of problem solving. Rather, it has the influence of other artefacts and other people sharing interests and meaning making through different forms of programming together (e.g. by creating narratives, by designing together).

Although not always referring to the early tradition of Logo, the revival of the subject, now with the nomenclature of "computational thinking" owns a lot to its origins, although our perception is that a very technical perspective is being taken on the subject. In our view there are many aspects of knowledge construction, including the informal and formal ones that, besides the technical, should be brought to the situation of programming; among them, the affective aspects of interaction, the social meaning and the creative engagement in a codesign process, to name a few. Thus, by social, we do not mean sharing the product of programming with others in the website of the community; rather, we analyze programming processes and programming environments as spaces for co-construction, i.e. for codesign of a "program".

In this work, we intend to revisit the early concepts, analyze the recent movements on studying 'computational thinking', and seek to understand the computational thinking from a socio-situated and systemic perspective [3, 4], drawing on a recent case study addressing the design of constructionist environments based on low cost tangible technologies.

The paper is organized as follows: Sect. 2 contextualizes and situates the object of study summarizing historical views of programming; Sect. 3 presents and discusses our view of programming as a social construction, the main concepts and principles. The following sections illustrate some ideas with a case study conducted with a low cost tangible programming environment. Finally, the conclusion section summarizes the main findings while suggesting further work on the subject.

2   Background – Computational Thinking

The expression 'computational thinking' has gained a revival as a movement to promote the early teaching of programming concepts in the schools, as a new discipline, adding to the math and the other regular ones. This resurgence came after the work of

Wing [24], who encountered a perfect timing to relaunch the idea of *"a universally applicable attitude and skill set everyone, not just computer scientists, would be eager to learn and use"* (p. 33). In the last decade, society in general have been making sense of the digital technology in different manners, and this same technology has provoked profound transformations in the way people live. These transformations encompass all aspects of life: working, learning, having fun, making business, communicating within social groups, and even communicating with things, participating in a world in which computer systems are underlying objects of the physical and social world, mediating our actions in society. Thus, this scenario reinforces the idea of a new literacy more and more demanded. This amplified view of the computational technology in our life brings to question the reach of the 'computational thinking' concept. Would computational tool users, procedures followers, digitally literate but not expert in computer science, be included in the target audience of the prospective benefits of computational thinking? or should the concept refer only to mental processes triggered by those creating new code?

Different communities, especially from the Computer Science and from the Education domains of interest seem not always agree on the concept, on the possible benefits of practicing this type of thinking, and on who benefits with the movement. In fact, to understand the expression and situate it in the current social context, a historical perspective on the concept from these different communities is needed. Nevertheless, this does not mean a consensus is necessary, as the different perspectives may add to our understanding of the subject.

2.1   The Origins and Evolution

In the early history of computing, computational thinking was related to the special style of reasoning about problem solving ultimately by 'coding' a solution to it. Even the pioneers of Computer Science as Dijkstra [9] and Knuth [14] inquired about the nature of computational thinking, comparatively relating it to its mathematical roots. As compared to mathematical thinking, both argued that the identity of the computing discipline originates from the unique mental processes it promoted.

To characterize the computational mental processes, Dijkstra [9] reflected on the intellectual demands the programmer faces that are typical of him/her. He starts arguing the programmer has to have the ability to express herself/himself in both a natural language and in formal systems. As it comes first, the natural language expression is a necessary 'tool for thinking' before any formalization also required, especially when new concepts have to be introduced. For him, the new concepts are not those occurring in the problem statement, but those necessary for the programmer to find, describe and understand his own solution to the problem; and this is an activity the programmer has to do all the time. In his words, *"(...) given the problem, the programmer has to develop (and formulate!) the theory necessary to justify his algorithm"* (p. 611). Although he recognizes this type of thinking exists in other knowledge domains, he argues that it is heavier in computer science. Besides precision and explicitness, what he thinks is typical of the programming activities is the concerns with 'size', for which the hierarchy is considered a key concept. In other words, he is speaking of the level of granularity one has to consider along the problem understanding and the development of its solution. What he considers the particular characteristic of the competent programmer, when compared to thinking in other domains is his/her abilities do navigate back and forth through different semantic levels in the hierarchy, between local and global considerations, microscopic and macroscopic concerns. To this intellectual agility, he named "mental zoom lens" (p. 611). When compared to what a mathematics standard curriculum provides, he suggests the programmer is demanded more on organizing his/her thoughts rather on organizing his/her symbols.

Based on examples of academic works from mathematicians and from computer scientists Knuth [14] studied and summarized two types of thinking patterns computer scientists use that were absent from the mathematicians works he analyzed: one related to the notion of 'complexity' and the other related to the notion of the dynamic *state*[1] of a process. By 'complexity', he meant the economy of operation; i.e. the mathematical works, although constructive, were not paying attention to the cost of construction in terms of the algorithmic efficiency. The second missing thinking pattern is related to the assignment operation, i.e. changing values of quantities. For him, changing states of affairs or seeing glimpses of a computation is typical of algorithms and algorithm thinking. The understanding of data structures for example, which are fundamental in computer science, relies on the ability to reason in terms of processes states and the interaction of processes acting in parallel. He considers dealing fluently with concepts that are inherently non-uniform, like different kind of steps found in an algorithm, a strength of the computer scientist way of thinking.

In the late 80's, with the formalization of Computer Science as a Discipline by ACM and IEEE, the understanding of computational thinking started to broaden with the definition of 9 (nine) subareas of computing. Besides algorithms, data structures and programming languages, other subjects appeared as core of Computer Science including architecture, numerical and symbolic computation, operating systems, software methodology and engineering, databases and information retrieval, artificial intelligence and robotics, and human-computer communication [8]. For Wing [24], computational thinking includes a group of mental tools that reflects the width of the Computer Science field and we should add it to children's education, in addition to their reading, writing and arithmetic analytic abilities.

More recently, as computing has been considered the third pillar of science, together with theory and experimentation, a broader description of the discipline is being considered, from the old study of algorithms to the study of (both natural and artificial) information processes [23]. Within this new perspective, along theory and abstraction, "design" skills have been considered central for creating the software systems currently demanded in terms of reliability, usability, security, etc. Thus, it seems we should consider a conceptual movement from programming (coding) to designing (a system).

---

[1] In italics as in the original text (p. 181).

2.2   Implications in Education

Many people valued the kind of thinking computer science promotes, starting from Knuth [13], who considered it a general-purpose mental tool with potential to aid the students in the understanding of other disciplines such as "chemistry, linguistics, or music" (p. 327). The assumption is that attempting to formalize things in algorithms, leads to much deeper understanding than being told about things or other traditional ways of learning. For Wing [24], among the mental tools experienced with the computational thinking are: using abstraction and decomposition, thinking recursively, heuristic reasoning, planning, choosing appropriate representations and modeling the problem, etc. All those aspects were already present in the works of Papert [17] and his colleagues with the Logo language in the 80's; the main difference lies in that Papert's ideas were not restricted to computing per se, rather he targeted a much more profound influence in the education of children.

The concept of "constructionism", brought with Papert and his colleagues, is a heritage of the Piagetian concept of "constructivism", supporting the idea that to build a knowledge "in the head" is facilitated when one can build something in the world (a computer program, a drawing, a story, etc.). By constructionism, Papert [16] refers to learning by "making things", and making them work in the real world, talking about them, and reflecting on our own doing. In his words, *"we learn better still if we combine our doing with talking and thinking about what we have done"* (p. vi). The constructed things must pass the "test of reality"; if they do not "work" they represent a challenge to understanding and overcoming the obstacles. What distinguish things build with Logo is the contact with "powerful ideas" that enable those things to serve as "transitional objects" for children's appropriation of the ideas. Logo as a "mathland" – an environment in which children could learn mathematics as naturally as they learn to speak their native language, i.e., without formal instruction, is an instantiation of the constructionist intentions. The "turtle geometry" was what provided the Logo environment with a more accessible way of approaching mathematics than the ways taught in schools.

Concerning technology in education, Papert [16] mentions the two "wings" of it he names "the technology as an informational medium" and "the technology as a constructional medium", stressing there is an imbalance on them, culture being dominated by the informational one, although both are important. Part of learning is related to getting information (from a book, from listening the teacher, for example), and part is related to building things valuable for the learners. For Papert, this imbalance may be the result of lacking suitable technology-based environments as constructional medium.

Besides being a theory of learning, the constructionism and Logo's philosophy represent a strategy of education, a way of thinking in computers and education, and a guide to the design of learning environments. The agency of the learner in the learning process and in the environment may be what best characterizes a constructionist approach to children's involvement with programming. Nevertheless, besides the informational and the constructional dimensions involved in those learning environments, we argue that a communicational medium is lacking if we want to consider widening the types of thinking to encompass also design; this medium would be necessary for a social shared construction in the learning environment.

3 Programming Systems and Socially Aware Environments

For Tedre and Denning [23], "*Design is the bridge between the technical and the theoretical realms of computing and the needs and problems of communities and customers*" (p. 124). A project for the inclusion of computing technology in a formal learning space (e.g. a school), in our view, must be built with the parties that involve that space as an organization, in its informal, formal, and technical aspects. As in a constructionist environment, they bring their own knowledge, experience and inventiveness to the situations at hand in the Project; at the same time, their participation in the process allow them the construction of meaning for the technological artefact, as well as more awareness of their own learning process.

The challenges of a project involving digital technology, education and society demand a systemic, socio-situated vision [3] and involve:

- At the societal level, to reduce disproportionalities in access to and use of knowledge;
- At the formal level, educate for/with the use of technology and new media; essential aspect to empower citizens with the skills necessary to guarantee the universal right to information and freedom of expression;
- At the technical level, create inclusive environments and systems that can support the constitution of a digital culture where the parties are also knowledge producers.

Implicit in our model is the recognition that communication among stakeholders and interested parties is a culturally defined social phenomenon and the artefacts constructed to mediate such communication must ensure their creative and collaborative use in order to lead to proposals for technology use that make sense to those involved.

Our framework draws on the "semiotic onion", adapted from Stamper et al. [21], as the conceptual basis of our understanding of designing information systems. It illustrates the structure of informal, formal and technical layers of meanings in the conceptual model we use for the socio-situated view of a problem/project understanding and the "solution" to be designed (Fig. 1).

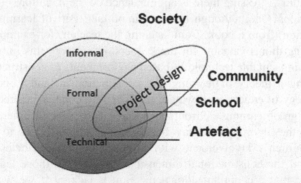

Fig. 1. The 'semiotic onion' model for designing a project [3, 4]

In our understanding, solving a problem (e.g. through the computer, but not restricted to it) involves a systemic thinking, situating the "program" in the nucleus of the "semiotic onion" in which informal, formal and technical levels of meaning of the social group coexist. At the outer (informal) levels, meanings and intentions are established, beliefs are formed and commitments are established and changed. At formal levels, forms and rules replace meanings and intentions of the outermost levels of the onion. At the technical levels (onion core), technical solutions (coding) are generated as consequence of meanings in the previous levels. Thus, designing a solution to the problem involves the articulation of the three layers of meanings related to the problem/project, by the involved parties.

In the proposed framework, understanding the problem, analyzing and proposing solutions, evaluating results of actions throughout the project are built by the action of the participants in workshop dynamics. The foundation of the whole process is the workshops, named Semioparticipatory [1, 3, 4] in reference to their bases, that articulate meanings of the (social) world towards the (technical) system and vice versa. Several artefacts are used in the workshops, such as a diagram of interested parties (DIP), an evaluation frame (EF) and a semiotic ladder (SL); other artefacts are customized to the aims of each workshop and its audience. The DIP supports the participants in raising awareness regarding the (other) parties direct or indirectly involved in the problem, the reach and impact of the solutions in not only technical terms, but social as well. The EF enables anticipation of problems the interested parties would face with the prospective technology, to propose solutions. The SL allows organizing and sharing the demands of the Project in six different layers of information, going from the physical world, to the social world, passing through the empirics, syntactic, semantic and pragmatic steps [22]. Figure 3 in the next section illustrates some artefacts and workshops conducted with the interested parties in the context of a tangible programming environment Project.

The proposed socio-situated framework represents computing technology as a social invention and, in a Project, promotes the sharing of responsibility in its reconceptualization, giving voice to the stakeholders in the design and development of the Project with its communicational mechanisms. The situations fostered in the Semioparticipatory workshops open space for this expressive manifestation of the parties and their understanding requires immersion of the facilitators in scenarios for which traditional methods of design do not fit.

Thus, instead of bridging the gap between the technical and the theoretical computing issues, in the perspective we bring with this framework, designing a computing system should be a continuous movement from social to the technical issues, and back to the social; the theoretical computing issues are underlying this movement.

4 Designing TaPrEC: A Low Cost Tangible Programming Environment for Children

Even recognizing the potential benefits of developing computational thinking, literature has shown that children have difficulties with the traditional form of programming, not only in learning the syntax of rigid symbols, but also in the use of complex programming environments [7]. There are authors [11] who affirm that programming languages based on TUIs (Tangible User Interfaces) [12] have the potential to facilitate the learning of complicated syntaxes, to promote collaboration, and to facilitate teachers to maintain a positive learning environment.

Nevertheless, tangible technology is considered delicate, expensive and non-standard [10]. This can be a problem in educational contexts where cost is a deciding factor when choosing a particular technology. Another important factor to consider is the process of including tangible programming environments already existing in an educational context different from which it was thought. Forcing a technology into a new educational context can be a slow and complicated process.

Considering the above, we have designed, created and evaluated the Tangible Programming Environment for Children (TaPrEC), involving the main stakeholders (researchers, teachers and students) in the design process to ensure that the solution created make sense to them. In this process, we used the Semioparticipatory Design Model [1, 3, 4], inspired by Organizational Semiotics, which articulates at the same time the development of interactive systems and social practices with stakeholders. In this model, the user concept does not fit and is replaced by "interested parties", as a way to respect values, interests and competences of those involved in the product and/or design process. This reconceptualization of roles implies recognizing in users the competence to design and enabling their creative and responsible involvement in design solutions.

TaPrEC allows children to create computer programs by organizing tangible objects, applying three basic programming concepts: Sequences, Repetitions, and Procedures [6]. The architecture of the TaPrEC consists of a Raspberry Pi [19], the RFID technology incorporated in the Programming Blocks and a Processing Software developed in the programming language Scratch [20]. We aimed at proposing an environment to enable children to learn basic programming concepts, which is a low-cost alternative to teaching programming in schools and potentially allowing a smoother transition to virtual learning environments and the world of computer programming.

4.1 Design Rationale

The vision of the TáPrEC environment is to promote the development of computational thinking in the context of elementary school students through the programming l based on tangible interfaces. Among the key requirements of the environment were: (i) users should be able to build 'physical' computer programs by organizing tangible objects and applying basic programming concepts such as Sequence, Repetition, and Procedures; (ii) the environment should require a minimum cost investment; (iii) the environment should have tangible objects using a simple, although robust technology, to allow easy maintenance, and personalization; (iv) the software used for data processing and the creation of learning scenarios should be as simple as possible to facilitate the customization and creation of new learning scenarios by the teachers themselves; and (v) in the design process, key stakeholders should be involved to ensure that the solution created makes sense to them.

One of the main motivations of our project is to use technology accessible to socioeconomically disadvantaged populations without making a huge investment, while maintaining the quality of the interaction. For this purpose, we chose to use Raspberry Pi 2 B Model, a low-cost single-board computer. The other technology used in TaPrEC is a Radio Frequency Identification (RFID). The operation of RFID systems is simple: the RFID tag, which contains the identification data, generates a radiofrequency signal with this data. This signal is detected by an RFID reader, responsible for reading the information and sending it in digital format for a specific application.

The second component of the environment is the Programming Blocks, which is a set of colored pieces of puzzle-like wooden blocks containing an RFID tag on one side and a graphical symbol on the other as label for the block. We embossed the symbols to enable a visually impaired person, for example, to build tangible programs. The colors of the programming blocks are inspired by the Scratch language to allow a smooth transition to its programming environment later.

The third component of the TaPrEC environment is the Processing Software, developed in the Scratch 1.4 programming language. The software stores the identifiers of the RFID tags of the Programming Blocks. Codes that represent the same functionality are grouped into a list. When the program receives a sequence of identifiers, it: (i) checks if the identifier matches any of the action lists; (ii) execute the Scratch code associated with this action; finally (iii) shows the results in the Scratch environment. Figure 2 illustrates the TaPrEC environment constructed, its components and the architecture of the system showing how its three components interact with one another.

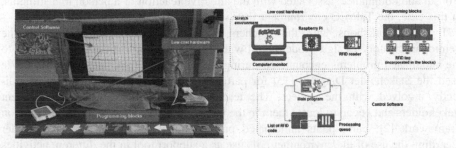

Fig. 2. TaPrEC physical environment (left) and system architecture (right)

The control blocks indicate the start and end of the program. The tangible program information is entered into the TaPrEC environment through the RFID reader. The environment has a limited number of basic commands. To construct a program in the TaPrEC environment it is necessary to organize the Programming Blocks in a specific sequence: first the start block, then the action blocks and finally the end block.

4.2   The TaPrEC Usage Experimentation

Context and participants

The TaPrEC project was developed with a partnership of the Division of Children's Complementary Education, which is an educational space inside the University of

Campinas, in Brazil, State of São Paulo aiming at supplementary education for the children of the university employees. In that educational physical space, we carried out the activities in the atelier room. The activities were formally scheduled by the coordinator of that Division in the set of weekly activities of the involved teachers and students. The Research Ethics Committee (CEP) of the university approved the project.

The practice of using the TaPrEC environment we are going to illustrate here occurred along the year of 2015. In the next subsection, we present some results of the workshops, conducted with both the teachers, and children separately within the TaPrEC environment. We worked with sixteen children between 7 and 10 years old, and with thirty eight teachers between 31 to 54 years old.

Method

Eleven (11) workshops were conducted along the semester, with teachers of the educational unit, and 10 with children and their responsible teacher. During this process, the system was being introduced and its design being yet refined. We conducted two types of workshops: Experimental Workshops (EW) and Semioparticipatory Workshops (SpW). We filmed all workshops, after the written consent of all participants or their respective representatives in the case of children. The videos allowed us to observe the behavior of the system environment, demands for improvements and for new functionalities along the process, and the participants' actions.

In addition to filming, at the end of each workshop all participants (children and teachers) filled the SAM (Self-Assessment Manikin) instrument [5]. SAM is a nonverbal instrument of self-assessment of emotions, specifically the level of pleasure, arousal and dominance, associated with the affective reaction of a person to a stimulus, in this case, the TaPrEC environment they were experimenting.

In two Workshops with the teachers, we worked with the artifacts of the Semioparticipatory Design Model [1, 3] with the objective of articulating solutions to the anticipated problems encountered during the use of the TaPrEC environment. We used the Stakeholder Diagram [15] for participants to identify those directly or indirectly involved with the project. The teachers talked and identified the different stakeholders and began to locate them in the layers of the diagram. With the Evaluation Framework [2], participants anticipated problems and issues of each stakeholder regarding the use of the environment, its use as a support tool in the different activities of the school and possible solutions. With the Semiotic Ladder [21, 22] participants were able to understand the different implications of the environment from the physical world to the social world.

During the Experimental Workshops, we worked with the teachers and the children separately. In each workshop, the participants formed teams to solve simple exercises of displacement of a character in a scenario, applying the programming concepts implemented in the TaPrEC (Sequences, Repetitions and Procedures) environment.

The dynamics of the workshops involved: first, a quick introduction on the concept of programming focus of the particular workshop, followed by the explanation on the operation of the tangible blocks associated with that concept. In the sequence, each team worked the proposed problems by planning a solution (in a paper), setting up the solution organizing the tangible objects, and finally inserting the tangible program into the TaPrEC environment using the RFID reader. The processing software was in charge of executing the tangible program and showing the results. The last step in the workshops involved the affective evaluation of their experience in the workshop, where teachers and children were invited to complete SAM. In Fig. 3 (top) we illustrate a SpW with teachers, and the three moments of the Experimental Workshop with children are illustrated in Fig. 3 (bottom).

Fig. 3. Semioparticipatory Workshops with teachers and artefacts being filled (top) and the three stages of the Experimental Workshops (bottom)

Results

From the Semioparticipatory Workshops

With the collaborative construction of the Stakeholders diagram (Fig. 3, top, the artefact hanging on the left) we sought to clarify the real scope of the project and its importance not only to those directly involved in its operation, but also to the entire community. The teachers raised the parts that direct or indirectly influence or undergo the influence of the project. Some stakeholders raised by the teachers were: trainees placed in the Contribution layer; the school management group placed in the Source layer; the pedagogical games on DVD placed in the Market layer; and non-governmental organizations placed at the community level.

Once teachers identified the parties involved in the project, teachers began to fill out the Evaluation Framework (Fig. 3, top, the artefact in the middle). The group discussed specific issues/problems of each of the Stakeholders for the use of TaPrEC and raised ideas or solutions envisaged. For example, in the Operation layer they raised the following question/problem: "In what type of activities would the environment be better utilized?" The answer/solution raised was: "the environment could be used to help math, literacy, socialization and motor development." The results of this discussion were essential to clarify the demands on each of those involved parties.

With the Semiotic Ladder (Fig. 3, top, artefact on the right), the different abstraction levels of the TaPrEC project were clarified, from the physical level where each of the devices used in the environment were identified and explained, to the social world where the development of computational thinking promoted by the environment was highlighted.

From the Experimental Workshops

During the Introduction phase of the Experimental Workshops we explained the syntax of programming blocks through a simple tangible program that illustrated the concept to be worked on in that Workshop. In the Execution phase, we visited each work team answering the doubts of the participants. The children collaborated with each other in solving the exercises, suggesting which programming blocks to use, as well as their order and quantity. The results of the work groups show that our dynamics allowed participants to learn the logic to construct a tangible program in the TaPrEC environment (beginning, sequence of actions and end) and programming concepts (Sequences, Repetitions and Procedures). In general, all teams were able to make a plan for their tangible solution and execute it with the blocks in the environment. The researchers helped the work teams by making suggestions or observations that helped them to find the mistakes of the tangible solution and thus manage to solve the exercise. We observed that the main difficulty some participants had in one of the Workshops was to understand that during the definition of a procedure the tangible program does not perform any action; only when the procedure is invoked by its name, it executes the actions previously defined. Despite this difficulty, other groups demonstrated that they understood the concept and operation of this programming concept. Regarding the symbols used in the tangible blocks, children sometimes confused the "End Repeat" symbol with the "End" from the control block. This is probably because both blocks used a similar (circular) symbol.

The solutions (algorithms) created by the groups of participants should result in a specific action (create a geometric figure, walk the right path in a labyrinth, etc.); we observed how the participants faced error correction situations until reaching the established goal. Some teams were able to get the correct solution on the first try (after planning), others faced with not expected responses, began the debugging process. First, they checked whether the paper solution matched the tangible solution. Sometimes it happened that they forgot to put some programming block or they had put one block in place of another. If both solutions coincided, they began to analyze the tangible program by sequentially comparing the tangible program blocks with the result shown on the monitor to find out the program error. During that debugging process the children talked with each other in the group raising suggestions to correct the tangible program, some suggested changing one block for another, others wanted to reduce or add the amount of a particular block. When the children took a long time trying to find the mistake, they became anxious and asked for help, but when they were able to solve the problem, they felt pride and joy.

The teachers were exposed to the same type of problems as the children and did not present difficulties in solving them. The objective of working separately with teachers was to enable them to operate the environment so that in the near future they could customize it and create their problem situations to work on different themes using programming concepts with children. We received many suggestions from teachers along the Workshops who helped us to improve the environment and the organization of the Workshops; one example of suggestion was "to improve the designs of the programming blocks labels to facilitate the interpretation".

From Affective Evaluation

The results of the Self-Assessment of Emotions were almost all positive with both children and teachers. Only the workshop addressing Repetition showed a neutral result regarding affective states with younger children (7 years), still in the process of literacy (with difficulty for the paper planning stage, for example). The Workshop addressing Procedures was conducted with older children (8 and 9 years old), which showed an excellent result (100% pointing out positive feelings).

5 Discussion

Incorporating the use of a new technological tool in the classroom is not limited to teaching how to use it simply; part of the process is to work out challenges related to technical issues (such as how to handle and maintain technology) as well as pragmatic issues (what to do with technology in activities related to school content). Similarly, including a programming environment in an educational context should not be disconnected of meaning the involved people (children, teachers, managers, parents) make of it. That is why our environment is not only focused on the technology used to create a tangible programming environment, but also on supporting the stakeholders, those people affected direct or indirectly by the Project. The Semioparticipatory Workshops conducted in the scope of this work resulted in several outcomes: (i) for the teachers to understand and reimagine how the inclusion of the TaPrEC environment in the daily life of the school could support different activities and skills developed with the children; (ii) for all the involved people to understand the influence of other stake-holders (e.g. trainees, director, coordinator) in the process; (iii) and for anticipating problems different parties could have regarding the technological environment and its use, and propose solutions.

When we planned the Semioparticipatory Workshops, we decided to carry them out after the Experimental Workshops, so that the teachers had a broader view of the functioning of the TaPrEC environment with the children and could better understand possible problems in the process of incorporating the environment into activities with their students. Teachers imagined the use of the TaPrEC environment as a support in the teaching of mathematics, space orientation, logic and literacy, not the programming *per se*. Nevertheless, they emphasized the opportunity for children to create their own programs and to know the computer from another point of view, not exclusively as users of applications.

In general, the preliminary results regarding the TaPrEC design as well as its use with the children were very encouraging. Nevertheless, it is worth analyzing Tedre and Denning [23] list of seven risks the new enthusiasm for computational thinking revival could bring and we should avoid. They are commented as follows, as an opportunity to reflect on our own work:

Lack of Ambition. The first risk they call our attention for is the scope of understanding for 'programming' in a world very much different from that of the 80's. The digital systems have become an integral part of everyday life, underlying our processes of communication, making business, working, learning, living in society. Thus, in this context, our conceptions of literacy must be revisited to include other forms of digital composition, besides coding. The analytical abstract world, as used to be seen in computing, should give place to a view that includes the (social) complexities of the (real) world. A socio-situated approach to systems design, illustrated by the design of TaPrEC - the tangible programming learning environment, involving the interested parties was carried out as an effort towards a new way of looking at programming practices and programming environments design for educational contexts.

Dogmatism. This risk is related to the claiming of computational thinking to be the "best" way of thinking in problem solving, over other forms of thinking, e.g. design thinking, science thinking, critical thinking, ethical thinking, etc. Instead, we should have Papert's spirit of epistemological pluralism to the subject, being open to alter-native approaches to problem solving thinking. In our proposal, a holistic and plu-ralistic view of 'computational thinking' is envisaged with the socially aware framework to the design of (software) systems, in which the interested parties are directly involved in socio-situated contexts of design. Their voices are brought together with the designers and other interested parties voices to the process of designing the environment and to the ways of using it.

Knowing versus Doing. The third risk, according to Tedre and Denning, concerns the assessment of the students for their competencies at designing computations. Those authors observe there is a difference on the concept of skill and of knowledge of facts or information, and the relationship between these knowledge progressions, as measured by formal frameworks available for K-12 education (in the USA), and skill or competencies acquisition is unclear. In our approach, the children are programming together, doing it in groups, in a participatory way; mutual learning is shown by the results the groups accomplish in interacting and communicating to solve a problem. They are learning not only by making things work in the programming environment, as in Papert's Logo projects, but also by communicating with their peers along the process of constructing the solution together.

Exaggerated Claims. This risk regards repeating the same mistakes of the past by not considering the historical view and the predecessors' studies in this subject. It regards also the still unsubstantiated claims that computational thinking confers problem-solving skills transferable to non-computational knowledge domains. This debate continues and the answers, in our view, are not reachable looking only into the cognitive processes (in the head) of those engaged with the types of mental processes specific of computer scientists, nor in the computation represented in the coding (in the program). Rather, it may be hidden as well in the way people affectively relates to the subject and work together to communicate and make sense of the solution in their situated contexts (in the world, in the life).

Narrow Views of Computing. This risk is concerned with considering "coding" as a central issue of the computational thinking and of the computer science. Tedre and Denning argue that reducing computing to programming is a myth from the 70's, never embraced by the pioneers of computer science; moreover, coding skills are less and less relevant to the design challenges and design tools of contemporary computing. A deep understanding of the discipline in its breadth in terms of computational thinking is needed to avoid that risk. The semiotic framework we draw upon enables to see programming as designing in different layers of sign system, bringing issues of the social and informal nature (culture, commitments) to the formal and technical levels of a computer system.

Overemphasis on Formulation. This risk regards the use of the word "formulation" in the descriptions of computing and the computational thinking. Tedre and Denning claim that while it can be understood as "designing computation", it also can be interpreted as "expressing commands calling a computation" and this second meaning does not necessarily regards computational thinking as people can issue commands (or push buttons) without engaging in computational thinking. They propose instead of "formulation", "design". While we agree with their proposal, we take a wider meaning for design, not restricting it to design of computation, but understanding design as a process that encompasses the informal, the formal and the technical levels of information if we are to construct computer-based applications that enrich human life in the world.

Losing Sight of Computational Models. The seventh risk regards the relationship computational thinking has with the behavior of (practical or theoretical) machines; one should not lose that insight for not risking an exaggerated claim about the computational thinking. In our work, TaPrEC offers a tangible (accessible, practical) but also subtle way of presenting the relationship between certain concepts and controlling a machine to have things (problems) done. Besides being a tangible programming environment designed for children to experience programming in their different and uncomplete levels of apprehension, it is also an 'object to think with' for us in designing programming learning environments. As so, TaPrEC is situated in the technical layer of the semiotic framework, embedding and supporting formal and informal issues considerations (e.g. cost).

6 Conclusion

In the last decade, the digital technology has provoked profound transformations in the way people live in society, certainly requiring attention to a new type of demanded literacy. Programming has been argued as a new discipline to support such technological fluency, due to the types of mental processes it triggers. The transformations we have experimented with the digital technology encompass all aspects of life as computer systems are underlying objects of the physical and social world, mediating our actions in society. This amplified view of the computational technology in our life brings to question the reach of the 'computational thinking' concept as it has been presented in literature. In this paper, we shed light on this subject by revisiting early studies on computing and computational thinking, as well as recent works discussing the matter. We added to the old debate in computer science, of those who question the 'coding' versus the 'systems' views for programming, by proposing an integration vision which recognizes a social nature in programming.

The approach presented in this work draws on a semiotic framework to see programming as designing in different layers of signs system, bringing issues of the social and informal nature (culture, commitments) to the formal and technical levels of a computer system. We illustrated the approach with the design of TaPrEC, a low cost tangible learning environment created to introduce programming ideas to children. The low cost requirement addresses the challenges of disadvantaged social contexts, and problem solving through programming in that environment is practiced as group work. The teachers and other interested parties were also involved along the design and use of the environment, having voice in it and sharing their concerns. Other works have been developed within the same conceptual framework, addressing alternative ways of getting in touch with programming ideas, as for example by constructing narratives [24], but are left out of the scope of this paper. Results so far encourages the openness search for fluency with digital information technology by reflecting on the social nature of computing.

Acknowledgement. The authors thank their institutions, research groups, colleagues and students. The first author has a productivity scholarship from CNPq (#308618/2014-9) and grant #2015/16528-0, São Paulo Research Foundation (FAPESP), the second from CAPES. The authors especially express their gratitude to all the participants of the research projects they have been working with and to GGBS-UNICAMP for funding support.

References

1. Baranauskas, M.C.C., Martins, M.C., Valente, J.A.: Codesign de Redes Digitais: tecnologia e educação a serviço da inclusão social. Penso Editora, Porto Alegre (2013)
2. Baranauskas, M.C.C., Schimiguel, J., Simoni, C.A.C., Medeiros, C.M.B.: Guiding the process of requirements elicitation with a semiotic approach. In: 11th International Conference on Human-Computer Interaction, pp. 100–111 (2005)
3. Baranauskas, M.C.C.: Social awareness in HCI. ACM Interact. 21(4), 66–69 (2014)
4. Baranauskas, M.C.C.: Uma abordagem sócio-situada para tecnologia e educação: concepção e método. In: Baranauskas, M.C.C., Martins, M.C., de Assis, R. (eds.), XO na Escola Construção Compartilhada de Conhecimento – Lições Aprendidas. NIED –Unicamp (2012)
5. Bradley, M.M., Lang, P.J.: Measuring emotion: the self-assessment manikin and the semantic differential. J. Behav. Ther. Exp. Psychiatry 25(1), 49–59 (1994)
6. Carbajal, M.L., Baranauskas, M.C.C.: TaPrEC: desenvolvendo um ambiente de programação tangível de baixo custo para crianças. In: Anais XX Congreso Internacional de Informática Educativa, Santiago, Chile (2015)
7. Cockburn, A., Bryant, A.: Leogo: an equal opportunity user interface for programming. J. Vis. Lang. Comput. 8(5), 601–619 (1997)
8. Denning, P.J., Comer, D.E., Gries, D., Mulder, M.C., Tucker, A., Turner, A.J., Young, P.R.: Computing as a discipline. Commun. ACM 32(1), 9–23 (1989)
9. Dijkstra, E.W.: Programming as a discipline of mathematical nature. Am. Math. Mon. 81(6), 608–612 (1974)
10. Horn, M.S., Jacob, R.J.: Designing tangible programming languages for classroom use. In: Proceedings of the 1st International Conference on Tangible and Embedded Interaction, pp. 159–162. ACM (2007)
11. Horn, M.S., Solovey, E.T., Crouser, R.J., Jacob, R.J.: Comparing the use of tangible and graphical programming languages for informal science education. In: Proceedings of the SIGCHI Conference on Human Factors in Computing Systems, pp. 975–984. ACM (2009)
12. Ishii, H., Ullmer, B.: Tangible bits: towards seamless interfaces between people, bits and atoms. In: Proceedings of the ACM SIGCHI Conference on Human Factors in Computing Systems, pp. 234–241. ACM (1997)
13. Knuth, D.E.: Computer science and its relation to mathematics. Am. Math. Mon. 81(April), 323–343 (1974)
14. Knuth, D.E.: Algorithmic thinking and mathematical thinking. Am. Math. Mon. 92(March), 170–181 (1985)
15. Liu, K.: Semiotics in Information Systems Engineering. Cambridge University Press, Cambridge (2000)
16. Papert, S.: Introduction in Logo Philosophy and Implementation. Logo Computer Systems Inc., Montreal (1999)
17. Papert, S.: Mindstorms. Basic Books, New York (1980)
18. Posada, J.E.G.: Interfaces tangíveis e o design de ambientes educacionais para co-construção de narrativas. Tese de doutorado. IC UNICAMP, Brasil (2015)
19. Raspberry Pi. https://www.raspberrypi.com
20. Resnick, M., Maloney, J., Monroy-Hernández, A., Rusk, N., Eastmond, E., Brennan, K., Millner, A., Rosenbaum, E., Silver, J., Silverman, B., Kafai, Y.: Scratch: programming for all. Commun. ACM 52(11), 60–67 (2009)

21. Stamper, R.K., Althaus, K., Backhouse, J.: MEASUR: method for eliciting, analyzing and specifying user requirements. In: Olle, T.W., Verrijn-Stuart, A.A., Bhabuts, L. (eds.) Computerized Assistance During the Information Systems Life Cycle, pp. 67–116. Elsevier Science, The Netherlands (1988)
22. Stamper, R.: Social norms in requirements analysis: an outline of MEASUR. In: Requirements Engineering, pp. 107–139. Academic Press Professional, Inc. (1994)
23. Tedre, M., Denning, P.: The long quest for computational thinking. In: Proceedings of the 16th Koli Calling Conference, 24–27 November 2016, Koli, Finland (2016)
24. Wing, J.: Computational thinking. Commun. ACM **49**(3), 33–35 (2006)

System for Measuring Teacher–Student Communication in the Classroom Using Smartphone Accelerometer Sensors

Naoyoshi Harada[1(✉)], Masatoshi Kimura[1], Tomohito Yamamoto[1], and Yoshihiro Miyake[2]

[1] Department of Information and Computer Science, College of Engineering, Kanazawa Institute of Technology, 7-1 Oogigaoka, Nonoichi, Ishikawa 921-8501, Japan
{b1356706,b6501725}@planet.kanazawa-it.ac.jp,
tyama@neptune.kanazawa-it.ac.jp
[2] Department of Computer Science, School of Computing, Tokyo Institute of Technology, 4259 Nagatsuta-cho, Midori-ku, Yokohama, Kanagawa 226-8503, Japan
miyake@dis.titech.ac.jp

Abstract. The quality of communication between a teacher and students is deeply related to the cultivation of students' motivation, autonomy, and creativity in a university education. It is important to evaluate such communication and improve it to enhance faculty development. In this study, a system for measuring this communication has been developed. To implement the system, an application for measuring students' body movements using the acceleration sensor of a smartphone was developed. At the same time, a server-side web system that visualizes the measured data was developed. Using this measurement system, the communication in a seminar of a university laboratory was measured. The results show that the activities of a presenter and audience can be clearly detected by the raw and frequency-analyzed accelerometer data. Moreover, the correlation between the sonograms of the presenter and of the audience members became stronger when they had constructive discussion. These results suggest that the synchronization between a presenter and the audience is related to their level of rapport.

Keywords: Communication · Class · Accelerometer sensor · Smartphone · Frequency analysis

1 Introduction

University education is now changing from a one-way teaching style to active learning, by which students learn various topics subjectively. As a backdrop to this transition, specialized knowledge is easily obtained from a variety of media, such as the Internet, at very low cost. In this situation, the most important thing for a university is to educate students in a self-learning style and provide a good learning environment. If this approach succeeds, students deepen their study spontaneously. In this kind of education

© Springer International Publishing AG 2017
M. Kurosu (Ed.): HCI 2017, Part II, LNCS 10272, pp. 309–318, 2017.
DOI: 10.1007/978-3-319-58077-7_24

style, the teachers' role is not that of a transmitter of specialized knowledge but that of a facilitator who studies deeply with students and creates something new with them. From this point of view, a university classroom is a co-creative field between teachers and students.

With this kind of education, its quality depends on the communication between teacher and students. Therefore, in the future, it will be very important to evaluate the quality of the communication and to improve it. There are some previous studies that have dealt with communication between teacher and students. Katsumata et al. investigated such communication by analyzing the relationship between the voice of the teacher and the movements of students, which were captured by a video camera [1]. In this study, they showed that there was a positive correlation between the correlation coefficient of the teacher's voice and the students' movements with the degree of interest of the students. Watanabe et al. also investigated the relationship between the movements of a teacher and those of the students for estimating the degree of students' understanding in the class [2, 3]. In their research, they showed that there were some periods when the teacher's movements synchronized with the movements of students and speculated that these periods were important for evaluating the degree of students' understanding. In another study, by Miura et al., the researchers analyzed the synchronization of body movements in a lecture-style experiment [4]. They reported that the nodding rhythm between a teacher and a student was more highly synchronized when the degree of the student's understanding was high. Moreover, they reported that the students, who were the listeners in this experiment, synchronized their nodding 10 ms earlier than the teacher's subconscious nodding.

In these studies, the relationship between the synchronization and the degree of students' understanding in the class was investigated by analyzing the rhythm of body movements or of the voice. However, in each of these studies, a video camera and accelerometer sensors attached to the forehead were used for measuring the body movements of the teachers and students. In the case of a video camera, there is a limitation in the amount of detail that can be measured in the body movements of many students. Additionally, in the case of accelerometer sensors, it is difficult to attach such sensors to students' foreheads in a real class. Therefore, in our research, we focus on the accelerometer sensor of a smartphone, whose use is widespread and which is owned by most of the students, for measuring the body movements of students in an actual classes. Recently, a group of researchers investigated the activity of an organization quantitatively using this kind of accelerometer, and they improved the activity of the organization by using the analyzed data [5].

In this study, we first developed and constructed a system to measure the body movements of students in a class using the accelerometer sensor of a smartphone. Next, we measured a seminar that was held in a university laboratory setting using this system and analyzed the data from the accelerometer sensor, utterance corpus, and body movements corpus. Using these data, we discuss the possibility of evaluating the communication between teacher and students.

2   Measuring System and Experiment

2.1   System Overview

Figure 1 shows an overview of the measuring system that was developed, composed of a server and client system.

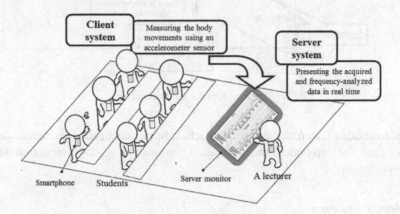

Fig. 1. Overview of measuring system

As the client system, Android and iOS devices are used, and they send the measurement data from the accelerometer sensor to the server system repeatedly using HTTP (Hypertext Transport Protocol). The server system receives the sent data and presents them to a browser in real time. Through these processes, a user can monitor the data for each student on site. In the following subsections, the client and server system are explained in more detail.

2.2   Client System

To take advantage of smartphones that are in widespread use, the client system was developed as an application for an Android or iOS device. In these devices, the application handles two tasks. One task is to measure the accelerometer value. In each device, the application measures the accelerometer X, Y, and Z values at a sampling rate of 100 Hz. After this measurement is taken, in order to acquire the norm value, the application sums the squared values for each axis and calculate square root of the result. The other task is to send the acquired data. In each device, the application sends the 50 calculated norm values and their time of measurement, including the ID of the device, to the server system every 500 ms.

Figure 2 shows the appearance of the measurement application on an Android device. There are setting windows for the IP address of the server, duration of measurement, and ID of the device. In this application, the dialogue box appears when there is an input mistake, and after the start of the measurement, the setting screen

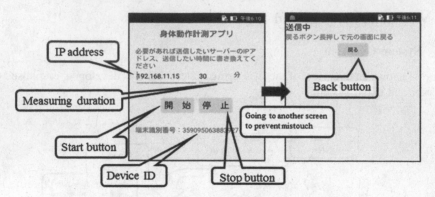

Fig. 2. Client system for an Android device

changes to another screen to prevent mistouches. In this application, as long as a user does not push the stop button, the application continues to send the measured data to the server system.

2.3 Server System

The server system was essentially developed as an HTTP server. The system receives the calculated norm data from the accelerometer, which are sent from the client system, and presents them to a web browser. Apache was used as the HTTP server program and PHP was used in the development of the receiving and presentation of the data.

Figure 3 shows a picture of the accelerometer data from the students as displayed by the server system. The server system first receives the 50 data from the clients and saves them to a text file every 500 ms. The system then retrieves the last 5 s of data to make the graph of each device. In the graph, the newest data are shown at the left. In the graphing, the data are properly presented by showing the ID of the device and the

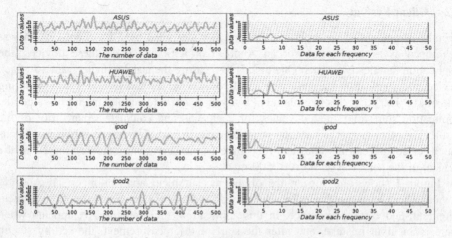

Fig. 3. Measurement data presented by the server system

time measured. In this system, not only the accelerometer's raw data but also the frequency-analyzed data are presented to allow recognition of the characteristics of the body movements.

2.4   Overview of Experiment

Using the system described above, the communication between a presenter and the presenter's audience in a seminar at the university's laboratory was measured as an example of a lecture at the university. After measurement, the accelerometer data, corpus of utterances, and body movements were analyzed. The presentation, given by a student, was measured five times, and for each presentation there were about 20 persons comprising the audience. The presenter and 4–6 members of the audience wore Android devices for measurement, and the scene of the presenter and audience were recorded by two video cameras.

Each Android device was hung from the neck of the presenter or audience member by a strap with a plastic case. The device was adjusted to be positioned at the solar plexus in order to measure the nodding that was often observed in the class.

One video camera was placed to capture the presenter and the other was placed to capture the entire audience. In video recording, two synchronized digital clocks were placed one in front of each camera to allow the time relationships between the accelerometer data, utterances, and body movements to be readily associated. All measuring devices, including these two clocks, were synchronized to under 100 ms by a time setting application.

For the data analysis, first, a frequency analysis of all measurement data from the accelerometer was conducted to investigate the relationship between specific body movements and specific frequencies. Next, sonograms of the accelerometer data were made to investigate the temporal change of body movements of the presenter and the audience. Moreover, the correlation between sonograms was analyzed to investigate the relationship between the body movements of the presenter and of each audience. Using recorded video data, corpuses of utterances of the presenter and audiences were made, and each utterance was tagged [6] to allow an analysis of dialogue structure. In addition, corpuses of body movements of presenters and audiences were made by describing the movements one by one; these were used to analyze the relationship between the accelerometer data and body movements. In this study, there are five sets of measurement data; because of space considerations, however, one representative set of results is used for explanation in the next section.

3   Results

3.1   Frequency Distributions of Accelerometer Data

Figure 4 shows the frequency distribution of the accelerometer data of the presenter, and Figs. 5 and 6 show those of two typical audience members. These frequency data were for the entire measurement period. In this measurement, the sampling frequency was 100 Hz, but the range of the graphs is 0–15 Hz because the object of measure was a human, who cannot move so quickly.

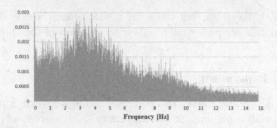

Fig. 4. Frequency distribution of accelerometer data of a presenter

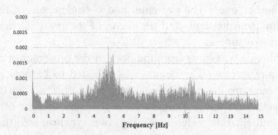

Fig. 5. Frequency distribution of accelerometer data for audience member A

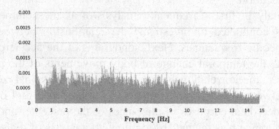

Fig. 6. Frequency distribution of accelerometer data for audience member B

In these figures, it is possible to recognize frequency peaks in the following three areas: 0–3 Hz, 3–7 Hz, and over 7 Hz. The relationship between the corpuses and the accelerometer data corresponding to these peaks was analyzed. The results show that the peaks at 0–3 Hz correspond mainly to major body movements such as the swaying of a shoulder. The peaks at 3–7 Hz correspond to small body movements such as normal nodding or a hand movement. The peaks above 7 Hz correspond to quick body movements such as laughing or speaking. In the case of Fig. 5, the audience member often nodded during the seminar. The audience member of Fig. 6, on the other hand, did not nod so much. As a result, in Fig. 5, there is a clear peak around 4–6 Hz. Additionally, in the case of Fig. 5, the audience member sometimes laughed during the seminar. As a result, there is a peak around 10 Hz that is not observed in Fig. 6 as this audience member did not laugh.

These results show that it is possible to detect specific body movements of a presenter or audience using the accelerometer of a smartphone that is hung from the neck.

3.2 Sonograms of Accelerometer Data and Relationship Between Sonograms

Figure 7 shows the raw accelerometer data and the corresponding sonogram for a presenter, and Figs. 8 and 9 show those of two audience members. The window of analysis for these sonograms was 4 s.

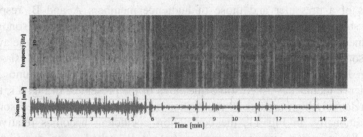

Fig. 7. Acceleration data (bottom) and corresponding sonogram (top) of a presenter (Color figure online)

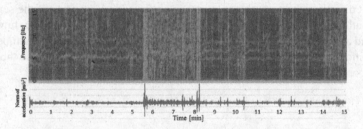

Fig. 8. Acceleration data (bottom) and corresponding sonogram (top) of audience member A (Color figure online)

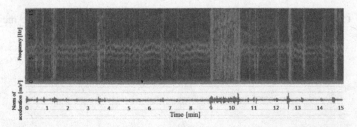

Fig. 9. Acceleration data (bottom) and corresponding sonogram (top) of audience member B (Color figure online)

In this seminar, the presenter talked for about 6 min. From Fig. 7, it is possible to recognize this period from the raw data of the accelerometer and the corresponding sonogram. After the presentation, audience member A asked a question of the presenter, and then audience member B asked a question. In Figs. 8 and 9, it is possible to recognize these activities by the accelerometer data and the corresponding sonogram. In particular, in the sonogram, some peaks (highlighted in yellow) are observed. In the previous subsection, it was seen that some body movements appear as a frequency peak. The sonogram data suggest that some specific body movements appear intermittently.

These results suggest that it is possible to detect the active period of the body movement of a presenter and an audience during communication and also to clarify the specific movements by using the frequency data of an accelerometer.

Figures 10 and 11 show the time series of correlation coefficients between the sonograms of a presenter and those of audience members A and B, respectively. Figure 12 shows the time series of correlation coefficients between the sonograms of audience members A and B. The coefficient values were calculated from the average of 1 min of sonogram data, and the window slides every 30 s for this analysis.

In Fig. 10, the correlation coefficient becomes relatively high around 7–8 min, when audience member A asked some questions of the presenter. In Fig. 11, the value becomes relatively high around 10 min, when audience member B asked some questions. Additionally, in Fig. 11, the correlation coefficient becomes relatively high around 7–8 min, when audience member A (not B) asked some questions of the presenter. As a result, in Fig. 12, the correlation coefficient between audience members A and B becomes relatively high around 7–8 min.

A tendency for a high correlation between the presenter and an audience member who is not directly uttering to the presenter is observed in later parts of the seminar. In Figs. 11 and 12, for example, the correlation coefficient becomes relatively high around 12 min and again around 14–15 min. In these parts, two other audience members asked some questions of the presenter. Audience members A and B were quiet at these times, but their correlations become high.

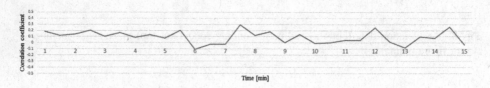

Fig. 10. Correlation between sonogram of the presenter and that of audience member A

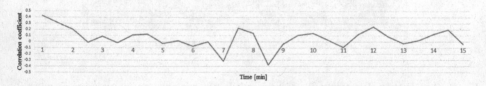

Fig. 11. Correlation between sonogram of the presenter and that of audience member B

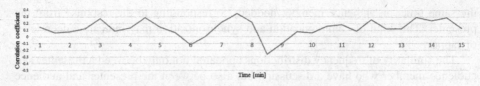

Fig. 12. Correlation between sonograms of audience members A and B

In these peak areas of high correlation, the corpuses of utterance data and body movements show that an audience member asked a question (tag: qh) or mentioned a suggestion (cs) or point of agreement (aa) to a presenter, or a presenter nodded in response to comments and sometimes mentioned a point of agreement (aap) to the audience.

4 Discussion and Conclusion

In this study, a measuring system using the accelerometer of a smartphone was developed to evaluate the communication between a teacher and students in the class. Moreover, the communication between a presenter and the audience in a seminar of a university laboratory was measured, and the accelerometer data and corpuses of utterances and body movements were analyzed. The results show that it is possible to detect the body movements of the presenter and audience members by the frequency characteristics of the accelerometer data and that the correlation between the frequency distribution of the presenter and that of the audience members becomes relatively high when a presenter has a discussion with them.

Our final purpose is to evaluate the quality of communication between a teacher and students using the accelerometer sensor of a smartphone in the class. The results of this measurement suggest that there is suitable potential for detecting the presenter's movements while speaking and the audience's movements while asking questions using the raw and frequency-analyzed accelerometer data. At present, the relationship between a specific movement and characteristics of the frequency distribution is manually associated using the corpus of movement data. However, in the future, it will be possible to detect specific body movements using a deep classifier system that is trained with the frequency data tagged with the body movements. Using such a learning method, it will also be possible to display the distribution of students' body movements in class in real time.

The results of the analysis of sonogram correlations show that the relationship between the frequency distribution of a presenter and that of an audience member becomes similar when they interchange comments with each other. This result may come about from the synchronization of body movements between presenter and audience. In previous studies, the synchronization between the voice of a teacher and body movements of students, or the synchronization of body movements between students, has been observed when students' level of understanding became high. In this study, we can observe the same phenomenon. In the high-correlation part of the seminar, the presenter nodded, corresponding to comments from the audience, and at the same time, an audience member nodded, corresponding to the response from the presenter. This kind of communication and synchronization may indicate a deep level of rapport.

The similarity of frequency distributions appeared not only between a presenter and audience member who have a discussion but also between the presenter and audience members with whom the presenter does not have a direct exchange. This result means that the synchronization of body movements was widespread among other audience members who were merely present in the room. This phenomenon might be important for classroom rapport. The nodding of students is important feedback for a teacher to sense the level of understanding in the class. If this feedback is widely synchronized among the class, both teacher and students could feel a sense of unity in learning something new. At the same time, this sense of unity would promote the involvement of students in the class. It is suggested that in a good class, this cycle of the synchronization of body movements, emergence of sense of unity, and subjective involvement might occur. In future work, the synchronization of body movements should be analyzed in more detail to evaluate the quality of communication between teacher and students. To carry out this analysis, subjective evaluations of teacher and students (e.g., levels of understanding, levels of interest) will be investigated and associated to the accelerometer data or corpuses of utterances and body movements. By such an analysis, the possibility of a method for class evaluation will be discussed.

References

1. Katsumata, G., Nagaoka, C., Komori, M.: Assessing students' interests in a lecture using speech-driven body movement entrainment. Trans. Hum. Interface Soc. **13**(3), 275–282 (2011)
2. Watanabe, E., Ozeki, T., Kohama, T.: Analysis of behaviors by students corresponding to behaviors by lecturers in lectures. IEICE Technical report, vol. 115, no. 36, pp. 85–90 (2015)
3. Watanabe, E., Ozeki, T., Kohama, T.: Relationships between understandings and noting behaviors by students for video lectures. IEICE Technical report, vol. 115, no. 149, pp. 25–30 (2015)
4. Miura, S., Yokozuka, T., Kwon, J., Chidchanok, T., Miao Sin Robin, Y., Ogawa, K., Miyake, Y.: Relationship between body motion synchrony and empathy in human communication. In: Proceedings of 28th SICE Symposium on Decentralized Autonomous Systems, pp. 126–129 (2016)
5. Asami, A., Ogawa, K., Ara, K., Yano, K., Miyake, Y.: Relationship between synchronization of body movements and transitivity of the communication network during face-to-face communication in real society. In: Proceedings of Human Interface Symposium 2015, pp. 953–958 (2015)
6. Dhillon, R., Bhaget, S., Carvey, H., Shriberg, E.: Meeting recorder project: dialog act labeling guide. ICSI Technical report TR-04-002, 9 February 2004

Situation-Awareness in Action: An Intelligent Online Learning Platform (IOLP)

Jasser Jasser, Hua Ming$^{(\boxtimes)}$, and Mohamed A. Zohdy

Oakland University, Rochester, MI 48309, USA
{jjasser,ming,zohdyma}@oakland.edu

Abstract. *Situation* is a computational abstraction that encapsulates human-centric contexts, which can be human-oriented behavioral contexts as well as the relevant environmental contexts. Its potential applications in computer science range from artificial intelligence, service computing, human-computer interaction, pervasive computing to software engineering and software systems. In this paper, we introduce a user-centric *situation-aware* Intelligent Online Learning Platform (IOLP) that aims to provide a personalized learning experience for those conducting online-learning activities. It joins the engineering techniques from Machine Learning, Intelligent Systems (IS) and Human-Computing Interaction (HCI) to offer highly personalized services to the users. It serves as an experimental subject for, as well as a real-world implementation of *situations*. Under the strength of the abstraction of *situation*, various elements drawn from different areas in computer science are seamlessly integrated towards a user-centric Intelligent Online Learning Platform (IOLP). Our discussions on the IOLP are further supported by an online class instance it currently hosts featuring Python Programming.

Keywords: Situation · Situation-awareness · Human-computer interaction (HCI) · Massive Open Online Course (MOOC) · Intelligent Systems (IS) · Online learning · Adaptive learning

1 Introduction

Information sharing by the internet has vastly extended the philosophy of learning and therefore, the means to pursue learning has drastly changed. The pervasive accessibility of the internet, escalated by the explosive growth of mobile platforms and mobile apps prepared necessary conditions for the further development of online learning services. People no longer need to attend a class to learn a specific topic; the internet is full of tutorials, videos, and discussion forums to help them obtain knowledge to master a specific subject. MIT OpenCourseWare spearheaded the sharing of high-quality university-level courses [18]. This led to the rise of Massive Open Online Courses (MOOC), opening the way to popular online learning services including Coursera, edX, and Udacity [23]. However, the existing MOOC-based services mainly provide recorded videos, navigation menus,

© Springer International Publishing AG 2017
M. Kurosu (Ed.): HCI 2017, Part II, LNCS 10272, pp. 319–330, 2017.
DOI: 10.1007/978-3-319-58077-7_25

and multiple-choice homework problems to facilitate independent student online learning activities. While having successfully migrated the learning experience from classrooms to the more open internet space, these existing services have been mostly recognized as one-size-fits-all [28] that provide less than sufficient capabilities to intimately interact with, guide and engage individual students. Indeed, there is an outstanding need for an infrastructure that is able to provide personalized online learning services based on individual clients, or client groups.

In this work, we present Intelligent Online Learning Platform (IOLP), an intelligent system-based online learning platform that aims to provide a fully personalized learning experience for each individual. IOLP and transitively all the services hosted on top of it are empowered by *situation-awareness* [7,8,21]. In addition, we present a concrete online class instance hosted by IOLP that features a personalized learning experience for Python Programming.

2   The Concept of Situation and Situation-Aware Computing

The concept of *situation* has its roots in mathematical logic [4,11,19] and analytical philosophy [5]. Over the years, it entered different areas in computer science including computational linguistics [12], logic programming [17], functional programming [20,21], artificial intelligence [19,25], human-computer interaction (HCI) [13,21], pervasive computing [26,27], service computing [8], software requirements engineering [2,3] and software evolution [8].

Of particular interest, [8] came up with a novel framework called *Situ*, empowered by the concept of situation, lends itself to defining situation as a rigorous computational abstraction towards automated service evolution. In [8], situation includes human-oriented cognitive and behavioral contexts, as well as the environmental contexts on a temporal basis. Indeed, *situation* thus defined is context-oriented [1,24] and in other words, a situation is a hub of context data lending itself to a wide spectrum of the-state-of-the-art machineries, such as machine learning techniques, during this age of big data and big data analytics.

Following the vein of work initiated by [8,21,22] further developed situation into a programmable abstraction that enables software reusability, as well as providing a straight-forward support for functional-programming originated, big data analytical tools such as MapReduce [10].

In particular, situation-awareness empowers IOLP with the following aspects:

1. Situation-centric design. The system scenarios are derived, combined and interchanged in the unified form of situations, which primarily consist of user's cognative, behavioral and environmental contexts. This design view ensures user-centric philosophy of the entire IOLP system, from macro level to micro level.
2. The underlying Intelligent Systems of IOLP are constructed based on situations, i.e., different user's are treated based on their collective context data that compose user-specific situations, which eventually leads to the generation of personalized learning experiences for individual users.

3. Dimensional situation analytics [22] was used to facilitate the information derivation and comprehension, while IOLP used situations to encapsulate and analyse user's raw context data.

3   The Intelligent Online Learning Platform (IOLP)

IOLP consists of two major Intelligent Systems (IS). The first is the Intelligent Assistant that provides real-time answers to student questions and tips for further exploration and study. It takes the student question as an input, compares it with a database full of related questions artificially trained using Bag-of-Words learning model, then provides an answer and a clue to what the student should ask about to understand the material in question. As a student progresses through the traditional videos, slides, homework, and exams, the history of his/her actions is tracked and recorded to generate individualized learning characteristics for each student. Our unsupervised machine learning techniques then cluster students based on his/her progress in the learning process among both current and previous students who took the same class. The second major IS is the Intelligent Advisor, which then directs students to enhance his/her performance in the areas where they are having difficulties, by recommending chapters for review, homework to retake, and topics to dedicate more focus. The IS will also generate exams containing questions related to areas where a student had trouble understanding and needed extra study time. We tested IOLP by designing a Python programming course, where our database is filled with videos, slides, questions, homework, and tests that are related to that material.

The main components of the IOLP are:

- The class view, which contains the lecture videos, presentation slides, homework and exam links, and extra resources to help the student.
- The Python Console, which is a full online Python Interpreter, where the student practices writing code.
- The Homework view, where the student is directed to write code for a specific homework using the Python Console.
- The *Student Help Portal*, where the student is directed if they are having difficulty solving a problem or want help regarding a specific topic.
- The Exam view, where the student is tested based on his/her knowledge of the current studied chapter.
- The Intelligent Assistant: The first major Intelligent System in IOLP where the students ask questions to get answers and hints.
- The Intelligent Advisor: The second major Intelligent System that assesses student performance to provide constructive feedback.

3.1   Intelligent Assistant

The Intelligent Assistant provides clear and efficient answers, and sometimes code examples about various topics regarding Python programming language. Figure 1 shows the Intelligent Assistant providing an answer to "How to write hello world." The Intelligent Assistant also provides Speech Recognition and Text-to-Speech features, where it takes a user voice as input, and provides an answer for the student like any other smart assistant, such as Apple's Siri, Microsoft's Cortana, Google's Assistant, or Amazon's Alexa.

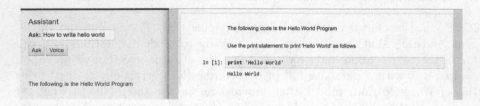

Fig. 1. The Intelligent Assistant

The question design is divided into three categories:

- **What** questions provide a core definition regarding the topic asked about, for example:
  - Q: What is the "Hello World" program?
  - A: Is a simple program that outputs the "Hello, World!" as-is to the standard output screen. It is usually the simplest working program, which can be written in most programming languages, to illustrate the basic syntax to write a computer program.
- **How** questions provide an explanation on how the topic is used and implemented with a real-life example, for example:
  - Q: How to write Hello World program?
  - A: The following is the Hello World program (with a code snippet on the side to show the code, as shown in Fig. 1)
- **Why** questions provide more explanation regarding a specific topic or a specific approach, for example:
  - Q: Why Hello World?
  - A: Hello World is considered the simplest form of a coding program and is used by many tutorials as the starting point to familiarize the student with writing code.

The hint module within the Intelligent Assistant suggests topics the students can explore deeper, in particular when a student asks a question that the system considers unconventional to his/her learning level based on the student's activity history. All questions in the database are connected in a k-ary tree structure, where within each level every node (question) contains 0 or k children (dependent questions) [6]. When a student asks a question, the IS will go through the tree path of the question history of the student. If it finds that the parent node of the current asked question is not registered in the student's question history, it will provide a hint to explore a topic that is related to the uncovered question node. Figure 2 shows an example. In the example, the student asked about Conditional

Statement. After the IS traced the student's question history, it discovered that the student didn't read, watch, or ask about Boolean Expressions, which is a prior topic to understanding Conditional Statements. Therefore, the IS provides a hint to the student to consider asking about this topic first.

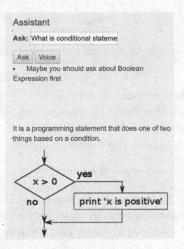

Fig. 2. The Intelligent Assistant hint module

The Bag-of-Words. Answers to student questions are retrieved from the database by measuring the similarity between the asked question and every question within the database. Together with a vector space model, the bag-of-words representation is used to define the similarity between the questions, where every question is presented as a multidimensional vector [9]. In this way, a vocabulary that contains all distinct terms after linguistic preprocessing is created. Each term, either in the student's question or database of questions, is weighted using w_{ij}, then both are expressed as t-dimensional vectors $d_j = (w_{1j}, w_{2j}, \ldots, w_{tj})$ where j represents the numbers of questions in the database, $j = 1, 2, 3, \ldots, n$. The database of all questions is represented by a term matrix (also known *term-frequency matrix*, as shown in Fig. 3).

To compute the weights, the frequency of a term i in question j is calculated using the formula (1), where the frequency is normalized by the frequency of the most common term in the document.

$$tf_{ij} = \frac{f_{ij}}{max_i(f_{ij})} \tag{1}$$

where f_{ij} represents the frequency of term i appearing in question j.

After calculating the term frequency, the inverse document frequency is used to specify the discriminative power of term i, as shown in formula (2).

$$idf_i = \log_2(\frac{n}{df_i}) \tag{2}$$

$$\begin{bmatrix} & T_1 & T_2 & \cdots & T_t \\ D_1 & w_{11} & w_{21} & \cdots & w_{t1} \\ D_2 & w_{12} & w_{22} & \cdots & w_{t2} \\ \vdots & \vdots & \vdots & \ddots & \vdots \\ D_n & w_{1n} & w_{2n} & \cdots & w_{tn} \end{bmatrix}$$

Fig. 3. Term matrix for database of n questions and t tems

where df_i is the document frequency of term i.

Finally, the weights are computed by multiplying the term frequency by the inversed document frequency as shown in formula (3). The terms that occur most in the question are assigned the highest weights.

$$w_{ij} = tf_{ij} * idf_i \tag{3}$$

The question with the highest weight is considered the question that is most similar to the question the student asked, the index of which will be used thereafter by the Intelligent Assistant to search and retrieve an answer that is most closely relevant.

3.2 Student Activities History

A powerful feature in IOLP is the student activities history. A student history is collected from four types of activities: the student's asked questions, the student's code sessions done in the Python Console provided in the platform, the student's homework sessions (like the code sessions), and the student's test records. Having a record of all the activities helps the IS to build each student report after assessing his/her performance. The student activities history is the base of the Intelligent Advisor, since every action committed by a student is translated into learning features the Intelligent Advisor will use to perform the student clustering algorithm. The platform main view, shown in Fig. 4, always provides a panel to remind the student of his/her latest activities.

3.3 Intelligent Advisor

After the learning features are collected from the students activities, the Intelligent Advisor clusters the students that share similar feature values together, meaning these students are performing at the same level. The Intelligent Advisor will then provide every group with the appropriate level homework, exams, and tips. Each student will receive his/her own dynamically generated report that contains tips and reviews based on his/her individual history that will suit his/her learning experience. The Intelligent Advisor does not evaluate the student's performance until they progress through the learning material. The following features are used in assessing students performance:

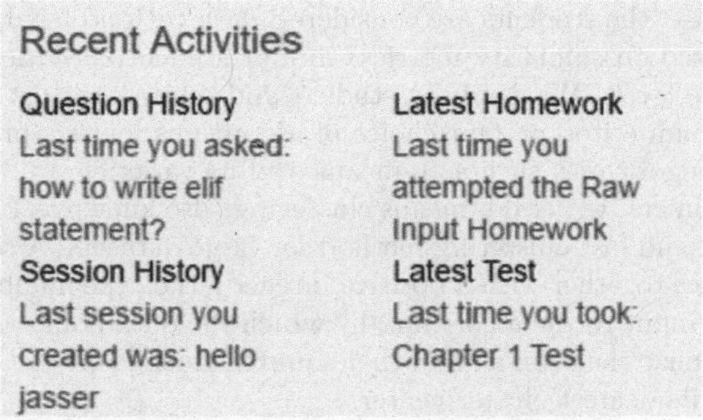

Recent Activities

Question History	Latest Homework
Last time you asked: how to write elif statement?	Last time you attempted the Raw Input Homework
Session History	**Latest Test**
Last session you created was: hello jasser	Last time you took: Chapter 1 Test

Fig. 4. The recent activities panel

1. **Attention to Details:** In this feature, the student's ability to deal with the Python Programming Language's syntax, i.e., the grammar, is measured.
2. **Breadth of Knowledge:** This feature measures the progress of the student's learning as they progress through the chapters.
3. **Problem Solving:** This feature measures the ability of the student to solve problems using the Python Programming Language.
4. **Abstraction:** This feature measures the ability of the student to learn advanced material and write complex code.
5. **Teamwork:** This measurement is for student participation on the student help portal.
6. **Creativity:** This measures a student's ability to provide new approaches to solving advanced problems.

These features are obtained as a student progresses through the online lectures, and by asking questions, writing code in the Python Console, doing homework, and passing exams. Each action the student takes is translated into points towards a specific feature. For example, asking *What is hello world program?* will gain the student a point towards the **breadth of knowledge** feature, since it is considered a general knowledge question, while asking *How to write hello world program?* will gain the student a point toward **attention to details**, since it deals with the obtaining the knowledge to write the syntax for this program. For the **creativity** feature, we follow a unique approach in determining the level of creativity in his/her work. For example, if the student is tasked to type the word *"hello"* 4 times (hellohellohellohello), it can be simply done by using the *print* statement, but a creative student would use the $*$ operation to multiply the string 4 times, since Python allows string operations such as multiplication:

- Normally: *print "hellohellohellohello"*
- With novelty: *print "hello" $*$ 4*

Unsupervised learning is also known as clustering, or class discovery. It is one of the major categories in machine learning, the other two being the Supervised Learning, and Reinforcement Learning. What makes unsupervised machine learning different than the other two is that it deals with data that does not have labels. In our case, the students are considered data with no label, because they are grouped based on similarity metrics; similar student activities lead to similar performance levels. We carefully studied and revised our list of features to ensure an optimum criterion. Our choice of algorithms for this problem are the centroid based algorithms, such as k-means and its varieties [14].

In our experiment, we used k-means clustering, also known as Lloyd's method [16], a versatile, and fast clustering method for large datasets. A set of points in a Euclidean space together with a positive integer k (i.e., the number of clusters) are provided as input to the algorithm, by which the data points are split into k clusters to minimize the total sum of the (squared Euclidean) distances between each point and its nearest cluster center.

Consider a set of data $X \subseteq \mathbb{R}$, and k clusters $C_1, C_2, \ldots, C_k$ with corresponding centroids $c_1, c_2, \ldots, c_k$. Then, for each element $x \in X$ assuming that the size of X is n, we need to find the value j that minimizes the Euclidean distance between x and c_j:

$$dist(x, c_j) = \sqrt{\sum_{i=1}^{n}(x_i - c_{ji})^2} \tag{4}$$

$$C_j = \{x : min_h dist^2(x, c_h) = j\} \tag{5}$$

To find the mean of all elements x that belongs to cluster C_j, we have:

$$c_j = \frac{1}{m}\sum_{x \in C_j} x \tag{6}$$

m_j is the number of elements in C_j.

Given formula (5), we minimize the summation of distance between each point in the cluster and the centroid in that cluster as follows:

$$\sum_{j=1}^{k}\sum_{x \in C_j} dist^2(x, c_j) \tag{7}$$

As an example, in Fig. 5 students are grouped into 3 clusters, (excellent students, good students, weak students), based on the student performance features.

In Fig. 5, the centroids are represented with grey dimension signs. *Excellent students* are represented by the blue dots. *Good students* are represented by the green multiplication signs. Finally, *weak students* are represented by the red asterisks. The Intelligent Advisor will provide all students in a cluster with the same homework and exams, but will also utilize **personalized** approaches to engage individual students to maximize their performances. For example, if a student demonstrates a lack of creativity, then the Intelligent Advisor will start providing them with more problems that they can solve with creative approaches.

3.4   Energy-Aware Situation in IOLP

We designed IOLP to be energy efficient whether working on PCs or mobile devices. Since the display is considered the most energy consuming component,

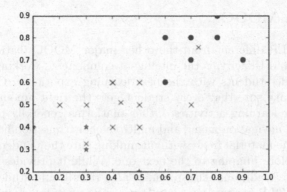

Fig. 5. Example: 20 students in 3 clusters by k-means

we implemented Li, Huyen, and Halford's approach [15] for automatically rewriting the Cascading Style Sheets (CSS) files that empower the webpages under IOLP. By this engery-aware feature, the light-colored background that consumes more energy is switched to more energy friendly colors, which are usually darker, without sacrificing the user experience. Figure 6 shows the usual user interface and the energy friendly user interface side by side.

Fig. 6. Standard interface. (left) vs. engergy-efficient interface (right)

4   IOLP vs. MOOC

What makes IOLP different from the other major MOOC platforms, such as Coursera, edX, and Udacity, is the intelligent components working in the background to provide students with the best learning experience. Our main goal in IOLP is to make sure that every student gets the right amount of feedback based on his/her learning activities. Other platforms generally provide only a recorded lecture, navigation menu, and multiple-choice question homework. Students navigate the material freely without making sure they understand the previous chapter before jumping to the next one. While it provides students with freedom from the traditional classroom, it also risks losing students who need more direction. IOLP has two vital intelligent systems to follow up with student progress and always direct them to the right track, an advantage that is missing in other platforms. There, the students need to wait for a feedback from the assistants monitoring the class, a response to his/her questions on the questions form, or not getting an answer at all due the massive amount of students participating in the class. Our platform also uses a student help portal so students can ask tough questions, such as code compiling errors, and code semantic errors, that are considered too advanced to our current state-of-art artificial systems to answer.

5   Conclustion and Future Work

Our future work is two-fold:

1. To facilitate students from all over the globe to use our platform to get as many question wording biases as possible, so that our platform can be fully trained to answer any question that is input from a student whose first language is not English. Also, we seek to have a dataset of student features that would help the Intelligent Advisor to accurately cluster the next batch of students based on his/her performance. We also plan to implement a massive online testing of the platform to verify its accuracy and efficiency.
2. To escalate the situation-awareness level the IOLP possesses. As the system grows more sophisticated, owning more features, this objective becomes especially challenging.

References

1. Abowd, G.D., Dey, A.K., Brown, P.J., Davies, N., Smith, M., Steggles, P.: Towards a better understanding of context and context-awareness. In: Gellersen, H.-W. (ed.) HUC 1999. LNCS, vol. 1707, pp. 304–307. Springer, Heidelberg (1999). doi:10.1007/3-540-48157-5_29
2. Alkhanifer, A., Ludi, S.: Towards a situation awareness design to improve visually impaired orientation in unfamiliar buildings: requirements elicitation study. In: 2014 IEEE 22nd International Requirements Engineering Conference (RE), pp. 23–32. IEEE (2014)

3. Atukorala, N.L., Chang, C.K., Oyama, K.: Situation-oriented requirements elicitation. In: 2016 IEEE 40th Annual Computer Software and Applications Conference (COMPSAC), vol. 1, pp. 233–238. IEEE (2016)
4. Barwise, J.: The Situation in Logic. Center for the Study of Langauge and Information. Stanford University, Stanford (1989)
5. Barwise, J., Perry, J.: Situations and Attitudes. MIT Press, New York (1983)
6. Black, P.E.: Dictionary of Algorithms and Data Structures. National Institute of Standards and Technology Gaithersburg, Gaithersburg (2004)
7. Chang, C.K.: Situation analytics: a foundation for a new software engineering paradigm. Computer 49(1), 24–33 (2016)
8. Chang, C.K., Jiang, H., Ming, H., Oyama, K.: Situ: a situation-theoretic approach to context-aware service evolution. IEEE T. Serv. Comput. 2(3), 261–275 (2009)
9. Cios, K.J., Pedrycz, W., Swiniarski, R.W.: Data mining and knowledge discovery. In: Cios, K.J., Pedrycz, W., Swiniarski, R.W. (eds.) Data Mining Methods for Knowledge Discovery, pp. 1–26. Springer, New York (1998)
10. Dean, J., Ghemawat, S.: Mapreduce: simplified data processing on large clusters. In: OSDI, p. 1 (2004)
11. Devlin, K.: Logic and Information. Cambridge University Press, Cambridge (1995)
12. Devlin, K.: Situation theory and situation semantics. Handb. Hist. Logic 7, 601–664 (2006)
13. Endsley, M.R.: Toward a theory of situation awareness in dynamic systems. Hum. Factors 37(1), 32–64 (1995)
14. Gentleman, R., Carey, V.: Unsupervised machine learning. In: Gentleman, R., Carey, V.J. (eds.) Bioconductor Case Studies, pp. 137–157. Springer, Heidelberg (2008)
15. Li, D., Tran, A.H., Halfond, W.G.: Making web applications more energy efficient for OLED smartphones. In: Proceedings of the 36th International Conference on Software Engineering, pp. 527–538. ACM (2014)
16. Lloyd, S.: Least squares quantization in PCM. IEEE Trans. Inf. Theory 28(2), 129–137 (1982)
17. Loke, S.W.: Representing and reasoning with situations for context-aware pervasive computing: a logic programming perspective. Knowl. Eng. Rev. 19(3), 213–233 (2004)
18. Martin, F.G.: Will massive open online courses change how we teach? Commun. ACM 55(8), 26–28 (2012)
19. McCarthy, J., Hayes, P.J.: Some philosophical problems from the standpoint of artificial intelligence. In: Readings in Artificial Intelligence, pp. 431–450 (1969)
20. Ming, H.: Situ^f: a domain specific language and a first step towards the realization of situ framework. Ph.D. dissertation. ProQuest Dissertations & Theses Global. UMI 3539397 (2012)
21. Ming, H., Chang, C.K.: Can situations help with reusability of software? In: Kurosu, M. (ed.) HCI 2016. LNCS, vol. 9731, pp. 598–609. Springer, Cham (2016). doi:10.1007/978-3-319-39510-4_55
22. Ming, H., Chang, C.K., Yang, J.: Dimensional situation analytics: from data to wisdom. In: 2015 IEEE 39th Annual Computer Software and Applications Conference (COMPSAC), vol. 1, pp. 50–59. IEEE (2015)
23. Pappano, L.: The year of the MOOC. New York Times 2(12), 2012 (2012)
24. Perera, C., Zaslavsky, A., Christen, P., Georgakopoulos, D.: Context aware computing for the internet of things: a survey. IEEE Commun. Surv. Tutorials 16(1), 414–454 (2014)

25. Reiter, R.: The frame problem in the situation calculus: a simple solution (sometimes) and a completeness result for goal regression. In: Artificial Intelligence and Mathematical Theory of Computation, vol. 27, pp. 359–380 (1991). Papers in honor of John McCarthy

26. Yau, S.S., Liu, J.: Hierarchical situation modeling and reasoning for pervasive computing. In: The Fourth IEEE Workshop on Software Technologies for Future Embedded and Ubiquitous Systems, and the Second International Workshop on Collaborative Computing, Integration, and Assurance (SEUS-WCCIA 2006), p. 6. IEEE (2006)

27. Ye, J., Dobson, S., McKeever, S.: Situation identification techniques in pervasive computing: a review. Pervasive Mobile Comput. **8**(1), 36–66 (2012). http://www.sciencedirect.com/science/article/pii/S1574119211000253

28. Yousef, A.M.F., Chatti, M.A., Schroeder, U., Harald Jakobs, M.W.: A review of the state-of-the-art. In: Proceedings of CSEDU 2014, 6th International Conference on Computer Supported Education, pp. 9–20 (2014)

Thoughts on Effective Learning Procedure for Tangible Learning Environment Based on Embodied Design

Hideaki Kuzuoka[1(✉)], Ryo Kimura[1], Yuki Tashiro[1], Yoshihiko Kubota[2], Hideyuki Suzuki[3], Hiroshi Kato[4], and Naomi Yamashita[5]

[1] Faculty of Engineering, Information and Systems, University of Tsukuba, 1-1-1 Tennoudai, Tsukuba, Ibaraki, Japan
{kuzuoka.hideaki.fa,s1420778,s1211144}@u.tsukuba.ac.jp
[2] Graduate School of Education, Utsunomiya University, 350 Minemachi, Utsunomiya, Tochigi, Japan
kubota@kubota-lab.net
[3] The College of Humanities, Ibaraki University, 2-1-1, Bunkyo, Mito, Ibaraki, Japan
suzukicity@gmail.com
[4] Faculty of Liberal Arts, The Open University of Japan, 2-11 Wakaba, Mihama-ku, Chiba, Japan
hkato@ouj.ac.jp
[5] Innovative Communication Laboratory, NTT Communication Science Laboratories, 2-4, Hikaridai, Seika-cho, Keihanna Science City, Kyoto, Japan
naomiy@acm.org

Abstract. Based on an observational study of astronomy education using a tangible globe system, this paper aims to elicit implications for effective learning procedure for tangible learning environments. By analyzing the experiment based on "embodied design" concept, we found that, when appropriate instruction is not provided, intuitive operability of tangible user interface at times rather disturbs learners' thinking opportunities. We also found that by properly limiting the information to show learners, the system can make learners be more conscious of the meaning of manipulating tangible objects and result in better understanding of the learning content.

1 Introduction

Grasping the concepts related to earth-sun relationships is difficult since students need to deal with immense scales and combine knowledge from various perspectives [15]. For example, they need to understand how the spatiotemporal relationships between the sun and the earth cause daily and seasonal variations to fully understand the sun's diurnal motion [8,11]. Atwood and Atwood reported that even some preservice elementary school teachers fail to understand these relationships [2].

© Springer International Publishing AG 2017
M. Kurosu (Ed.): HCI 2017, Part II, LNCS 10272, pp. 331–340, 2017.
DOI: 10.1007/978-3-319-58077-7_26

In this paper, we adapt a tangible user interface (TUI) approach to support astronomy education. Since globes effectively help students grasp basic astronomy concepts [2,8,14], we believe that expanding the tool's capability to provide multiple perspectives is a promising approach for astronomy education. While many studies have applied TUIs for educational purposes (e.g., seismology [7], basic programming [12,17], and vocational training [10]) and demonstrated their benefits in collaborative learning [5,16], few have applied them to astronomy education [8].

With the TUI approach, we developed a tangible learning environment (TLE) called the tangible globe system (Fig. 1) to support the learning of earth-sun relationships. Our system consists of a tangible globe, a tangible avatar, an electric light, and a PC screen that shows a computer-simulated view from the tangible avatar. The spatial arrangement of these components fosters learners to observe multiple perspectives of such earth-sun related phenomena as a birds-eye-view of the solar system and a computer-simulated ground-level view.

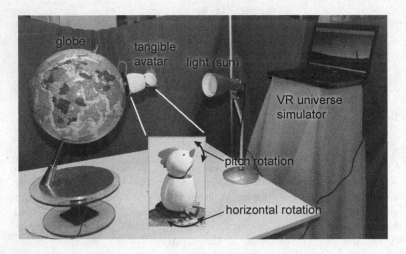

Fig. 1. Overview of tangible globe system

We have been empirically applying our system in regular/extracurricular junior high science classes. Although most of the students and teachers were enthusiastic about the system, we also observed instances where it was not embraced. Our controlled experiments have barely shown its clear benefit over traditional methods that only use a simple globe.

To better understand our system's problems and to propose design implications to improve them, we chose a design-based research approach [3] and observed how the system impacted learning practices. Through these experiments, we came to realize that not only the system but also the study method is important. Based on these experiences, this paper aims to discuss the effective learning procedure design which can make use of the TLE more effectively.

2   Framework

2.1   Design-Based Research

Design-based research (DBR) was developed to compensate for the limitations of traditional laboratory studies. According to Collins et al., "Laboratory studies are effective for identifying effects of particular variables, but they often neglect critical values to the success of" [3] educational intervention. To compensate for this limitation, design-based research is carried out in actual learning environments, and ethnographic techniques are often used to understand what is happening in the field and how.

The goal of design-based research is twofold: designing effective learning environments and developing general theories of learning. "Continuous cycles of design, enactment, analysis, and redesign" [4] allow researchers to effectively achieve these goals.

2.2   Embodied Design

Abrahamson and Lindgren proposed 'embodied design' concept to guide designing learning environment for science, technology, engineering, and math [1]. According to them, when one cannot achieve the desired effect despite a trial to achieve a certain goal using a physical tool, he/she conciously reflect on how we used the tool and recalibrate the usage of the tool to achive the goal. Such thinking and re-adujusting process is certainly a learning. The important thing about the learning tool is not to let learners use the tool unconsciously without thinking of the meaning of the operation, but to let them analyze how they are interacting with the tool themselves and to make them understand concretely and quantitatively. By doing this, the behaviors with respect to the tool is gradually internalized within the learners. Then, even without the tool, it becomes possible for them to simulate the behavior against the tool, or even to simulate the motion in their mind.

What is important here is to design a learning tool that makes it possible to understand its meaning during performing trial and error process on an artifact, and gradually internalize the body motion. Furthermore, it is pointed out that a teacher's proper scaffolding is important in making the learning tool effective.

Based on these ideas, this paper clarifies how the learners' actions to the tangible globe system affect the understanding of learning contents. We then discuss the appropriate learning procedure that makes the tangible learning environment effective.

3   Past Studies with Tangible Grobe System

3.1   Tangible Globe System

Based on the concept of TUI, the authors developed the tangible globe system to support the learners to understand the spatio-temporal relationship between the sun and the earth [13].

Our TLE, called the tangible globe system, was designed to support the learning of the relation of the sun's diurnal motion and the earth's rotation. It consists of a doll-like figure (tangible avatar or avatar), a globe, a rotating table, an electrical light, and a laptop PC (Fig. 1). The electrical light represents the sun. The laptop runs a publicly available VR universe simulator, Mitaka [18] to show the diurnal motion of the sun in the celestial sphere (ground-level view).

The globe is rotated around the earth's axis either forward or reverse during the simulation to change the sun's position in the celestial sphere. Rotation of the globe is detected by a rotary encoder inside the globe. DIN type connectors are embedded at the locations of Japan, Australia, and Honduras to plug the avatar into those places and to change the location of the ground-level view. The avatar's body rotation angle and pitch rotation angle are detected by potentiometers embedded in the avatar. The information of the globe rotation, the avatar's position, and the avatar's posture is captured by a PIC16F876 microcontroller and wirelessly sent to a note PC using ZigBee protocol.

With this mechanism, the simulator's line of sight can be changed by the horizontal rotation of the avatar's body and its head's pitch rotation. The clock time in the simulator, the compass point names, and the azimuth altitude of the line of sight are displayed on the PC screen.

To see the sun in the simulator, a learner simply rotates the globe and reorients the avatar's body and its head toward the light. With this configuration, learners are expected to naturally relate the earth's rotation, the avatar's posture, the relative position of the earth and the sun, and the sun's diurnal motion.

3.2 Remaining Issues

Following the DBR process, we have been invesitigating the effect of tangible globe system on learning activities. Especially, based on the Price's framework [9], we raised a few issues to be solved [6].

The first issue is about *location* of information. Since the time and orientation are shown on the display, the learners tended to focus only on the display and they did not pay atention to the positional relationship of the globe, avatar, and the sun.

The second issue is about *manipulation* of tangible objects. To observe the sunrise and the sun's culmination, the learners had to adjust the rotation of the globe and the head of the avatar so that the sun could be seen in the center of the PC screen. However, the learner seemed to manipulate the these objects randomely without thininking of the meaning of manipulation.

To alleviate these issues while satisfying the requirements for the embodied design, we decided to apply following two improvements to the system:

- Improve the avatar so that the learners can understand that the avatar is their surrogate and they have to pay attention to its line of sight.
- Imporve the study procedure so that the learners can manipulate the avatar while contemplating the meaning of the manipulation.

3.3 Improvement of the Avatar

As the first improvement, we changed the avatar from chicken like appearance to a person like appearance, and made it have a long nose like Pinocchio to make it easy to recognize the gaze direction.

As a second improvement, we embeded motors in the avatar so that its neck can tilt back and forth for 90°, and the whole body rotates in the pan direction infinitely. Below the avatar, we attached a orientation board which denotes eight azimuth orientations so that learners can easily recognize the avatar's current orientation. The avatar has two control modes, a manual operation mode in which the avatar is operated by hand, and a body motion synchronization mode in which the avatar moves synchronously with the learner's body motion (Fig. 2). We used a tablet PC (Microsoft Surface Pro 3) for body motion synchronization mode.

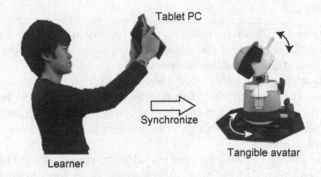

Fig. 2. Body motion synchronization mode of the avatar

4 Experiment

We conducted an experiment at a junior high school in Tsukuba, Japan. Eight second grade male students (learners) participated in the experiment.

4.1 Study Procedure Design

We applied pretest and posttest to examine the knowledge level of the participants. In the pretest, we asked questions on the orbit of the sun's diurnal motion, the direction of the rotation of the earth, directions of east, west, north, and south on the globe, the sun's trajectory at the sunrise and sunset in Japan. As for the posttest, in addition to the same questions as the pretest, questions about the orbits of the diurnal movement in Australia was asked.

After the pretest, we instructed how to use tangible glove system. Then, the learners became a group of two and worked on the two tasks written on the worksheet using the system. The tasks asked the learners time, elevation angles, and directions at the sunrise, mid-day, and sunset in June 21 (summer solstice) both in Japan and in Australia. The Learners attached the avatar to Japan or to Australia first. Then by taking the relative position of the avatar with the sun into consideration, they rotated the globe so that the avatar was brought to sunrise, sunset, and midpoint positions. Then, while manipulating the avatar, they observed the movement of the sun on the tablet PC screen and answered the questions in the worksheet.

We conducted the fist experiment in the morning with four learners and second experiment in the evening with other four learners. Since the study procedure for the first experiment was similar to our past experiments, we still saw the similar issues that was observed previously (see Sect. 3.2). Thus, following the DBR approach, we redesigned our study procedure for the second experiment.

In the second experiment, the learners performed the following procedure for Japan and Australia when observing sunrise, culmination, and sunset in manual operation mode.

1. Laied the tablet PC's screen down so that the screen is not visible.
2. Manipulated the avatar and the globe to the appropriate positions to observe sunrise, culmination, and sunset respectively.
3. After the learners determined that they adjusted the avatar to the correct position and orientation, they turned the tablet PC over to see that the simulator showed the expected time and the sun was at the expected position (in case of the sunrise, for example, the learners made sure that the sun was near the east horizon).
4. Brought the sun at the desired position while finely adjusting the globe and the avatar, and recorded the time and orientation on the worksheet.

Next, the learners performed the following procedure for each Japan and Australia. During the following two steps, the learner who manipulated the tablet PC stood on a orientation indicator mat (Fig. 3) so that the learner can always be aware where he was oriented to.

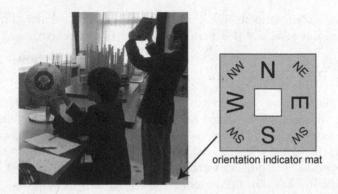

orientation indicator mat

Fig. 3. Manipulating the tablet PC on the orientation indicator mat

1. First, the system was set to manual operation mode, let the learners hold a tablet PC with blank display, and move the tablet PC to simulate the sun's diurnal motion both in Japan and in Australia.
2. Start the simulator on the tablet PC, set the body motion synchronize mode, let the learners observe sunrise, sunset, and culmination, and record the time and orientation in the worksheet.

5   Results

The correct answer rate of the pretest was 50% on average and the correct answer rate of the posttest is 82% on average. We observed that learners were making projections while thinking about relationship between the avatar, the globe, and the sun. Figure 4 is a scene that the learners were speculating the posture of the globe and avatar at the time of culmination in Australia. After P1 and P2 manipulated the avatar together, they confirmed that the avatar's gaze direction was heading toward the sun by seeing it from the avatar's face position.

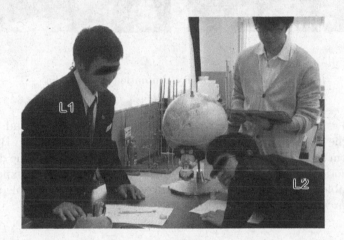

Fig. 4. Learners focusing on the relation between the avatar and the sun

Figure 5 is a scene where another group was trying to observe the culmination in Australia. First of all L3 thought that avatar should face to the south to observe the sun at noon, so while saying "south", he manipulated the avatar to face the sun. At this time, L4 was also paying attention to the avatar, but by seeing the orientation board at the avatar's feet, they simultaneously noticed that the avatar was facing to the north. Then, as L4 pointed at the orientation board, asked L3 "North?" (Fig. 5 (a)). After that, L4 rotated the avatar to the south and tried to lift the neck up to make it look to the sun. However, since the avatar's neck stopped at its 90°, the avatar's line of sight did not reach the sun (Fig. 5 (b)). As a result, it was impossible to make the avatar see the sun in

Australia if the avatar faced the south, which made both L3 and L4 understand that the sun culminates to the north in Australia.

From these examples, by employing a stage where participants predict only from the postures of avatar and the globe without looking at the tablet PC, both of the groups could focus on the avatar and the globe. Such focus seemed to led them to be conscious of the relative positions of the globe, the avatar, and the sun. Furthermore, by applying various manipulations to them, the learners seemed to better understand the phenomena.

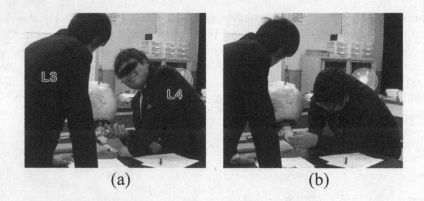

(a)   (b)

Fig. 5. Discussing about culmination in Australia

Figure 6 is the scene when L2 was working on the posttest and trying to remember the movement of the sun at the time of sunrise and sunset. By swingin his arms from right to left, L2 seemed to reproduce the action that he did during the body motion synchronization mode. Since the learners had an experience to move the tablet PC to follow the sun's diurnal motion, it is possible that such an operation was internalized.

6   Discussion

Through our previous experiments [6] as well as the first experiment in this study, we obtaned an implication that **"In the case where an appropriate learning procedure is not provided, the intuitive operability of the tangible user interface may rather impede the learner's thinking."**

On the other hand, in our second experiment, we first made the learners predict the result without seeing the display of the tablet PC. This process seemed to made them contemplate how the avatar's posture should be in relation to the positions of the globe and the sun. Furthermore, as an example of the Fig. 5 shows, when the learners found that the result was different from their predictions, they tried to understanding the phenomena while manipulating the avatar. The example of Fig. 6 shows the possibility that the learner internalized

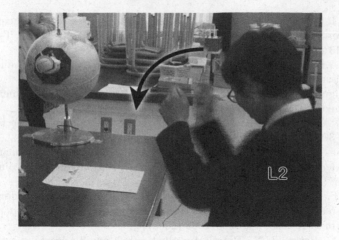

Fig. 6. Simulating the motion

the manipulation of the tablet PC. Therefore, the study procedure in our experiment seemed to support embodied design concept to some extent. From these discussions, we propose an implication that **"it is effective for the learners to restrict the information to be provided first, then, let them perform trial and error as they manipulate objects, and let them predict the result."**

7   Result

In this paper, by analyzing the experiment of astronomy education using the tangible globe system, we aimed to obtain implications about the learning procedure that enables to use the tangible learning environment effectively. We conducted observational study and analyzed the results based on the idea of embodied design. Based on the analysis, we proposed two implications, (1) if an appropriate learning procedure is not provided, the intuitive operability of the tangible user interface may rather hinder the learner's thinking, and (2) it may be effective to restrict the information to be offered to the learners first, let them try trial and error while manipulating artifacts, and let them predict the result. In the future, further experiments should be conducted with various learning procedures. It is also necessary to clarify what kind of scaffolding is effecitve for embodied design.

References

1. Abrahamson, D., Lindgren, R.: Embodiment and embodied design. In: Sawyer, R.K. (ed.) The Cambridge Handbook of the Learning Sciences, 2nd edn, pp. 258–376. Cambridge University Press, Cambridge (2014)

2. Atwood, R.K., Atwood, V.A.: Effects of instruction on preservice elementary teachers' conceptions of the causes of night and day and the seasons. J. Sci. Teach. Educ. **8**(1), 1–13 (1997)
3. Collins, A., Joseph, D., Bielaczyc, K.: Design research: theoretical and methodological issues. J. Learn. Sci. **13**(1), 15–42 (2004)
4. The Design-Based Research Collective: Design-based research: an emerging paradigm for educational inquiry. Educ. Res. **32**(1), 5–8 (2003)
5. Gokhale, A.: Collaborative learning enhances critical thinking. J. Technol. Educ. **7**(1), 22–30 (1995)
6. Kuzuoka, H., Yamashita, N., Kato, H., Suzuki, H., Kubota, Y.: Tnagible earth: tangible learning environment for astronomy education. In: Proceedings of HAI 2014, pp. 23–27 (2014)
7. Moher, T., Hussain, S., Halter, T., Kilb, D.: RoomQuake: embedding dynamic phenomena within the physical space of an elementary school classroom. In: Proceedings of CHI 2005, pp. 1655–1668 (2005)
8. Morita, Y., Setozaki, N.: Practical evaluation of tangible learning system: lunar phase class case study. In: Proceedings of SITE 2012, pp. 3718–3722 (2012)
9. Price, S.: A representation approach to conceptualizing tangible learning environments. In: Proceedings of TEI 2008, pp. 151–157 (2008)
10. Schneider, B., Jermann, P., Zufferey, G., Dillenbourg, P.: Benefits of a tangible interface for collaborative learning and interaction. IEEE Trans. Learn. Technol. **4**(3), 222–232 (2011)
11. Shelton, B., Hedley, N.: Using augmented reality for teaching earth-sun relationships to undergraduate geography students. In: Proceedings of ART 2002, 8 p. (2002)
12. Suzuki, H., Kato, H.: Interaction-level support for collaborative learning: AlgoBlock-an open programming language. In: Proceedings of CSCL 1995, pp. 349–355 (1995)
13. Yamashita, J., Kuzuoka, H., Fujimon, C., Hirose, M.: Tangible avatar and tangible earth: a novel interface for astronomy education. In: CHI 2007 Extended Abstract, pp. 2777–2782 (2007)
14. Vosniadou, S., Skopeliti, I., Ikospentaki, K.: Modes of knowing and ways of reasoning in elementary astronomy. Cogn. Dev. **19**(2), 203–222 (2004)
15. Young, T., Farnsworth, B., Grabe, C., Guy, M.: Exploring new technology tools to enhance astronomy teaching & learning in grades 3 classrooms: year one implementation. In: Annual Meeting of the Association for Science Teacher Education, pp. 4556–4567 (2012)
16. Zakaria, E.: Promoting cooperative learning in science and mathematics education: a Malaysian perspective. Eurasia J. Math. Sci. Technol. Educ. **3**(1), 35–39 (2009)
17. Zuckerman, O., Arida, S., Resnick, M.: Extending tangible interfaces for education: digital montessori inspired manipulatives. In: Proceedings of CHI 2005, pp. 859–868 (2005)
18. 4D2U Project. http://4d2u.nao.ac.jp/html/program/mitaka/index_E.html

Learning by Tangible Learning System in Science Class

Yusuke Morita[1]([⊠]) and Norio Setozaki[2]

[1] Faculty of Human Sciences, Waseda University, MIkajima 2-579-15,
Tokorozawa, Saitama 359-1192, Japan
ymorita@waseda.jp
[2] Faculty of Education, Nagasaki University, Bunkyo-machi 1-14,
Nagasaki, Nagasaki 852-8131, Japan
setozaki@nagasaki-u.ac.jp

Abstract. Tangible User Interfaces are one of the ideas to develop a learning materials as an invisible computing system. First, we developed a tangible learning system for learning Solar System that allows the users themselves to manipulate astronomical models of the sun, earth, and moon, which exist as visible tangible bodies. Second, the tangible learning system was implemented in an elementary school science class and twenty 6th grade students from a public elementary school participated in this practical study. The results clearly showed that the comprehension test scores of students who scored high on mental rotation test increased greatly following the class using the tangible learning system.

Keywords: Tangible user interface · Science class · Mental rotation

1 Introduction

The astronomy area of science courses is one of the most difficult contents for teachers to teach in classroom. In the same way, it is not easy for students to understand the positional relationships of celestial bodies rotating in relative motion [1–3]. To imagine the movement of the relative positional relationships with an awareness of the positional relationships of celestial bodies, it is necessary to mentally shift their viewpoint and shape dynamic images into a mental model [4–7].

There has been research into the effectiveness of astronomy learning materials using physical models and video contents in order to indicate the scenes in space. Computer simulations can be presented a virtual space as three-dimensional (3D) dynamic images that cannot be observed in the real world, so students can learn the phenomena from a variety of angles in the space [8–11].

However, the previous astronomy learning materials that formed the basis for celestial body simulations were unable to touch and operate the 3D computer graphics (CG) relative positional relationships of the sun, earth, and moon. The learners can become observers of natural phenomena within the virtual space;

© Springer International Publishing AG 2017
M. Kurosu (Ed.): HCI 2017, Part II, LNCS 10272, pp. 341–352, 2017.
DOI: 10.1007/978-3-319-58077-7_27

however, in many cases, they are unable to actively interact with the CG model, or observe after shifting to different viewpoints. For elementary school students, manipulating models in physical space and actively observing the phenomena from various angles will provide a more effective learning environment.

A tangible user interface (TUI) is technology that makes it possible to operate models in physical space to promote learning [12–15]. As for studies of astronomy learning to which TUI was applied, there is the development of a tangible globe system supporting viewpoint shifts in a learner using an avatar [16–18]. Also, an astronomy learning content that could be operated intuitively were developed for science classes [19].

Morita *et al.* [20] applied augmented reality technology to develop a tangible learning system in which virtual models in the virtual learning environment and physical models in the real learning environment seamlessly move in conjunction. There has also been practical research where the systems have been introduced in elementary school and junior high school classrooms [21,22]. In this paper, we focus on the relationship between the mental rotation ability of 6th grade elementary school students and comprehension tests, and discuss the benefits and problems of the tangible learning system.

2   Development

2.1   Design

The tangible learning system was designed to support collaborative learning in classroom [20]. The learners operate concrete objects on a table in physical space, while shifting their viewpoint in virtual space, and discussing the waxing and waning of the moon, and the positional relationships between the sun, earth, and moon. Furthermore, the learners themselves are able to recreate the movement of the celestial bodies, rotating in relative motion, and the phenomena they cause (for example, the eclipse) in their own mental space, and carry out activities such as shifting viewpoints to the desired position and performing observation.

The thing given most attention to during system design was not the simulation, but the reproduction of learning focusing on shifting viewpoints within the simplified virtual space. The astronomical 3D CG model in this system does not fix the positional relationships in the virtual astronomical model as shown in the previous simulations and does not perform rotational linking of rotating and revolving. For this reason, learners can move the model actively while searching for astronomical positional relationships and rotating and revolving manually.

Furthermore, the earth's axis in the global model within the virtual space is set vertically in relation to the revolving surface (inclined at a 23.4° angle in relation to the physical revolving surface of the earth's axis. For this reason, although the seasonal changes in the south altitude and meaning of tropics cannot be demonstrated to the learner, it is possible to focus learning on the phase of the moon. In addition, in this system, it is set so that the revolving orbit plane of the earth and revolving orbit plane of the moon do not overlap, to present a full moon or new moon. For this reason, when reproducing phenomena such as a solar eclipse or lunar eclipse, the operation of lifting the celestial bodies from the table to the air is required.

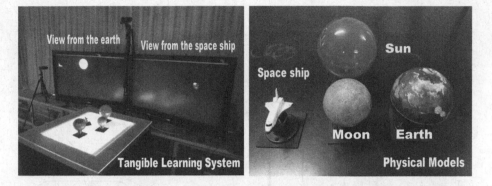

Fig. 1. External appearance of the tangible learning system and physical models

2.2 Hardware

Figure 1 shows the external appearance of the developed tangible learning system and the physical models used in manipulations by the students. In this paper, we call the model that they can actually touch the physical model, and the 3D CG objects within virtual space the virtual model. The reason for adopting a table-top interface is that a scenario is envisaged in which the students learn collaboratively and exploratorily in groups while operating the physical models. The physical models envisage learning of the waxing and waning of the moon in the science class, and the models has prepared the sun, earth, moon, and a space ship. The reason for including the space ship model is to encourage exploratory activities and set viewpoints for observing celestial bodies in outer space.

The respective sizes of the physical models, in the same way as other simulation learning materials, was not scaled down based on the physical size. Sizes that were considered to be suitable to be physically operated by elementary and middle school students were selected.

2.3 Software

Figure 2 shows an overview of the processing carried out by the tangible learning system. The system recognizes the black and white rectangular image known as the marker, stuck to the reverse side of each physical model placed on the table, and determines the global coordinates in the virtual space and the local coordinates for each marker. It then calculates how it is viewed from virtual cameras (invisible and not displayed as images on the display) installed in each virtual model within the virtual space and outputs that image to the display. As these processes are processed in real-time, they are linked to the operations of the physical model and enable interactive operations of the virtual model. Furthermore, to realize multi-viewpoint learning, images seen from any two viewpoints at the same time can be presented respectively on two displays.

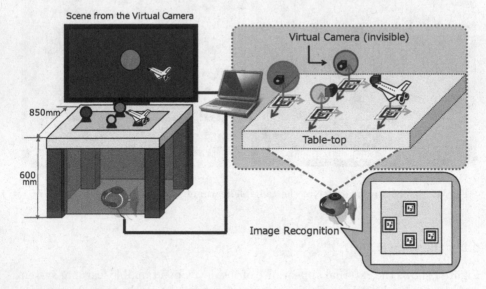

Fig. 2. Processing of tangible learning system

3   Evaluation

3.1   Practical Research in Science Classes

Overview of Target and Procedure. In this study, we carried out science classes on the waxing and waning of the moon using the developed tangible learning system aimed at twenty 6th grade public elementary school students (13 boys and 6 girls).

Figure 3 shows the procedure of practical research in the science classes. The classes were held three times, for two class period (90 min) each, over approximately four weeks. Furthermore, all practical classes were conducted by a full-time elementary school science teacher. For group activities using the tangible learning system, teacher instruction and student activities were recorded from the top of the table and left the side of the display.

Group Activities Based on Image Presentation. The first class was a teacher-centered class mainly using video and CG contents. Firstly, the teacher indicated a hi-vision video captured by lunar probe *Kaguya* on a large-scale liquid crystal display to make the students consider the positional relationship between the sun and the earth. Next, in order to compare the size of the sun,

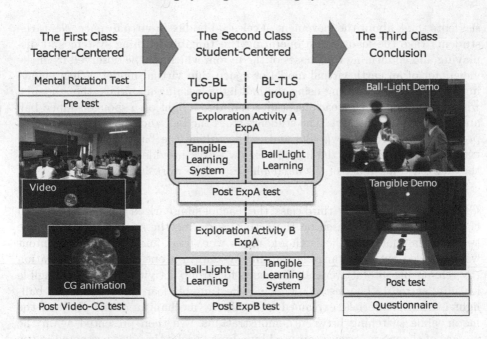

Fig. 3. Procesure of practical research in 6th science class

earth, and moon, CG images of the solar system planets were presented on the display. Then, revolving and rotating images of the earth and moon was presented to explain the positional relationships with the sun. Finally, the phase of the moon presented by CG animation.

Exploratory Learning in Groups. In the second class, the students were divided into two groups and using tangible learning system configured four physical models and two displays and ball-light learning materials using a light. They learned the mechanism of the waxing and waning of the moon in an explorative way. The students were divided into two groups because, when the tangible learning system was designed, it was envisaged that it would involve collaborative and explorative activities by up to a maximum of 10 people. The group first learning in an explorative way using the tangible learning system, and then using ball-light learning materials was named the TLS-BL group, and the group learning in the reverse order was called the BL-TLS group. The exploratory activities carried out in the first half were called "ExpA" and when carried out in the second half, the exploratory activities were named "ExpB."

The exploratory learning with the tangible learning system and the exploratory learning using the ball-light learning materials were each carried out for 30 min. With the exploratory learning using the tangible learning system, the science teacher moves physical models of the sun, earth, moon, and space ship by hand for the students, while performing an experiment to make students think about the movement of celestial bodies in virtual space. Next, the students take the lead role in operating the tangible learning system and displaying and confirming the phases of the moon, which can be observed from the viewpoint of an earth virtual model or space ship virtual model. When engaging in exploratory learning using the ball-light learning materials, the students, with the support of the teaching staff, irradiated a light on a sponge-shaped ball and observed the shadows. The students fixed the ball and light (their own eyes provide a bird's eye viewpoint) and, while taking the ball in their hands and rotating this in front of the light (their own eyes provide an earth viewpoint), they sketched an image of the lunar phases on the worksheet.

Class Summary. In the third class, the teacher summarized the first and second classes. At this time, based on the activities during the second class, only the two physical models of the earth and moon were used, and the learning content was provided with the tangible learning system in a one display configuration (by referencing interactive analysis results for group activities using the tangible learning system). The instructor, using the tangible learning system and ball-light learning materials, explained in detail the mechanism of the phase of the moon while switching between demonstrations. We then presented again the images of the moon surface captured by a lunar probe that was presented in the first class, to make the students reconsider the positional relationships of the sun, earth, and moon.

3.2   Measurement

We executed a Mental Rotation Test (MRT) [23, 24] consisting of 20 questions at the start of the first class to measure the ability of the individual learners to mentally rotate shapes. Also, a comprehension test has performed a total of 5 times and all had the same questions. The first test was performed at the start of the first class (Pre test), and the second one was done after the class in which the image materials and CG materials are presented in the first class (Post Video-CG test). After the exploratory activities A (TLS-BL group used the tangible learning system, and the BL-TLS group using the ball-light learning materials) in the second class, the third test was performed (Post ExpA test), and the forth test (Post ExpB test) was done after the exploratory activities B (TLS-BS group using the ball-light learning materials and the BL-TLS group using the tangible learning system). In the third class, students took the last test after the summary (Post test). To answer the respective questions correctly, it was necessary to imagine the classroom activity scenarios, shift viewpoints within mental space, and operate mental models dynamically.

In the comprehension test, we used two questions for six points in regard to shifting viewpoints exhibiting a ball shadow in physical space, two questions with four points exhibiting the earth's shadow (static image) in virtual space, two questions with four points exhibiting the shadows of an physical model of the moon observed between an physical model of the earth and physical model of a space ship placed on a table in physical space (static image) and 2 questions with four points with selective answers on the phases of the moon seen from the earth in virtual space in relative rotational motion, for a total of 18 points.

3.3 Analysis

The mean values of MRT points were calculated, and the students were divided into the MRT upper group and MRT lower group. Then, three-way analysis of variance (ANOVA) was performed the groups during exploratory activities and relationship with the comprehension test scores. The first factor was MRT (upper and lower groups), the second factor was exploratory activities (TLS-BL and BL-TLS groups), and the third factor was the test period (Pre test, Post Video-CG test, Post ExpA test, Post ExpB test, and Post test).

3.4 Results

Comprehension Test. Figure 4 shows the result of the mean scores for the both TLS-BL and BL-TLS divided into the MRT upper and lower groups. The results of the three-way ANOVA show that the secondary interaction effect was insignificant at the 5% level ($F = 0.72$, $df1 = 4$, $df2 = 64$, n.s.). Furthermore, the primary interaction effects between MRT and exploratory activities and the exploratory activities and test period were not significant either ($F = 0.05$, $df1 = 1$, $df2 = 16$, n.s.; $F = 0.14$, $df1 = 4$, $df2 = 64$, n.s.). The main effects of the exploratory activities were significant at the 5% level ($F = 4.70$, $df1 = 1$, $df2 = 16$, $p < .05$). Based on this, it is clear that there was a significant difference between the TLS-BL group and BL-TLS group, regardless of factors such as MRT and test period.

On the other hand, the primary interactive effects between MRT and the test period was significant ($F = 4.35$, $df1 = 4$, $df2 = 64$, $p < .01$). Therefore, the result of performing lower level analysis using Ryan's Method was that in the test, after the exploration activity A, the test after the exploration activity B, and in the post test, there was a significant difference between the mean values in the MRT upper and lower group comprehension test scores ($F = 6.12$, $df1 = 1$, $df2 = 16$, $p < .05$; $F = 5.79$, $df1 = 1$, $df2 = 16$, $p < .05$; $F = 4.58$, $df1 = 1$, $df2 = 16$, $p < .05$). In other tests, there was no significant difference between the MRT upper group and lower group. Furthermore, in the MRT upper group, a significant difference was seen between the scores for the test after the exploration activity A, the test after the exploration activity B and post test and the respective pre tests ($Mse = 2.80$, $df = 64$, $p < .05$). In the MRT lower group as well, a significant difference was seen between the post test scores and pre test scores ($Mse = 2.80$, $df = 64$, $p < .05$).

The following four points are clear based on the above results; The BL-TLS group, when compared to the TLS-BL group, had significantly high comprehension test scores from those before the class. After receiving the classes in which Video and CG are presented, the comprehension test scores were significantly improved. The students in the MRT upper group after performing exploratory learning, using the tangible learning system or ball-light learning materials, had significantly improved test scores. The MRT lower group, after taking 3 classes, had improved comprehension test scores.

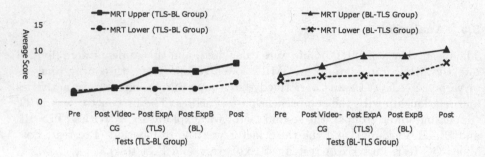

Fig. 4. Comprehension test scores

Group Activities. We analyzed the interaction during group activities using the tangible learning system. From these results, we learned that, with the 2-screen configuration tangible learning system, it took time for the students to understand what images were being presented from which viewpoint by which display. Furthermore, in the dialogue shown below, the following three points have been clarified: the prompting of collaborative learning, the issue of the sun model being a point light source, and the fact that there are students that play with the physical model of the space ship.

The Prompting of Collaborative Learning. The students collaboratively explored positional relationships with images in groups, with images of the new moon, the crescent moon, half-moon, and full moon. At this time, using this system, a dialogue took place to understand the phenomena of the moon phases. An example of the dialogue is shown below as the evidence of collaboration.

Student A: It's a full moon.
Student C: Yes, if you move it more that way...
Student A: It's a full moon, this.
Student E: Not yet.
Student A: I think it is OK now.
Student C: Full moon.
Student A: A perfect full moon.

Issue of the Sun Model as a Point Light Source. As, in this system, the sun was set as a point light source, it was not possible to reproduce a half-moon accurately. Therefore, cognitive conflicts might occur in some students, and some scenarios in which understanding was not promoted were seen. This is shown in the following dialogue.

Student N: Hey, this is a full moon.
Student L: How about a half moon? Or crescent moon?
Student N: <u>Half-moon... I don't know what a half moon is</u>.
     I could do a crescent moon, though.
Student L: Where did the space shuttle go? OK, then I will be the space
     shuttle.
Student K: Crescent moon? Half-moon... like this, see...
Student N: <u>Hey, this is not half</u>. Do a bit more... a bit more <unclear>.
...
Student L: Hey, space shuttle. <u>This isn't working out to be a crescent moon.</u>
Student N: Right next to it.
Student O: Like this?
Teacher: Yes, yes, yes
Student M: So, <u>this is not a half moon</u>.

Students that Play with the Physical Space Ship Model. The physical space ship model was introduced as a viewpoint to project, with a bird's eye view, the phenomenon of the phases of the moon. However, there were students who were interested in the physical space ship model and who engaged in actions that were completely unrelated to the classes. An example of the dialogue is shown below.

Student M: It's broken... No, no, no.
Student L: Stop, <u>moon, moon, moon</u> ...come on!
Teacher: Hang on···. I'm feeling sea sick. Stop it.

Above, we described some of the dialogue of the students operating the tangible learning system. The students conducted exploratory activities related to the phases of the moon. This system could prompt collaborative learning among the learners. On the other hand, the model of the sun in this system impeded students' understanding. Additionally, it is clear that there were many scenarios where the physical space ship model was used for objectives other than those related to the class.

4   Discussion

4.1   Effectiveness of the Tangible Learning System

From the results of the comprehension test, it can be said that the tangible learning system was effective for students with mental rotation skills, but not so much for students without such skills. Below, the TLS-BL group and the BL-TLS group will be discussed separately.

In the TLS-BL group, after taking the first class with Video and CG animation contents, the scores for the comprehension test were not significantly improved. In the second class, after the exploratory activities using tangible course materials, the comprehension of the MRT upper group students was significantly improved. From this fact, it is suggested that exploratory activities using the tangible learning system are effective. However, following this, an improvement in comprehension was not seen using the ball-light learning materials.

For the BL-TLS group, in the same way, after taking the first class with Video and CG animation contents, the comprehension test scores were not significantly improved. In the second class, after the exploratory activities using the ball-light learning materials, the comprehension in the students in the MRT upper group was significantly improved. This suggests that the exploratory activities using the Ball-Light course materials are effective; however, there was no improvement in comprehension seen through activities(ExpB)using the tangible learning system after this.

From these results, in regard to the MRT upper group, it is suggested that there may be an impact on the learners on the improvement in active and exploratory activities. The fact that no improvement was seen in ExpB for either the TLS-BL group and BL-TLS group may be due to the ceiling effect. This point requires careful discussion. On the other hand, in regard to the MRT lower group as well, there was no improvement in comprehension level even when using Video and CG animation teaching materials, tangible course materials, and light materials. In regard to the summary in the 3rd class, as a result of the detailed explanation by the teaching staff, comprehension was improved in comparison to before the class. This suggests that a certain amount of time for repeating an explanation may be required to improve the comprehension of students with comparatively low mental rotation skills.

4.2   Points of Improvement for the Tangible Learning System

From the interactive analysis results, it is clear that there are some light source issues and physical model issues in the tangible learning systems. We shall move forward with the discussion of both of these respectively.

The issue with the sun model as a point light source is essentially the same issue with the tangible learning system and ball-light learning materials. Differences in the sun and earth were taken up in the first class. However, they are different to the point light sources of model and light; there were students who could not imagine light as a parallel light source from large fixed stars such as the sun. As shown in the dialog, this was thought to cause cognitive conflicts in the students so comprehension could not be promoted. In this implementation, this issue was noticed when executing the second class. Therefore, in the third class, the class was carried out with the physical solar model excluded. Furthermore, the instructors emphasized and explained that the sun is much bigger than the earth and the moon and that it exists as a parallel light source in relation to the earth and the moon.

The issue with the space ship physical model is not essentially a problem and not a problem with the system. This was physically a problem with the physical model in front of us. In the case of elementary school students, the space ship model was attractive as a toy. It was clear that there was an essential problem we had not grasped in that this may have distracted attention from the content of the class. In the same way as the sun model, the issue in the space ship physical model was learned while conducting the second class. In the third class, the class was executed with the sun model excluded.

5 Summary

In this paper, we investigated the effectiveness of the developed tangible learning system in an elementary school science class on the phase of the moon. The results of ANOVA were that for students with comparatively high mental rotation skills, the learning content could be understood through active and exploratory activities using the tangible learning system. Improvements in comprehension test scores meant that a mental model had been formed in the mental space. It was considered that the group with high MRT scores, that is to say, students who, comparatively, had acquired the mental rotation skills, learned in an exploratory way, linking real space and virtual space, and formed a mental model related to the waxing and waning of the moon. Comprehension improvements in students with comparatively low mental rotation skills required a certain amount of time and repetition of explanation. Issues moving forward include long-term views, from elementary school to junior high school, investigating learning using the tangible learning system.

Acknowledgments. This study received the support of the Grant-in-Aid for Scientific Research (KAKENHI Grant JP21680053 and JP26350337). We would like to express our sincere gratitude for the great cooperation of Mr. Yasushi Ito. Part of this paper was published by the authors in SITE International Conference 2012.

References

1. Nussbaum, J., Sharoni-Dagan, N.: Changes in second grade students's preconceptions about the earth as a cosmic body resulting from a short series of audio-tutorial lessons. Sci. Educ. **67**(1), 99–114 (1983)
2. Vosniadou, S.: Conceptual development in astronomy. In: Glynn, S., Yearny, R.H., Britton, B.K. (eds.) The Psychology of Learning Science, pp. 149–177. LEA, NJ (1991)
3. Suzuki, M.: Conversations about the moon with prospective teachers in Japan. Sci. Educ. **87**(6), 892–910 (2003)
4. Taylor, I., Barker, M., Jones, A.: Promoting mental model building in astronomy education. Int. J. Sci. Educ. **25**(10), 1205–1225 (2003). doi:10.1080/09500069022000017270a
5. Shen, J., Confrey, J.: From conceptual change to transformative modeling: a case study of an elementary teacher in learning astronomy. Sci. Educ. **91**(6), 948–966 (2007). doi:10.1002/sce.20224
6. Plummer, J.D., Wasko, K.D., Slagle, C.: Learning to explain daily celestial motion: understanding astronomy across moving frames of reference. Int. J. Sci. Educ. **33**(14), 1963–1992 (2011). doi:10.1080/09500693.2010.537707
7. Türk, C., Kalkan, H., Kiroğlu, K., İskeleli, N.C.: Elementary school students mental models of formation of seasons: a cross-sectional study. J. Educ. Learn. **5**(1), 7–30 (2016). doi:10.5539/jel.v5n1p7

8. Barnett, M., Yamagata-lynch, L., Keating, T., Barab, S.A., Hay, K.E.: Using virtual reality computer models to support student understanding of astronomical concepts. J. Comput. Math. Sci. Teach. **24**(4), 333–356 (2005)
9. Morita, Y., Iwasaki, T., Takeda, T., Fujiki, T.: Portable immersive projection technology system for 3D visual learning. In: Proceedings of ED-MEDIA, pp. 2585–2588 (2006)
10. Setozaki, N., Morita, Y., Takeda, T.: Examination for the practical use of screen presentation systems and VR teaching material. In: Proceedings of the SITE International Conference, pp. 3488–3494 (2007)
11. Sun, K.L., Wang, S.C.: A 3-D virtual reality model of the sun and the moon for e-learning at elementary schools. Int. J. Sci. Math. Educ. **8**(4), 689–710 (2010)
12. Ishii, H., Ullmer, B.: Tangible bits: towards seamless interfaces between people, bits, and atoms. In: Proceedings of CHI, pp. 234–241 (1997)
13. Schneider, B., Wallace, J., Blikstein, P., Pea, R.: Preparing for future learning with a tangible user interface: the case of neuroscience. IEEE Trans. Learn. Technol. **6**(2), 117–129 (2013)
14. Schneider, B., Blikstein, P.: Unraveling students' interaction around a tangible interface using multimodal learning analytics. J. Educ. Data Mining **7**(3), 89–116 (2015). doi:10.1109/TLT.2013.15
15. Cuendet, S., Dehler-Zufferey, J., Ortoleva, G., Dillenbourg, P.: An integrated way of using a tangible user interface in a classroom. Int. J. Comput.-Support. Collab. Learn. **10**(2), 183–208 (2015). doi:10.1007/s11412-015-9213-3
16. Yamashita, J., Kuzuoka, H., Fujimon, C., Hirose, M.: Tangible avatar and tangible earth: a novel interface for astronomy education. In: Proceedings of CHI, pp. 2777–2782 (2007). doi:10.1145/1240866.1241078
17. Yamashita, J., Nishikawa, S., Kuzuoka, H.: Tangible earth: a novel interface for astronomy education. In: Proceedings of ASIAGRAPH, pp. 206–209 (2008)
18. Kuzuoka, H., Suzuki, Y., Yamashita, N., Kato, H., Suzuki, H., Kubota, Y.: Thoughts on design principles for tangible learning environment for astronomy education. J. Sci. Educ. Japan **38**(2), 65–74 (2014). doi:10.14935/jssej.38.65. (in Japanese)
19. Kawasaki, T., Iwane, N., Matsubara, Y., Okamoto, M.: Development of a VR-based astronomy learning environment using intuitive manipulation and switching of the view corresponding to user's body movement. Educ. Technol. Res. **34**(1/2), 173–180 (2011)
20. Morita, Y., Setozaki, N., Iwasaki, T.: Development and evaluation of a tangible learning system for astronomy education: a pilot study. In: Proceedings of ED-MEDIA, pp. 3666–3671 (2010)
21. Morita, Y., Setozaki, N.: Practical evaluation of tangible learning system: lunar phase class case study. In: Proceedings of SITE International Conference, pp. 3718–3722 (2012)
22. Morita, Y., Setozaki, N.: Science class using interactive multimedia and tangible learning system: a pilot study. In: Proceedings of ED-MEDIA, pp. 2929–2934 (2012)
23. Shepard, R.N., Metzler, J.: Mental rotation of three-dimensional objects. Science **171**, 701–703 (1971)
24. Samsudin, K., Rafi, A., Hanif, A.S.: Training in mental rotation and spatial visualization and its impact on orthographic drawing performance. J. Educ. Technol. Soc. **14**(1), 179–186 (2011)

Toward Interest Estimation from Head Motion Using Wearable Sensors: A Case Study in Story Time for Children

Ayumi Ohnishi[1], Kaoru Saito[2], Tsutomu Terada[1,3(✉)], and Masahiko Tsukamoto[1]

[1] Graduate School of Engineering, Kobe University, Kobe, Japan
tsutomu@eedept.kobe-u.ac.jp
[2] Graduate School of Frontier Science, The University of Tokyo, Tokyo, Japan
[3] PRESTO, Japan Science and Technology Agency, Kawaguchi, Japan

Abstract. Learning activities were evaluated using questionnaire survey, video, or audio. However, these methods have the following problems. First, writing on the questionnaire paper is difficult, especially for little children. Second, because the answering questionnaires was performed after the experiments were finished. They were different temporally and spatially from the scene to be evaluated. Moreover, sometimes participants has forgot the part of the contents. Finally, by recording video or audio, we can look back at each scene and evaluate them, however, video or audio analysis takes a very long time. This research aims to solve these three problems and evaluate natural reactions; first, for children of a low age group, second, including changes in the state of participants during an activity, and third, as much as possible without wasting time and effort. In this paper, during storytelling events for children, we attempted to obtain the values of acceleration and angular velocity sensors with sensors placed on the participant's heads, and tried to estimate their motions and degree of interests. Motions were calculated using the F-value, with accuracies of 0.66 in "Sitting state", 0.26 in "Sitting again", 0.47 in "Wriggling", and 0.93 in "Playing with hands". From these results, "Playing with hands" had the highest degree of interest, with a motion recognition rate of 0.93 in F-value. Comparing the proposed method with the video evaluation later, the proposed method can obtain the evaluation result during the learning activity. Therefore, by feeding back the estimation result in real time, we can make improvements while doing activities.

Keywords: Motion recognition · Interest estimation · Book reading to children · Wearable sensing

1 Introduction

After conducting learning activities such as lessons and little learning, by evaluating these activities and designing based on the evaluation results, the next activities are further improved. To evaluate methods of these activities are generally used questionnaire surveys, video, and audio recordings. However, as shown in Table 1, there are three problems described as follows.

© Springer International Publishing AG 2017
M. Kurosu (Ed.): HCI 2017, Part II, LNCS 10272, pp. 353–363, 2017.
DOI: 10.1007/978-3-319-58077-7_28

Table 1. Score sheet of each evaluation method in learning activities

	(a) Evaluation of children	(b) Evaluation dividing scenes	(c) Time and effort to evaluate
Questionnaire	Difficult	Difficult	Quickly, and easily
Video, or audio	Evaluable	Evaluable	Taking a long time
Wearable sensing	Evaluable	Evaluable	Quickly, and automatically

(a) Questionnaire surveys can analyze trends against many participants at a time, however, it is difficult for little children to answer.

(b) The participants are evaluated after the objective is done. Therefore, it is different temporally and spatially from the scene to be evaluated. As a typical questionnaire method, people participate in some event and answer the questionnaire after all event contents are over. Therefore, in this method, people may be more impressed with the contents of the last one than the first one. As a result, some questionnaire answers are influenced by the contents of the last one.

(c) In participant observation, an analysis after the examination is a waste of time. Furthermore, there is a possibility of giving an oppressive feeling to participants by increasing the number of cameras used to record personal detailed movements from multiple angles. It is common to receive data related to physical appearances, facial expressions, and gestures from images obtained by video cameras.

This research aims to solve these problems and evaluate natural reactions; (a) for children of a low age group, (b) including changes in the state of participants during an activity, and (c) as much as possible without wasting time and effort.

Then, consider which method is actually suitable as an evaluation method of activities. Yamashita et al. attempted to evaluate activities by implementing Sounding Board. This system records a person's assessments in real activities such as conversations [1]. However, it is difficult to use it on a daily basis, because it is necessary to point the PDA terminal to the participant to be assessed, and to operate it. By accumulating everyday casual person's gestures, such as nodding or neck cranking, we can analyze the data from that content. However, these evaluations are improvised and not recorded. Therefore, if we record this casual evaluation, it possibly can be used as an indicator of interest during learning in addition to the conventional evaluation such as a questionnaire. Therefore, we propose a method to analyze evaluation activities by wearable sensing. As shown in Table 1, wearable sensing can solve (a) to (c) problems. In details, (a) it becomes possible to evaluate from the reaction of children, (b) time series analysis is possible, and (c) applications using this analysis method can evaluate quickly and automatically. In this paper, during storytelling events for children, we acquired acceleration and angular velocity from the subjects that participated with a cap with a motion sensor attached. At the same time, one movie recorded for annotation. Using the acceleration and angular velocity data, we attempted to recognize their reactions and estimate degree of interests from these natural motions. We evaluated by the following steps. First, we calculated the recognition accuracy of the motion seen in the story time. Second, we created five degrees of interest indicators. Additionally, two observers judged the degree of interest of the children to the story time from the recorded movie. Finally, the correspondence between observers' judgements and index of interest were compared, and the expressivity of the index was considered. By calculating the interest estimation rate by such a procedure, we evaluated whether each motion is effective as index of the degree of interest.

This paper is organized as follows. Section 2 describes related works. Section 3 explains the system requirements. Section 4 describes the evaluation. Finally, Sect. 5 provides the conclusion and mentions future work.

2 Related Works

Various systems that analyzes people's behaviors in conversation and recognition of head movements have been proposed. As an analysis of multiparty interaction, the sociometer implemented by Choudhury et al. is a portable device consisting of a microphone, acceleration sensor, infrared module, and GPS. They aimed to visualize the social relationships of multiple people from data obtained from gestures and conversation [2]. The Augmented Multi-party Interaction (AMI) project aims to develop meeting browsing and analysis systems. His meeting corpus is recorded by using a wide range of devices including close-talking and far-field microphones, individual and room-view video cameras, a projector, a whiteboard, and individual pens, and so on [3]. SUMI et al. developed IMADE environments to collect various kinds of information during a conversation, such as a subject's motion, gaze, voice, and biological data [4]. Tung et al. implemented a multimodal system, which consists of a large display attached to multiple sensing devices, to obtain individual speech and gazing directions [5]. Mana et al. proposed a multimodal corpus system with automatic annotation of multi-party meetings using multiple cameras and microphones. They investigated the possibility of using audio-visual cues to automatically analyze social behaviors and to create a system to predict personality characteristics [6]. Okada et al. attempted to classify nonverbal patterns with gestures, e.g., utterance, head gesture, and head direction of each participant, by using motion sensors and microphones. In this research, we are targeting events that already exist, therefore in order to take as much natural behaviors as possible, it is necessary for it to be a location- independent system. We determined that more natural evaluation behavior would be acquired by using wearable sensors. As mentioned above, there was much research conducted for estimating interests and the degree of concentrations from estimations using the camera images and motion sensors. However, a few studies evaluated behaviors and interests of young or low-grade school children. It is difficult to evaluate quantitatively for children by using a questionnaire because of the difficulty filling them. Therefore, in this research, we aim to use a story time activity targeted to such children of such an age and determine what evaluation behaviors should be measured with wearable sensors.

3 System Requirements

The assumed activity is a storytelling of picture books, which is one of the learning activities for young children, for example, like a story time. An experiment at a story time event for children held monthly was conducted at The Mount Fuji Research Institute, Yamanashi Prefectural Government. During in this story time, individual children determined their seating positions and some infants sat on their part's lap. Obtaining images from the front of each person's face with the video camera would be difficult.

To evaluate the natural behavior of children, it was necessary to bring them closer to their usual activities. As a result, wearable sensors, independent on the location were adopted. In this research, children from various elementary school lower grades, who could not answer the questionnaire, were targeted. An experiment was conducted during the story time part of the event aimed at enhancing interest in nature, with 'interest' in this activity being the main focus. Actions indicating aggressiveness and passivity from the children's behavior were detected, assuming them as an evaluation behavior, and whether it is an index of interest or not were examined. To clarify actions that could be indicators for the interest from actions the following experiments were conducted.

4 Evaluation

To estimate the degree of interest for contents, this study aims to examine behaviors which can be an index of interest in the activity during story telling. In other words, actions associated with the degree of interest and actions that can be detected with a high level of accuracy using a wearable sensor were considered.

4.1 Procedure

Evaluation experiments were conducted in the story time period cooperated with this research, which contained three different stories and time to play with hands. This event was approximately 20 to 30 min in total. Participant's children wore a cap with ATR's TSND121 sensor [8] as shown in Fig. 1 and attached acceleration and an angular velocity sensors to the right side of the cap. Moreover, as shown in Fig. 2, the children sit facing the storyteller, the staff member who reads picture card's and shows large picture books at the front. Five caps with sensors were prepared and motions of up to five heads of participants were acquired. The measurement frequency of the sensor was 20 mm/s. Table 2 lists the subjects that participated in the experiment. Test subjects included 14 children from kindergarten or lower grades of elementary school. 11 out of 14 children wore the cap until the last story. A movie for confirmation was taken by a video camera. The data was annotated from the video using Elan software [9], and correct answer data were collected. The correlation between motion recognition results based on the acceleration value/angular velocity value and correct answers was compared and evaluated.

Acceleration and Gyro sensor

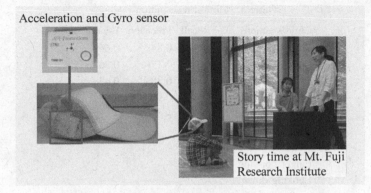

Story time at Mt. Fuji
Research Institute

Fig. 1. Sensor position

Fig. 2. Snapshot of experiment environment

Table 2. Breakdown of the subjects in experimentation

	June 21, 2015		July 12, 2015	
	1st time	2nd time	1st time	2nd time
All subjects [persons]	5	1	5	3
Valid subjects [persons]	2	1	5	3

*Valid subjects mean full data acquired. Some children took off their
caps with the sensor during the story time.

4.2 Result

Motion Recognition

Table 3 shows the motion recognition rate by acceleration/angular velocity, against a
list of all actions seen during the story time. Evaluation items were six-dimensional
feature values, (1) three-axis acceleration, (2) three-axis angular velocity, (3) three-axis

Table 3. Motion recognition rates

Child's actions	Recall	Precision	F-value
Sitting state	0.54	0.84	0.66
Sitting again	0.61	0.17	0.26
Wriggling	0.63	0.38	0.47
Playing with hands	0.96	0.90	0.93
Looking around	0.33	–	–
Clapping	–	–	–
Nodding	–	–	–
Finger pointing	–	–	–
Looking down	–	–	–

acceleration composite, (4) average of the composite value over one second, (5) variance of the average values, and (6) inclination angle of three-axes. The recognition rate was evaluated by 10 using division cross with validation with Weka's J48 algorithm [10]. Motions were calculated using the F-value, with accuracies of 0.66 in "Sitting state", 0.26 in "Sitting again", 0.47 in "Wriggling", and 0.93 in "Playing with hands". It was not possible to acquire gestures with occurrence frequencies less than 1% of the total time. To resolve this issue, an algorithm, which could recognize more accurately the motions seen in this experiment was needed.

Interest Judgement from Observers

Table 4 summarized the five interest degree evaluation criteria and the actual observed actions. The degree of interest from the children was evaluated continuously in five levels by two observers. Figure 3 shows the distribution of the observers' evaluations. The interest level 3, which was positioned between the high and low levels, occurred for approximately 20% the experiment duration. Figure 4 compares the evaluation of the interest degree of two observers in time series. In this case, the interest level could be used as an interest indicator; because the observer's judgements were almost always level 5 during the period of playing with hands. Degrees of interest are subjective and it is necessary to ascertain whether they are consistent with each other. Therefore, Cohen's secondary weighted kappa statistics [11] were used to confirm the reproducibility between the two evaluators. The reproducibility between the two evaluators was 0.93. It could be said the rate was almost matched in this case.

Table 4. Stage of five interest levels and participant's behavior observations

	5	4	3	2	1
Interest level	Obviously interested	Listening, seems interesting	Undecided	Does not seem to be listening	Obviously not interested
Observed actions	Joining, answering the questions, nodding	Listening, watching the speaker, clapping	Sitting state, undecided	Looking down, sitting again, wriggling	Looking around

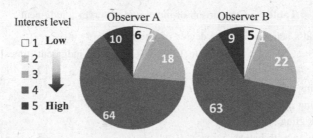

Fig. 3. The distribution of observers' evaluation

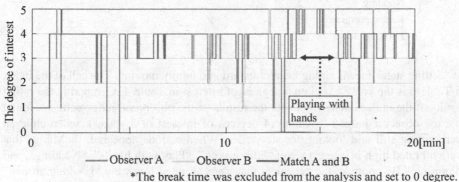

Fig. 4. Interest degree evaluated from observers

Interest Estimation by Motion Recognition

The correspondence between subject's behaviors and index of interest were compared, and the expressivity of the index in Table 3. was considered. In other words, the judgment accuracy of interests in this section was evaluated. Table 5 shows the calculated results of the interest estimation accuracy from motions. Moreover, Table 6 lists the number of interests with which the index and observer's judgment matched.

Table 5. Accuracy of interest determination from motions

Child's actions	The degree of interest	Recall	Precision	F-value
Sitting state	4	0.96	0.86	0.91
Sitting again	2	0	0	0
Wriggling	2	0	0	0
Playing with hands	5	1	0.36	0.53
Looking around	1	0.38	1	0.55
Clapping	4	0	0	0
Nodding	5	0	0	0
Finger pointing	5	–	–	–
Looking down	2	–	–	–

Table 6. Comparison of index and observer's judgment

Child's actions	The degree of interest					
	Index in Table 3	Observers' judgment [times]				
		5	4	3	2	1
Sitting state	4	1	25	–	–	–
Sitting again	2	3	1	8	–	–
Wriggling	2	2	2	29	–	–
Playing with hands	5	–	–	–	5	3
Looking around	1	–	–	–	–	–
Clapping	4	–	–	4	–	–
Nodding	5	–	1	–	–	–
Finger pointing	5	1	–	–	–	–
Looking down	2	–	–	–	–	1

"Sitting state" means sitting facing forward and hardly moving. The cell of the index in Table 6 is the value based on 5 degrees of interest in Table 4. Comparing the rating results of the indices in Table 5 with the results of the observers' judgement, we found that the observer judged 'listening (4 degrees of interest of 5 stages)' when children were sitting still and looking for storyteller. When actions appeared, the things that were all rated high in interest were; "Sitting state", "Play with hands", "Nodding", and "Pointing". By contrast, the behaviors that were all rated low were "Looking around" and "Looking down". In addition, comparing index and judgment, the results for the number of "Sitting again" and "Wriggling" were scattered. For both of these motions, any positive judgment occurred before the playing with hands time. As a result, it is thought that sitting again, like the preliminary action of the play, is rated as interesting. Because it is thought that this can be seen in the children who are motivated to play, the observer judged it as interested. As for the other "Sitting still" and "Wriggling", it appeared collectively in the degree of interest 3, therefore, it could be used as an indicator of the degree of interest 3. From the results of this experiment, comparing the interest degree estimation rates of Table 5 with the motion recognition rates of Table 2, children's action, "Sitting state" and "Playing with hands" were considered to be effective as an indicator of interest. To summarize the results, the indices shown in Table 7 were obtained from the results obtained in this paper.

The correspondence between the actual actions and the indices of interest was organized, and we investigated whether it could be an indicator of interest. The

Table 7. New index based on evaluation results

	5	4	3	2	1
Interest level	Obviously interested	Listening, seems interesting	Undecided	Does not seem to be listening	Obviously not interested
Observed actions	Joining (ex. playing with hands), pointing	Sitting state, nodding	Wriggling, sitting again, clapping	Looking down	Looking around

situation in "Sitting state" and in playing with hands were effective as action indices. The hand-playing action seemed to be adopted intentionally in this event to prevent children getting bored. However, it was considered that recognition of actions in the participatory situation, besides the hand-playing action, using the wearable sensors was effective as a method of evaluating the degree of interest.

4.3   Discussion

The recognition accuracy of motion in Table 2; F-value 0.66, for "Sitting state" was lower than expected. It was influenced by the low in difference between "Sitting state" and "Wriggling". The situation observers saw in the video and judged as "Wriggling" was primarily when participants were swinging or moving their fingers. The low recognition accuracy value was caused by the position of the sensors on the participants, which did not reflected the information from their hands or fingers. In this experiment, it was not possible to use all of the motions for judging the degree of interest in the evaluation of the motion and the interest; because there were cases in which there were combined reactions such as answering while wriggling. Analysis of the state "Wriggling" was needed in detail. The state of the subject observed from the video is described as follows. First, co-occurrence relationships between the voice and the motion were seen in each subject, in many cases, some actions against sounds were recorded in the scene observers selected. Second, from the time series showing the variance of the acceleration and the degree of interest, shown in Fig. 5, changes in behavior were seen when the rating of the degree of interest changed. Finally, during this story time, the number of occurrences of actions considered to have an interest, such as agreement, was low. In regard to storytelling, improvement of the recognition rate of particular motions as indicators and judging those who clearly behave differently from the other children by

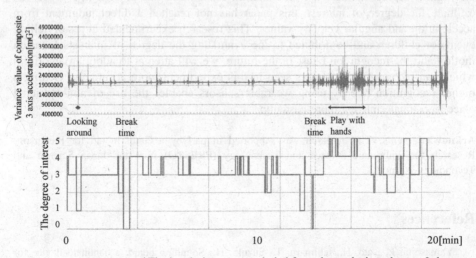

*The break time was excluded from the analysis and set to 0 degree.

Fig. 5. Comparison of acceleration value and degree of interest

using the degree of movement as an index are needed. The degree of the interest was not directly judged by the sensor values. To determine whether children were really interested in the content, further experiments were needed, for example, measuring the reaction when people showed the children obviously funny or stupid content. However, we suggested that motion recognition from acceleration and angular velocity could be used for interest estimation for the playing with hands. This research performed experiments at storytelling events for children and contributed to evaluating the degree of interests for each motions and the recognition rates of each.

5   Conclusion

In this paper, we proposed a method to acquire head movement measurements using wearable sensors and estimate interest based on its acceleration and angular velocity. As a case study, we evaluated the recognition accuracy of storytelling events targeted for children. We obtained video for confirmation, and used it to create a correct answer label of motions and degrees of interest. We then attempted to estimate the behavior and degree of interest of participants from the features of acceleration and angular velocity. Correct answer data of interests were evaluated by two observers in five levels from the video. From this experiment, ratings of the two observers' evaluation data matched by Cohen's Kappa coefficient.

As a result of the evaluation, nine motions were observed from the video data as follows; "Sitting state", "Sitting again", "Wriggling", "Playing with hands", "Looking around", "Clapping", "Nodding", "Finger pointing", and "Looking down". Moreover, four out of nine motions were recognized by using wearable sensor values, whose F-values were accuracies of 0.66 in "Sitting state", 0.26 in "Sitting again", 0.47 in "Wriggling", and 0.93 in "Playing with hands". In this case, "Playing with hands" was the highest degree of interest, with a motion recognition rate of 0.93 in F-value. To estimate the degree of interest, this paper has not reached a direct judgment from acceleration and angular velocity values. This research experimented at a storytelling event for children and contributed to the evaluating the degree of interests for each motion and the recognition rates. In the future, we will attempt to adopt an algorithm which can recognize the motions seen in this experiment more accurately. Getting a higher recognition rate by using wearable sensors enables the use of non-restricted place to estimate interest more casually.

Acknowledgments. This research was supported in part by a Grant in aid for Precursory Research for Embryonic Science and Technology (PRESTO) from the Japan Science and Technology Agency.

References

1. Yamashita, J., Kato, H., Ichimaru, T., Suzuki, H.: Sounding board: a handheld device for mutual assessment in education. In: Extended Abstracts on Human Factors in Computing Systems (CHI 2007), pp. 2783–2788 (2007)

2. Choudhury, T., Pentland, A.: Sensing and modeling human networks using the sociometer. In: Proceedings of 7th IEEE International Symposium on Wearable Computers (ISWC 2003), p. 216 (2003)
3. Carletta, J., et al.: The AMI meeting corpus: a pre-announcement. In: Renals, S., Bengio, S. (eds.) MLMI 2005. LNCS, vol. 3869, pp. 28–39. Springer, Heidelberg (2006). doi:10.1007/11677482_3
4. Sumi, Y., Yano, M., Nishida, T.: Analysis environment of conversational structure with nonverbal multimodal data. In: Proceedings of International Conference on Multimodal Interfaces and the Workshop on Machine Learning for Multimodal Interaction (ICMI-MLMI 2010), p. 44 (2010)
5. Tung, T., Gomez, R., Kawahara, T., Matsuyama, T.: Multiparty interaction understanding using smart multimodal digital signage. IEEE Trans. Hum.-Mach. Syst. **44**, 625–637 (2014)
6. Mana, N., Lepri, B., Chippendale, P., Cappelletti, A., Pianesi, F., Svaizer, P., Zancanaro, M.: Multimodal corpus of multi-party meetings for automatic social behavior analysis and personality traits detection. In: Proceedings of International Conference on Multimodal Interfaces and the 2007 Workshop on Tagging, Mining and Retrieval of Human Related Activity Information (ICMI-TMR 2007), pp. 9–14 (2007)
7. Okada, S., Bono, M., Takanashi, K., Sumi, Y., Nitta, K.: Context-based conversational hand gesture classification in narrative interaction. In: Proceedings of 15th ACM on International Conference on Multimodal Interaction (ICMI 2013), pp. 303–310 (2013)
8. ATR-promotions. http://www.atr-p.com/products/TSND121.html
9. ELAN. https://tla.mpi.nl/tools/tla-tools/elan/
10. Weka 3, The University of Waikato. http://www.cs.waikato.ac.nz/ml/weka/
11. Cohen, J.: A coefficient of agreement for nominal scales. Educ. Psychol. Measur. **20**(1), 37–46 (1960)

Development of a Tangible Learning System that Supports Role-Play Simulation and Reflection by Playing Puppet Shows

Hiroshi Sasaki[1(⊠)], Toshio Mochizuki[2], Takehiro Wakimoto[3],
Ryoya Hirayama[2], Sadahide Yoshida[2], Kouki Miyawaki[2],
Hitoki Mabuchi[2], Karin Nakaya[2], Hiroto Suzuki[2], Natsumi Yuuki[2],
Ayaka Matsushima[2], Ryutaro Kawakami[2], Yoshihiko Kubota[4],
Hideyuki Suzuki[5], Hideo Funaoi[6], and Hiroshi Kato[7]

[1] Information Science and Technology Center, Kobe University, Kobe, Japan
sasaki@kobe-u.ac.jp
[2] School of Network and Information, Senshu University, Kawasaki, Japan
tmochi@mochi-lab.net, {ne220151,ne230116,ne230145,
ne240227,ne240152,ne240108,ne200060,ne200201,
ne200152}@senshu-u.jp
[3] Faculty of Education and Human Sciences, Yokohama National University,
Yokohama, Japan
t-wakimoto@ynu.ac.jp
[4] Graduate School of Education, Utsunomiya University, Utsunomiya, Japan
kubota@kubota-lab.net
[5] Faculty of Humanities, Ibaraki University, Mito, Japan
hideyuki@suzuki-lab.net
[6] Faculty of Education, Soka University, Tokyo, Japan
funaoi@umegumi.net
[7] Faculty of Liberal Arts, The Open University of Japan, Chiba, Japan
hkato@ouj.ac.jp

Abstract. This paper describes the development of a tangible puppetry role-play simulation system called "EduceBoard", which enables students to role-play, based on various character's voices, in role-play simulation. It is to be noted that students are unable to play the diverse roles of children due to psychological inhibition and other factors in face-to-face self-performed role-play. EduceBoard is a tangible puppetry role-play simulation system that assists improvisational role-play, such as microteaching, by enabling students to play using puppets. It also provides web animation and comment functions for reflecting upon their play, recorded in a server. This paper describes the design specifications and implementation of the EduceBoard system, and discusses the current and future system applications.

Keywords: Role-play simulation · Puppetry · Computer-supported collaborative learning (CSCL) · Real-world oriented user interface

© Springer International Publishing AG 2017
M. Kurosu (Ed.): HCI 2017, Part II, LNCS 10272, pp. 364–376, 2017.
DOI: 10.1007/978-3-319-58077-7_29

1 Introduction

Role-play provides an effective way for participants to "dive in" to a particular situation, enabling them to learn to adopt other perspectives, often that of another person, in a simulated situation [1, 2]. In social- and medical-study activities, role-play is recognized as a suitable technique for the study of social situations including dynamic, complex, and non-routine situations such as decision-making training. Crisis management training [3, 4], nursing or medial situations [5, 6], and classroom teaching [7] are good examples that adopt role-play for decision-making training. Decision-making in a crisis is critical; however, it is ill-structured, involving communication among multiple people or parties and considerable information from various sources. Nursing and medical training often adopt case-based simulations in real complex situations. For quality service, nursing and medical staff should learn methods for dealing with hysterical patients or other stressful situations during bedside care through role-play. Pre-service teacher training often uses "microteaching" as a teaching simulation for learning teaching techniques before practical training in actual schools. Teachers work in ill-structured, dynamic, and non-routine environments, focusing on communication with their students, in classroom teaching. They need to estimate the student capacities, and contrive and decide teaching methods to enable better student understanding and satisfaction.

One interesting aspect of these kinds of role-play in complex situations is that they often emphasize on improvisations than the use of scripted scenarios to enable the participants change their fundamental belief system. Improvisation in role play is a particularly powerful learning strategy because it provides the participants a safe opportunity to undertake character roles or parts, in a particular situation [8]. Such role-play can be structured to be counter-attitudinal such that biases can be overcome through the development of the new beliefs fostered during role-play. The improvisations created during role-play are reflections of the agency's daily life, based on the role players' experience and require the participants to pay attention to all forms of feedback available in the role environment [9].

The importance of such improvisation in role-play for learning decision-making and communication in complex situations can be explained in terms of Bakhtin's theory of dialogism. According to Bakhtin [10], all utterances can be seen as replies to the voice of the preceding person, as the speaker takes into account his listener's background knowledge, previous utterances, gestures, etc. in predicting the listener's likely refutation, and, in order to avoid the same, will fashion his argument accordingly [11]. Hence, one's utterances will be formed with the anticipated words of the listener in mind; at the same time, the follow-up response of the listener will also be foreseen. In this sense, utterances in themselves, can be said to constitute dialogue. Bakhtin termed this essential character of utterances as multivoicedness. In this dialogic view, decision-making and negotiations in complex situations are the process of forecasting the reactions of the actors in the situation, engaging in hypothetical dialogues, and incorporating the results into the method of dealing with the situation. From this point of view, involving improvisation in role-play is crucial because the situation is multivoiced and role-play requires the ability to vividly imagine diverse actor voices that are rooted in the individual values and background of each participant. Therefore, engaging the participants in imagining the situation from the standpoint of the actors, as "others", is central to role-play.

However, it is not easy, particularly for novice students or citizens, to envision the reaction of the actors to ones' dealing strategy, in the situation. Even though role-play is more effective in enabling shy students to participate in learning activities than the usual lectures, some of the participants cannot play their roles effectively due to self-consciousness [12] or evaluation apprehension [13]. For example, microteaching role-play in pre-service training requires the participants to play their roles collaboratively as a teacher and young pupils, and to simulate an actual classroom themselves, in order to demonstrate his/her teaching in a real context, as far as possible. However, reactions and feedback provided by the colleagues acting as pupils are sometimes out of context, although they play the role of considerably younger people. Further, their reactions and feedback cannot be ensured to be serious, honest, or realistic due to embarrassment or hesitation. Such ineffective microteaching cannot directly improve a pre-service teacher's ability to imagine possible learner reactions.

For scaffolding the participants' dialogic imagination in role-play, we argue that puppetry can be a catalyst for enabling people to engage in the face-to-face conversation and for eliciting various realistic reactions or responses (multivoices) from the participants, enabling the perspective-taking of a wide variety of people during role-play. Puppetry allows each participant to obtain a participant-observer balance by creating a clear separation between the self (puppeteer) and non-self (puppet), as well as the character (puppet) and observer (puppeteer), while playing a puppetry story; therefore, participants can use informal/irregular discourse more in puppetry, similar to a realistic situation, than in self-performed role-play [14].

This paper describes a tangible puppetry-based role-play system, which decreases the participants' anxiety of acting each role sufficiently, enabling them to reflect the role-play effectively. The design and features of the system, and its applications in practical education are presented.

2 System Design and Implementation

2.1 Overview of the EduceBoard System

The EduceBoard system was designed such that users can achieve and dramatize the possible insights of the various characters in a role-play with puppets. The system has two functions: (1) engaging-in and recording the actions and conversations of puppetry-play on a tabletop system, and (2) playing the recording online to enable the participants to reflect upon their performance [15].

The system comprises of puppets, which represent characters (such as students, patients, etc.) on a transparent table that is the arena for the puppetry, a small microphone to recode the puppetry conversation, small lights to adjust the lighting, and a server to store the puppetry data and generate a puppetry animation movie for reflection.

Figure 1 shows the overview and architecture of the system; Figs. 2 and 3 depict the actual positioning of the system and the puppets, and Fig. 4 displays the players playing puppetry using the tabletop system collaboratively with the small puppets.

The system records the actions and conversations of the participants (hereafter, the "characters") on a transparent table. Figure 2 depicts the system, when it is ready to conduct the puppetry role-play. Each puppet or prop is attached to a transparent box with an augmented reality (AR) marker on the bottom. Each character can express his or her puppet's condition by manipulating a switch to change the color of the LED to red or blue (Fig. 3); in microteaching role-play, for instance, a red LED may represent a sleeping or careless student and a blue LED an attentive/note-taking student. We can assign various statuses for the characters, as per the situation played by the participants (for example, if they play nurses and patients in a hospital, these statuses might be illness, anger, hunger, etc.). A web camera and microphone, under the table, record the puppet movements and conversations (i.e., the behavior of the characters), by detecting the AR markers. After role-play (Fig. 4), the system sends all the recorded data, including the puppet movements, conversation, and conditions, to the web server to enable the participants to view the recorded puppetry and reflect upon it (Fig. 5). The webpage displays the role-play in an animated form, from a bird's-eye view. The users can stop and resume the animation, as desired and can also manipulate the seek-bar to find appropriate points to discuss or to include comments for reflection, on the timeline located next to the animation.

The application programming languages are Visual C++ 2008, Action Script 3.0, and Javascript; Microsoft Visual Studio 2008 and ARToolKit were used for the development environment. MySQL was used for the database and PHP was implemented as the interface for connection with the database. We discuss the implementation of the EduceBoard system in detail, in the following sections.

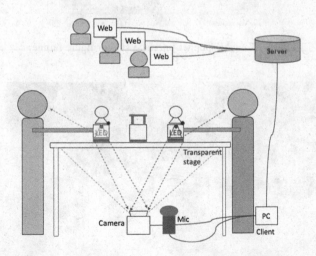

Fig. 1. Tangible puppetry simulation system overview

Fig. 2. Tangible puppetry simulation system

Fig. 3. Tangible puppet interface (Color figure online)

Fig. 4. Tangible microteaching puppetry (Color figure online)

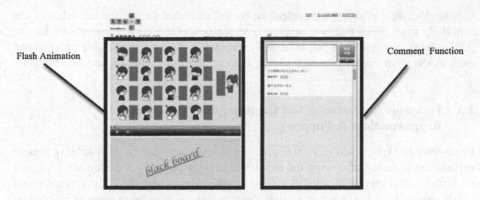

Flash Animation

Comment Function

Fig. 5. Web-based reflection-support system

2.2   Functions for Capturing and Recording the Locations of the Puppets and Furniture

We have adopted a tabletop interface [16] for implementing the technical support of the puppetry-based role-play simulation. This interface enables all the players to access to the puppetry arena such that the players can interact with each other without physical barriers, offering an open collaboration environment for fruitful collaboration [17]. Although various implementations for a tabletop computing interface have been proposed, vision tracking is a promising implementation, which enables the system to identify the locations of the objects on the table. Markers and the image processing technology for vision tracking that identify each marker location, enable the identification of the various puppet locations on the tabletop; thus, many studies for tabletop collaborative learning systems adopt this solution [18, 19].

We have adopted the ARToolKit [20] as the tool for vision tracking, attaching a marker at the bottom of each puppet box (see Fig. 3). Each marker represents a character in the puppetry; for example, in microteaching puppetry, boy student A, boy student B, girl student C, girl student D, female teacher E, etc. In addition, some of the markers represent furniture. Each piece of furniture is distinguished such that all the characters and furniture are depicted correctly in the reflection animation. All the data regarding the assignment of the characters and markers are stored in a database, in the webserver in which the reflection animation is generated.

The tracking system requires the calibration and establishment of a coordinate system defined by locations with known coordinates within the acquisition region. Hence, users must locate a puppet with a standard marker on the four corners of the tabletop, the first time, at the start of the puppetry; with this, the system can know the fixed points and edges to identify the size of the stage for calculating the relative positions of the characters to generate the reflection animation. The ARToolKit records the coordinates of the markers with the bottom left corner of the captured image as the origin, parallel to the x-y plane in which the moving markers are located; no data regarding the z-coordinates is used. In addition, the attitude or direction of each puppet or furniture is captured from $-180°$ to $180°$. at a negative clockwise and counterclockwise positive with reference to the direction facing the top edge of the captured stage. Note that we suspect certain unexpected error recognitions by the ARToolKit; thus, we have implemented a procedure to omit impossible movements, such as the short appearance of a certain marker and immediate distant movements.

2.3 Functions for Fostering and Capturing the Non-verbal Representations in Puppetry

Users need to express and recognize non-verbal representations also to achieve a more realistic communication among the characters, during puppetry. In addition, replaying such non-verbal communication is crucial in recognizing realistic communication and for discussing user participation in such communication, in order to promote participant reflection, after the puppetry, to achieve effective experiential participatory simulation.

Hence, we have included another function that lights-up colors on the markers; each human character puppet has LED color lights that are projected onto the marker at the bottom of the transparent box and there is a switch on top of the box to manipulate the light status. This allows users to manipulate the non-verbal status of the puppet, such as an emotion or concentration, as a visible expression, both for the puppetry players and for the camera under the tabletop for capturing the location and status of each puppet (see Figs. 3 and 4, for example). The transparent box permits the projection and reflection of the LED color on the back of the AR marker, enabling the observation of the non-verbal status of each puppet during puppetry and displays the color of the status for the camera. Each box has red and blue LEDs to enable the users to express three different statuses, for the abovementioned purpose.

The allocations of the color and status are stored in the database in the webserver; hence, the reflection animation can include the non-verbal representation of each human character. For example, for microteaching puppetry, we have assigned three typical pupil reactions during class hours: distraction (such as sleeping), concentration (such as note-taking), and a normal reaction. We believe that these reactions can assist the teacher in distinguishing student attitude, during class hours. This color allocation must be defined based on the context of each role-play situation (i.e., microteaching, nursing, or crisis management), similar to the character definition in the database to generate the effective reflection animation described in the next section. Before starting the puppetry simulation, the facilitator should explain this function and the non-verbal expression indicated by each color.

The client software of the EduceBoard system, with the ARToolKit processes, includes the following: It detects the color information in the RGB colorimetric system within each square area of the AR marker pattern captured by the camera and records the state of each character, as well as its location. In this procedure, the software distinguishes two image systems, the AR marker system and the visible light identification system; the former processes the location information of each AR marker, whereas the latter, the non-verbal representation information of each character. For processing the visible light identification image, the image processing system detects the number of pixels that fall within the threshold value of the red or blue in the RGB colorimetric system, when the red or blue LED is turned on. If the ratio of the blue or

Table 1. Marker information table

id	session_id	tid	mid	TS	X	Y	Z	Color	Direction	Status
Log ID	Session ID of puppetry	ID of puppetry trial	Marker ID	Time stamp	x-coordinate	y-coordinate	z-coordinate	LED color	Direction or attitude of puppets or furniture	(not used)
int	int	int	int	datetime	double	double	double	int	int	int

red color exceeds a certain value, the system judges and records it as the lighting-up of the respective color, else it is recognized as an off-state (i.e. normal). This threshold value can be configured in the client software, based on the influence of ambient light at the installation location, such as a classroom. While playing puppetry using the EduceBoard system, the software captures, analyzes, and integrates the information from both the image systems into a single file, and then sends and records it to a table in the database, as shown in Table 1.

2.4   Interface for Reflection by Playing the Recorded Puppetry Role-Play

After the role-play, reflection confirming what the participants experienced as players, discussions on their actions and how they would change it in the next trial, including the self-performed role-play, is critical for the participants to acquire skills, competencies, attitudes, and strategies that can be learned through role-play simulation [12, 21].

Video-recording is the most common way to support such reflection, for role-play simulation. However, capturing the puppetry on a small tabletop can be difficult because there are several obstacles in capturing the puppet movements correctly, including the players around the tabletop, their hands and arms, when moving the puppets or switching the LEDs, etc.

Instead of video-recording the actual puppetry, the EduceBoard's Web system provides a bird's-eye view of the animation of the puppetry simulation, using the data and voices captured by the camera and the microphone in the tabletop system. This system captures the locations and non-verbal expressions of each puppet character so that the animation can provide trajectories, including the verbal and non-verbal actions of each character, to effectively foster player reflection [22]. Further, the system also provides review and comment functions for mutual asynchronous reflection outside the classroom or school, particularly for learners who were immersed in acting during the simulation. This animation is generated using Adobe Flash technology.

Figure 5 shows a sample of the Flash animation, reflecting the movements of the puppets; the recorded sounds can be played simultaneously. When a user opens the Web reflection interface by selecting his/her experienced simulation, the Flash module calls two PHP modules with the simulation information (i.e., session number and trial number described in Table 1) via HTTP. Then, one of the PHP modules retrieves the recorded puppetry information such as the time, location, attitude, and status of each puppet from the database and organizes them into an XML; whereas, the other retrieves

Fig. 6. Character images according to the non-verbal information and directions of the figures

the captured voice data of the corresponding puppetry on the server. The Flash module loads and caches this data and waits for the user's action.

When the user clicks the play button, the Flash module starts to generate the animation, presenting images of the characters and furniture assigned to each marker, according to the database. As described above, the database stores the allocations of the markers and characters or furniture images, which include all the status/attitudes of the character/furniture. Figure 6 depicts examples of the character images according to the non-verbal information and directions, in the case of microteaching puppetry. The Flash module depicts these character images according to the information in the timing, described as timestamps in the XML, thereby, generating an animation. When the information indicates that a character's status or direction changes, the Flash module starts to use the appropriate image, when necessary. If a character's status does not change for a while, the Flash module displays the same image for that character, according to the information on the XML. To present a natural trajectory, the Flash module uses the motion tween function to generate a smooth movement, adjusting the timestamps provided by the ARToolKit.

Users can review this animation by manipulating a seek bar on the bottom of the Flash movie interface in order to confirm/replay the puppetry role-play. The seek bar is generated based on the length of the puppetry voice data and the Flash animation is linked to the seek bar so that the Flash module can reload the XML data and reallocate the character images according to user manipulation on the seek bar. Thus, the users can replay the animation correctly, when required, and reflect upon a specific part of their play.

Reflecting upon the puppetry by watching the animation movie requires more time than the actual time of the experienced puppetry. For educational purposes in schools or classes, providing an opportunity to reflect upon the conversations and actions later at a set time period is crucial for considering the communication and strategies, in accordance with the simulation. The comment function beside the Flash animation field enables users to add comments interactively in the timeline. While watching the animation, users can write a comment with a time tag. When reviewing the animation, all the comments are listed as per the attached time and the comment linked to the current time being played in the animation blinks to attract user attention. Users can also observe the viewpoints of the other participants in the puppetry simulation, deepening their reflection.

2.5   3D Animation for Promoting Deeper Perspective-Taking

Transfer to self-performed role-play or actual practice, after tangible puppetry, is an important issue. For self-performed role-plays, we determined that the transfer of

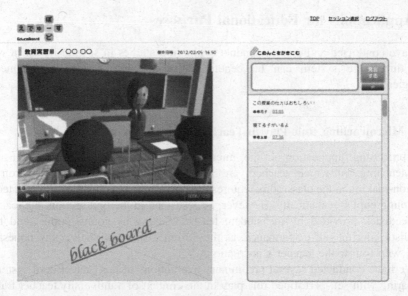

Fig. 7. Character's point of view for reviewing tangible puppetry role-play in microteaching

multi-voiced perspective-taking was not effective, even immediately after the tangible puppetry role-play [6]. One promising way of fostering deep perspective-taking may be a complete shift of viewpoint. Lindgren [23] indicated that experiencing a first-person perspective in a virtual world can generate person-centered learning stance and perspective-taking, discussing the possibility and efficacy of inter-identity technology (IIT) for learning from the viewpoint of a virtual learning environment such as the MUD or MR (mixed realities). They discussed that the IIT enables the learner to see through the avatar's point of view and this blurs the boundaries between the self and the other; hence, the players can gain novel perspectives.

We consider this to be a potentially effective method for eliciting more discussion not only on the performance of the various characters in the role-play, but also on the content of the reflection and on the conversation regarding this performance from the viewpoints of the diverse characters.

Therefore, we developed an additional system function, which allows participants to reflect upon their role-play by combining the wide and thorough (bird's-eye view) views of all the dialogues, and the various participant views (character points of view), using Unity3D technology (Fig. 7). From the bird's-eye view (Fig. 3), the participants can examine the overall situation, whereas, from the character points of view, they can consider the possible reactions (communication and behavior) of specific characters. The participants can switch the interface, while watching the role-play animation; hence, they can consider the first-person perspective of each character, when necessary.

3 Applications for Educational Purposes

We have conducted and plan to conduct evaluation studies in several fields, in which the EduceBoard system can be beneficial for learning various communication strategies.

3.1 Microteaching Role-Play in Teacher Education Program

One promising application is the microteaching role-play in teacher education. Microteaching, in which teachers are trained to engage in communication and decision-making in the classroom, requires the participants to play the roles of a teacher and young pupils, realistically. However, as described in the first section, the reactions and feedback provided by the student teachers acting as young pupils tend to be unrealistic, during self-performance, as they often disproportionally play honest students, who follow the teacher's instructions.

We have conducted several preliminary evaluations of the EduceBoard system by comparing with self-performed role play in the context of a university teacher training course with microteaching practices; this demonstrated that the system enables the participants to play various roles in the role-play and assisted them in reflecting upon their role-play from several perspectives [15].

3.2 Nursing Education

Another promising application is in nursing education, particularly for nursing involving multiple duties with interruptions. This training is usually conducted with a scenario-based scripted simulation [24], enabling nurses to reflect upon their own actions and observe optimal nursing practices including the realization of the importance and difficulty of priority management, efficient operations, and collaborative problem solving. However, this training lacks the various viewpoints of patients, which cause interruptions. Understanding these viewpoints through tangible puppetry is a promising way to understand the patients' feeling regarding the nurse's decisions and to reflect upon such practices.

Fig. 8. Patient and nurse puppets for nursing education

We have developed new types of characters and puppets that are appropriate for nursing education (Fig. 8). Before implementing these characters on the system, we plan to conduct a case study of the puppetry role-play in a situation involving multiple duties with interruptions; this kind of role-play training entails significant costs and efforts such as room reservations, patient players, facilitators for reflection, considerable time for reflection by reviewing the video recording, etc. We believe that even by using only puppets, the training can be achieved, with reduced costs.

4 Conclusion

This paper describes the implementation of a tangible puppetry role-play support system that fosters perspective-taking and discusses several system applications. The use of puppets in role-play as transitional objects that prompt a projection of the self (puppeteer) on the non-self (puppet), elicited a variety of informal discourse, rarely used in self-performance, but useful for studying the various perspectives in a possible scenario. The EduceBoard system is a tangible puppetry role-play simulation system that assists improvisational role-play such as microteaching by enabling the students to play using puppets. It also provides web animation and comment functions for reflecting upon the role-play recorded in the server.

The issues to be addressed in future are as follows. (1) Auto adjustment for ambient light in various learning environments. Due to the nature of vision tracking, ambient light significantly affects image recognition accuracy. An auto adjustment function for the ambient light is required, in this system, in a general setting in the dissemination phase. (2) We need to consider the use of the tabletop as the display in the reflection animation movie to support timely trial-and-error simulation, during puppetry. This can achieve a different type of reflective learning experience in role-play simulation, enabling the participants to stop the simulation and discuss, and conduct another simulation from the interrupted point. This is not yet included in the scope of our research, but would be challenging from the technical point of view.

Acknowledgement. This work is supported by the JSPS KAKENHI Grants-in-Aids for Scientific Research (B) (Nos. JP26282060, JP26282045, JP26282058, and JP15H02937) from the Japan Society for the Promotion of Science.

References

1. Resnick, M., Wilensky, Y.: Diving into complexity: developing probabilistic decentralized thinking through role-playing activities. J. Learn. Sci. **7**(2), 153–172 (1997)
2. Forsyth, D.R.: Group Dynamics, 3rd edn. Wadsworth, Belmont (1999)
3. Kleiboer, M.: Simulation methodology for crisis management support. J. Conting. Crisis Manag. **5**, 198–206 (1997)
4. Leung, L., Law, N.: Online role play simulation to tackle groupthink—case study of a crisis management training. In: Connecting Computer-Supported Collaborative Learning to Policy and Practice: CSCL 2011 Conference Proceedings, vol. 1, pp. 208–215 (2011)

5. Chan, C.S.Y., Wun, Y.T., Cheung, A., Dickinson, J.A., Chan, K.W., Lee, H.C., Yung, Y. M.: Communication skills of general practitioners: any room for improvement? How much can it be improved? Med. Educ. **37**(6), 514–526 (2003)
6. Chan, Z.C.Y.: Role-playing in the problem-based learning class. Nurse Educ. Pract. **12**(1), 21–27 (2012)
7. McKnight, P.C.: Microteaching in teacher training: a review of research. Res. Educ. **6**, 24–38 (1971)
8. Friedman, S.: Learning to make more effective decisions: changing beliefs as a prelude to action. Learn. Organ. **11**(2), 110–128 (2004)
9. Feinstein, A.H., Mann, S., Corsun, D.L.: Charting the experiential territory: clarifying definitions and uses of computer simulations, games and role play. J. Manag. Dev. **21**(10), 732–744 (2002)
10. Bakhtin, M.M.: Speech Genres and Other Late Essays. University of Texas Press, Austin (Originally Published in 1979). (Edited by, C. Emerson and Translated by, M. Holquist, W. McGee)
11. Wertsch, J.V.: Voice of Mind: A Sociocultural Approach to Mediated Action. Harvard University Press, Cambridge (1991)
12. Ladrousse, G.P.: Role Play. Oxford University Press, Oxford (1989)
13. Cottrell, N., Wack, D., Sekerak, G., Rittle, R.: Social facilitation of dominant responses by the presence of an audience and the mere presence of others. J. Pers. Soc. Psychol. **9**(3), 245–250 (1968)
14. Aronoff, M.: Puppetry as a therapeutic medium. In: Bernier, M., O'Hare, J. (eds.) Puppetry in Education and Therapy, pp. 109–115. Authorhouse, Bloomington (2005)
15. Mochizuki, T., Wakimoto, T., Sasaki, H., Hirayama, R., Kubota, Y., Suzuki, H.: Fostering and reflecting on diverse perspective-taking in role-play utilizing puppets as the catalyst material under CSCL. In: Lindwall, O., et al. (eds.) Exploring the Material Conditions of Learning – The Computer Supported Collaborative Learning Conference 2015, vol. 2, pp. 509–513 (2015)
16. Dillenbourg, P., Evans, M.: Interactive tabletops in education. Int. J. Comput.-Support. Collab. Learn. **6**(4), 491–514 (2011)
17. Kato, H., Mochizuki, T., Funaoi, H., Suzuki, H.: A principle for CSCL design: emergent division of labor. In: Cantoni, L., McLoughlin, C. (eds.) Proceedings of EdMedia: World Conference on Educational Media and Technology 2004, pp. 2652–2659 (2004)
18. Leitner, J., Haller, M.: Geckos: combining magnets and pressure images to enable new tangible-object design and interaction. In: Proceedings of ACM CHI 2011 Conference on Human Factors in Computing Systems, pp. 2985–2994 (2011)
19. Cuendat, S., Bonnard, Q., Do-Lenh, S., Dillenbourg, P.: Designing augmented reality for the classroom. Comput. Educ. **68**, 557–569 (2013)
20. ARToolKit. http://www.hitl.washington.edu/artoolkit/ (2005)
21. Allen, D., Ryan, K.: Microteaching. Addison-Wesley, Reading (1969)
22. Collins, A., Brown, J.S.: The computer as a tool for learning through reflection. In: Mandl, H., Lesgold, A. (eds.) Learning Issues for Intelligent Tutoring Systems, pp. 1–18. Springer, New York (1988)
23. Lindgren, R.: Generating a learning stance through perspective-taking in a virtual environment. Comput. Hum. Behav. **28**, 1130–1139 (2012)
24. Toyomasu, K., Kato, H.: Video analysis of reflection scenes on the scenario simulation nursing training involving multiple duties with interruption. Poster presented at 5th International Nurse Education Conference, Noordwijkerhout, The Netherlands (2014)

Investigation of Learning Process with TUI and GUI

Natsumi Sei[1(✉)], Makoto Oka[2], and Hirohiko Mori[1]

[1] Graduate Division, Tokyo City University,
1-28-2 Tamadutumi, Setagayaku, Tokyo, Japan
G1581815@tcu.ac.jp
[2] Tokyo City University, 1-28-2 Tamadutumi, Setagayaku, Tokyo, Japan

Abstract. In this paper, we investigate the effect of the types of user interfaces on human cognitive processes of learning. We built the systems of making logic circuits with TUI and GUI. In the initial stage of learning, the participants took the same strategy and the behaviors of problem solving were very similar. However, as the learning proceeded, we found that the behaviors got different between each interfaces. Moreover, we found that the strategies adopted with each interface are different. When the subjects learn with GUI, they keep considering by predicting the results with only the already obtained knowledge, and, if they cannot apply the knowledge because of being difficult problems, they just repeat the process of the trials and errors. On the other hand, when the subjects learn with TUI, they use various strategies and think from various viewpoints. If they face to some difficulties, they try to find new rules or knowledge to overcome the difficulties.

Keywords: Tangible User Interface (TUI) · COCOM · Verbal protocol · Cognitive process · User interface

1 Background

Computers are widely used in various situations throughout the society, and various kinds of user interfaces have been proposed. Tangible User Interface (TUI) has been studied widely so far, because a computer can be controlled by touching a physical object directly by hand and the user can use a computer intuitively. Because of this advantage, TUI can be employed in the field of the learning. However, learning systems using TUI are not popular, because the effects of the types of user interfaces on human learning are not well known.

2 Purpose

In this paper, we focused on the effects of Tangible User Interface and Graphical User Interface on human learning process and aims to investigate how the types of user.

M. Kurosu (Ed.): HCI 2017, Part II, LNCS 10272, pp. 377–384, 2017.
DOI: 10.1007/978-3-319-58077-7_30

3 Related Works

Various user interface are adopted to learn same subject. For example, Light-bot [1] is a system of learning programing with Graphical User Interface (GUI). Light-bot allows the users to learn programming with PC screen and mouse. On the other hand, Osmo coding [2] is a system of learning programming with TUI. The user with Osmo coding can program the movements of the character on the screen by arranging the function panels by hand. Though they share the same goal of learning programming, they adopt the different interfaces and the effects of the user interfaces on human learning are not considered. We, therefore, focus on what type of user interface is suitable for the leaning subjects (Fig. 1).

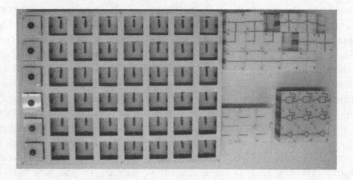

Fig. 1. Experiment system (TUI)

Some research have been done about the difference among the devices using in learning. Akahori [3] investigated the features of human learning among PC, tablet, and paper. The subjects with paper got the best results in the foundational problems. The subject with using tablet obtained the good results in the practical problems. The subject with PC got the worst results. In this way, the types of devices are caused the difference effects in learning, but they did not make it clear the effects of the types of interface in learning process (Fig. 2).

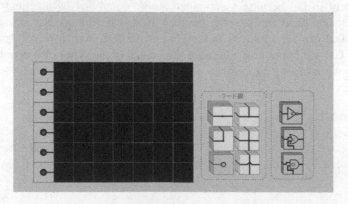

Fig. 2. Experiment system (GUI)

4   Experiment

4.1   Objective of Experiment

We conducted the experiment to clarify the effect of TUI and GUI on human learning processes according to the types of user interfaces.

4.2   Procedure

The types of the user interface used in this experiment are GUI and TUI for learning. We chose logical circuit building as learning tasks that are easy to be implemented the tasks in the same appearance with GUI and TUI. The subjects are required to build a logical circuit watching a truth table by connecting some logic circuit. The three logical symbol used in this experiment was the "AND", the "OR" and the "NOT". In addition, the lead wire objects and the lamp objects, to connect among each gate and to confirm the output of the circuit respectively, were also prepared.

In GUI condition, all operations for the logic circuit are "click" and "drag" on the icons with a mouse. In TUI, each logic gate is represented as a cube- shaped block which is grasp-able. The circuit can be created by arranging the blocks in 2-dimensional place.

The subjects asked to "think aloud", and, their behavior and verbal protocol data were recorded by VCR.

4.3   Methods

The subjects asked to solve the problem of the logic circuit. The instruction manual about each interface and about the logic circuit are printed on the paper and the subjects were permitted to read them at any time during the experiment. The experiment was conducted for 6 weeks (6 times) for one subject and the subjects were asked to solve 6 problems in one hour per every week.

The tasks were gradually got difficult over the weeks. In the first week, we conducted the personality test to know whether each subject usually consider things logically or intuitively and divided all subjects equally into each condition to eliminate the effects of the personality types. After the second week, the subjects learned about the logic circuits and asked to build logic circuits from truth tables. In only the second week, they created truth tables from the given logic circuits to accustom the tasks.

The problems of 3th are make logic circuit from truth table. Logical symbol of 3th is 2 pieces, 4th is 3 pieces, 5th and 6th are no specified pieces for increase the difficulty level.

The problems of 6th are used 2 lamps of output. The problems of 6th are application problems.

5 Methods of Analysis

We analyzed the obtained data from two aspects. The subjects' behavior data are analyzed based on Contextual Control Model proposed by Hollnagel. We also conducted the verbal protocol analysis.

5.1 A Contextual Control Model

We analyzed the behavior of the subject based on a Contextual Control Model proposed by Hollnagel [4].

We classify the behaviors of the subject into 5 modes of Contextual Control Model as follows:

- *Scramble control:* The state that the user has no idea of what to do to solve the problem.
- *Explorative control:* Their sub-goal is not clear and not to go toward the goal directly but to just try to find something tentatively.
- *Opportunistic control:* Though the subjects think looking at only one or a few sub-goals toward the goal, they do not know what kind of action should be done to achieve them.
- *Tactical control:* Subjects think several sub-goals sweeping some part of path to the goal and knows what kind of action is needed to achieve sub-goals though they have not found the whole path for the goal yet.
- *Strategic control:* The path toward the goal is established more detail than tactical control, and subjects know what action are required to achieve it.

We focus on the frequency of each mode. Which mode the subjects stay is determined by the logic circuit itself they built and the state of its validation, and is done by following three steps. In the first step, the mode were determined by whether the subject tried to build the whole circuit or only the parts. In the second step, it was done by he/she validate all connections among its inputs and outputs. In the third step, it was determined by the how many times he/she validated the connection between one input and one output.

6 Results of the Analysis

6.1 Probability of Occurrence of Mode by COCOM

We analyzed the subjects' mode transition based on COCOM by dividing the whole period of the experiment into 3 stages to focus on their learning process as follows:

Initial stage: The third week
                    The subjects learn the basis of the logic circuits.
Latter stage: The 4th and 5thweeks
                    The subject becomes accustomed to solve the problems of the logic circuit.
Practical stage: The 6th (using 2 lams)
                    The subjects are asked to solve some advanced problems.

Here, no Scramble mode were observed because we did not restrict the time to solve one problem. Furthermore, we do not adopt the Strategic control mode in our analysis because it appeared in solving only very easy problems.

Tables 1 and 2 show the rates of which the subjects stayed each mode with each interface in each stage. Though, in the initial stage, the subjects with TUI and GUI stayed the same mode, in the latter and practical stage the rates of the modes they stayed were changed. While, with GUI, the subjects stayed the tactical control mode many times in the initial stage, they gradually increased to stay the opportunistic control mode in latter stage and practical stage (Table 1). On the other hand, with TUI, though in initial stage their behavior was very similar to the condition with GUI, the modes they stayed appeared evenly in later stage and practical stage (Table 2).

Table 1. Probability of occurrence of mode with GUI

	Opportunistic control	Explorative control	Tactical control
Initial stage	0.19	0.13	0.68
Later stage	0.54	0.07	0.39
Practical stage	0.62	0.01	0.37

Table 2. Probability of occurrence of mode with GUI TUI

	Opportunistic control	Explorative control	Tactical control
Initial stage	0.34	0.15	0.51
Later stage	0.33	0.40	0.27
Practical stage	0.34	0.36	0.30

This means that, in initial stage, the subject with both interfaces thinks and creates a logic circuit logically. It must be caused because the subject does not have accustomed to the relationship between the logic circuits and the truth tables and can adopt only the manner they have already learned.

In later stage and practical stage, the different behaviors were observed between the conditions. The subject with GUI only uses and persists in the manners of already learned approaches. And, when he/she faces to some difficulties, he/she tries to establish a simple and local sub-goal and, tries to accomplish it by trials and errors. The subject with TUI, on the other hand, tries to solve the problem from various viewpoints.

6.2   Protocol Analysis

To investigate why the difference of their behavior occurred between both conditions, we focused on their strategies in problem solving using the verbal protocol analysis.

During solving one problem, they repeated that they adopted one strategy to approach the goal, and if it did not work well, then they abandoned it and try to adopt another strategy. The strategies they tried to adopt can be classified into three types as follows:

Strategy 1: Trying to achieve a local solution
Strategy 2: Trying to discover new rules
Strategy 3: Trial and error.

Table 3 shows a typical example of a Strategy 1. At No.2, the subject talked "This is no good" because the obtained result was different from the expected one. Actually, observing from No.1 to No.3, it can be said that the subject establish a local sub-goal and try to accomplish it. This can also confirmed At No. 7. The subject talked "I have done it" and this indicates that he kept the local sub-goal, and finally accomplished it. After it, he kept adopting the same strategy. In this way, in Strategy 1, the subject established the local sub-goal by considering the truth table, and tried to create the logic circuit while predicting the result, and, if the obtained the results were wrong, he/she repeated the same process until they reached the correct result.

Table 3. Subject C the 6th 4th question

No.	Start	Action	Utterance	Protocol analysis
1	13:48	Move object		The subject created the logic circuit
2	13:58		This is no good	while predicting the results, but notice
3	14:48	Operation check		it was wrong
4	14:53		I should remove this object from the board	
5	14:54	Move object		The subject created logic circuit while
6	15:22	Operation check		predicting the result
7	15:31		I have done it	
8	15:40	Move object		The subject tried to expand the last
9	15:47	Operation check		result to build whole correct circuit
10	15:53	Move object		The result was wrong
11	15:55	Operation check		
12	16:00		What?	
13	16:04	Move object	How about this	The subject makes the logic circuit
14	16:10	Operation check		while predicting the results
15	16:51	Watch the ploblem		

Table 4 shows a typical example of the Strategy 2. At No.1 and No.2, the subject talked "I want all lights are "ON"" and "Try "OR"". Here, the subject decided which gates he would use without estimating the results. Then, he tried to a circuit. Here, looking at the talk of No. 8, "How does it work if I reverse these gates?" clearly shows that he build the circuit to know how it worked and tried to obtain a new rules or knowledge about the logic circuit. In this way, in Strategy, the subjects tried to acquire new knowledge or rules by build a circuit as a trial.

Table 5 shows the typical example of the Strategy 3. At No.1 to No.3, the subject decided which logic gates he would use in advance to considering the behavior circuit.

Table 4. Subject F the 5th 5th question

No.	Start	Action	Utterance	Protocol analysis
1	03:19		"I want all lights are "ON""	
2	03:25		"Try "OR"	
3	03:32	Move object	Both using AND and using OR at the last position will be fine because I can reverse their position	The subject tried to build a circuit to know how it works
4	03:40		Before this	
5	03:43	Operation check		
6	03:46		Which are the lamp that should be turned off?	
7	03:56		Both are "OFF"?	
8	04:00	Move object	How does it work if I reverse these gates?	The subject confirmed the result
9	04:06	Operation check		

Table 5. Subject E The 5th 4th question

No.	Start	Action	Utterance	Protocol analysis
1	03:31		I will use two "NOT" gates	The subject decided which gates will use in advance
2	03:41		How about "OR" with "NOT"	
3	03:55		How about "NOT" and "AND"	
4	04:06	Move object		The subject is making the circuit only with the gated decided to use in advance
5	04:29	Operation check		
6	04:36	Move object		The subject is making the circuit only with the gated decided to use in advance
7	04:40	Operation check		

Then, he just built the circuit only with the gates. In this way, the subject, in strategy 3 made the logic circuit by trial and error without predicting result.

In Tables 6 and 7 shows the frequency rates of each strategy in each condition. These table indicates, while the subjects learned with GUI tend to adopt Strategy 1 (Table 6) mainly and increase the Strategy 3 as the leaning proceeded, the subjects with TUI adopted all strategies and the rates of Strategy 2 are significantly higher and the rate of Strategy 3 are significantly lower than with GUI.

Table 6. Frequency rates of strategies (GUI)

	Strategy 1	Strategy 2	Strategy 3
Initial stage	0.86	0.00	0.14
Later stage	0.63	0.09	0.28
Practical stage	0.68	0.04	0.28

Table 7. Frequency rates of strategies (TUI)

	Strategy 1	Strategy 2	Strategy 3
Initial stage	0.31	0.46	0.08
Later stage	0.24	0.59	0.18
Practical stage	0.26	0.53	0.14

These mean that when we learn with GUI, we keep considering by predicting the results with only the already obtained knowledge, and, if we cannot apply the knowledge because of being difficult problems, we just repeat the process of the trials and errors.

On the other hand, when we learn with TUI, we use various strategies and think from various viewpoints. If we face to some difficulties, we try to find new rules or knowledge to overcome the difficulties. Actually, the correction rates with TUI in the practical stage is high despite no subjects with GUI could complete questions in the practical stage.

In addition to this, we also found the relationships of the transition patterns among the modes of COCOM and the strategies. In adopting the Strategy 1, the subjects almost repeat the transition between the opportunistic control and the tactical control mode. In Strategy 2, they frequently moved from explorative control mode to other 3 modes. In Strategy 3, they just stayed the opportunistic control mode.

7 Conclusions

We investigated the types of user interfaces effect the human learning by using the cognitive model and protocol analysis, and found that there are some differences in learning process and strategy between GUI and TUI.

The subject with TUI solved the problem by building a new rule. The subject with GUI solved the problem by using already-obtained knowledge.

The type of user interface determines the common strategy in all stage and it causes the different behaviors in learning process. The subject with TUI solved the problem by stayed evenly 3 modes, and the subject with GUI solved the problem by stayed one mode.

References

1. Lightbot (2016). http://lightbot.com/
2. Osmo coding (2016). https://www.playosmo.com/
3. Akahori, K., Wada, Y.: Characteristics comparison of iPads, paper and PCs as learning devices **6**(1), 15–34 (2012). Hakuoh University
4. Hollnagel, E.: Human Reliability Analysis: Context and Control. Academic Press (1994)

Exploiting Bodily Movement to Regulate Collaborative Learning by Designing a Tablet-Based CSCL System

Hideyuki Suzuki[1(✉)], Hideo Funaoi[2], and Yoshihiko Kubota[3]

[1] Faculty of Humanities and Social Sciences, Ibaraki University,
2-1-1 Bunkyo, Mito, Ibaraki, Japan
hideyuki@suzuki-lab.net
[2] Faculty of Education, Soka University,
1-236 Tangi-Machi, Hachioji, Tokyo, Japan
funaoi@umegumi.net
[3] Graduate School of Education, Utsunomiya University,
350 Minemachi, Utsunomiya, Tochigi, Japan
kubota@kubota-lab.net

Abstract. This paper describes the design of XingBoard (Crossing Board) system from the viewpoint of bodily control of interaction. XingBoard is a tablet-based tool that supports a bi-directional transition between personal and collective activities in collaborative learning process. For this purpose, this system provides a shared space for discussion comprised of multiple, connected tablet terminals and allows users to move post-it like cards from one terminal to another. In addition, the system can copy cards from a shared space to each learner's tablet for individual work, which consists of reflection on or revision of the results of the group discussion. To evaluate the system from an interaction perspective, we record scenes where a group of 4 subjects use XingBoard. As a result of interaction analysis, it turns out that XB, by its tangible nature, supports collaborative work by enabling learners to use their bodily movements as interaction re-source.

Keywords: CSCL system · Tablet terminals · Personal-collective activity transition · Tangible interface · Bodily movement · Interaction analysis

1 Introduction

This paper describes the design of XingBoard (Crossing Board) system from the viewpoint of bodily control of interaction. XingBoard is a tablet-based tool that supports a bi-directional transition between personal and collective activities in collaborative learning process. Design of XB system takes advantage of the tangible nature of a tablet terminal in order to support learners to regulate collaborative activity through their bodily movement. This paper is divided into three parts. Firstly, educational context of the XB system is discussed. In that part, the significance of transition between personal and collective activity in a collaborative learning session will be shown. Secondly, the concept and functions of XB system, which is a tablet-terminal based CSCL system

© Springer International Publishing AG 2017
M. Kurosu (Ed.): HCI 2017, Part II, LNCS 10272, pp. 385–397, 2017.
DOI: 10.1007/978-3-319-58077-7_31

designed for supporting transition between personal and collective activity, is described. Finally, the authors discuss how this system takes advantage of the tangible nature of a tablet terminal in order to regulate collaborative activity with enabling learners to exploit their bodily movements to control and organize collaboration.

2 Educational Background

It is very common to design a collaborative learning session in the way that it starts from a personal activity and then to proceed to group activity. In the group activity, learners are expected to share each idea generated through the personal activity and then to discuss in order to reach collective result or understanding. In many collaborative learning sessions, a plenary discussion that functions as an overall summary is placed in the very last phase of the learning and there is no chance to return to a personal activity again. The flow is one way. The authors believe that making learners engage in a personal contemplation based on the result of group discussion is very important for learning.

One of the reasons is the effect of review/reflection in learning [1, 2]. By reviewing the results of a collective activity again, learners can notice points that they missed in the discussion and identify any points that need to be covered further. In addition, the personal contemplation makes learners to anchor the conclusion of discussion onto their personal experiences or preexisting knowledge. Trying to rephrase the collective words into personal words is expected to lead the learners to deeper understanding. Another reason is based on the limitation of group work. As Johnson et al. pointed out, in group learning, there are differences in the degree of learners' attendance to work and the contribution from each learner, and it is possible that each learner's role is fixed [3]. Some learners may not be able to express their opinions in a discussion, and others may not be able to understand the discussion because of its rapid pace. Reviewing the material individually after the group work can provide an opportunity for each learner to think carefully about the results of the collective activity. Based on above discussion, the authors propose the "back and forth model" for collaborative learning. With this model, learners transit between individual and collective activity. Typically, learners begin learning with individually, and then proceed to collaborative activity, after the collaboration they return to the phase of individual reflection, finally they gather again in order to share their personal contemplations and discuss based on it.

The benefit of this model is that students are led to generate ideas interactively to arrive at a deep understanding. The learning process begins with a personal activity, in which each learner is expected to develop his/her own ideas while keeping in mind others' viewpoints. Because they would anticipate that their outputs of this individual activity will eventually be shared in a collective activity with other learners. With anticipation for future collective work, learners necessarily develops a sense of accountability for the output of their own works. In the collective activity, multiple viewpoints and values are to be compared. Any differences or discrepancies can prompt learners to develop new ideas. When they bring the results of their collective activity back for their own individual review, they are required to re-examine the results of the preceding discussion by applying them to an individual context and trying to explain them in their own words. This change of contexts may enable them to identify points that were not fully discussed in the collective discussion or that need to be further elaborated. If the learners gather again to share the results of their individual contemplations, they will consider the ideas from multiple viewpoints, thereby arriving at a deeper understanding of the theme.

3 ICT Tool for "Back and Forth" Collaboration

3.1 Requirements

In this section, we examine what is needed to support "back and forth" learning using ICT. To support personal activity the tool needs to offer learners an exclusive personal field and functions to record and edit (add, delete, and move) information on the field individually. This will help them develop their own ideas about the lesson theme and organize the results of their investigation. For supporting the collective activity of "back and forth" learning, the tool should offer functions to combine and share the results of the preceding personal activity. In addition, the tool should support transition from working collectively to working individually. For this transition, it must be able to distribute the output of the group work to all the group members so that they can examine the results individually in the following personal activity. Again, the functions of recording and editing information are needed for the learners to re-examine the distributed results and input new ideas.

3.2 Development of XingBoard System

The authors developed XingBoard (Crossing board) system as a tool that fulfills the requirement shown above. XingBoard is a system that uses cards, similar to sticky notes, to share ideas in order to support "back and forth" learning. Figure 1 shows the overall concept. In the following, we will explain the concept by following the learning flow.

Personal Activity I. Each learner is given a tablet terminal to record ideas and results obtained from his/her individual work. The ideas can be written on a "card", which resembles a sticky note. The cards can then be organized or summarized.

Card Input and Moving a Card. When the learner touches the tablet screen with two fingers, an input screen appears. Letters can be input using the on-screen keyboard. The learner can choose/change the card color or drag the card (using a finger) to any group.

Grouping Cards. Learners can select cards by using their fingers to trace around them. They can group the selected cards by touching any place on the screen with two fingers. Groups can be nested. Figure 2 shows screen image with grouped cards.

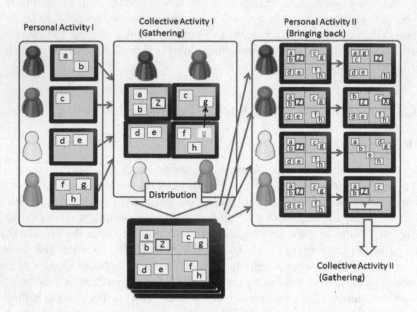

Fig. 1. Concept of XingBoard

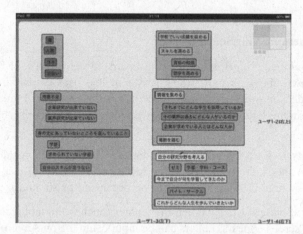

Fig. 2. Screen image of XingBoard

Collective Activity I. Collective Activity I. The learners report each other the results of their personal activity and then discuss in a group. Placing their tablet terminals side by side or end to end (see Fig. 1(center)), they can create an enlarged shared field where they can make a summary of the group results by moving and editing cards.

Moving Cards Between Terminals. Learners can move a card from one terminal to another using the motion shown in Fig. 3.

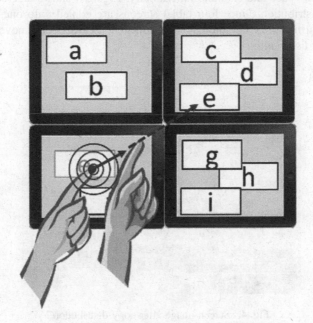

Fig. 3. Moving a card between terminals

When a learner touches a card with one finger, a red ripple will appear, and he/she can move the card to another terminal screen by flicking the finger in the desired direction, as illustrated in Fig. 3. It is possible to move a card from one screen to another in a diagonal direction and even to move grouped cards. Using this function, learners can organize the cards on their own terminals and then integrate them with other group members' cards.

Turning Cards Upside Down. Touching the screen with three fingers will make the cards turn upside down. This function makes it easy for learners to read each other's screens when they are seated in a circle or across from each other. Touching the screen again with three fingers will return the cards to their original orientation.

Personal Activity II. Each learner reviews the results of the collective activity individually and then reedit cards in order to revise the group's result based on his/her own
understanding.

Copy Distribution. The results of the collective activity are recorded on a sheet of
domain which is com-posed of four tablet terminals. "Copy distribution" is a function
that copies the output of the group work, which is recorded on a field comprised of
gathered four tab-lets, onto each tablet terminal so the group members can bring it back
to their personal space and examine individually. Figure 4 shows a screenshot image
after a copy distribution. Since four tablet screens are copied onto one terminal, the
spaces between the cards are automatically adjusted. Learners can move and edit the
cards after the distribution.

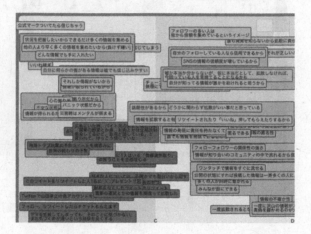

Fig. 4. Screen image after copy distribution

With this function, a learner can review the results of the group discussion individually and make further revisions if needed. Note that copy distribution is possible
only when all four group members agree to it.

System Configuration. This system is configured as a client-server type. The development environment for a tablet terminal on the client side is Mac OS 10.6 and Adobe
Flash CS6.0. It is an AIR application; therefore, it is possible for the system to be
published as an iOS application and an Android application, respectively, and it runs in
each environment. Also, when it is published as an SWF file, it can run in a web
browser. The development environment in the server side is Windows 7 (Professional),
Apache 2.2, PHP 5.3, and MySQL 5.5. In terms of the execution environment, if
equivalent service is available, the system runs not only in Windows, but also in other
OS such as Linux. Note that for the management of information such as a user and a

sheet, the type of OS (including iOS for iPad and Android) does not matter, as long as the web browser works and text input is possible.

4 Interaction Support and Tangible Nature of XingBoard

In this section we discuss how XingBoard, tablet-based CSCL system, enables users' exploitation of their bodily movements in controlling collaboration as well as transition between personal and collective activity and then provides natural collaborative environment. Firstly, tablet terminal can be grasped by a hand and carried to any-where in the classroom. This enables learners switch between private and collective activity by physically placed tablet terminals in the learning space; scattered tablets makes scattered individual work spaces, assembled tablets in one place makes space of collective work. In short, spatial structures of work can be visually marked/formed by physical configuration of terminals. Secondly, tangible feature of tablet terminals enables learners to utilize their gaze and pointing action to control interactions as Goodwin has shown through analysis of everyday conversation [4]. Tablet terminals inevitably evoke users' gaze and pointing action while making them available for others. With tablet terminals, a group of learners can look into together a horizontally placed screen at a time. In this situation, the learners are naturally leaded to point an object on the screen while talking about the object. Importantly, the move of pointing can be monitored by the other learners. It is also natural in this situation that learners direct his/her line-of-sight to an object on the screen. That can also be noticed by others and therefore the eye-line functions as a social marker of attention. In this way, learners' gaze and pointing which are evoked naturally in the process of discussion or collaborative work are utilized as resources to control their collective attention, thus collaboration is supported naturally. That is impossible when using a laptop computer with an upright LCD that always constructs enclosed personally space [5]. Finally, tablet terminals, which can be set on a tabletop and surrounded physically by users, enables learners to utilize their body configuration to construct/dismiss a collective working space: orienting each other's body toward same direction together, that is forming F-formation [6], creates an overlap of attention foci and then construct shared working space. On the other hand, by drawing one's body from the shared workspace, the person's disengagement from the cooperative work is marked and therefore constituted. In this way, physical feature of tablet terminals helps learners to control their collabo-ration through their bodily movement.

4.1 Evaluation

We performed an evaluation experiment to see how XB supports learners to use their bodily resource to carry out discussion and transition between personal and collective phase of their activity.

Session Design. Four university students participated in the evaluation. They engaged in a discussion activity using XingBoard, and we videotaped the process. The discussion theme was "How to deal with hoaxes and lies circulated on SNS at times of disasters". The tablet terminal model was the Apple iPad2. After introduction (which included time to learn how to operate XB), the experimental session was organized as followed: (1) Personal activity, in which they individually work on the following questions; (a) why people believe in rumors in the event of a disaster, (b) why people complicit to circulate the rumors, and then (c) what possible measures to avoid that is. (2) Group discussion, (3) Personal activity where they obtain the result of the discussion using distribution copy function of XB and revise it based on personal reflection. (4) Group discussion based on the results of each other's personal contemplation.

4.2   Analysis

In this section, we discuss how XB facilitates learners' interaction using body resources based on videotaped data. In the following transcript; parentheses indicate unclear utterance, angle brackets indicate description of action, single left square bracket connecting two utterances indicates overlapped talk, square brackets show markers for explanation, and curly brackets indicate annotations by the authors.

Making Foci of Conversation by Social Markers of Attention. Transcript 1 demonstrates how XB supports learners to utilize their gaze and pointing action to control conversation. Here, they have just started discussion by mutually seeing each other's result of preceding personal activity. Student H starts speaking with pointing at a card on S's screen (H01-[a]). His pointing indicates the direction of his attention socially. Subsequently, S and Y move their body forward and look into the spot where Student H is pointing (Y02-[b], S03-[c]). This creates overlap of transactional segment and then constructs the foundation of discussion. Here we can observe smooth starting up of discussion exploiting pointing action and gaze as resources for interaction.

Transcript 2 shows conversation following the transcript 1. They are talking about their experiences about a fraud tweets which coax people into re-tweet by offering attractive bait. Student Y talks about her experience (Y02, Y04). At the end of her talk H points to a card on the V's screen ([a]). This pointing action can be considered as a social display of H's intention to start up discussion on V's card. However, at the very moment, the other participants are laughing aloud at Y's talk that Y retweeted even in the toilet and they do not respond H's intention, i.e., they do not look at the card H is pointing. H canceled the pointing once ([b]). As the laughter ends, he restarts, i.e., points to the same card again saying "This" (H06-[c]). At this time, as a response to H, Y asks "Which one?" (Y07) with looking at the direction of the card pointed by H ([d]). Almost simultaneously, S also leans forward and looks into the same card ([e]), and thus overlap of their transactional segments is formed on the card ([e]). Therefore, they can start up discussion on the contents of the card.

In these transcripts, we observed learners using pointing action and gaze as resources to control collaborative work. These actions are generated naturally by working with tangible tablet terminals which can be placed horizontally on the table. In this sense, it can be considered that the tangible characteristics of the tablet terminal made it possible to use the pointing action and gaze as interaction resources.

Transcript 1

H01: I agree with this. <points at S's card: "You can get a
      theme park ticket only if you retweet this" > [a]
Y02: What? [b]
S03: <leans forward> [c]
H04: If you retweet that (   )

Transcript 2

S01: Actually no one get a Disneyland ticket.
Y02: Right. It's a lie. Absolutely. But I retweet it.
S03: hhhh
⌈Y04: Yesterday, I took out [my phone] in restroom [and
      retweeted]
⌊H05 <Points V's screen> [a]

⌈<Everyone laughs>
⌊<H puts back his hand [b]>

H06: This. [c]
Y07: Which one? <looks at V's terminal>[d]

<Everyone look into V's terminal>[e]
V08: Well, when I was in Hiroshima.

Making Transition from Individual to Collective Activity by Body Configuration. Transcript 3 shows the scene of transition from personal task to group discussion.

In this scene, they have been engaging in individual task. First, V utters "OK?" (V01) and then in response to this utterance, Y and H answer "Ok" (H02, Y04) with moving their bodies off their terminals and setting their upper body upright ([b], [d]). By this posture, the attention to the terminal is canceled, and as a result, their remarks "OK" can be heard as approval for suspension of current task.

Transcript 3

< Everyone is looking into each one's terminal >[a]
V01: OK? (For now, we should   )

H02: Yeah, OK. <makes his upper body upright>[b]
S03: OK.<still looks into his terminal>[c]
Y04: I'm OK.<makes her upper body upright>[d]
V05: <makes her upper body upright>[e]

V06: Hey, OK, OK, OK, OK, OK? <Looks at S>[f]
S07:   OK, OK, OK, OK.

Y08:This way? Which one? All right.
<Each person pushes his/her terminal forward>[g]

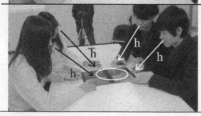

<Everyone looks into terminals>[h]
V09:OK, Then?

Thus, the relevant transitional point to the next phase of work is constructed. On the other hand, although answering "OK" (S03), S continues operating his terminal ([c]). While V hurries him (V06-[f]), Y and H did not return to work while maintaining their upper body stood up. Here appears the scene where three people including Y, H and V are waiting for S to finish his individual work. After that, Y, H and V starts to move their terminals toward the center of the table without waiting S to finish ([g1]). S also begins to move his terminal to the same direction a little late ([g2]). When four terminals are gathered in the center of the table and four participants orient their bodies toward the terminals, the transactional segment of each person overlaps on the terminals ([h]). As a result, a shared space for collaborative work is constructed here. This is apparently observable from everyone, so V could start up discussion by saying "OK, then". In this transcripts, we observed learners accomplished the transition from individual activity to collective activity very naturally through utilizing their body configuration.

Starting Up/Closing Local Discussion Using Tablet Terminal as Substitute for Body. Transcript 4 show how local discussion between Y and H is constructed. They have been engaging in individual work. Y and H exchange words (Y01, H02, Y03) but keeping the body arrangement suitable for individual work. By this body configuration, the conversation between Y and H here appears as a temporary one. But next moment, Y pushes her terminal in the direction of H ([a]) saying "This" (Y04). At the same time Y looks at H. This behavior can be seen as an invitation for some sort of collaborative work. Thus, H's utterance "I see," (H05) can be interpreted as approval of that invitation. After that, Y gets bent forward a little, looks into the terminal of H ([c]), and reads one of the cards on H's terminal (Y06). Since the terminal placed in the work area of an individual is exclusively owned by individuals, some "request for permission" is necessary to look into others' screen. However, Y is accessing the card on the terminal of H without asking for permission in particular. Also, H will not blame it. From this, it can be said that a shared space where Y and H can access from both sides is generated here. Within this space, Y and H can keep on talking about the contents of the card written on the Y's terminal (H07-H11). In this conversation, H is paying attention to the card that Y wrote: "kind of tweet urging you to re-tweet within 10 s". Y explains in detail the contents of the card she wrote while giving an example (Y08, Y10). Immediately after H said "I see" (H11), Y pulls back her terminal in front of her ([e]). As a result, the shared space between Y and H is released, and the termination of the discussion can be observed. Immediately after that, Y and H turn their bodies and eyes toward S and V ([i]), and Y says "We are waiting for you" (Y12). In this scene, they appear as those who are finished their work together and waiting for S and V to finish their work.

The process of starting up and closing the local discussion analyzed here can be seen as a process of formation and breaking up of F-formation by two participants. Interesting point is that the terminal plays a role of body substitution. When Y pushes his terminal towards the center of the table, the upper body of Y stays still standing and thus her transactional segment does not overlap with that of H. In spite of that, Y and H begin conversation about cards on each other's terminal. It was not the bodies of Y and H but the terminals that approached each other (of course, as the inevitable consequence of looking into the terminals, the two bodies are tilted slightly ahead and take a posture that is oriented towards each other). From the fact that Y terminates the discussion by returning the terminal to the original position, we can consider that the terminal has replaced her body, which has its unique transactional segment. A tablet terminal belongs to an individual, even if it is temporally, and the individual's ideas are recorded on it. In that sense it has relatively stronger nature of "extended self". Tablet terminals, at least in this experimental session, probably have both "extended self" and mobility integrated inside, and this would be the reason why the tablet terminal functions as a substitute for the body as resource for interaction.

Transcript 4

Y01: ah, can I edit these?
H02: (in yellow   )
Y03: This, perhaps this seems to be same.

Y04: Oh, in this case, this is it. This!
       < Pushes forward her terminal>[a]
H05: I see. <looks into Y's screen>[b]

Y06: Mentally weak hhh, Oh, I see::, mental factor is.
       <looks into H's screen>[c]

H07: I never pass information to someone in 10 seconds.
       <looks into Y's terminal>[d]
Y08: hhh Haven't you seen that kind of information, you
       know, that says you can be rich only if you pass it to
       someone?
H09: Yes, certainly.
Y10: It is apparently a lie. They send us a scary picture
       urging us to circulate to others.
H11: I see.

<Y returns her terminal to the original position>[e]
Y12: We are waiting for you two. <looks at V&S >[f]
<H looks at V&S>[f]

5   Conclusion

This paper described the design of XingBoard system, tablet-based tool that supports a bi-directional transition between personal and collective activities in collaborative learning process, from the viewpoint of bodily control of interaction. For that purpose, we recorded scenes where a group of 4 subjects used XingBoard. As a result of interaction analysis, it turned out that XB, by its tangible nature, supports collaborative work by enabling learners to use their bodily movements as interaction resource. Firstly, XB supports learners to make foci of conversation by utilizing bodily actions such as pointing and gaze as social markers of attention. Secondly, XB helps learners to transit from individual to collective activity through forming/breaking F-formation surrounding the tablet terminals. Thirdly, the tablet terminal of XB system is used by learners as substitute for body to control collaboration. Detailed analysis of collaborative work using XB is our further work.

Acknowledgments. This work was supported by JSPS KAKENHI Grant Numbers JP26282045, JP23300295.

References

1. Moon, J.: Handbook of Reflective and Experiential Learning: Theory and Practice. Routledge, Abingdon (2004)
2. Pirolli, P., Recker, M.: Learning strategies and transfer in the domain of programming. Cogn. Instr. **12**, 235–275 (1994)
3. Johnson, D.W., Johnson, R.T., Holubec, E.J.: Circle of Learning: Cooperation in the Classroom. Interaction Book Company, Edina (1993)
4. Goodwin, C.: Conversational Organization Interaction Between Speakers and Hearers. Academic Press, Cambridge (1981)
5. Alvarez, C., Brown, C., Nussbaum, M.: Comparative study of netbooks and tablet PCs for fostering face-to face collaborative learning. Comput. Human Behav. **27**, 834–844 (2011)
6. Kendon, A.: Conducting Interaction: Patterns of Behavior in Focused Encounters. Cambridge University Press, Cambridge (1990)

Plugramming: A Tangible Programming Tool for Children's Collaborative Learning

Tomohito Yashiro, Yasushi Harada, and Kazushi Mukaiyama[✉]

Graduate School of Computer Science, Future University Hakodate,
116-2 Kamedanakano-cho Hakodate, Hokkaido 041-8655, Japan
{g3115003,haraday,kazushi}@fun.ac.jp

Abstract. This paper describes a tangible programming tool named Plugramming that promotes collaborative work and reports on how learning this tool can have beneficial effects on children. In recent years, there have been many programming workshops for children. However, ordinal computers are designed to be operated by only one person. This means it is difficult for children to collaborate with other children in the workshop. Therefore, Plugramming is focused at enabling collaboration among children when compared to the other tools. It consists of module blocks and plug cables; a user can create a program by connecting module blocks with plug cables. Plug is an important concept of this tool. To evaluate this tool, we held a workshop and observed various children. We determined that there was physical advantage of making a program with tangible blocks. In the future, we will continue the development while discussing the possibility of enabling various studies.

Keywords: Design thinking · Information design · Children education · Computer-aided instruction · Interaction design · Tangible user interfaces

1 Introduction

This paper describes a tangible programming tool for children that promotes collaborative work and reports on how learning this tool can have beneficial effects on children.

Many children's programming classes have been held in a workshop style. Then this tangible programming tool is focused on taking advantage of this style when compared to the other tools. We report on children who used our tool in the workshop.

2 Background

In recent years, there have been many programming workshops for children. And, Scratch [1] is the most widely used programming tool in these workshops. The activities with Scratch are increasing yearly, and many educational organizations

© Springer International Publishing AG 2017
M. Kurosu (Ed.): HCI 2017, Part II, LNCS 10272, pp. 398–409, 2017.
DOI: 10.1007/978-3-319-58077-7_32

not only schools but also independent volunteers choose Scratch in their workshop. This is because Scratch can create programs like building blocks on the computer screen. As there is no need to type difficult words, children can easily create their own works such as character animations and games. In addition, children can publish their work to the official site and get comments on them by other people who use Scratch. The number of new comments is increasing, and we can see that programming by children is active all over the world [2].

In a workshop, it is said that collaborators or cooperative work among children is important. Brooks-Harris and Stock-Ward cited the following six features of a workshop: (1) Short-term intensive learning, (2) Small group interaction, (3) Active involvement, (4) Problem solving, (5) Behavioral change as outcome, and (6) Application to new learning. Particularly, in (2), cooperative work by several groups is very important in many activities of a workshop [3].

However, as seen from the one display, one keyboard, and one mouse, ordinal computer machines that are used in the workshop are designed to be operated by only one person. This means it is difficult for children to collaborate with other children in the workshop. Therefore, this situation leads to a disintegrated sharing of knowledge among children. In addition, like educational toys such as building blocks, it is also important for children to touch and use a tool directly. Therefore, we have developed a tangible programming tool to support collaborative work so as to encourage a child's ingenuity.

3   Related Researches

From previous researches, we have found that many tangible programming tools were examined technically and evaluated for small groups. Therefore, we decided to examine the function and the shape of physical blocks that can be applied to many groups. Typical researches are listed as follows:

AlgoBlock is a tangible programming tool developed by Suzuki and Kato [4]. AlgoBlock consists of programming blocks with built-in computers; children use the blocks to program submarines to pass through a maze in the sea displayed on the computer screen.

Tern is a tangible programming tool developed by Horn and Jacob [5]. The programming block is made of wood and has markers to detect through an image processing camera. This tool can control a robot-driven car. To control it, the user needs to take a picture of the built blocks.

Tangible Programming Bricks is a programming tool developed by McNerney [6]. A user can program by stacking up like bricks. Through this tool, it is possible to create a flexible program that performs calculations of numerical values and to connect external devices. In each brick, an IC microcontroller is embedded to operate as a program.

In addition, we have to think about our tools for workshops where a lot of people attend. Most of the previous researches adopted a method of combining blocks as program commands. At that time, there were many technical considerations to be made to get the connection status of the block by a computer. The technical consideration is roughly divided into two approaches: block recognition by camera and electronic components.

The advantage of an approach using a camera is low cost and obtaining an unlimited shape of blocks. However, a disadvantage of using a camera is that it is affected by the amount of ambient light. In order to avoid this problem, there is a method of fixing the camera area to take images of blocks [7] and another method of taking images of each block by a user with camera [8] and so on.

The advantage of an approach using electronic components [9] is that the recognition accuracy is high and that it is not necessary to limit the place to operate the block. However, the disadvantage is that the material cost and production time of block production increase. This can be avoided if you only perform nonprofit activities. Therefore, we decided that an approach using electronic components is appropriate in a workshop where multiple people perform activities.

4   Preparing

To develop our tools, we investigated some other tools and checked problems related to children's learning. For example, one is the prototyping tool named MESH [10] and another is Scratch. A prototyping tool is a kind of tool that supports the prototyping of new products. By using prototyping tools, users can quickly prototype products without having to deeply learn specialized technologies such as electronic work and programming.

MESH consists of module blocks that are close to our proposal, and it connects every block wirelessly. There are modules blocks used to work the LEDs, sensors, switches and so on, and users can create an application program to control using the tablet. This allows the module block of the switch to wirelessly turns on the module blocks of the LED. In addition, because these blocks are small, it is easy to embed into a house appliance. Despite it is being convenient to embed into appliances or products, we cannot see the program flow of blocks quickly because the connection of each block is invisible. Therefore, the wireless connection is difficult for children to share the entire program structure directly in a collaborative workshop.

In addition, in the workshop using Scratch, children do not look at each other because they concentrated more on the computer screen. The workshop using Scratch revealed a special support in learning programming. As an example, we describe a programming game using characters on the screen as follows. Every child could understand and handle the character animation realized by combining blocks. However, it was necessary to program conditional branches such as "move to the left if the left arrow key is pressed" to control the character with the keyboard. In this case, children with little experience in Scratch only mimic the examples, and never thought about the meaning of conditional branches. Therefore, they could reach the improved part only if they spends a lot of time with their random attempts. However, when conditional branches became necessary again, they were looking for that part from the beginning, as they moved to the next task without thinking about why the character could be controlled by conditional branches. On the other hand, children who had a lot of experience in Scratch and understood conditional branches made their games without checking the examples. This observation shows that an understanding of program execution procedure flows such as conditional branches is important in learning programming.

Next, we examined the way to visualize the structures and execution procedures of a program. Many visual programming languages such as Scratch express commands as virtual blocks and combine them like building blocks. This way the troublesome key input can be forgotten and the users can operate naturally. In addition, the text portion of the final assembled blocks can be read like a program code written in a text-style programming language like C (Fig. 1). However, the order of the blocks is expressed only as if they are arranged in one row from the top like program code by text. In order to encourage children's understanding of the program execution flow, we needed to find a new way rather than using expressions that are arranged in a line in an order from the top as text. Flowchart [11] can be cited as expressions of programs other than text. In the flowchart, symbols and lines represent the program execution flow. Therefore, compared to visual programming tools like Scratch, the program structure and execution flow can be confirmed at once (Fig. 2). The representation of symbols and lines like flowchart can be applied to the shape of a tangible programming tool.

Therefore, we decided to develop a tool that allows users to easily list the structure and execution procedure of a program and collaborate with each other.

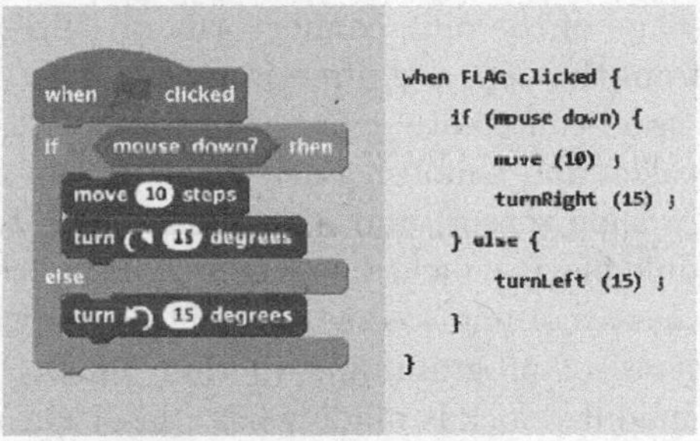

Fig. 1. Scratch and program codes.

5   "Plugramming"

Plugramming is a tangible tool for computer-program learning that we developed (Fig. 3). We coined the term, and it is a combination of "plug" and "programming." Plug is an important concept of this tool. Plugramming consists of module blocks and plug cables. Module blocks represent programming elements

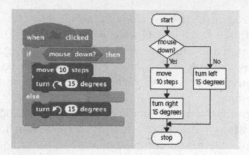

Fig. 2. Comparing Scratch and flowchart.

such as conditional branches. A user can create a program by connecting module blocks with plug cables. On this tool, a user can see the structure and flow of the entire program on a desktop. Additionally, as multiple users can create a program like making building blocks, this tool leads users to collaborate among each other. For example, it can represent a conditional branch with two plug cables (Fig. 4).

When a program is executed, module blocks are executed as one step in order. For each step, the connected plug cable between the module blocks blinks and users can see the flow of execution. Both the step execution time and the cable blinking time are 1.5 s. This speed is set such that children can observe how the program executes. Each module block sends data with serial communication through the plug cable and determines the timing of program execution. In addition, this plug cable has an LED inside that blinks following a program execution flow. The shape of the plug connector is of USB A-B type, so that a user cannot connect from the opposite direction.

In Plugramming, users can create a program for operating electronic parts such as an LED, a speaker, and a motor. Further, users can attach a sensor such as an optical sensor, a slide sensor, and a volume sensor to a specific module block. By using a module block attached to a sensor, users can create a program whose behavior branches according to environmental conditions.

There are three types of programming module blocks: START, POWER, and CASE blocks. A module block is made with a laser-cut acrylic resin and an electric circuit board. Every block has a PIC microcontroller and USB connectors for input and output (Fig. 5). The START block is a green block. This block is always used at the beginning of the program. It has a button in the center to execute the program. The POWER block is a red block. This block is used to operate the electronic parts. Therefore, in addition to the USB connector for input and output, there is another connector to connect the electronic parts. This extra connector has a general-purpose configuration to connect various electronic parts. In addition, It has a dial that can change the operation of the electronic parts. The CASE block is a blue block. This block can branch into the next execution flow depending on the value of the attached sensor. Therefore, it has one USB connector for input and two USB connectors for output. Additionally,

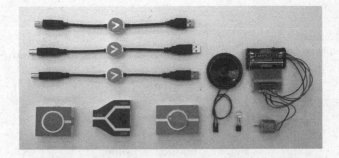

Fig. 3. Plugramming's modules and cables.

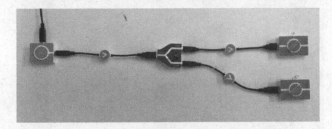

Fig. 4. An example to change LED by the conditional branch.

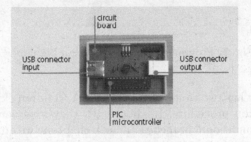

Fig. 5. Inside the Red Power Block. (Color figure online)

it has an extra connector to attach the sensor. As same as the POWER block, this extra connector uses a general-purpose configuration, and so it is possible to use various sensors with a user's own electric circuit.

6 Workshop

We held a workshop and observed children who used Plugramming. The purpose of this workshop was to encourage children to understand the program execution procedure. Of the 19 participants, 11 were boys and 8 were girls. In addition, they were all elementary school students aged 9 to 12 years old.

Children performed two learning activities in the two-day workshop (Fig. 6). One is the activity using Plugramming and another one is Scratch. The activity

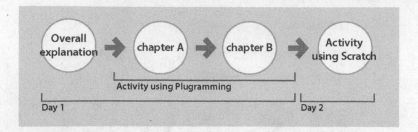

Fig. 6. Workshop schedule.

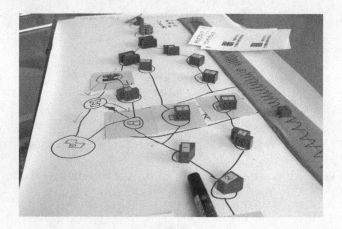

Fig. 7. Programming mimics with a big paper.

using Plugramming has two chapters. In chapter A, children experienced the flow of program execution procedure. In chapter B, they experienced the changing flow as a result of conditional branches. In both chapters, we adjusted the average age by dividing the children into four groups.

In chapter A, we gave the children a big paper, a few pens, Lego blocks and cards, and let them perform their activities without a computer. At first, the children drew a flowchart of program on the big paper, and then placed the Lego blocks over the flowchart (Fig. 7). Subsequently, we let the children pass the pen as a baton according to the flowchart drawn by them. At this time, the child who had the baton must pretend to be a program command. The program commands are Lego blocks placed over the flowchart. And the command content is written on the card related to each block. For example, "Say Hello!" is the content on the card of "speaking" command. Through this activity, we let the children know that the program was a group of commands and there is a procedure flow in execution (Fig. 8).

In chapter B, we let the children use Plugramming to reproduce the programs that they experienced in chapter A (Fig. 9). For the POWER block, some LEDs, speakers, and motors were arranged. In addition, optical sensors were arranged

Fig. 8. Body exercises of the flow of program execution.

Fig. 9. Plugramming workshop.

for the CASE block. Plugramming could perform conditional branches through the condition of a sensor in the CASE block. Therefore, children took much time to understand how to operate the program by using the CASE block. When part A's program finishes, we gave the children the trial time to create another program. In particular, we encouraged them to try the CASE block where the flow of program execution changes depending on the sensor response.

In the activity using Scratch, children made an animation that performs various actions depending on conditional branches. At this time, we arranged every child a PC and a sensor board to detect light, sound volume and so on. Desks were allocated in such a manner that two children faced each other. In addition, we permitted that the group members of Plugramming to sit close. At the beginning of this activity, we explained the basic usage of conditional branch to link the sensor board and animation. Subsequently, each child started to create a character animation by programming. We did not provide any assistance or instructions for animation production unless the children asked for it. However, we told the children to move freely in the room and we recommended that they discuss with their neighbors. The presentation showing each other's works was at the middle and the end of the activity time.

7   Conclusion

As intended, the physical advantage of Plugramming, that is, making a program with tangible blocks, could be confirmed. The children's confirmed activities are as follows. Children worked together collaborating and sharing their roles during the creation and execution of the program. In addition, at the time of the program execution, we confirmed that they discussed why their program did not work properly.

The children were judging whether the program execution was what they thought by observing the plug cables blinking and the action of electronic parts of the POWER block. In particular, some children confirmed the flow of execution at every step of execution by pointing their figure or saying "worked." The programs that did not work were caused by the conditional branch on the CASE block. At this time, their discussion point was mainly on how the sensor responded by covering the light using their hands. After the discussion, roles were assigned to those who reacted to the sensors, those who pushed the execution buttons, etc.

The children had to collaborate with others in order to create their program smoothly. This is because users must connect their cables to create a program in Plugramming, and it requires a large amount of workspace on the table. Every group finished creating a program through trial and error on the execution procedure of a program. Their trial and error work was to observe whether their program correctly branched when using the CASE block. At this time, we found two groups: a group where someone took the initiative such as inserting and removing the cables, and giving instructions, and another group where everyone worked closely with each other and finally integrated their programs. Neither group seemed to be unable to create a program unless they cooperated with other groups for a wide workplace.

In addition, the children aggressively integrated their programs without the staff's advice. Subsequently, they had finally combined all their small programs into one big program (Fig. 10). When their integrated program worked successfully, all children shouted to cheer their program. While running their program, some children chased the plug cables blinking. In addition, if the trial failed, the children themselves found the part of the problem and the solution for it.

On the other hand, in the workshop using Scratch, we confirmed that the children concentrated on their own work. Most of the children did not stand in the room to see other's work. Some children continued to pursue their own works even during other's presentation. In addition, in the workshop using Scratch, despite constantly recommending discussion with other children, the children simply depended on instructions from the staff and never discussed among each other.

We also confirmed an interesting conversation between the teaching staff and the children. In each work, the children were challenging to change the animation through conditional branch according to the theme of the workshop. However, some children found difficulty in understanding Scratch's conditional branch. Therefore, the staff reminded them of using Plugramming as an example. Subsequently, the children could understand the conditional branch used in their own program, once Plugramming's CASE block was applied.

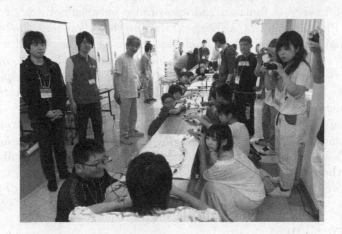

Fig. 10. An integrated program of Plugramming.

8   Consideration

It was confirmed that tangible module blocks and plug cables made children understand the program structure and execution flow and encouraged collaborative work. Even in a small space, we could develop a programming tool if we used virtual blocks in the computer screen. However, this tangible tool requires a wide workspace as one person alone cannot reach the blocks. We do not think that this is a disadvantage, and rather believe that this leads to aggressive collaboration. To that proof, children were themselves responsible for each block and discussed the behavior of the program with others.

In the role sharing, it was interesting to know the person responsible for checking the sensors. This was attributed to the feature that the optical sensor used at this workshop constantly changed with ambient lights. The children were discussing the optical sensors as follows: "whether they are covered by hand." It appears that role sharing originated because someone had to cover the optical sensor by their hand at all times. We consider that role sharing is difficult to occur only by slide volumes, turning the switches on or off, etc. This is because these sensors can maintain its state even if they are not touched by hand.

Connecting the fact that children prefer integrating the programs by every group rather than enjoying the block action such as LED blinks, we understand that children wanted to check the execution order in all their programs. This result is because of the visualization of the flow of program execution owing to the cable's blinking. We also consider setting the program execution speed to a speed that can be observed by humans.

In the activity using Scratch, it appeared that the children understood Scratch's conditional branch syntax through staff's assistance. At that time, the staff's aid was to encourage an understanding by comparing the experience using the Scratch's conditional branch and Plugramming's CASE block. There is a difference in function and appearance between Scratch's conditional branch and Plugramming's CASE block. Despite the differences, the reason why children could understand conditional branch was that they could understand the abstract concept of "what will be changed next depending on conditions." Therefore, we consider that Plugramming's CASE block and the plug cables were effective for promoting the understanding of the flow of program execution and the structure of the program.

From the above description, we have concluded that Plugramming has induced learning acts that can solve problems through discussions and collaborative work with physical movements. In addition, the Plugramming style of connecting the module blocks through plug cables was effective for experiencing and understanding the flow of program execution and the structure of programs.

9   Future Plan

Currently, Plugramming can only operate electric parts such as LEDs, speakers, and motors at a fixed speed and order. In the future, we will continue the development while discussing the possibility of various other studies, as tangible programming tools have potential extensions to use in not only children's workshops but also flexible situations. For example, we are planning to develop a module block that can adjust the execution speed of programs; we are also planning to develop module blocks that allow LEDs, speakers, and motor operation to be set in more detail.

References

1. Resnick, M., Maloney, J., Monroy-Hernandez, A., Rusk, N., Eastmond, E., Brennan, K., Millner, A., Rosenbaum, E., Silver, J., Silverman, B., Kafai, Y.: Scratch programming for all. Commun. ACM **52**(11), 60–67 (2009)
2. The Lifelong Kindergarten Group at MIT Media Lab: Scratch Statistics - Imagine, Program, Share, 25 December 2016. https://scratch.mit.edu/statistics/
3. Brooks-Harris, J.E., Stock-Ward, S.: Workshops: Designing and Facilitating Experiential Learning. Sage, Thousand Oaks (1999)
4. Suzuki, H., Kato, H.: AlgoBlock: a tangible programming language, a tool for collaborative learning. In: Proceedings of the 4th European Logo Conference, Greece (1993)

5. Horn, M., Jacob, R.J.K.: Tangible programming in the classroom with tern. In: Proceedings of CHI 2007 ACM Human Factors in Computing Systems, San Jose (2007)
6. McNerney, T.: From turtle to tangible programming bricks: explorations in physical language design. Pers. Ubiquit. Comput. **8**, 326–337 (2004)
7. Wang, D., Zhang, C., Wang, H.: T-Maze: a tangible programming tool for children. In: Proceedings of the 10th International Conference on Interaction Design and Children, IDC 2011. ACM (2011)
8. Sullivan, A., Elkin, M., Bers, M.U.: KIBO robot demo: engaging young children in programming and engineering. In: Proceedings of the 14th International Conference on Interaction Design and Children, IDC 2015. ACM, pp. 418–421 (2015)
9. Zuckerman, O., Arida, S., Resnick, M.: Extending tangible interfaces for education: digital montessori-inspired manipulatives. In: Proceedings of the SIGCHI Conference on Human Factors in Computing Systems, CHI 2005. ACM, pp. 859–868 (2005)
10. Sony Corporation: With MESH: Anything Can Become a Smart Device! Sony, 17 November 2016. http://meshprj.com/en/
11. Hartree, D.: Calculating Instruments and Machines, vol. 112. The University of Illinois Press, Champaign (1949)

HCI in Complex Human Environments

DTMi – A New Interface for Informed Navigation

Tamara Babaian, Ren Zhang, and Wendy Lucas$^{(\boxtimes)}$

Bentley University, Waltham, MA 02452, USA
{tbabaian, zhang_ren, wlucas}@bentley.edu

Abstract. We introduce an interactive, dynamic visualization aimed at improving navigation in complex systems, including but not limited to Enterprise Resource Planning (ERP) systems. Users of these types of industrial behemoths are typically presented with a multilayered menu structure for navigating the various task interfaces. The vast number of options and paths tends to overwhelm users rather than encourage system exploration. Experienced users prefer memorizing transaction codes that take them directly to the page for that task, leaving them with a fragmented understanding of how tasks fit together. The Dynamic Task Map with information (DTMi) addresses these issues by providing an interactive, dynamic mapping of the tasks supported by the system and the connections between them. A laboratory evaluation involving an earlier version of this interface, referred to as DTM, revealed that users were at least twice as fast at finding transactions with DTM than with a standard SAP interface and were correct nearly twice as often in their answers to questions concerning those transactions. Outcomes from that study, including feedback from participants, led to improvements that were incorporated into DTMi. In this paper, we present this new interface, describe how it extends the earlier version, compare it to alternative approaches, and discuss our plans for user evaluations and future research in this area.

Keywords: Interactive visualizations · Dynamic visualizations · Usability · User experience · ERP

1 Introduction

One of the most daunting tasks facing users of complex systems is figuring out how to navigate to the desired task interface. This is particularly true for users of large enterprise systems, such as Enterprise Resource Planning systems [1–5]. These systems encompass hundreds of interfaces supporting a wide variety of business tasks (also called transactions) and processes. Difficulties with navigation are mainly due to the fact that the number of interrelated transactions supported by the system is very large, yet each individual organization typically uses only a subset of these transactions. For individual users, the situation is more severe, as they are involved in an even smaller fraction of the total number of supported tasks.

The standard navigational tool for these systems takes the form of nested menus, which offer an overwhelming number of possible paths. Many of the menu options

M. Kurosu (Ed.): HCI 2017, Part II, LNCS 10272, pp. 413–423, 2017.
DOI: 10.1007/978-3-319-58077-7_33

sound the same, and may indeed lead to the same task interface, though that is not always the case. The sheer number of often unfamiliar choices makes it difficult for the user to proceed with confidence and operate with a sense of competency. User confusion and intimidation are further exacerbated by difficulties with piecing together how transactions are related to the overall process or goals of the individual organizational units. As a result of these issues, novice users often turn to their colleagues for help, while more experienced users memorize the shortcut codes for the transactions they use most frequently. Both types of users rely on notes and other paper-based aides [6] in performing their work with the system. While all of these methods make it possible for users to accomplish what needs to be done, they also serve to limit the potential for system exploration and hinder even experienced people from using the system to its fullest potential.

In this paper, we present a novel interface component for navigating between tasks that is designed to alleviate the problems mentioned above. The *Dynamic Task Map with information*, or *DTMi*, is an extension of the DTM interface, which we presented earlier [7, 8]. DTM is an interactive graph constructed from transaction usage logs containing information about transactions performed with the system. Labeled nodes represent a set of system transactions; this set can be adjusted to include all transactions, or any subset of all transactions. For the version presented here, we chose to include all transactions that were used at least once by at least one user. The transaction that the user is currently engaged in is highlighted and linked to other transactions that users typically perform immediately after or in parallel with it. DTM also allows the user to search for a transaction node by its label. In a laboratory comparison of DTM with a standard SAP menu and search tools, in which users were asked to first locate a transaction and then find a related transaction, users were able to perform the navigation tasks faster and with greater success and accuracy using DTM [8].

DTMi extends the original DTM interface in the following ways:

1. Tasks belonging to the same functional module (e.g. Financial, Human Resources, etc.) are grouped together in distinctly colored convex hulls. The goal of this grouping is to support user exploration and understanding of the different system modules.
2. It includes a dedicated panel on the right side for displaying task information that is not communicated by the graph itself but might be useful in choosing what task needs to be done next. This information may include the names or identifiers of users who have performed the selected task, the date the task was last performed, and additional, pertinent data obtained from the usage logs or other relevant system components.
3. An improved search interface is located in the top bar that, upon request, pans between partially matching transactions and zooms in on each one in turn. This aids in the selection process by enabling the gradual exploration of transactions.

In the next section of this paper, we discuss the outcomes of user studies and interviews with users of enterprise systems that motivated the original and updated versions of the DTM interface. We then summarize the results from a user study with the original interface and discuss our approach in light of related work. In Sect. 3, we present the DTMi interface, which was designed to address the issues raised in prior user studies. We then discuss future plans for evaluating DTMi, followed by our conclusions.

2 Related Work

2.1 Background and Motivation

Many recent research studies have pointed out system navigation as being one of the bottlenecks in successful and effective utilization of enterprise systems [2–5]. Figure 1 shows three different approaches to navigation from popular commercial systems. The nested menu structure, exemplified by the *SAP Easy Access Menu* shown on the left in this figure, expands as users drill down through the menu options. While this approach preserves the path taken by the user, it can quickly become overwhelming. New users are intimidated by the massiveness of the menu structure and often do not know where to start looking; experienced users memorize the transaction codes they use most frequently, thereby bypassing this cumbersome menu entirely.

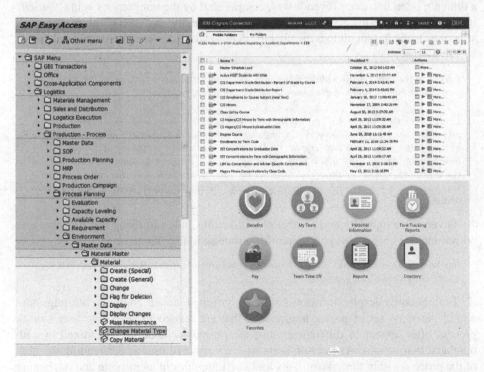

Fig. 1. Three menu structures, with an SAP nested menu structure on the left, an IBM Cognos single-level menu with breadcrumb trail on the upper right, and a Workday graphical menu on the lower left (Color figure online)

A flat menu structure augmented with a breadcrumb trail is illustrated by the *IBM Cognos* screenshot appearing in the upper right of the figure. While this approach can be less intimidating, it can be even more difficult to find the correct option because only one menu level can be viewed at a time; the user must click back through the breadcrumb trail to view other paths. Lastly, a graphical approach is illustrated by the *Workday* menu in the lower right of Fig. 1. While this appears to be the least threatening of the three, it too presents challenges to the user. The user's expectation of where a particular option will be may not be aligned with the icon-with-label depiction. Once the user has selected the appropriate icon, they will again be presented with a list of options. Selecting the Reports icon for the interface instance shown here, for example, reveals a list of over 400 reports.

In our own studies, we have found that users have a difficult time finding desired transactions. A usability study involving 20 novice users performing tasks with SAP revealed that navigation through the main menu was a significant usability issue [9]. It was found to be responsible for 6% of all detected usability incidents and experienced by 65% percent of all study participants.

Users in a field study in which we interviewed employees working with three different enterprise systems reported that finding the functionality that they needed was a difficult, often unsuccessful endeavor, complicated by the transactions being "buried" under layers of nested structures [10]. The complexity and sheer volume of these structures made it difficult to remember the path to take to even common tasks, as noted by these employees:

User1: So you could easily wander down some menu path and get lost and never find that again for another month. And not even know how you got there, right?

User2: And then things will be buried, you know, under something. You'll think it's an accounting thing but it will be under IS, and then it's another thing they call environment. Some of these menu paths are a little cryptic. And so it's hard to sort of get the lay of the land just by looking at it. And it's like if you were brand new to this, it's been so long, but I suspect you could drill down many of these paths wondering, you know, where does this end? And then if you found what you wanted, you know, you might think, "I'm never going to find that ever again."

Given the complexity and number of transactions, it is surprising that the interfaces do not include an easy way to search for a transaction by its name.

Interviewer: So what would you do if you can't find something that you really had to do?
User3: Just keep clicking around.

Furthermore, despite transactions being grouped under common headings and within the same set of pages, transactions that are related to a specific user's work process often appear in different groups, are placed far apart, or are mixed in with unrelated transactions. As a result, users have a very hard time understanding the flow of the process within the system. This leads to difficulties in identifying and navigating to a transaction that is related to or must follow the one they are currently working on, as noted by the following user:

User4: There's a transaction for 'A', transaction for 'B' and a transaction for 'C' and nothing links them…

To overcome this difficulty, users create notes that range in complexity from simple lists of transaction codes on a post-it to elaborate flowcharts supporting them and their colleagues in their work [6]. Figure 2 depicts one example of informal notes created within an organization; the flowchart in the figure presents a process, which is annotated with references to specific transaction codes. These kinds of notes, along with other observations from field studies, motivated our innovative approaches to supporting users of complex enterprise systems.

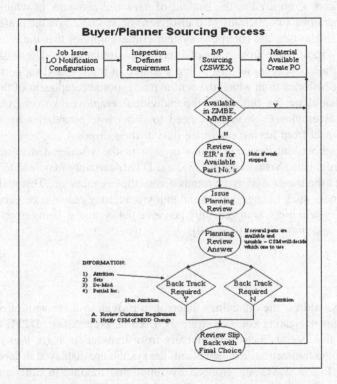

Fig. 2. A flow chart created by users of an enterprise system, depicting the flow of a business process with references to the corresponding transactions referenced by transaction codes

2.2   Adaptive Menus and Visual Approaches to Navigation

In our previous work, we developed and evaluated a dynamic visualization-based approach to navigation in enterprise systems called DTM [7, 8]. When compared in a user study to the transaction search and navigation facilities within SAP, users overwhelmingly preferred DTM, noting its ease of use and its appealing and more informative nature [8]. In terms of performance measures, users who were asked to locate transactions by name were, on average, three times faster and 1.6 times more accurate with DTM compared to SAP. Users' suggestions for improving DTM included adding groupings of transactions and refining the visual layout of the graph and labels for improving the readability of the transaction nodes.

DTM, along with its successor DTMi that is presented here, can both be viewed as a type of adaptive menu because they are constructed from usage logs, making the composition of the graph dependent on the use of the system within an organization. User evaluations of adaptive menus have yielded mixed results in the published literature [11, 12]. Most studies, however, have been focused on the effectiveness of adaptive approaches to creating toolbars and split menus in personal productivity software. Adaptation accuracy, stability, and predictability of adaptive interface features have been cited [12] as important factors in achieving user efficiency gains with such adaptations. Compared to the context of *personal* software, in which the adaptation (whether done automatically or user-driven) occurs based on the preferences and history of a single user, the enterprise system context implies that the relevant transaction history must come from a set of users with similar goals. Users of enterprise systems cite their colleagues as their primary source of training and support. It follows that the usage histories from which the central navigational component of the system is composed should not be limited to the individual employee's workgroup or even department, as employees sometimes need to cross role boundaries to achieve the maximum impact from having enterprise data at their disposal.

Learning about and detecting trends present in the visualized data are potential advantages from using visualizations [13], and DTMi certainly may lead to employees learning about the transaction usage trends across the organization. This and other user experience goals, such as engagement and enjoyment, may prove to be very beneficial to enterprise system users, who generally perceive the system as being overly complex, intimidating, and unforgiving [5, 6, 10].

3 DTMi

DTMi aims to address the difficulties inherent in providing users with effective, intuitive means for navigating complex systems. Like its predecessor, DTMi is an interactive graph that is constructed dynamically from transaction usage logs. When first loaded, all of the transactions available from the system are displayed as labeled nodes, as shown in Fig. 3. Tasks are grouped by functional module in differently colored convex hulls. The darker green grouping, for example, represents the Sales and Distribution (SD) module, while the Financial (FI) module is depicted in dark pink. These groupings help the users understand which tasks constitute the different modules in the system. To reduce congestion, links between tasks are not shown in this view.

To assist in user exploration of tasks within modules, both zooming and panning actions are supported: moving two fingers towards each other/away from each other on the mouse pad will cause the mapping to zoom out/zoom in; panning is enabled by pressing one finger on the mouse pad while moving another along the pad. The user can also hover the mouse over a particular task; additional details concerning that task are then displayed in a dedicated panel located on the right side of the DTMi. These details are provided by the usage logs and other relevant components of the system.

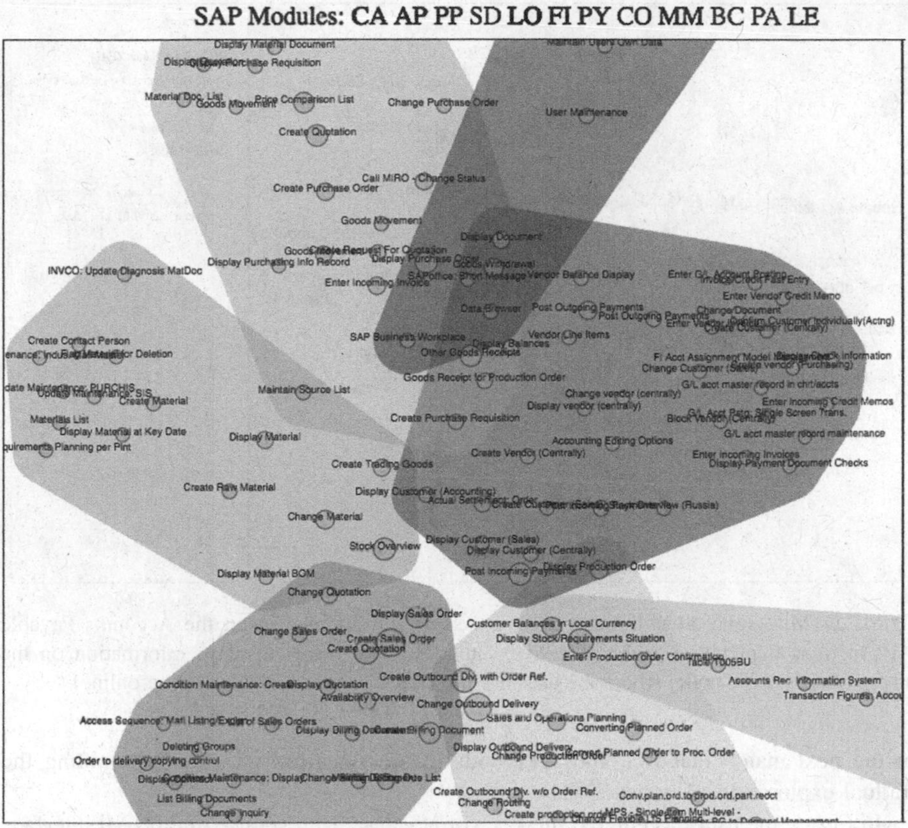

SAP Modules: **CA AP PP SD LO FI PY CO MM BC PA LE**

Fig. 3. A partial snapshot of the initial Dynamic Task Map with information (DTMi) showing all transactions available in the system. Tasks belonging to the same module are grouped together in colored hulls, identified by the legend at the top of the screenshot. (Color figure online)

Figure 4 shows the results of the user panning to the lower left corner of the display, zooming in on the Accounts Payable (AP) module, and hovering the mouse on the "Display Sales Order" node. Among the information displayed in the right panel is the identity of the person who last performed this task, when it was performed, and that person's department. This information could be helpful to the current user if they have questions concerning this task. Any data from the logs could potentially be displayed in this panel; ideally the contents would be configured to best meet the needs of the particular organization.

DTMi also includes a search interface. After the user enters a search term, the display updates to highlight a transaction whose label is at least a partial match with that term. Connections are shown between that node and any nodes depicting transactions that are performed concurrently or immediately after it. The color intensity of each transaction node indicates the frequency with which transitions are made to it from the highlighted transaction, as determined from the usage logs collected by the system. Each time the user clicks the "next" button, the display will pan to and zoom in

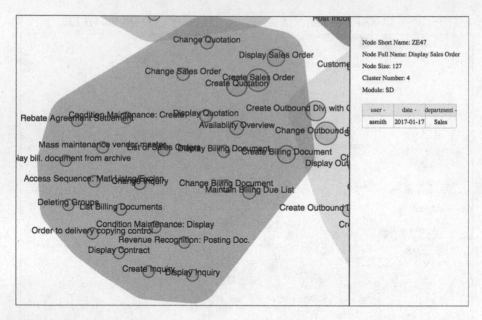

Fig. 4. DTMi display after the user has panned to and zoomed in on the Accounts Payable (AP) module, depicted as a green, convex hull. The side panel displays information on the Display Sales Order node, where the user has hovered the mouse. (Color figure online)

on the next match that is found. This aids in the selection process by enabling the gradual exploration of transactions.

In Fig. 5, the user has entered the keyword "sales." In response, the DTMi interface has highlighted one of the 11 matching transactions, "Display Sales Order," which appears in the center of the screen. This transaction is shown as being connected to several other transactions. The nodes with the strongest color intensity include "Create Sales Order," "Create Quotation," and "Create Outbound Div. with Order Ref.," indicating that these transactions are performed most frequently in parallel or immediately following the "Display Sales Order" task. The user has hovered the mouse over the "Change Sales Order" transaction, revealing additional information about it in the right panel that may be useful in determining which transaction to perform next.

4   Discussion

We have designed and developed DTMi based on our understanding of the needs and work practices of users of enterprise systems, which we gained through field studies and analysis of ERP usability literature. While the original design of DTM as an interactive, searchable graph based on the SAP system log proved effective and well-liked by novice users in a laboratory study [8], the new design must be validated with real users of enterprise systems in the field.

Search for: `sales`   **found 11 results** `Next`

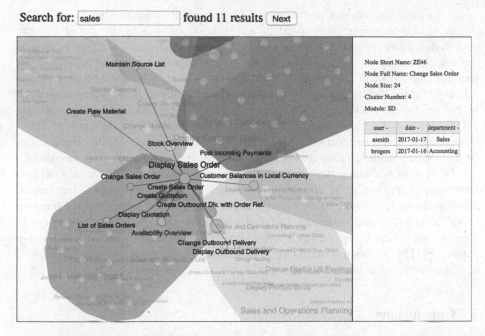

Fig. 5. A snapshot of DTMi including the search interface, in which the user has entered the keyword "sales." The side panel displays information on the Change Sales Order node. (Color figure online)

As we discussed in Sect. 2.2, DTMi fits into the paradigm of adaptive user interfaces, as it presents transactions connected to those that follow them, based on the usage logs that record sequences of transactions as they are executed by users. Brusilovsky et al. [14] have demonstrated that, since interface adaptation is performed by combining a user model with interaction features augmented by this model, results of an "as-a-whole" evaluation of an adaptive interface may not reveal the real value of adaptation. This is because an end-result-focused evaluation does not distinguish between the effects of choosing the right model and choosing the appropriate presentation and interaction techniques to go with it. Instead, the authors argue for a *layered* approach to evaluation, in which the usefulness and accuracy of the model underlying the adaptation is evaluated separately from the way the model is employed in the interface. These arguments are corroborated by the experimental results reported by Gajos et al. [11], who have tested three different adaptive menu designs, all based on the same usage model. In their study, they found significant differences in user preferences regarding different versions of the interfaces, as well as significant differences in the average time it took users to locate menu items using those interfaces. These considerations point to the necessity of investigating specific design choices within DTMi, such as whether the model of transaction "relatedness" that connects a transaction to the ones following it in a user's history is the right model for enterprise system users. Alternatives include linking two transactions if they are related in a document flow.

In terms of the chosen presentation and interaction characteristics, we need to assess if, for example, the grouping of transactions should be based on the system-defined characteristics or on specific organizational practices. That is, should the colored blocks separate transactions by system modules or by the organizational unit that employs them? Another important question concerns the selection of the usage threshold for the displayed transactions: should infrequently or never used transactions be hidden and only revealed when they are explicitly searched for? Lastly, since the DTMi informational side panel can be configured to present different kinds of information, what would be most useful to include here? These aspects of the interface can be assessed by demonstrating and discussing DTMi in focus groups with real users.

Along with evaluating user performance and satisfaction with DTMi, it would be interesting to find out if the visualization will help organizational users detect trends, promote the understanding of the organizational practices and processes, and improve users' attitudes toward using the system by reducing their perceptions of its complexity. Since users in our previous study were very enthusiastic about the interactive nature of DTM, employing the DTMi interface may aid in the successful adoption of complex industrial systems by some of the more reluctant users.

5   Conclusions

In this paper, we have presented DTMi – a visual interactive interface for transaction search and navigation in enterprise systems. DTMi extends a previous version (DTM) with features that include the grouping of transactions, iterative search based on a partial keyword match, and a panel for displaying task- and navigation-related information. DTMi presents a new approach to navigation, which can be configured to present a variety of detailed information that can aid in task selection. We plan to interview enterprise system users regarding:

- the usefulness of our chosen model of connecting transactions based on usage history, and
- the informational content that should accompany each transaction in the side panel.

We expect that the visual nature of DTMi will contribute to an enhanced user experience through greater enjoyment, increased engagement with the system, and the potential for greater learning and trends discovery. These expectations will need to be verified in practice.

References

1. Iansiti, M.: ERP End-user productivity: a field study of SAP and Microsoft (2007)
2. Topi, H., Lucas, W., Babaian, T.: Identifying usability issues with an ERP implementation. In: Proceedings of the International Conference on Enterprise Information Systems (ICEIS-2005), pp. 128–133 (2005)

3. Singh, A., Wesson, J.: Evaluation criteria for assessing the usability of ERP systems. In: Proceedings of the 2009 Annual Research Conference of the South African Institute of Computer Scientists and Information Technologists, pp. 87–95. ACM (2009)
4. Parks, N.E.: Testing & quantifying ERP usability. In: Proceedings of the 1st Annual Conference on Research in Information Technology, pp. 31–36. ACM, New York (2012)
5. Lambeck, C., Fohrholz, C., Leyh, C., Müller, R.: (Re-) Evaluating user interface aspects in ERP systems - an empirical user study. In: Proceedings of the 47th Hawaiian International Conference on System Sciences. IEEE Computer Society (2014)
6. Topi, H., Lucas, W., Babaian, T.: Using informal notes for sharing corporate technology know-how. Eur. J. Inf. Syst. **15**, 486–499 (2006)
7. Babaian, T., Lucas, W., Li, M.: Modernizing exploration and navigation in enterprise systems with interactive visualizations. In: Yamamoto, S. (ed.) HIMI 2015. LNCS, vol. 9172, pp. 23–33. Springer, Cham (2015). doi:10.1007/978-3-319-20612-7_3
8. Babaian, T., Lucas, W., Chircu, A., Power, N.: Interactive visualizations for workspace tasks (2017, forthcoming)
9. Babaian, T., Lucas, W., Oja, M.-K.: Evaluating the collaborative critique method. In: Proceedings of the 2012 ACM Annual Conference on Human Factors in Computing Systems, CHI 2012, pp. 2137–2146. ACM, New York (2012)
10. Babaian, T., Lucas, W., Xu, J., Topi, H.: Usability through system-user collaboration. In: Winter, R., Zhao, J.L., Aier, S. (eds.) DESRIST 2010. LNCS, vol. 6105, pp. 394–409. Springer, Heidelberg (2010). doi:10.1007/978-3-642-13335-0_27
11. Gajos, K.Z., Czerwinski, M., Tan, D.S., Weld, D.S.: Exploring the design space for adaptive graphical user interfaces. In: Proceedings of the Working Conference on Advanced Visual Interfaces, pp. 201–208. ACM (2006)
12. Findlater, L., McGrenere, J.: Comprehensive user evaluation of adaptive graphical user interfaces. In: CHI-2008 Extended Abstracts, Florence, Italy (2008)
13. Saket, B., Endert, A., Stasko, J.: Beyond usability and performance: a review of user experience-focused evaluations in visualization. In: Sedlmair, M., Isenberg, P., Isenberg, T., Mahyar, N., Lam, H. (eds.) Proceedings of the Sixth Workshop on Beyond Time and Errors on Novel Evaluation Methods for Visualization (BELIV 2016), pp. 133–142. ACM, New York (2016)
14. Brusilovsky, P., Karagiannidis, C., Sampson, D.: Layered evaluation of adaptive learning systems. Int. J. Contin. Eng. Educ. Life Long Learn. **14**, 402–421 (2004)

Game of Drones: How to Control a UAV?

Jan Conrad[✉], Dieter Wallach, Fabian Kalweit, Patrick Lindel,
and Stefan Templin

University of Applied Sciences Kaiserslautern,
Amerikastr. 1, 66482 Zweibruecken, Germany
jan.conrad@hs-kl.de

Abstract. Unmanned aerial vehicles (UAVs) so-called drones are getting more and more popular in the civil sector as well as in the military scope. One of the main challenges is the interaction of the pilot and the drone. This paper explores the usage of different game controllers as input device to control an UAV. In an explorative study, participants fulfill a predefined flying task and report their expectations before and experiences after performing the flight with different gaming controllers. The resulting insights are a basis for further interaction research activities.

1 Introduction

Since the beginning of aviation, airplanes are controlled by the help of a control stick. It was already used in the first motorized aircrafts and is still standard in actual aviation. So, unmanned aerial vehicles (UAVs) so-called drones are typically operated by a control stick as well. Also virtual airplanes in the gaming section are often controlled by Joysticks too. But for gaming purposes, many other interaction devices exist beside the Joystick and a huge community is familiar in using them.

Since drones are getting more and more popular, this paper explores the usage of different game controllers for operating a leisure sector drone. Therefore, three wide-spread input devices are selected:

1. A Joystick is a quite usual way to interact with a drone
2. A Xbox console gamepad represents a very common interaction devices for console gamer but it is rather unusual to control UAVs
3. A Wii Balance Board is very unusual to control a UAV and it exposes the user to a physical challenging operating situation

These input devices are used to control a drone to fulfill a predefined task. This task is carried out in an empirical study and reviews different aspects including gaming know-how, gender, sportiness and age.

© Springer International Publishing AG 2017
M. Kurosu (Ed.): HCI 2017, Part II, LNCS 10272, pp. 424–432, 2017.
DOI: 10.1007/978-3-319-58077-7_34

1.1   Technical Realization

The following technical adaptions are conducted to connect different input devices with the drone. So, the user is enabled to control the direction and speed of the UAV. The flight intelligence and stabilization algorithms of the drone are still active and working.

The used technical setup is based on a student's work in the lecture "Advanced Interactive Systems" in 2016. As UAV, the drone Bebop 2 of the French manufacturer Parrot is used. It was chosen, since it is a comparatively compact, stable and powerful quadcopter with an open programming interface. As SDK, the currently newest software version ARDroneSDK 3 is utilized. A special feature of Bepop 2 is the connection via Wireless Lan, which allows an easy and simple connection of self-programmed control software. The central element of the used setup is a laptop or PC, which acts as a control station (tower). It serves as a central interface between the controlled drone and the used input devices. This experimental setup, in combination with geofencing and the continuous intervention facility of the 'tower'-PC, allows safe flights even with inexperienced participants. The application logic is written in JavaScript and executed with NodeJS. Both, the drone and the various input devices are embedded by corresponding node modules. As input devices, a joystick, a gamepad, a keyboard and a Wii Balance Board are used. Thereby the joystick and the gamepad are connected via USB-ports and the Balance Board over Bluetooth. Due to the missing NodeJS implementation for the Balance Board, a Java application is used to connect the main program and the board via UDP sockets.

The used software is publicly available under github.com/fog1992/AIS-Drone. A schematic representation of the technical implementation is shown in Fig. 1.

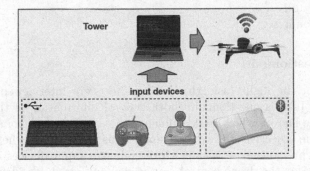

Fig. 1. Technical realization

2   Related Work

Due to the importance of the pilot and drone interaction, there are several studies that focus on the question, how a UAV can be controlled. Higuchi et al.

introduced a control mechanism that transforms head motion to UAV movements [HR1]. A Brain Computer Interface is used by Kos'myna et al. in their research about an optimal BCI architecture for controlling a UAV [KT1].

Ballas evaluated different methods of direct manipulation in aviation. In modern airplanes fly-by-wire systems separate the pilot from direct control of the wing surfaces [BH1]. This is also suitable for most UAVs: the control device allows to steer in several directions and the UAV reacts appropriately, but the user does not need to know how this motion is achieved.

Some studies try to design new interfaces and/or controllers for airplanes, drones, etc. For example, Won et al. created GUI guidelines for UAV ground control stations in [JH1]. Witheside concluded that usability depends more on a specific interface design than the interface style [WJ1].

This paper explores and discusses how suitable different game controllers are to interact with a drone. Among others, Skalski discussed the naturalness of game controllers and the use of different input devices [ST1]. Recent work in the area of games has shown that beyond simply performing a task, users want to engage with an interactive system, allowing them to have a playful and joyful experience [B1]. User experience in games considers that the users should enjoy their activities while interacting with the computer and that this enjoyment can be one of the main goals they want to achieve [BB1].

3   Study Method and Participants

To achieve an evaluation before and after the flight task, the study was divided into three parts:

- pre-questionnaire,
- field study, and
- post-questionnaire.

3.1   Pre-questionnaire

Before starting the flight task, the participants were interviewed by using a questionnaire. In this questionnaire both general information of the person as well as possible factors which could influence the ability to control a drone were questioned. The objective of the questionnaire was to elaborate whether the participants have previous experience with the relevant input devices and whether synergy effects for the drone control can be demonstrated. To identify synergy effects, some questions deals with sport activities, driving license, gender, and age of the participants. In addition, the expectations regarding the personal knowledge and their usefulness during the execution of a flight task were asked. The participants estimated furthermore how suitable the different devices for flying the drone will be.

3.2   Field Study

The field study took place at the university sports ground by moderate weather. While carrying out the study, participants had to cope with various flight tasks. Among other challenges, the participants had to direct the drone several times through a predefined course (cf. Fig. 1), using each of the available input devices. The task was to maneuver the drone around three bars, fly through a gate and return in a straight line to the starting point. The flight altitude was predefined and could not be altered by the participants. This simplification reduced the risk of crashes and improved the comparability (Fig. 2).

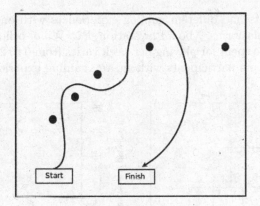

Fig. 2. Course sketch

The flight time was measured between a predefined start area and end area. The elapsed time for the pass with each device was measured separately with the order Joystick, Gamepad, Balanced Board. This order was chosen to minimize learning effects by ordering the devices from familiar to unfamiliar. The distance of the drone to each obstacle during the flights was not determined, since the resulting time for conducting the task describes the performance of each pass sufficiently.

3.3   Post-questionnaire

In the post-questionnaire a subjective assessment of the task difficulty with each input device was determined. The participants answered how suitable each input devices for the control of the drone was. Furthermore, the question was asked whether the participants believed that the personal knowledge had a positive effect on the performance in the study task.

3.4   Participants

For the study, 25 adults were selected as participants. The group consisted of 18 males and 6 females, aged from 21 to 64 years (cf. Fig. 3).

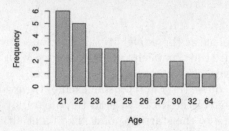

Fig. 3. Age of participants

The participants had different gaming experiences with one or more of the following gaming platforms: Xbox, Playstation, PC, Wii or others. This is shown in Fig. 4b. The time spent for playing per week varies from 0 to 25 h per platform. There were almost no participants without any gaming experience.

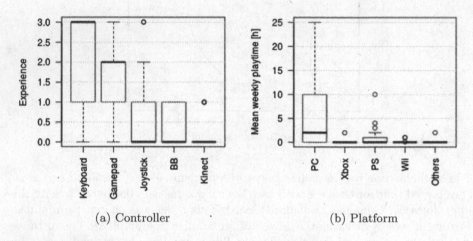

(a) Controller   (b) Platform

Fig. 4. Participant experience

4   Analysis

This section explains the executed statistics in more detail. The data is analyzed concerning the expected and actual performance of the three controls, the measured course times and correlations in gaming experience and drone flight performance.

4.1   Ratings of Expected and Actual Performance of the Three Controls

All three controls (gamepad, joystick, Balance Board) were rated regarding their expected performance (before task execution) and the actual performance (after execution). The differences of the two ratings for each control were compared with a paired two-sample t-test. The gamepad was rated significantly better after the testing than before. The two other controls ratings also improved, however the differences were not significant (cf. Fig. 5). The gamepad's mean rating improved, with a mean rating of 2.8 ($MD = 1.3$) before and a mean rating of 3.7 ($MD = 0.2$) after the testing ($t(23) = -4.2, p < .001$). The joystick received a mean rating of 2.4 ($M = 1.3$) before, and a mean rating of 2.7 ($MD = 0.7$) after the testing ($t(23) = -1.0, p = n.s.$). The Balance Board received a mean rating of .9 ($MD = 0.8$) before, and a mean rating of 1.3 ($MD = 1.2$) after the testing ($t(23) = -1.2, p = n.s.$). The ratings for the three controls were compared to each other with two one-way ANOVAs, one for the ratings of expected performance and one for the ratings of actual performance. The assumption of sphericity was violated, therefore degrees of freedom were corrected using Greenhouse-Geisser correction. The ratings significantly differed between the three conditions before ($F(1.5, 345) = 31.4, p < 0.001$) and after the testing ($F(1.5, 345) = 55, p < 0.001$). Planned contrasts revealed, that the gamepad's performance ratings after the actual testing were significantly better than those for the joystick and the Balance Board ($F(23) = 142.3, p < 0.001$) Furthermore, the Balance Board was rated significantly worse than the joystick ($F(23) = 24.8, p < 0.001$). Furthermore the joystick and the gamepad's ratings of expected performance did not significantly differ ($F(23) = 1.9, p = n.s.$). However the Balance Board was rated as significantly worse than the gamepad and the joystick ($F(23) = 57.1, p < 0.001$). This can be interpreted in a way that the gamepad's actual performance outperformed initial expectations, while the other two controls performed as expected. When rating the expected performance, the participants expected the Balance Board to perform worse than the two other controls, and this expectation was confirmed in the actual testing.

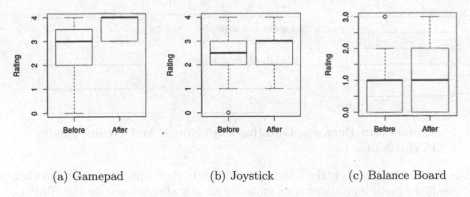

(a) Gamepad   (b) Joystick   (c) Balance Board

Fig. 5. Participant expectations

4.2   Performance Differences Between the Controls

The performance differences were analyzed with a between-subjects repeated measures ANOVA. The assumption of sphericity was violated, therefore degrees of freedom were corrected using Greenhouse-Geisser correction. The performance significantly differed between the three conditions ($F(1.6, 34.8) = 73.0, p < 0.001$). Planned contrasts revealed a nonsignificant difference between the joystick condition and the gamepad condition ($F(1) = 1.4, p = n.s.$). The joystick condition showed a mean performance time of 30.5 ($SD = 4.3$), while the gamepad condition revealed a mean performance time of 29.4 ($SD = 5.5$). This is shown in Fig. 6. However, the Balance Board condition showed a significantly decreased performance with a mean performance time of 40.8 ($SD = 5.8$), which was significantly longer than in the two other conditions ($F(1) = 97, p < 0.001$). While the joystick and gamepad seem to be equally suitable for controlling a drone, the Balance Board seems to be less efficient when it comes to performance times.

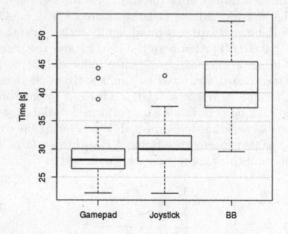

Fig. 6. Course times

4.3   Connection Between Gaming Experience and Drone Flight Performance

The correlation between the participants' weekly time spend gaming and their drone flight performance was not significant for any of the three controls (Balance Board: $r = -0.24$, Joystick: $r = -0.18$, Gamepad: $R = -0.19$, $p = n.s.$). Although a null-effect should be interpreted with care, the result suggests that previous gaming performance might not have a strong influence on one's ability to fly a drone.

4.4 Comments of Participants After Flight

Below, some of the most meaningful comments of the participants after flying with the controllers are listed:

Comments on the Gamepad

P4 *'Very good control, reacts fast and precise.'*
P5 *'Familiar precision, nice usage as controller, fits better pilots as well'*
P8 *'Very enjoyable. The only controller that is portable. Furthermore has many usable buttons.'*
P15 *'Astonishing precise flight behavior.'*
P18 *'The Controller was the easiest to handle, because the type of controlling is formally known. Doesn't matter if XBOX- or Playstation Controller, they are all used alike.'*
P25 *'Very intuitive.'*

Comments on the Joystick

P6 *'Very intuitive. Forgives controlling mistakes. Very good for beginners.'*
P8 *'Flying with one hand is advantageous.'*
P18 *'The Joystick is the most difficult to use, what actually surprised me.'*
P20 *'Needs to get used to, but works very well after that.'*
P21 *'Some kind of imprecise.'*
P22 *'Easy to handle, but it feels delayed. Reacts very sensible.'*

Comments on the Balance Board

P12 *'Required getting used to. You have be careful to not fall down.'*
P15 *'Very imprecise.'*
P16 *'Easy to balance, but delayed.'*
P18 *'Takes a lot sense of balance, After a short testing time you quickly get how it's done.'*
P19 *'The way of controlling was actually pretty good. If the board would have been more precise controlling would have been easier.'*
P20 *'Needs a lot of practice. Very unintuitive.'*
P22 *'Easier than expected but the coordination was difficult, you have to get used to it.'*

5 Conclusion

The main conclusion of the conducted study is that both, the gamepad and the joystick are equal suitable to control a drone. The third tested input device, the Wii Balance Board is rather unsuitable to execute sophisticated flight tasks. This result emerged directly from the collected data as shown in the analysis section. In addition to the worst elapsed times for the course, the Balance Board has earned low suitability rates before as well as after the flight.

The joystick and the Balance Board satisfied the expectation of the participants, whereby the gamepad surpassed its expectation. It was assumed that the joystick was rated comparatively high before the field study, because the participants knew of its usage in aviation. This expectation was met by the actual flight experience. The Balance Board was significantly less familiar in comparison to the other devices. This and the fact that the Balance Board is usually not used to control motion supposedly leaded to its poor rating and actual flight performance. The gamepad is one of the most known gaming controllers, especially in racing games, therefore most participants already knew it (cf. Fig. 4a) and were aware of its purpose to control first or third person motion. This implies that using a gaming controller for controlling a highly interactive device is a promising topic for further investigations.

As mentioned in Sect. 4 there is no evidence, that the gaming experience (respectively gaming hours per week) of the participants have any impact on their UAV flight skills. Though the collected data show interesting possibilities for further investigation. Two of the participants have no driving license and performed very badly controlling the UAV. This suggests that the driving experience enables the participants to control the UAV more precise. In a follow-up study will be tested a group consisting of 50% with and 50% without a driver license.

The influence of a first person view compared to observing the drone is another thread for further investigation.

References

[B1] Bernhaupt, R.: User Experience Evaluation in Games. Springer, Heidelberg (2010)

[BB1] Bernhaupt, R., Boy, G., Faery, M., Palanque, P.: SIG: engineering automation in interactive critical systems. In: CHI 2011 SIG (2011)

[BH1] Ballas, J.A., Heitmeyer, C.L., Pérez, M.A.: Evalating two aspects of direct manipulation in advanced cockpits. In: CHI 1992 (1992)

[HR1] Higuchi, K., Rekimoto, J.: Flying head: a head motion synchronization mechanism for unmanned aerial vehicle control. In: CHI 2013 Extended Abstracts, pp. 2029–2038 (2013)

[JH1] Won, J., Lee, H.: UAV ground control station GUI guidelines: for the designer, developer and operator's needs. In: HCI KOREA 2015 (2015)

[KT1] Kos'myna, N., Tarpin-Bernard, F., Rivet, B.: Bidirectional feedback in motor imagery BCIs: learn to control a drone within 5 minutes. In: CHI 2014, pp. 479–482 (2013)

[L1] Lu, W.: Evolution of Video Game Controllers: How Simple Switches Lead to the Development of the Joystick and the Directional Pad

[ST1] Skalski, P., Tamborini, R., Shelton, A., Buncher, M., Lindmark, P.: Mapping the road to fun: natural video game controllers, presence, and game enjoyment. New Media Soc. **13**, 224–242 (2011)

[WJ1] Whiteside, J., Jones, S., Levy, P.S., Wixon, D.: User performance with command, menu, and iconic interfaces. In: ACM CHI 1985 Human Factors in Computing Systems, New York, pp. 185–191 (1985)

Acquiring Disaster Prevention Knowledge from Fieldwork Activities in a Region

Hisashi Hatakeyama[1,2(✉)], Masahiro Nagai[3], and Masao Murota[4]

[1] Library and Academic Information Center, Tokyo Metropolitan University,
Tokyo, Japan
hatak@tmu.ac.jp
[2] Department of Human System Science, Graduate School of Decision Science
and Technology, Tokyo Institute of Technology, Tokyo, Japan
[3] University Education Center, Tokyo Metropolitan University, Tokyo, Japan
mnagai@tmu.ac.jp
[4] Institute for Liberal Arts, Tokyo Institute of Technology, Tokyo, Japan
murota@ila.titech.ac.jp

Abstract. There has been increasing awareness of the need for disaster prevention in Japan. The aim of this research is to ascertain whether a basic knowledge of disaster prevention can be acquired through fieldwork learning activities for purposes of creating a disaster prevention map. We developed a disaster prevention learning support system that facilitated the task of recording information at real locations, and then aggregated it. Using this system, we conducted a classroom exercise at a high school to help students identify the kinds of hazards that are likely to develop in specific areas—based on their features—in the event of a large earthquake. After conducting fieldwork, they returned to the classroom. Under the guidance of their teachers, they referred to the information they had recorded and the knowledge they had acquired to postulate a scenario in which a large earthquake occurred. They further assumed that this earthquake had occurred while they were outdoors. The students then devised evacuation measures using paper simulations. The results of this exercise revealed that the knowledge of disaster prevention acquired through this exercise had practical applications.

Keywords: Disaster management · Disaster prevention · Mobile learning · System development

1 Introduction

Damage caused by natural disasters is reported from around the world every year. Japan is no exception. This country has suffered extensive damage from disasters such as earthquakes, typhoons, and heavy rains. In the Great East Japan Earthquake that occurred in 2011, the earthquake and tsunami inflicted enormous damage mainly on the Pacific coast of the Japanese archipelago, and resulted in more than 15,000 victims. The Kumamoto earthquake that occurred in 2016 and wreaked havoc on many houses is still a fresh memory. The occurrence of multiple class 7 seismic intensities exceeds

M. Kurosu (Ed.): HCI 2017, Part II, LNCS 10272, pp. 433–442, 2017.
DOI: 10.1007/978-3-319-58077-7_35

our conventional assumptions. Since these events have occurred recently, there has been an increasing awareness of the need for disaster prevention in Japan.

Especially at educational sites, students' safety and possible evacuation routes have been examined. Following the earthquake, the Ministry of Education, Culture, Sports, Science and Technology Japan organized a meeting of experts—called the "Council on Disaster Prevention Education and Disaster Management"—to have them present their recommendations on this aspect of disaster prevention. According to a proposal in which their recommendations were summarized, "disaster prevention learning" is not only necessary for protecting oneself in the case of a natural disaster, but also for acquiring a systematic understanding of the regional disasters that are likely to occur in the future [1]. However, in school education, disaster prevention learning programs—in the form of general lectures and repetitive training for viable evacuation procedures—have been largely implemented. We believe that there is a need to devise programs and activities that will interest learners in developing a better understanding of disaster prevention. However, we also believe that not much practical training has been offered, in the context of situations in which a disaster might strike students on their way to and from school [2].

Learning about local disaster prevention requires the development of a disaster prevention map, in which learners gather information about an area by walking through the area, or examining information on a hazard map. They then assume that a disaster has stricken the area, and organize information according to whether specific areas are safe or in danger. Disaster prevention maps display this information. These types of activities are frequently conducted as part of children's elementary and secondary school education, and are positioned as part of regional study. Disaster prevention maps are typically drawn on paper, but there are also some examples in which computers have been used for this purpose [3, 4].

The disaster prevention map and the hazard map are used in a method called DIG (Disaster Imagination Game), which imagines a disaster and depicts it on paper [5]. Desirable characteristics of DIG are its simplicity and interactive nature. Assuming a disaster, learners will work in the cause of the presented targets, such as disaster relief, think about solutions, and summarizing their analyses on a map. This paper training method is arranged variously, and is widely practiced as part of disaster prevention activities in local community.

The aim of this research is to ascertain whether basic knowledge of disaster prevention acquired through fieldwork learning activities can be applied to disaster prevention for mitigate the harm done by the disaster such as using to create a disaster prevention map. Learners observe normal situations, and consider a possible disaster occurrence using disaster prevention knowledge. They record the risks that have been depicted on a disaster prevention map, and collaboratively reflect on each viewpoint. We expect that their participation in the outdoor activities and group reflections will inspire students' further interest in disaster prevention learning at school. To conduct this learning, we developed a mobile system that supports learning outdoors.

2   System Development

2.1   System Concept

Basic Design. To proceed with learning, a system is needed to record the disaster assumptions that emerged as a result of learners' outdoor activities. We developed a disaster prevention learning support system called "Sonael" that facilitates the task of recording information at a real location and aggregating it for presentation on a disaster prevention map. The basic concept of Sonael is based on the prototype "FaLAS" [6]. Sonael consists of a client system that operates with an Android tablet computer and a server-side system that stores client data.

The client application is implemented as an Android application installed on the Android tablet device the learner carries while conducting fieldwork and learning outdoors. Tablet devices generally support network connections with Wi-Fi, but there are not many models that can be connected to a cellular phone network alone. Even devices that permit data communication may lose speed or be disconnected, depending on outdoor radio wave conditions. For this reason, to allow outdoor learning to proceed without relying on a network, the client application included a mechanism that would enable recording information in a local database (SQLite) in such a way that it could even operate stand-alone.

The server application aggregates data asynchronously and shares it among the client applications. It is implemented by Ruby on Rails and uses MySQL as a data store. The client application communicates via the API corresponding to the JSON format. There is also a screen that can be viewed from some web browsers. For functions not required by client applications, such as the ability of teachers to view information, the server application has a screen that can be used from a browser.

Utilization. The learner carries the tablet device outdoors, and the application provides instructions for the learners on how to take pictures at a point, record classifications indicating safety or danger, and input comments that explain the basis for the classifications. This record is stored in a local database, together with the GPS coordinates for that point. Using this system outdoors engenders learners' interest in conducting surveys outdoors, and focuses their interest on disaster prevention learning.

These records are transmitted to the server in the classroom over the network and aggregated when communication is established. The aggregated data is redistributed to the devices from which learners can share information and view the merged records on maps. Once the photos and comments have been consolidated, learners can consider the relative safety of areas without conducting fieldwork. Also, they can expect to evaluate their judgments objectively, by comparing them with those of other learners (Fig. 1).

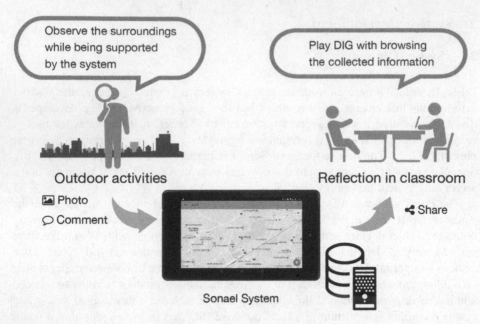

Fig. 1. Image of Sonael system

2.2 Helping Learners Use the System

Quiz for Applying Knowledge. Even if a learner is encouraged to investigate the outdoors at his/her own discretion, there is a possibility that he/she may not know where to go. To mitigate this possibility, we adapted a technique from the sport of Orienteering. The teacher preliminarily set a plurality of "mission areas" in the area where the field study was being conducted. A circle with a radius of about 100 m represented this mission area. The data was stored in the client application's local database, and presented to the learner as a circle on the map. Multiple checkpoints can be set inside the mission area. A checkpoint is like a quiz. It provides an example of how the teacher would respond to a question, according to the learning goal, and describes the event the student wants to discover or record, by applying his/her disaster prevention knowledge. The data consists of locational information that has not previously been presented to the learner—including the type of location, the assumed situation, and a hint for the learner—that is stored in the client application's local database. In addition to the positional information of latitude and longitude, a hint can be provided for each checkpoint. Hints have content that will help remind students of their disaster prevention knowledge when searching for checkpoints. By demarcating mission areas that include these checkpoints in the area to be analyzed, it is expected that the learner will move over the whole area by going around the points and answering the questions in each quiz. Once the learners' responses to a quiz have been recorded for the mission area, whether or not they correspond to a checkpoint is verified, and if they do, the learner receives feedback.

Position Tracking. In learning activities outside of the classroom, teachers must secure the learners' safety. Under one method the teacher always leads, but doing so is difficult when there are many learners. To address this limitation, we developed a mechanism that would identify the learners' positions in real time, based on the current position of the device.

For the client application, we always acquired locational information using a GPS to verify the mission area. Although the network on the learner's device was not always valid, its current location was sent periodically as communication was possible. A screen displaying the current position of the device on the map was included in the server application. Using Web Socket, it was possible to update current locations in real time, without reloading the browser. The environment in which the teachers' devices was being operated functioned in general modern browsers, including those of smartphones.

User Management for Data Sharing. In order to safeguard the learners' data, we implemented a mechanism that could manage users' authentication and users' data. Before commencing learning activities, the teachers inputted the master data necessary for learning—such as the mission area and the learners' information—into the server. At the same time, the teachers linked a learner's information with the mission area that would be presented to that learner. User authentication was required prior to using the client application. Once the user's authentication had been confirmed, the client application received the master data associated with the user from the server via API. Throughout the learning process, the device's locational information and survey records were sent to the server, along with the user's information. To save the transmitted information without duplication, a universally unique identifier (UUID) was applied to all data exchanged between the client application and the server application. This facilitated the detection of duplicate records, and enabled updating the differences safely (Fig. 2).

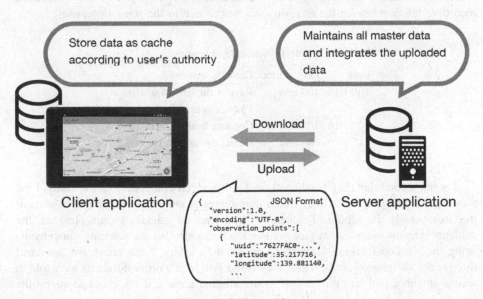

Fig. 2. The roles of client and server system

Since the review of field survey results might be conducted on a class-by-class basis, it was necessary to have controls for each group. Therefore, the "user" was the group's class. Only the records pertinent to the user group to which the user belonged were acquired from the server.

3   Classroom Practice

3.1   Outline

Using this system, we conducted hands-on lessons at a high school to help students learn about the types of hazards that can be expected in a specific area, based on its features, when a large earthquake occurs. These lessons were conducted for first-year high school students during the Integrated Study period. The school is near Tokyo Bay in the western part of Chiba Prefecture, inland from the sea. A river flows next to the school. There is extensive topographic relief here, which includes a small hill close to the school. For purposes of this learning activity, the study area was set as being a range of about 1 km between the school and the coast.

3.2   Learning Contents

Four teachers in four classes conducted a total of three lessons from October 2016 to November. The complete schedule is shown in Table 1. On the first day the students confirmed that they were responsible for securing their own safety, depending on the situation present in the area when a disaster occurred, which was the overall learning objective. With the help of their teacher, they reviewed their basic knowledge. To help students familiarize themselves with the operation of the system, they practiced recording information for the mission area for practice in the school premises.

Table 1. Schedule of lessons

Day	Date	Lesson time	Learning content
1	10/11/16	100 min	Review the basic knowledge
			Practice operating the system
2	10/17/16	100 min	Conduct fieldwork survey
3	11/28/16	60 min	Depict the information on paper

On the second day they conducted the field research component of the study. First they formed groups of four, after which they surveyed and recorded various aspects of the area outside the school. Teachers did not lead the student groups. Instead, the students acted as independent groups. The teachers patrolled the students' movements using the position tracking function to ensure their safety. Each group was assigned three of the six mission areas, which they could visit in any order. Students were told to record anything that was not limited to the mission areas and the checkpoints on the system.

On the last lesson day the students assumed that a large earthquake had occurred. Assuming that the large earthquake had occurred while they were outdoors, by referring to the recorded information and their learned knowledge, under the guidance of their classroom teacher, the students worked out evacuation measures using paper simulations such as DIG. These paper simulations created two scenarios: One scenario involved encountering an earthquake in the middle of a school road typically used by students, and another involved encountering an earthquake near the coast, in an area that was less familiar to students. The purpose of the exercise was to identify an appropriate evacuation site, and consider possible escape routes to that place. Students first considered each scenario independently, after which group discussions were held. This was followed by a summary discussion and final analysis that involved the class as a whole.

To facilitate the use of this system, we lent one Android tablet device to each group on each lesson day. The device used was either a ASUS Nexus7 (2013) or a Lenovo YOGA2. Since YOGA has a SIM card slot, it was set so that each user could communicate data independently. In addition, because Nexus is not compatible with the SIM card, we installed portable Wi-Fi router on each device, in preparation for pairing and communication. Consequently, we created an environment in which communication could be carried out in the field from all devices. We also installed a Sonael client application on each device, so that we could view the records.

4 Results

4.1 Questionnaire Survey

Following the investigative learning completed in the field on day 2, we conducted a subjective survey of the students on their use of the system. The results are shown in Table 2. Each item was phrased as a question, allowing responses on a five-point Likert scale (from "very little" to "completely"). Items that received scores of 3 or more were considered to be high scores.

Table 2. Summary of the responses to self-efficacy questions

	N	M	SD
Was the tablet device easy to operate?	109	3.35	1.158
Was the system easy to operate?	109	3.37	1.086
Was the map displayed on the system easy to see?	109	3.47	1.167
Was the hint of the mission displayed on the system easy to understand?	109	3.07	1.176
Was it easy to understand how to record the investigation results on the system?	109	3.29	1.165
Was it easy to see how to check the information recorded on the system?	109	3.31	1.136

Before and after learning, we investigated students' self-efficacy with regard to disaster prevention. Each item being evaluated was phrased as a question, allowing responses on a five-point Likert scale (from "very little" to "completely"). Table 3 summarizes the responses to the questions relating to self-efficacy. These results showed improvements in the average scores for all of the items surveyed. Using a t-test, changes in the scores were found to be significant for all questions. These results show that the students' self-efficacy in terms of disaster prevention had been developed through the practice.

Table 3. Summary of the responses to questions evaluating the system

	Before			After	
	N	M	SD	M	SD
Can you judge a dangerous place outside the school when an earthquake occurs?**	99	3.22	1.121	4.06	0.890
Could you protect yourself should an earthquake occur outside the school?**	97	3.58	1.029	4.02	0.924
Can you explain in detail how you should act after the earthquake has settled, if you feel a strong tremor outside the school?**	98	2.99	0.947	3.71	0.952
Can you explain in concrete terms how I should act to protect my own safety when I feel a strong tremor outside the school?**	97	2.89	0.967	3.60	1.047

**Significant at $p < 0.01$

4.2   Record of Learning

The GPS traces acquired in these outdoor field activities shows how the learner group in class moved. When examining the GPS traces, many groups moved around the area to visit specific mission areas. The number of records differed from 1 to 15, depending on the group, and many gathered information on places that would be dangerous in the event of a disaster.

5   Discussion

According to the results of the subjective survey, the learners' summary evaluation of the system's operation was positive. In the comments' section of the questionnaire completed after investigative learning in the field on day 2, multiple opinions were as follows: "I felt that there were quite a few dangerous places on the way walking to school," and "I was able to confirm dangerous places and safe places." From these comments, it is evident that a new awareness can be created by conducting field surveys in the areas where students live. It is thought that the system was able to support the students' learning in the field. In addition, from comparisons made before and after learning, it was confirmed that students' self-efficacy in terms of being able to protect themselves in the event of a disaster had improved through learning achieved using this system.

In the paper simulations there were many instances in which students' chose nearby evacuation sites, and some in which they chose evacuation sites with the highest altitude, even at some distance. However, after some of these students had learned about specific evacuation sites, they selected different evacuation destinations, considering events that might occur on that route. A learner initially thought, when confronted by an evacuation scenario on the coast, that it would be best to evacuate to the station. However, because the preferred evacuation route passed through a narrow alley, we introduced the possibility that a house had collapsed and it would be difficult to go around it, so after a discussion with group members, we then chose to evacuate to the hill. Routes were also revised, to enable passage on relatively wide roads. Although this is only one example, in the lesson on retrospective learning, activities were conducted that necessitated considering and judging various possibilities based on the appearance of a locality—something that is hard to decipher from a map. A learning method that uses a system that shares its records and outdoor activities is thought to have had a positive effect on the application of knowledge to disaster prevention learning.

The function of tracking the learner's position received a positive evaluation from the teachers. Since there is a range of learning and there are differences in elevation, it was difficult to confirm all the learners' actions at specific sites. We were also moving around the field by car. Sometimes we could not locate them, when a learner was passing through a narrow alley for example. However, using the system, teachers could check the current positions of the students with their own smartphones. We received one comment that this support was carried out smoothly, because it was possible to remind learners of the time available to collect data by looking at their positions, so that all groups conducting the field survey could return to school by the end of the class.

6 Conclusion

We aimed to ascertain whether basic knowledge about disaster prevention could be acquired through outdoor learning activities. We developed a disaster prevention learning support system called Sonael that enables recording information from a real location and aggregating it. We conducted a classroom exercise at a high school using this system to help students learn what kinds of hazards can be expected when a large earthquake occurs, based on the features of a specific area.

As reported above, it was confirmed that students' self-efficacy for protecting themselves at the time of a disaster improved, along with the effectiveness of the system. We received a positive evaluation of the operation and functioning of the system. This learning method, which allows records and data summarizing outdoor movements to be shared, is thought to have had a positive effect on disaster prevention learning, and so the application of knowledge. It remains a challenge for future research to objectively evaluate what learners learned as adaptable knowledge.

Acknowledgements. We would like to thank Amaha High School for its support of the training exercises described here. This work was supported by JSPS Grant-in-Aid for Scientific Research Grant Numbers 15H02933, 16K21262.

References

1. MEXT - Ministry of Education, Culture, Sports, Science and Technology: Final Report of the "Council on Disaster Prevention Education and Disaster Management" (2012). (in Japanese). http://www.mext.go.jp/b_menu/shingi/chousa/sports/012/toushin/1324017.htm
2. Shizuoka Prefecture: Survey on actual condition on school disaster prevention (2016). (in Japanese). https://www.pref.shizuoka.jp/kyouiku/kk–120/bousai/documents/jittaityousa27.pdf
3. Abukawa, M., Tnew, C., Yoshimoto, S.: Consideration of assistive application for elementary school safety mapping activity. JSiSE Res. Rep. **29**, 27–32 (2015). (in Japanese)
4. Mitsuhara, H., Inoue, T., Yamaguchi, K., Takeuchi, Y., Morimoto, M., Ikawa, K., Kozuki, Y., Shishibori, M.: Support system for creating digital disaster map and its use in class. JSiSE Res. Rep. **30**, 89–96 (2016). (in Japanese)
5. Komura, T., Hirano, A.: On disaster imagination game. In: Papers of Annual Conference of the Institute of Social Safety Science, vol. 7, pp. 136–139 (1997). (in Japanese)
6. Hatakeyama, H., Nagai, M., Murota, M.: Educational practice and evaluation utilizing disaster prevention map creation support system "FaLAS". In: Research Report of JSET Conferences, vol. 15, pp. 1–6 (2015). (in Japanese)

Research on Foreground Color Adaptive System of Aircraft Head-Up Display Based on the Background Real-Time Changes

Yu Hu, Chengqi Xue, Haiyan Wang, and Lei Zhou[(✉)]

School of Mechanical Engineering, Southeast University, Nanjing, China
zhoulei@seu.edu.cn

Abstract. This paper use the interface of airplane HUD as object and based on the color design theory and visual perception theory to study the HUD foreground color adaptive system. First, selecting the best appropriate color model and put forward the best matching color scheme based on the color adaptive theory, color design theory and visual perception theory. Second, proposing the way of background master color extraction by study the color processing theory. Finally, typical aircraft background environments selection and processing results. In this paper, the research provides background color processing method and HUD foreground color adaptive scheme. There are positive contributions to improving HUD interface color design. A better HUD interface can strengthen cognitive abilities of pilots and make more correct decisions or judgments during the process of flight mission.

Keywords: Head-up display (HUD) · Background real-time changeable · Color extraction · Color matching · Human cognition · Foreground color adaptive

1 Introduction

With the development of aerospace and computer technologies, the digital visual interfaces have been used into the avionics system. Head-up display (HUD) is the main flight display of the modern aircraft [1]. HUD as a new display, it can project flight data onto the transparent display in front of the pilots, and so that pilots could Head-Up get more airplane flying information. HUD as a transparent display interface, it is particularly important to accurate and clearly overlay information to a complex and real-time environment. It plays a huge role in getting flying information especially during the emergency condition.

The information of the existing HUD interface is generally presented with single green color, while the background environment will change because of the time and region. During the process of actual use, the display information will be affected by the external background color and light conditions [2]. So there is a serious problem that the cognition of flying information projected to the HUD interface will be affected in the green environment such as grassland and forest. This condition make the pilots not easy to distinguish information clearly, even lead them missing information or take in

© Springer International Publishing AG 2017
M. Kurosu (Ed.): HCI 2017, Part II, LNCS 10272, pp. 443–451, 2017.
DOI: 10.1007/978-3-319-58077-7_36

something wrong and then may make airplane in danger. Due to the change of background environment, HUD foreground color becomes an important research in the HUD interface design. In developed countries like America, certain research has been conducted in pertinent fields. Such as the HUD of F-15C has (red/yellow/green; two kinds of color depths) six color modes. But the study of foreground color adaptive system of aircraft HUD is very less. In consideration the importance and insufficiency of this problem, this study is aimed to explore the way of extracting main color from the background image and then give the appropriate HUD foreground color.

2   Basic Theory of HUD Color Design

2.1   Color Space

Processing color images, the most basic job is to choose the right color space. Color space is a color model that represented by mathematical method. With the development of color image processing technology, the common color space are RGB, HSV, NTSC, YCbCr. They have their own characteristics during image processing. HSV (Hue, saturation, value) is one of the color systems used by people to choose colors from the palette or color wheel, HSV system is more approximate to people's experience and perception than others, and thus more close to the characteristics of human observation. So in this paper, HSV model is used in the main color minutia extraction. HSV color space is created by A. R. Smith based on the intuitive nature of color. It can also be called a hexagonal pyramid model [3].

2.2   Human Cognition

The Relationship Between Hue and Cognition. Hue is one of the main properties of a color. In the system of color, usually use twelve ring hue circle to present color hue (Fig. 1). The twelve ring is composed of 12 basic colors, including the first three primary colors.

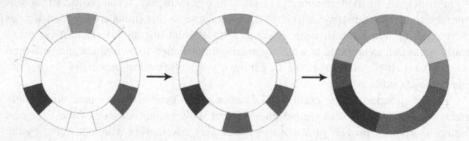

Fig. 1. Hue circle (Color figure online)

Two colors separated by 180° are called complementary colors. Complementary color combinations have strongest contrast, allowing users to produce a sense of irritation and instability. Colors separated by 15° are called analog color. Analog colors are low contrast and user will be in a calm mood. Colors separated by 60° are called adjacent colors. The combination of adjacent colors is elegant and gentle and has a good recognition [4].

The Relationship Between Value and Cognition. Value is the feeling of brightness and it also can represent the brightness of color [4]. Value can exist independently, even if there is no hue, value can also show without color (Fig. 2).

| White hightest | light gary high | medium gary medium | dark gary low | black lowest |

Fig. 2. Value change

Any kind of color in nature has value. And the way that improve or reduce the value is also suitable for color. In other words, adding black will reduce the lightness and adding white will improve the brightness. In real life, a color will appear dark color in the weak light and will appear bright under the glare of the light (Fig. 3).

Fig. 3. Green value change (Color figure online)

The Relationship Between Saturation and Cognition. Saturation refers to the degree of color. The saturation of color is calculated based on the degree of gray, and it will become low if color mixed with black or white (Fig. 4).

Fig. 4. Color saturation change (Color figure online)

The color with high saturation is bright and have strong visual impact. It easy to cause the visual attention but if long-time visual easily lead to visual fatigue and then increasing user load. On the contrary, the color with low saturation only has weak visual impact on user. Although it is suitable for long-time attention but not easy to cause the user visual attention.

2.3   Color in Avionics System

Color is one of the basic elements of avionics system interface design. On the one hand, color can highlight the important information in the avionics interface to guide the pilots to complete their tasks well and improve the efficiency of the system, on the other hand, user psychological feeling is affected by different color significantly.

The HUD color design should follow the standard of color application in avionics system. At early 1980s, many countries began to explore the colorful head-up display, and carried out some relevant researches. At present, the color head-up display technology is mature. The different information should be expressed in different color. Such as for the abnormal information showing, the red is better than yellow and green is not appropriate [5]. For this study is about the main color of HUD, we should avoid the warning color and fluorescent color.

Through the analysis of the relationship between hue and cognition (2.2.1), this paper choose the color separated 60° with the background color as our mainly color. In addition, after the exclusion of alarm color we could get the following figure with color (Fig. 5).

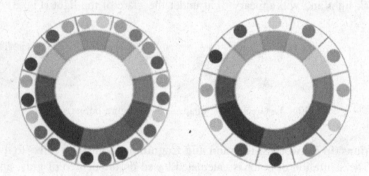

Fig. 5. Color matching diagram (Color figure online)

3   Color Processing Method

3.1   Image Partition

Aircraft head-up display interface have different information layout, including the flight mode notification area, the airspeed indicator, the attitude guidance area, the height and glide deviation area and the course beacon deviation area [6]. (Figure 6) In this paper, we choose the HUD interface size of 480*600 px.

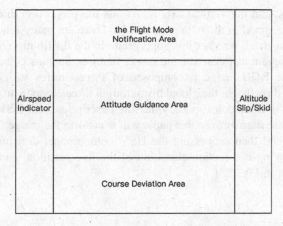

Fig. 6. The layout of HUD

Depend on the Rockwell Collins Flight Dynamics Head-Up Guidance System (HGS®) installed on an in-service aircraft [7], we divide the aircraft HUD interface and the background image into the following dimensions (Fig. 7). The separated five parts correspond to the five functional areas of HUD interface. Part 1 is airspeed indicator, part 2 is the flight mode notification area, part 3 is the attitude guidance area, part 4 is course deviation area and the part 5 is altitude & slip/skid area. There are different kinds of information required by the pilots in different flight stages, so pilots need to observe the information in different regions of the HUD interface to guide their task execution.

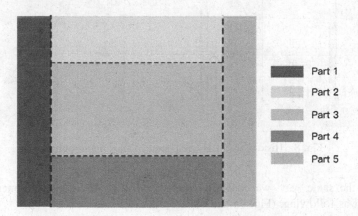

Fig. 7. Image dimension partition

3.2 Image Partition Main Color Extraction

Color histogram is one of the most widely used color feature extraction methods. Color histogram is the statistical distribution of color value for the image. The color range is the horizontal axis, and the vertical axis represents the proportion that the number of the same color accounted in the whole image [8]. There are many kinds of histogram, gray histogram can check whether it is appropriate in the distribution of available gray range; global histogram can describe the image features, such as color image in RGB space, because the RGB image is composed of three images with monochromatic brightness, can be directly get the global histogram in three component (RGB). Most of the color image is in RGB color space, while the description with HSV space is closer to human visual characteristics, so this paper will transform the image from RGB space into HSV space, and then processing the HSV color image, drawing the color histogram. The following is a section algorithm of the five partition, and the histograms obtained as shown in Fig. 8.

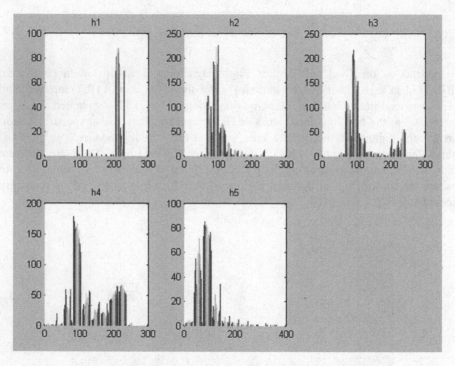

Fig. 8. Histograms of H component (Color figure online)

Using the same way, we could drawing the histograms of S component and V component as following. (Fig. 9a and b)

Next, calculate the average value of the three largest H, V, S value that obtained by histograms of H, S, V component. The average value is the H, S, V value of main color for this partition. For this Figure, the three largest H, V, S, and their average values were obtained by the histogram, and the HSV value of dominant color was obtained. Contrasting Fig. 5, it is concluded that the following color matching (Fig. 10).

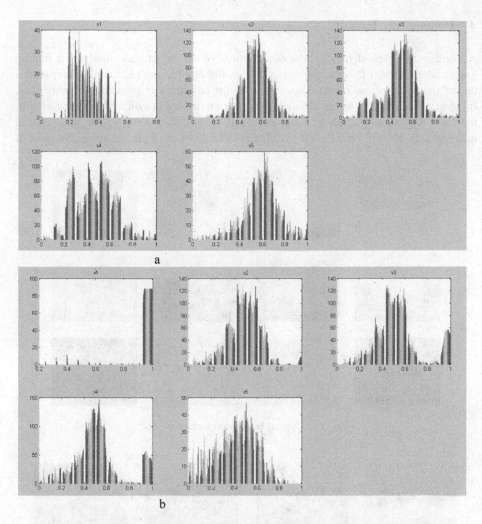

Fig. 9. (a) Histograms of S component, (b) Histograms of V component (Color figure online)

Fig. 10. Color processing and matching (Color figure online)

4 Processing Result

According to different regions, the environment of the forest and grassland is mainly green; when aircraft fly over the sea or a lake, the environment is mainly blue; over a desert, the environment is mainly yellow; over the city, the environment is mainly gray. In addition, according to the different time, the environment color of morning is soft, the color will become bright at noon, and it will appear dark at night. The same area in different seasons will be reflected in different colors, for example, in spring, because of

Fig. 11. Typical background environment

Fig. 12. The foreground color matching result

the recovery of all things, the background gives a fresh feeling; in summer, everything becomes flashy; in the autumn, background is vicissitudes of environment, most things become yellow; in the winter, snow white is everywhere. The following Fig. 11 shows the typical task environment.

Using MATLAB software to extract the main color of this group figure, then according to the color matching diagram (Fig. 5) to determine the foreground color of HUD interface (Fig. 12).

5 Conclusion

This study put forward foreground color adaptive system of aircraft Head-Up Display based on the background real-time changes. And according theory of color design, this paper propose the color matching plans and an image main color partition extracting way based on the HUD interface information layout. The conclusion of this paper can guide the color design of aircraft HUD interface, but it can be only used as preliminary process. If it is to be practical application, it still need to be research deeply and verified with experiments.

Acknowledgement. This paper is supported by Natural fund of Jiangsu Province (No. BK20150636) National Natural Science Foundation of China (No. 71471037, 71271053, 51405514).

References

1. Du, J., Yu, S., Lu, Y.: Attention study of perception and application in visual display interface. Manuf. Inf. Eng. China **35**(3), 59–62 (2006)
2. Xiong, D., Liu, Q., Guo, X., Zhang, Q., Yao, Q., Bai, Y., Du, J., Wang, Y.: The effect of one-color and multi-color displays with HUD information in aircraft cockpits. In: Long, S., Dhillon, B. (eds.) Man-Machine-Environment System Engineering. LNEE, vol. 406, pp. 389–398. Springer, Singapore (2016)
3. Su, H.: Study of color theory and its application—analysis of the color design of Beijing taxi. **22**(2), 232–233 (2008)
4. Xue, C.: Product Color Design, pp. 21–34. Southeast University Press, Nanjing (2007). (in Chinese)
5. Xiao, X., Wanyan, X., Zhuang, D., et al.: Ergonomic design and evaluation of visual coding for aircraft head-up display. In: 2012 5th International Conference on Biomedical Engineering and Informatics, BMEI 2012, pp. 748–752 (2012)
6. Qin, H., Lu, G.: GJB301 -87. People's Republic of China national military standard aircraft under visual display character. National Defense Science and Technology Commission, the Ministry of Military Standard Press, Beijing (1987). (in Chinese)
7. Wood, R.B., Howells, P.J.: Head-up displays. In: Spitzer, C.R. (ed.) Digital Avionics Handbook. CRC Press, Boca Raton (2007)
8. Huang, D.S.: Radial basis probabilistic neural networks: model and application. Int. J. Pattern Recogn. Artif. Intell. **13**, 1083–1101 (1999)

Development of Sightseeing Support System with Emphasis on Scenery and Detours in Strolls

Junko Itou[1](✉), Takaya Mori[2], and Jun Munemori[1]

[1] Faculty of Systems Engineering, Wakayama University,
930, Sakaedani, Wakayama 640-8510, Japan
{itou,munemori}@sys.wakayama-u.ac.jp
[2] Graduate School of Systems Engineering, Wakayama University,
930, Sakaedani, Wakayama 640-8510, Japan
s175056@center.wakayama-u.ac.jp

Abstract. This paper proposes a sightseeing support system that uses pictures and location information to guide tourists to of interest when they take a stroll during the free time available in sightseeing tours. This system allows the selection of a place that the user wants to visit by displaying various pictures of nearby interesting places on a map. This enables the user to choose a course freely, and enjoy detours at one's own leisure. The system thus helps tourists in visiting multiple places of interest other than their predetermined destination within the limited time available for sightseeing. The results of experiments on 30 min strolls using the proposed system suggest that in choosing the places of interest, the pictures displayed on the map were found to be very useful, and comparing the actual scenery with the pictures helped the subjects reach their destination easily. They were also able to change their destination to a different one easily during the strolls.

Keywords: Sightseeing support system · Stroll · Photograph · Location information · Vacant time

1 Introduction

In this article, we propose a sightseeing support system that helps tourists use the free time available in sightseeing tours effectively.

Combining GPS with SNS has become useful in collecting information and providing navigation to sightseeing spots as a tourist moves from one place to another during a tour. However, existing sightseeing support systems are tailored to famous sightseeing spots only, and many of them do not provide any information on other sightseeing spots nearby [1–4]. There is a lack of information regarding places of interest worth visiting and the type of experience that one may enjoy in such places. This is especially so for tourists who want to visit other places of interest near their destination, or want to explore the area around the destination within a certain time without selecting a specific spot. Furthermore, it is difficult for tourists to obtain information to plan how to spend unscheduled vacant time around their destination.

© Springer International Publishing AG 2017
M. Kurosu (Ed.): HCI 2017, Part II, LNCS 10272, pp. 452–463, 2017.
DOI: 10.1007/978-3-319-58077-7_37

Therefore, we focus on effective utilization of unexpected vacant time at unfamiliar travel destinations and many scenic photographs around sightseeing spots. The purpose of this study is to develop a smartphone service to support about 20–30 min of strolls around sightseeing spots using pictures of nearby places of interest and location information.

Our system displays pictures taken around the current location on a map in a smartphone, enabling the user to set a tentative destination based on the impressions derived from the pictures and remaining time. A user freely takes a stroll through multiple places of interest around a sightseeing spot within a limited period of time.

This paper is organized as follows: in Sect. 2, we describe the related service for sharing sightseeing information. In Sect. 3, we explain our proposed system, which supports strolls in a travel destination using photographs. A validation test for our system will be given in Sect. 4. Finally, we discuss conclusions and future work in Sect. 5.

2   Related Works

2.1   Optimal Route Recommendation

A common trend among existing sightseeing support services is to determine the most efficient way to travel by providing an optimal route to the destination. This results in a lack of information about other places around the sightseeing spots, for a user who may want to enjoy some free time or explore the surrounding area. Google Places is one of information-sharing service that uses a map [1]. Users share information such as addresses, photographs, and comments about popular locations. Most of the information relates to shops, and especially to restaurants, and users can evaluate the shops on five levels. In some cases, a lot of information may overlap so users cannot easily locate the information they are trying to seeking.

2.2   Recommendation Based on Information on the Web

Approaches using geotagged photo data posted to a photo-sharing service are proposed [2,3]. They analyzed large quantities of photograph and extracted travel information such as activities or typical patterns of sightseeing. These systems provide users visual analysis result about attractive areas or example itineraries. In these systems, the emphasis is on famous places of interest within an area, or providing an efficient route to move around. Therefore, there is a lack of information along the routes connecting one place of interest to another, and the walking routes provided are also limited. Accordingly, with respect to the inability to change a tentative destination or the route in the middle of a stroll, these services are not much different from existing navigation systems.

Tiwari et al. proposed a tourist spot recommender system using enrichment information including weather conditions and traffic conditions [4]. They assemble a database that contains location data and contextual information registered by users. Users could obtain detailed graphical information about a tourist area using these systems. Fujii et al. propose a method to analyze tourists' behaviors automatically from travel blog entries [5]. By using this method, tourist information on souvenirs and sightseeing spots was extracted with high accuracy. This result can also be applied to automatic construction of tourist information link collections. In these systems, recommended sightseeing routes are provided to the user based on relevant information collected on route preferences from other users. However, these systems find it difficult to provide route recommendations for the not-so-famous sightseeing spots because of the lack of data, as sharing of such data depends on user preference.

CT-Planner introduces routes starting from a specific point and moving within a certain area without a predetermined destination [6]. Users can design their tour interactively. The systems allows users to register new tourism resources with recommendation reasons, so attractive tourism information can be provided sufficiently. However, it is not clear whether the place that the traveler actually wants to visit is included in the recommended route.

2.3 Utilization of a Vacant Time

Service that utilizes a vacant time have also been proposed. Layover with a Local is an application that gives opportunities to interact with local residents during the layover time [7]. The target user is passengers arriving in the Amsterdam Schiphol airport, who stay for more than six hours until the next transfer. Travelers are matched with an Amsterdam local based on languages and social interests. The application provides travelers with clear instructions to lead Amsterdam's city centre, where they hook up with the local. Although tourists can use their vacant time efficiently for sightseeing, this service is only helping to directly lead people's interpersonal exchanges. Therefore, it may be assumed that travelers fail in matching or direct negotiation.

2.4 Approach of this Study to the Problems

In response to these problems, we propose a sightseeing support system that pictures taken around the current location are displayed on a map in a smartphone, enabling the user to set a tentative destination by themselves based on the impressions derived from the pictures. Users can grasp the required time from displayed information on the map while they set a place that they are interested in as a temporary destination. It also allows the tentative destination to be changed at any arbitrary time, allowing for easily changing the route. This way the system allows a user to freely take a stroll through multiple places of interest around a sightseeing spot within a limited period of time. In Sect. 3, we describe the system's details.

3 System Framework

3.1 Goal

Our goal is to realize a system that uses pictures and location information to guide tourists to places of interest when they take a stroll during the free time available in sightseeing tours. Our target user is not familiar with the sightseeing area or not collecting tourist information in advance.

In contrast to conventional navigation systems that display the shortest route to the sightseeing destination, our system provides scenery pictures to guide tourists to places of interest when a user take a stroll and information to plan how to spend unscheduled vacant time around a user's travel destination. The user can choose a course freely, and enjoy detours at one's own leisure. In our system, it is assumed that the vacant time is about thirty minutes to about two hours.

3.2 Design Method

The system is implemented as a web service that can be accessed from a smart-phone. Google Maps API is used to display maps on the web, and the pictures are placed as markers on the map. The following section describes the system design method.

1. Setting the destination based on pictures
   The user sets the destination of interest based on the impressions derived from the pictures of nearby places displayed on the map of the current location. The time, date, and location information of each picture are also displayed in the application. Pictures of scenery other than those at the sightseeing spots are also displayed at times. This lets the user to select a destination that appears to be intuitively attractive, since no explanatory text is displayed.
2. Displaying a list of pictures taken around the current location
   As the destination is set, the shortest route is not displayed; instead, a list of pictures of nearby places is displayed, along with the date, time, and place the picture was taken at. This is also accompanied by a rough estimate of the time required to reach the place on the picture from the current location. This enables visual selection of a route as the user looks for places of interest other than the destination.
3. Setting and changing the candidate destination
   As the user selects a picture of a place of interest, the selected location is recorded as a candidate destination on the map. The selection of a stroll route or a destination is made easier as the user can visually confirm the candidate spot displayed on the map.
4. Displaying pictures at a branching point on a route
   The route selection at a branching point is assisted by displaying a list of pictures along each possible route beyond the branching point.

3.3 System Overview

The system is implemented as a web service that can be accessed from a smartphone so that users can easily access our service even if they suddenly have unexpected free time outdoors. The clients in the system are smartphones running on iOS or Android, with GPS and PHP-enabled web browsers installed. Google Maps API[1] is used to display maps on the web, and the pictures are placed as markers on the map. All map data in this article is based on Google Maps.

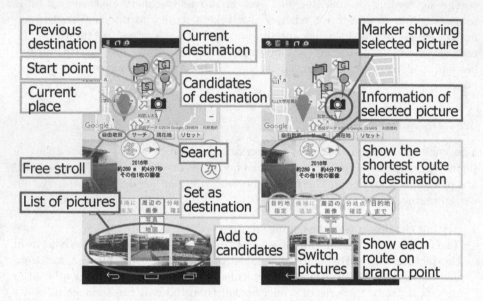

Fig. 1. Screenshot of the proposed system in operation.

Figure 1 shows the screenshot of the proposed system in operation. The map with markers for the current location and the destination is displayed in the upper part of the screen. Just below that, the "free stroll", "search", "display current location", and "reset" buttons are displayed. In the middle of the screen, the selected picture along with the information on time, season, and direction the image was captured from, is displayed. Moreover, the operations available on the selected picture are also concurrently displayed. The pictures of nearby places are listed at the bottom of the screen.

The usage patterns are shown in Fig. 2. The system displays the pictures along the path from the current location to the final destination as thumbnails or markers on the map, or in the form of a list. The user can decide on the next destination (or transit point) after browsing the pictures. The user can also have a good view of the scenery at different places through the pictures displayed by the system.

---

[1] Google Maps API: https://developers.google.com/maps/.

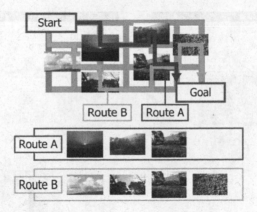

Fig. 2. Usage patterns in deciding the stroll route.

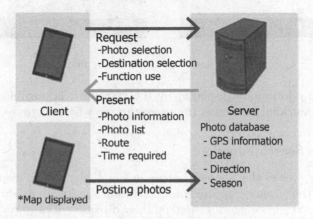

Fig. 3. Server and clients.

3.4   Presentation of Photograph Information

Figure 3 provides an illustration of the server and the clients. A client selects a picture on the map, then a request is sent to the server.

Photographs are placed on the map as a marker or a thumbnail. Figure 4 shows screenshots that a picture on the map is selected. The left side of Fig. 4 uses arrow markers and the photo information is displayed in the balloon with thumbnail. The photo information includes the direction in which the picture was taken, the date and the season. The direction of the arrow means that the picture were taken in which direction from the current location. The right side of Fig. 4 uses thumbnails of each photo. The photographs with characters that means the direction are placed in groups on the map. Users can switch the representation.

Users check each picture and set a marker indicating a picture of interest as a tentative destination based on the photograph information. From the photo

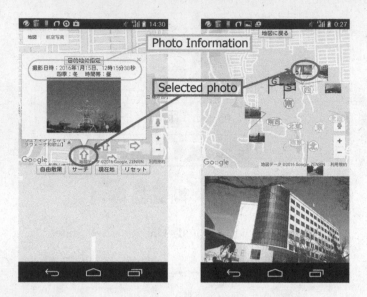

Fig. 4. Photograph data on the map.

and the photo information displayed by the system, it is possible for users to easily grasp what kind of scenery the users can see where to go.

3.5   Picture Search Function

When the user presses the "search" button in Fig. 1, the system displays a list of thumbnails of the pictures captured around the current location. The thumbnails are grouped into eight categories based on their direction of capture. This feature enables the application to display all the pictures of other sceneries in the same direction as that of the image selected by the user from the thumbnails displayed.

The "search" button can also be used to determine the route while checking the detailed information on the pictures by selecting the arrow marks displayed on Google Maps. The arrow itself points to the direction of the camera in which the image was captured, and by tapping on it, the date, season, and time of the day when the image was captured, and its thumbnail gets displayed.

3.6   Listing Stroll Spots Function

When the user presses the "set as destination" button in Fig. 1 during marker selection, a flag marker with the letter G is displayed on the location of the picture. The picture is set as the tentative destination.

Once the destination is set, the pictures of different spots between the current location and the destination are displayed as a list at the bottom of the screen. The screenshot of the photograph list is shown in Fig. 5. In Fig. 5, the photograph at the second row and the third column is selected. The distance from the user's current location to this photo location and required time are displayed next to the photo.

Fig. 5. List of photographs between the current location and the destination.

This function enables the user to select detour spots while keeping track of the remaining stroll time, the distance to the destination, and contents of the images. If more than one place of interest is found, the application allows them to be stored as candidate destinations for subsequent visits.

3.7 Reviewing Branch Point Function

When the route being followed reaches a branching point, the user can check the pictures along the different routes beyond the branching point. The direction of different routes at the branching point can be displayed as markers on the map by pressing the "show each route on the branching point" button. As shown in Fig. 2, if the user chooses the marker that points to the right, then route A is selected, and if the marker pointing down is chosen, then route B is selected, and the pictures along the selected route are listed starting from the one nearest to the current location. Since the list of pictures for each route is different, the user can select a preferred route, either by selecting the shortest route to the destination or by selecting a route that include detours to the places of interest to the user, before reaching the destination.

Figure 6 shows the screen of a result of using this function. The photographs are placed in order of distance. The user can review in advance the scenery pictures seen by going in the selected direction.

3.8 Free Stroll Function

The "free stroll function" has been designed to enable the user to stroll freely with the user's current location set as the final destination. The target is the

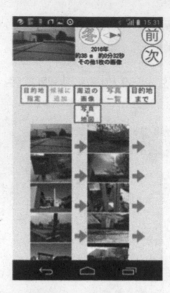

Fig. 6. List of photographs to the destination in order of distance.

users who want to walk around without setting the final destination, or who want to stroll around the current location while they want to search for new experiences. This function can also be used when the user plans to return to the original location after a stroll around any particular area.

4   Evaluation Experiments

4.1   Experimental Overview

An experiment was conducted with 7 university students to test the proposed system for strolling within a limited period of time. The site for the experiment was the university campus where the participants studied. The participants used their own Android phone or iOS phone equipped with a GPS function in the experiment. The participants confirmed beforehand that the system will operate on the web browser of their own smartphone.

We explained the functions and usage of the system in advance to the participants. Although all the participants started the stroll from the same point, they were allowed to freely stroll without setting any particular destination or route. The participants were subsequently asked to fill out a questionnaire after completing the experiment.

It is to be noted that pictures within the campus were recorded in the system prior to the experiment. The students used several sets of pictures along roads mostly frequented by the students, places along less trodden alleys, as well as places around research buildings other than their own. This was done to enable the participants to discover new sceneries that they may have never seen in their day-to-day campus life.

: Set as goal

: Set as candidate

: Start

: Main street

Fig. 7. Distribution of the number of times the destinations were set.

4.2 Experimental Results

Figure 7 shows the distribution of places that were selected as destinations or candidate destinations. The figures within the circles denote the number of times a particular place was selected. The values in Table 1 are the number of times that each function was used. The experimental results are presented in Table 2.

The average number of places marked by the participants as destination and candidate destination was 9.7 and 3.4 per person, respectively. It was observed that many of the participants used the markers for places near the current location as destinations and not as candidate destinations. In contrast, the number of markers for candidate destinations increased for places that were farther from the current location. The results suggest that this is likely due to the fact that the participants tended to move gradually from the marker closest to the current location to the ones further away as they adjusted the time to stroll around.

The results of questions (i), (iv), and (vi) in Table 2 suggest that although there was no written information available such as pamphlets describing sightseeing spots, the participants were able to select their destinations based solely on the information provided by the pictures. Moreover, the results of questions (ii), (v), and (vi) suggest that it is likely that regarding guidance in selecting a destination for strolling, introducing routes solely using pictures was adequate for most of the participants.

The existing tourism support service can guide users with less operation since the voice guidance are played back and the instruction are displayed on the screen only by setting the destination. On the other hand, in this system, many operations such as setting of destinations and candidate places are required. Therefore, there were some comments in the free description fields on the questionnaires regarding the improvement of the interface. One of them is screen design tailored to small screens like smartphones; "I want to freely change the size of the photos in the list", or, "It will be hard to see each photo if the markers are overlapped".

Table 1. Number of times that each function was used.

Operation contents	No.	Avge.	SD
Set as a destination	68	9.7	8.4
Set as a candidate destination	24	3.4	2.6
Route search at branch point	30	4.3	3.0
Free stroll	22	3.1	2.1

Table 2. Average values from the posting questionnaire.

Questionnaire item	Median	Mode
(i) Selecting the next destination based on the pictures was easy	4.0	4
(ii) There were no concerns about getting lost despite the absence of any voice guidance	5.0	5
(iii) The number of pictures displayed in the list was appropriate	3.0	3
(iv) The pictures in the list were effective in advancing the stroll	4.0	4
(v) The scenery at different places could be confirmed using the pictures displayed	4.0	4
(vi) The scenery of interest was easy to find	4.0	4
(vii) An enjoyable stroll was realized within the limited time available	4.0	4

Additionally, there were opinions on the functions that they wanted to add such as "I want a warning for the narrow street that it is hard to pass."

The screen of the smartphone is very small, so complicated operation forces users to bear the burden. However, we think that it is important to adopt a format that displays maps and photo information at the same time. Therefore, in the future, it is necessary to improve the interface that can comfortably provide photograph information on the map and select a destination while minimizing operation.

5   Conclusion

This study proposed a system that supports strolls to a destination using maps and pictures. Unlike the existing sightseeing support systems where voice assistance and current location information are used, the proposed system enables the user to freely select the destination or the route to the destination from pictures and location information displayed on maps and complete the stroll within a limited time.

An experiment was conducted to verify whether an enjoyable stroll can be undertaken within a limited time, guided by pictures and sceneries using the proposed system. The results suggest that the users, despite not being presented with any text-based route guidance or introduction to the sightseeing spots, were able to select the stroll route and destination based solely on information provided through pictures. It must be noted that the participants, through their daily activities, were already very familiar with the area where the experiment was conducted. This may have likely affected their evaluation. It is believed that implementing improvements in the user interface by adjusting the number of pictures displayed and conducting verification experiments in an area that the participants are unfamiliar with are necessary in the future.

References

1. Google Developers: Google Places API. https://developers.google.com/places/. Accessed 28 Feb 2017
2. Kisilevich, S., Krstajic, M., Keim, D., Andrienko, N., Andrienko, G.: Event-based analysis of people's activities and behavior using Flickr and Panoramio geotagged photo collections. In: 2010, 14th International Conference on Information Visualisation (IV), pp. 289–296 (2010)
3. Popescu, A., Grefenstette, G., Moellic, P.: Mining tourist information from user-supplied collections. In: Proceedings of the 18th ACM conference on Information and knowledge management (CIKM), pp. 1713–1716 (2009)
4. Tiwari, S., Kaushik, S.: Information enrichment for tourist spot recommender system using location aware crowdsourcing. In: IEEE 15th International Conference on Mobile Data Management (MDM), vol. 2, pp. 11–14 (2014)
5. Fujii, K., Nanba, H., Takezawa, T., Ishino, A., Okumura, M., Kurata, Y.: Travellers' behaviour analysis based on automatically identified attributes from travel blog entries. In: Workshop on Artificial Intelligence for Tourism (AI4Tourism), PRICAI 2016 (2016)
6. Kurata, Y.: Collecting tour plans from potential visitors: a web-based interactive tour-planner and a strategic use of its log data. In: Egger, R., Gula, I., Walcher, D. (eds.) Open Tourism, Open Innovation, Crowdsourcing and Co-Creation Challenging the Tourism Industry. TV, pp. 291–297. Springer, Heidelberg (2016). doi:10.1007/978-3-642-54089-9_20
7. KLM Royal Dutch Airlines: Social airline KLM connects travellers and Amsterdam locals. Amstelveen, 18 February 2016, Newsroom. http://news.klm.com/social-airline-klm-connects-travellers-and-amsterdam-locals. Accessed 28 Feb 2017

Time-Aware Recommender Systems: A Systematic Mapping

Eduardo José de Borba[1], Isabela Gasparini[1(✉)], and Daniel Lichtnow[2]

[1] Graduate Program in Applied Computing (PPGCA),
Department of Computer Science (DCC),
Santa Catarina State University (UDESC), Joinville, SC, Brazil
eduardojoseborba@gmail.com,
isabela.gasparini@udesc.br
[2] Polytechnic School, Federal University of Santa Maria (UFSM),
Santa Maria, RS, Brazil
dlichtnow@politecnico.ufsm.br

Abstract. A Recommender System (RS) provides personalized suggestions of objects of users' interest or that they may like. Traditional RS techniques consider only aspects related to users and items to recommend and ignore contextual information. Context-Aware RS (CARS) consider information about the user's context to improve the recommendation process. Time is a dimension of context that has the advantage of being easy to collect, since almost any system can record the interaction timestamp. Moreover, time can serve as valuable input for improving recommendation quality. Therefore, this work aims to investigate how time is being applied in CARS and, for this purpose, we used a Systematic Mapping methodology. In total, 88 papers were considered to answer the research questions defined. Initially we observed that the papers' distribution by year have been increased in the last years. As a result, we also defined seven categories of how CARS uses the time in recommendation process.

Keywords: Recommender System · Context-Aware · Time-Aware · Systematic Mapping

1 Introduction

Recommender Systems (RS) are computational tools that supports users in finding items of their interest, especially when the amount of available items is huge. According to Burke [1] a RS is any system that provides personalized recommendation or that has the effect of guiding the user in a personalized way to interesting or useful items among several possible options.

Traditional RS consider only the users and available items, not taking into ac-count the context where these items are inserted [2]. Context is any information that can be used to characterize the situation of an entity [3]. An entity, in the domain of a RS, could be the users of the system or the items to be recommended.

© Springer International Publishing AG 2017
M. Kurosu (Ed.): HCI 2017, Part II, LNCS 10272, pp. 464–479, 2017.
DOI: 10.1007/978-3-319-58077-7_38

Among possible context information, time is being explored in RS in several application domains, e.g., movie recommendation [4], tourism domain [5, 6], restaurants recommendation [7, 8] and in e-commerce [9, 10]. The recent interest in this area is observed by Campos et al. [11] in their state-of-the-art review.

This work aims to identify how time is used in Context-Aware RS (CARS) of diverse application domains. For this purpose, the methodology chosen is a bibliographic study through a systematic mapping defined by Petersen et al. [12].

The paper is organized as follows. Section 1 presents the introduction. In Sect. 2 the theoretical background is described. In Sect. 3 the related work is presented. Section 4 presents the Systematic Mapping Process. In Sect. 5 the classification of time is proposed, where we defined seven categories based on how the time is used in CARS. In Sect. 6 is presented the results of the Systematic Mapping and a discussion about these results. Section 7 contains the final remarks.

2 Theoretical Background

Recommender Systems (RS) algorithms are usually divided in the following approaches [13, 14]: Content-based, Collaborative Filtering, Knowledge-based and Hybrid.

According to Lops et al. [15], Content-based approach is the one that recommends to the user items similar to what he had interest in the past. It consists of comparing the similarity between an item and the user's interests. This approach is strongly related to Information Retrieval area, due to the fact that the item and the user's interests are usually represented by a set of keywords [13]. The main advantages of this approach are: (a) it does not need an active community of users to recommend and (b) the possibility to recommend new items in the system that any user used or rated. The main drawbacks are the User Cold Start (new users in the system do not have a defined profile) and the Overspecialization (user can always receive items very similar to what he already saw).

In Collaborative Filtering approach, user receives as recommendation items that users with similar tastes had interest in the past, i.e., it is the automatization of the word-of-mouth process [16]. This approach assumes that people who have had similar preferences in the past tend to agree in the future [14]. As this approach considers only users with similar tastes to recommend and not the items description, the main advantage of this approach are the serendipity (phenomenon of finding valuable or agreeable things not sought for) and that the quality of the item is considered (not only its description). The main drawbacks of this approach are the need of an active community to recommend, the User Cold-Start (new users will not receive recommendation because not rated any item yet), the Item Cold-Start (new items will not be recommended because were not rated by anyone yet) and the difficulty to recommend to users with unusual interests (called black sheep).

Knowledge-based approach recommends items to users based on the knowledge the system has about how the item's characteristics matches the user needs and how useful this item would be [17]. This approach is mostly used together with others approach aiming to improve recommendation quality or to avoid some drawback. Knowledge-based RS are developed where the knowledge about the domain is available in some structured machine-readable form, e.g., an ontology [13]. The main advantage of this approach is that it usually improve recommendation quality when applied together with others approaches. The main drawback of this approach is that it needs the knowledge acquire and representation, and it is not always possible.

Hybrid approach combines two or more approaches to recommend items to users. Its goal is to gather the advantages of each approach and tries to avoid its drawbacks [1]. Some examples of this combination are [1]: Feature augmentation, where one approach is applied first and the result is applied in the next. Switching, where there is an alternation between the approaches and the RS has criteria to decide which one to use. Mixed, where the approaches are used separately and the result of each one appears in the same ranking, but this hybridization is most used if it is practical to make large number of recommendations simultaneously.

CARS considers context information where the item is going to be consumed, beyond the information already used by traditional approaches. According to Adomavicius and Tuzhilin [18], there are three paradigms in which context can be part of the recommendation process: Contextual Pre-Filtering, Contextual Post-Filtering and Contextual Modeling. In Contextual Pre-Filtering contextual information drives data selection or data construction for that specific context and then traditional approaches are used. In Contextual Post-Filtering initially traditional approaches are used without any contextual information, and then the resulting set of recommendations is adjusted for each user using the contextual information. In Contextual Modeling contextual information is used directly in the recommendation technique as part of rating/ usefulness estimation.

Context dimensions are categories of contextual information, where each of them are defined by set of attributes, in different levels of granularity. For example. Location is a context dimension that could assume values like Brazil (less granular) or "200 Paulo Malschitzki Street, Joinville" (more granular). There are different set of dimensions that could represent context [19–21]. In this work, we follow Schmidt et al. [22] that defines the following dimensions:

- Information on the user, e.g., users' habits, users' emotional state, etc.;
- User's social environment, e.g., co-location with others users, social interaction in social networks, etc.;
- User's tasks, e.g., general goals, whether it is a defined task or random activity, etc.;
- Location, e.g., absolute position, whether the user is at home or office, etc.;
- Physical conditions, e.g., noise, light, etc.;
- Infrastructure, e.g., network bandwidth, type of device, etc.;
- Time, that could be categorical, e.g., Time of the day (Morning, Afternoon, Evening), or continuous, e.g., a timestamp like "June 1st, 2016 at 17:14:36".

According to Adomavicius and Tuzhilin [18], depending on the application domain and the available data, at least some contextual information might be useful to improve the recommendation process. Among all context dimensions, time has an advantage to be easy to capture, considering that almost every device has a clock that could capture the timestamp when an interaction occurs. Besides that, works in this area showed that the context of time has potential to improve recommendation quality [11]. This kind of RS is called Time-Aware Recommender Systems (TARS).

According to Campos et al. [11], time dimension can be represented in continuous format (e.g., as a timestamp like "June 1st, 2016 at 17:14:36") or in categorical format (e.g., Days_of_the_week = {Monday, Tuesday, Wednesday, ..., Sunday} or Time_of_ the_day = {Morning, Afternoon, Evening}.

3 Related Work

In order to understand the TARS field, this work conducts a systematic research and analysis of papers to identify how the time is used in Context-Aware RS in several application domains. We identified two works that also uses literature review with similar objectives: Pereira et al. [23] and Campos et al. [11].

Pereira et al. [23] executes a systematic mapping to identify which context dimensions are used in Context-Aware RS in e-learning domain. This study considered 30 papers and showed that the most used context dimension in this domain is Information on the user (with 22 papers), followed by Infrastructure (with 14 papers). Time appears in the 4th place, with 8 papers. This studied also identified that time is represented in this 8 papers as Timetable or Time interval, both as continuous format.

Campos et al. [11] presents a literature review of Time-Aware RS.In this research it is explained the main recommendation strategies and algorithms using time, and evaluation methods to this kind of RS. Then, the authors proposed a framework on how to evaluate Time-Aware RS.

The work of Pereira et al. [23] is limited to recommendation in e-learning environments, while Campos et al. [11] is more focused to evaluation of Time-Aware RS, although it makes a review of the main algorithms of the area. In this way, this paper presents a Systematic Mapping looking to identify how the time is used in Context-Aware RS in several application domains (not only e-learning) and thus describe the area. It is worth saying that, on how the time is used in RS, classification of Time-Aware RS is proposed based on the works studied and is a contribution of this work.

4 Methodology: Systematic Mapping Process

In this work was executed a Systematic Mapping based on Petersen et al. methodology [12]. This methodology is frequently used in medical research, but can be applied in others domains too, allowing a structured research (that could be replicated) and quantitative results in order to answer the research questions [12]. That's why the results of a systematic mapping are usually represented by visual charts and maps of the desired domain.

The essential steps of the Systematic Mapping, as seen in Fig. 1, are [12]: (1) Definition of Research Questions, where are defined the research goal and results in the Review Scope. (2) Conduct Search, where all potentially relevant papers are identified. (3) Screening of papers, based on selection criteria only papers relevant to the research remains. (4) Keywording using Abstracts, where researchers look for keywords and concepts that reflects the contribution of the each paper and the set of

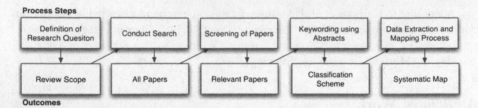

Fig. 1. Systematic Mapping process [12].

keywords from different papers are combined together to develop a high level understanding about the nature and state of the field. (5) Data Extraction and Mapping of Studies, based on the classification made in step 4 the papers are categorized and relevant information are extracted and represented visually.

4.1 Research Questions

The Main Research Question (MRQ) that this work aims to answer is:

- **MRQ:** How the time is used in Context-Aware Recommender Systems?

In order to answer the MRQ, three Secondary Research Questions (SRQ) where defined below. Answering all SRQ make this work answer the MRQ.

- **SRQ1:** How recommender algorithms use time?
- **SRQ2:** What are the differences about the use of time in different application domains?
- **SRQ3:** What others context dimensions are used to be applied together with time dimension?

4.2 Conduct Search

Take into account the research questions, it was defined the main keywords related to this research. The identified keywords used as the search arguments are (time-aware OR context-aware) AND ("recommender system"). These search arguments were used in three Academic Search Engines (ASE): IEEE Xplorer, Scopus and Springer Link. These ASE were chosen because they have a huge amount of content in Computer Science and have the necessary search and filtering mechanisms.

The defined search arguments intent to find for papers about Time-Aware Recommender Systems or about Context-Aware Recommender Systems, that could use time dimension to recommend. This search argument were used in each one of three ASE, looking for papers that presents these keywords in the Title, Abstract or Keywords (also called Topic in some ASEs).

Three constrains were defined to filter more relevant papers to our research. These constrains are called Objective Criteria (OC). As the first OC was defined that we will consider only papers published in the last ten years from beginning of this work, i.e., from 2006 to 2016. As the second OC was defined that, we will consider only papers fully available to download. This constrain is also related to the ASE. The third OC is the language, where only papers in English were considered. This last constraint were applied manually by the authors, although some ASE allows to filter for language.

4.3   Screening of Papers

After conducing search on all ASE, Inclusion and Exclusion Criteria must be applied to obtain only papers relevant to answer the research questions. The Inclusion Criteria (IC) and Exclusion Criteria (EC) are:

- IC1: Include only papers that aims to describe a strategy (i.e., algorithm, framework, method, model, etc.) to recommend.
- EC1: Exclude papers that do not use time to recommend or do not explain how time is used.
- EC2: Exclude duplicates or different papers related to the same work.

For a paper be considered for the research it must be accepted by IC1 and not be eliminated by EC1 neither EC2. The process was documented, registering which criterion eliminates each paper.

4.4   Classification Scheme and Data Extraction

After selecting all relevant papers, next step involves reading and classifying papers to answer the research questions. The results of this step are the categories defined in Sect. 5 and the charts and analysis in Sect. 6. The main data extracted of the papers were: (1) Publication Year; (2) Paper's authors; (3) Application Domain; (4) If time is used as Categorical or Continuous; (5) how the time is applied (i.e., Pre-filtering, Post-filtering or Modeling); (6) In which use of time category the recommendation are classified; (7) what others dimensions are used in the recommendation process. First, only Abstracts was read, as directed by Petersen et al. [12]. But, when it was necessary, a superficial reading of the full paper was executed, trying to answer the research questions.

5   Use of Time Categories

During the Systematic Mapping process, it was observed patterns of the use of time in the Recommender Systems (RS) studies. The works that use time in a similar way were grouped together, based on when the time appears in the recommendation process and how time affects the recommendation. Seven categories of how the time is used in RS were defined. The names to these categories were given by the authors of this paper trying to find the nomenclature that best represents each category. Using these categories, we aim to summarize how the time can be used in RS. The categories are:

- Restriction: the time is used to restrict which items are recommended, take into account the available of items in a certain time and the user's available time with time required to use the item. Examples: recommend only restaurants that are open when user's going to have lunch [24].
- Micro-profile: the user has different profiles for each time. Here, time is usually categorical. Thus the user has a profile for weekdays and a profile for weekends, or the user has a profile for morning, a profile for afternoon and another for evening. Example: recommend a mobile app to the user at Sunday morning based only in apps used by this user in past Sunday mornings [25].
- Bias: time is the third dimension of a User x Item matrix. So, collaborative filtering has more information for identifying similar users and to predict user's rating to a non-viewed item. Example: Koren [4] uses a similar strategy at the Netflix Grand Prize, where he proposes a Tensor Factorization strategy using a User x Item x Time tensor.
- Decay: it uses time as a decay factor, in which old interactions are less important than new ones, but are not discarded. Example: in E-commerce, it considers items the user searched recently more important when deciding what products to recommend, and give older searches less impact at recommendation [26].
- Time Rating: time supports the RS to understand user's preferences, e.g., the more the user stays at the item, more he likes it. It means that time gives feedback to an item implicitly to a user, i.e., without need of user rate the item. Example: in Smart TVs, consider that TV programs the user watches more often and for longer are the ones he likes, helping the RS to find others programs to recommend [27].
- Novelty: only new items will be recommended. The RS has a threshold and items older than a specific timestamp it will not recommended. Example: in news website, it's better to recommend news of, at most, one day ago [28].
- Sequence: the RS observe items that are usually consumed following a sequence. Thus, if the first of the sequence is consumed, the second should probably be consumed too. Example: in music recommendation, songs of the same album are most likely to be heard together, so if the user selects one of them, the next one should be recommended [29].

6   Results

The search for relevant papers, as described in Sect. 4, were done in June 2016. Table 1 show all selection process executed in this search. At beginning, 561 papers were accessed from the three ASE. After applying OC, 556 papers remains. From these

Table 1. Papers selection.

ASE	Downloaded	After OC	After IC1	After EC1	After EC2
IEEExplorer	213	212	183	58	53
Scopus	71	69	49	20	18
SpringerLink	277	275	101	23	17
Total	561	556	333	101	**88**

papers, 333 papers matched IC1 and were keep. After applying EC1 e EC2, 88 papers that are relevant to this research were kept. In the next subsections the analysis of these 88 papers and the answers to the research questions are presented.

6.1 Analysis

Figure 2 presents the distribution of the 88 papers by year. The results indicate that the use of time in recommender systems is a subject with increasing interest by researchers. The year of 2012 was the one with more papers published (16 papers), and from 2011 to 2015 the number of publications is almost uniform (between 13 and 16 papers). On 2016, the number of publications was less than the previous year, but it is necessary to observe that the research was executed in June 2016. The growing between 2006 and 2011 shows RSs considering context (time context, in this case), information that were not considered in the pioneering RS.

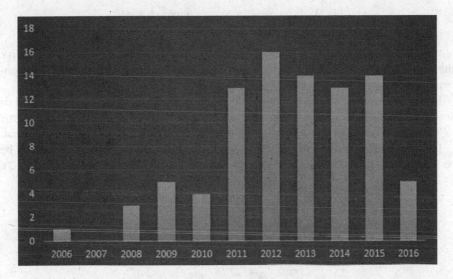

Fig. 2. Papers distribution by year.

6.2 How Recommender Algorithms Uses Time?

In order to answer the Main Research Question (MRQ) and understand how the time is used in Context-Aware Recommender Systems, it was necessary to answer three Secondary Research Questions (SRQ). The first SRQ involves how recommender algorithms use time. In this sense, Fig. 3 presents which RS approach (described in Sect. 2) is used in Time-Aware RS. It is possible to observe Collaborative Filtering is the most used approach, appearing in 41% of all papers. This number probably bigger, because most of Hybrid algorithms combines Collaborative Filtering with other approach. All other approaches appear with almost the same percentage. It is worth

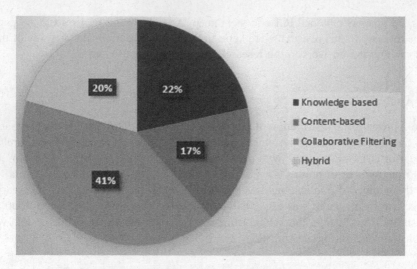

Fig. 3. Recommender System approach used.

pointing out that Knowledge-based approach is not as traditional as Collaborative Filtering or Content-based, but it is often used, maybe because many RSs use contextual information through ontology inference.

Figure 4 shows how time is represented in the analyzed papers, i.e., categorical or continuous (described in Sect. 2). It is possible to see that the majority represents time in Continuous format, with 63%, while only 37% represents it in a Categorical format.

It was also analyzed how time is applied in recommendation process, and could be Pre-Filtering, Post-Filtering or Modeling (this distinct process are described in Sect. 2).

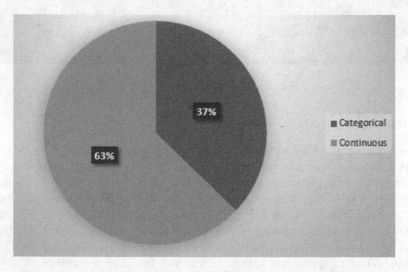

Fig. 4. Time format.

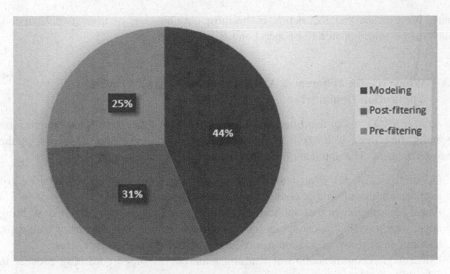

Fig. 5. Time application.

Figure 5 shows that Modeling is the most common application way (44% of the papers), followed by Post-Filtering (31%) and Pre-Filtering (25%).

Another analysis were made considering the use of time, i.e., how the time influences the recommendation process. To do this analysis, seven categories were observed and are explained in more detail in Sect. 4. Figure 6 shows how the papers analyzed in the work uses time, take into account the categories defined in the Sect. 6. Some papers use of time in more than one way, because of this there are more 88 papers listed in the

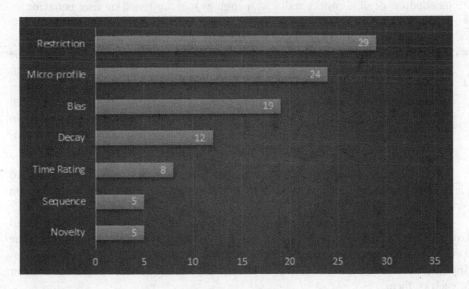

Fig. 6. Use of time.

chart. We can see that Restriction is the most common use of time (in 29 papers), followed by Micro-profile (24 papers) and Bias (19 papers).

6.3   What Are the Differences About the Use of Time in Different Application Domains?

To answer SRQ2, about the difference between the use of time in different application domains, first there is a need to define the applications domains identified in the analyzed papers. The applications domains identified are:

- Generic: works not related to a specific application domain. These works just propose an algorithm that could be applied in any domain.
- Apps: recommendation of applications that the user may be interested, like walking apps, weather apps, investing apps, etc. The apps include mobile apps or web apps.
- E-commerce: recommendation of products in electronic commerce sites.
- E-learning: recommendation of learning materials to support learning process in e-learning environments.
- Scientific Events: presents recommendation of presentations to watch in a scientific event, e.g., an academic conference.
- Multimedia: recommendation of multimedia resources, e.g., music, movies, videos, images, etc.
- Museum: recommendation of artwork or others exhibitions to visitors inside a museum.
- News: recommendation of news to users.
- Points-of-Interest: recommendation of points-of-interest, e.g., touristic attractions, events, shows, restaurants, hotels, etc. These papers are usually related to tourism.
- Advertising: recommendation of advertisement to the user, similar to ads recommended in social networks and search engines that are based on user behavior.
- Social Network: recommendation of content (e.g., posts) or other users (e.g., new friends) in social networks.
- Walking route: papers that presents recommendation of routes to walking, from the actual position.
- Others: this category represents application domains that appear in just one paper. In summary, there are seven applications domains joining in this category: physical activity recommendation, movie sessions recommendation, recommendation in sharing economy app, social events recommendation, cook recipes recommendation, sales recommendation in a mall and tasks recommendation.

Figure 7 shows that the most common application domain is Multimedia (with 16 papers), followed by Point-of-Interest (with 15 papers) and Apps recommendation (with 13 papers).

The application domains aforementioned were analyzed separately to understand how the time is used in each of them. Figure 8 shows the analysis about the time format, i.e., how the time is represented in each domain. The chart shows that continuous format overcome categorical in all domains, being in equal of greater number in each of them.

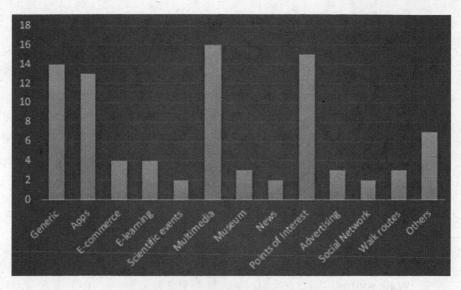

Fig. 7. Application domains.

Domain	Time Format	
	Continuous	Categorical
Generic	9	6
Apps	8	5
E-commerce	2	2
E-learning	4	0
Scientific events	2	0
Multimedia	8	8
Museum	3	0
News	1	1
Points of Interest	9	6
Advertising	2	1
Social Network	2	0
Walk routes	2	1
Others	4	3

Fig. 8. Domain vs. time format.

Figure 9 shows the comparison of each of the 13 application domain with how the time is applied. It is possible to observe that, depending on the application domain one paradigm is more used than the others, but there is not one that dominates the others for all domains. For example: in Apps recommendation, Pre-Filtering is most common

Domain	Contextual Paradigm		
	Pre-filtering	Post-filtering	Modeling
Generic	4	3	10
Apps	8	0	5
E-commerce	2	2	1
E-learning	0	2	2
Scientific events	0	2	0
Multimedia	7	2	9
Museum	0	3	0
News	1	0	1
Points of Interest	3	8	7
Advertising	0	1	3
Social Network	0	0	2
Walk routes	0	3	0
Others	0	4	3

Fig. 9. Domain vs. contextual paradigm.

way to apply the time, while in Point-of-Interest recommendation the most common is Post-Filtering and in Multimedia recommendation Modeling is the most used. It is important to analyze and use this information to implement a new RS for a determined domain.

It was also analyzed the application domain with the Use of Time category defined in Sect. 5. Figure 10 shows this analysis. It is possible to observe that certain domains

Domain	Use of Time						
	Sequence	Novelty	Time Rating	Decay	Bias	Micro-profile	Restriction
Generic	2	1	0	3	4	4	2
Apps	0	1	3	1	2	8	0
E-commerce	0	0	1	1	1	2	1
E-learning	0	0	0	2	0	0	2
Scientific events	0	0	0	0	0	0	2
Multimedia	1	1	1	2	5	7	1
Museum	0	0	0	0	0	0	3
News	0	1	0	0	0	1	0
Points of Interest	1	0	2	1	2	2	11
Advertising	0	0	1	1	1	0	1
Social Network	1	1	0	0	0	0	0
Walk routes	0	0	0	0	1	0	2
Others	0	0	0	1	3	0	4

Fig. 10. Domain vs. use of time.

have higher trend to use the time according to some of the defined categories. For example: in Point-of-Interest recommendation the most common use of time category is Restriction, maybe due to this kind of recommendation worry whether the establishment possible to recommendation is open or closed at the time the user arrives there. In Apps recommendation the most common category is Micro-Profile, due the strategy of this domain of comparing the current time of the user (e.g., time of the day, day of the week, month of the year, season, etc.) with that the user have done in similar conditions and so recommend more personalized to the user. In E-learning, the recommendation uses Decay (recommending more based on what the user last studied) and Restriction (recommending items with duration that matches the user available time).

6.4 What Others Context Dimensions Are Used to Be Applied Together with Time Dimension?

To answer the last SRQ were extracted from the papers which others context dimensions are used, based on the definition of Schmidt et al. [22] (described in Sect. 2). Figure 11 shows this analysis. It is possible to see that location appears in most papers (70 papers out of 88), followed by Information about the user (46 papers) and Social environment (24 papers). From the 88 papers, 10 use just time dimension or do not specify the others context dimensions used.

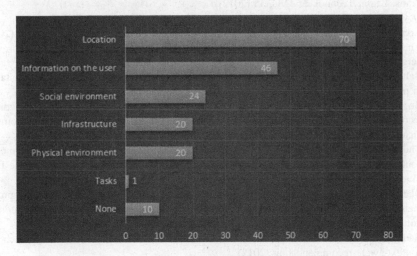

Fig. 11. Others dimensions used together with time.

7 Conclusion

In this work, were executed a Systematic Mapping to investigate the Time-Aware Recommender Systems in several application domains. The goal of this work is identify how the algorithms of this area are used, answer the research question defined (How the time is used in Context-Aware Recommender Systems?). With this

Systematic Mapping, we hope to support other researches to understand this research area and how the algorithms are being used.

The use of time (categories defined in Sect. 5) most common are Restriction, Micro-profiles and Bias. The format of time most used is continuous and the paradigm of time application most used is Modeling. The dimension most used together with time is location that appears in almost all papers. We consider that this fact occurs because nowadays it is easy to obtain user's location using mobile devices.

One of the contributions of the present work, through the Systematic Mapping, is related to the fact that we have identified that depending on the application domain the way the time is applied is very distinct. This information can be useful for researchers who want to develop a RS's in a specific domain (e.g. is it value to recommend an old new to users of a SR that recommend news?). Besides, it is possible to think in use the dimension time in a different way.

References

1. Burke, R.: Hybrid recommender systems: survey and experiments. User Model. User-adapt. Interact. **12**, 331–370 (2002)
2. Verbert, K., Manouselis, N., Ochoa, X., Wolpers, M., Drachsler, H., Bosnic, I., Duval, E.: Context-aware recommender systems for learning: a survey and future challenges. IEEE Trans. Learn. Technol. **5**, 318–335 (2012)
3. Dey, A.K.: Understanding and using context. Pers. Ubiquit. Comput. **5**, 4–7 (2001)
4. Koren, Y.: The bellkor solution to the netflix grand prize. Netflix Prize Doc. **81**, 1–10 (2009)
5. Anacleto, R., Figueiredo, L., Almeida, A., Novais, P.: Mobile application to provide personalized sightseeing tours. J. Netw. Comput. Appl. **41**, 56–64 (2014)
6. Baltrunas, L., Ludwig, B., Peer, S., Ricci, F.: Context relevance assessment and exploitation in mobile recommender systems. Pers. Ubiquit. Comput. **16**, 507–526 (2012)
7. Bedi, P., Richa, S.: User interest expansion using spreading activation for generating recommendations. In: 2015 International Conference on Advances in Computing Communication Informatics, ICACCI 2015, pp. 766–771 (2015)
8. Chu, C.H., Wu, S.H.: A Chinese restaurant recommendation system based on mobile context-aware services. In: Proceedings of IEEE International Conference on Mobile Data Management, vol. 2, pp. 116–118 (2013)
9. Blanco-Fernández, Y., López-Nores, M., Pazos-Arias, J.J., García-Duque, J.: An improvement for semantics-based recommender systems grounded on attaching temporal information to ontologies and user profiles. Eng. Appl. Artif. Intell. **24**, 1385–1397 (2011)
10. Haddad, M.R., Baazaoui, H., Ziou, D., Ghezala, H.B.: A model-driven approach for context-aware recommendation (2012)
11. Campos, P.G., Díez, F., Cantador, I.: Time-aware recommender systems: a comprehensive survey and analysis of existing evaluation protocols. User Model. User-adapt. Interact. **24**, 67–119 (2014)
12. Petersen, K., Feldt, R., Mujtaba, S., Mattsson, M.: Systematic mapping studies in software engineering. In: 12th International Conference on Evaluation Assessment in Software Engineering, vol. 17, p. 10 (2008)
13. Adomavicius, G., Tuzhilin, A.: Toward the next generation of recommender systems: a survey of the state-of-the-art and possible extensions. IEEE Trans. Knowl. Data Eng. **17**, 734–749 (2005)

14. Ricci, F., Rokach, L., Shapira, B.: Introduction to recommender systems handbook. In: Ricci, F., Rokach, L., Shapira, B., Kantor, P.B. (eds.) Recommender System: Handbook, pp. 1–35. Springer, Heidelberg (2011)
15. Lops, P., de Gemmis, M., Semeraro, G.: Content-based recommender systems: state of the art and trends. In: Ricci, F., Rokach, L., Shapira, B., Kantor, P.B. (eds.) Recommender System: Handbook, pp. 73–105. Springer, Heidelberg (2011)
16. Jannach, D., Zanker, M., Felfernig, A., Friedrich, G.: Recommender Systems: An Introduction. Cambridge University Press, Cambridge (2011)
17. Felfernig, A., Friedrich, G., Jannach, D., Zanker, M.: Developing constraint-based recommenders. In: Ricci, F., Rokach, L., Shapira, B., Kantor, P.B. (eds.) Recommender System: Handbook, pp. 187–215. Springer, Heidelberg (2011)
18. Adomavicius, G., Tuzhilin, A.: Context-aware recommender systems. In: Ricci, F., Rokach, L., Shapira, B., Kantor, P.B. (eds.) Recommender System: Handbook, pp. 217–253. Springer, Heidelberg (2011)
19. Schilit, B., Adams, N., Want, R.: Context-aware computing applications. In: IEEE Workshop Mobile Computing Systems Applications, pp. 1–7 (1994)
20. Chen, G., Kotz, D.: A survey of context-aware mobile computing research (2000)
21. Zimmermann, A., Lorenz, A., Oppermann, R.: An operational definition of context. In: 6th International Interdisciplinary Conference Context 2007, vol. 1, pp. 558–571 (2007)
22. Schmidt, A., Beigl, M., Gellersen, H.W.: There is more to context than location. Comput. Graph. 23, 893–901 (1999)
23. Pereira, C.K., Campos, F., Braga, R., Ströele, V., David, J.M.N.: Elementos de Contexto em Sistemas de Recomendação no Domínio Educacional: um Mapeamento Sistemático. In: XIX Conferência International sobre Informática na Educ, vol. 19, pp. 10 (2014)
24. Gallego, D., Woerndl, W., Huecas, G.: Evaluating the impact of proactivity in the user experience of a context-aware restaurant recommender for android smartphones. J. Syst. Archit. 59, 748–758 (2013)
25. Rho, W.H., Cho, S.B.: Context-aware smartphone application category recommender system with modularized bayesian networks. In: 2014 10th International Conference on National Computation ICNC 2014, pp. 775–779 (2014)
26. Limbeck, P., Suntinger, M., Schiefer, J.: SARI OpenRec–Empowering recommendation systems with business events. In: 2nd International Conference on Advances Databases, Knowledge, Data Applications DBKDA 2010, pp. 111–119 (2010)
27. Vildjiounaite, E., Kyllönen, V., Hannula, T., Alahuhta, P.: Unobtrusive dynamic modelling of TV program preferences in a household. In: Tscheligi, M., Obrist, M., Lugmayr, A. (eds.) EuroITV 2008. LNCS, vol. 5066, pp. 82–91. Springer, Heidelberg (2008). doi:10.1007/978-3-540-69478-6_9
28. Montes-García, A., Álvarez-Rodríguez, J.M., Labra-Gayo, J.E., Martínez-Merino, M.: Towards a journalist-based news recommendation system: the wesomender approach. Expert Syst. Appl. 40, 6735–6741 (2013)
29. Pálovics, R., Benczúr, A.A.: Temporal influence over the Last.fm social network. Soc. Netw. Anal. Min. 5, 1–12 (2015)

LifeRescue Software Prototype for Supporting Emergency Responders During Fire Emergency Response: A Usability and User Requirements Evaluation

Vimala Nunavath[✉] and Andreas Prinz

CIEM Research Group, Department of ICT,
University of Agder, Grimstad, Norway
{vimala.nunavath, andreas.prinz}@uia.no

Abstract. For an efficient emergency response, emergency responders (ERs) should exchange information with one another to obtain an adequate understanding and common operational picture of the emergency situation. Despite the current developments on information systems, many ERs are unable to get access to the relevant information as the data is heterogeneous and distributed at different places and due to security and privacy barriers. As a result, ERs are unable to coordinate well and to make good decisions. Therefore, to overcome these difficulties, a web-based application called LifeRescue was developed for supporting easy information access during emergency search and rescue operation. The goal of the paper is to test the developed LifeRescue system against the user requirements. We conducted a workshop with nine participants i.e., six ERs from fire protection service and three ERs from police service. First, the workshop session started with prototype demonstration and trial, then a System Usability Scale (SUS) questionnaire was given, and finally a semi-structured interview was conducted to collect data on the user requirements validation. The results presented in this paper combine both qualitative and quantitative data from a semi-structured interview and a survey conducted after the prototype demonstration and trail. The interview results indicate that our developed system fulfils the user requirements of 6 ERs from fire protection and 3 ERs from police services. Furthermore, the survey results indicate that the participants would like to use our developed system frequently as they felt that it was easy for them to get access to information with a simplified view.

Keywords: Emergency management · Search and rescue operation · User requirements evaluation · Usability evaluation · 'User-centered design · Emergency response information system · SUS-questionnaire · Qualitative and quantitative data analysis · Information awareness · Information accessibility · Nvivo tool · Human computer interaction

1 Introduction

Information is considered as a key requirement for managing any kind of emergencies [1]. When an emergency happens, a complex network of emergency responders (ERs) from various emergency response organizations (EROs) such as police service,

© Springer International Publishing AG 2017
M. Kurosu (Ed.): HCI 2017, Part II, LNCS 10272, pp. 480–498, 2017.
DOI: 10.1007/978-3-319-58077-7_39

fire protection service, hospital service and municipality officials are involved in emergency response operations to alleviate both property and human losses. Furthermore, among these involved ERs, few ERs work on-site and others off-site (Control and Command Center). In addition, the involved ERs are often fragmented into different teams to carry out different tasks (such as evacuation, finding victims, firefighting, preventing property and so on) at different geo-locations [2]. Due to geographical dispersion, these fragmented teams must get access to relevant information such as location of the victim, location of the fire, location of the resources, location of the exits and so on to share within or among (intra-inter) teams to obtain or help to get the overview of the situation, to cooperate effectively and for decision-making [3].

When an emergency occurs, a lot of data is generated from various places. The volume and velocity of generated data tend to be extremely high, making it hard for ERs to process it [2, 4]. Without having enough and the right type of information, it is difficult to gain situational awareness [5–7]. Particularly, in dynamic and time critical situations, it becomes difficult for the first response teams to adequately decide which information might be relevant for other teams to support overall coordination. Despite the rapid development of ICT for emergency management [8, 9] information on-site is still typically collected manually.

In addition, each organization stores data in different formats in their own databases, making retrieval and sharing difficult. Consequently, the responders, both onsite and remotely face a lot of difficulties in getting an overview of the situation. The time pressure and the urge to respond worsen the problem and information may be ignored, even though it is available [10]. Therefore, to overcome these difficulties, the authors of this paper proposed and implemented a Model-driven data integration framework for emergency management. So, the research question that we want to answer is *"Does the developed information system which can be used in any emergency response meet the user requirements of various ERs?"*.

As this research question is generic and difficult to answer, we have formulated the above question to a specific case i.e., indoor fire emergency search and rescue operation. The goal of this paper is to address the following research question: *"Does the developed information system (LifeRescue) which can be used during indoor fire emergency search and rescue operation meet the user requirements of different ERs?"*.

To address the formulated research question, the authors of this paper developed a prototype named LifeRescue and conducted a workshop session by following a three-step process: (1) prototype demonstration and trail session, (2) semi-structured interview, and (3) individual questionnaire. The results presented in this paper were analyzed after the workshop session. The significance of this work lies on providing a holistic way to access information for supporting different ERs during indoor fire emergency search and rescue operation with a developed software prototype consisting of a GUI.

The remaining sections of this paper are organized as follows: we first begin with presenting the proposed data integration framework Sect. 2. Then, in Sect. 3, we describe the research methodology that was used for evaluating the user requirements and also describe the developed LifeRescue prototype. We then present our findings in the results part and the findings of the prototype evaluation are discussed in Sect. 4. Finally, contribution and conclusion of this research are discussed with directions for future research in Sect. 5.

2 Data Integration Framework for Emergency Management

To overcome the above-mentioned challenges, we proposed a framework for supporting different ERs. This proposed framework supports a holistic way of improving information availability and accessibility for sharing information among various ERs during emergency response by using Model-driven data integration approach which can be seen in the Fig. 1. In Fig. 1, the data integration framework consists of three components. The complete details of the proposed framework can be found in our previous research [11].

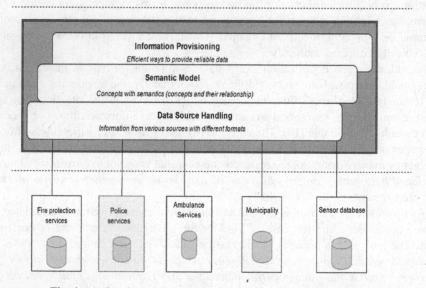

Fig. 1. A data integration framework for emergency management

To develop an information system based on the proposed framework, the authors of this study could not get permission to access different EROs' databases and applications. So, we used an indoor fire in educational building emergency scenario as a use-case and different university applications for data integration. This is because, to develop an effective Information System (IS), a detailed analysis of end-users' information needs is required in order to make the system consistent [12]. In addition, the usability of such application is crucial for the continuous, efficient and satisfactory use of the system. In the system development, the approach of Human-Centered Design (HCD) involves end-users in each stage of the development cycle [13–15]. So, indoor fire emergency use-case scenario was used to capture the user requirements of different ERs. The details of user requirements elicitation can be found in our previous research [16].

3   Research Methodology

As mentioned in [17], evaluation of the system is necessary to analyze the user requirements and usability requirements. Therefore, in this section, we present the methods and material that were used to analyze the user requirements and usability requirements.

3.1   Emergency Scenario and Used User Requirements

The indoor fire emergency scenario which was used during workshop session was as follows.

"Fire accident happened inside the third floor of A' block of the university building. The building consisted of many students (who might be normal, physically challenged, and sick), library, laboratories and storage rooms. Most of the students noticed smoke, flames, and screams inside the building. Some of the victims also report fire intensification. Due to the fire, the emergency site became rampageous and many students inside the building were wounded and traumatized. The number of people inside the building was unknown. But, the people who were running out of the building were giving information about the seen victims. To respond to the emergency, ERs did not know how many people are still inside the building and also their location [2]". This emergency scenario was also used for user requirements elicitation, for convenience, these requirements are shown in the Table 1.

3.2   Developed LifeRescue Prototype

Based on the proposed data integration framework, we developed a prototype as a proof-of-concept. According to the suggestion given in [18] and described in our previous paper [19], we followed an HCD process for developing the LifeRescue system and it's GUI. During entire software development process, different ERs from both police and fire protection services have been involved at several stages (for an example, indoor fire in a university building scenario creation, knowing user requirements for performing the search and rescue operations, mock-up GUI design and so on) to increase the usefulness and acceptance of the system, and to provide feedback and their requirements for the GUI features with us [20].

The GUI of the LifeRescue can be seen in Figs. 2 and 3. Figure 2 represents the login page for the developed application. Figure 3 presents relevant information to different ERs. However, to provide relevant data to different ERs for prior emergency scenario, the authors have used university systems' applications for data integration. The prototype architecture, description of each data source, its metadata and implementation can be found in our previous research [19].

Table 1. Used user requirements of different emergency responders

User requirement ID	User requirement description	Stakeholders	
		Firefighters	Police
1	The user should connect to the system from at any place and at any time	✓	✓
2	The user should get data from diverse sources in a structured form	✓	✓
3	The user should know the victims' count and their location who are inside the building	✓	✓
4	The user should know the resources' location and its details	✓	✗
5	The user should get the building related information	✓	✓
6	The user should get the hazardous materials' location and its details	✓	✓
7	The user should get real time information access to the other emergency response organizations' databases	✓	✓
8	The user should get family information of the victims	✗	✓
9	The user able to know information related to victims' details	✓	✓
10	User should get trustworthy information	✓	✓
11	Users should not face information overload on the screen	✓	✓
12	Users should understand the language that is visualized on the UI including acronyms, signs and symbols	✓	✓
13	User shall see the rescuers location inside the building	✓	✗

LifeRescue web based application for University of Agder	
User Name	admin
Password	•••
Login	Reset

Fig. 2. Log-in page of LifeRescue prototype graphical user interface

The developed LifeRescue provides both static and dynamic information to the ERs. Here dynamic information means the information which gets changed over time during fire emergency and static information means the information which remains unchanged all the time during fire emergency. Both types of information are provided to the ERs with the following features which are listed below.

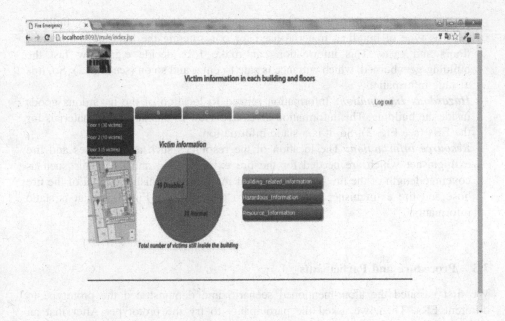

Fig. 3. Main page of the LifeRescue prototype graphical user interface [19] (Color figure online)

– *Pie-chart:* In this chart, ERs can understand the total number of victims who are still inside the university building in a pie chart format. When the victims are rescued and out of the university building, then the count on the pie chart will be changed automatically (see Fig. 3). So, it is a dynamic information. This information can make the ERs get awareness of the situation and help them in making decisions.

– *Floor map:* In GUI, the floor map represents each floor. The location of the victims' is displayed on the map of each floor of each building block. The icons on the map (red and blue) represents location of the victim and their details (such as full name, age, gender and medical status) on a specific floor and the color of the icon helps the ERs to distinguish whether the victim is a normal or a physically challenged person. In this floor map, ERs can also see the fire related information with heat map (i.e., state of the fire in each room). The heat map is updated every second to consider the latest development of the fire. The colors on the floor map (in Fig. 3) go from green to red depending on the intensity of the fire. In the same floor map, ERs can also have a chance to see information related to the movement of the victims (i.e., moving from one location to other). So, this information is dynamic information. With this information, ERs get awareness of the victim location and can decide what should be done to rescue the victims.

– *Tabs:* Tabs represent each block (such as A, B, C, D) which is located inside the university building. In each tab, the total number of floors can be seen. For an example, Block A has three floors (e.g., Floor 1, Floor 2, Floor 3) (see Fig. 3). In each floor, information related to the total number of victims can also be seen in the GUI. So, it is a dynamic information.

- **Building related information:** This information is related to university building such as type of building, material used for constructing the building, number of floors and exits. This information can make ERs decide e.g., how fast the building-gets burned, which entrance is safe to enter and so on (see Fig. 3). So, it is a static information.
- **Hazardous Information:** Information related to location of the hazardous goods inside the building. This information gives overview of the hazardous materials for the ERs (see Fig. 3). So, it is a static information.
- **Resource information:** The location of the resources such as fire hoses and fire extinguisher which are needed for the fire extinguishing and its details such as coverage length of the fire hose, capacity of the fire extinguisher, model of the fire hose and fire extinguisher also provided to the ERs (see Fig. 3). So, it is static information.

3.3   Procedure and Participants

We first narrated the afore-mentioned scenario and demonstrated the prototype to different ERs. Then, we asked the participants to try the prototype. After that an individual SUS questionnaire was given to scale their opinion on the system usability and finally a post-test group interview was conducted with ERs to know whether the system fulfilled their information requirements.

The evaluation of the system was made with 6 ERs from fire protection and 3 ERs from police service departments in their respective organizations. The facilities had a meeting room with external screen and keyboard. In the meeting room, all the ERs gathered and the authors of this paper narrated an indoor fire in the university building scenario. After narrating the scenario, the developed prototype was demonstrated on the external large screen after connecting with a laptop where the prototype was running on. All features of the LifeRescue GUI were explained thoroughly to the ERs for 30 min. Then, participants tried the LifeRescue.

Among the participated 6 ERs of fire protection service, one works as fire chief (FC) who acts as an on-scene commander, 1 person as crew manager (CM), one as smoke diver leader (SDL), and three persons as smoke divers (SD). Whereas, 3 ERs from police service, 2 work as police chief (PC) at emergency site, and 1 as control room supervisor (CRS). The experience of the involved participants in responding to the emergency situations ranges from 4 to 20 years' experience. The entire workshop session carried out for 2 h (120 min). During the session, participants were encouraged to ask questions and comment on the LifeRescue prototype.

3.4   Data Collection

The data collection was done by using audio recording of the post-test group interview and with SUS questionnaire.

Semi-Structured Interviews. After the SUS questionnaire, a semi-structured interview session was held with all participants to obtain in-depth feedback in relation to the user requirement fulfilment and to get any suggestions for the system improvement. The whole interview session was audio recorded for the content analysis.

System Usability Scale Questionnaire. After the prototype demonstration and trail, a System Usability Scale (SUS) questionnaire [21] which consists of 10 questions was given to each participant to evaluate the usability and performance of the system. The SUS questionnaire, is composed of 10 statements that are scored on a 5-point scale of strength of agreement.

The SUS was developed by Brooke [21] as a "quick and dirty" survey scale that would allow the usability practitioner to quickly and easily assess the usability of a given product or service [22].

Although there are a number of other excellent alternatives surveys available such as After Scenario Questionnaire (ASQ) [23], Computer System Usability (CSUQ) [23], Post-study System Usability (PSSUQ) [24], Software Usability Measurement Inventory (SUMI) [25], System Usability Scale (SUS) [21], Usefulness, Satisfaction and Ease of Use (USE) [26, 27] and Web Site Analysis and Measurement Inventory (WAMMI) [28], the SUS has become a good choice for general usability practitioners. The reason for this is the initial paper of Brooke [21] where the SUS questionnaire was first published has been cited over 3500 times, and studies have confirmed the reliability of the SUS with Cronbach's alfa 0.91 [22] with the conclusion that SUS can positively supplement a usability test and evaluation program.

In the study [22], all the above mentioned surveys were compared and the results summarized that the SUS survey was the most reliable one. Therefore, in this paper, SUS survey has been used to evaluate the user satisfaction and usability of the system. In SUS, final scores range from 0 to 100, where higher scores indicate higher user satisfaction and better usability.

According to the researchers in [29, 30], the researchers used an adjective scale by dividing the SUS scores as follows: score of 0–25: worst, score of 25–39: poor, score of 39–52: OK, score of 52–85: excellent, and score of 85–100: best imaginable. So, in this paper we have adapted the same adjective scale in our study. The used SUS questionnaire format and questions can be seen in Fig. 4.

3.5 Data Analysis

After the workshop session, all the data from SUS questionnaires and audio recordings of the group interview were transcribed into excel sheet. After transcribing, the scores of the each SUS questionnaire were calculated. The score calculation was based on the details of scoring the SUS which was explained in the article [21]. The recordings data were imported into QSR NVIVO 10 tool [31] for transcription and a qualitative content analysis.

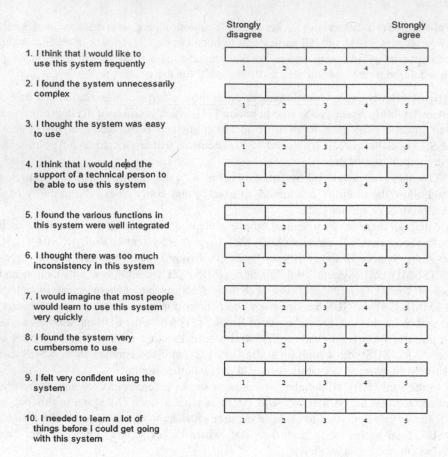

Fig. 4. System usability scale © digital equipment corporation, 1986 (Source: [21])

4   Results

In this section, the results of the system evaluation are presented with the help of qualitative and quantitative analysis.

4.1   Qualitative Analysis

During workshop session, participants got access to the LifeRescue GUI. After getting access to the GUI, they went through the GUI features thoroughly. Then some questions were asked to the participants. Their answers were audio recorded and later encoded into Nvivo tool. The coded content organized into 4 groups: User Requirement Evaluation, GUI Placement, GUI Features Recommendations, and Existing Systems vs LifeRescue GUI.

User Requirement Evaluation. During the interview, all the participants from fire and rescue service mentioned that *"after reaching the emergency site, we have no idea how many people are still inside the building and their location. This information we generally collect manually from either security personnel or from floor responsible person"*. With this statement, it is apparent that there is no ICT (decision-support) system used in Norway to support ERs' information needs during an indoor fire emergency at university.

We then asked the participants about their first impression after seeing our developed system. All participants stated and agreed that *"the system is very well integrated and gives relevant information to us"*. We then asked the participants whether the developed system fulfils the user requirements that they stated at the beginning of the system creation. Answer to this question was given by FC and PC1 that *"it is easy to login to the GUI and the screen was useful to get overview of the inside situation i.e., victims and their location"*.

Another four participants (1 SDL, 1 CM, 1 SD and PC2) positively commented on the pie chart feature of the GUI, *"it helps to get the overview of the number of victims still inside the building"*. Based on the responses to the questions, we have categorized the participants' responses into YES or NO (i.e., if user requirements are met then answered as 'YES' and if user requirements are not met then answered as 'NO'). The results of the user requirements evaluation are presented in Table 2.

Table 2. Results for the user requirements evaluation

User requirement ID	User requirement description	Participants' responses	
		YES	NO
1	The user can connect to the system from at any place and at any time	✓	–
2	The user can get data from diverse sources in a structured form	✓	–
3	The user can know the victims' count and their location who are inside the building	✓	–
4	The user can know the resources' location and its details	✓	–
5	The user can get the building related information	✓	–
6	The user can get the hazardous materials' location and its details	✓	–
7	The user can get real time information access to the other emergency response organizations' databases	✓	–
8	The user can get family information of the victims	✓	–
9	The user able to know information related to victims' details	✓	–
10	User can get trustworthy information	✓	–
11	Users can not face information overload on the screen	✓	–
12	Users can understand the language that is visualized on the UI including acronyms, signs and symbols	✓	–
13	User can see the rescuers location inside the building	✓	–

GUI Features. All participants found that features that got incorporated in the GUI were very well integrated and useful for supporting their information needs to perform emergency response activities. They also mentioned that navigation was very easy and the information that was displayed on the GUI was with good visibility. However, they have provided some recommendations to improve the current GUI features by adding some extra information i.e., adding phone number to the victim details. With this information, either police or fire personnel can send mass messages to the trapped victims. Furthermore, the participants also mentioned that adding information related to room and corridor dimension (such as width, breadth and length size) will be helpful for the fire fighters.

Participants have also stated that displaying all information in a single browser with a single click was an outstanding idea, because, participants have lot of thing to perform at the same time at the emergency site. So, if they are given with multiple browser windows, that would be overloading for them to remember the information that they get from the LifeRescue GUI.

Participants have also commented that getting fire related information on the LifeRescue GUI was an excellent feature. However, they recommended that "*coloring whole room would be better instead of showing this information in a dot form on the LifeRescue GUI*". All the firefighters agreed and specified that "*instead of showing which room has hazardous materials in a list form, better to show them on the LifeRescue GUI with a symbol form*".

GUI Placement. During the interview, the authors of this paper were interested to know answers to the following questions: "*where can the system be placed during emergency and who should have access to the LifeRescue*".

All the participants responded to these questions as follows: "*access to the GUI should be given to the ERs who are working at the emergency site*". The reason for this statement was given by the fire chief "*he/she does not get orders from the support room (110 room). Fire chief just asks the support room to provide additional resources whenever he/she needs during emergency response*".

FC has also mentioned "*he is the one who takes decisions at the emergency site. So, he is the one who is suitable for having the GUI access*". Furthermore, participants who work as CM and SDL mentioned "*we would also like to get access to the GUI as they should also obtain the awareness of the situation to guide SDs*". However, SDs mentioned "*if we carry small tablets with us, then we will get the information about the victims and their location. However, carrying the tablet would hinder our performances*".

When it comes to police service participants, the police chief mentioned that "*access to the LifeRescue GUI should be given to both control room (112) and police chief who are at emergency site*". The reason for this statement was given by the police chief as "*he/she get orders from the control room (112). Police chief informs the control room and wait for their decisions during emergency response process*". Police chief also mentioned that "*he waits for the decisions that are taken by the superiors at the emergency site. However, having access to the GUI can make him to recognize the suspected person*".

Existing Systems vs LifeRescue GUI. Firefighters do not use any kind of ICT system that can help them to acquire the needed/relevant information automatically from the emergency site. Usually, they take notes manually from the emergency site and later use the collected information to make reports in "Microsoft word document" after any kind of fire emergency. These reports are then sent to Directorate for Civil Protection and Emergency (DSB) [32]. All this process is done through electronic mail.

Whereas, police use lots of ICT (decision-support) systems during emergency response, but they also do not have any kind of ICT system that can help them to acquire the needed information automatically from the emergency site. However, social media like twitter, Instagram and so on are being used by the police department to help them getting the awareness of the situation. However, this channel does not completely give the awareness of the situation. Generally, they collect information either manually from the emergency site or get from the fire chief. This information is then used in emergency reports that are created in the "Microsoft word document".

From our interview with the participants revealed that mainly 2 ICT systems in Norwegian crisis management have been used i.e., A crisis incident management (CIM) tool used by the police, and (2) LOCUS used by the fire and rescue service, and the health service.

CIMtool [33] is a software program for crisis management support, produced by One Voice AS, a company delivering crisis management solutions for a variety of organizations. It supports aspects of crisis management such as quality assurance, risk and vulnerability analyses, emergency planning, training, and evaluation. The purpose of this tool is to notify police personnel when major incidents occur. It supports notification and alerting of personnel through distribution lists for sending messages by email, SMS, and phone. The system provides the receiver with several response alternatives which are logged, so that the sender of a message can keep track on the status of each alerted individual [34]. It is currently used by many organizations that the police collaborate closely with, among others, the Directorate for Civil Protection and Emergency Planning (DSB), The Norwegian Civil Defense, and all Norwegian municipalities and county governors.

Whereas, LOCUS is a company delivering mission-critical solutions and products to the fire and rescue service as well as to the health service, among others (e.g. transport and logistics, security service companies). Its solutions are designed to reduce time constraints through being a tool for the emergency agencies to make the right decisions in relation to resource allocation. LOCUS' solutions are used by the 110 and 113 emergency call centrals (TransFire for the fire and rescue service and TransMed for the health service) and mobile devices installed in vehicles for the tactical personnel (TransMobile 7). The detailed information about the solutions can be found in [34]. However, both ICT systems, do not provide the information requirements (see Table 1) of the different ERs automatically from the emergency site as LifeRescue provides.

When we asked the participants for their opinion on the LifeRescue system, one participant stated as *"I like this new system and would find it helpful. In LifeRescue GUI, there are not many clicks and acquiring the relevant information is not complicated at all."* Another participant commented: *"Anyhow, I think this system would be useful. Usually, I should search a lot for information during emergency response. But, in this LifeRescue, I like the visibility of the key information".*

4.2 Quantitative Analysis

During workshop session, a SUS questionnaire has been used to document the participants' opinion on system usability. The results of the SUS responses are presented in Table 3.

Table 3. SUS scores (higher score implies better performance)

SUS questions	Mean agreement	SD
Q1. I think that I would like to use this system frequently	4.4	0.72
Q2. I found the system unnecessarily complex	1.4	0.81
Q3. I thought the system was easy to use	4	0.7
Q4. I think that I would need the support of a technical person to be able to use this system	1.4	0.52
Q5. I found the various functions in this system were well integrated	3.7	0.83
Q6. I thought there was too much inconsistency in this system	1.8	0.78
Q7. I would imagine that most people would learn to use this system very quickly	4.1	0.6
Q8. I found the system very cumbersome to use	1.8	0.63
Q9. I felt very confident using the system	3.7	0.44
Q10. I needed to learn a lot of things before I could get going with this system	1.4	0.83
Learnability dimension (Q4 and Q10)	1.4	
Usability dimension (other 8 questions)	3.11	

The SUS responses in Table 3 are described as follows. If the mean agreement scores are ≥ 4 out of 5, that means the participants Strongly Agreed that they felt confident using the LifeRescue prototype, it was easy to use and ERs would like to use. If the mean agreement scores are <3 out of 5, then the participants generally Disagreed with statements that the LifeRescue prototype was: unnecessarily complex or cumbersome (or required technical assistance), or inconsistent in format (i.e., the mean of the dissatisfaction ratings were on the range of Agree, Strongly Agree or Neutral for most answers to the positively enunciated questions and in the range of Disagree, Strongly Disagree or Neutral for most of the answers for the negatively enunciated questions).

Adjective Rating. The researchers in [29, 30] used an adjective scale by dividing the SUS scores as follows: *score of 0–25: worst, score of 25–39: poor, score of 39–52: OK, score of 52–85: excellent, and score of 85–100: best imaginable.* Authors of this paper also adapted the same adjective scale in our study. The results of the overall SUS scores of each participant response are presented in the Fig. 5. Based on the responses

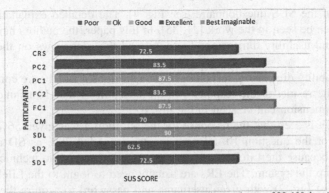

* Score of 25–39: poor, score of 39–52: OK, score of 52–85: excellent, and score of 85–100: best imaginable.
* SD = Smoke Diver, SDL= Smoke Diver Leader, CM = Crew manager, FC = Fire Chief, PC = Police Chief,
CRS = Control Room Supervisor.

Fig. 5. SUS scores based on each participant's response

given to the SUS questionnaire, the results show that all the participants have given rating above 60%. Therefore, the LifeRescue achieved "*Excellent and Best imaginable*" SUS rating. However, the SUS scores calculation can be found in [21]. From the Fig. 6, it is observed that SDL, FC1, PC1 and PC2 rated that the LifeRescue is "*best acceptable*" system which can be used to support their work during the indoor fire emergency search and rescue operation. The other participants also rated the system as "excellent" to be used to support their work during the indoor fire emergency search and rescue operation.

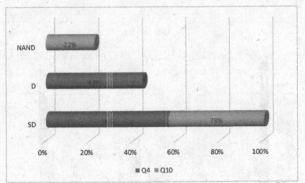

* SD = Strongly Disagree, D = Disagree, NAND = Neither Agree Nor Disagree.

Fig. 6. Responsesto learnability dimension

Learnability and Usability Dimensions. In the seminal work of [35], the researcher conducted factor analysis on the SUS statement and then defined two dimensions, i.e., learnability and usability. As per their analysis, the learnability dimension includes the statement 4 and 10, while the usability dimension includes the statements 1, 2, 3, 5, 6,

7, 8, and 9 of the SUS questionnaire (see Fig. 4). The detailed explanation of these dimensions can be seen in the work [21, 35]. In this paper, the authors have also used learnability and usability dimensions to understand the user views on the developed LifeRescue.

For learnability dimension, responses to the questions 4 and 10 are considered and calculated. The results of the responses to the questions 4 and 10 to understand the learnability dimension can be seen in the Fig. 6.

In Fig. 6, it is seen that the response for the question 4 was given 56% as SD and 44% as D. For the question 10, all participants responded 78% as SD and 22% as NAND. It is because the LifeRescue was very easy to use and no technical person is needed to setup the system. The ERs are usually need to login to the LifeRescue web application (see Fig. 2) with given username and password to acquire the emergency related information on the main screen (see Fig. 3). Therefore, with the responses, it is perceived that the LifeRescue was not much difficult to learn.

Whereas, for the usability dimension, the other 8 questions are considered. The responses to these 8 questions can be seen in the Fig. 7. Results reveal that all the participants responded as either SA or A or NAND for positive questions and SD, D or NAND for negative questions. From the results, it is again perceived as LifeRescue was easy to use. In an overall view, participants mentioned "the system is easy to learn, use and support them to achieve their goals during search and rescue operation". The participants also commented that the colors which are being used in the GUI are good enough to differentiate the different kind of victims and fire related information (see Fig. 3). Participants did not face any kind of usability problems.

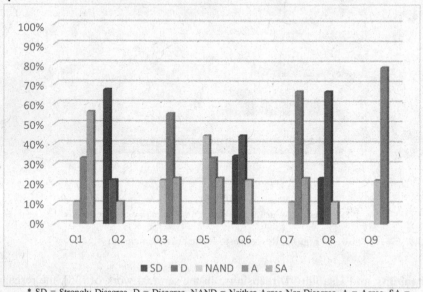

* SD = Strongly Disagree, D = Disagree, NAND = Neither Agree Nor Disagree, A = Agree, SA = Strongly Agree.

Fig. 7. Responses to usability dimension

5 Discussion and Conclusions

Emergency response operations demand well information access to support search and rescue tasks and decision-making at the emergency site and at the command and control center, because, the availability of the needed information is one of the bottlenecks [36]. However, in any kind of emergency response, upon arrival at an emergency location, first responders usually use lot of time gathering information to obtain an overview of the situation. The time for which first responders spend on gathering static and volatile situational information from affected people as well as from responsible persons at the emergency site can be reduced if they are given with accessibility or availability of the needed information [16]. Therefore, an approach was proposed which is a holistic way to access information during emergency search and rescue operations. Based on the approach, a LifeRescue information management system was developed to support different ERs for enhancing their response activities during fire emergency in a university building.

When a software system's development is complete, it is necessary to ensure that the outcome is successful. To check that, the design team must check whether the system satisfies the needs and wants of the user. To achieve this, user needs should not only be elicited by techniques such as surveys, focus groups, interviews etc., but they should also be reflected back to users via simulations in order to prototype the user requirements [37]. Therefore, in this paper, we present an evaluation of a developed LifeRescue information management system to ensure that user requirements (of different ERs in case of a fire emergency in the educational building) are met. In addition, we present the usability of the developed prototype.

To evaluate the user and usability requirements of the system, a workshop session was being held with 6 participants from fire and 3 from police departments for testing the developed LifeRescue. The workshop session was incorporated with a prototype demonstration and trail, semi-structured interview and a SUS questionnaire. The findings show that the participants felt that the developed system fits to their purposes and showed their satisfaction that the system fulfils the requirements. All participants mentioned that accessing diverse information from diverse sources was very easy. This information accessibility and availability can make them achieving the situational awareness. The participants also acknowledged that *"they prefer to use this system during any kind of fire emergency response"*.

Furthermore, the SUS questionnaire results reveal that all participant gave rating above 60%. That means that the LifeRescue achieved *"Excellent and Best imaginable"* SUS rating. The results show that participants SDL, FC1, PC rated that the LifeRescue is *"best acceptable"* system which can be used to support their work during the indoor fire emergency search and rescue operation. The other participants rated the system as *"excellent"* to be used to support their work during the indoor fire emergency search and rescue operation. When it comes to learnability and usability dimensions, results of the responses to the SUS questionnaire concludes that LifeRescue that the system is easy to use and learn. So, with this obtained results, answer the sub question which was mentioned at the beginning of the paper.

Based on the results of our study, it is anticipated that our methodology can be used for all types of emergencies and fulfils user requirements. Moreover, the lessons learned from this study are two-fold: Firstly, any emergency information system should be easy to use and fast enough to provide relevant/needed information to the involved ERs upon arrival at the emergency site. Another lesson is that ERs information requirements should be met with the support of ICT i.e., integrating diverse data sources, presenting, and sharing the right information to the right people in the right format at the right time which is critical in any emergency response situation.

There were some limitations associated to this study, such as the use of a simulated test environment and a reduced number of end-users. Firstly, the workshop session was carried out with a prototype demonstration and trail in a simulated setting instead of a real emergency response environment. So, testing the system in a real emergency settings through a field trial would be recommended. Secondly, the reduced number of participants in the user requirement and usability evaluation can be seen as an impediment of the applicability of the findings in a larger scale. However, the participants meaningfully represented the end-users of the system and in qualitative usability studies, a small number of participants can be sufficient for having valid results [38].

Our potential future research directions will be to develop the LifeRescue by adding the features that are recommended by the participants and test the implemented prototype in a realistic fire emergency response setting for making further improvements of the system.

Acknowledgements. We would like to owe our gratitude to the Grimstad fire and rescue service personnel, and Kristiansand police staff who supported and allocated their time for participating in the workshop session and semi-structured interviews. We would also like to appreciate Tina Comes and Jaziar Radianti for providing their support and help throughout our research.

References

1. Comes, T., Vybornova, O., Van de Walle, B.: Bringing structure to the disaster data typhoon: an analysis of decision-makers' information needs in the response to Haiyan. In: Proceedings of the AAAI Spring Symposium Series (SSS-15) on Structured Data for Humanitarian Technologies: Perfect Fit or Overkill (2015)
2. Nunavath, V., Prinz, A.: Taking the advantage of smartphone apps for understanding information needs of emergency response teams' for situational awareness: evidence from an indoor fire game. In: Kurosu, M. (ed.) HCI 2016. LNCS, vol. 9733, pp. 563–571. Springer, Cham (2016). doi:10.1007/978-3-319-39513-5_52
3. Nunavath, V., et al.: Representing fire emergency response knowledge through a domain modelling approach. In: Norsk konferanse for organisasjoners bruk av IT (2016)
4. Netten, N., et al.: Task-adaptive information distribution for dynamic collaborative emergency response. Int. J. Intell. Control Syst. 11(4), 238–247 (2006)
5. Endsley, M.R.: Theoretical underpinnings of situation awareness: a critical review. In: Situation Awareness Analysis and Measurement, pp. 3–32 (2000)
6. Kuusisto, R.: Common operational picture to precision management. In: Manage-Mental Information Flows in Crisis Management Network. Publications of the Ministry of Transport and Communications, Helsinki (2005)

7. Toner, E.S.: Creating situational awareness: a systems approach. In: Medical Surge Capacity: Workshop Summary. National Academies Press, Washington (2009)
8. Comes, T., et al.: Decision maps: a framework for multi-criteria decision support under severe uncertainty. Decis. Support Syst. **52**(1), 108–118 (2011)
9. Van de Walle, B., Turoff, M.: Decision support for emergency situations. Inf. Syst. E-Bus. Manag. **6**(3), 295–316 (2008)
10. Turoff, M., et al.: The design of a dynamic emergency response management information system (DERMIS). JITTA: J. Inf. Technol. Theory Appl. **5**(4), 1 (2004)
11. Nunavath, V., Prinz, A.: Reference architecture for emergency management operations. In: 8th IADIS International Conference on Information Systems. IADIS, Madeira (2015)
12. De Leoni, M., et al.: Emergency management: from user requirements to a flexible p2p architecture. In: Proceedings of 4th International Conference on Information Systems for Crisis Response and Management (ISCRAM 2007) (2007)
13. Lazar, J.: Web Usability: A User-centered Design Approach. Pearson Addison Wesley, Boston (2006)
14. Gulliksen, J., et al.: Key principles for user-centred systems design. Behav. Inf. Technol. **22** (6), 397–409 (2003)
15. Nielsen, J.: Usability engineering at a discount. In: Proceedings of the Third International Conference on Human-Computer Interaction on Designing and Using Human-Computer Interfaces and Knowledge Based Systems, 2nd edn., pp. 394–401. Elsevier Science Inc., Boston (1989)
16. Nunavath, V., Prinz, A., Comes, T.: Identifying first responders information needs: supporting search and rescue operations for fire emergency response. Int. J. Inf. Syst. Crisis Response Manag. (IJISCRAM) **8**(1), 25–46 (2016)
17. Lazar, J., Feng, J.H., Hochheiser, H.: Research Methods in Human-Computer Interaction. Wiley, Hoboken (2010)
18. Maguire, M.: Methods to support human-centred design. Int. J. Hum. Comput. Stud. **55**(4), 587–634 (2001)
19. Nunavath, V., Prinz, A.: LifeRescue: a web based application for emergency responders during fire emergency response. In: 2016 3rd International Conference on Information and Communication Technologies for Disaster Management (ICT-DM). IEEE (2016)
20. Frassl, M., Lichtenstern, M., Angermann, M.: Disaster management tool (DMT)-usability engineering, system architecture and field experiments. In: Farshchian, B.A., Divitini, M., Floch, J., Halvorsrud, R., Mora, S., Stiso, M. (eds.) The Workshop on Ambient Intelligence for Crisis Management, Pisa, Italy (2012). http://ceur-ws.org/
21. Brooke, J.: SUS-a quick and dirty usability scale. Usability Eval. Ind. **189**(194), 4–7 (1996)
22. Bangor, A., Kortum, P.T., Miller, J.T.: An empirical evaluation of the system usability scale. Int. J. Hum.-Comput. Interact. **24**(6), 574–594 (2008)
23. Lewis, J.R.: IBM computer usability satisfaction questionnaires: psychometric evaluation and instructions for use. Int. J. Hum.-Comput. Interact. **7**(1), 57–78 (1995)
24. Lewis, J.R.: Psychometric evaluation of the PSSUQ using data from five years of usability studies. Int. J. Hum.-Comput. Interact. **14**(3–4), 463–488 (2002)
25. Kirakowski, J., Corbett, M.: SUMI: the software usability measurement inventory. Br. J. Edu. Technol. **24**(3), 210–212 (1993)
26. Igbaria, M., Nachman, S.A.: Correlates of user satisfaction with end user computing: an exploratory study. Inf. Manag. **19**(2), 73–82 (1990)
27. Lund, A.M.: Measuring usability with the USE Questionnaire12.". Usability Interface **8**(2), 3–6 (2001)

28. Kirakowski, J., Claridge, N., Whitehand, R.: Human centered measures of success in web site design. In: Proceedings of the Fourth Conference on Human Factors & the Web (1998)
29. Bakhshi-Raiez, F., et al.: A usability evaluation of a SNOMED CT based compositional interface terminology for intensive care. Int. J. Med. Inform. **81**(5), 351–362 (2012)
30. Bangor, A., Kortum, P., Miller, J.: Determining what individual SUS scores mean: adding an adjective rating scale. J. Usability Stud. **4**(3), 114–123 (2009)
31. Nvivo: Nvivo Qualitative Content Analysis Tool (2015). http://www.qsrinternational.com/product
32. DSB: Directorate for Civil Protection and Emergency (2017). https://www.dsb.no/. Accessed 23 Jan 2017
33. OneVoice: Crisis Incident Management Tool (2016). https://onevoice.no/en/focus/crisis. Accessed 06 Sep 2016
34. Boden, A., Buscher, M., Zimmermann, M.L.A.: Domain Analysis II: User Interfaces and Interaction Design (2013). http://www.sec-bridge.eu/content/d02.3_domain_analysis_ii.pdf
35. Lewis, J.R., Sauro, J.: The factor structure of the system usability scale. In: Kurosu, M. (ed.) HCD 2009. LNCS, vol. 5619, pp. 94–103. Springer, Heidelberg (2009). doi:10.1007/978-3-642-02806-9_12
36. Seppänen, H., Virrantaus, K.: Shared situational awareness and information quality in disaster management. Saf. Sci. **77**, 112–122 (2015)
37. Maguire, M., Bevan, N.: User requirements analysis. In: Hammond, J., Gross, T., Wesson, J. (eds.) Usability. ITIFIP, vol. 99, pp. 133–148. Springer, Boston, MA (2002). doi:10.1007/978-0-387-35610-5_9
38. Nielsen, J.: Estimating the number of subjects needed for a thinking aloud test. Int. J. Hum. Comput. Stud. **41**(3), 385–397 (1994)

Usability Evaluation of Newly Developed Three-Dimensional Input Device for Drone Operation

Michiko Ohkura[1](✉), Hiroya Sano[1], and Yuya Mochiyoshi[2]

[1] Shibaura Institute of Technology, 3-7-5,
Toyosu, Koto-ku, Tokyo 135-8548, Japan
ohkura@sic.shibaura-it.ac.jp
[2] Mochiyoshi Engineering Development Co., Ltd., 1078-6, Oaza Imafuku,
Kawagoe-City, Saitama 350-1151, Japan

Abstract. As an input device suitable for operation in VR space, we developed a prototype in 2003. Comparison experiment results with other input devices, including game controllers, showed that our prototype had learnability and memorability advantages; that is, this device is suitable for intuitive operation in VR space. After the improvement of the device, it was placed on the market under the name Cyberbird. Moreover, we experimentally proposed the best combinations between a 3-DOF analog stick and two buttons on Cyberbird and six movements of drones: pitch, roll, yaw, throttle, take-off and landing. This article introduces the results of the experiment evaluating the usability of Cyberbird for older people and students unfamiliar with playing TV games using a game controller.

Keywords: Usability · Input device · Intuitive operation · Drone · Older users

1 Introduction

As an input device suitable for VR spaces, we developed a prototype in 2003. Comparison experiment results with other input devices (including game controllers) showed that our prototype had learnability and memorability advantages; that is, this device is suitable for intuitive operation in VR space [1]. Then, the device, which was named Cyberbird [2], was improved and placed on the market.

At the same time, drones used for rescue operations emerged, with advantages of no spatial restrictions. They have also begun to be used for entertainment. The Drone Race was held in California in 2015 [3], and a Bebop Drone [4] was developed for use with Oculus Rift. However, when operators control the drones that are currently available on the market, their controllers must be grasped with both hands and operators must be trained to control them.

We addressed this training requirement with Cyberbird, as it can provide intuitive drone operation. Then, we began to study how to apply Cyberbird to the intuitive operation of a drone.

Generally, there are six movements involved in flying drones: pitch, roll, throttle, yaw, take-off and landing. On the other hand, Cyberbird has 3-DOF movements with an analog stick and two buttons. Since drone operation is impossible by just using an

© Springer International Publishing AG 2017
M. Kurosu (Ed.): HCI 2017, Part II, LNCS 10272, pp. 499–511, 2017.
DOI: 10.1007/978-3-319-58077-7_40

analog stick, we had to examine drone-operation methods using Cyberbird to discover the best combination of drone movements and Cyberbird operations. Therefore, we performed an experiment to determine the best combination.

During the experiment, we recognized the necessity of improvement for better operability of Cyberbird. Thus, we improved its shape, and performed a comparative experiment to evaluate the usability of the improved version of Cyberbird. This article describes these experiments and improvements in detail.

2   Cyberbird Operation Methods

Figure 1 shows how to hold Cyberbird. The operator's thumb is placed on the analog stick, and both of her pointer and middle fingers are on specific buttons. Operators can control drones with these analog sticks and buttons.

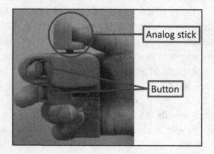

Fig. 1. Holding cyberbird

A drone has four flight control inputs: pitch, roll, yaw, and throttle (Fig. 2). The pitch input is the horizontally front and back movement parameters, and the roll is the horizontally left and right movement parameters. The yaw turns the drone left or right. The throttle moves it up or down.

Forward & backward   Left & right   Turn left & turn right   Up & down
(Pitch)   (Roll)   (Yaw)   (Throttle)

Fig. 2. Drone flight movements

First, we designed operation methods 1 and 2. Their differences are shown in Fig. 3. In operation method 1, when the operator turns the analog stick left or right, the drone moves horizontally left or right. When the operator pushes the buttons, the drone turns left or right. In operation method 2, when the operator turns the analog stick, the drone rotates. When the operator pushes the button, it moves horizontally.

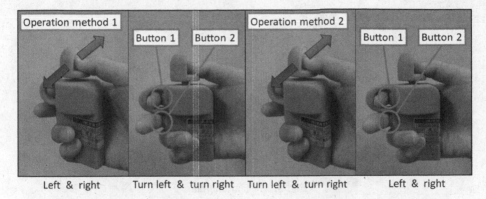

Left & right   Turn left & turn right   Turn left & turn right   Left & right

Fig. 3. Differences of operation methods 1 and 2

We designed operation methods (a) and (b). For example, in operation method 1(a), if the operator pushes button 1, the drone turns left, and it turns right when button 1 is quickly pushed twice. In operation method 1(b), when the operator pushes button 1, the drone turns left, and it turns right when button 2 is pushed. We designed four operation methods: 1(a), 1(b), 2(a), and 2(b). Their common operation methods are shown in Fig. 4.

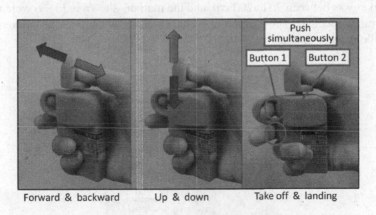

Forward & backward   Up & down   Take off & landing

Fig. 4. Common operation in all methods

3 Experimentto Determine Combination of Operations

3.1 Experimental System

A diagram of our system is shown in Fig. 5. The drone we used is the Parrot AR. Drone 2.0 [5]. The PC is connected to Cyberbird via USB and to the drone by Wi-Fi. The drone 2.0 has a front- and bottom- mounted cameras; we used the front camera and those images appeared on the PC. The operator manipulates the drone using Cyberbird

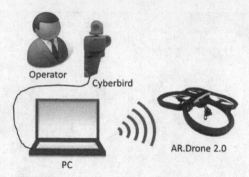

Fig. 5. System diagram

while looking at the image on the PC. The system sends control commands to the drone 2.0 based on input from Cyberbird. The library we used to control the drone is ARDroneForP5 [6].

3.2 Experimental Method

The operator sequentially captured four markers using the drone camera. Figure 6 shows the numbered markers targeted on a pole extending to the ceiling. The height of each marker was between 70 to 200 cm, and the markers shown in Fig. 6 were used for both operation methods. The operator also confirmed the position of the markers before starting the capture operation.

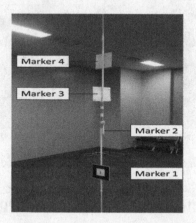

Fig. 6. Marker positions and orientations

First, the operator controls the take-off of the drone from 2.1 m away. A few seconds later, the operator starts to capture the markers. In the normal state, the image from the drone's inner camera with the black square is shown on the PC (Fig. 7). When

Fig. 7. Capturing markers (Color figure online)

the marker is in the black square and the drone is in the marker's range, a green box is displayed on the marker (Fig. 7). This is the successful-capture state. After the operator successfully captures the marker, he starts to capture the next marker. After capturing the fourth marker, he lands the drone. This experiment's methodology is based on Higuchi and Rekimoto [7].

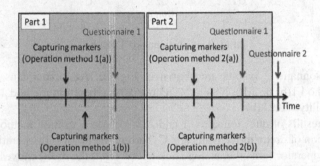

Fig. 8. Experimental procedure

An example of our experimental procedure is shown in Fig. 8. We divided our experiment into parts 1 and 2. At the end of part 1, the participants answered questionnaire 1. After finishing part 2, they answered questionnaire 2. Table 1 shows the items in questionnaire 1. We also changed the combination of operation methods in each part for every participant. In questionnaire 2, participants explained which operation method they preferred and explained why.

Table 1. Items for questionnaire 1

Number	Question
Q1	Which operation method was easiest to understand?
Q2	Which operation method was simplest to use?
Q3	Which operation method did you use most confidently?

3.3   Experimental Results

Our participants were 12 male students in their 20 s at the Shibaura Institute of Technology. Figure 9 shows the results of questionnaire 1. Operation method 1(b) showed the best score among the four methods because it is more intuitive for rolling with an analog stick than with buttons. It is also easier to assess left-right orientation using buttons 1 and 2.

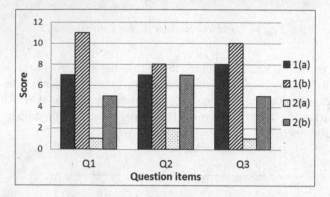

Fig. 9. Questionnaire 1 result

The questionnaire 2 results are shown in Fig. 10. All participants chose either operation method 1(b) or 2(b). Nine of 12 chose 1(b). Operation method 1(b) has more general versatility than 2(b).

From the results of questionnaires 1 and 2, we chose operation method 1(b) as the best combination of drone movements and Cyberbird operations. In operation method 1 (b), when the operator turns the analog stick left or right, the drone moves horizontally left or right. When the operator moves the analog stick forward or backward, the drone moves horizontally forward or backward. When the operator moves the analog stick upward or downward, the drone moves horizontally upward or downward. Also if the

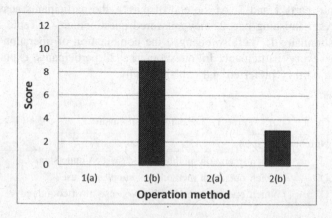

Fig. 10. Questionnaire2 result

operator pushes button 1, the drone turns left, and it turns right when button 2 is pushed. Also, if the operator pushes buttons 1 and 2 simultaneously, the drone takes off or lands.

4 Improvement of Cyberbird

During the above experiment, we noticed a problem with Cyberbird in that it was difficult to transmit the force of the fingers when pressing down the analog stick or pushing buttons. Based on the knowledge that the grasping force increases as the contact area between the hand and the cylindrical object increases [8], we made new parts with a 3D printer and attached them to Cyberbird to increase its contact area with the hand. We will call this "improved Cyberbird" from here on (Figs. 11 and 12).

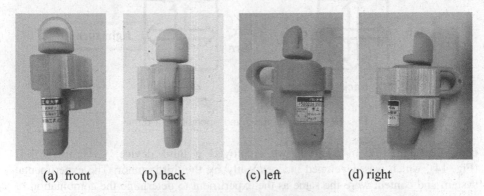

(a) front   (b) back   (c) left   (d) right

Fig. 11. Cyberbird with new attachments

Fig. 12. Top view of holding Cyberbird with new attachments

5 Experiment for Usabilityevaluation

5.1 Experimental Method

To evaluate the usability of improved Cyberbird for drone operation, we performed an experiment, in which we compared two devices, the improved Cyberbird and a game

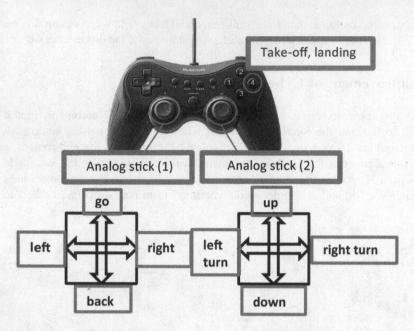

Fig. 13. Game controller and operations of drone

controller (Fig. 13). In addition, we employed a third device, Cyberbird Mk-II (Fig. 14), which was developed independently by the third author. The experimental system and content were the same as the experiment to determine the combination of operations described in Sect. 3. The operator captured four markers while operating a drone with the improved Cyberbird, and then with a game controller. The order of using the two devices was counter-balanced.

A questionnaire and required time for capturing markers were employed for evaluation. Operators were asked six questions on a five-point Likert scale as shown in Table 2 after operation. Required time was measured from take-off to landing of the drone.

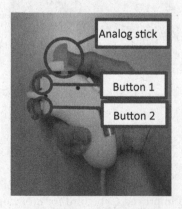

Fig. 14. Cyberbird Mk-II

Table 2. Items for questionnaire

Number	Question
Q1	Was the operation simple?
Q2	Was the operation easy?
Q3	Were you able to memorize the operation?
Q4	Were you able to do what you wanted?
Q5	Did you enjoy the operation?
Q6	Did you satisfy the operation?

5.2   Experimental Results

The experiment was performed employing eight older people in their 60's and 70's with no video game experience, eight male students in their 20's with less experience of video game, and eight male students in their 20's with more video game experience. "With less experience" means that they play video games fewer than five times a month, and "with more experience" means that they play video games often. Figure 15 shows an experimental scene. In the experiment for older users, only Cyberbird and the game controller were employed for comparison because Cyberbird Mk-II had not been produced at that time.

Fig. 15. Experimental setting

The questionnaire results for older users are shown in Fig. 16. Because of the significant differences between the two devices in Q2 and Q3 ($p < 0.05$, $p < 0.01$), the improved Cyberbird has significantly better learnability and memorability than the game controller for older users. Figure 17 shows the required time for each task. The time in the case of using the improved Cyberbird is significantly shorter than that in the case of using the game controller.

The questionnaire results for the students are shown in Figs. 18 and 19. Although there are no significant main effects of devices for "with less game experience" students, there are significant main effects in Q1, Q4, and Q5 for "with more game experience" students. From the results of multiple comparisons, the game controller is

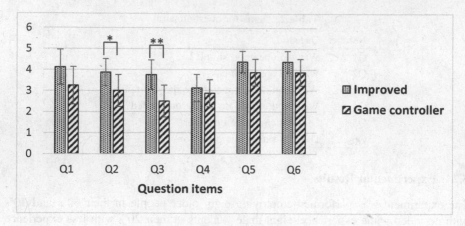

Fig. 16. Questionnaire results for older users

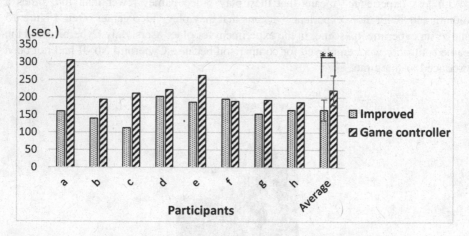

Fig. 17. Required time for each device for older users

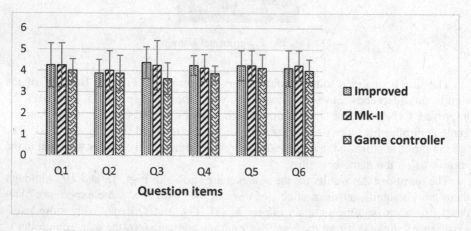

Fig. 18. Questionnaire results for students with less game experience

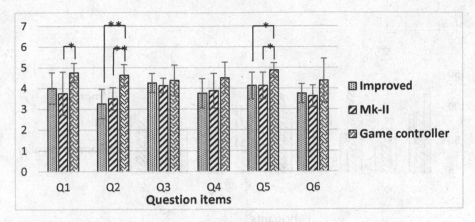

Fig. 19. Questionnaire results for students with more game experience

significantly simpler, has significantly better operability, and is significantly more enjoyable for "with more game experience" students. Figures 20 and 21 show the required times. There are no significant main effects of devices for both student groups.

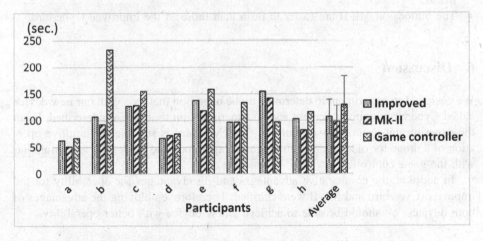

Fig. 20. Required time for each device for students with less game experience

We obtained the following results.

- The improved Cyberbird has better usability than the game controller for older users with no game experience.
- The improved Cyberbirdand Mk-II show no difference with the game controller for students unfamiliar with the game controller.
- The game controller has better usability than the improved Cyberbird and Mk-IIfor students familiar with the game controller.

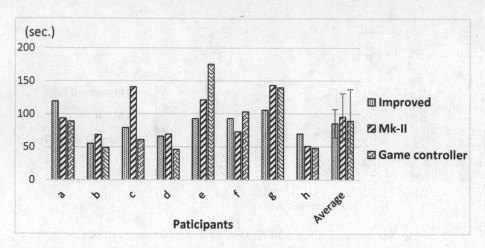

Fig. 21. Required time for each device for students with more game experience

In addition, the students familiar with the game controllers commented in the questionnaire as follows.

- The analog stick of the improved Cyberbird has better operability than that of Mk-II.
- The buttons on Mk-II are easier to push than those of the improved Cyberbird.

6 Discussion

We designed an experiment to determine drone operation methods with our new device called Cyberbird; its improvement and an experiment on usability are described. From the experimental results, it was clarified that Cyberbird is suitable for intuitive operation of a drone for older users with no game experience and those who are unfamiliar with the game controller.

In addition, the comparative advantages and disadvantages for operability for the improved Cyberbird and Mk-II were clarified. Therefore, employing the advantages of both devices, we should be able to achieve a new device with better operability.

7 Conclusions

To apply the device we developed for intuitive operation in VR space to drone operation, we performed the following.

- Experiment to decide the combinations of drone movements and Cyberbird operations.
- Improvement of Cyberbird by new attachments for better transmission of force from fingers.
- Evaluation experiment to compare the usability of improved Cyberbird with the game controller.

Finally, we reached the conclusion that the improved Cyberbird is suitable for intuitive operation of a drone for older users with no game experience and those who are unfamiliar with the game controller.

In addition, combining the advantages of the improved Cyberbird and Mk-II should allow us to achieve a new device with better operability.

References

1. Ohkura, M., Mochiyoshi, Y., Nakayama, K.: Development of a device for manipulation in immersive 3-dimensional space. J. Hum. Interface Soc. **6**(4), 371–377 (2004). (in Japanese)
2. Mochiyoshi Engineering Development Co., Ltd.: Mochiyoshi Engineering Development Co., Ltd. http://www.mochiyoshi.co.jp/
3. Ground Flight, Inc.: National Drone Racing Championships. http://dronenationals.com/
4. Parrot.: Parrot Bebop Drone. http://www.parrot.com/usa/products/bebop-drone/
5. Parrot: AR.Drone 2.0. Parrot new wi-fi quadricopter (2015). http://ardrone2.parrot.com/
6. Engineering Navi: ARDroneForP5: Processing, You can control AR.Drone frome Processing. http://kougaku-navi.net/ARDroneForP5/index_en.html
7. Higuchi, K., Rekimoto, J.: Flying head: a head motion synchronization mechanism for unmanned aerial vehicle control. In: Proceedings of CHI EA 2013, pp. 2029–2038 (2013)
8. Yakou, T., et al.: Force transmission between hand and cylindrical objects at the grip states. Trans. Jpn. Soc. Mech. Eng. C **60**(573), 1721–1726 (1994). (in Japanese)

A Feedback Delivery System for Communal Energy Consumption Practices

Mina Rahimian[✉] and Lisa Domenica Iulo

Penn State, University Park, State College, PA, USA
{Mxr446,ldil}@psu.edu

Abstract. In recent years, a pervasive shift of thinking has emerged in distributing the existing electrical grid in urban areas from centralized power generations to decentralized local power infrastructures, as a promising contribution to the energy resiliency of cities. Communities and neighborhoods adopting distributed energy resources as a means towards decentralization are designated to communal energy co-generation practices. Along with the co-generation of energy in such communities, it is as important to view energy consumption more than a personal decision but as a response to shared experiences and resources. Re-visioning energy consumption requires re-defining users as an indispensable element of a community through their participation in groups. This paper explores the benefit of computational means of energy feedback delivery, structured upon a collaborative incentive program, as an effective intellectual means of performing a participatory energy sharing dynamics within users of a community. We use the word "participatory" rather deliberately to place emphasize on humans as the end users of community-scale local power infrastructures, and on the institutional forces that reimagine the role of human action on constructing energy resiliency in such communities.

Keywords: Participatory · Persuasion design · Feedback delivery system · Social resiliency · Energy sharing

1 Introduction

Urban areas and the building sector have proven to be a major source of energy consumption and waste. Industrialization, urbanization, along with the electrification of cities with fossil fuel based power plants [3] have resulted in 75% of global energy use and 80% in global greenhouse gas emissions to occur in urban areas [2, 6]. As an approach addressing these effects, researchers have suggested transforming to self-sustained and dispersed urban settlements by benefiting from the concentration of people and industries in communities [14].

Community microgrids are a result of this approach applauding sustainable patterns of local urbanization by communal means of supplying and utilizing energy. Herein, community microgrids are defined as building-integrated, decentralized, clean energy systems that are situated within clearly defined electrical and regional urban boundaries. Within these boundaries, community microgrids interconnect a certain number of buildings and energy loads with on-site renewable and clean energy co-generation

© Springer International Publishing AG 2017
M. Kurosu (Ed.): HCI 2017, Part II, LNCS 10272, pp. 512–521, 2017.
DOI: 10.1007/978-3-319-58077-7_41

technologies (i.e. solar, wind, fuel cells, etc.) and storage facilities (i.e. batteries). The uniqueness of such urban energy systems is their technical ability to disconnect ("island") from the larger power grid and sustain based on independent energy generation for a couple of hours to several days, providing resilience in the face of natural or human events.

Energy resiliency in community microgrids depends on two major factors; first are the consisting digital technologies at the microgrids' operational system which technically enable the integration of distributed energy resources, and facilitate networking and communications among all its energy generation, transmission and distribution subsystems [11–13]. Second are the energy users dwelling in these communities which benefit from the existing technologies to manage their energy consumption [4]. Energy metering devices and feedback delivery technologies are the immediate tools for users of community microgrids to deal with on a daily basis. These tools are designed to give information on energy pricing throughout the day, deliver quantified feedback on the users' energy consumption pattern, and provide users the basis for controlling their energy consumption and employing energy management practices [7, 8].

Energy metering devices act as a medium for communication between each individual user and the grid by making the grid transparent and filling the gap of energy illiteracy. The concept of delivering feedback on users' energy consumption is based on the assumption that users lack a tangible awareness and understanding about the quantity of energy consumed by their daily rituals. It is widely accepted among researchers that energy consumption unawareness limits the consumers' capacity on deciding to take conservation actions [5, 9]. Although some challenge the concept of changing people's energy behavior as being a non-effective and non-laudable strategy for promoting energy conservation actions [1, 10], several studies suggest that delivering high quality energy-related information on users' activities and consumption patterns has the potential of motivating users in adopting energy conservation behaviors in the long run [15].

2 Problem Statement

Building occupants of a community microgrid are the ultimate end users of these local energy infrastructures. Energy is generated from communal resources in community microgrids and is shared among the community members. Therefore, users' energy actions not only to shape their individual consumption history, but also influence the way that energy is utilized and managed as a common good in such shared energy systems. While community microgrid technologies are building efficiencies, and bolstering the resilience of energy systems, it is necessary and vital to view community members as more than just passive energy/service users.

Co-generation practices of supplying energy also calls for collective strategies of energy co-consumption for community members to be aware of and to employ. While benefiting from conventional energy metering devices in community microgrids form a good strategy for raising energy consumption awareness among individual energy users, its utilization in community microgrids is limiting when users are treated as passive energy consumers - neglecting the collective modes of energy consumption.

Studying users' experiences in consuming energy in community microgrids requires re-defining users as 'active,' recognizing that their energy consumption behaviors directly influences the community entity while considering their communal modes of living, working and interactions. This follows a longer tradition of participation and signals new opportunities for collective action in the making of communities and cities at large.

3   System Overview

Studying the demand side in community microgrids, this paper recommends a shift in focus on the community's energy use rather than individual energy consumers as the key unit of analysis. The stimulus of a community wide energy co-consumption proposed in this paper is structured upon an incentive-based energy exchange mechanism, incentivizing users to share energy among each other. The proposed energy exchange mechanism is a collective persuasion model aiming to accomplish persuasion design objectives by actively engaging users in treating energy consumption as a community endeavor. This model is manifested through the design of effective mobile and associated web portals. In the next section, the two underlying constituents of the energy exchange mechanism are explained through a simple use case scenario that presents the operation of the system (Fig. 1).

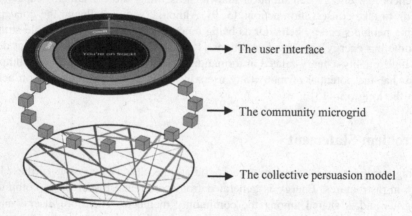

The user interface

The community microgrid

The collective persuasion model

Fig. 1. A conceptual figure of the energy exchange mechanism and its constituents

3.1   The Collective Persuasion Model

User Environment: The context for implementing the energy exchange mechanism is a conceptual prototype of a residential community microgrid that is home to a diversity of intense energy users. The variegation of users in this community plays an important role in driving the system since their different energy consumption patterns intensifies the possibility of energy exchanges to take place.

Operation: In this conceptual prototype the operation of the energy exchange mechanism results from a pro-environmental cap-and-trade strategy incentivizing user's participation and collaboration for saving energy in the community. This strategy provides targeted incentives for users of a microgrid to manage their actions on utilizing energy based on the energy pricing throughout the day and the community's overall energy fluctuations and demand.

The energy of the hypothesized community microgrid is provided and shared by a common source of power generated on-site via renewable and clean energy technologies (i.e. solar, fuel cells, combined heat and power). A customized currency for the energy transaction taking place; *"energy-tokens (eT),"* is defined as an established value for energy based on its pricing throughout the day and the average energy use per capita. Energy-tokens are assigned to each household of the community monthly based on the number of family members. Three shares of energy-tokens are available for allocation and transaction:

- Debit-eT (Debit-tokens): represents the first and main share of energy that each household receives every month according to their number of family members. The specific quantity of the allocated debit-tokens is anticipated to be enough for the family's monthly usage based on their history of energy use, users' demographic analysis, and the environment's energy demand specificities.
- Credit-eT (Credit-tokens): represents the second share of energy assigned to each household on a monthly basis as a trading mechanism for obtaining extra energy. In this case by using from the credit-tokens share, the household gets charged by energy-tokens.
- Community-eT (Community-tokens): represents a third share of energy-tokens belonging to the entire community households. It's a system for purchasing and selling extra energy-tokens when individual households have already used their limited share of debit and credit tokens. By using from the community-tokens the household gets charged both energy-tokens and actual money.

As mentioned, each month every household receives two constant shares of debit-energy tokens and credit-energy tokens. The household's monthly energy usage is tracked using debit-energy tokens first. In a typical scenario, household energy can be managed through the use of debit and credit tokens. If a household's consumption goes beyond the limits of the second share of energy-tokens (credit-energy tokens) in a month, leaving the user in need of extra energy-tokens, the shared community-token account can be borrowed against, providing household's access to additional energy tokens. By using energy-tokens from this shared account, the user owes the community both energy-tokens and actual monetary amounts due at the end of the following month. In order to prevent users from continuously depending on the credit and community energy accounts for purchasing extra energy, the energy price follows an ascending pattern.

Diverse households with different energy consumption patterns increases the probability that, at the end of a month, some users will have performed efficiently and other users performing more or less inefficient in terms of energy consumption. This means every month there are some users selling their extra energy-tokens to the community, some buying the energy-tokens, some staying in the limits of their debit-energy share and receiving monetary rewards and some crossing the lines of efficiency and paying back money to the system. Through this cap-and-trade energy exchange mechanism it is expected that energy and money transactions constantly occur in the scale of the community and become the main driver of the community's collective consumption efforts.

3.2   The User Interface

Below, the proposed collective persuasion model have been merged with current mobile product/services, including an application for phones, tablets, and home dashboards (Fig. 2).

In the design of the energy feedback delivery interface, information is presented in combination with elements of persuasion design geared towards positive community engagement and collective energy consumption practices. User-centered user-experience design principles were followed, including the use of:

- easily perceived and remembered metaphors conveyed through words, signs, and images;
- appropriate organization of data;
- high quality visualization of information;
- efficient movement within different tabs, menus, and control panels for the formation of a mental model;
- modes of interaction for an effective input and output feedback sequencing;

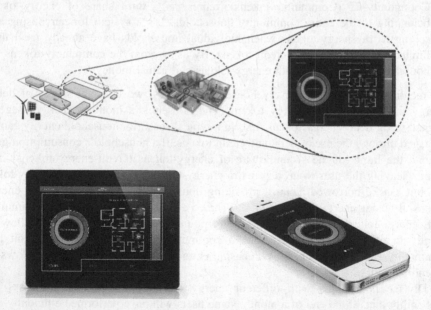

Fig. 2. The energy exchange system is presented in many manifestations through home dashboards, tablets, and phones.

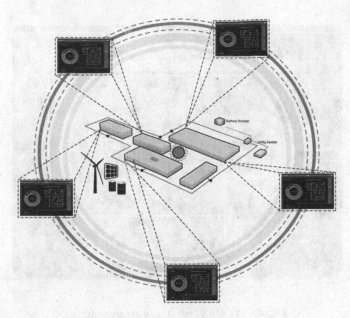

Fig. 3. The interface in this strategy is a communicative web-service device serving as a medium between the users, the community, and the grid

- high quality visual appearance; and
- high quality visual design principles such as scale, proportion, rhythm, symmetry and balance.

Additionally, effective principles of environmental psychology for inducing collective behavior among community members were adopted:

- Self and else comparison as an effective stimulus for taking action
- Monetary and ethical rewards and penalties as consequence motivation techniques coming after a behavior (Fig. 3).

The interface graphically displays three different, but related set of data on the household's personal and communal energy information under three separate tabs. The information displayed in these tabs help users perceive their personal and group benefits of making more efficient energy consumption decisions and understand the payoffs of taking conservation actions for themselves and for their community. The "YOURS" tab displays personal information on each household's debit and credit-energy accounts, the "OURS" tab is specified to community's energy information including displaying the community-energy account, and the "TIPS" tab" is designed for recommending energy conservation actions and tips based on the household's overall consumption pattern and energy pricing during the day.

"YOURS" Tab: As mentioned, this tab represents household's personal energy information and includes graphics and information on:

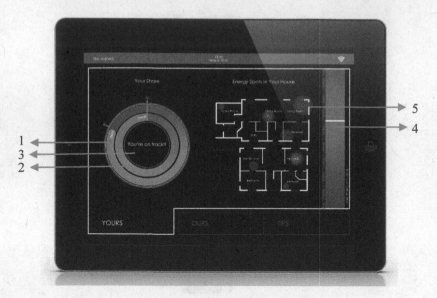

Fig. 4. "YOURS" tab (Color figure online)

1. Debit-energy account and the user's status in terms of using the associated energy-tokens.
2. Credit-energy account and the user's status in terms of using the associated energy-tokens.
3. Informative messages on the user's personal energy accounts.
4. Overall energy efficiency status of the house.
5. A simplified plan of the user's house displaying color-coded spots in the house that are consuming energy i.e.by specifying the location of electrical equipment. The intensity of the energy consumed is signaled through graphically keyed displayed color. For instance, red signals high energy consumption and green signals low energy consumption (Fig. 4).

"OURS" Tab: This tab displays information mainly on the community's energy status. The graphics displayed in this tab include:

6. The community's overall stance of community's energy performance (Fig. 5).
7. The user's contribution to the community as a member as an ethical incentive.
8. The community-energy account and the community's status in terms of using community-energy tokens.
9. The user's usage from community-energy tokens.
10. Informative messages on the community's energy account and the user's position within.

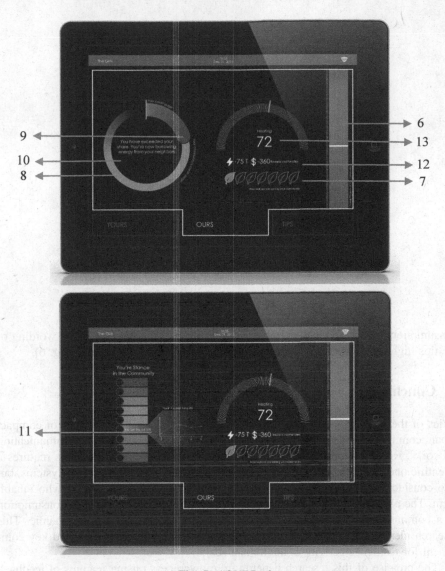

Fig. 5. "OURS tab

11. Visual evaluation of each household's current and past energy behavior in addition to graphically displaying the user's stance in the overall community's energy consumption.
12. The user's status on monetary rewards and penalties.
13. The house's temperature setting.

"TIPS" Tab: Displays recommended energy conservation suggestions and tips for the user. The suggested recommendations are based on the household's energy

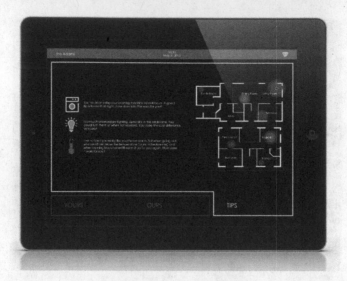

Fig. 6. "TIPS" tab

consumption history and the energy pricing during the day. Moreover, the wording of the tips highlight the personal benefits of taking the suggested actions (Fig. 6).

4 Conclusion

Cities of the future are envisioned to be comprised of a plentiful number of compact urban communities with shared energy facilities and concentrated communication networks. Resilient approaches to energy production in such communities requires a scientific understanding of not only the deployed technologies and digital systems, but also consideration of communities as built environments and the people who inhabit them. The purpose of this research is to advance a novel view on energy consumption as a community endeavor by fostering a cooperative energy-sharing dynamic. This research identifies co-production and co-consumption as the interconnected key component for resilience activity at the human scale.

The premise of this research benefits from awareness-raising features of feedback delivery technologies as means for information and communication facilitation. Therefore, the focus is on the user as the smartest component of a community microgrid system rather than any so-called smart technological device. Users' co-consumption behavior, collaboration and participation in a community microgrid, shapes the use of shared-energy resources, linking energy resiliency to a community's collective intelligence.

Acknowledgements. The authors are grateful for the contributions that Daniel Cardoso Llach made to this research. The support of the Penn State Department of Architecture, Stuckeman School, and the Stuckeman Center for Design Computing (SCDC) in the development of this work and the work to follow is also appreciated.

References

1. Aune, M.: Energy comes home. Energy Policy **35**(11), 5457–5465 (2007)
2. Bastiononi, S., Pulselli, F., Tiezzi, E.: The problem of assigning responsibility for greenhouse gas emissions. Ecol. Econ. **49**(3), 253–257 (2004)
3. Dodman, D.: Blaming cities for climate change? An analysis of urban greenhouse gas emissions inventories. Environ. Urbanization **21**(1), 185–201 (2009)
4. Farhangi, H.: The path of the smart grid. IEEE Power Energy **8**(1), 18–28 (2010)
5. Froehlich, J., Findlater, L., Landay, J.: The design of eco-feedback technology. In: Proceedings of the SIGCHI Conference on Human Factors in Computing Systems, pp. 1999–2008, Atlanta (2010)
6. Grubler, A., Bai, X., Buettner, T., Dhakal, S., Fisk, D., Ichinose, T., Keirstea, J.E., Sammer, G., Satterthwaite, D., Schulz, N.B., Shah, N., Steinberger, J., Weisz, H.: Urban energy systems (Chap. 18). In: Global Energy Assessment. Toward a Sustainable Future, pp. 1307–1400. International Institute for Applied System Analysis, Cambridge, UK and New York, NY, USA. Cambridge University Press, Laxenburg (2012)
7. Ipakchi, A., Albuyeh, F.: Grid of the future. Are we ready to transit to a smart grid? IEEE Power Energy **7**(2), 52–62 (2009)
8. Kang, S.J., Park, J., Oh, K., Park, H.: Scheduling-based real time energy flow control strategy for building energy management system. Energy Build. **75**, 239–248 (2014)
9. Lutzenhiser, L.: Social and behavioral aspects of energy. Ann. Rev. Energy Environ. **18**(1), 247–289 (1993)
10. Mostavi, E., Asadi, S., Boussaa, D.: Development of a new methodology to optimize building life cycle cost, environmental impacts, and occupant satisfaction. Energy **121**, 606–615 (2017)
11. Paglia, T.K.: Energy improvement districts and local energy production. Dissertation Master of Regional Planning Dissertation, Cornell University, Ithaca, NY (2011)
12. Rahimian, M., Cardoso-Llach, D., Iulo, L.D.: Participatory energy management in building networks. In: Sustainable Human-Building Ecosystem, pp. 27–35. American Society of Civil Engineers, Pittsburgh (2015)
13. Sherman, G.R.: Sharing local energy infrastructure - organizational models for implementing microgirds and district energy systems in urban commercial districts. Dissertation Masters of City Planning, Massachusetts Institute of Technology, Cambridge, MA (2007)
14. Steadman, P.: Energy and patterns of land use. Energy Archit. **30**(3), 62–67 (1977)
15. Yu, Z., Fung, B., Haghighat, F., Yoshino, H., Morofsky, D., Shenoy, P.: A systematic procedure to study the influence of occupant behavior on building energy consumption. Energy Build. **43**(6), 1409–1417 (2011)

Development of a Concept for Evaluation User Acceptance and Requirements for NFC Based E-ticketing in Public Transport

Gertraud Schäfer[✉], Andreas Kreisel, Denise Rummler, and Ulrike Stopka

Technische Universität Dresden, Dresden, Germany
{gertraud.schaefer,andreas.kreisel,denise.rummler,
ulrike.stopka}@tu-dresden.de

Abstract. In frame of OPTIMOS project (Open, Practical Infrastructures for Mobile Services) an open practical ecosystem based on Near Field Communication (NFC) will be developed and demonstrated by different implemented use cases in the field of public transport services in two German regions. One of the main objects is e-ticketing. For the generic definition of the OPTIMOS application (APP) user requirements are surveyed among the recruited friendly user group. Based on the results of different research studies and a conducted pretest among a student group an evaluation concept with a user-centred approach is developed and discussed.

Keywords: Mobility application · User requirements · Usability · Public transport · Evaluation concept · User-centered design

1 Motivation

Digital applications and services increasingly determine economic, social and personal life. Nowadays the smartphone as a personal device acts more and more as key and access for all kind of digital services, so also in public transport. Already in 2013, more than 50% of public transport passengers used mobility APPs on their smartphones searching for travel information or purchasing e-tickets [14]. They can enable an easy and comfortable way to navigate through the public transport network, because users do not have to deal with complex timetables or complex tariff information. The German public transport sector is traditionally organized regionally by some hundreds transport operators with different pricing schemes, fare conditions, e-ticket infrastructure and systems. For users it is nearly impossible to know all the regional specifics and to use public transport services on the spot without studying detailed information and to purchase ticket in advance. Till now passengers are used to be provided with real time schedule information, routed and navigated to a destination, or informed about ticket purchase. In 2015 the Innovation Centre for Mobility and Social Change in Germany tested 74 mobility APPs available at Google Play Store or at Apple Store. Almost all provide information about intermodal transport connections

© Springer International Publishing AG 2017
M. Kurosu (Ed.): HCI 2017, Part II, LNCS 10272, pp. 522–533, 2017.
DOI: 10.1007/978-3-319-58077-7_42

but only half could calculate ticket fares [9]. Purchasing and paying electronic tickets via a personal access by smartphone application has been established in different regions but is still not realized as an unique service in public transport all over Germany. To increase customer acceptance for public transport services it is necessary to implement an open ecosystems for mobile services, which can be used without discrimination by service and technology providers as it has been well-known and used for airline or railway services for years. NFC mobile devices are seen as generic platforms that should support Public Transport e-ticketing worldwide.

With respect to usability and user experience for mobility APPs different problems can be assumed e.g. users are often not sufficiently supported in their current context and too many concepts from the desktop area are still used for mobile applications. One challenge for the accompanying research is to actively involve the potential users in the development process of the mobile APPs in order to communicate their requirements and feedbacks in the development process of the open system.

Therefore friendly users in two German test regions are recruited and provided with NFC mobile devices or NFC Universal Integrated Circuit Card (UICC). For testing the new implemented services the specific APPs in the test regions have to be defined and developed. In this context TU Dresden surveys user requirements for generic definition of the OPTIMOS APPs and will afterwards evaluate the user acceptance in field tests with the friendly user group. Based on desktop research results and a conducted pretest among a student group an evaluation concept is developed.

2   Project Presentation

OPTIMOS research project defines an open, practical ecosystem connecting the world of public transport with the world of mobile communication. It will be developed, tested and defined use cases will be evaluated. This approach uses open standards. Therefore the project collaborates with international standardization bodies like the European Committee for Standardization (CEN), GSM Association (GSMA), NFC-Forum to ensure acceptance for passengers, public transport provides and device manufacturers. The project work is funded from the German Federal Ministry of Economic Affairs and Energy and includes relevant stakeholders and associated partners from all parts of the ecosystem like IT-system and -security provider, mobile network operators, handset makers, public transport industry.

3   Desktop Research on Customer Requirements on Digital Services and Mobility Application

For analysing public transport passengers' needs and requirements on digital services and especially on mobility APPs a desk top research was carried out by focusing on two different objectives. First we reviewed four general mobility studies in Germany and secondly the results of customer requirements on mobility APPs, evaluated in the frame of four research project.

By summarising the result of four general mobility studies [4–6,15] we detected that digital services and digital cross linkage between different transport modes will be more and more important for realising public transport in the next decades and will influence the user behaviour. Multi- and intermodal services need mobility platforms with digital information, routing, navigation and e-ticketing services supporting the individual transport chains. A big challenge is the creation and the commitment on interoperability by creating technical standards and interfaces for digital services. Implementing improved information and communication technology (ICT) access barriers to public passenger transport can be reduced. At the same time additional mobility offers can develop the public transport system as the backbone of the future multimodal system supporting the digital service chain: information – navigation – ticket purchasing – ticket control.

As the result of the further four research studies [1–3,17] concerning user requirements on mobility application five usability meta-categories [1] could be underlined with the aspects shown in Table 1.

It can be clearly seen users expect simple and intuitive mobile applications with clear and comprehensible visualization and reliable real-time information.

Those results are going to be validated for definition the OPTIMOS APPs. Therefore, a workshop concept is developed by the principles of Design Thinking with the tools personas, scenarios and journey mapping.

4   Pretest

In preparation of the usability study for definition a generic concept for the OPTIMOS APP a pretest was conducted with a non-representative student group. Aim was to collect first ideas about specific requests on mobility APPs. On the one hand we get first impressions what kind of functions are known, often used and appreciated. On the other hand we wanted to find out, which additional functions could be useful or even requested.

4.1   Brainstorming

We started with a brainstorming session about general requirements on APPs and on specific requirements in the field of mobility APPs. Mobility APPs are generally seen as a good and useful door opener for public transport services. A trustworthy issuer of a mobility APP is even very important for the purchase decision and using the APP for information, planning, navigation or ticketing services in context of transport services.

In Fig. 1 we structured the collected results into a mind map. Students wish generally simple, intuitive, fast, well-structured and smooth applications. Mobility APPs should not be overloaded but customisable e.g. with a user profile.

Table 1. User requirements surveyed for mobility application of public transport services

Function	User requirements
Technical usability	– Fast and easy menu-driven handling – Comprehensibility – Reliability – Consistency – Realistic mapping of real transport and mobility situation by high quality – Unique and comparable information provision across all media

Wording	–Consistency of terms between digital and real services, wrong choice of words could lead to irritation, e.g.:
	  • Searching connection vs. timetable
	  • Travel companion not used in regional public transport only in long-distance travel
	–Interpretation of real time
	– Descriptions or words in foreign language
	–Textual information

Structuring	– Simple and intuitive navigation – Traceability and transparency – Visibility of navigation options
Visualization/Frontend design	– Clear presentation (preference of symbols instead of text) –Legibility – Intelligible icons and symbols Well-structured and designed forms of presentations –Appropriate size of the several elements –Assembling elements according to use routine –Appropriate contrast between text, symbol, background
Interactive elements	– Expedient error messages –At sensible points out-put with two-step function, e.g. "Are you sure you want to quit the app?" –Visible interaction elements

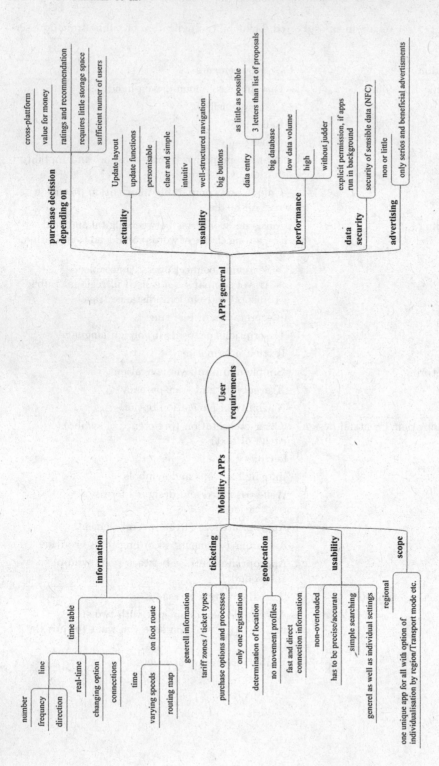

Fig. 1. User requirements - results of brainstorming process

The main function of mobility APPs are seen in connection information added by the option of electronic ticket purchase. By using public transport also the location function is appreciated. At the same time, there are concerns about data protection, the creation and misuse of personalized movement profiles and the misuse of the NFC interface concerning e-ticketing and mobile payment services. No clear picture was seen, if there is a preference for a unique Germany-wide application or for different regional ones. A solution could be a unique APP with the option for regional customization especially under the focus of the desired preselection list of starting point and destination input.

During the brainstorming process only known and already used aspects and application functions were mentioned. Barriers or problems were actively communicated, but not additional requirements and wishes. Even by encouraging the group to think about new aspects, approaches or issues to be taken in consideration for better usability and function design, no creative and innovative ideas were given.

This brainstorming method provided first insights for the researcher about customer behaviour and gives the basis for further research and analyses.

4.2   Conjoint Analysis

In the second step we carried out a conjoint analysis among the non-representative student group with the goal to understand customers' preferences of different product features. For this purpose product bundles were evaluated to determine user benefits by decomposing the values of the different functions and their attributes [11].

Since OPTIMOS project especially focusses on e-ticketing for public transport via NFC media such as smartphones or smartcards we chose the following four application functions: registration process, login procedure, payment system, and payment process. In Table 2 the function with different attributes are indicated.

16 different product bundles were created and 27 students were asked to rank them, according to their preferences with the results shown in Table 3.

The login procedure as well as the payment system seem not to be very important. The attributes of those function shown negligible values even taken in account the standard error. The highest benefit for the pretest group is the registration process by manual data input followed by the payment process by direct withdrawal at public transport operator and payment via financial service provider.

The quite high utility estimate for the attribute direct withdrawal at public transport operator by the function payment process underlines the importance of data security and provider confidence. By analogy of brainstorming the conjoint results show that those attributes were ranked best, which the study participants are most familiar with.

Nevertheless the results must be questioned critically, because we did not rotate the product bundles. All test persons valued all product bundles with the

Table 2. User requirements surveyed for mobility application of public transport services

Function		Feature attributes
Registration process		Electronic transmission of the personal data by eID of the ID card
		Manual entry of personal data
		Transfer of personal data from external service providers (Facebook, Google, ...)
Login procedure		Login once and stay logged in
		Re-login for each session
Payment system		Prepaid (using previously charged credit)
		Pay-per-Use (on each trip)
		Postpaid (billing weekly, monthly, quarterly)
Payment system		Cash (ticket machines, selling point, ...)
		Payment via mobile phone (carrier-billing)
		Financial service provider (credit card, paypal, ...)
		Direct withdrawal at public transport operator

same choice set order. So there might be a bias in favour on the first positioned registration process.

Considering the results of the brainstorming and the conjoint pretest we conclude that both methodologies are suitable for validation already known and experiences features, but not for detecting user requirements which are not yet explicitly known by customers. Those ones are difficult to communicate and to rank. Therefore we assume a different study design for evaluating user requirements for application usability.

5   Development of a Concept for User Acceptance and Requirement Research

In our pretest we detected difficulties for test persons to express and to evaluate specific feature requirements which are not yet used or the persons are not familiar with as it is with mobile payment services on German public transport market via NFC technology today. Because of this a multi-perspective approach by a user-centered design in four steps should be followed (Fig. 2).

5.1   Defining Personas

First, we create ideas of different target groups by defining personas. They are created on the basis of primary research, taking into account that they are not an average person, but hypothetical, specific individuals with desires, goals and expectations [12]. Personas describe a typical representative of a specific target group as "archetypical user, whose needs are determined as close as possible to reality" [10]. However they allow study participants to empathize and understand different target groups.

Table 3. User requirements surveyed for mobility application of public transport services

Function	Feature attributes	Utility estimate $\hat{\beta}$	Standard error
Registration process	Electronic transmission of the personal data by eID of the ID card	−0, 167	0, 204
	Manual entry of personal data	3, 296	0, 174
	Transfer of personal data from external service providers (Facebook, Google, ...)	−3, 130	0, 204
Login procedure	Login once and stay logged in	0, 111	0, 131
	Re-login for each session	−0, 111	0, 131
Payment system	Prepaid (using previously charged credit)	−0, 432	0, 174
	Pay-per-Use (on each trip)	0, 272	0, 204
	Postpaid (billing weekly, monthly, quarterly)	0, 160	0, 204
Payment system	Cash (ticket machines, selling point, ...)	−1, 426	0, 226
	Payment via mobile phone (carrier-billing)	0, 019	0, 226
	Financial service provider (credit card, paypal, ...)	0, 685	0, 226
	Direct withdrawal at public transport operator	0, 722	0, 226
Absolute term		7, 784	0, 144

Designing personas within the scope of the OPTIMOS project we make use of the defined ones of IP-KOM-ÖV project. They had been created by an extensive research with regard to mobility APPs by combining statistical analyses, expert interviews, focus groups and interviews reflecting the classification and the behaviour of public transport passengers adequately [13]. Those seven personas will be analysed, refined and if necessary complemented. Therefore it is necessary to check whether IP-KOM-ÖV-personas correspond to OPTIMOS target groups. A division into primary, secondary, complementary and non-personas (explicitly not considered target groups) can be helpful taking in consideration the different defined project use cases. The personas should focus specific user groups and prioritize their requirements by designing the OPTIMOS APP [8].

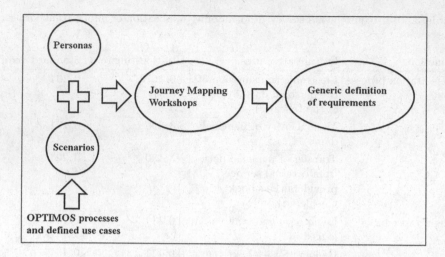

Fig. 2. User requirements - results of brainstorming process

5.2 Development of Scenarios

In a second step user scenarios must be developed based on the different defined personas. They are dependent on detailed research questions. Use cases are already developed during the OPTIMOS project. They focus on the following different processes:

- Mobile management of the personal account
- Classical sales and maintenance
- Mobile authentication
- Mobile sales and maintenance
- Personal point of sales
- Registration of customer media

The scenarios are the basis for the user-centered design discussion, analyses and evaluation in the workshops. According to Richter and Flückiger [8] user scenarios have to show the following features:

- Design for a specific user group
- Representation a specific case of an APP
- Showing deployment in real environment
- Illustrating the aspects relevant to the development of the new solution
- Describing exemplary exceptional and fault situations.

5.3 Workshop Journey Mapping

Based on the developed personas and scenarios workshops are being prepared in two test regions. Therefore potential workshop participants out of the project's friendly user group will be invited. Aim of the workshop is to work out and to define user requirements for the OPTIMOS APP by using the Journey Mapping (also called Customer Journey) methodology. "The Customer Journey is a systematic approach designed to help organizations understand how prospective and current customers use the various channels and touch points, how they perceive the organization at each touch point and how they would like the customer experience to be. This knowledge can be used to design an optimal experience that meets the expectations of major customer groups, achieves competitive advantage and supports attainment of desired customer experience objectives." [7].

Under consideration of the different use scenarios a workshop guideline has to be developed for possible touch points by using the OPTIMOS APP. The workshop participants are asked to put themselves in the situation of a specific persona and scenario. By going through the different touch points needs, specific requirements but also fears will be communicated. On the one hand the workshop guideline allows a target-orientated moderation to ensure that the participants are aware of important issues and take note of them. On the other hand the participants can easily move into the process flows from the perspective of their persona [16]. For visualisation and structuring the discussion poster-templates with two dimensions are prepared. The horizontal shows the different touch points and the vertical the potential function fields regarding the specific scenario and use case. Furthermore, prepared facilitation cards with typical features of the individual situations and functions will help to complete the posters by the individual workshop participants respective their persona. Thereby it is desired to communicate what the persona might think, feel and actually do, and what opportunities and risks are seen.

The workshop leader moderates the process by asking target-oriented questions for user requirements regarding APP functionality and usability. It should be also examined which symbols, terms and error messages are understood in which way. These questions could be as follows:

- What information is expected?
  - Absolutely
  - Nice to have
  - Superfluous
- How should this information be presented?
  - Words
  - Figure
  - Icon
  - Image
- What kinds of processes are accepted?
  - Accepted best
  - Still accepted
  - Not accepted
- What could particularly interfere the usability of the APP in a particular situation?
- What are the chances of the APP in a particular situation?

As a result, a Customer Journey Map is created for each scenario, which takes into account all areas deemed to be relevant. In addition, the spoken word as well as specific questions can be used to extract the user requirements and required functions at each touch point.

5.4 Generic Definition of Requirements

Based on the workshop results and in consideration of the general usability categories guidelines and style guides for test regions' APPs will be developed and surveyed by iterative acceptance tests using generic mock-ups among the friendly user groups. Up to three innovation cycles are planned. The survey will take place by online-tool as well as in a moderated user workshop in the test regions. This will lead to develop the generic concept supporting all use cases and processes tested in OPTIMOS in order to ensure a user-friendly mobile APPs.

6   Conclusion

The described concept will ensure a generic user-centered approach by developing and designing user friendly mobile APPs for the open NFC-based system in frame of OPTIMOS project. In the subsequent field tests the APPs will be proved by the friendly users and their acceptances surveyed with the aim of identifying usage and acceptance barriers and potentials for improvement as well as to indicate best case scenarios.

References

1. Beul-Leusmann, S., Habermann, A., Ziefle, M., Jakobs, E.M.: Unterwegs im ÖV. Usability mobiler Fahrgastinformationssysteme. In: Prinz, W., Borchers, J., Ziefle, M. (eds.) Mensch und Computer. Gesellschaft für Informatik e.V. (2016)
2. DYNAMO: Dynamische nahtlose Mobilität - Schlussbericht der Technischen Universität Dresden (2016)
3. HaCon Ingenieurgesellschaft: Cairo - context aware intermodal routing: Abschlussbericht (2013)
4. Hans-Böckler-Stiftung: Branchenanalyse: Zukunft des ÖPNV (2015)
5. Institut für Mobilitätsforschung: Die Zukunft der Mobilität - Szenarien für Deutschland 2035 (2015)
6. Karlsruher Institut für Technologie - Institut für Verkehrswesen: Deutsches Mobilitätspanel. http://mobilitaetspanel.ifv.kit.edu/
7. Nenonen, S., Rasila, H., Junnonen, J.M., Kärnä, S.: Customer journey - a method to investigate user experience. In: Proceedings of the Euro FM Conference Manchester, pp. 54–63 (2008)
8. Richter, M., Flückiger, M.D.: Usability Engineering kompakt: Benutzbare Produkte gezielt entwickeln. Springer, Heidelberg (2013)
9. Scherf, C.: Vom Verkehrsmarkt zum Mobilitaetsmonitor. Motive, Instrumente und Aufbau. Internationales Verkehrswesen (2015)
10. Semler, J.: App-Design. Rheinwerk Verlag GmbH, Bonn (2016)

11. Skiera, B., Gensler, S.: Berechnung von nutzenfunktionen und marktsimulationen mit hilfe der conjoint-analyse (teil i). WiSt-Wirtschaftswissenschaftliches Studium **31**(4), 200–206 (2002)
12. Spieß, M.: Branded Interactions: Digitale Markenerlebnisse planen und gestalten. Verlag Hermann Schmidt, Mainz (2012)
13. Technische Universität Ilmenau: Das Begleitheft für den Entwicklungsprozess Personas, Szenarios und Anwendungsfälle aus AK2 und AK3 (2011)
14. Infratest, T.N.S.: Fahrgäste öffentlicher Verkehrsmittel nutzen immer häufiger Verkehrs-Apps (2013). https://www.tns-infratest.com/presse/presseinformation.asp?prID=3259
15. TÜV Rheinland Consulting GmbH: Digitale Vernetzung im öffentlichen Personenverkehr - roadmap (2016). http://www.bmvi.de/SharedDocs/DE/Artikel/G/initiative-digitale-vernetzung-im-oepv.html
16. Uebernickel, F., Brenner, W.: Design thinking. In: Hoffmann, C.P., Lennerts, S., Schmitz, C., Stölzle, W., Uebernickel, F. (eds.) Business Innovation: Das St. Galler Modell. BIUSG, pp. 243–265. Springer, Wiesbaden (2016). doi:10.1007/978-3-658-07167-7_15
17. Verband deutscher Verkehrsunternehmen: Kommunikation im ÖV (IP-KOM-ÖV) - Szenarien & Personen sowie deren Anforderungen an die Kundeninformation. VDV-Mitteilung 7023. Ausschuss für Kundenservice, -information und -dialog (K3) (2012)

Cloud Computing Security and Privacy: An Empirical Study

Farid Shirazi[1(✉)], Adnan Seddighi[2], and Amna Iqbal[2]

[1] Ted Rogers School of ITM, Ryerson University, Toronto, Canada
f2shiraz@ryersion.ca
[2] Ted Rogers School of Management, Ryerson University, Toronto, Canada
{adnan.seddighi,amna.iqbal}@ryerson.ca

Abstract. Cloud computing allows organizations to deliver better and faster services at reduced cost. Moreover, cloud also enables organizations to expand or contract based on market demand and requirements. Despite many benefits, concerns around security and privacy challenges in cloud are on the rise.

In this paper we have developed a cloud security and privacy taxonomy which is used to capture the traditional security challenges with the divergence cloud technology. The content analysis revealed that cloud security and privacy inherits most of the challenges existing in traditional security, however it also introduces several new challenges around virtualization, trust, legal, privacy and data interoperability issues. The paper identifies also the gaps found in literature around Security as a Service. Finally, it introduces Privacy-by-Design (PbD) framework integrated with cloud security. We developed a control matrix based on the literature review integrated with PbD to offer organizations, developer, business architects, and decision makers a mechanism for assessing security and privacy concerns before adopting a new cloud solution.

Keywords: Cloud computing · Security as a service · Privacy by Design · Control matrix

1 Introduction

In the last two decades, we have witnessed the exponential growth of internet and the emergence of an ever-connected and intertwined world. This has paved the road for the fourth industrial revolution encompassing the cyber-physical era. In such a world, organizations have no choice but to become more agile in order to cater the growing clients' demands. Two decades ago and before the emergence of smart phones, our connectivity to the world through the internet was relatively limited. We communicated with friends primarily via telephone and emails. We worked in physical offices and communicated directly with corporate administration and the physical resources. Fast forward to the present day, it is evident that communication makes heavy use of smart phones and social media platforms. The concept of the office has undergone substantial transformation to the point at which we are able to access resources from anywhere without being physically in the office.

© Springer International Publishing AG 2017
M. Kurosu (Ed.): HCI 2017, Part II, LNCS 10272, pp. 534–549, 2017.
DOI: 10.1007/978-3-319-58077-7_43

The concept of cloud computing is not a new concept. The creation of ARPANET project in 1969, was the first step toward building cloud computing. The ARPANET (Advanced Research Project Agency Network) project was designing and implementing a network through which different kind of computers connect and communicate with each other within cloud known also as Internet. As Internet bandwidth and communication speed grew, more computers were able to connect to each other over a wide area network. Moreover, the advancement of virtualization technologies allowed computers to share their resources more effectively and efficiently. The development of grid computing made it possible for advanced parallel computing and CPU resource sharing. In addition, Web 2.0 technology provided a two-way communication system and paved the way for the rise of social media networks (SMNs). All of this has helped to shape cloud computing technology as we know today. Companies such as Salesforce.com and Amazon Web Services (AWS) were among the first companies to offer commercial cloud services. AWS provides services such as storage and computation via websites allowing a diverse set of devices access cloud resources by the means of a thin client application. Major IT companies such as IBM, Microsoft, Google and VMware among others offer cloud services.

Cloud Computing enables organizations to expand or contract on demand and provide services at reduced cost. By migrating to such solutions, organizations can reduce capital and operational expenditures and at the same time be more efficient. Although cloud solutions provide many advantages there remain serious challenges ahead. As per a survey done by International Data Corporation (IDC) in 2009, security was found to be the main concern that organizations have in adopting a cloud solution [1]. In this paper, we will investigate various privacy and security challenges organizations face in adopting cloud solutions in quest for developing a robust security and privacy framework. Specifically, we intend to identify the main differentiators of a cloud and a traditional security through the lens of Privacy-by-Design (PbD) framework.

Our main research questions are as follow: (a) are there any differences between privacy and security issues in a cloud environment and a non-cloud environment? and (b) how PbD framework can improve the design and implementation of the next generation cloud.

To answer the questions outlined above, we provide an extensive literature review to identify and map the work done by other researchers and practitioners in the field. The output of this research will help organizations focus on the relevant security and privacy concerns when adopting a new cloud solution.

1.1   Research Methodology Overview

The content and data sources of this study come from four main sources as outlined below: (a) peer reviewed articles and literature, (b) reports from industry research organizations such as Gartner, IDC, CSA, SANS, NIST and others, and (c) survey and studies conducted by consulting firms such and Deloitte, EY, PWC among others.

For the sake of content analysis we used NVIVO software (version 11.0). NVIVO provides features such as matrix coding that help researchers to code text documents or further analysis. In total, we've studied 121 documents from the above list in which 84 relevant literature and articles were chosen for further analysis.

2 Cloud Computing Market Overview

Although the concept of cloud computing has been around for some time, mainstream adoption of cloud services did not start until late 1990 and early 2000. Cloud computing first appeared on the Gartner hype cycle in 2008. Hype cycle is a well-known industry graph which presents emerging technologies and estimates time period required for such technologies to mature and become main stream. In 2008, Gartner estimated that it would take 2 to 5 years for cloud computing to be adopted as a mainstream technology. To identify the adoption state of cloud computing, we have tracked the movement of cloud computing on the Gartner hype cycle from the year 2008 to 2014. The graph below shows the way in which cloud computing moved on the hype cycle during these years. It can be seen from the graph that cloud computing has passed the peak of inflated expectation and it is on its way to become a mature technology. However, even in 2014, Gartner expected that the time required for mainstream adoption of cloud computing would be 2 to 5 years. From Gartner's estimation, cloud computing is still not a mature technology and will continue to evolve in the coming years (Fig. 1).

Cloud computing can impact various sections of the IT ecosystem from infrastructure to platforms to services. Moreover, cloud computing can impact various

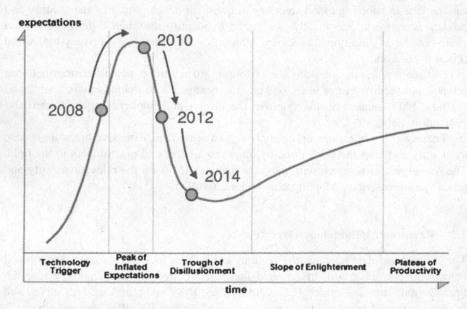

Fig. 1. State of cloud computing on Gartner hype cycle from 2008–2014

organizations and end user based on the type of applications and services they use. When evaluating the market value of cloud computing it is important to understand what aspects of cloud computing are being evaluated. For example, is the evaluation looking at services offered via Software-as-a-Service (SaaS) or Platform-as-a-Service (PaaS) and/or in combination of Infrastructure-as-a-Service (IaaS)? Or is it also taking into consideration other factors such as cloud advertising cost and the cost of cloud management? As per Gartner the public cloud services is forecasted to reach $204 Billion in 2016 [2]. Beside SaaS, PaaS, and IaaS, Gartner also includes among others, cloud business process services, cloud management and security as a service. For example cloud management and security services has shown an increase of 24% from 5.0 billion dollars in year 2015 to 6.2 billion in 2016 [3].

The second source from which market value estimates were collected was IDC. IDC estimated the public IT cloud services at $57.8 billion in 2015 (IDC 2015). If we add up the Gartner market value for SaaS, PaaS, and IaaS for 2015 we get $51.4 billion which is close to IDC's evaluation of $57.8 billion. Hence, it can be concluded that IDC is only including three main cloud services i.e. SaaS, PaaS, and IaaS when estimating the cloud market value. IDC also predicts that the cloud spending will grow to $112 billion in 2019 [4]. Cisco Global Cloud Index (CGI) provides also valuable forecasting data for the future market distribution of cloud services categorized by service models and deployment modes. This index attempts to forecast and map the global cloud-based IP traffic. Table 1 below summarizes CGI's predictions for 2019 [5].

Table 1. Cisco Global Cloud Index 2019

Public vs. Private Cloud (by 2019)
Public: 56%, Private: 44%
Global Cloud Traffic (by 2019)
Annual Global IP traffic will grow more than quadruple from 2.1 ZB (Zettabyte) per year to 8.6 ZB per year
1 Zettabyte = 10^{21} bytes
Cloud Service Delivery Model (by 2019)
59% SaaS, 11% PaaS, 30% IaaS

By looking at the market size estimation and the future prediction of cloud, it is clear that cloud computing is not only here to stay, but will also shape the future of the IT world. Many organizations and businesses have started to embrace cloud solutions. As per a survey done by KPMG in 2011, 81% of businesses were in early or advance stages of experimentation or full implementation of cloud solutions [6]. Among the companies which are adopting cloud solutions, small and medium enterprises (SMEs) are the ones which are realizing the most benefit [33]. This is primarily because smaller companies can adopt cloud solutions faster with fewer hurdles. AMI Partners predicted that SMEs will spend up to $100 billion on cloud computing by 2014 [7].

Data Security and Privacy Challenges

Online cybercrime activities are not only increasing day by day, but they are also becoming more sophisticated and targeted. Cyber war does not recognize any borders and cyber criminals are targeting organizations across the globe because of various financial, political, or even personal reasons. In a data breach study conducted by IBM and the Ponemon Institute in 2016, it was estimated that on average the cost of a data breach is estimated $4 USD and that the cost of each stolen record has increased from $154 in 2015 to $158 in 2016 [8].

To demonstrate the financial, privacy and social impact of a data breach, we have provided some examples of the most famous breaches in the recent years. Examples below are just some of many incidents which occur on a daily basis across the world. The aftermath of a data breach can sometime affect individuals and organizations for many years. Organizations affected by data breach lose their trust among their clients which will eventually result in loss of business (Table 2).

Given that many organizations have started to shift their services to cloud, cloud environments have become an attractive target for hackers. Hence, organizations should be extra cautious of the security and privacy measures when moving their services to the cloud.

3.1 Cloud Security and Privacy

As discussed above, the use of cloud computing is on the rise. Organizations have to face the fact that their employees will be using cloud-based services regardless of organizations' policies [9] As per cloud survey done by IDC in 2015, more than 43% of organizations expect that within five years the majority of their IT services will be delivered through cloud. The same report predicts that by 2018 half of the IT spending will be cloud based and that by then industry cloud creation will be seen as a top market entry strategy for IT providers [4]. In addition, a survey conducted by IDC in 2009 indicates that security is among of the main challenges facing the adoption of cloud [10]. Similar concern was echoed by other surveys conducted by Deloitte, Forrester, EY, and KPMG. For example a survey conducted by EY in 2013 shows that 43% of organizations indicate that their information security budgets are on the rise [11].

Within security, issues around trust and privacy are becoming CIOs top concerns. A survey by Deloitte in 2013 revealed that 78% of IT managers considered that the lack of trust in security was the biggest barrier to the adoption of cloud technologies [12]. The same survey showed that insufficient data security and risk of data availability, open compliance and legal issues, and the risk of losing governance or control over data [12] to be the main challenges of cloud adoption. A KPMG survey in 2014 revealed that 53% of organizations believe that data loss and privacy risk are the main challenges of doing business in cloud [13]. The same survey showed that in 2014 security and data privacy was identified to be of greater concern than cost when adopting a cloud solution [13]. Another research survey by Forrester in 2013 indicated that 50% of businesses in Europe and North America view security as the number one

Table 2. Some examples of recent data breaches

Organization	Description
MySpace, 2016	In May 2016, the hacker named Peace (same person who sold the record of more than 164 million LinkedIn users) claimed to have 360 million emails and passwords of MySpace users. This claim was verified by LeakedSource [33]
Anthem, 2015	In February 2015, the giant healthcare provider Anthem was hacked where hackers stole up to 80 million user records. This hack was estimated to be "worth 10 times the amount of credit card data" [36]
AshleyMadison, 2015	In July 2015, the online meeting website Ashly Madison was hacked by a group called The Impact Team. This hack potentially exposed 37 million private records (Krebs on Security 2015). This hack had significant social effects, impacted the personal and private life of many people
Sony, 2014	In December 2014, hackers used phishing techniques to enter Sony network. In this attack, hackers erased data from Sony data bases, stole personal and sensitive information, and released pre-released movies. The financial impact of this attack was estimated at $100 million dollars [36]
JP Morgan Chase, 2014	In this attack more than 83 million household and business account information was compromised. Hackers used this information to perform money laundering and fraud wire transfers through which they made over $100 million [36]
Home Depot, 2014	This attack targeted Home Depot's payment terminal units, which compromised 56 million credit card and debit card numbers. The direct and indirect financial cost of this breach was estimated at $837 million [36]
Yahoo, 2013	In December 2016 Yahoo admitted that one billion of its user account credentials were stolen by an unauthorized third party, in August 2013 [32]. This is one of the biggest breaches of all times. This breach is said to have ripple effects well beyond Yahoo, including hijacking of tens of thousands of other [35] and the $4.8 billion Verizon-Yahoo take over deal [37]
Target, 2013	Similar to Home Depot attack, attackers infected Target's POS (Point of Sale) with a malware through which they got access to identities of 70 million customers and 40 million credit cards [36]
American Banks, 2005–2012	This attack was carried out by Russian and Ukrainian attackers for a period of seven years. During this period the attackers targeted American financial organizations and got access to more than 160 million credit and debit card information. The financial impact of this attack was estimated at $300 million [38]

reason for not adopting a cloud solution [11]. Similarly, EY's global information security survey in 2013 indicates that 25% of organization admit that cloud computing has changed their risk exposure in the last 12 months [11].

Literature Review and Related Work

clear majority of reviewed research articles were associated with to the following categories.

1. Threats and vulnerabilities in cloud
2. Issues around privacy, compliance, audit, legal, and trust in cloud
3. Challenges organizations face in adopting a cloud solution
4. Solutions and recommendations for cloud security concerns and issues

A list of all keywords and phrases associated with our literature review has been generated, but due to the page limitation we excluded the list from our appendix.

We could not find any literature during the time of this study (2015–2016) that considered cloud computing design and implementation from the perspectives of the PbD framework. In fact those articles dealing with cloud security have considered privacy as subset of overall cloud security but not as its own specific domain.

4 Data Analysis and Results

In this section we will present the results of our content analysis. In total, we have reviewed over 121 academic and industry reports. For the purpose of content analysis, 84 of the most relevant literature were selected and analyzed by using NVIVO software package. NVIVO software was very helpful in performing thematic analysis and data comparison. Out of 84 papers chosen for this study, 51 focused on cloud security issues, 13 focused on cloud adoption issues, 17 articles focused on cloud security business adoption issues (including the e-commerce), and 3 papers were focused on privacy issues.

4.1 Methodology in Action

In order to perform content analysis, it was crucial to identify the themes which were relevant to this research study. To do so, we needed a well-defined taxonomy presenting a complete anatomy of security issues in cloud computing. The development of such taxonomy was very paramount to this study as it provided a common framework through which we could do the content analysis. Hence, we have used the open coding technique in the first round of literature review for the purpose of building such taxonomy.

Using the keywords generated through relevant industry and academic research studies, initially we ended up with more than 20 categories related to cloud security issues. However, through continuous revision of categories and literature review, we managed to merge and amalgamate relevant categories. As such, we ended up with 11 categories which could not be reduced any further. As per process outlined by [14], we had to continuously sanity check our categories to ensure they addressed this study's security and privacy questions. The categories identified, presents a holistic taxonomy of the cloud security issues based on the reviewed literature. The list of this taxonomy is outlined in table below. The coding agenda table below which was generated using NVIVO tool outlines how coding was done based on each category defined (Table 3).

Table 3. Classification of cloud security domains

Category	Definition	Example
C1: Network and infrastructure security	This category focused on issues related to network and infrastructure security as it related to cloud computing	"Network security: Problems associated with network communications and configurations regarding cloud computing infrastructures" [15]
C2: Software and application security	Any security issue related to software and application, this could be security issues related to web services or any other application used at SaaS layer (like email, photo sharing)	"Security concern #7: Users must keep up to date with application improvements to be sure they are protected" [16]
C3: Virtualization security	Any security issue arising from the virtualization and multi-tenancy technology	"Multi-tenancy issue: this issue poses a challenge to protect user data against unauthorized access from other users running processes on the same physical servers. This is in fact not a new issue taking into consideration the current concern with web hosting services. However, with the widespread use of cloud computing and with the fact that users store more important data in the cloud, this issue needs to be reconsidered seriously." [17]
C4: Data security	Data security category encompasses issues related to confidentiality, integrity, and availability of data	"Confidentiality and integrity of data transmission need to ensure not only between enterprise storage and cloud storage but also between different cloud storage services. In other words, confidentiality and integrity of the entire transfer process of data should be ensured" [18] "Organizations worry about whether Utility Computing services will have adequate availability, and this makes some wary of Cloud Computing" [19]
C5: Data storage, recovery, and backup	Security issues around location of stored data, data isolation, how data is backed up and recovered in an event of disaster	"end-users use the services provided by the cloud providers without knowing exactly where the resources for such services are located" [17] "Another important research area concerns determining apt granularities for isolation." [18]

(continued)

Table 3. (*continued*)

Category	Definition	Example
C6: Identity and access control	Security issues around authentication, authorization, identity management, access to data, credentials, privileged user access, etc.	"Security is always a popular topic and there are the following areas of specializations for Clouds: identity management, access control, single sign-on and auditing" [18] "In many application scenarios, such as those in enterprises or organizations, users' access to data is usually selective and highly differentiated. Different users enjoy different access privileges with regard to the data. When data are outsourced to the cloud, enforcing secure, efficient, and reliable data access among a large number of users is thus critical" [17]
C7: Compliance, audit, and legal issues	Issues around data transfer between different jurisdictions, how data can be audited and logged as per various security compliance requirements. Also this category addresses issues related to forensic and investigation shortcomings in cloud	"There is currently no regulation in place to determine how to keep track of the use of the cloud system and what is required to be audited and logged" [20] "Given that cloud computing is a relatively new technology, the current cyber laws do not yet cover the requirements posed by it" [21] "Regulatory compliance: Is the cloud vendor willing to undergo external audits and/or security certifications?" [22] "Legal issues: Aspects related to judicial requirements and law, such as multiple data locations and privilege management." [15]
C8: Privacy and trust	Issues around client's trust with CSPs and handling of users privacy in cloud	"Cloud computing raises new privacy issues that require clear standards for custodians of this information who receive government requests for access to that information." [20] "Lack of consumer trust is commonly recognized as a key inhibitor to moving to Software as a Service (SaaS) cloud models" [18–20]

(*continued*)

Table 3. *(continued)*

Category	Definition	Example
C9: Threat and vulnerabilities	This category relates to any vulnerabilities and threats identified in IaaS, PaaS, and SaaS	"Bugs in Large-Scale Distributed Systems. One of the difficult challenges in Cloud Computing is removing errors in these very large scale distributed systems. A common occurrence is that these bugs cannot be reproduced in smaller configurations, so the debugging must occur at scale in the production datacenters." [19] "Cloud provider vulnerabilities. These could be platform level, such as an SQL-injection or cross-site scripting vulnerability in salesforce.com." [23]
C10: Security governance and risk management	Issues around governance and risk management in cloud	"Governance: Issues related to (losing) administrative and security controls in cloud computing solutions" (Gonzalez et al. 2012)
C11: Standards	Issues around security standards in cloud. Also this category addresses interoperability between CSPs and data lock-ins	"Cloud standards: standards are needed across different standard developing organizations to achieve interoperability among clouds and to increase their stability and security" [15] "there are many general computing standards that may be reused in the cloud, but for the moment, there are to our knowledge no dedicated cloud standards." [17]

4.2 Comparing Traditional and Cloud Security

By taking a closer look at the cloud security taxonomy derived from literature, we can see that nine out of eleven cloud security issues identified are in fact issues which are also addressed by traditional security. The security issues that were uniquely associated to cloud were mainly associated with virtualization, web interface issues and data storage; particularly the issues related to storage locality. This observation alone indicates that cloud security and traditional security have a lot in common.

Although the literature points to the similarities of cloud and traditional security, there are still some major differences. Based on the literature review with argue that due to the complexity of cloud architecture and lack of visibility, traditional security solution cannot address today's cloud security challenges. So although most of the security issues are the same, as mentioned by Chen and Zhao [18] the traditional security mechanisms are no longer suitable for applications and data in cloud. For example, performing some tasks such as forensic investigation in cloud will become much more difficult as investigators might not be able to access system hardware physically [17]. Such differences introduce new challenges and calls for new solutions specific to the cloud.

Another point to note is the differences that exist around the privacy and trust issues in traditional and cloud environments. In traditional computing, since the data resides on clients' premise, there are controls built around securing the data. However, it is assumed that the client is to be trusted with their data as they are the custodian and guardian of that data. In cloud environment however, clients' data is hosted at a third party Cloud Service Provider (CSP). This shift of data storage introduces new challenges around privacy and trust.

The lack of standards and legal issues are two other challenges which should be looked at from a different angle when operating in cloud environments. As discussed above, these issues have much wider impact and expose data to a higher level of risks in cloud environments as opposed to traditional environments.

5 Privacy Concerns in the Cloud

According to [24], privacy is the ability of the persons to decide when, how and to what extent information about themselves is communicated to other people. There are four states of being private: (1) Solitude – physical separation from the group; (2) Intimacy – participation in a small unit that achieves corporate solitude (3) Anonymity – freedom from surveillance (4) Reserve – creation of psychological barrier that protects the individual from unwanted intrusion [24].

As discussed above, the main topics discussed in literature were mainly associated with security threats compromising customers' data. The risk of private data violation is much higher for data stored on the cloud. Cloud providers can deliberately or unintentionally misuse or disclosure sensitive user information that resides within a provider's premises. There are different aspects of the violation of data privacy. For example, the storage location may be a serious data privacy issue. When users start using cloud services, their data is located in cloud. While some providers explicitly specify where the data are located, others do not provide such information. In this case the data can be moved from location to location or even from country to country without a user's knowledge. Because legal regulations may be different in other countries, other privacy laws may apply that users unknowingly have to comply with. In most cases, users do not have full control over their sensitive data once placed in the cloud. According to [25, 26], there are many legal concerns that companies should be worried about. They relate to the privacy and security of the data as well control of the data ownership. Many details depend on the service agreements which still aren't nearly robust enough compared to SLAs in traditional manufacturing industries. Additional issues arise from cloud datacenters being located in different geographical locations which can result in confusion over which law has to be applied. Then there are concerns related to cloud provider declaring bankruptcy – it is not clear what will happen to the data belonging to the companies.

Bowen [25] first looks at data privacy and security issues. There are multiple laws that protect personal data enacted in USA and EU that cloud providers have to comply with. Some laws force cloud providers to notify their users when data breach of personal unencrypted information has occurred. The notable laws are Patriot Act in USA and European Union Data Privacy Directive (EUDPD). The US Patriot Act basically allows government to intercept any electronic information as well as compel any company to disclose such information to the government. The only requirement is government's certification that this information is relevant to the ongoing investigation. This fact is usually used to caution companies about storing their data in clouds located in USA and in promotion of European providers [27]. However, most European countries have analogous anti-terrorism laws as well. There are multiple Mutual Legal Assistance Treaties (MLATs) that require participants to share third-party information upon the formal request. This basically makes actual geographic location of servers storing the data in the cloud immaterial [26, 27]. EUDPD's key feature is its extraterritorial effect – any data from EU can only be sent to countries with compatible data protections.

Next are the jurisdictional issues related to virtualization and data location in which users' data can be stored in multiple countries while in the cloud. One problem is that once EUPDP law is applied to the data it becomes attached to it so from that point it can be sent only to compatible countries as discussed before. This may result in the conflict if initial contract with the cloud provider stipulated that it is done under, say, USA laws which can contradict European Union Directive. In addition, different countries will have different laws regarding government access to the data. As mentioned above the US Patriot Act allows government to access any data it wants. This may not be something that Amazon's customer residing in Europe wants to be exposed to.

A special problem might be with data retention: which policy is in place? how is it implemented? and how long data is retained in the cloud? After the retention period, a user's data have to be destroyed. The cloud provides high data availability by keeping a few copies of the data, sometimes at different locations. The issue here is how to make sure that all copies are destroyed correctly. Cloud users should know and act accordingly, and data privacy regulatory requirements effective data managing policies should be applied to the cloud. While auditing and monitoring cloud service providers it is essential to guarantee that business privacy requirements are not violated, and that sensitive user personal information is not leaked or misused. It is also important to be proactive rather than reactive when it comes to data privacy. To do so we offer a new approach in monitoring and assessing cloud privacy by implementing PbD as a control mechanism in protecting users' private data.

5.1 Privacy by Design

The privacy by design (PbD) framework was originally developed by Cavoukian [28]. This framework contains seven fundamental principles such as: Proactive not Reactive; Privacy as the Default Setting; Full Functionality; End-to-End Security; Visibility; Transparency; and User Privacy and Privacy Embedded into Design. The latter in particular is an important part of this study. The PbD framework offers an approach that is characterized by a proactive privacy measures rather than a reactive ones, it assures that all stakeholders (cloud stakeholder in this case) whether the business practice or technology involved, operate according to the stated promises and objectives and subject to independent verification [28]. Privacy by Design requires architects and operators to keep the interests of the individual uppermost by offering such measures as strong privacy defaults. As such we offer a cloud control matrix integrated with PbD to ensure clients' privacy. Figure 2 below was generated based on the eleven security domains discussed above. It integrates PbD as a control mechanism as integral part of cloud design and implementation.

In other words PbD offers a dynamic approach in which the legacy framework of security-privacy-usability triangle [29, 30] is modified so that the user-centric design principle of PbD is fulfilled.

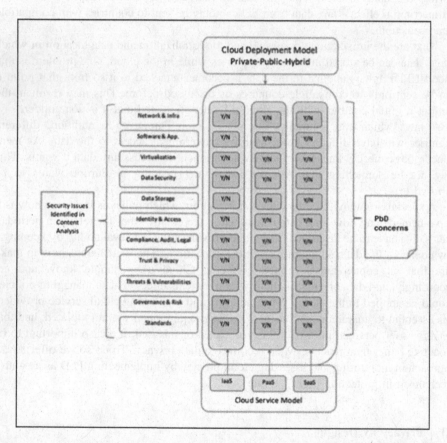

Fig. 2. Cloud security control matrix integrated with PbD

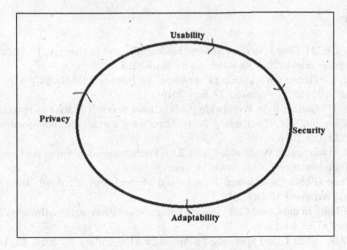

Fig. 3. Privacy, security, usability, and adaptability

As shown in Fig. 3, this integration highlights the vital links between privacy, security and usability in building organization's credibility and trust [31]. The updated model takes into account the dynamic nature of privacy. In addition, it addresses the need for flexibility and adaptability in the process. This paves the way for a richer and smoother user experience.

6 Conclusion

In this study we have focused on identifying differences of cloud and traditional security. Although cloud computing offers many advantages over conventional computing such as reduced cost, elasticity, rapid growth potential, among others, it has several challenges among which security and privacy concerns were the main focus of this study.

Our analysis revealed that cloud computing introduces new challenges on issues around privacy, trust, legal, virtualization and data interoperability. Organizations need to be aware of these new challenges as they move their services to the cloud. The cloud security and privacy taxonomy developed in this paper offers a framework in which the principles of privacy as outlined in PbD has been integrated into the deployment of cloud. Depending on the cloud model being used, organizations can use the matrix offered in this study to ensure whether or not the cloud solution they want to adapt addresses the main concerns associated with cloud privacy and security.

With the current speed of cloud adoption, organizations need to be more vigilant with their data when outsourced to cloud. Organizations should view cloud security and privacy through new lenses and use new frameworks and tools to assess CSPs security.

References

1. Gens, F.: IDC IT Cloud Services Survey: top benefits and challenges, 15 December 2009. http://blogs.idc.com/ie/?p=730. Accessed 27 Sept 2016
2. Stamford, C.: Gartner: Worldwide IT spending, 18 January 2016. http://www.gartner.com/newsroom/id/3186517. Accessed 27 Sept 2016
3. Stamford, C.: Gartner Says Worldwide Public Cloud Services Market Is Forecast to Reach $204 Billion in 2016, 25 January 2016. http://www.gartner.com/newsroom/id/3188817. Accessed 13 Oct 2016
4. IDC. IDC FutureScape: Worldwide Cloud 2016 Predictions—Mastering the Raw Material of Digital Transformation (2015). www.idc.com
5. Cisco. Cisco Global Cloud Index: Forecast and Methodology, 21 April 2016. http://www.cisco.com/. Accessed 13 Oct 2016
6. KPMG. Clarity in the Cloud (2011). www.kpmg.com/SG/en/IssuesAndInsights/Documents/ICE-ClarityInTheCloud.pdf
7. Hickey, A.R.: SMB Cloud Spending To Approach $100 Billion By 2014, 12 August 2010. http://www.crn.com/
8. Ponemon Institute. 2016 Cost of Data Breach Study: Global Analysis, June 2016. http://www-03.ibm.com/security/data-breach/
9. ENISA. Cloud Computing-Benefits, risks and recommendation for information security, 9 November 2009. https://www.enisa.europa.eu/
10. IDC New IDC IT Cloud Services Survey: Top Benefits and Challenges, 15 December 2009. http://blogs.idc.com/ie/?p=730
11. EY. Under cyber attack EY's Global Information Security Survey 2013, October 2013. http://www.ey.com
12. Deloitte. How to ensure control and security when moving to SaaS/cloud applications, October 2013. www.deloitte.com
13. KPMG. Elevating business in the cloud (2014). www.kpmg.com/cloudsolutions
14. Mayring, P.: Qualitative Inhaltsanalyse. Grundlagen und Techniken, 7th edn. Deutscher Studien Verlag, Weinheim (2000). First edition 1983
15. Gonzalez, N., Miers, C., Redigolo, F., Simplicio, M., Carvalho, T., Näslund, M., Pourzandi, M.: A quantitative analysis of current security concerns and solutions for cloud computing. J. Cloud Comput.: Adv. Syst. Appl. 1(1), 11 (2012)
16. Popović, K., Hocenski, Ž.: Cloud computing security issues and challenges. In: Proceedings of the 33rd International Convention, pp. 344–349. IEEE Xplore, Opatija, May 2010
17. Rong, C., Nguyen, S.T., Jaatun, M.G.: Beyond lightning: a survey on security challenges in cloud computing. Comput. Electr. Eng. 39(1), 47–54 (2013)
18. Chen, D., Zhao, H.: Data security and privacy protection issues in cloud computing. In: 2012 International Conference on Computer Science and Electronics Engineering (ICCSEE), vol. 1, pp. 647–651, March 2012
19. Armbrust, M., Fox, A., Griffith, R., Joseph, A.D., Katz, R., Konwinski, A., Zaharia, M.: A view of cloud computing. Commun. ACM 53(4), 50–58 (2010)
20. Marston, S., Li, Z., Bandyopadhyay, S., Zhang, J., Ghalsasi, A.: Cloud computing—the business perspective. Decis. Support Syst. 51(1), 176–189 (2011)
21. Fernandes, D.A., Soares, L.F., Gomes, J.V., Freire, M.M., Inácio, P.R.: Security issues in cloud environments: a survey. Int. J. Inf. Secur. 13(2), 113–170 (2014)
22. Ramgovind, S., Eloff, M.M., Smith, E.: The management of security in cloud computing. In: 2010 Information Security for South Africa, pp. 1–7. IEEE, August 2010

23. Chow, R., Golle, P., Jakobsson, M., Shi, E., Staddon, J., Masuoka, R., Molina, J.: Controlling data in the cloud: outsourcing computation without outsourcing control. In: Proceedings of the 2009 ACM Workshop on Cloud Computing Security, pp. 85–90. ACM, November 2009

24. Katzan, H.: On the privacy of cloud computing. Int. J. Manag. Inf. Syst. (IJMIS) 24(2), 1 (2010)

25. Bowen, J.A.: Cloud computing: issues in data privacy/security and commercial considerations. Comput. Lawyer (2011)

26. Bender, D.: Privacy and security issues in cloud computing. Comput. Internet Lawyer (2012)

27. Wolf, C.: Privacy and data security in the cloud: what are the issues? IP Litig.: Devoted Intellect. Prop. Litig. Enforc. 18(6), 19–28 (2012)

28. Cavoukian, A.: Privacy by Design: The 7 Foundational Principles. Implementation and Mapping of Fair Information Practices. Information and Privacy Commissioner Ontario, Canada (2009)

29. De Cristofaro, E., Wright, M. (eds.): PETS 2013. LNCS, vol. 7981. Springer, Heidelberg (2013). doi:10.1007/978-3-642-39077-7. See also Security and Privacy http://www.parc.com/work/competencies.html

30. Balfanz, D., Durfee, G., Smetters, D.K., Grinter, R.E.: In Search of usable security: five lessons from the field. IEEE Secur. Priv. 2(5), 19–24 (2004). http://www.parc.com/work/competencies.html

31. Casalo, V.L., Flavian, C., Miguel Guinaliu, M.: The role of security, privacy, usability and reputation in the development of online banking. Online Inf. Rev. 31(5), 583–603 (2007)

32. Yahoo 2016. Recognize and secure a hacked Yahoo Mail account. https://investor.yahoo.net/releasedetail.cfm?ReleaseID=1004285

33. Tehrani, S.R., Shirazi, F.: Factors influencing the adoption of cloud computing by small and medium size enterprises (SMEs). In: Yamamoto, S. (ed.) HCI 2014. LNCS, vol. 8522, pp. 631–642. Springer, Cham (2014). doi:10.1007/978-3-319-07863-2_60

34. Motherboard.: Hacker Tries To Sell 427 Million Stolen MySpace Passwords For $2,800, 27 May 2016. http://motherboard.vice.com

35. Satter, R.: And this password breach could have ripple effects well beyond Yahoo (2016). http://www.theglobeandmail.com/

36. Sporck, L.: 8 of the Largest Data Breaches of All Time, 17 January 2016. https://www.opswat.com/

37. Leswing, K.: Yahoo confirms major breach—and it could be the largest hack of all time, 22 September 2016. http://uk.businessinsider.com

38. Beekman, D.: Hackers hit Nasdaq, 7-Eleven, others for $300 million: Feds, 26 July 2013. http://www.nydailynews.com

Augmenting Smart Buildings and Autonomous Vehicles with Wearable Thermal Technology

Matthew J. Smith[1]([✉]), Kristen Warren[1], David Cohen-Tanugi[1],
Sam Shames[1], Kelly Sprehn[2], Jana L. Schwartz[2], Hui Zhang[3],
and Ed Arens[3]

[1] EMBR Labs, Cambridge, MA, USA
matt@embrlabs.com
[2] Draper, Cambridge, MA, USA
[3] University of California, Berkeley, Berkeley, CA, USA

Abstract. Smart buildings and autonomous vehicles are expected to see rapid growth and adoption in the coming decades. Americans spend over 90% of their lives in buildings or automobiles, meaning that 90% of their lives could be spent interfacing with intelligent environments. EMBR Labs has developed EMBR Wave™, a wearable thermoelectric system, for introducing thermal sensation as a connected mode of interaction between smart environments and their occupants. In this paper we highlight applications of wearable thermal technology for passengers in autonomous vehicles and occupants of smart buildings. Initial findings, collected through partnerships with Draper and UC Berkeley, respectively, are presented that illustrate the potential for wearable thermal technology to improve the situational awareness of passengers in autonomous vehicles and improve personal comfort in smart buildings.

Keywords: Smart home · Autonomous vehicles · Thermal · Wearable · Multimodal interface · Real life environments · Internet of things

1 Introduction

The average American spends 87% of her or his time in buildings and 6% in vehicles, amounting to 93% of their life inside [1]. In the next decade, rapid technological disruption is expected to bring new levels of intelligence to both automobiles and buildings, which will have a transformative impact on our interactions with these technologically sophisticated environments. There will be thousands of autonomous vehicles deployed in the U.S. by 2020 and it is forecasted that 21 million autonomous vehicles will be sold in the U.S. in the next 20 years [2]. The smart building market is expected to grow from $6B in 2016 to $25B by 2021, affecting lighting, HVAC, communication, and security systems [3]. The rapid deployment of smart technologies in buildings and automobiles means that, in less than 20 years, Americans could be spending over 90% of their lives interfacing with intelligent environments.

The incentive for this rapid adoption of smart technologies is two-fold: First, it is the urgent need to improve the systems-level efficiency of our buildings and automobiles in the face of a resource-constrained world. Second, smarter environments

© Springer International Publishing AG 2017
M. Kurosu (Ed.): HCI 2017, Part II, LNCS 10272, pp. 550–561, 2017.
DOI: 10.1007/978-3-319-58077-7_44

present opportunities to meaningfully improve the experience of the occupants in automobiles (safety) and buildings (environmental quality). In this proceedings, we discuss the potential systems- and occupant-level benefits of integrating wearable thermal technology, connected wearable accessories that deliver precise sensations of heating or cooling, with smart buildings and autonomous electric vehicles. In Sect. 2, a wearable thermoelectric system, EMBR Wave^{TM}, is presented that has been designed specifically for integrating personalized thermal sensations into the internet of things. In Sect. 3, we utilize EMBR Wave^{TM} to demonstrate the ability of wearable thermal technology to improve the situational awareness of passengers in autonomous vehicles. Finally, in Sect. 4, we will discuss the value that can be unlocked by integrating wearable thermal technology with Smart HVAC systems. Together, these examples highlight the new opportunities for human-computer interactions enabled by the convergence of intelligent environments and wearable technology. By introducing thermosensation into the internet of things, new channels of interaction are created that can improve the operation of the complex systems while simultaneously enhancing the experience of the occupants.

2 Wearable Thermal Technology

Wearable thermal technology, the concept of wearable technology that is designed to deliver precise, localized thermal sensations, is now feasible and attractive as a wearable human computer interface due to the significant technological and scientific progress of the last 20 years. Wearable thermal technology has become technologically feasible owing to the same advances currently enabling the Internet of things: Energy-efficient wireless communication, the miniaturization of computational systems, and the increasing energy and power density of batteries. In parallel with these technological advancements, scientific advancements have elucidated astounding relationships between the human body and the experience of thermal sensations that suggest thermal sensations can be used to convey information [4], relieve personal discomfort [5] and even influence the experience of emotions [6]. In this section, we present EMBR Wave^{TM}, a wearable platform technology for integrating personalized thermosensation with smart environments and the Internet of things.

2.1 EMBR Wave^{TM}: A Smart Platform for Wearable Thermal Technology

EMBR Wave^{TM} is a platform technology developed at EMBR Labs for introducing precise, localized, and personalized thermal sensations into connected and wearable accessories. EMBR Wave^{TM} utilizes a thermoelectric module to generate precise and dynamic temperature profiles directly on the wearer's skin. Thermoelectric modules are conventionally considered inefficient and high-power devices, but through iterative prototyping (Fig. 1) we have demonstrated a custom thermoelectric element with size and power specifications that enable wearable form factors with battery included. In previous attempts at wearable heating and cooling, power consumption and thermal

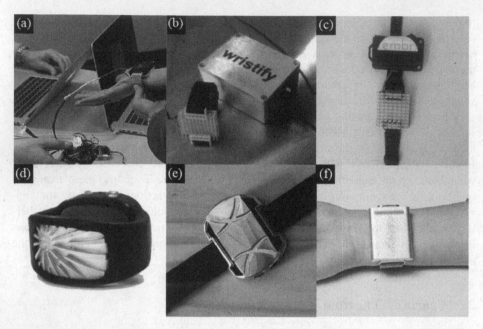

Fig. 1. (a) Original EMBR Wave™ demonstration at MADMEC competition in 2013 (Cambridge, MA). (b–e) Examples of wrist-worn prototypes developed 2014 - 2016. (f) Current wrist-worn adaptation of EMBR Wave™, called Wristify, being commercialized in 2017.

dissipation have been major obstacles to designing devices that are sufficiently small and light for everyday use. EMBR Wave™ can be powered from a lithium battery, comparable to what is currently used in smartphones and smart watches (250–1000 mAh), and uses under 2 W of power. Furthermore, the heat generated can be dissipated using natural convection and a passive aluminum heat sink.

EMBR Labs has developed patent-pending architectures for this comprehensive system that are robust and enable all components to be packaged into wearable form factors appropriate for everyday use. The thermoelectric heat pump is packaged with multiple temperature sensors that provide a resolution around 0.1 °C and the thermal system can controllably create rapid temperature profiles at the skin in the range of 0.1–1 °C/s. Finally, EMBR Wave™ heating and cooling modules are equipped with wireless communications and onboard computing to enable sophisticated systems-level integration with Smart Environments.

2.2   The Power of Thermal Sensations

When you feel something warm or cold, a lot more is going on than just a thermal sensation. When we wrap our hands around a warm mug of tea, or a cool breeze blows across our face, the temperature changes are detected by two different kinds of receptors in the skin, known as cold and warm thermoreceptors. These thermoreceptors send signals to the brain, which translates the thermal stimuli into thermal sensations through the same neural networks that are also responsible for touch, pleasure, thermoregulation, emotion, and the balance of the autonomic nervous system [7].

Through this complex network of regions in the brain, localized thermal sensations have the unique potential to influence the human experience through both exteroceptive and interoceptive pathways. Like conventional haptic devices, thermal sensations can be used to convey information [4], albeit with limited information density and temporal resolution compared to audio or visual feedback. Thermal sensations, however, can offer occupants much more meaningful interactions than just notifications. For example, experiencing localized thermal sensations can influence the experience of emotions [6, 8, 9] and personal comfort (See Sect. 4) [5]. Integrating wearable thermal technology with smart environments unlocks new potential value through these relationships between temperature and human psychophysiology. In the following sections we present two ongoing collaborations in which, utilizing EMBR Wave^{TM}, wearable thermal technology is being used to improve the functionality of smart environments and the experience of the occupants or passengers.

3 Improving Situational Awareness in Autonomous Vehicles with Wearable Thermal Technology

Ninety percent of automobile collisions are due to human error with 20–40% of those collisions resulting from driver distraction [10]. The adoption of autonomous vehicles is expected to significantly reduce automobile crashes by removing or reducing the potential influence of human error [11]. Autonomous vehicles present new challenges, however, because as vehicles become increasingly autonomous the passengers may pay less direct attention to their surroundings. An important component of interfacing within an autonomous vehicle is the ability of the vehicle to capture the driver's attention and provide her or him with the necessary information to rapidly and accurately respond to unexpected events.

Multiple resource theory states that communicating information over multiple channels can help individuals better perform multiple tasks [12]. As the number of sensory features given to a piece of data increases, the amount of information a person can receive also increases [13]. Multimodal information presentation has demonstrated clear benefits, such as faster reaction time combining audio and visual alerts [14]. In this study we investigate the potential value of conveying situational information to passengers in autonomous vehicles through multimodal sensory inputs, including thermal sensation.

The Immersive Situation Awareness system (isaWear), developed at Draper (Cambridge, MA), includes visual, auditory, thermal, and haptic feedback. (Figure 2) Thermal feedback is provided on the inside surface of each wrist by two EMBR Wave^{TM} wristbands, allowing for directional information to be intuitively conveyed by thermal cues. Our hypothesis is that imbuing situational information with features across multiple human senses will increase human capacity for information perception, which translates to faster and more accurate responses by the driver when presented

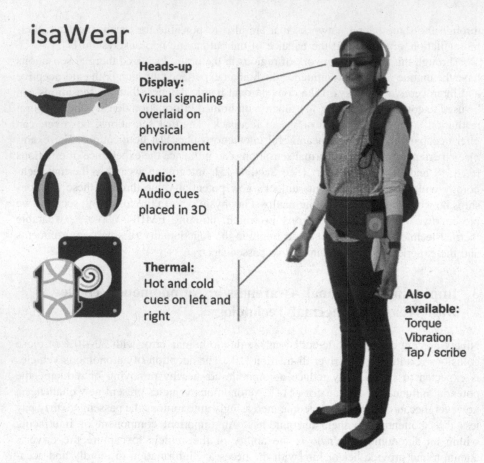

Fig. 2. The Immersive Situation Awareness system (isaWear), including augmented reality in a heads up display, 3-dimensional audio, and EMBR Wave™ wearable thermal technology on each wrist.

with unexpected events that require attention and rapid decision making. Two experiments will be presented that evaluate the use of multisensory information to convey situational awareness and aid human response and decision-making.

The first experiment was an object identification test. Participants were placed in the middle of eight large screens with a forest scene projected on all sides (Fig. 3). Users received signals through auditory, thermal, and a combination of auditory and thermal channels that were counterbalanced to account for learning and ordering effects. All signals had dangerous and benign signals associated, and were presented in all conditions. Their task was to turn to the source screen and identify whether the source was dangerous or benign. We collected response time and accuracy. After experimenting with a 3 × 2 experiment design over 24 participants, the single presentations of information performed worse than the combined signals, both in reaction

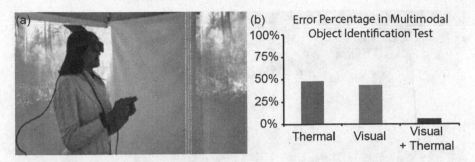

Fig. 3. (a) The experimental setup of a hand-held response, augmented reality glasses, and the EMBR Wave™ heating and cooling wristbands. (b) The chart demonstrates the percentage of incorrect responses for each condition. The paired-presentation experiment compared error rates using a presentation device using single channels (either thermal or visual) to a paired presentation of visual and thermal presentation. The paired presentation resulted in a 10× error reduction.

times and in accuracy. Figure 3 presents the experiment set-up (a) and the accuracy results (b). Overall, by pairing visual and thermal signals, there was an order of magnitude reduction in error in identifying dangerous or benign signals.

The second experiment was a driving simulator in which participants wearing isaWear had to react to obstacles encountered en route to arriving at a goal location (Fig. 4(a)). The participants were instructed to drive through a maze with various objectives, including avoiding animals, dealing with vehicle overheating, and getting to the goal within a certain time. Participants received visual signals through augmented reality goggles simulating a heads up display, auditory signals through earphones that placed sounds in a three-dimensional location, and directional thermal signals from EMBR Wave™ wristband worn on each wrist. Signals were presented alone, in pairs, and in a combination of three to understand any combinatory effects of the signals. All users saw all instances of the obstacles and all of the designs of the signals. The ordering of these conditions was counterbalanced between participants to account for learning or effects of overwhelming the user. Researchers measured performance of the participants by time to react to the signal. Figure 4(b) shows the average reaction time of participants in response to combinations of sensory signals. The experiment demonstrates that combinations of signals across modalities can improve reaction times in high-stress environments. This trend is consistent with Multiple Resource Theory and supports the feasibility of leveraging wearable thermal technology as a complementary interface between passengers and autonomous vehicles.

The aforementioned investigations utilizing isaWear and EMBR Wave™ wearable thermal technology highlight the potential value that multisensory feedback systems could have in ensuring the situational awareness of the passengers of autonomous vehicles. Directional thermal cues, delivered by wearable thermal technology, have several practical advantages in the context of interacting with autonomous vehicles. First, wearable thermal technology was found to pare favorably with augmented reality (Fig. 4(b)), which was meant to imitate the type of heads up displays expected to be

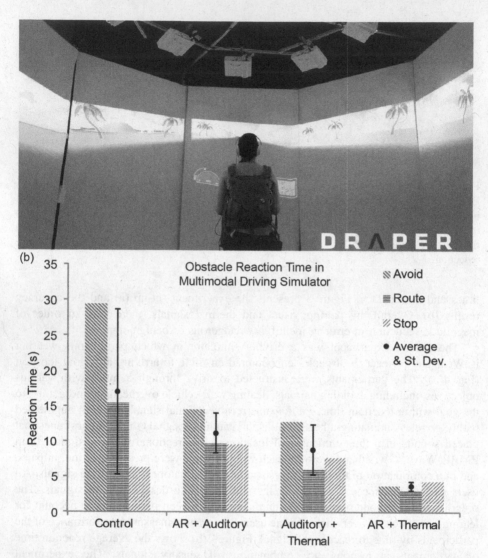

Fig. 4. (a) Driving Simulator with isaWear kit and 5-panel 180° display. (b) Reaction time to different categories of obstacles presented in multimodal driving simulation. Comparing control (no isaWear, visual and dashboard-only signals) to different combinations of sensory inputs.

prevalent in autonomous vehicles. Second, relying on wearable technology to provide sensory feedback ensures that the occupant receives the notifications independent of their hand or body locations. Third, thermal cues can be provided without obfuscating other visual or auditory information that is necessary for situational awareness.

There are limitations to temperature as a haptic medium that make thermal cues better suited to be a complementary sensory input than a primary input. First, the resolution of information that can be conveyed by thermal signals is limited compared to auditory or visual cues. In this study, a thermal system was worn on each wrist and this allowed directional information to be intuitively included in the thermal cues. Even under high-stress environments, participants were able to consistently distinguish warm from cold and assign directional information to the cues. However, when additional information was encoded in the thermal stimulus, such as varying intensity or temporal profiles, subjects exhibited difficulty differentiating between temperature profiles during the immersive and high-stress simulation. Second, the meaning ascribed to thermal sensations is often mixed and context dependent [15]. We found that the interpretation of thermal signals varied depending on many variables: user preconceived notions, expectations relating to the scenario, environmental cues, and implicit associations with heat and cold. Combining thermal cues with other sensory inputs reduces the ambiguity of thermal cues and allows for a broader range of affective tones when providing haptic feedback [16]. Cross-modal matching and the effective pairing of thermal cues with other sensory inputs for clear meaning is an area of ongoing research.

4 Reducing Energy Consumption and Improving Occupant Comfort and Productivity in Smart Buildings with Wearable Thermal Technology

Current approaches to building-scale heating and cooling are causing both environmental and economic damage. Every year over 12 Qbtu of energy, more than 12% of all energy used domestically, is used to heat or cool spaces with the goal of maintaining occupant comfort [17]. Despite enormous energy consumption put into tight environmental control in the built environment, more office occupants are dissatisfied (42%) than satisfied (39%) with their office environment [18]. In a study focused on thermal comfort, 50% of the subjects preferred a change in their thermal state, 38% of subjects in winter were dissatisfied with thermal conditions, and almost 50% of the thermal conditions during summer were outside of the thermal comfort zone [19].

The smart building market is expected to grow from $6B in 2016 to $25B by 2021, [3] and this trend has the potential to significantly reduce the amount of energy used to condition our indoor environments and improve occupant comfort. In Smart HVAC, this is being demonstrated [20–23] by integrating a combination of sensors that can provide information about the environment and the occupants, the collection of self-reported comfort data from occupants, and developing sophisticated models for aggregating this data and using it to optimize HVAC operation. It is important to recognize, however, that building-scale solutions are incapable of solving the core issue underlying occupant dissatisfaction: Different people have different standards for what environmental conditions are comfortable at any given time. Current ASHRAE guidelines suggest that, even under "ideal" conditions, only 80% of occupants will be comfortable [24]. Building-scale HVAC systems, whether intelligent or not, face fundamental challenges with regard to maintaining comfort across populations of people.

Introducing wearable thermal technology as a human-computer interface in smart buildings has the potential to both improve occupant comfort and further reduce the energy consumption of building-scale heating and cooling. Contrary to mainstream belief, improving personal comfort in moderate environments does not require changing the heat balance equation of the body. Personal comfort, while closely related to thermoregulation, is a distinct psychophysiological concept [25]. The most significant advancement in the field of comfort science in the past 20 years has been the shift from a physical, steady state and deterministic model of comfort to an adaptive comfort model [26]. The adaptive comfort model recognizes that personal comfort is not just a heat balance equation but depends on more complex mental and adaptation processes [27, 28]. Accordingly, the ASHRAE Standard 55 defines thermal comfort as: "that condition of mind that expresses satisfaction with the thermal environment" [24].

Leveraging this full psychophysiological model of thermal comfort, it has been demonstrated that localized, transient thermal sensations can improve personal comfort [5]. In this comfort model, if a local thermal sensation is experienced, so long as the occupant has some control over their thermal experience and the thermal experience is transient, then the overall comfort experienced by the user becomes the average of the 2 most uncomfortable regions and the maximum comfort vote (the transient thermal sensation) [29]. By taking a personalized and transient approach to thermal sensations, there is an opportunity to improve whole-body comfort while using much less energy than is necessary to heat or cool the entire body.

EMBR Labs is developing a wearable personal comfort system that can provide up to 8 h of use (1 work day) and could expand a building occupant's thermal comfort zone by 1–3 °C. Such personalized comfort performance would have a transformative impact on both building-scale energy consumption and occupant productivity: The energy required to heat or cool a building is reduced by 7-10% for every 1 °C that the occupants' float zone is extended, [30] suggesting a potential for greater than 20%+ reduction in building energy consumption. Analyses have suggested that personalizing temperature in a ±2 °C range would lead to a building-wide increase of 3% in the performance of both logical thinking and very skilled manual work and a 7% increase in typing performance [31].

Equipping occupants with a connected and wearable personal comfort system creates a new channel for interacting with Smart HVAC systems. The use of a personal comfort system, whether in heating or cooling, is in itself an indicator of personal discomfort that can be immediately communicated to the Smart HVAC system. Tracking occupants' behavioral response to discomfort will provide a rapid and accurate form of comfort reporting to complement Smart HVAC operation. The smart HVAC system (or facilities manager) will know at any given time how many people are hot or cold and to what degree, giving them high-resolution insight into the most important HVAC performance criteria: occupant comfort. Wearable thermal technology has the potential to provide instantaneous thermal relief, allow occupants to suit their own comfort needs, and provide real-time comfort data to help inform more intelligent building-scale HVAC operation. For these reasons, it has the potential to be the defining experience of the smart building of the future.

5   Summary

The last 20 years of progress in mobile technology and in the science of thermal sensations are converging to enable wearable thermal technology that serves as a tool for the wearer and an interface for interacting with smart environments. We have demonstrated the feasibility of wearable thermal technology through EMBR Wave™, a wearable thermoelectric platform designed for integrating thermosensation with the Internet of things. In collaboration with Draper, we have validated the capability of EMBR Wave™ for improving situational awareness in autonomous vehicles, in particular when thermosensation is integrated with a multisensory system such as IsaWear. In the built environment, wearable thermal technology has the potential to improve occupant satisfaction and productivity while reducing the energy consumed heating and cooling buildings. EMBR Labs, together with UC Berkeley, has received a Phase I NSF STTR to demonstrate wearable personal comfort systems that can improve occupant comfort and generate real-time comfort data for smart buildings. These examples highlight the new opportunities for human-computer interactions enabled by intelligent environments and connected wearable thermal technology. Introducing thermosensation into the Internet of Things creates new channels of interaction that can improve the operation of the complex systems while simultaneously augmenting the experience of the occupants. Potential collaborators interested in using EMBR Wave™ to introduce thermosensation into their connected systems should contact the corresponding author at EMBR Labs.

Acknowledgments. EMBR Labs and UC Berkeley gratefully acknowledge the support of the National Science Foundation through a Phase I STTR #1622892.

References

1. Klepcis, N.E., Nelson, W.C., Ott, W.R., et al.: The national human activity pattern survey (NHAPS): a resource for assessing exposure to environmental pollutants. J. Expo. Anal. Environ. Epidemiol. **11**, 231–252 (2001). doi:10.1038/sj.jea.7500165
2. IHS: IHS clarifies autonomous vehicle sales forecast – expects 21 million sales globally in the year 2035 and nearly 76 million sold globally through 2035. In: IHS Markit (2016). http://news.ihsmarkit.com/press-release/automotive/autonomous-vehicle-sales-set-reach-21-million-globally-2035-ihs-says. Accessed 1 Feb 2017
3. Marketsandmarkets.com: Smart Building Market by Building Automation Software (2016). http://www.marketsandmarkets.com/Market-Reports/smart-building-market-1169.html. Accessed 1 Feb 2016
4. Singhal, A., Jones, L.A.: Dimensionality of thermal icons. In: IEEE World Haptics Conference on WHC 2015, pp. 469–474 (2015). doi:10.1109/WHC.2015.7177756
5. Zhang, H., Arens, E., Huizenga, C., Han, T.: Thermal sensation and comfort models for non-uniform and transient environments, part III: whole-body sensation and comfort. Build. Environ. **45**, 399–410 (2010). doi:10.1016/j.buildenv.2009.06.020
6. Bargh, J.A., Shalev, I.: The substitutability of physical and social warmth in daily life. Emotion **12**, 154–162 (2012). doi:10.1037/a0023527

7. Farrell, M.J.: Regional brain responses in humans during body heating and cooling. Temperature **3**, 220–231 (2016). doi:10.1080/23328940.2016.1174794

8. IJzerman, H., Coan, J.A., Wagemans, F., et al.: A theory of social thermoregulation in human primates. Front. Psychol. **6**, 1–17 (2015). doi:10.3389/fpsyg.2015.00464

9. Rotman, J.D., Lee, S.H.M., Perkins, A.W.: The warmth of our regrets: managing regret through physiological regulation and consumption. J. Consum. Psychol. (2016). doi:10.1016/j.jcps.2016.08.008

10. Singh, S.: National Motor Vehicle Crash Causation Survey Data Book (2008)

11. Fagnant, D.J., Kockelman, K.: Preparing a nation for autonomous vehicles: opportunities, barriers and policy recommendations. Transp. Res. Part A: Policy Pract. **77**, 167–181 (2015). doi:10.1016/j.tra.2015.04.003

12. Wickens, C.D.: Multiple resources and performance prediction. Theor. Issues Ergon. Sci. **3**, 159–177 (2002). doi:10.1080/14639220210123806

13. Miller, G.: The magical number seven, plus or minus two: some limits on our capacity for processing information. Psychol. Rev. **101**, 343–352 (1956). doi:10.1037/h0043158

14. Hines, K.P.: Exploration of alerting methods on vest-worn systems. Virginia Polytechnic Institute and State University (2016)

15. Wilson, G., Dobrev, D., Brewster, S.A.: Hot under the collar: mapping thermal feedback to dimensional models of emotion. pp. 4838–4849 (2016)

16. Wilson, G., Brewster, S.A.: Multi-moji: combining thermal, vibrotactile and visual stimuli to expand the affective range of feedback. In: CHI 2017: CHI Conference on Human Factors in Computing Systems, Denver, CO, USA, 6–11 May 2017 (2017). ISBN 9781450346559

17. United States Department of Energy: Buildings energy databook. Energy Effic. Renew. Energy Dep. 286 (2011)

18. Huizenga, C., Abbaszadeh, S., Zagreus, L., Arens, E.: Air quality and thermal comfort in office buildings: results of a large indoor environmental quality survey. Proc. Heal. Build. **III**, 393–397 (2006)

19. Schiller, G., Arens, E.A., Bauman, F., Benton, C., Fountain, M., Doherty, T.: A field study of thermal environments and comfort in office buildings. ASHRAE Trans. **94** (Part 2) (1988). http://escholarship.org/uc/item/4km240x7. Center for the Built Environment, UC Berkeley

20. Jazizadeh, F., Becerik-Gerber, B.: Toward adaptive comfort management in office buildings using participatory sensing for end user driven control. In: BuildSys 2012, pp. 1–8 (2012). doi:10.1145/2422531.2422533

21. Jazizadeh, F., Kavulya, G., Klein, L., Becerik-Gerber, B.: Continuous sensing of occupant perception of indoor ambient factors. In: Computing in Civil Engineering, pp. 161–168. American Society of Civil Engineers (2011)

22. Laftchiev, E., Nikovski, D.: An IoT system to estimate personal thermal comfort. In: 2016 IEEE 3rd World Forum Internet Things (WF-IoT), pp. 672–677 (2016)

23. Ghahramani, A., Jazizadeh, F., Becerik-Gerber, B.: A knowledge based approach for selecting energy-aware and comfort-driven HVAC temperature set points. Energy Build. **85**, 536–548 (2014). doi:10.1016/j.enbuild.2014.09.055

24. Ansi/Ashrae: ANSI/ASHRAE 55:2013 Thermal Environmental Conditions for Human Occupancy. Ashrae (2013). doi:10.1007/s11926-011-0203-9

25. De Dear, R.J., Akimoto, T., Arens, E.A., et al.: Progress in thermal comfort research over the last twenty years. Indoor Air **23**, 442–461 (2013). doi:10.1111/ina.12046

26. Knecht, K., Bryan-Kinns, N., Shoop, K.: Usability and design of personal wearable and portable devices for thermal comfort in shared work environments. In: Proceedings of British HCI 2016 (2016)

27. De Dear, R.: Thermal comfort in practice. Indoor Air **14**(Suppl. 7), 32–39 (2004). doi:10. 1111/j.1600-0668.2004.00270.x

28. Brager, G.S., De Dear, R.: Thermal adaptation in the built environment: a literature review. Energy Build. **27**, 83–96 (1998). doi:10.1016/S0378-7788(97)00053-4

29. Zhang, H., Huizenga, C., Arenas, E., Wang, D.: Thermal sensation and comfort in transient non-uniform thermal environments. Eur. J. Appl. Physiol. **92**, 728–733 (2004). doi:10.1007/s00421-004-1137-y

30. Hoyt, T., Arens, E., Zhang, H.: Extending air temperature setpoints: simulated energy savings and design considerations for new and retrofit buildings. Build. Environ. **88**, 89–96 (2015). doi:10.1016/j.buildenv.2014.09.010

31. Wyon, D.P.: Individual microclimate control: required range, probable benefits and current feasibility. In: Proceedings of Indoor Air, vol. 1, pp. 1067–1072 (1996)

Gathering and Applying Guidelines for Mobile Robot Design for Urban Search and Rescue Application

Ekaterina R. Stepanova[1]([✉]), Markus von der Heyde[2],
Alexandra Kitson[1], Thecla Schiphorst[1], and Bernhard E. Riecke[1]

[1] School of Interactive Arts and Technology, Simon Fraser University,
Surrey, BC, Canada
{erstepan,akitson,thecla,berl}@sfu.ca
[2] Archiact Interactive, Vancouver, BC, Canada
markus.von.der.heyde@archiactvr.com

Abstract. Robotics technology can assist Urban Search and Rescue (USAR) by allowing to explore environments inaccessible or unsafe for a human team [1]. This creates the need to develop a better understanding of the USAR procedures and specific requirements in order to guide the design of the robotics technology which will be accepted by USAR professionals. The current paper explores the specific requirements for the assistive technology, and extracts design guidelines for development of the robotic technology to be used during USAR operations. Design guidelines are derived from both literature review and from a qualitative study performed with Vancouver Heavy Urban Search and Rescue Task Force (HUSAR), focusing on usage scenarios and specific requirements for communication, control and user experience. The study revealed that the most crucial factors for the design of the robot are speed, robustness, reliability, weight, affordability, and adaptability to different environments and tasks, as well as ability to provide a two-way audio/video communication. For the interface, the most important characteristics are its learnability, immersiveness, and ability to afford a high sense of spatial presence. We further discuss how the above requirements were implemented though a case-study of the development of the "TeleSpider" (a hexapod tele-operated walking robot), and assess its effectiveness during the field testing at the Vancouver HUSAR warehouse. Failing to meet a number of the discussed requirements will likely result in the technology to be rejected by the USAR team, and never being used during actual deployments as has happened with a number of existing technologies.

Keywords: Urban Search and Rescue · Participatory design · Design guidelines · Robotics · Telepresence

1 Introduction

Search and Rescue (SAR) and Urban Search and Rescue (USAR) are important, often dangerous, life-saving operations. The assistance of modern technology can substantially improve the speed and safety of these operations. SAR is an operation of search

© Springer International Publishing AG 2017
M. Kurosu (Ed.): HCI 2017, Part II, LNCS 10272, pp. 562–581, 2017.
DOI: 10.1007/978-3-319-58077-7_45

for missing people, often in large natural areas, such as forests and mountains. Robotics technology could be sent out to explore the potential area, where the missing person might be located, which is faster and cheaper than sending a human search team or a helicopter [2]. USAR is an emergency response to a natural or mankind induced disaster, such as an earthquake or a terrorist attack, which destroys urban structures, resulting in people being buried under heavy and unstable debris. In this scenario, a USAR team will be deployed to the site of the disaster to locate, extricate and provide with the initial medical aid the victims. Robotics technology is of a great assistance in USAR operations, as it can go into places, which would be considered unsafe for a human to enter [1, 3]. A robot could be sent to scout the area, identify locations of victims, establish a communication channel with victims, or deliver items like water, snacks or blankets. Robotic technology has also been evaluated to be effective for Marine search and rescue, which is a smaller scale search and rescue operation of extricating victims from ships that sank nearshore [4].

Urban Search and Rescue operations are very time- and error-sensitive, and they impose a lot of stress and cognitive and physical exhaustion on the team – the delays and errors can cause human lives. Technology seems an obvious choice to provide assistance for the USAR team and make the operation go more efficiently. However, this introduces a very challenging task for the designers of the technology, as during USAR operation there is very low tolerance for unreliability of technology or the cognitive demands it imposes on the operator. In other words, there is a high responsibility put on the designers of the technology to make it perfectly suitable for the USAR domain, or otherwise it will get immediately rejected by the users. Technology can be useful for USAR at different stages of the operation: acquiring initial information of the state of the environment, search for victims, providing victims with support, while they are being rescued, and extricating victims [5]. A lot of the technology designed for USAR, is designed with the search stage in mind. That is an important stage to focus on, given that the safety of the USAR team members is of high priority, so the team will not be sent inside the buildings to look for victims until the supporting structures are built and it is ensured to be safe to go in and search for survivors. This delays the rescue process, which can potentially cost victim's lives. However, the robotics technology is disposable, and can be sent into the unsafe environment to scout for survivors, before the collapsed structure was stabilized, and made safe to enter, thus allowing to start the search earlier [6, 7].

The robot, which will be sent to search for the survivors buried under debris, will replace a search and rescue professional, who would have gone into the environment if it were safe enough. That is, the operator can via a tele-presence robot virtually explore the environment – "extend the sense into the interior of the rubble or through hazardous material" while staying in the safety of the base [8]. This can possibly be best achieved if the interface for the robot focuses on creating a sense of "telepresence" - an experience on being present in a distant environment through the medium of technology, thus the experience of actually physically being in that environment [9].

Search and Rescue forces have some technology in their disposal, including some robotic technology, assisting them in the search component [8]. However, a lot of the robotic technology currently used in Urban Search and Rescue is borrowed and then appropriated from a different domain like cameras from construction or lifedetectors from military, and as a result it does not fit the search and rescue environment perfectly. To the best of our knowledge there was not any participatory design reported in the literature for robotics for urban search and rescue. As a result, technology currently available to be used in urban search and rescue does not always meet the requirements of the stakeholders. This motivates a clear need for a deeper understanding of the practices and needs of the USAR professionals by the developers of the technology to be used in USAR operations. To this end, we designed and report here a qualitative pilot study conducted to develop a set of guidelines for the design of the robotics technology for USAR. We collected interview and observations data about USAR practices and experience with technology, to motivate and guide the design of the TeleSpider robot and the interface, which is then analyzed as a case-study.

2 Related Literature

When analyzing research on technology for urban search is rescue, it is important to keep in mind the limitations associated with the methodologies researchers have to use. Due to the nature of the domain, such research is challenging to perform since each disaster cite and conditions are always very different from the previous one, so technology has to be highly adaptable, and the testing environments need to be able to assess that. Another challenge comes from the difficulty to acquire real-world usage data, or to even create a realistic simulation of a USAR operation with comparable levels of stress and exhaustion, and, thus, most of the research may be lacking ecological validity. The opportunities to do on-site research are very rare, but provide very valuable data [3, 7], which still may not generalize to a different disaster scenario. Other data comes from robotic competitions [10–12], which assess the task performance capability of the robot fairly well, however less attention is paid to the usability of it, and how it will fit into the procedures of USAR response.

Hancock and colleagues [13] reported that the most important factor determining the trust in and, consequently, the usability of the robot is the reliability of its performance. It is important to keep the technology very intuitive and fast to learn because the USAR members do not have a lot of time to dedicate to learning a novel interface for the new technology. And, giving the stress level and cognitive exhaustion at the time of the operation, USAR team will not use the technology that requires them a lot of cognitive effort to figure out how to control [3]. Many of the existing robots for USAR were also found to require multiple people to operate, which previous research unanimously considered to be a major disadvantage [3, 14]. Another common issue with the existing technology was its size, because a number of robots were cumbersome, heavy, and may require multiple people to carry them [3], which can be addressed with a solution where a larger "mother" robot carries smaller robots to the site [15].

When operating a robot for search and rescue, it was also reported that some participants would find it hard to perform both the navigation and the search tasks at the same time [16]. This last finding highlights the importance for better interface for navigation, which can reduce the cognitive load required for staying oriented and controlling the movement, and free up the resources for the search process. Another solution would be to create a partially autonomous robot, which receives some direction from the human, but still allows the operator to mostly focus on the search [17–19]. Besides shifting the navigation tasks mostly onto an autonomous robot, it was shown to be beneficial to design the robot to assist with the search as well, by providing cues to the human operator of possible locations of the victim based on heat, skin color, color contrast and motion [20]. Tejada and colleagues [21] explored different levels of robot autonomy used in search and rescue, and reported the level of autonomy will depend on the particular role the human-robot team is performing, and therefore the optimal setup is to have the capability to switch between the modes.

Another problem was associated with the position of the robot – most of the robots designed for search and rescue are low to the ground making it harder for the user to feel immersed and maintain spatial awareness because they look at the environment from an unusual angle for a human. Burke and colleagues [14] have suggested that users need to develop a new cognitive model in order to comprehend the environment in terms of the robot. Also, spatial and situational awareness was challenging to maintain because of the fast or large rotations of the camera, or the operator not keeping track of the relative orientation of the camera to the body of the robot – both led to a loss of orientation [22]. Adding different components to the interface can moderate this situational awareness problem, indicating various states of the robot: relative location, orientation of the robot body and camera, camera used, health state of the robot, etc. [23]. There was also a difference in the case of learning of the new interface. Novel users have less problems with learning a new interface, while experienced users will prefer the interface to be similar to something they are already familiar with [22, 24]. This is important to consider when modelling an interface for a robot for USAR from an existing interface used for modern video games and other entertainment technology, and as such hoping to increase the familiarity and shorten the learning curve. A lot of USAR team members are likely to have little experience with modern video games, and will not have an extensive experience with popular controllers. This is because most of the USAR members are over the age of 30, because prior to becoming a USAR specialist they have to get training and work experience in another field (e.g. firefighting), and only then go through the specialized training for USAR: as a result, they will have little experience with modern interfaces, because the technology was less available or common when they were children, and now their work and training schedule makes it challenging to explore it at their spare time.

There is a number of factors to consider, when developing technology for the domain of USAR: reliability, cognitive load, human-robot ratio, access to information about the state of the robot, position of the camera, and stakeholders experience with modern technology.

3   Study Methodology

In order to inform the development of a robot and the interface for it, which will fit the practices of USAR the best and maximize the ease of use, we used a participatory design method. For this preliminary pilot study which aims to gather functional requirements for the robot and the interface, we conducted a semi-structured interview and informal group interview with USAR professionals. This allows us to develop a better understanding of the possible usage scenarios and functional requirements for the robotic technology. Understanding how urban search and rescue team members navigate through the emergency site, how they search for the victims, and how they communicate with their colleagues, will give suggestions on how to integrate the exiting strategies being used by the USAR Task Force into TeleSpider design and make it more intuitive and easy to learn. We also sought information about the existing technology being used by USAR, what works well, and what kind of issues they encounter, in order to minimize these problems in the design.

3.1   The Interview Guide

For conducting the semi-structured interview, we developed an interview guide (see Appendix), focusing on particular areas of USAR practice, which are important to understand in order to inform particular aspects of the robot design (see Fig. 1 for the relationship between interview questions and design implications). The Interview Guide contained three sections: introduction, questions about the practice and the procedures of a USAR operation, and questions related to the use of technology. The guide was designed to develop an understanding of the practices and experience of the USAR team, which will motivate our design decision for the robot and the interface. See the full interview guide in the appendix.

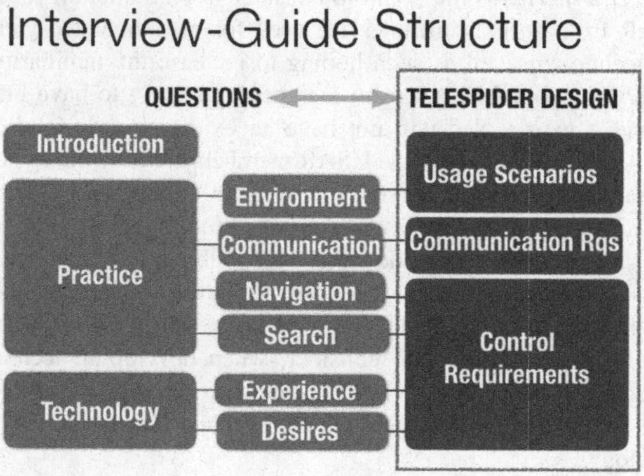

Fig. 1. Power distribution of channel at 1555 nm along the link of 383 km (Source: LNCS 5412, p. 323)

3.2   Participants

We contacted Vancouver Heavy Urban Search and Rescue and went to visit their warehouse where we conducted a semi-structured interview and observations with fields notes with six Urban Search and Rescue professionals. We had one participant for semi-structured interview and five participants for observation and informal group interview. All participants were males and have a background in firefighting. They participated voluntarily and have not received any monetary compensation for their time.

4   Findings

We report the findings as the summary from the background research, field notes and audio recordings from the interviews.

4.1   The Team

The search and rescue is a very complex multi-staged operation. In the Vancouver Urban Search and Rescue Task Force there are about 120 professionals of various expertise. Team members are coming from the following departments:

- Vancouver Fire and Rescue Services
- Vancouver Police Department
- City of Vancouver Engineering Department
- Vancouver Park Board
- BC Ambulance Service

Then, they undergo specialized training for urban search and rescue, on top of their original training in firefighting, paramedics, etc. As a result, different team members will have various expertise and different roles. On a particular deployment about 70–120 team members are sent, and a few people may coordinate the operation from the warehouse in Vancouver.

4.2   USAR Procedure

When there is a big disaster somewhere in the world, the Vancouver Urban Search and Rescue team may be sent there on a deployment along with USAR teams from other countries. When going on a deployment, USAR will ship most of their warehouse with them to create an autonomous base near the disaster site.

Once the Task Force arrives at the destination of their deployment, they first do a "360" – they walk around the collapsed structures to get a sense of the environment. After the "360", the engineering team assesses the structure and the level of damage. Then, the search team will proceed to searching for survivors. However, because the safety of the team is the highest priority, no team members will be entering any buildings until supportive wooden structures are built to ensure that nothing is going to collapse any further.

Once a general location of a survivor is identified and confirmed, which usually requires two independent positive signals unless its unambiguous, the search team will start gathering the more detailed information regarding the specific position and the state of the victim. Based on that information and with the help of the engineering team, the plan for making a safe access to the survivors will be created. The rescue process usually involves slow and careful cuts through concrete, and therefore takes a long time (i.e., multiple hours), depending on the complicatedness of the case. If the environment allows for that, then there will be an attempt to pass water, protein bars and blankets to the victims, to help them survive while they are waiting to be rescued. The team tries to maximize the number of saved victims in the shortest time, and, as a result, the USAR team will first make a quick assessment of the amount of the required effort for a particular rescue, and may make a sacrifice of not proceeding with this rescue, if there is a different area, requiring less time and resulting in higher number of people saved.

4.3   Practice

Environment
The environment, in which search and rescue operations are held, can differ a lot. As most of the USAR operations are responds to natural disasters, such as earthquakes and floods, the affected areas tend to be of a big scale (one or several towns), however after terrorist attacks the area will usually be smaller. The level of the destruction can vary a lot, however usually it will be a very challenging terrain for the robot (See Fig. 2 for an example of the training environment). Often the team does not have to dig deep under the destroyed concrete of a building, as it is assumed that there are unlikely to be any survivors any deeper than a few meters. Often there might be a lot of noise in the environment, especially once the rescue starts, accompanied with drilling through and cutting the concrete. When the Task Force is sent on a deployment, they are getting some minimal crucial information about the state of the site they are being sent to. Therefore, the interviewees have expressed an interest in getting a better overview of the site prior to the deployment, which could be realized, for example, through sending drones to the site in advance.

Design Implications: Considering the scale of the area that needs to be investigated for potential survivors, the speed and the range of search becomes a very critical parameter of the assistive technology. Adaptability to different terrains is also of high importance.

Communication
Communication was reported to be a very crucial part of the USAR practices. Communication is usually performed through radio or texting, and tends to be succinct and periodical. A person in the field will report to their captain the main information, such that he is going in or detecting a survivor. Once a survivor is located, the team will try to have a constant communication with them if possible. The team cannot always rely on having service in the area of disasters, so radio is the default medium of communication. Once a victim is located, if the environment allows for that, the rescue team will try to establish a continuous periodical communication with him/her to check on their needs and state and keep them calm, while they are being rescued.

Fig. 2. The training environment at Vancouver HUSAR.

Design Implications: Robot should have a good connection with it's control interface independent of having service in the area and be powerful enough to send signals through a level of obstruction (i.e., usually layers of concrete), as well as being robust to occasions of loss of signal. It may be worth exploring incorporating autonomous backtracking through the path a robot walked in case of the connection loss until it is re-established. One of the interviewees also expressed an interest for a 2-way audio and video connection to the robot, allowing a multimodal conversation with victims. In this usage scenario, a robot will seat with the survivor it found until the survivor is being extricated.

Navigation

USAR team uses the system similar to cardinal directions: they will assign letters to the sides of the building and will refer to them to communicate directions and locations. They will also leave tape marks on the building, if they need to note and later refer to a specific location. The interviewees reported rarely to have problems with getting lost in the environment, which often can be explained by the fact that the environment in most cases does not allow for a human to walk inside the building and explore it for a long time, and most of the search happens from the surface. However, one participant reported getting lost once in an underground parking in a fire, where he could not see the environment because of the smoke. He found his way out by going in the direction of the voices of his team members.

When the location of a survivor was identified, the search team will find an existing or drill a new hole to put a camera through and gather information about the surroundings of the survivor. In order to do that, the team member will have to manipulate the camera (see Fig. 5) by turning it around and try to derive from the image from the camera the actual specific location of the objects on the other side of the hole. The interviewees have reported to have difficulty sometimes remaining oriented when using those cameras after making multiple turns. To cope with this issue, they will usually have to take the camera out and put it back in to reconfirm their understanding of the positions of the objects, as well as using a landmark (e.g. a chair) on the camera stream to map the relative positions of everything else. So, they will "home" all of the key objects they find to the landmark they have chosen. One of the interviewees has expressed an interest for those cameras to have some kind of display of the specific camera rotation on the handlers.

Design Implications: Having a mini map view on the interface for the robot may help with disambiguating its position and orientation in the environment. Specifying customized "cardinal" directions and landmarks on the map would help keep it consistent with the established system in the USAR, which will allow for easier communication of spatial information to other team-members, who are not using the robot. The robot could have a functionality of leaving marks on landmarks on the map analogously to the tape marks used by the team. The rotation of the camera in relation to the body of the robot should also be clearly identified on the interface. The camera on the robot should also be equipped with a light, since the environment is usually very dark.

Search

A significant portion of the search is performed from the surface, and relies on the responses from the survivors. Search teams will work around the disaster area and yell to let the survivors know that the USAR team is there and then listen for any responses and cries for help from the victims. Survivors are advised to knock, if they cannot respond vocally, so the search team listens to a rhythmic knocking as well as voices.

Design Implications: If the robot is used for this initial stage of the search, it should have the functionality to broadcast the message that it is there on the rescue mission to the potential survivors to encourage them to start signalling that they need help. It should also be able to listen for the sounds in the environment, and be able to identify the direction from which the sound is coming from, to continue the search in that direction. Having the 3rd sound system would be especially important for this purpose. Having an automatic system for identifying voices or knocking could be an asset.

4.4   Technology

Experience

Most of the technology used in USAR is borrowed from a different field, e.g. construction and then appropriated to the needs of USAR. Some technology gets inherited from military: when military gets new technology, they can pass the older models to USAR. The lack of USAR specific technology is partially explained by relatively low budget of HUSAR and high costs of technology designed specifically for USAR, when analogous gadgets from a different field can have a lower price.

Technology used for the search can be divided into 3 functional groups:

(1) Assisting with detecting survivors (large range)
(2) Assisting with determined specific position and condition of a survivor once they have been detected (small range)
(3) Assisting the interaction with survivors, while they are being rescued

For the first function USAR uses: K-9 units (search and rescue trained dogs), life detectors (acoustic) and life detectors (vital signals).

K-9 units are the fastest and most efficient, however they can get tired and there are only two of them in the Canadian HUSAR.

Sound life detectors were reported to be somewhat slow to use, and they do not work that well if the noise level gets too high.

Life detectors, based on vital signals such as heart rate, have yet to be used by the interviewees in the field. But, they see a lot of potential in this technology. It is likely to be slower than K-9 units, but faster than sound detectors.

Some of the interviewees also mentioned drones, that they do not have at the warehouse, but have seen presentations with them. Drones were evaluated as a potentially very helpful piece of technology that can significantly speed up the search process at the very initial stages even prior to the deployment. Drones can provide a quick overview of the whole site of the operation and they will not have to overcome the obstacles of the harsh terrain as any on-land technology. One of the participants also mentioned the immersiveness of the technology as an interesting and enjoyable experience.

For the second function USAR team is equipped with a variety of cameras, which can be pushed through a small hole, which is usually made by drilling through the concrete), and then turned around to get an understanding of the details of the immediate surroundings of the survivors, his/her relative position and physical and emotional condition. All of the above is important to assess in order to refine the rescue plan, to ensure that the survivor does not get hurt through the process of rescue.

At the third stage, depending on what the environment allows for, a K-9 units may be sent to deliver blankets, water and power bars to the survivor. A communication through radio or audio-visual device like Facetime™ may be established with a survivor to ensure that they know that they are being rescued and inquire them regarding their needs.

Design Implications: The robot design should concentrate on a particular function to ensure it's best fitness. The participants saw the potential for the robot to be used in any of those three stages. However, for the first functional application the speed and robustness to the terrain will need to be the main focus of the design. For the second function, the focus should be more on the smaller size and good video stream and lighting. For the third function it will be important to find the optimal size to allow the robot to carry small loads but still fit through narrow holes, as well as have a reliable two-way audio and video communication. For this function also some attention should be put on the appearance of the robot, as well as affordability.

Requirements and Assets
Interviewees have emphasised the following criteria as being the most important for a new piece of technology:

(1) Fast to operate
(2) Fast to learn
(3) Robust (hard to brake)

(4) Light to carry
(5) Affordable price

All of the participants have reported preference to a low-level control of a robot to the level of whole robot-body movement over the options of the control of limbs, or high-level control of the end location. However, we should note that the literature has suggested the advantage of partially autonomous robots [17–19].

When the participants were asked to brainstorm freely about what they would want the robot to do in the "ideal world", they have suggested the following ideas:

- lifting itself up to fly over obstacles
- bring water, protein bars and blankets to the survivors
- leave a metronome (a device producing knocking sound) at the location where victims are found so they can be located more easily later on
- have a two-way video camera (e.g., facetime) to talk to victims
- assess the quality of the air
- have life detectors (vital signals)
- have a real-time language translator (as most of the deployments are international)
- have a "mind-control" mode

More Details on the Used Technology

K-9 Units (Specially Trained Dogs for Search and Rescue)

K-9 unit (See Fig. 3) is a team of an USAR professional and a specially trained dog who uses her sense of smell to locate the victim. Once the victim is located, the dog will bark to draw attention to the area where they found them. K-9 units will only respond to a stationary victim, as otherwise, they will assume that the person is fine and does not require a rescue. This way, K-9 units will not respond to finding other search team members. False-positive signals are relatively frequent. So, before making a decision to proceed to the rescue stage after one positive signal from a K-9 unit, the team will bring the second dog to reconfirm the location. In the case where a dog can reach the victim, they may be used to bring a blanket, water bottle and a protein bar to the survivor to help them sustain themselves before they get rescued, which may take hours. K-9 units are very fast and efficient, and there is currently no technology in

Fig. 3. K-9 unit – specially trained dog.

which USAR would prefer to use over K-9. However, a different assistive technology is required as well, as dogs get tired, or they can die during a rescue. K-9 s are also expensive and take half a year to get trained. As a result, USARs do not have enough K-9 resources to perform search with their help only. Another issue with K-9 units is that no one except for the dog has any knowledge of the environment the dog has searched through. Our interviewees express an interest in putting a robot or a camera on the K-9 unit, so that a human team member can see the environment the dog is navigating through. However, the problem with that suggestion is that dogs usually have to work "naked", to ensure that they do not get stuck in the debris or get caught on a strap.

Delsar Life Detectors (Acoustic)
Sound based detectors (See Fig. 4) are used to refine the location of the victim based on the vocal signals or knocking. A search team member will place the detectors to encompass the area of the search, and listen to the acoustic signals from victims. Then, he will slowly narrow down the area of the sound source by moving the detectors closer together. This method is very slow, but it could be used when K-9 units are not available, or when a more precise location is required.

Fig. 4. Acoustic life detectors.

Cameras
Once a general location of a victim is determined, the rescue team will drill a hole in the concrete and they will put a camera (See Fig. 5) through the hole to examine the environment and the precise condition and position of the victim. The cameras are equipped with diodes to light up their view and a monitor either on the handle or in a separate box, which is carried on a strap around the neck (the monitor get placed at a belt level). One of the camera types also has a second monitor that is left in the base,

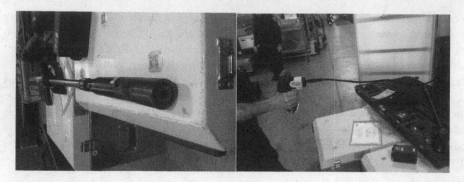

Fig. 5. Cameras. The left camera is designed specifically for USAR. The right camera is normally used in construction.

and often is not used. However, in some cases a second person looking at the monitor may use the radio to point out to the person in the field that he has missed something.

5 Summary of Requirements

From the collected data we suggest the following guidelines for the development of the technology to assist in USAR operations:

1. Identify the specific stage(s) and functions of the operation, where the robot will be able to assist the team. Preferably a niche where it can outperform alternative solutions.
2. Maximize the speed, robustness and adaptability to different environments.
3. Minimize the price, as the robot won't be rescued if it gets stuck or buried.
4. Use iterative participatory design to get feedback on the prototypes at different stages of the development from the stakeholders.

Vancouver HUSAR has shown a lot of interest in the project and further collaboration.

6 Case Study

To test and refine the described requirements, we designed and built a hexapod robot ("TeleSpider") that was after several in-lab design iterations brought out to a local USAR training environment for testing. The Telespider design is focusing on implementation of a biologically inspired hexapod locomotion system allowing for better adaptability to challenging unpredictable terrain than wheel-based robots [25–27] and telepresence enhancing interface. Due to constraints in the context of student projects and funding the requirements were not implemented in the order of priority, but in the order of complexity of the task. Therefore, our first approach was to design a hexapod robot that can perform robust walking patterns in unknown environments including debris and obstacles.

After a brief market review, the initial design decision fell onto off the shelf components for the mechanical design (due to low cost) with a minicomputer (Raspberry PI) due to having both a flexible programming environment as well as many connectors to sensor equipment.

The first prototype was brought on a field trip to the USAR training site in Vancouver (see Fig. 6) to perform under best available real world conditions. This demonstrated the inability of the robot to walk uphill on loose material, which had not been tested under lab conditions beforehand. However, the robot could:

Fig. 6. First functional TeleSpider prototype on the USAR training site inside a tube.

1. Walk over and climb across smaller obstacles, but failed with steps higher than approx. 8 cm.
2. Walk in uneven terrain (a concrete tube) and return.
3. Carry a stereo camera and a variable set of batteries.
4. Carry additional loads about its own weight (2.5 kg) during the operation (tested under lab conditions)
5. Be controlled by a custom build radio controller with an effective distance up to 100 m.
6. Be robust to some environmental hazard as having mostly water resistant electronics.
7. Walk at a speed of about 2 cm per second with a battery life time of about 20 min.

The transmitted video stream was technically stable but contained all the vibrations and jitter from the walk pattern. In addition, the latency in the control for gaze direction motivated us to shift towards 360-degree camera alternatives.

Under lab conditions, the smallest passage the robot can currently cross with the appropriate gait-pattern measures 75 × 260 mm (height x width). The biggest step it can go up keeping still an upright position and not touching ground is about 180 mm. Potentially, the robot can cross gaps with a size up to 350 mm. The gait patterns for those behaviors are still under development and these estimates are based on the mechanical design of the robot construction.

The combination of speed, payload and battery lifetime of 20 min needs improvement, since normal operations would last much longer and the operators should not have to spend time to change batteries. The overall payload of about 3 kg suggests that the robot could extend the operating time up to 3 h given additional battery packs. In lab conditions, we could produce walking speeds up to 4 cm/sec which would allow a distance up to 50 m over the lifetime of one set of batteries (~ 20 min with 2200 mAh).

However, the first prototype also failed on some requirements, which were thus shifted towards later implementation stages: Supporting reorientation, transmission of audio signals, form a map layout during exploration. Further necessary improvements were gathered to improve the design:

1. Stabilize the body during walk behavior and during stationary periods to smooth the video signal.
2. Make the user see the transmitted video in first person perspective while controlling the robot, thus making use of the effortless self-orientation proclaimed by the project.
3. Carry a 360° camera system (not tested on USAR training site) and transmit control signals alongside the pictures over standard Wi-Fi.

Actually building and testing the robot in a fairly realistic yet safe USAR environment allowed us to not only better understand necessary next steps to designing a more suitable USAR robot, but also allowed us to come up with the revised and refined requirement and design recommendations described above.

7 Conclusions

This initial study expanded on our understanding of the current practices in Urban Search and Rescue and their challenges and needs. The USAR has also expressed an interest in the TeleSpider, even though it is currently only in an early stage of its development with a number of yet to be resolved issues. Our procedure has highlighted the high importance of the field testing of the technology, as the controlled in-lab environment cannot provide the same range of challenges as a real world scenario. There is a number of challenging trade-offs to balance when developing technology for USAR, as it needs to be both highly reliable and low-maintenance, while also remain low-cost since there is a high risk of it to be stranded and abandoned on top of a generally low budget of USAR departments.

For the future studies we will refine the research methodology, and develop a more targeted interview guide to explore specific parts of the search and rescue procedures with members of the corresponding sub teams. We will also perform user testings of teleoperation interfaces with the USAR team accompanied by interviews and observation in order to gage an understanding of the specific factors in this particular demographic, that would have an influence on the use of the telepresence technology.

In order to ensure that an assistive robotic technology fulfills the needs of the stakeholders, we need to focus on making it robust to harsh and fluctuating terrains and also fast. Another important consideration is to determine a specific scenario, where the robot will have a competitive advantage over other technology and K-9 s, e.g. going through very small holes into the environment, which is otherwise unreachable for anything as big as a dog, or environments where the level of oxygen and toxins is not determined. The robotic technology has a high potential of improving the efficiency of search and rescue operations and contributing to a lot of humans lives saved, but it has to be designed to meet the specific needs and practices of a USAR team in order to be adopted in the team.

Acknowledgments. Our thanks go to Archiact Interactive for their partnership on this project and to Vancouver Heavy Urban Search and Rescue for providing us with an opportunity to visit the warehouse. This research was funded by an NSERC ENGAGE grant.

Appendix

Interview Guide – Example Questions

Introduction

Personal story/Understanding the interviewee

- Why did you decide to become a search and rescue professional?
- What do you love and not so much about your work?
- Who would you have become if you were not a search and rescue worker?
- Tell me about your most challenging rescue?
- Was there a significant moment in your work experience, which you would not mind sharing?
- Describe how you feel when you save a person?
- How often do you get calls?
- How do you spend your time when there are no emergency calls?

Usage Scenarios/Transition

Environment and process of urban search and rescue operations

- Describe the **setting** of a typical search and rescue operation?
- How do you **asses the condition** of the environment?
- What is the **noise** level like normally?
- How **long** does the operation take on average?
- How does a search and rescue operation normally progress?
- How **many people** are usually involved?

- What kind of **information** will you need to **gather** about the space/environment in the emergency state?
- What kind of information would you **ideally** like to have, but which is hard to get currently?
- What are some of the **main challenges** you face during a search and rescue?
- What are some of the important things **to do first** once you arrived at a place of emergency?
- Do you have any formal **safety procedures**?
- How do you deal with stress and **cognitive exhaustion**?

Dangerous situations

- What type/levels of dangerous situations can occur during USAR?
- How do you assess them? How do you deal with them?
- How do you ensure your own and your partner's **safety**?

Communication Requirements

Collaboration and inner team interaction

- How do you **communicate** with your colleagues during a search and rescue operation?
- How do you provide and receive **support** from your team?
- What is the **relationship** between team communication and a **successful** rescue operation?
- Any interesting stories about how an interaction went? Examples of **seamless** communication? **Communication failure**?

Interaction with Victims

- What do you **feel & think** once you have just spotted a buried victim?
- What **procedures** do you need to follow?
- What some of the important things to **communicate to a victim**, once you found him?
- If a victim is conscious, how do you ensure their physical and **emotional safety**?

Navigation Control Requirements

Movement and Navigation

- How do you **move** through a collapsed building?
- How do you **navigate**? Do you study the **map** of the building before going in?
- How do you know where to go?
- How do you remain oriented?
- Is it easy to get **lost**? If so, why?

– Is there an information you wish you had in those situations?
– How do you **communicate** the plan of the collapsed building to your colleagues?

Process of Search for survivors

– How do you perform a **search** in a collapsed building?
– What kind of things do you need to pay attention to?
– How do you ensure the thoroughness of the search?
– Is there any information you **ideally** would like to have to assist you in the search process which is not currently available for you?
– Can you **compare a search experience** to any other activity?
– How do you **communicate the location** of a victim to the rest of the team?
– Do you often find yourself getting **false positive signals**?
– What type of things make the search harder?

Technology Specific Requirements

Use of technology to assist Search and Rescue operations

– Have you ever used any **technology** to assist you in search and rescue?
– Could you describe your experience?
– What did you like/ dislike about it?
– What kind of **features** did it have and what worked/ did not work?
– Do you think technology (such as robots) could be useful for search and rescue operation?
– What **kind of tasks** could it be useful for? Where you don't think that it may be used?
– **How much control** would you want to have over navigation of a remote robot?
– How would you like to control it ideally?
– How should it **feel** like to operate a remote robot?
– Have you ever felt fully **immersed** in some kind of virtual experience? What was it? Can you describe your experience? What were the factors invoking the sense of immersion?

Final Questions

– Quick introduction of the TeleSpider concept
– What are your first thoughts?
– From what we have discussed, what in your opinion are the most important aspects to be considered in the design of the TeleSpider robot?

References

1. Lima, P.U.: Search and rescue robots: the civil protection teams of the future. In: 2012 Third International Conference on Emerging Security Technologies (EST), pp. 12–19 (2012)
2. Bogue, R.: Search and rescue and disaster relief robots: has their time finally come? Ind. Robot Int. J. **43**, 138–143 (2016). doi:10.1108/IR-12-2015-0228
3. Casper, J., Murphy, R.R.: Human-robot interactions during the robot-assisted urban search and rescue response at the world trade center. IEEE Trans. Syst. Man Cybern. Part B Cybern. **33**, 367–385 (2003). doi:10.1109/TSMCB.2003.811794
4. Yeong, S.P., King, L.M., Dol, S.S.: A review on marine search and rescue operations using unmanned aerial vehicles. World Acad. Sci. Eng. Technol. Int. J. Mech. Aerosp. Ind. Mechatron. Manuf. Eng. **9**, 396–399 (2015)
5. Murphy, R.R., Tadokoro, S., Kleiner, A.: Disaster robotics. In: Siciliano, B., Khatib, O. (eds.) Springer Handbook of Robotics, pp. 1577–1604. Springer, Cham (2016). doi:10.1007/978-3-319-32552-1_60
6. Statheropoulos, M., Agapiou, A., Pallis, G.C., et al.: Factors that affect rescue time in urban search and rescue (USAR) operations. Nat. Hazards **75**, 57–69 (2015). doi:10.1007/s11069-014-1304-3
7. Nagatani, K., Kiribayashi, S., Okada, Y., et al.: Emergency response to the nuclear accident at the Fukushima Daiichi Nuclear Power Plants using mobile rescue robots. J. Field Robot **30**, 44–63 (2013). doi:10.1002/rob.21439
8. Murphy, R.R., Tadokoro, S., Nardi, D., et al.: Search and rescue robotics. In: Siciliano, B., Khatib, O. (eds.) Springer Handbook of Robotics, pp. 1151–1173. Springer, Heidelberg (2008)
9. Minsky, M.: Telepresence. Omni, 45–50 (1980)
10. Sheh, R., Jacoff, A., Virts, A.-M., Kimura, T., Pellenz, J., Schwertfeger, S., Suthakorn, J.: Advancing the state of urban search and rescue robotics through the RoboCupRescue robot league competition. In: Yoshida, K., Tadokoro, S. (eds.) Field and Service Robotics. STAR, vol. 92, pp. 127–142. Springer, Heidelberg (2014). doi:10.1007/978-3-642-40686-7_9
11. Osuka, K., Murphy, R., Schultz, A.C.: USAR competitions for physically situated robots. IEEE Robot. Autom. Mag. **9**, 26–33 (2002). doi:10.1109/MRA.2002.1035211
12. Schneider, F.E., Wildermuth, D., Wolf, H.L.: ELROB and EURATHLON: improving search amp; rescue robotics through real-world robot competitions. In: 2015 10th International Workshop on Robot Motion Control RoMoCo, pp. 118–123 (2015)
13. Hancock, P.A., Billings, D.R., Schaefer, K.E., et al.: A meta-analysis of factors affecting trust in human-robot interaction. Hum. Factors **53**, 517–527 (2011)
14. Burke, J.L., Murphy, R.R., Coovert, M.D., Riddle, D.L.: Moonlight in miami: field study of human-robot interaction in the context of an urban search and rescue disaster response training exercise. Hum.-Comput. Interact **19**, 85–116 (2004). doi:10.1080/07370024.2004.9667341
15. Mashrik, T., Baized, A.M., Iftekhar, L., Ahmed, N.: Urban search and rescue mission: the use of marsupial robots. J. Mod. Sci. Technol. **4**, 27–35 (2016)
16. Yanco, H.A., Baker, M., Keyes, B., Thoren, P.: Analysis of human-robot interaction for urban search and rescue. In: Proceedings of PerMIS (2006)
17. Bruemmer, D.J., Boring, R.L., Few, D.A., et al.: I call shotgun!: an evaluation of mixed-initiative control for novice users of a search and rescue robot. In: 2004 IEEE International Conference on Systems, Man and Cybernetics, vol. 3, pp. 2847–2852 (2004)
18. Wegner, R., Anderson, J.: Agent-based support for balancing teleoperation and autonomy in urban search and rescue. Int. J. Robot Autom. **21**(2), 120 (2006)

19. Liu, Y., Nejat, G.: Robotic urban search and rescue: a survey from the control perspective. J. Intell. Robot. Syst. **72**, 147–165 (2013). doi:10.1007/s10846-013-9822-x

20. Murphy, R.R., Casper, J., Micire, M., et al.: Mixed-Initiative Control of Multiple Heterogeneous Robots for Urban Search and Rescue (2000)

21. Tejada, S., Cristina, A., Goodwyne, P., Normand, E., O'Hara, R., Tarapore, S.: Virtual synergy: a human-robot interface for urban search and rescue. In: AAAI Mobile Robot Competition, Chicago, pp. 13–19 (2003)

22. Maxwell, B.A., Ward, N., Heckel, F.: Game-based design of human-robot interfaces for urban search and rescue. In: Computer-Human Interface Fringe (2004)

23. Scholtz, J., Young, J., Drury, J.L., Yanco, H.A.: Evaluation of human-robot interaction awareness in search and rescue. In: 2004 IEEE International Conference on Robotics and Automation, ICRA 2004, vol. 3, pp. 2327–2332 (2004)

24. Baker, M., Casey, R., Keyes, B., Yanco, H.A.: Improved interfaces for human-robot interaction in urban search and rescue. In: 2004 IEEE International Conference on Systems, Man and Cybernetics, vol. 3, pp. 2960–2965 (2004)

25. Baisch, A.T., Sreetharan, P.S., Wood, R.J.: Biologically-inspired locomotion of a 2g hexapod robot. In: 2010 IEEE/RSJ International Conference on Intelligent Robots and Systems (IROS), pp. 5360–5365 (2010)

26. Billah, M.M., Ahmed, M., Farhana, S.: Walking hexapod robot in disaster recovery: developing algorithm for terrain negotiation and navigation. In: Proceedings of World Academy of Science, Engineering and Technology, pp. 328–333 (2008)

27. Hoover, A.M., Steltz, E., Fearing, R.S.: RoACH: an autonomous 2.4g crawling hexapod robot. In: IEEE/RSJ International Conference on Intelligent Robots and Systems, pp. 26–33 (2008)

NFC-Enabled eTicketing in Public Transport – Aims, Approaches and First Results of the OPTIMOS Project

Ulrike Stopka[✉], Gertraud Schäfer, and Andreas Kreisel

Technische Universität Dresden, Dresden, Germany
{ulrike.stopka,gertraud.schaefer,andreas.kreisel}@tu-dresden.de

Abstract. The comprehensive digitalization of the economy requires efficient actions from all market partners involved. This also applies to public transport sector. Proprietary solutions and closed systems are inefficient and hamper interoperability, harmonization, competition and market success. The paper presents the planned establishment of an NFC-based open ecosystem to offer secure identification for mobile services, which is demonstrated in the eTicketing domain of public passenger transport. Objectives, approaches and initial results of the OPTIMOS project are discussed, as well as further steps of action and expected results. In the run-up, the paper deals with the characteristics of the NFC technology, the NFC enabled mobile devices, the necessity of standardization and the new developed specifications in cooperation with NFC Forum, GSMA, ISO and other standardization bodies. The use cases to be implemented within the scope of the customer mobile life cycle are presented as well as the first results of interoperability tests between NFC-enabled smartphones and reader devices in public transport vehicles. At the same time, user acceptance, a high level of usability and ease of use is at the focus of the project and has to be evaluated.

Keywords: eTicketing in public transport · Near field communication · NFC enabled mobile devices · Interoperability · Standardization · Authentication · Use cases · KA provisioning system · Open ecosystem

1 Motivation

The increasing use of mobile services is one of the leading social trends worldwide. Service providers are obliged to follow this trend in order to remain competitive.

Leading international corporations implement and use mobile infrastructures on the basis of proprietary electronic identities or proprietary payment methods. Furthermore, using Near Field Communication (NFC) smartphones for public transport worldwide seems difficult due to the diversity of different eTicket infrastructures. National service providers and technology suppliers are, however, dependent on non-discriminatory and open infrastructures, accessible for all and interoperable with different existing systems. Therefore, the research

© Springer International Publishing AG 2017
M. Kurosu (Ed.): HCI 2017, Part II, LNCS 10272, pp. 582–597, 2017.
DOI: 10.1007/978-3-319-58077-7_46

project OPTIMOS (acronym for Open PracTical Infrastructure for MObile Services) in the frame of the German federal government's NFC initiative aims to create a NFC-based open ecosystem using secure identities for mobile services. The project focusses on national e-ticketing in public transport to define and test NFC based applications. The findings will contribute to international NFC standardization with the goal to ensure the global interoperable use of NFC devices in the medium term.

2   Characteristics of NFC Technology in Comparison to Other Wireless Short Distance Communication Technologies

NFC is a technology for the contactless exchange of data over short distances which is particularly suitable for mobile applications such as mobile payment or mobile ticketing. NFC was developed in 2002 by NXP Semiconductors and Sony, mainly based on two already established technologies (radio frequency identification and electronic chip cards). With the Mikron Fare Collection System (MIFARE) from NXP Semiconductors and Felicity Card (FeliCa) from Sony, both manufacturers brought their experience in the field of contactless radio frequency identification (RFID) smart-card systems into the NFC world. However, the market breakthrough did not come until 2011, when around 30 million NFC-enabled mobile phones in more than 40 different handset models were delivered worldwide [1]. These are mostly being used in Asia (especially South Korea and Japan), where NFC applications are already very popular. In Europe, however, NFC has been less successful. Forecasts for the world-wide number of NFC-enabled smartphones expect approx. 1.9 billion by 2018 [7]. This equals circa 57% of the global number of smartphones estimated at 3.3 billion for 2018 [5].

The NFC technology is based on classical RFID systems. A special reader generates a constant electromagnetic field and asks whether a NFC chip is in range [13]. Figure 1 shows the development from RFID and smart card to NFC technology.

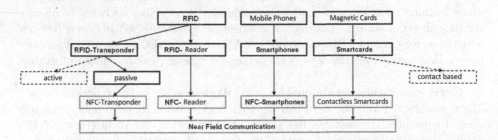

Fig. 1. Evolution from RFID to NFC technology (based on [2, p. 43])

NFC transponders, readers, contactless smartcards and NFC-enabled smartphones form the basis for today's application of NFC technology. However, there is no physical contact ("touch") between the devices required for communication. This makes NFC particularly attractive for the installation in smartphones and smart cards.

A fundamental feature that distinguishes NFC technology from RFID is that the strict separation between reading devices that carry out the active part and transponders that behave passively is canceled. Accordingly, NFC devices can alternately take on the role of an active reader (also called initiator) and act as a passive transponder (also called target device) in the next moment. This offers more flexibility in use due to the possibility of switching between the active and passive communication mode. For data transmission, NFC devices use inductive coupling in a magnetic field in the frequency range of 13.56 MHz. This frequency is license-free and can therefore be used worldwide. The maximum data transfer speed that can be achieved is 424 kbit/s and the transmission range is limited to 10 cm or less (in case of NFC enabled smartphones ca. 4 cm) [10] to ensure trouble-free operation], whereas RFID-Systems can bridge much more greater distances between reader and transponder (in the 2.45 or 5.8 GHz range up to 10 m) [9]. Because of the extremely short range, NFC does not compete with Bluetooth or wireless LAN. NFC operates at slower speeds than Bluetooth, but consumes far less power (similar to Bluetooth low energy protocol). [5] Another benefit of NFC technology comes in its ease of use. When a NFC-enabled smartphone, for example, is hold up to the contact surface of the terminal, the electromagnetic field activates the NFC chip in the smartphone, and the two devices exchange data. Unlike Bluetooth or Wi-Fi, there is no need to connect the device or log in [13].

NFC devices can be deployed in different modes of operation: peer-to-peer-mode, read/write mode, card emulation mode (see Fig. 2).

In the **peer-to-peer operation mode**, also called active mode, two connected NFC devices can exchange small amounts of data and communicate with each other to exchange information in an ad hoc fashion. In this case, one NFC device carries out the role of the initiator, generates a magnetic field and can thereby be perceived by a second NFC device supplying it with energy (target device). The next step is to swap the roles of both devices. The previous target becomes the initiator and generates the carrier signal for the transfer to the previous initiator. The communication between the two devices is therefore always reciprocal. By so-called "pairing", a connection is established between devices which are, for example, Bluetooth or W-LAN capable. NFC ensures that all necessary information on the set-up is exchanged quickly, easily and comfortably [2, p. 131].

Card emulation mode enables NFC devices such as smartphones to act like a smart card and the data can be exchanged with a RFID reader, allowing users to perform transactions like payment or ticketing. Accordingly, the NFC device emulates functions of contactless chip cards whereby the power supply is realized via the electromagnetic field of the reader. That is, the NFC device operates in passive mode.

In **read/write mode**, the NFC-enabled smartphone takes on an active role and is able to read different transponders such as smart labels, eTickets, etc. or to write on.

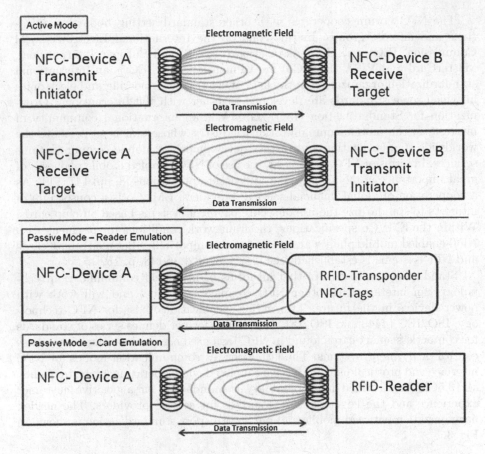

Fig. 2. NFC modes of operation (based on [4, p. 75])

A key advantage of the NFC technology is the increased security in communication between the devices. Much of the potential attacks (eavesdropping, data corruption, data modification, data insertion) are already avoidable by pairing the devices, e.g. the establishment of a secure connection between them. However, "man-in-the-middle" attacks could be used. This type of attack, in which an attacker attempts to switch between the initiator and the target device, can be practically prevented by the different operating modes and the types of data transmission of NFC [6].

3 Standardization

The standardization activities for NFC technology are mainly based on the NFC Forum which was founded in 2004 by NXP, Sony and Nokia and currently consists of more than 190 members.

The NFC Forum cooperates with other standard setting bodies organizations and interest groups. In this context, the International Electrotechnical Commission (IEC), the GSM Association (GSMA) and Europay International, MasterCard and VISA (EMVCo) are to mention. The IEC is an international standardization organization in the field of electrical engineering and electronics in which some standards are developed together with the International Organization for Standardization (ISO). GSMA is an international community of interests in the mobile communications industry whose aim is to promote the worldwide standardization and further development of mobile communications services. In terms of NFC technology, the use of NFC-enabled mobile phones is of great importance in mobile payment and ticket applications [8, pp. 147–149]. As a cooperation of global financial services providers, EMVCo is a consortium of interests to standardize the use of secure payment systems based on chip cards. Within the EMVCo specifications, the framework conditions for payment with NFC-enabled mobile phones are created and compatibility between smart cards and NFC systems is established (see [2, pp. 80–82] and [8, p. 152]).

Standards exist to ensure that all forms of near field communication technology can interact with other NFC compatible devices and will work with newer devices in the future. Two major specifications exist for NFC technology: ISO/IEC 14443 and ISO/IEC 18092. The former defines series of standards for contactless smart cards found in NFC tags used e.g. for identification, access control or payment systems. The latter defines communication modes for NFC interface and protocol using inductive coupled devices operating at the frequency of 13.56 MHz. Certified interoperability is mandatory for a positive customer experience and the key to business success for service providers. The needed harmonization between mobile and public transport standardization is shown in Fig. 3.

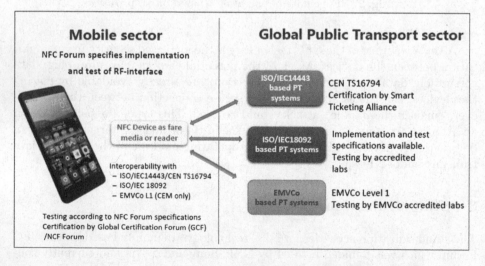

Fig. 3. Introduction to the interoperability initiative [11, p. 6]

4   NFC Enabled Smartphones

In order to ensure the functionality of the NFC technology, smartphones must be equipped with four elements on the hardware side. Figure 4 illustrates the integration of NFC in mobile terminals.

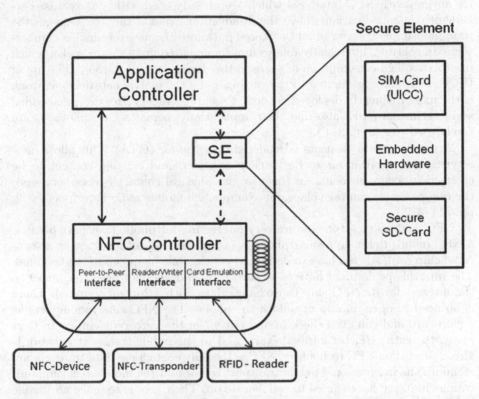

Fig. 4. NFC components in mobile terminals (based on [2, p. 84] and [8, p. 147])

The application controller, also known as a host or baseband controller, is needed for managing peripherals, communication interfaces, and user interfaces. It thus represents the central element in a mobile phone. The NFC controller provides the interface for the NFC components enabling communication in the different operating modes. There is a connection between application controller and NFC controller via the application controller interface.

Within mobile terminals, one or more secure elements take over the task of providing a secure environment for storing and executing safety-related data and applications [8, p. 155]. The connection between the NFC controller and the secure element can be realized via single wire protocol (SWP) and NFC Wired Interface (NFC-WI) [8, p. 153].

Figure 4 provides an overview of different ways in which secure elements (SE) can be integrated into mobile terminals. A simple possibility is the use of SIM cards based on Universal Integrated Circuit Card (UICC) which exist in GSM terminals anyway. Furthermore, interchangeable elements, e.g. Memory cards equipped with a chip (Secure Memory Card), can be applied. Unlike SIM cards and memory cards, secure elements can be incorporated in the device. For embedded hardware (eSE), the smart card chip is incorporated in the device (see [4, pp. 518–519]). Secure elements allow the use of the same security standards for devices with NFC interfaces which are already used with smartcards. Permanently installed variants have the disadvantage that if the user changes the terminal, simple transfer of all the stored data into the new terminal is cumbersome. In contrast, interchangeable secure elements require a slot or socket which results in a high consumption of space in the device (see [8, p. 156]). The use of UICC, which are distributed to the customers by the mobile network operators, is the most frequently deployed version of secure elements. However, embedded secure elements (eSE) also find their application whereas secure SD cards are rarely used (see [3, p. 3–4]).

Access to secure elements is rendered over the air (OTA). This allows new services and applications to be wireless uploaded and existing content to be changed to secure elements. In this case, no physical contact is necessary since the remote access can take place, for example, via mobile radio networks (see [2, pp. 311–312]).

NFC enabled smartphones are very interesting for public transport because a NFC mobile ticket on a smartphone is just as easy to authenticate as a separated chip card. All you have to do is hold your mobile phone up to the terminal. The smartphone does not have to be turned on and does not need to connect to the internet for its NFC chip to exchange data with a control terminal. There is no need to open an app or unlock the phone. The NFC smartphone acts as a chip card and can even check in and out when the battery is empty. In Germany, the entire eTicket-infrastructure used in the public transport network is already based on NFC technology. NFC is the only contactless data transmission standard the international public transport sector and the mobile telecommunications industry have agreed to collaborate on. Their goal is to make all mobile NFC devices globally compatible with the NFC infrastructure used in public transport. Roughly two years from now, passengers will be able to use their NFC-enabled smartphone as a ticket in Berlin, Paris and Tokyo. NFC-enabled smartphones are an additional customer-friendly way of combining information, reservation, payment and proof of payment [13].

In the following explanation, a research project, which aims at the use of NFC enabled smartphones for secure eTicketing functions within an open ecosystem, will be presented.

5   General OPTIMOS-Project Objectives

OPTIMOS defines an open, practical ecosystem for the use of secure identities in mobile services and implement it as a prototype based on the national public transport e-ticketing system. It is intended to demonstrate the suitability for daily use and the advantages of an open ecosystem in comparison with proprietary concepts [12, p. 6]. Ecosystems in the economic sense describe the interaction between different market players in a self-organizing business community. Often, a collaborative, technological platform or a common market forms the basis for an ecosystem, which is characterized by the exchange of information, resources, products or services. The relevant stakeholder groups, which constitute the public transport mobile service ecosystem are standardization bodies, mobile device manufacturers, system suppliers, mobile operators, eID technology and service providers, trusted service manager, transport service platform operators, transport service companies and transport associations.

The findings of the OPTIMOS project will contribute essentially to international NFC standardization with the objective of ensuring the global interoperable use of NFC devices in the medium term. The most important targets are [12, p. 6]:

- Creating an interoperable NFC interface as a "communication hub" of advanced mobile fare management systems, connecting NFC mobile devices with the existing readers in public transport vehicles and cards according to ISO/IEC 14443 and ISO/IEC 18092, eID cards or authentication tokens, ePayment and service control infrastructures. This should work both very steady because no battery is required for cards or tokens as well as very secure due to strong crypto mechanism and short operating range in line with privacy and data protection obligations of current systems.
- Connecting the world of public transport with the world of mobile communication by creating a special NFC system world, known as the already mentioned NFC ecosystem, that uses open standards and is accessible for every service provider.
- Collaborating with the NFC Forum and conducting the proof of concept (PoC) to achieve the implementation and interoperability of the NFC interface on mobile devices.
- Implementing internationally relevant use cases in the PoC to demonstrate the viability, the user acceptance and the business value of the open ecosystem.
- Performing research on the security requirements of mobile applications and the security architecture of mobile devices with the aim of preparing the launch of additional innovative services in connection with secure identities in other branches and application fields outside of the public transport, e.g. car or bike sharing.

6   State-of-the-Art of Science and Technology

There is no green-field situation in public eTicketing and fare management systems today. Billions of contactless cards and millions of readers have been deployed. The envisaged open ecosystem will consist subsystems which are already existing. Important administrative functions such as the "Trusted Service Manager", the NFC-UICC and interface standards for the data exchange as well as IT security and data protection considerations for different individual subsystems are available. For example, in the "Suica" system of the Tokyo metropolitan area, NFC mobiles and NFC-cards have been successfully used for public transport ticketing since 2006. However, today there is no implementation that satisfies the above requirements for an open ecosystem for mobile services which shall support competition between suppliers and the freedom of choice for transport companies and their customers (e.g. for eID or payment services, technical equipment). There are, however, gaps in interoperability as three different standards of contactless interfaces (ISO/IEC 14443, ISO/IEC 18092 and EMVCo L1) are currently being used in existing infrastructures. They differ in detail among themselves and from the actual standards of the NFC Forum for mobile devices.

In addition, there is a lack of system components and open interfaces that enable service and technology providers to have open access to the ecosystem and users to switch between providers easily (see [12, p. 11]).

The innovations of the OPTIMOS-project compared to the state-of-the-art of science and technology are as follows (see [12, p. 13]):

- It establishes interoperability between the various standards of contactless interfaces for NFC mobile devices and the standards of contactless infrastructure in public transport, mobile communications and banking and defines further open interfaces.
- With the open, central KA[1] provisioning system[2] a new concept is introduced that makes it significantly easier for all kind of service providers to get access or to support a specific application. Today, individual interfaces between more than 300 public transport companies and the mobile network operators on the German market have to be agreed. The KA provisioning system solves this problem by providing the needed functions centrally via open interfaces. The KVP[3] can use this interface to configure NFC mobile devices of all MNOs participating in the nationwide network and the MNO does not have to use application-specific sequences in its' system.
- It pursues research and development activities on security architectures for NFC mobile devices. Currently, only a few NFC mobile device types have a defined level of protection from attacks on inputs (e.g. PIN), display information, boot process, etc. OPTIMOS analyzes the protection requirements of innovative use cases of mobile payment, authentication, etc. and defines appropriate protection measures.

---

[1] The VDV-KA is the open and secure German standard for electronic fare management system (EFM) which enables passengers to move freely and easily between public transport companies without having to deal with different fare zones.

[2] The KA provisioning system comprehends the transport service providers' online service and ticket platforms and connects the mobile network operators, the VDV-KA and the public transport companies via open interfaces. It frees the public transport companies and mobile service operator (MNO) from complex adaptations of their systems.

[3] KVP = Kundenvertragspartner (customer contract partner). This can be every kind of public service provider like a transport company, transport association, ticket reseller, etc.

7 Project Phases

The OPTIMOS project includes 2 major phases (see Fig. 5). The main activities in these two project phases include [12, p. 7–8]:

1. Development, implementation and evaluation of essential use cases which should be available to the user according to the most advanced status of standardization of mobile services in public transport.
2. Integration and harmonization of the three technical system landscapes (1) identification and authorization solutions, (2) eTicketing and (3) NFC mobile devices with the infrastructure of the MNO.
3. Improvement and development of innovative security features for mobile devices, SIM-cards and other components in such a way that applications and services, which are due to their protection requirements not carried out

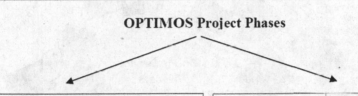

OPTIMOS Project Phases

First Phase (2016 – 2017)	**Second Phase** (2017 – 2018)
Preparation for field introduction of the NFC-enabled open ecosystem - Proof of concept (PoC)	*Research for a future generation of mobile ecosystems - development of innovative security architectures for mobile devices*
First stage:	· using eID-function of the identity card
· evaluation of interoperability between NFC mobile devices and ISO-conformant public transport readers and cards	· using Fast Identity Online (FIDO) NFC Universal Second Factor (U2F), FIDO Universal Authentication Framework (UAF) function and other authentication mechanisms
· validation of interoperability solutions that have been developed by the NFC Forum in practice	· wallet-based online payment with mobile devices
Second stage:	· online payment by using NFC mobile devices as a mobile terminal for contactless credit/bank cards
· documented use cases for NFC mobile devices in public transport are made available to friendly users in test regions	⇨ in cooperation between the leading mobile device manufacturers, IT-security experts and technology suppliers
· evaluation of the user acceptance and the implications for the service providers	

Fig. 5. Content of the OPTIMOS project phases

on mobile devices today, can be added to the ecosystem. This opens up the rare opportunity to define standards with regard to IT security and the technical protection of mobile devices in cooperation with leading manufacturers.

8   Description of Use Cases

The open ecosystem is intended to reflect the entire "mobile life cycle" a customer of mobile services is going through (see Fig. 6).

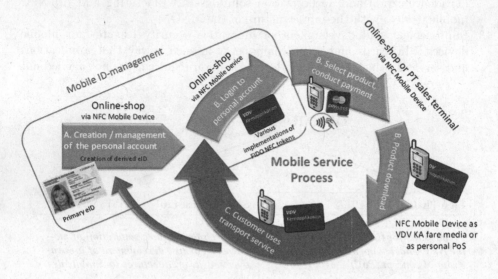

Fig. 6. Mobile service life cycle in public transportation [12, p. 9]

This can be seen as a set of business processes divided in different use cases and functions in the domain of mobile eTicketing in public transport. The following steps will be implemented in the project:

1. Customer downloads the needed smartphone app and creates, manages and enters a personal account at the online service and ticket platform of a customer contract partner (KVP) by using the German identity card with eID function and NFC mobile device.
2. Customer selects products, pays for and downloads the ticket on fare media or smartphone. For authentication and login to the account the German ID card or a FIDO NFC Universal Second Factor (U2F) token can be used.
3. Customer uses the transport services with the NFC mobile device as KA-conformant fare media, with VDV KA card as fare media or NFC tags as access points to travel information.
4. The KVP online system cares for the purchase of entitlements (season cards, single- or multi-journey tickets etc.), maintenance of fare media and management of the personal account.

The open, central KA provisioning system will enable the cooperation of the more than 300 public transport providers in Germany which issued more than 10 million PT chip cards to customers with all national mobile phone network providers via a standardized interface.

The customer of the KVP will be able to handle all steps in the KVP online system and the KVP-App with the NFC smartphone from any place and any time. This includes the following use cases (see [12, p. 9]):

– **Secure creation and management of a user account in the online sales system of the customer contract partner (KVP online system)**
  The open ecosystem is intended to allow the customer and the KVP to use electronic identities from different providers. In the PoC, the eID function of the German ID card is used as an example. This means for the customer only one time to request a service with the electronic ID card safely and reliably and then use it conveniently by derived identities in external tokens or in the NFC mobile devices. This is a combination that has not yet existed so far and will significantly increase the spread of secure electronic identities in the mass application "public transport ticketing".
– **Secure login to the online account**
  It will be rendered by means of 2-factor authentication (2FA) as a user-friendly alternative to classic, but in the meantime unsafe methods for log in with username and password. Though it should be possible to use different methods here as well. As already mentioned in the PoC-phase will be implemented the eID function of the German ID card and the FIDO U2F method. Authentication media from different manufacturers are used to test openness and interoperability in practice.
– **Configuring the NFC mobile as a public transport user medium**
  The SIM card (NFC-UICC) of the user's NFC mobile devices has to be prepared for storing entitlements and tickets. This should be carried out online at the request of the user.
– **Selection and purchase of tickets in the KVP Online System**
  The open ecosystem is designed to support a wide range of payment procedures in order to avoid dependencies on payment service providers and open up the largest possible user group.
– **Loading and management of entitlements and tickets into the NFC mobile device**
  In addition, the user of a NFC mobile device is supposed to be able to load the ticket on public transport chip cards or to have a look at it. This makes the 10 million already issued chip cards of the VDV-KA usable for mobile services.

As a result of the previous steps, NFC mobile devices and KA chip cards can be used as media for mobile services in national public transport. The existing infrastructure, e.g. reading devices for sales and control, can be used furthermore.

9   The Specific Tasks of the Dresden University of Technology Within the OPTIMOS Project

As part of the OPTIMOS project, the Dresden University of Technology is taking on the scientific accompanying research. In doing so, scientifically based concepts are developed for the user-friendly implementation of the use cases into practical applications. On the basis of neutral, scientific principles requirement analysis and acceptance studies are conducted among ca. 200 friendly users and the public transport partners. The main scientific and technical work objectives of the subproject are:

- exploration of customer and supplier requirements in the test regions of Berlin and Düsseldorf,
- development of guidelines, style guides and checklists for the KVP-Apps that need to be developed,
- the generic definition of the KVP-Apps and optimization of the operating concepts, usability and ease of use,
- elaboration of concepts for the user-friendly implementation of the KVP-Apps and KVP online systems,
- development of test concepts and evaluation scenarios for usability tests of the PoC stages 1 and 2,
- evaluation of both the benefit and the acceptance of users and the public transport companies relating to NFC-based services in the context of the implemented use cases.

10   First Evaluation Results of the Interoperability Between NFC Mobile Devices and ISO-Conformant Public Transport Readers and Cards

In August 2016, live interoperability field tests took place in public transport vehicles in the regions of Berlin and Düsseldorf. Project staff members and friendly users were equipped with NFC UICC mobile devices (smartphones). The technical tests were based on the preliminary implementation of CEN TS 16794 Edition 2 specification on reader devices and NFC Forum Analog 2.0 test cases[4] on smartphones. The aim was to check to which extent these specifications enable interoperability in practice and allow user oriented ease of use. Since devices according to the above mentioned specifications are not yet on the market, the devices could not be fully tested. Only the compliance of selected critical parameters of the physical layer were examined, but no higher layers, e.g. protocol level (time outs, timing shifts). One stationary and two mobile readers from two different suppliers were tested. The technical tests of the physical parameters of three different NFC enabled smartphones were focused on

---

[4] See test library of NFC Forum Analog; http://www.micropross.com/NFC-FORUM-TESTING-forum-Analog-22-29-m.

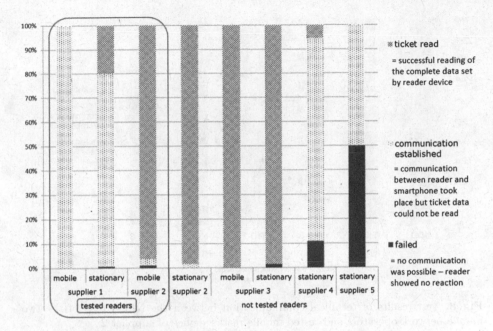

Fig. 7. Test interoperability results between reader devices and smartphones in operation mode (in total)

the Load Modulation Amplitude-scenario where the smartphone is in the card emulation mode. The smartphone status was changed during the tests between on mode and flight mode. Also, the distance between the reader and smartphone was modified from less than 1 cm to about 2 cm. Approximately 1,100 tests in operation mode were carried out and reported. Furthermore, two mobile network operators were involved in the tests. The results are shown in Figs. 7 and 8.

In nearly all test cases, the mobile and stationary readers were able to detect the complete ticket data set or at least establish a communication between the reader and the smartphone without reading the complete implemented ticket data set. For stationary reading devices, it was assured that most tickets could be read in a distance of about 2 cm. Only a very few did not show any reaction at this distance. We assumed that this was not a problem of the technical interface but more or less a software problem. Cases of incomplete data detection also happened when the position of the smartphone antenna did not correctly match with the position of the reading field or when the smartphone and the reader antenna overlapped so that a very strong coupling lead to a high load of the reading devices.

In summary, the first tests have shown that a successful technical interoperability between NFC smartphones compliant to NFC-Forum Analog 2.0 standard and PTO readers according CEN TS 16794 Edition 2 seems to be realistic. These are, however, first temporary results. Specifications have to be completed and released. The tests will be continued in Berlin and Düsseldorf with valid

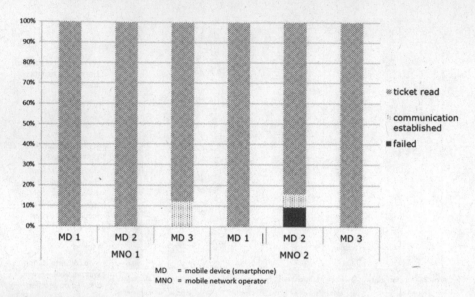

Fig. 8. Test results of technical communication between the NFC-UICC of the two mobile network operators and tested mobile reader device of supplier 2

electronic tickets and special test tickets in order to be refined and to get final statements. Not all public transport readers today have a practicable certification according to the above mentioned CEN standard so that implementation and upgrading of such readers is necessary. The planned 200 subjects in the two test regions need to get more familiar with the use of NFC smartphones for ticketing. The intuitive ease of use and customers' usability should be improved (e.g. identification of antenna position).

11   Outlook

In stage 2 of the PoC-phase (see Fig. 5), beginning in the second half of 2017, the different use cases described in Sect. 8 will be made available to friendly users in the test regions and tested. In order to be able to develop usage routines for the different activities, training workshops are offered. The user behavior as well as the user acceptance and the usability of the KVP-App must be evaluated. Therefore, empirical and analytical evaluation methods as well as quantitative and qualitative surveys will be conducted in the two test regions. These include:

- focus group interviews
- expert interviews
- user tests under observation (thinking aloud)
- free user tests in combination with standardized questionnaires
- logfile-surveys
- tests by experts

The analysis and evaluation of these investigations will show the best case scenarios, as well as acceptance and utilization barriers.

Furthermore, the acceptance, benefits and obstacles of the implemented use cases for the KVP and the implications on the complete open NFC-based ecosystem in public transport are objects of the evaluation. This will be done by guided expert interviews, workshops and elaboration of a scoring model. Explanations to the methodical approaches of the mentioned investigations are included in the paper Schäfer et al. "Development of a concept for evaluation user acceptance and requirements for NFC based e-ticketing in Public Transport" in the same proceedings volume.

References

1. Insight, B.: Shipments of NFC-enabled handsets reached 30 million units in 2011 (2012). http://www.berginsight.com/News.aspx?m_m=6&s_m=1
2. Coskun, V., Ok, K., Ozdenizci, B.: Near Field Communication (NFC): From Theory to Practice. Wiley, Hoboken (2011)
3. de Reuver, M., Ondrus, J.: When technological superiority is not enough: the struggle to impose the SIM card as the NFC secure element for mobile payment platforms. Telecommun. Policy (2017)
4. Finkenzeller, K.: RFID-Handbuch: Grundlagen und praktische Anwendungen von Transpondern, kontaktlosen Chipkarten und NFC. Carl Hanser Verlag GmbH Co KG (2015)
5. Abendblatt, H.: Bis 2018 gibt es 3,3 Milliarden Smartphones weltweit (2012). http://www.abendblatt.de/wirtschaft/article111354027/Bis-2018-gibt-es-3-3-Milli arden-Smartphones-weltweit.html
6. Harnisch, M., Uitz, I.: Near Field Communication. In: Informatik Spektrum Jahrgang 36, p. 101 (2013)
7. IDATE: Prognose zum weltweiten Bestand an NFC-fähigen Mobiltelefonen von 2013 bis 2018 (2014). https://de.statista.com/statistik/daten/studie/320924/umfrage/weltweiter-bestand-an-nfc-faehigen-mobiltelefonen/
8. Langer, J., Roland, M.: Architektur mobiler NFC-Geräte. Anwendungen und Technik von Near Field Communication (NFC), pp. 145–186 (2010)
9. Lipinski, K.: RFID-Frequenz (2017). www.itwissen.info/RFID-Frequenz-RFID-freq uency.html
10. NearFieldCommunication.org: Near Field Communication Technology Standards (2017). http://nearfieldcommunication.org/technology.html
11. Sourgen, L.: Introduction to the interoperability initative, presentation at OPTI-MOS' Interoperability Event (2016)
12. VDV eTicket GmbH & Co. KG: OPTIMOS Project: Gesamtvorhabensbeschreibung - Grundlagen für offene, praxistaugliche Infrastrukturen für mobile Services (2016)
13. VDV eTicket Service GmbH & Co. KG: Why NFC? (2017). http://www.eticket-deutschland.de/en/optimos/why-nfc/

Scratchpad: Lightweight Data Capture Tool to Support Mission Planning

Erika von Kelsch$^{(\boxtimes)}$, Stephanie Kane, Chris Muller, and Chris Hogan

Charles River Analytics, Cambridge, USA
evonkelsch@cra.com

Abstract. Pilots use powerful and complex tools to support the mission planning process. However, during the mission planning process, pilots need tools that support the capture and referencing of common mission data objects. Specifically, pilots need to capture data objects, such as key waypoints, to reference across individual planning user interface (UI) components. Pilots also need methods for capturing actions and tasks on key mission data objects. To address these needs, Charles River Analytics designed and developed a software component that enables lightweight capture of data objects for reference across mission planning components and track pending actions on data objects. In this paper, Charles River Analytics presents our overall approach and solution to address these needs and create software that better supports the mission planning process.

Keywords: Mission planning · User interface components · Data management

1 Introduction

Navy pilots have access to robust software tools to support their mission planning process. However, these tools frequently require the manual input of mission data across multiple mission planning components. This manual input of mission data across diverse planning components is complex and rote and has a high learning curve. As mission data objects are referenced by pilots across multiple mission planning components, the risk of the propagation of errors is increased. These errors can impact data that other pilots and mission controllers depend on, like airspace traffic and fuel use, leading to emergency and dangerous situations in flight. Furthermore, there is no way to capture highly precise data for use across planning components, nor methods to document tasks on mission data objects themselves.

Because of these challenges, pilots have developed a number of workarounds to current systems to fulfill this need. During our observations of training events, two main workarounds were observed during the mission planning process. First, pilots recorded mission data on their hands or on pieces of paper for later reference. These were often high precision values, such as −60.827364. This approach introduces the potential for human error as the notes can become altered when transposed and the piece of paper can be lost. Second, as pilots had questions about specific mission data elements, such as the validity of a waypoint's latitude for their particular mission, pilots

© Springer International Publishing AG 2017
M. Kurosu (Ed.): HCI 2017, Part II, LNCS 10272, pp. 598–607, 2017.
DOI: 10.1007/978-3-319-58077-7_47

input egregiously invalid values, such as "000000.000000," as a cue to return and correct the mission waypoint later. This workaround creates a significant risk that these invalid mission data values will flow forward through the system. To support pilots during the mission planning process, two requirements were identified. First, pilots need lightweight capture methods that they can use across mission planning components to store commonly used mission data. Second, pilots need methods to formally flag mission data when questions arise.

To address these issues, Charles River Analytics worked with a team of pilots to identify functional requirements for a lightweight data capture tool in an iterative design process. Through lightweight prototyping, cognitive walkthroughs, and lightweight testing, Charles River Analytics designed a tool that fulfills necessary pilots' needs which fits into their current mission planning workflow.

2 Related Work

We performed a literature review to identify approaches to task management and related areas. Previous work in the areas of task management systems has been advantageous in identifying the tools and their strategies to aid in completing work and locating or storing useful information. Task management systems attempt to fulfill similar needs to those of the pilots Charles River Analytics observed, such as storing lightweight information for the purpose of task completion.

Successful task management systems include convenient placement of task-related information [1], continuously visible to-do items [2], and flexible task representation, as they "may be represented at any level of abstraction or detail" [3]. Notes are a critical component of personal task management, as they can be any level of preciseness in relation to a task, remind the creator of useful information, and create a safe spot for the keeping of important information [4]. Min et al. describes these kinds of messages people write to themselves as "micronotes": this distinguishes them from formal notes taken during meetings or lectures, which are associated with a multi-part lifecycle [4]. These notes are many times personal and most useful to the creator, as many times they are only a couple of words in length [4]. Notes are a flexible and critical part of the task management process. Many times this kind of information is written on paper similar to workarounds observed during training events, post-its, or even inputted into a non-descript text file, which circumvents systemic storage even when it is available. Bernstein et al. refer to these kinds of recordings as "information scraps". He suggests that information management tools should provide the user with a lightweight way to enter notes that are unconstrained content, be flexible and adaptable, and visible and mobile [5].

Related to note-taking is list-making, in which cues are recorded for incomplete tasks [3]. Task lists can be thought of as a subset of notes [4]. Task lists are characterized by being very flexible in nature. A worker may have an overall to-do list of tasks that must be completed for the day, but the tasks themselves may not have any relationship to one another. Conversely, a worker may have a to-do list that specifically falls under the umbrella of a larger task, with the to-do items acting as sub-tasks. Notes and lists can be clustered and grouped together, and the combinations can fall under a single objective for organization and convenience, as Bellotti et al. showed in the functionality of Taskmaster, creating "thrasks" within an email inbox [2]. However, no singular task management tool is one-size-fits-all, as demonstrated by the great variance in approach, form, and function of these tools [2, 3, 6].

We also reviewed commercial applications for task management, including Wunderlist™ [7], Google Keep™ [8], and Microsoft OneNote® [9]. These applications all offer broad and flexible solutions to note-taking and list-making in a large, single app window. The Wunderlist task view is easy to scan and action-oriented. Some of the tools Charles River Analytics explored were highly glanceable, like Google Keep's card-based view of items. This view provides a high-level overview showing how many items are pending completion and the items' main subject by utilizing large type sizes, card user interfaces (card UIs) and medium to high contrast of color. Search and automation functionality, like the search bar in Microsoft OneNote, facilitate information lookup across the task management system. Similar support tools would allow pilots to look up important mission data quickly and gain confirmation on the mission data from the system rather than typing mission data by hand.

3 Scratchpad Design and Use

To address the needs of pilots during mission planning process, a combination of note-taking and list-making functionality was employed to facilitate mission data object capture and reference. Based on our initial observations and review of related work, Charles River Analytics designed a component called Scratchpad. Similar to a bulletin board, the Scratchpad component enables pilots to collect mission data objects, reference the collected mission data objects, and create tasks in the context of the collected mission data objects.

Throughout the mission planning process, pilots are frequently manipulating waypoints, or key locations in space. A waypoint includes data like latitude, longitude, altitude, time of arrival, and speed of the plane when arriving to the location. Waypoints frequently are associated with a waypoint type to indicate the type of activity that will occur. For example, a 'rendezvous' type waypoint involves multiple aircrafts meeting or joining together. One critical component of the Scratchpad is to assist in the capture and reference of waypoints throughout the mission planning process.

Figure 1a shows an empty Scratchpad component with no mission data objects. At the top of the component is a header with the Scratchpad title and a label ("0 mission objects") indicating the number of objects in the Scratchpad component. As elements are added to the Scratchpad, this label changes to reflect the updated count. The arrow icon in the top right corner of the Scratchpad component allows the entire panel to be collapsed, which shows just the Scratchpad component's header. The collapsible nature of the Scratchpad component minimizes the screen space used by the component. Scratchpad screen minimization is an especially important feature as pilot screen space is at a premium with many other tools present for mission planning Below the header, a gray search field provides support text on how to use the component.

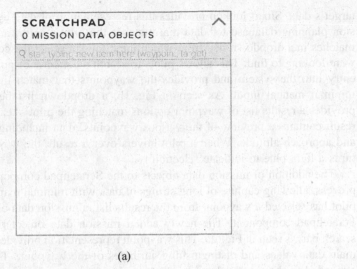

(a)

(b)

Fig. 1. The Scratchpad component, with no mission data objects saved, prompts pilots to type into the gray search field (a, left) in order to prompt the smart lookup feature (b, right). The smart lookup feature to display a drop down list of waypoints that match the pilot's search query. This allows pilots to find waypoints they are looking to add to the Scratchpad component with minimal manual data entry, and a low barrier entry process. (Color figure online)

In Fig. 1b, the pilot has begun to type "rendezvous" into the gray input field. As the pilot begins typing, the helper text drops below the input field to continue providing instruction even when the search field has been engaged. This prompts the Scratchpad component's smart lookup feature to activate. The smart lookup feature allows a pilot to quickly search and select the mission data object without manually typing the target's data. Smart lookup provides this representation of data by searching the mission planning database for data that matches the pilot's entry, and then displays the matches in a dropdown list, from which the pilot can select the correct waypoint they were looking to find. This allows pilots to search a database of possible waypoints for entry into the system and provides the waypoints that match the pilot's entry with minimal manual input. As seen in Fig. 1b, a dropdown list below the search bar provides a results list of waypoint options matching the pilot's text entry. Each search result contains a preview of the various waypoints' data including latitude, longitude, and approach altitude. When a pilot hovers over a result, the waypoint's background turns a light blue to indicate selectibility.

The addition of mission data objects to the Scratchpad component is a lightweight process, allowing capture of long strings of data with minimal manual effort. Once the pilot has selected a waypoint from the results list, a mission data object is added to the Scratchpad component. The newly added mission data object populates below the search bar, as seen in Fig. 2a. This waypoint representation provides an overview of the main data values and distinguishing attributes of the waypoint. The waypoint can be expanded to show more detail by clicking the blue arrow icon in the upper left of the waypoint bar, as seen next to Waypoint 5 in Fig. 2a. Now the pilot can quickly reference the waypoint's associated data values, like latitude and longitude by copying and pasting or dragging and dropping into the appropriate mission planning components. Mission data objects are collapsible by the blue arrow icon to the left of the mission data object's title and provides summary detail of the most important information for identification. Collapsed waypoint bars display a mission data object's general type, the mission it belongs to, and how many active tasks are associated with it. This is aided by abbreviations like and WP (Waypoint) and TGT (Target) which allow more information to exist in the small title space. Figure 2b shows Waypoint 5 expanded by clicking the arrow icon left of the mission data object's title to show the complete data set. This eliminates the process of typing out values manually and greatly reduces the risk of entering typographical errors.

As seen in Fig. 2b, the waypoint mission data object has been expanded and shows additional details on the waypoint data, such as time of arrival and speed. In this expanded view pilots can add individual tasks onto the mission data objects. As shown in Fig. 3a, the pilot can create a task on Waypoint 5 by clicking the blue circle plus sign icon next to "add task to waypoint 5". This action creates a new field for the pilot to start typing their task. Figure 3b shows the results of a pilot creating a specific task, "Confirm latitude with leader", including a counter of incomplete tasks. Once a task has been created, it is marked with a time stamp below the typed note to provide context for when the task was created. The ability to make actionable tasks on mission data objects provides pilots with a place to store important reminders for checks on information so that it can be attended to at a later time.

As the pilot completes the tasks they can mark tasks as complete by clicking the blue checkbox to the left of the task. Figure 4 shows two different pending tasks on Waypoint 5, with one task marked by the pilot as complete. Once the pilot clicks on the blue checkbox, the task's timestamp updates with additional information on the time when the task was marked as complete. Once a task is checked, the task counter located

(a)

(b)

Fig. 2. Waypoint 5 has been added to the Scratchpad component (a, left). By using the arrow icon next to the mission data object's title, the data can be displayed or hidden to save space in the interface and reduce clutter (b, right). Expanded mission data objects' titles turn blue in order for expanded data objects to be easily recognizable. (Color figure online)

in the header is updated to reflect the new number of remaining tasks. The pilot can delete both complete and incomplete tasks by using the gray "x" icon to the right of the task or keep it for later reference. If the pilot decides at a later point that the task was not substantially completed or needs to be revisited, they can send the task back to the active task list by clicking on the checked blue box and 'un-check' the task.

(a)

(b)

Fig. 3. The blue plus icon has been clicked in order to add a task corresponding to Waypoint 5 (a, left), which creates a task slot with cursor focus so the pilot can type a task. Once the task is recorded by clicking outside of the task box (b, right), a note is added to the end of the mission data object's title to indicate that the mission data object includes an active, unresolved task. (Color figure online)

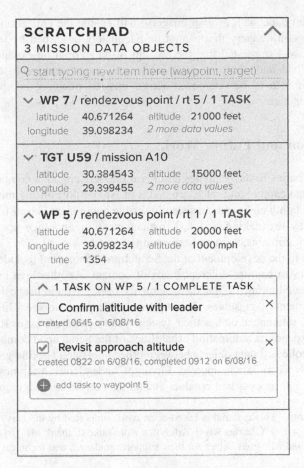

SCRATCHPAD
3 MISSION DATA OBJECTS

Q start typing new item here (waypoint, target)

˅ WP 7 / rendezvous point / rt 5 / 1 TASK
latitude   40.671264   altitude   21000 feet
longitude   39.098234   *2 more data values*

˅ TGT U59 / mission A10
latitude   30.384543   altitude   15000 feet
longitude   29.399455   *2 more data values*

˄ WP 5 / rendezvous point / rt 1 / 1 TASK
latitude   40.671264   altitude   20000 feet
longitude   39.098234   altitude   1000 mph
time   1354

˄ 1 TASK ON WP 5 / 1 COMPLETE TASK

☐ Confirm latitiude with leader   ✕
created 0645 on 6/08/16

☑ Revisit approach altitude   ✕
created 0822 on 6/08/16, completed 0912 on 6/08/16

⊕ add task to waypoint 5

Fig. 4. Multiple tasks have been added to Waypoint 5, with one already marked as complete. Once a task is marked as complete by clicking the checkbox to the left of a task, the timestamp is updated to display the time when the task has been marked as complete. (Color figure online)

4 Preliminary Informal Evaluations

To evaluate whether the Scratchpad component addressed the needs of pilots, Charles River Analytics performed informal evaluations with representative uses, including screen-by-screen walkthroughs. Preliminary results and feedback indicate that the Scratchpad component will support pilots and facilitate lightweight mission object capture. Additionally, the Scratchpad component would decrease the number of occurrences that pilots need to interrupt their workflow in order to receive answers and confirmation on questions and concerns they may have for team leaders. Instead, they can store and ask multiple questions while using the Scratchpad component.

Based on feedback from our representative users, key areas for investigation and extension include the incorporation of other types of media besides text to the Scratchpad component and the expansion of data included. The incorporation of media beyond waypoint data, such as map imagery, will enable the collection of visual data objects and mission imagery that cannot be adequately described by text data alone. Additionally, it was suggested that the breadth of data could be expanded to include call signs, payload and platform parameters, and sensor settings to enable a more extensive set of data to be referenced across mission planning components by the Scratchpad component.

5   Conclusion and Future Work

In this paper, Charles River Analytics described the Scratchpad, a component tool that addresses the data capture and reference needs of Navy pilots during mission planning The design of a lightweight and consistently visible component is transferrable to other domains such as list-making and task management in an office setting and other knowledge work domains, such as performing research.

Future steps in the development of the Scratchpad component include the extension of its capabilities to capture different kinds of content. Another area of investigation include the direct linking of the data elements back to their usage in the mission planning components themselves. This would enable pilots to see when, where, and how this data is referenced across their system. Additionally, Charles River Analytics would like to expand the automation capabilities of the Scratchpad component to allow pilots to share collected data objects between other pilots and specific groups of pilots, for cases such as when data is updated. Finally, Charles River Analytics will continue our iterative design process and conduct evaluations on these design approaches.

Acknowledgements. This material is based upon work supported by the Navy under Contract No. N68335-15-C-0158. **Charles River Analytics** would like to thank Mr. Bryan Ramsay, Mr. Lohn Schneider, and Mr. Fred Selzer for their support, guidance, and technical feedback.

References

1. González, V., Mark, G.: Constant, constant, multi-tasking craziness: managing multiple working spheres. In: CHI 2004. Association for Computing Machinery, New York (2004). https://www.ics.uci.edu/~gmark/CHI2004.pdf
2. Bellotti, V., Ducheneaut, N., and Howard, M.: Taking email to task: the design and evaluation of a task management centered email tool. In: CHI 2003. Association for Computing Machinery, New York (2003). https://www.ischool.utexas.edu/~i385q/spring2005/readings/Bellotti_Ducheneaut-2003-Taking.pdf
3. Bellotti, V., Dalal, B., Good, N., and Flynn, P.: What a to-do: studies of task management towards the design of a personal task list manager. In: CHI 2004. Association for Computing Machinery, New York (2004). http://www2.parc.com/csl/members/nicolas/documents/CHI2004-to-do.pdf
4. Lin, M., Lutters, W., and Kim, T.: Understanding the MicronoteLifecyce: improving mobile support for informal note taking. In: CHI 2004 Connect: Proceedings Conference on Human

Factors in Computing Systems, Vienna, Austria, New York, 24–29 April 2004. http://userpages.umbc.edu/~lutters/pubs/2004_CHI_Full_Lin,Lutters,Kim.pdf

5. Bernstein, M., Van Kleek, M., Karger, D., Schraefel, M.: Information scraps: how and why information eludes our personal information management tools. ACM Trans. Inf. Syst. (TOIS) 26(4), 24 (2008)

6. Robertson, G., Van Dantzich, M., Robbins, D., Czerwinski, M., Hinckley, K., Risden, K., Thiel, D., Gorokhovsky, V.: The task gallery: a 3D window manager. In: Proceedings of the SIGCHI Conference on Human Factors in Computing Systems, pp. 494–501. ACM (2000). https://www.microsoft.com/en-us/research/wp-content/uploads/2000/01/taskgallery-submitted.pdf

7. Wunderlist. https://www.wunderlist.com/home

8. Google Keep. https://play.google.com/store/apps/details?id=com.google.android.keep&hl=en

9. Microsoft OneNote. https://www.onenote.com/

Multi-method Approach to Identify Acceptance-Relevant Characteristics of Renewable Energy Infrastructure

Barbara Sophie Zaunbrecher[✉] and Martina Ziefle

Chair of Communication Science, Human-Computer Interaction Center (HCIC),
RWTH Aachen University, Aachen, Germany
{zaunbrecher,ziefle}@comm.rwth-aachen.de
http://www.comm.rwth-aachen.de

Abstract. Despite the general positive attitude towards renewables, protests against renewable energy infrastructure continues in Germany. The study aims to explore acceptance-relevant aspects of renewable energy sources and their infrastructure to gain a better understanding for argumentation lines of protesters and supports of renewables. The research followed a two-step procedure, beginning with an extensive focus group study. In the focus groups, participants discussed which aspects of renewables they perceived as problematic or advantageous. Based on the results, an ACA (adaptive conjoint analysis) study was designed as an online study, which 109 people fully completed. The most important attributes which resulted from the study were those that represented direct impact on nature and humans. The studies confirmed current research on energy-related infrastructure, which stress the importance of communicating about possible local impacts on the environment and residents. Methodologically, the study exemplified a user-centered research design based on bottom-up principles, in which qualitative analyses were used to determine attributes relevant to laypersons.

Keywords: Social acceptance · Renewables · Mixed-method approach · Focus group · Conjoint study

1 Introduction

To achieve the goal of a share of 80% renewables for the electricity supply by 2050, a drastic change of the energy landscape in Germany is required. While there is widespread support of renewables in the general public in Germany [1], single infrastructure projects face resistance by local residents. The rejection of energy infrastructure can seriously hinder the diffusion of renewable energy technologies by delaying or even hindering the completion of these projects altogether [2]. Thus, it has been recognized that a socially supported energy transition is needed. Still, the social responses to energy infrastructure are not yet fully understood. This might be due to several reasons: First of all, well-established research

© Springer International Publishing AG 2017
M. Kurosu (Ed.): HCI 2017, Part II, LNCS 10272, pp. 608–627, 2017.
DOI: 10.1007/978-3-319-58077-7_48

models of technology acceptance (TAMs) (such as TAM [3]) are not applicable to acceptance of energy infrastructure, as they were developed for small-scale technologies in the workplace and differ to a great extent from renewable energy infrastructure. Therefore, traditional TAMs cannot explain the complexity of acceptance levels in energy infrastructure and other, new approaches are needed. Second, because renewable energy infrastructure is often widely visible and thus impacts the surrounding landscape, it interferes to a much larger extent with peoples' personal spaces. Research suggests that local acceptance towards energy infrastructure is in fact to a large part dependent on non-technical issues such as trust in stakeholders [4] and also needs to be understood against its local background, as "[v]iews are developed in the context of immediate surroundings" [5]. Nevertheless, there are recurring argumentation patterns which frequently occur in the debate about renewable energy infrastructure acceptance in general, many of which are also reasons on which local opposition is based. Among those are, for example, the impact of renewable energy infrastructure on landscape, local flora and fauna, or issues relating to the choice of location. Although these topics have been extensively discussed with regard to specific energy infrastructure projects, only few approaches have been made in which the characteristics and their relative importance for energy source preferences have been discussed independently of the specific energy infrastructure (as advocated in [6,7]).

This paper seeks to contribute to the current research on energy acceptance by empirically analyzing acceptance-relevant characteristics of energy sources across different technologies and by identifying which characteristics contribute most to the preference for an energy source. The research focuses on technology-inherent characteristics to (a) gain a better understanding about acceptance or rejection of energy technologies independent of local context, and (b) provide developers of future energy technology infrastructure with ideas which characteristics could become problematic. An empirical bottom-up procedure is adopted, in which in a first step, the acceptance-relevant characteristics are identified using focus groups, and subsequently quantified with regard to their importance for preferences for energy sources using a choice experiment.

2   Acceptance-Relevant Factors of Renewable Energy Infrastructure

Research on the social acceptance of renewable energy infrastructure shows that there are crucial topics for peoples' acceptance or rejection of renewable energy infrastructure. In the following paragraphs, an overview about the most prominently debated topics with regard to renewable energy infrastructure acceptance will be given in a cross-technological approach, focusing on the three renewable energy sources with the highest shares of produced electricity in 2016 [8], wind energy, photovoltaics (PV) and biomass.

2.1 Landscape Impact

This factor is by far more extensively researched for wind power plants than for biomass or PV [9], although research indicates that the two latter technologies face a similar barrier. The fact that the landscape impact, in visual terms, plays such a big role in the renewable energy infrastructure discussion, particularly for wind energy, is explained on the basis of the invisibility of past energy production. The "energy landscapes", which arise from the change towards more renewables, in contrast, make energy production more visible [10]. For wind energy, visual impact has been identified as acceptance-relevant and is extensively researched, and the importance of an integration of wind power plants in the landscape has been stressed [11]. Studies on collaborative virtual environments and their role in an acceptable wind power planning have taken a practical approach to this potential barrier [12]. The visual impact is not merely an aesthetic issue, but also an economic one, as the influence of wind farms on nearby property prices shows [13].

Although more prominent in the wind energy debate, studies have identified the issues of location choice and visual impact also in the context of biomass plants. A location near an industrial estate is favored over one close to residential areas, as the visual impact on the landscape, here due to the chimneys of the plant, is perceived to be negative [14]. Like in the context of wind energy, this also resulted in the fear of decreasing property values [14].

While the installation of PV on rooftops is not as drastic a change to the landscape compared to biomass plants or wind power plants, still, the installation also has a visual impact and could also indirectly affect the surrounding landscape, for example when trees need to be cut or are not allowed to be planted because of possible shadowing [9]. When large-scale PV systems are considered, similar siting issues with regard to landscape impact arise like for wind power and biomass plants. Because of the larger size of the construction and the placement in the landscape, the choice of location can then also affect the social acceptance of a PV plant [1,15]. This parallel is further underlined by efforts to transfer visual impact assessment known from wind power plants also to PV plant planning [16].

2.2 Environmental Impact

Related to questions of landscape impact and siting decisions are impacts on the environment, flora and fauna, by renewable energy infrastructure. Although generally a means to protect the environment by using more renewables instead of fossil fuels, renewable energy sources and their associated infrastructures are not unanimously viewed as environmentally friendly when their direct surroundings are concerned. This is termed "green-on-green conflict" [17] and especially prominent in the wind power debate. In this context, the protection of birds and bats is cited as a reason to oppose to wind farm projects [18,19], but environmental concerns, such as a negative impact on the local ecosystem and wildlife, have also been documented in the context of biomass [14,21] and PV plants [1].

2.3   Impact on Humans/Physical Wellbeing Concerns

Besides impact on landscape and the natural environment, local residents have displayed concerns regarding their physical wellbeing in the direct surroundings of renewable energy infrastructure, for example because of acoustic, odor, or visual emissions. While the issues of health and wellbeing in the context of PV has predominantly been covered from a theoretical perspective in relation to occupational health [23] or potential EMF hazards [24], it is not known to occur in acceptance-related discourses. This is different for wind energy, for which acoustic emissions [25,26], shadow cast [26] or infrasound [27] are frequently cited as reasons for non-acceptance of wind power plants by local residents [28]. Also for biomass plants, "long-term uncertainties about the general health impacts caused by the plant" [14] play a role for social acceptance. There are concerns about the waste used in the incineration plant being hazardous to humans [20], as well as odor [14,20,22] and noise emissions [14] that could disturb local residents.

2.4   Social Context

While the factors introduced above refer to inherent qualities of the renewable energy sources and associated infrastructure, other factors which have been identified to play an important role in the local acceptance of renewable energy infrastructure refer to the social context in which the development of a renewable energy plant is embedded. This concerns the stakeholders involved, the decision making process, ownership of the plant and also the relation of residents to the site in question (referred to as "place attachment", [29]).

Trust in stakeholders and a perceived procedural fairness of the decision making process, both closely intertwined [30], have been identified as important drivers for the acceptance of local renewable energy developments, most notably in the wind power context [31]. It has been shown that these motives outplay so called "backyard motives" (NIMBY: not in my backyard) as reasons to oppose [32]. The strong relation between fairness, trust and local acceptance has also been identified in the context of biomass [20] and case studies showed indeed that a lack of trust, missing information and transparency and can lead to the failure of aspired projects [14,21]. One reason for this is the lack of involvement of the local communities in the decision process, resulting in top-down decisions, in which the local community is left with a feeling of bearing the costs of other people's benefit [14,33]. This is closely connected to issues of ownership: In the context of wind energy, Warren and McFayden came to the conclusion that community ownership of wind power plants can significantly increase acceptance [34], and this was also advocated in regard to renewable energy projects in general [35]. Besides the relation of the local community to the project and the project developers, the relation to the location of the renewable energy plant has recently gained importance in the discussion about renewable energy acceptance. It is argued that rather than NIMBY, the threat of disruption of the relation to the landscape which provides identification for those closely attached to a place can explain opposition to renewable energy projects [29].

2.5 Conclusive Derivation of Research Questions and Empirical Procedure

Considering the research on the social acceptance of renewable energy sources and their infrastructure, it is evident that there are common acceptance-relevant aspects across technological contexts. This is supported by empirical studies which have compared different renewable energies with regard to specific attributes [1,36]. It can be concluded that social acceptance aspects are of great importance for the success of the energy transition, also for future energy technology development, and that a closer analysis and understanding of these factors independent of the specific technological context is needed. This refers for example to the empirical weighting of the factors, to gain a better understanding of the relative importance of the aspects. To this end, an empirical choice-based questionnaire is applied as research method in this paper.

A second aspect that is evident from the literature review is the nature of the acceptance-relevant factors. There are factors which focus more on the specific integration of renewable energy projects within the local context, and there are factors which refer to technology-inherent characteristics, independent of the local context (e.g., onshore wind power plants will always emit noise from rotating blades, and PV plants will require specific resources for their production, regardless of where they are located). This paper focuses on technology-inherent characteristics, to analyze those aspects which make a technology preferable or not, independent of the local context. In this sense, the analysis is aimed at technology developers, in order to provide indicators about potentially problematic aspects, also for future energy infrastructure development. Consequently, the definition of social acceptance in this paper refers to broad socio-political acceptance of a technology rather than community acceptance [9].

3 Explorative Identification of Acceptance-Relevant Factors of Energy Infrastructure

The aim of the study was to identify factors or characteristics of renewable energy sources and their corresponding infrastructure which are discussed with regard to their social acceptability and to analyse their relative importance. The first step of the empirical research thus comprised of a explorative phase in which a broad range of factors was collected in a bottom-up approach, adding to the results of the literature review, to ensure that the attributes selected for the choice tasks in the second stage of the research procedure reflected the general public's concerns.

3.1 Method

As method to capture publicly discussed characteristics of renewable energy infrastructure, focus groups were chosen. Focus groups are used in initial stages of research, in which it is important to provide participants an open format to voice their concerns and wishes rather than providing predefined answering formats. In focus groups, a group of interested participants discusses the research topic in an open talk moderated by an experienced researcher along guiding questions. The results of the focus groups then served as basis for the choice of attributes in the conjoint study.

Research Design. Interested laypersons were invited to participate in discussion groups, which were moderated by an experienced researcher and voice-recorded. In the focus groups, they discussed perceived benefits and drawbacks of renewable energy infrastructure, mostly focusing on photovoltaics, wind energy and biomass. The recorded discussions were later analyzed based on qualitative content analysis [37].

Structure of Discussion. The general procedure was as follows: first, participants were introduced to renewable energies and the relevance of their public acceptance. It was explained to them that to develop sustainable sources of energy, the public opinion is important in order to facilitate their widespread diffusion and achieve a socially supported energy revolution with the public's interest in mind. To develop socially acceptable technology, public interests should be integrated as early as possible in the technology development process, and the participant's involvement in the discussion groups would help researchers understand their concerns. The discussion then started with general questions on renewable energy infrastructure. In this introductory phase, groups 1 and 2 were asked for their experience with renewable energy infrastructure (focusing on wind energy, solar energy and energy from biomass) and groups 3, 4 and 5 were asked for spontaneous associations with different types of energy sources (wind energy, solar energy, water energy, energy from biomass, geothermal energy, nuclear energy, fossil fuels). Groups 1 and 2 were subsequently asked for their impression on the usefulness of the different types of renewables, as well as advantages and disadvantages. Groups 3, 4 and 5 were asked to list the most important characteristics of different types of renewables. Finally, both groups were encouraged to imagine that they could choose renewables to supply their home(town) with electricity. They were asked which renewables they would choose for this purpose and why.

3.2   Sample

In total, five focus groups (FG) were conducted, the number of participants of each group ranged from 5 to 7. In total, 27 persons took part. The participants covered various demographic groups based on gender, age, educational background and residential situation (Table 1).

3.3   Results

As the research focus was laid on the aspects participants used for their evaluation of different energy sources, the results will be structured according to

Table 1. Demographic details of focus group participants (Numbers in cells indicate to how many participants per FG a criterion applied, some participants did not disclose all demographic information)

		FG No. 1	2	3	4	5
Gender	Male	3	2	2	1	2
	Female	4	3	3	4	3
Age range	<20				2	
	21–30 years	1	5	3	1	3
	31–40 years					1
	41–50 years	1				
	51–60 years	5			1	
	61–70 years			2		1
Educational background	Basic school leaving certificate	1				
	Vocational training	2				
	Qualification for university entrance		3	3		3
	University degree	3	2			2
Residential situation	Countryside				5	
	Town	6				
	City	1	5	5		5

the characteristics participants used to compare and evaluate different types of renewables. The characteristics reported below were used in reference to wind energy, energy from biomass, solar energy (PV), water energy and geothermal energy.

Recycling and Production: Participants discussed in how far the technologies required for the generation of electricity and heat from renewables would be sustainable with regard to their production and recycling. Here, it was for example argued that wind, geothermal energy, solar energy and water energy would not produce any waste during operation and were thus seen as favorable (FG 3 and 4). On the other hand, the problem of recycling specific components such as the PV panels and rotor blades of wind turbines was also discussed (FG 1, 2 and 5). For PV, the need of rare material for production (such as silicon) was mentioned as disadvantage (FG 2 and 5). In contrast to this, it was seen as an advantage of biomass that it could serve as a recycling method for waste itself (FG 3 and 4).

Emissions: A large part of the discussion centered around optical, acoustic, and olfactory "emissions" which would be disruptive to the direct surroundings, most notably neighbors, of a renewable energy plant. Flickering shadows were mentioned as a disadvantage of wind energy (FG 1, 2, 3 and 4), as well as the noise from rotating wind turbines (FG 1, 2, 3, 4 and 5). Ultrasound was also attributed to wind energy, which could harm animals and humans in the vicinity (FG 1 and 4). For biomass, possible odor nuisance was discussed (FG 1 and 2). In contrast to this, it was seen as an advantage of PV that no such emissions were to be expected (FG 2).

Use of Resources During Operation/Operation Costs: For wind energy, it was seen as an advantage that it does not "use up" resources during operation (FG 2, 5). Geothermal energy, on the other hand, was believed to cool the earth (FG 3 and 5). Using resources during operation was seen as a major disadvantage of biomass (FG 1, 2), the discussion here also focused on the resources itself, whether they could also be used as crops to produce food or how the resources in turn need space in the landscape to grow (FG 2). Another concern connected to the use of resources was their transport to the biomass plant, which would lead to a lot of traffic (FG 2).

Choice of Location/Dependence on External Factors: Another argument which was discussed by the participants of the focus groups was the choice of a location for the energy infrastructure and how, depending on which type of renewable energy was chosen, this depended on various external factors. The independence from specific conditions was rated an advantage for a biomass power plant, because it was argued that it could be fueled with different resources (FG 1). In contrast to this, wind and PV are more dependent on natural, local conditions, such as wind speed and solar radiation. Especially for wind farms, participants argued that finding location is difficult because wind farms needed to be away from residential and nature conservation areas (FG 1, 2). The dependence on local conditions was also mentioned as a counterargument for geothermal energy (FG 3).

Efficiency/Costs: Although the participants expressed a lack of knowledge about the costs of energy that would result from the different sources, they found wind energy to be favorable because it was regarded cheap (FG 3 and 5), apart from offshore wind parks (FG 2). Biomass was also considered cheap (FG 2), in comparison to PV, similarly hydropower was found to have low costs (FG 3 and 5). PV, wind and geothermal energy were considered inefficient (FG 5), although some also thought wind energy to be the most efficient of the sources discussed (FG 1 and 2). Geothermal energy was perceived as very expensive, especially because of high investment costs (FG 5). PV was considered inefficient for the north of Germany (FG 1 and 2). Participants argued that because of less hours of sunshine than in more southern countries, it would not be of much practical use.

Space Requirement: A further issue which participants discussed with regard to the acceptability of an energy source was the space which the corresponding infrastructure would need. It was, for example, discussed critically that for the usage of biomass to generate electricity and heat, large fields of, e.g., corn are needed (FG 1). Also for PV, the large space that was assumed to be needed was considered a major disadvantage (FG 1 and 2, 5), although it was also argued that sheep could still graze between the PV panels (FG 2). When PV would be installed on roofs, the fact that no additional space would be needed was seen as positive (FG 1). It was regarded as an advantage of wind farms that the space which is sealed permanentely was small and that the space inbetween the single turbines could still be used for farming (FG 1 and 2). The space needed was also considered a major disadvantage of hydropower, participants referred to large dam projects, for which they knew that residents were relocated (FG 4 and 5). Geothermal energy was rated with mixed results regarding space, while some participants argued that large space was needed (FG 5), others knew that only little boreholes were necessary (FG 5).

Baseload Capability/Security of Supply: The ability to provide energy to secure the baseload energy supply was discussed as advantage of several renewable energy sources. Biomass, for example, was rated positively in this respect, as most participants argued that there would always be waste to fuel the plant (FG 2 and 4), although others were skeptical if this was the case (FG 5). For PV, on the other hand, although generally perceived positively, the fact that it cannot secure supply any time of the year was seen as a negative characteristic (FG 1, 2, 3 and 4), the same was true for wind energy (FG 1, 2, 4 and 5). In FG 4 and 5, it was discussed, however, that a combination of wind energy and PV would probably generate enough electricity, as there would "sometimes [be] a bit more, sometimes a bit less, but never nothing at all". In this context, the possibility of electricity storage was also discussed. The ability to supply energy to cover the baseload was seen as a positive trait of hydropower, although not all participants were convinced this was true for hydropower (FG 5). In FG 3, geothermal energy was rated positively because of its "constant availability" (FG 3).

Visual Appearance/ Impact on Landscape: The question if and how a specific type of energy plant would impact the landscape was frequently discussed in the focus groups, most notably with regard to wind energy. For large-scale PV on open fields, its visual impression was seen as negative (FG 1, 2, 5), as a "disruptive element in nature" (FG 2). The possibility to install PV on rooftops was thus regarded an advantage (FG 1), but overall, PV was seen as having a rather low visual impact and thus not be too disturbing (FG 1, 2, 4). For wind energy, the impact on landscape was more decisive, as participants also felt it could have a negative effect on property value (FG 1). Opinions were mixed with regard to the perceived beauty of wind turbines in the landscape, ranging from "ugly" to "beautiful" (FG 1 and 2), while in other groups, they were unanimously criticized for their negative impact on landscape (FG 3, 4 and 5). For hydropower, on the other hand, its visual appearance was a fact that contributed to the positive image, it was regarded "aesthetic" (FG 3), although large-scale projects like pumpwater storage were also mentioned, which, according to the participants, impact landscape to a great extend (FG 3 and 4).

Construction: Furthermore, when evaluating the different renewable energies, the effort required for the construction of the plant was taken into account by the participants of the focus groups. For biomass, they assumed that it would be cheaper than building a PV plant (FG 2), while for PV, they argued that "you need lots of material to built it" (FG 1). For wind power plants, they discussed that the construction of the turbines and the transport of the single components of the turbine as complex (FG 1 and 2). In opposition to PV, however, no rare materials would be used for construction (FG 2). Geothermal energy, which was perceived positively because of its unobtrusive nature, was attributed to a very complex and expensive construction procedure (FG 3), which some participants mentioned as the reason to reject this technology (FG 3).

Ecological Effects: Despite being considered "green" themselves, some of the renewable energy technologies were associated with major effects on the nature surrounding them, animals as well as plants. An increasing focus on corn as fuel for biomass plants was feared to produce monocultures (FG 2, 3, 4), as well as heavily impacting landscapes ecologically that were formerly used for different purposes. PV plants in the open landscapes were also thought to impact nature, especially natural growth of plants, because "nature that grows between the panels is not really natural" and it was discussed whether the space could still be used for letting animals graze (FG 1, 2). The impact on animals was mostly discussed for wind turbines, harm to birds and bats was considered a major drawback for this technology (FG 1, 3, 4, 5), as well as the possible impact of offshore wind power on sea animals (FG 1, 4). In opposition to this, the fact that relatively little ground would be sealed was seen as an advantage of wind power (FG 1 and 2, see also "Space requirement"). The negative impact on animals was also one of the drawbacks that was associated with hydropower: participants worried about fish being harmed by the turbines (FG 4). In addition, nature would be changed on a large scale when dams would be built (FG 3). Concerning geothermal energy, participants were unsure whether groundwater quality would be at risk in those areas as some feared "leaking fluids which contaminate the groundwater" (FG 5). Besides, "cooling down" the earth (FG 3 and 5) was associated with changed to the ecosystem.

Further factors which were discussed only with relation to single technologies or mentioned by single participants included the *lifetime of a plant*, the *trust in the technology*, the *possibility to use it at household level* (PV), the *maturity of the technology* (geothermal energy) and the *effect of incidents* (e.g., breaking rotor blades on wind turbines).

Summarizing the results of the prestudy, it was apparent that many different factors were taken into account when renewable energy technologies were discussed. The discussion revealed insights in this variety of arguments, however, to identify trade-offs between the different factors and quantify preferences, a large-scale quantitative survey approach was needed as a second step.

4   Confirmative Weighting of Acceptance-Relevant Factors of Energy Infrastructure

As a follow-up on the qualitative prestudy the aim of the study was to quantify preferences and to analyse which of the factors was most important.

4.1   Method

Rather than a traditional survey, a conjoint survey was chosen. Conjoint analysis was developed in the 1960ies by Luce and Tukey [38]. In conjoint analyses, participants rate entire products consisting of different attributes rather than single attributes in isolation. This way, real-life decisions are more closely mimicked than in traditional surveys, where attributes are often rated in a stand-alone manner, without acknowledging possible trade-offs between attributes. By presenting several different products to participants, they are forced into a choice situation in which they have to state their preference for one (or none) of the products. All products consist of the same attributes (e.g., size, price, color), however, the levels in which the attributes are manifested can be different between products (e.g., for attribute color, product 1 is blue and product 2 is red). By analyzing participants' choice behavior, the importance of an attribute for the choice and the impact of specific levels of this attribute on the overall attractiveness of a product can be calculated. Market Simulator tools furthermore allow for a specification of the overall most preferred product and the simulation of market shares of different products.

Research Design. For the conjoint analysis to adequately reflect consumers' wishes, a careful selection of attributes is required in order to include the relevant decision factors. Attributes for the conjoint analysis were therefore based on the results of the qualitative prestudy rather than theoretically derived. The attributes were also chosen according to a second criterion, which was operational practicability. This refers to the requirement that the attribute needs to be translatable in a (visual) form which can easily be understood by survey participants. This second requirement led to the exclusion of the factors *Efficiency/Costs*, *Visual appearance* and *Construction*. *Costs* were excluded because participants showed difficulties in assessing costs of energy infrastructure and it was also not clear if they referred to total costs or costs that the consumer needs to pay. Resulting, the attributes presented in Table 2 were included in the conjoint analysis.

As a specification of the conjoint survey, the adaptive conjoint analysis (ACA) was chosen. "Adaptive" refers to the trait that the choice-questions asked are adapted to each respondent individually, so that subsequent questions built on the previous answers of the participant. The ACA is superior to a choice-based conjoint study when a large number of attributes (more than five [39]), is analyzed, because the choice-task would become too complex if all attributes are involved at the same time. In an adaptive conjoint analysis, all attributes are first evaluated separately, while the choice tasks in the later stage of the survey only include those attributes which were evaluated as most relevant in the first part. This way, the attributes that need to be processed at the same time in the choice task are kept at a minimum. Besides being more easily processable, the adapted choice task is more relevant to participants, as they only need to take into account those attributes which are important to them. Additionally, because

Table 2. Attributes and levels used in the ACA study

Attributes	Levels
Space requirement	High, medium, low
Recycling and production	Environmentally friendly, partly environmentally friendly, not environmentally friendly
Autarky	High degree, medium degree, low degree
Resources needed during operation	High amount, medium amount, low amount
Choice of location	Free choice, depending on climatic factors, depending on regulations and climatic factors
Emissions	No emissions, noise, odor, noise and odor
Immediate environmental effects	No effects on plants and animals, harmful for animals, harmful for plants, harmful for animals and plants

the tasks the respondent has to solve vary, ACA are more divers compared to CBC analysis, where respondents solve the same task type several times.

Questionnaire: The questionnaire consisted of the conjoint analysis part, as well as questions on demographics and user characteristics.

Demographics: To be able to interpret the results of the choice-tasks against the sample characteristics, participants were asked for their age, gender, educational degree and current or most recent occupation. Furthermore, they were asked whether there was an energy plant (such as wind turbines, biomass plant etc.) within view of their home (yes/no), whether they were engaged in an animal or environmental protection action group (yes/no), and where their permanent place of residence was located (urban or rural area).

Attitudinal Characteristics: The questionnaire also included several questions on participants attitudes, e.g., towards the environment or technology in general, which are not part of the following analysis.

Conjoint Analysis: In the beginning, participants were given a short information text about the scenario which they should imagine. They were asked to imagine themselves in the situation of a major of a municipality, who needs to decide which renewable energy plant should supply the municipality with electricity in future years and thus be newly built in the municipality. Rather than choosing the new energy plant directly, however, they should decide which characteristics of the renewable energy plant are most important for this choice. Subsequently, the participants were introduced to the attributes and their levels, while at the same time demonstrating the icons which would be used in the conjoint tasks.

In the following rating task, the participants rated the desirability of each level of an attribute on a seven-point scale (1 = not desirable at all, 7 = very desirable).

Then a choice task was presented, in which participants had to indicate how strong they preferred one of the two alternative energy sources presented to them on a 9-point scale (1 = strongly prefer option A, 9 = strongly prefer option B). The energy sources were defined by two attributes, with all other (not presented) attributes being equal, based on the participants' previous choices of desirability (Fig. 1). Participants had to solve seven of such choice tasks.

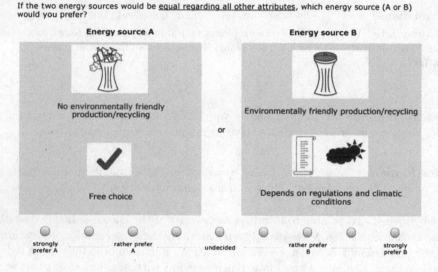

Fig. 1. Choice task with two attributes

Following, participants solved seven more choice tasks, where the energy sources presented were defined by three attributes. A final choice task consisted of indicating a preference for one of two energy sources defined by four attributes. For the choice tasks, a prohibition was installed that prevented the levels "Odor and noise emissions", "odor emissions" and "noise emissions" from appearing together with the level "free choice of location", based on the theoretical assumption that whenever an energy infrastructure would produce those emissions, legislations would be in place which, for example, define safety distances to residential areas or natural conservation areas.

4.2   Sample

Originally, 152 participants had taken part in the study. Because the data quality increases when complete sets of answers are used, only the 109 complete questionnaires were considered for further analysis. Among those, 57.8% were female, 42.2% male. Respondents were between 17 to 65 years old (Mean = 32.6 years). 75% had completed university education.

4.3 Results

The results of the ACA analysis are presented in Tables 3 and 4. The ACA analysis showed that overall, the local impact of renewable energy sites was most important for the preference of a renewable energy source (Table 3. This is shown by the fact that the attributes "environmental impact (local)" and "emissions (local)" were the two most important attributes for choosing a presented energy source. The two attributes represent an impact on both, nature and humans in the direct surroundings of the energy source facility. They were followed by the attributes "Recycling and production" and "Resources during operation". Least important were the "Space requirement", "Autarky" and "Choice of location".

Regarding the specific part-worth utilities of the levels (Table 4, the preferences showed a natural preference pattern where the most positive level received the highest preference and the least positive level received the lowest preference. This applied to the attributes "Space requirement", "Recycling and production", "Autarky" and "Resource consumption during operation", as well as "Choice of location". For the attribute "Emissions (local)", the least preferred level was "Noise and Odor", followed by "Noise emission" and "Odor emission", respectively. The most preferred level was "no emissions". Thus, unsurprisingly, a combination of both emissions, noise and odor, had the most negative impact on the overall preferability of a scenario. Additionally, noise annoyance was perceived more negatively than odor emissions. Concerning the environmental impact, a similar pattern emerged like for the emissions: a combination of harm to animals and plants was the least desired option, and "No effects" was the most preferred option. "Harm to animals" was less preferred than "Harm to plants".

Summarizing the results of the empirical study, it was found that the relative importance of the local impact on environment and humans (operationalized by "emissions") was the most important criterion for participants regarding their preference for an energy source.

5 Discussion

The aim of the study was to quantify the relative importance of acceptance-relevant attributes of energy sources and their corresponding infrastructure. The conjoint study revealed "local environmental impact" followed by "local emissions" as most important criteria for the preference of an energy source. The importance of environmental impact supports findings by Alvarez-Farizo and Hanley, who identified a negative impact on flora and fauna as "significant social costs" [44]. Regarding the ecological impact in detail, harm to animals was less accepted than harm to plants. It is likely that this result reflects peoples concerns for birds and bats in the vicinity of wind turbines. This topic was not only frequently mentioned in the focus groups, it is also often cited as a

Table 3. Average importances of attributes

Attribute	Importance (%)	SD[a]	Lower 95% CI[b]	Upper 95% CI
Space requirement	11.19	2.75	10.67	11.71
Recycling and production	15.87	2.77	15.35	16.39
Autarky	10.62	3.64	9.94	11.31
Resources during operation	15.60	2.98	15.04	16.16
Choice of location	8.35	3.29	7.74	8.97
Emissions (local)	16.76	3.96	16.01	17.50
Environmental impact (local)	21.61	3.86	20.88	22.33

[a]Standard deviation
[b]Confidence interval

drawback to the acceptance of wind turbines [15, 18]. Thus, a negative impact on local wildlife by renewable energy infrastructure should be avoided, as it is very likely to evoke opposition. On a different note, it has been shown that the active engagement of environmental protection groups in the planning process of wind turbines can foster acceptance [40]. Contrary to previous findings, ecological impacts on plants, such as a threat to species diversity, were mentioned in the focus groups and discussed as a potential barrier to widespread acceptance, while Upham and Shackley found this aspect to be of marginal importance [41].

Local emissions (noise and odor) were the second most important criterion for the choice of an energy source which corroborates the intense focus group discussions in this regard. It seems surprising that this factor, which concerned humans, was regarded less important than ecological impacts. One explanation for this mismatch could be that participants might be aware of planning regulations which ensure a certain distance to residential areas, for example for wind power plants, and thus the noise and odor emissions would not affect residents as badly. Still, it is known from other infrastructure contexts that human wellbeing is critical for social acceptance [42, 43], which is underlined by the importance given to this attribute and the discussion of nuisance through emissions by energy sources in the focus groups. Planners should thus be aware of the high impact of fear of health and wellbeing concerns on the acceptance of new (energy) infrastructure. While these emissions had only been operationalized as "noise" and "odor" in the conjoint study, local air pollution (from traffic) also presents a type of emission which was identified as an important reason to object to a biomass plant [41]. A follow up study should therefore expand the attribute emissions to include also air pollution.

Regarding the use of resources during the operation, it is interesting to note that this was only perceived as a *negative* aspect (in both, focus groups and choice task). Conversely, in the context of a biomass plant, the use of resources such as wood from local forests, that helps to maintain these, was seen as an additional local value [20].

Table 4. Part-worth utility values

Attribute	Level	Utility	SD[a]	Lower 95% CI[b]	Upper 95% CI
Space requirement	Large	−40.54	12.39	−42.86	−38.21
	Moderate	4.35	10.37	2.40	6.30
	Small	36.19	10.93	34.14	38.24
Recycling and production	Environm. friendly	51.62	10.55	49.64	53.60
	Partly environm. friendly	7.11	10.45	5.15	9.07
	Not environm. friendly	−58.73	11.87	−60.96	−56.50
Degree of autarky	High	31.60	19.75	27.89	35.31
	Moderate	5.35	9.12	3.64	7.06
	Low	−36.95	16.78	−40.10	−33.80
Resource consump.	High	−56.73	13.35	−59.24	−54.22
	Moderate	5.41	9.81	3.57	7.25
	Low	51.32	12.58	48.96	53.68
Choice of location	Legislation and climate	−16.40	21.92	−20.51	−12.28
	Climatic conditions	−0.68	12.02	−2.94	1.57
	Free choice	17.08	30.20	11.41	22.75
Emissions (local)	Noise and Odor	−49.58	15.43	−52.48	−46.69
	Noise	4.58	14.30	1.90	7.27
	Odor	−20.37	16.92	−23.55	−17.19
	No emissions	65.37	17.68	62.05	68.69
Environm. impact (local)	Harmful for plants and animals	−62.56	12.96	−64.99	−60.12
	Harmful for animals	−20.84	12.42	−23.18	−18.51
	Harmful for plants	−4.90	10.89	−6.95	−2.86
	No effects	88.30	17.71	84.98	91.63

[a]Standard deviation
[b]Confidence interval

Considering the results from the literature which emphasize the importance of trust in the stakeholders involved, it can be deduced that for existing projects, a transparent communication about ecological impacts and local emissions is of vital importance. For future technology development, non-obtrusive energy technologies with little to no impact on their immediate surroundings are to be preferred.

Methodological Discussion: In the choice tasks, the impact on landscape was not translated in a single attribute, as it was not feasible to depict and describe this factor independent of the specific energy source and independent of a specific location. Landscape impact had been extensively discussed in the focus groups as advantage or disadvantage of certain energy sources and is in line with the literature that has also identified landscape impact as important for acceptance. Contrary to expectations, the two attributes related to landscape impact ("space requirement" and "choice of location") were only of minor importance in the choice tasks. This could mean that the aspect of landscape impact was not operationalized ideally in the choice task and thus received less attention than expected.

Additionally, our choice task did not involve the factors referring to the social context, such as procedural issues like involved stakeholders, trust in these and the experience of a fair decision process. The focus on characteristics of the technology itself rather than the circumstances of the implementation process was due to the focus of technology development in this paper, thus addressing issues which can be influenced by technology developers. Procedural issues occur in the specific implementation phases of a project, in which the technology development is already finished, thus they are out of scope of engineers working in technology development. On the one hand, the results of the study can thus contribute to the research on the general acceptability of specific renewable energy technologies, independent of local circumstances. On the other hand, they can provide insight for technology developers for future (energy) infrastructure by identifying the most important characteristics of an energy technology. Still however, it will be a future research duty to include procedural issues as they have been identified as crucial to the local acceptance of renewable energy infrastructure.

The rather biased sample presents a further limitation to the results, which should be taken into account for the interpretation. Focusing on a young sample in the ACA study, however, had the unintended benefit on focusing on a generation which will live with this energy infrastructure in their surroundings in the future, thus providing an informative target group.

6   Conclusion

The conjoint study showed that for the general acceptance of energy sources, environmental impact plays the most important role, followed by impact on humans by emissions such as noise and odor. In the focus groups, landscape impact and visual appearance of the site were also intensively discussed as critical. Future development of energy infrastructure should take these findings into account and aim at developing non-obtrusive technologies. For existing technologies, the results support findings that impacts on humans and nature are sensitive topics which need to be communicated in carefully designed communication strategies.

Acknowledgments. Thanks to Valerie Scharmer, Jonas Hemsen and Anika Linzenich for research support. This work was funded by the Excellence Initiative of the German federal and state governments (project "Urban Future Outline" (UFO)).

References

1. Zoellner, J., Schweizer-Ries, P., Wemheuer, C.: Public acceptance of renewable energies: results from case studies in Germany. Energy Policy 36(11), 4136–4141 (2008)
2. Cohen, J.J., Reichl, J., Schmidthaler, M.: Re-focussing research efforts on the public acceptance of energy infrastructure: a critical review. Energy 76, 4–9 (2014)
3. Venkatesh, V., Bala, H.: Technology acceptance model 3 and a research agenda on interventions. Decis. Sci. 9(2), 273–315 (2008)
4. Friedl, C., Reichl, J.: Realizing energy infrastructure projects-a qualitative empirical analysis of local practices to address social acceptance. Energy Policy 89, 184–193 (2016)
5. Futák-Campbell, B., Haggett, C.: Tilting at windmills? Using discourse analysis to understand the attitude-behaviour gap in renewable energy conflicts. Mekhanizm Rehuluvannya Economiky 1(51), 207–220 (2011)
6. Devine-Wright, P.: Beyond NIMBYism: towards an integrated framework for understanding public perceptions of wind energy. Wind Energy 8(2), 125–139 (2005)
7. Haggett, C., Benson, J.F.: The attitude-behaviour gap in renewable energy conflicts: a theoretical and methodological review. In: 2nd Workshop of the Economic and Social Research Council's Environment and Human Behaviour Programme, London (2003)
8. Germany's Power Generation Mix 2016 - Market share of Germany's gross power generation (2016). http://strom-report.de/renewable-energy/
9. Wüstenhagen, R., Wolsink, M., Bürer, M.J.: Social acceptance of renewable energy innovation: an introduction to the concept. Energy Policy 35(5), 2683–2691 (2007)
10. Hirsh, R.F., Sovacool, B.K.: Wind turbines and invisible technology: unarticulated reasons for local opposition to wind energy. Technol. Cult. 54(4), 705–734 (2013)
11. Johansson, M., Laike, T.: Intention to respond to local wind turbines: the role of attitudes and visual perception. Wind Energy 10(5), 435–451 (2007)
12. Bishop, I.D., Stock, C.: Using collaborative virtual environments to plan wind energy installations. Renew. Energy 35(10), 2348–2355 (2010)
13. Hoen, B., Wiser, R., Cappers, P., Thayer, M., Sethi, G.: Wind energy facilities and residential properties: the effect of proximity and view on sales prices. J. Real Estate Res. 33(3), 279–316 (2011)
14. Upreti, B.R., van der Horst, D.: National renewable energy policy and local opposition in the UK: the failed development of a biomass electricity plant. Biomass Bioenergy 26(1), 61–69 (2004)
15. Wolsink, M.: The research agenda on social acceptance of distributed generation in smart grids: Renewable as common pool resources. Renew. Sustain. Energy Rev. 16(1), 822–835 (2012)
16. Chiabrando, R., Fabrizio, E., Garnero, G.: On the applicability of the visual impact assessment OAI SPP tool to photovoltaic plants. Renew. Sustain. Energy Rev. 15(1), 845–850 (2011)
17. Warren, C.R., Lumsden, C., O'Dowd, S., Birnie, R.V.: 'Green on green': public perceptions of wind power in Scotland and Ireland. J. Environ. Plann. Manag. 48(6), 853–875 (2005)
18. Krewitt, W., Nitsch, J.: The potential for electricity generation from on-shore wind energy under the constraints of nature conservation: a case study for two regions in Germany. Renew. Energy 28(10), 1645–1655 (2003)

19. Wolsink, M.: Wind power and the NIMBY-myth: institutional capacity and the limited significance of public support. Renew. Energy **21**(1), 49–64 (2000)
20. Rösch, C., Kaltschmitt, M.: Energy from biomass–do non-technical barriers prevent an increased use? Biomass Bioenergy **16**(5), 347–356 (1999)
21. Magnani, N.: Exploring the local sustainability of a green economy in alpine communities: a case study of a conflict over a biogas plant. Mt. Res. Dev. **32**(2), 109–116 (2012)
22. Soland, M., Steimer, N., Walter, G.: Local acceptance of existing biogas plants in Switzerland. Energy Policy **61**, 802–810 (2013)
23. Bakhiyi, B., Labrèche, F., Zayed, J.: The photovoltaic industry on the path to a sustainable future-environmental and occupational health issues. Environ. Int. **73**, 224–234 (2014)
24. Safigianni, A.S., Tsimtsios, A.M.: Electric and magnetic fields due to rooftop photovoltaic units. J. Basic Appl. Phys. **3**(2), 76–80 (2014)
25. Pedersen, E., van den Berg, F., Bakker, R., Bouma, J.: Response to noise from modern wind farms in The Netherlands. J. Acoust. Soc. Am. **126**(2), 634–643 (2009)
26. Musall, F.D., Kuik, O.: Local acceptance of renewable energy–a case study from southeast Germany. Energy Policy **39**(6), 3252–3260 (2011)
27. Crichton, F., Dodd, G., Schmid, G., Gamble, G., Petrie, K.J.: Can expectations produce symptoms from infrasound associated with wind turbines? Health Psych. **33**(4), 360–364 (2014)
28. Songsore, E., Buzzelli, M.: Social responses to wind energy development in Ontario: the influence of health risk perceptions and associated concerns. Energy Policy **69**, 285–296 (2014)
29. Devine-Wright, P.: Rethinking NIMBYism: the role of place attachment and place identity in explaining place-protective action. J. Community Appl. Soc. **19**(6), 426–441 (2009)
30. Aitken, M.: Wind power and community benefits: challenges and opportunities. Energy Policy **38**(10), 6066–6075 (2010)
31. Gross, C.: Community perspectives of wind energy in Australia: the application of a justice and community fairness framework to increase social acceptance. Energy Policy **35**(5), 2727–2736 (2007)
32. Wolsink, M.: Wind power implementation: the nature of public attitudes: equity and fairness instead of 'backyard motives'. Renew. Sus. Energy Rev. **11**(6), 1188–1207 (2007)
33. Pasqualetti, M.J.: Opposing wind energy landscapes: a search for common cause. Ann. Assoc. Am. Geogr. **101**(4), 907–917 (2011)
34. Warren, C.R., McFadyen, M.: Does community ownership affect public attitudes to wind energy? A case study from south-west Scotland. Land Use Policy **27**(2), 204–213 (2010)
35. Walker, G., Hunter, S., Devine-Wright, P., Evans, B., Fay, H.: Harnessing community energies: explaining and evaluating community-based localism in renewable energy policy in the UK. Global Environ. Polit. **7**(2), 64–82 (2007)
36. Visschers, V.H., Siegrist, M.: Find the differences and the similarities: relating perceived benefits, perceived costs and protected values to acceptance of five energy technologies. J. Environ. Psychol. **40**, 117–130 (2014)
37. Mayring, P.: Qualitative content analysis: theoretical foundation, basic procedures and software solution, Klagenfurt (2014)
38. Luce, R.D., Tukey, J.W.: Simultaneous conjoint measurement: a new type of fundamental measurement. J. Math. Psychol. **1**(1), 1–27 (1964)

39. Software, S.: The ACA/Web v6.0 Technical Paper. Sawtooth Software Technical Paper Series (2007). https://www.sawtoothsoftware.com/support/technical-papers/aca-related-papers/aca-technical-paper-2007
40. Jobert, A., Laborgne, P., Mimler, S.: Local acceptance of wind energy: factors of success identified in French and German case studies. Energy Policy **35**(5), 2751–2760 (2007)
41. Upham, P., Shackley, S.: Local public opinion of a proposed 21.5 MW(e) biomass gasifier in Devon: questionnaire survey results. Biomass Bioenergy **31**(6), 433–441 (2007)
42. Arning, K., Kowalewski, S., Ziefle, M.: Health concerns versus mobile data needs: conjoint measurement of preferences for mobile communication network scenarios. Hum. Ecol. Risk Assess. **20**(5), 1359–1384 (2014)
43. Zaunbrecher, B.S., Linzenich, A., Ziefle, M.: A mast is a mast is a mast..? Comparison of preferences for location-scenarios of electricity pylons and wind power plants using conjoint analysis. Energy Policy **105**, 429–439 (2017). doi:10.1016/j.enpol.2017.02.043
44. Álvarez-Farizo, B., Hanley, N.: Using conjoint analysis to quantify public preferences over the environmental impacts of wind farms. An example from Spain. Energy Policy **30**(2), 107–116 (2002)

HCI Case Studies

Measuring and Evaluating the User Experience Strategy Maturity of Spatial Web-Based Projects: A Case Study of Tehran Web-Based Map

Kaveh Bazargan(✉), Ali Rezaeian, and Hamidreza Hafeznia

Shahid Beheshti (National) University (of Iran), Tehran, Iran
{k_bazargan, a-rezaeian}@sbu.ac.ir,
h.hafeznia@gmail.com

Abstract. The design and implementation of spatial Web-based projects has been driving much research and development interest from the global community of practice over the past 10 years. The user centered evaluation of such projects outputs should be a vital part of the overall system development lifecycle. Continuously measuring and improving the User Experience (UX) of the output systems is a key factor driving better usage and enhanced user engagement.

Our research objective was first to track real-time and real-world usage of Tehran web based map, developed by TMICTO (Tehran Municipality ICT Organization), then to perform a usability test on selected tasks within a defined context of use and finally, to evaluate the UX strategy maturity of Tehran web based map based on existing maturity models.

We used mixed user research methods, including remote and on-site user research methods, to understand the context of use, usage behavior patterns in terms of actions and engagement, then we designed and performed usability testing and finally we evaluated the UX strategy maturity of Tehran web based map. Concrete and practical recommendations to improve the level of UX strategy maturity of Tehran web based map oriented towards short term, medium term and long term visions are formulated at the end of our research.

Keywords: User experience (UX) · UX strategy · UX maturity · Usability · Spatial web-based projects

1 Introduction

From a Human Computer Interaction (HCI) perspective, the availability of personal computers from the late 1970s was quite a disruptive technological innovation from the time when the only users who interacted with computers were ICT experts and professionals. Personal software and personal computer platforms made very basic literate human being a potential computer user. As non ICT professionals started to use personal computers and systems, usability and user experience (UX) challenges surfaced and became major barriers to user adoption and improved uptake [5].

According to the ISO 9241-11 standard, "usability is the degree to which software can be used by specified consumers to achieve quantified objectives with effectiveness,

© Springer International Publishing AG 2017
M. Kurosu (Ed.): HCI 2017, Part II, LNCS 10272, pp. 631–644, 2017.
DOI: 10.1007/978-3-319-58077-7_49

efficiency, and satisfaction in a quantified context of use". Usability is a subjective measure because levels of usability depend on the user and the context of use [2].

Customized experimental design, defining usability measure and usability measurement techniques for complex products, systems and services is difficult [15].

Although usability is a well-established concept with proven measure and measurement methods, HCI researcher and practitioners have different level of understanding of UX operational definition, metrics and measurement methods [13].

The international standard on ergonomics of human system interaction, ISO 9241-210, defines user experience as "a person's perceptions and responses that result from the use or anticipated use of a product, system or service" [10].

Beside the broad range of proposed definitions for UX, there is a consensus of opinion among HCI researchers and practitioners that UX as a concept is the result of the interaction between three elements: the user, the system and the context [13]. No one can predict for certain how a system will be perceived by the end users. Informed decisions can be made about UX during each phase of the overall system development lifecycle by using a mix or relevant user research and UX design methods and tools [7].

The level of interest for UX designers and researchers within organizations is constantly growing in most developed countries across the globe. Hence, competitive organizations and specifically multinational corporations compete for recruiting skilled UX consultants and experts that would be able to have a holistic impact.

The "2017 UX and User Research Industry Survey Report" published by UserTesting [1], indicates a positive trend toward early, frequent research positive trend toward early, frequent research positive trend toward early, frequent research throughout the design, development, and optimization of digital products. The majority of 2238 surveyed UX professionals reported that their testing frequency has increased moderately or significantly.. The number of UX professionals who do user research on their competitors has more than doubled year-over-year [1].

A strategy can be defined as approach or plan of action to achieve a major goal resulting in advantageous conditions. UX strategy applies this definition to UX design [4]. A UX strategy can be used as a basis for UX design to predict the future. A UX strategy builds a common vision in terms of user standpoint and based on organization business and product strategy.

This research tried to analyze, understand and evaluate the UX of spatial web-based projects by considering Tehran online map[1] as a case study. The Web-based map of Tehran is subset of Tehran Spatial Data Information (SDI) project which provides spatial services for users such as citizens, scholars, public sector and private partners. The main objective of this research is to answer the following research questions:

- How do existing and new users interact and engage with Tehran web-based map?
- What is the role of UX in Tehran web-based map?
- Which models and methods can be used to evaluate it's UX strategy maturity?
- How mature is Tehran web-based map in terms of UX strategy?
- What key recommendations can be formulated to improve the level of Tehran web-based map UX strategy maturity?

---

[1] Tehran online map <http://map.tehran.ir>.

2 Review of Literature

While performing extensive review of literature on topics related to the UX strategy maturity of Web-based map projects, we realized that much research has been performed on the connected topic of GIS[2] and online maps usability.

Harding (2009) provides a research methodology which established a reference base of qualitative data on user needs for geographic information with respect to context of use. The key elements which contribute to geographical information systems usability are namely: (1) information content, (2) information quality, (3) information structure and interoperability, (4) information file format, (5) information volume, (6) information presentation, (7) information cost, (8) information delivery and (9) information selectability [8].

Nivala et al. (2007) studied the level of usability methods' familiarity among map application and systems developers. The results showed that although usability engineering is slowly being incorporated into design of map applications, knowledge on how to execute the methods is still very low or almost non-existent. Many companies are actually interested to implement such methods, but one key problem is the lack of resources and applied knowledge on how to implement an approach [19].

Ingensand and Golay (2010) evaluated the task-oriented usability of a Web GIS. They realized there are different strategies for interacting with Web GIS and that users perform differently according to selected personal strategies. These differences in performance are related to the users' experience and expertise with respect to similar systems usage and to specific user interface key functions and features [9].

Different models to design a UX strategy and assess its maturity within organizations have been proposed in the past few years. Jaime Levy (2015) suggests a quadruple tenet to design a UX strategy framework. Levy's UX strategy framework is composed of: (1) Business Strategy, (2) Value Innovation, (3) Validated User Research and (4) Killer UX Design [14].

Stern (2014) has also proposed the CUBI model for achieving improved UX competitiveness. The CUBI model includes 4 main layers: (1) Content, (2) User goals, (3) Business Goals and (4) Interaction [20]. Each layer has dedicated sub-layers.

Kalbach (2014) has designed the UX Strategy Blueprint which is a simple tool to help define a given UX strategy. The elements within the UX Strategy Blueprint are: (1) Challenges, (2) Aspirations, (3) Focus Areas, (4) Guiding Principles, (5) Activities and (6) Measurements [11].

Nielson (2006) also defined an eight stages process for achieving Corporate UX Maturity [16]. In the initial stages developers and corporations show hostility towards usability. Most companies realize the value of making designs easier for human end users. In the next stages a fixed budget is dedicated and there shall be an official usability group, led by a UX manager in the company. Then, there should be an integrated user-centered design team incorporated within the corporation.

And finally the last stage should be a user-driven corporation. At this final maturity level, the usability methods will affect corporate strategy and activities [17].

---

[2] Geographic Information System.

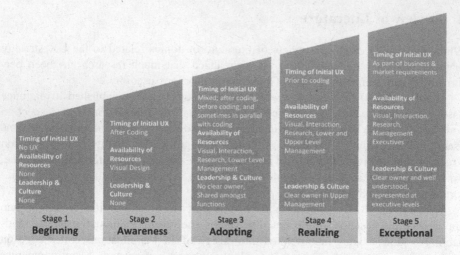

Fig. 1. Five Stages of UX Maturity [6]

Chapman and Plewes (2014) have developed a UX Maturity Model composed of 5 stages [6]. This model can help understanding any organization's UX level of maturity. The model provides six key indicators of UX maturity as follow: (1) the timing of UX (2), the UX expertise and resources, (3) the usage of appropriate techniques, (4) the leadership and culture in the company, (5) the degree of integration of UX with other corporate processes and finally (6) applying design.

The five stages toward improved maturity are illustrated in Fig. 1 namely:

(1) Beginning, (2) Awareness, (3) Adopting, (4) Realizing and (5) Exceptional [6].

3 Research Methods

To answer our research questions, we used selected complementary research methods. Initially, for 30 days, quantitative data related to users of Tehran map portal were logged and analyzed. We also used heatmap tools. Then based on the analysis of user behaviors, we did proper experimental design towards planning usability tests. Figure 2 provides a visual insight about how data sources were used to inform the experimental design towards defining relevant usability testing tasks.

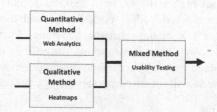

Fig. 2. Collecting quantitative and qualitative data via multiple user research methods

3.1 Quantitative Data

Online real-time and real-world user's behavior quantitative data was collected by using professional Web Analytics tools for a period of 30 days. We identified users to analyze and understand the way they interacted with Tehran online map portal[3]. Our analysis included segmentation of users based on key factors such as visitors, time, frequency, actions, content and engagement. This part of research, also known as web analytics, was performed over one month period. We used Google Analytics to generate specific Java Script tracking codes and embedded the codes in the proper source code with the assistance of a partner company in charge of Tehran Web-based map.

3.2 Qualitative Data

Online real-time and real-world user's behavior qualitative data was collected by using professional remote heatmapping tools, provided by SIGCHI Iran Chapter [21], for a period of 30 days. Heatmaps represent where the visitors concentrated their clicks and how frequently they clicked on a given screen zone. Generally, a color scale moving from blue to red indicates the frequency of clicks. Thus, a red spot over an area of a webpage might indicate that a participants clicked on this part of a webpage much frequently than other areas [18]. In the qualitative part of the research we analyzed selected screen heatmaps for specific visual elements to analyze and understand usage behaviors and possible design challenges as barriers to usage.

3.3 Mixed Method

Based on the data analysis performed on quantitative and qualitative data, we identified selected tasks to be performed in given context of use by selected users in a lab based environment on a desktop computer screen. The usability testing tasks were selected based on the newly available online sculpture database of Tehran Municipality. Table 1 provides a description of five selected user tasks to be performed by users.

The usability test session were conducted in a customized office of the Tehran Beautification Organization transformed into a usability lab for one full day. All usability test participants were staff members of Tehran Beautification Organization including 8 women and 10 men. A specific participant selection procedure and protocol was used to selected relevant participants based on previous knowledge and experience with Tehran online map portal and sculpture database widget. Informed consent forms, pre-test questionnaire, observer recording sheet, system usability scale (SUS) questionnaire and professional time and video recording software were used.

---

[3] Tehran online map portal < http://map.tehran.ir > .

Table 1. List of usability testing tasks

Task no.	Task description
T1	Use the sculpture database widget to identify a statue in Region 1 "*Niavaran*" neighborhood and orally state the artwork's name and used material
T2	Use the sculpture database widget by operating the "yes or no" selector to orally state whether the "*Garshasb*" statue is lighted or not. Identify and orally name the lighting equipment used to light-up this specific statue
T3	Use the sculpture database widget to identify and orally state the district of Tehran in which the "Bolbol" sculpture is located. Also identify and orally name the artist who created the "Bolbol" sculpture
T4	Use the sculpture database widget and the distance widget to orally state the distance between the "Garshasb" statue and the closest subway station
T5	Use the sculpture database widget and the street view widget to identify and orally state the type of urban furniture next to the "Roftegar" statue

4   Results

4.1   Existing and New User Interactions and Engagement with Tehran Web-Based Map

To understand how users interact with Tehran online web-based map, quantitative data was collected and analyzed with Google Analytics.

Quantitative Data Analysis (Using Web Analytics). Table 2 displays Tehran online web-based map key data about visitors during a period of 30 days (10 April 2015 – 10 May 2015).

Visitors accessed Tehran online web-based map via different sources. Namely, 59.1% of visitors came via search engine, 33.9% of visitors came by directly typing the <http://map.tehran.ir> URL and 7% came from links. In term of geographical origin of users, 94.2% of visitors were from Iran, 3% from the USA, 0.7% from the UK, 0.4% from The Netherland, 0.3% from Germany and the rest from other countries.

Table 2. Tehran map portal visitors' information (in a month)

No.	Title	Amount
1	No. of unique visitors	275320
1.1	No. of new visitors	133524
1.2	No. of returning visitors	141796
2	Actions (Clicks)	392291
2.1	Number of page views	390039
2.2	Downloads	1878
2.3	Outbound links	374
3	Average Actions	1.2
4	Total Time on portal	1776 days 23 h
5	Average time per visit	8 m 7 s
6	Bounce rate	6%

One of our quantitative metrics was the engagement rate of visitors with the portal. This metric is measured in terms of user's actions or clicks and visit duration.

Most visitors spent less than 10 min in Tehran map portal. A total of 19.78% of visitors engaged between 9 and 10 min and 19.44% engaged less than one minute. So, the engagement time for 12% of visitors is less than one minute which can be specified by two groups of users. Regarding bounce rate of 10–30% for service sites [12], a 6% bounce rate indicates the most visitors are in need of information and very much willing to engage with the map.

Qualitative Data Analysis (Using Heatmaps). Given the technical architecture of Tehran online map is single screen and all services are shown on the main screen, it was only possible to produce a heatmap for that screen. Figures 3 and 4 display the main homepage of Tehran online Web-based map and it's associated heatmap.

Figure 4, generated over 30 days or visitor heatmapping, displays red (hot) areas that are visitors "focus zones" on the main screen and colder colors (yellow, green) display a lower level visitor interaction and engagement. The "routing" and "Tehran key places" widgets located on the left side toolbar and the "search" and "more information" widgets located on the top toolbar got very high level of user interactions. Figure 4 provides a key insight about visitors not willing to access or read the "user manual" via the "help" section and to "register" with the map located on the top bar.

Mixed Data Analysis (Using Lab Based Usability Testing). To determine to what extent the usability test participants were familiar with online map service, a dedicated

Fig. 3. Tehran online Web-based map main homepage (Color figure online)

Fig. 4. Tehran online Web-based map main homepage generated heatmap (30 days data) (Color figure online)

questionnaire was distributed between them before the usability test. Among a total of 18 usability test participants, 8 were women and 10 were men.

Figure 5 displays a very low level of GIS and online maps usage by the participants for business purposes over a week period. In addition, participants were more familiar with Google map rather than Tehran map. A total of 45.8% of participants used online maps to find streets and public places. Routing features, urban traffic monitoring and

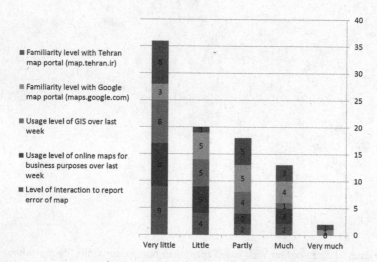

Fig. 5. Usability test participants pretest results (N = 18) (Color figure online)

Table 3. Average time of task (task duration) for usability test participants (N = 18)

Tasks	Duration (Seconds)
T1	92.44
T2	76.94
T3	121.17
T4	102.22
T5	99.78

street view functions were also mostly used by participants. A total of 72% of participants used a personal computer and 22% a smart phone to access online maps.

Table 3 displays the average time on task (task duration) as performed by participants for each of the five tasks presented in Table 1.

Based on the usability testing protocol the maximum time on task was 180 s. Figure 6 displays how users performed on each task. Half of the participants well performed on task T1. One-third of participants could get T1 completed with help and two participants didn't manage with T1 and failed. Task T2 got the highest success rate among all five tasks during the usability testing sessions. Quick observation of the sculpture's picture is one major explanation for the high speed of T2 completion.

Task T3 was the most failed task by participants with an average completion time of 121.17 s as the longest recorded time among all five tasks. One underlying explanation is that as most participants didn't manage to find and use the «Tehran city neighborhoods» selector so they would need to zoom out and in to identify the neighborhoods.

Almost 28% of the usability test participants were able to successfully perform task T4 that required using the horizontal toolbar at top of the screen as well as using the

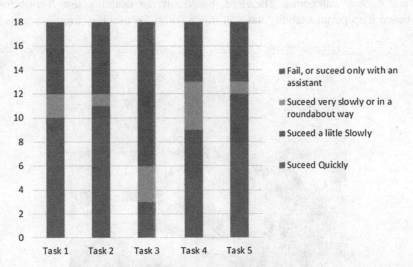

Fig. 6. Tasks T1 to T5 completion status by usability test participants (N = 18) (Color figure online)

«distance calculation» widget. One of the reasons participants' failed completing task T4 is that they were didn't understand how to use and operate this widget.

A total of 8 participants managed to successfully complete task T5 that required using «Street view» widget. One of the participants did a shortcut by using the picture of sculpture could to complete this task. Two participants also didn't manage to figure out and understand how to use and operate the widget.

Recurrent improvement suggestion for this map designers made by most of the usability test participants was to add simple and short usage guidelines, to use different color codes to identify the widgets and use simple unambitious icons on toolbars.

The usability test results confirm that although Tehran online Web-based map is full of advanced features and widgets, users have a hard time understanding how to usage and operate them. In addition, one of our participants looked into the available "help" section to learn how to use the widgets. Some usability test participants reported that the waring messages and text used inside the dialogue box were confusing.

Figure 7 displays the setting of one of the offices at Tehran Beautification Organization that was converted to a usability testing lab for one full day. The usability test participant is looking at the computer screen, the moderator is sitting on the side, the first observer is looking at the notebook screen (remote observation using recoding software) and the second observer (direct observation) is taking notes as well.

4.2   What Is the Role of User Experience in Tehran Web-Based Map?

A standard System Usability Scale (SUS) questionnaire was distributed to each participant right after the end of the usability test sessions. The Tehran online Web-based map obtained a SUS final score of 66.5. Based on Bangor (2009) adjective rating and acceptability ranges [3], 66.5 is an acceptable SUS score than is positioned in between "ok" and "good" categories. Therefore, based on our usability test, Tehran online Web-based map portal usability has still much room for usability improvements.

Fig. 7. Usability testing lab setting used to record participants interactions (N = 18)

Apart from the usability tests we performed with the participants, we also reviewed and analyzed the initial Request for Proposal (RFP) written for Tehran online Web-based map by TMICTO. The RFP we analyzed didn't include any minimum requirements for key human factors such as accessibility, usability and user experience factors. Our understanding is that TMICTO is either not aware of a user centered system development lifecycle method or no resources are dedicated to human factors.

4.3 Which Models and Methods Can Be Used to Evaluate It's UX Strategy Maturity?

Different methods and patterns have been proposed for evaluating the UX strategy maturity within organizations. In this research, Chapman & Plewes (2014) model was used to evaluate the UX strategy maturity of Tehran online Web-based map portal. As discussed in literature review section, Chapman and Plewes (2014) proposed a 5 stages model that drives an organization from an "immature" toward a mature "stage" [6]. This model can help organization with defining each stage indicators quite distinctively, so that they would be able to evaluate each maturity stage based on clear metrics.

4.4 How Mature Is Tehran Web-Based Map in Terms of UX Strategy?

Based on our findings we can affirm that the level of UX literacy and UX strategy maturity at TMICTO is very low. TMICTO would definitely benefit from learning and applying a user-centered system development lifecycle methodology. It also appears that there is a very low level of applied knowledge about usability, UX and human factors at TMICTO. Based on chapman & Plewes (2014) model, this organization is at the very beginning stage. This first stage is where the organization just thinks of UX as end-user product add-on or a service visual design enhancement.

4.5 What Key Recommendations Can Be Formulated to Improve the Level of Tehran Web-Based Map UX Strategy Maturity?

Improving the level of UX literacy and institutionalization within organization requires driving through each and every stage of the maturity model. According to Nielson (2006) and based on the literature, reaching the ultimate stage of maturity might take as long as 40 years [17]. Therefore, organization must have short term, medium term and long term planning with regard to understanding and continuously improving the level of UX strategy maturity. Based on our research findings, key recommendations are proposed as follows for all the team members of Tehran online Web-based map based at TMICTO:

- Taking advantage of professional user research experts and UX consultants outside the organization,

- Learning and applying the foundations of Human-Computer Interaction (HCI) including User-Centered Design (UCD), usability and UX by all researchers, designers and managers working at TMICTO,
- Understanding the importance of incorporating key human factors and metrics to each and very future Request for Proposal (RFP) related to Tehran online web-Based map and other information systems
- Performing continuous rapid and rigorous user research with a wide mix of analytical and empirical methods

The following key recommendations are proposed for the medium term:

- Defining and incorporating usability requirements and UX targets to each and every project at TMICTO,
- Ensure that all users and those who will be affected by an existing or future system have their needs clearly articulated during the assessment and design of requirements; later the system must be validated to meet requirements via usability testing

Long term recommendations are as follows:

- Prioritizing UX as a key success and competitiveness factor in each new project,
- Sponsoring user research and UX design for the very first day of each new project,
- Partnering and networking with local world-class professional communities of practice such as the AM SICHI Iran Chapter [21] for actionable professional training, applied and basic combined experience sharing towards better interactions.

5   Conclusion

In this research we aimed at investigating the UX of spatial web based projects and the level of UX strategy maturity within projects and more specifically organizations in charge of those projects. The Tehran online Web-based map owned by TMICTO was taken as our case study.

First, we tracked real-time and real-world usage of Tehran online Web-based map by collecting quantitative and qualitative data during 30 days. Quantitative data was also collected and analyzed with dedicated web analytics tools such as Google Analytics during the same 30 days. Qualitative data was collective via dedicated remote user research tools such as heatmap tools. The "routing" and "Tehran key places" widgets located on the left side toolbar and the "search" and "more information" widgets located on the top toolbar got very high level of user interactions. Based on the collected and analyzed data from 275320 unique visitors, we defined specific tasks for a specific context of use and conducted usability testing sessions with 18 participants including 8 women and 10 men from Tehran Beautification Organization.

Based on the results of the usability testing session, the Tehran online Web-based map obtained a SUS final score of 66.5. Based on our research findings we can affirm that the level of UX literacy and UX strategy maturity at TMICTO is very low.

The comparative survey of TMICTO and Tehran online Web-based map portal with respect to Chapman & Plewes (2014) UX Maturity Model's indicators showed the

TMICTO is still at the very beginning stage in terms of UX literacy, UX strategy and UX maturity. Much has to be done to incorporate UX from the overall lifecycle.

We proposed short term, medium term and long term practical recommendations for improving the current state of TMICTO UX literacy, maturity and Tehran online web-Based map UX strategy maturity. TMICTO should prioritize UX as a key success and competitiveness factor in each new project towards improved UX maturity.

Our research findings also highlight the negative outcomes of low usability and user experience as very strong barriers to improved end-user engagement. Sponsoring user research and UX design for the very first day of each new project and programs can be key driver towards overcoming such barriers. Finally, we strongly recommend partnering and networking with local world-class professional communities of practice such as the AM SICHI Iran Chapter <http://www.sigchi.ir> for actionable professional training, applied and basic combined experience sharing towards better interactions.

6 Limitations

One of the limitations of this research is the time constraint of 30 days (one month) during which the remote user research with web analytics and heatmap tools were performed. Extending this period of time to 6 or 12 months would provide us with richer real-time and real-world data towards improved research insights and findings. The authors also acknowledge that the context of use, selected tasks and participants with respect to the usability tests are domain specific and linked to Tehran Beautification Organization.

References

1. UX and User Research Industry Survey Report 2017 by UserTesting. (2017). http://info.usertesting.com/ux-industry-survey-2017.html. Accessed Feb 2017
2. Allanwood, G., Beare, P.: User Experience Design: Creating Designs Users Really Love. Bloomsbury, New York (2014)
3. Bangor, A., Kortum, P., Miller, J.: Determining what individual SUS scores mean: adding an adjective rating scale. J. Stud. 4(3), 114–123 (2009)
4. Bryan, P.: What is UX Strategy? (2014) http://www.uxstrat.com/blog/what-is-ux-strategy. Accessed Feb 2007
5. Myers, B.A.: The Encyclopedia of human-computer interaction. In: Soegaard, M., Dam, R. F. (eds.) The Interaction Design Foundation, 2nd edn. (2014). http://interaction-design.org. Accessed Feb 2017. ISBN 978-87-92964-00-7
6. Chapman, L., Plewes, S.: A UX maturity model: effective introduction of UX into organizations. In: Marcus, A. (ed.) DUXU 2014. LNCS, vol. 8520, pp. 12–22. Springer, Cham (2014). doi:10.1007/978-3-319-07638-6_2
7. Cousins, C.: Why Does User Experience Matter? (2013). http://designshack.net/articles/why-does-user-experience-matter. Accessed Feb 2017

8. Harding, J.: Usability of geographic information e Factors identified from qualitative analysis of task-focused user interviews. Appl. Ergon. **44**, 940–947 (2013)
9. Ingensand, J., Golay, F.: Task-oriented usability evaluation of a WebGIS for a real-world community. URISA J. **22**, 41–53 (2010)
10. ISO 9241-210: Ergonomics of human-system interaction – Part 210: Human-centred design for interactive systems. ISO (2010)
11. Kalbach, J.: UX Strategy Blueprint (2014). https://experiencinginformation.wordpress.com/2014/08/12/uxstrategyblueprint. Accessed Feb 2017
12. Kelly, K.: What is Bounce Rate? Avoid Common Pitfalls (2012). http://www.blastam.com/blog/index.php/2012/02/what-is-bounce-rate. Accessed Feb 2017
13. Lallemand, C., Gronier, G., Koenig, V.: User experience: a concept without consensus? exploring practitioners' perspective through an international survey. Comput. Hum. Behav. **43**, 35–48 (2015)
14. Levy, J.: UX Strategy: How to Devise Innovative Digital Products That People Want. O'Reilly Media (2015)
15. Miki, H.: Reconsidering the notion of user experience for human-centered design. In: Yamamoto, S. (ed.) HIMI 2013. LNCS, vol. 8016, pp. 329–337. Springer, Heidelberg (2013). doi:10.1007/978-3-642-39209-2_38
16. Nielsen, J.: Corporate UX Maturity: Stages 1–4. (2006). https://www.nngroup.com/articles/usability-maturity-stages-1-4. Accessed Feb 2017
17. Nielsen, J.: Corporate UX Maturity: Stages 5–8 (2006). https://www.nngroup.com/articles/usability-maturity-stages-5-8. Accessed Feb 2017
18. U.S. Dept. of Health and Human Services. The Research-Based Web Design & Usability Guidelines, Enlarged/Expanded edition. Government Printing Office, Washington (2006) https://www.usability.gov/how-to-and-tools/methods/eye-tracking.html. Accessed Feb 2017
19. Nivala, A., Sarjakoski, L., Sarjakoski, T.: Usability methods' familiarity among map application developers. Int. J. Hum.-Comput. Stud. **65**, 784–795 (2007)
20. Stern, C.: CUBI: A User Experience Model for Project Success (2014). https://uxmag.com/articles/cubi-a-user-experience-model-for-project-successAccessed Feb 2017
21. Bazargan, K., Kujala, T.: SIGCHI's Iran chapter: empowering local HCI to create a better shared sociotechnical future. Interactions **23**(2), 86 (2016). doi:10.1145/2890102

Effect of Animated and Non-animated Pictograms for a Non-lingual Disaster Management Application

Luis Ernesto Dominguez-Rios[✉], Tomoko Izumi, Takayoshi Kitamura, and Yoshio Nakatani

Graduate School of Information Science and Engineering, Ritsumeikan University, Kusatsu City, Shiga 525-8577, Japan
gr0186kv@ed.ritsumei.ac.jp, {izumi-t,ktmr}@fc.ritsumei.ac.jp, nakatani@is.ritsumei.ac.jp
http://www.sc.ics.ritsumei.ac.jp

Abstract. The creation of tools that can be used by the people in case of disaster, had been our main topic since two years ago. We created a system that generated aid links between the communities of people interconnected inside a Social Network Service. The system provides them gives the opportunity to start the relief efforts in advance and in a well organized way. As part of this platform, it is necessary the creation of a user front application. We always kept in mind that this platform should be easy to use. This may be possible with the use of a non-lingual interface with the help of a set of pictograms that should be related to the disaster field. These pictograms were collected, evaluated and animated to enhance their concept. In this paper, we will discuss about all the process that was conducted to get the set of pictograms that will be used in our user interface.

Keywords: Non-lingual interface · User interfaces · Disaster mitigation system · Design evaluation · Pictogram · Animated pictograms

1 Introduction

As part of our research, we developed a platform that can be used in a disaster as a tool for communication and disaster management. The principal feature of this system is the use of an algorithm that generates links between people. This makes them able to help each other taking advantage of their skills for a positive outcome in an emergency. That platform can be used by not only the people who cares about protection, but also the people who needs help. This can be possible gathering the current position via Global Positioning Systems (GPS), special skills or disabilities of each individual that uses this system. Generated aid links includes people, government and other organizations. As part of the implementation, we are looking for the use of an application with a non-linguistic interface. This addition will improve the usability of the platform by the users.

© Springer International Publishing AG 2017
M. Kurosu (Ed.): HCI 2017, Part II, LNCS 10272, pp. 645–663, 2017.
DOI: 10.1007/978-3-319-58077-7_50

To have better integration of a system with their users it is necessary the use of a friendly and easy interface. For that reason, we will add to this system, a non-linguistic interface that can be used by a wider number of people, eliminating the language barrier. In that case instead of words, we suggest the use of pictograms. These will allow the users to set their alerts, use the system, or even have communication inside it. The main purpose is to eliminate some common interface problems. That includes, not knowing the language, having different education levels among others. In a system dedicated to provide assistance in case of disaster, there is a big importance in give access to all types of people.

1.1 Graphical Representations Through History

During several stages of human history, it is possible to observe different ways of communication. There are inscriptions with more than 40,000 years old, being the picture-based inscriptions the most used. Important examples include hiero-glyphs, cuneiform, Chinese characters among others. Most of these examples allowed to those civilization an important role at that time [1]. All these historical references are important because they allowed the communication of ideas between people. In the case of this research we are looking for something similar.

Considering the definition of pictogram as: A form of writing employing shapes that have meaning in order to convey the meaning. One of the principal characteristics of the pictograms is that there is not a gap between the recognition and action [1]. With the use of pictograms, the people have the ability to understand or follow instructions as fast as they recognize the pictogram meaning. It is also important to consider that the pictograms can be understood regardless of any language, education or even age differences.

One of the most recognizable examples of the beginning of the usage of graphic expressions is the one created under the guidance of Dr. Otto Neurath in 1930. His idea was to express the social economic problems after world war. His designs had to follow several basic principles to have an understandable design being used most frequently in the Social Museum of Vienna. This museum became the center of the "Vienna Method". Created to become a new medium of communication using graphic expressions [2]. After ten years, this method started to be called Isotype, which means International System of Typographic Picture Education. The principal idea behind these graphic expressions was to unify the languages with visual terms. For example for the word man, about five different designs were created to be able to represent different types of man from different societies [3]. Without a doubt his ideas of having an international graphical representation of concepts were a breakthrough at that time. Giving us a clear example of the possibilities of using a common set of graphical expressions.

Otto Neurath work can be simplified by his own phrase: *Worten trennen, Bilder verbinden* (Words separate, pictures unite) [4]. From these words we can catch two important ideas. The first one is related to the big amount of languages that still exist around the world. Every language uses a different word to express the same thing. In this case it is very difficult to learn all the different concepts from the different languages. However, if we try to use a graphical representation of the same word. It can be understood by more people at first sight. His excellent work allows to have better explanations, if we compare them with the use of simple words. However, into his ideas he believed that pictures and words should be complementary and should not be used one or the other [5].

Another important person in charge of the design of pictograms is Rudolf Modley. He was the founder of US Pictorial Statics, Inc. His major collection of pictograms can be found in his handbook on pictorial symbols that included 3,250 examples that can be used as a source for graphical references [4].

1.2 Usage of Pictograms in Practical Cases

Pictograms are widely used in the medical field as part of the explanation of information related to medicines taken by patients. The consumption of medicines requires a correct understanding of the instructions. Keeping the patient aware of any unfortunate situation. In Katri et al. performed a research to see the effectiveness of pictograms on medicine leaflet [6]. In this research it was possible to have an identification of 15 evaluated pictograms. In this case kids from elementary school were required to answer questions about the pictograms' meaning. As part of the results obtained, kids from 6th and 5th grade made a faster recognition meanwhile the kids from 1st grade required previous explanation to understand the correct meaning of the pictogram. This allows us to understand the importance of education that may be considered as a generator of experience with general knowledge of the evaluation subjects.

The use of pictogram to express simple phrases can be observed in In Shiojiri et al. research [7], in which they create animation of pictograms that can represent simple phrases such as "I want water." With the usage of the pictograms provided by the Japanese standard known as JIS T0103 it was possible to represent these phrases. With their idea, it is possible to understand them without the usage of an specific language. Shiojiri et al. research continued with the visual communication system created to convert weblog texts into pictograms. As part of the results of that research, they conclude that the understanding of the generated group of pictograms was 40 percent more accurate [8].

1.3 Pictograms on Disaster Management Applications

To understand the impact of using pictograms in a system for disaster management, it is necessary to refer to the elements that are used by our system. These elements include the recorded information, the use of a social network and the sharing of information. In the case of our platform, we devise our platform with the potential to contain all important groups in case of disaster assembled in a common system. Likewise, Our platform goes further providing an interconnection of communities, allowing the mutual help between people with the use of an algorithm that generates aid links that can create a helped-helped bond between the people of a community in a disaster. To make this possible, we require both of the victims and the helpers to input into their profiles, information related to their skills and also their weak points. In case of a disaster, the system can determine who can be helpful, and who will require help.

The constant exchange of information and the constant communication between the organizations and communities, allow the communities the ability to perform their activities. For that reason, the use of the social network services can be helpful as the facilitator. Social network structure makes possible the interconnection of the people, allowing the collection of that information [9]. The use of the information exchanged by the communities and other important participants can be found in software implementation such as TWRsms. This system is described by Landwehr P. as a system able to collect information from twitter as their major source from community users and other technical supporters. Helping in the support of disaster planning, warning and response [10]. The need of the support or skills provided by other people within the community or from other locations is helpful in case of a disaster [11]. However as D. Schmalzried et al. suggested in their review of website's communication during disasters, this exchange of information can be improve communication in those situations [12]. One idea is the usage of standardized template, similar visuals, colors and fonts that should be easy to read and understand. Nevertheless this don't solve the complete problem. Specially if we are trying to scope into any person that is facing a disaster. For example, those individuals involved that want or need help and don't speak the same language. Those without the same cultural or educational background. There are several situations that can make difficult the communication. For those cases it is necessary to provide them an system with a more understandable user interface.

1.4   Disaster Management Application Interface

In our initial platform, we considered the usage of multiple languages depending on the user. However, after doing out some tests we found that some users are not familiar with some terms. There were some users that felt overwhelmed with the big amount of text. Leading to a constant request of explanation about the usage of the system. Coming back to the idea of having a system that should be used by a big amount of people with different ages, cultural background, education background, or other characteristics. It is clear that an increase in the usability of the system is required. With the use of pictograms, the system can be more understandable in its explanations and other information that may be needed in case of disaster. For that reason it is necessary to find a set of pictograms that can be used in our user interface.

This system's front-end user application is being developed to be used as a smartphone application. In Fig. 1, it is possible to observe the main screen of this application. Here, the user can find important information about the disaster and they have the possibility to set an alert to request for help. Additionally in Fig. 1, it is possible to observe the initial idea of the new user interface. In this new version we are looking for simplicity in the design. With the usage of pictograms to represent the information displayed by the system. Fortunately with big advances on smartphone hardware, it is possible to add non animated and animated pictograms that will improve the user's understanding and operation of the application.

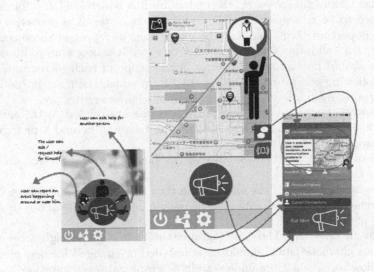

Fig. 1. New and previous user's main screen

2 Resources for User Interfaces: Pictograms

To be able to perform the pictograms' evaluation in this research. It was necessary to make a review of other evaluations performed previously by other researchers. After making this review it was possible for us to determine which are the most important points to be evaluate. Additionally to this, it was necessary to collect the necessary pictograms from different resources. Taking in consideration terms or graphical expressions necessary for a platform designed for the disaster management field.

2.1 Importance of the Design and Evaluation of Pictograms

Into the literature reviewed, most of the research that use graphical representations is related to the medical field. We based our pictogram design and evaluations following the points marked in those researches. Starting from the evaluation performed by Mok et al. with the validation and design of pictogram in a pediatric action plan [13]. Their methodology use five steps followed by our research as:

1. Pictogram Design: The main purpose of our research is the inclusion of pictograms in our user-end application. Into the main purposes of the application are: 1. The communication between the users and the communication of any important information during a disaster, and 2. Providing the user a possible

solution to his problem, connecting with someone that can give that help. These two actions should be performed without the use of any particular language, but giving enough information with the use of pictograms. Setting as the first task of this research, the task of finding which kind of information is required to be transmitted to the users. For this step it is necessary to find those important terms and find the pictograms to represent those concepts.

2. Pictogram Validation (evaluation): For this step it is necessary to know which points should be evaluated in terms of the scope of each pictogram. In this case following several researches as [13,14], in which the main purpose is the pictograms' evaluations. The most common characteristics are:

    (a) Transparency or Guessability: Both terms are related to the same idea which is to get the user to identify the meaning behind a pictogram by using simple words [15].

    (b) Translucency: Is the capability of the pictogram to represent accurately its meaning [16].

    (c) Recall: Retrieval of the information that is intended to be collected, comprehended and interpreted by the person who is looking at one or a group of pictograms [17].

3. Pictogram redesign: Those pictograms that can't get a high score on the previous characteristics, should be redesigned or changed for new ones. This will allow to have a more understandable graphical representation.

4. Population and setting: Refers to the group of people that in this case is intended to use our application.

5. Data analysis: After the performance of the evaluations it is necessary to check out the feedback and results obtained from each evaluation.

2.2   Pictogram Base

To set our first pictogram base, it was necessary to remember this interface will be used in disaster management. In that case we had to find at first, a complete set of pictograms that can represent a wide variety of disaster types. In that case, we refer to the classification provided by Keith Smith in his book Environmental Hazard [18]. There are 10 different disaster categories and in each category there are different disaster names. However, for the initial evaluation of a set of pictograms. We focused on the most recurrent disasters that occurred in the world in the last 10 years. This allow us to handle a small sample between 15 to 20 pictograms for the initial set. Allowing us to support our hypothesis in a small sample that can be easy to understand.

Information related to the most recurrent disasters that had happened in the last 10 years around the world, was obtained using EM-DAT (Emergency Events) database created by CRED (Center on the epidemiology of Disasters) available via online (http://www.emdat.be). Resulting in 14 pictograms related to disasters. Additionally to them, we decided to use 5 more pictograms which include human actions and human affectations in a disaster. This addition was made because it is important to have in our set human representation that require the human to be animated. The final set had a total sample of 19 pictograms expressed in Table 1.

Table 1. Pictogram set for evaluation

Disaster pictograms	Human pictograms
Fog	Calling for help
Avalanche	Food scarcity
House collapse	Lifting objects
Landslide	Bending and twisting
Hail	Lost child
Epidemic disease	
Heat wave	
Earthquake	
Drought	
Cold wave	
Winter storm	
Tsunami	
Tropical storm	
Storm	

2.3   Pictogram Resources

Once we have the complete list of concepts to be represented by pictograms. We propose the utilization of pictograms that are already in use for each concept. following our first hypothesis as:

Hypothesis 1 (H1): Already designed and normally used pictograms will be recognized by this study subjects. The score will satisfy the minimum score required to consider it as suitable. Due to these pictograms are already in use, we suppose that their designers already made the corresponding test to use them.

As we can observe in Fig. 2, there are five main sources of pictograms which includes important pictorial catalogs such as, the symbol sourcebook by Henry Dreyfuss [19]. Another is the handbook of pictorial symbols by Rudolf Modley [20]. To those cases in which the pictograms were not found on those sources we used the database created by the Research Center for Disaster Reduction Systems of Kyoto University that is available via online (http://picto.dpri.kyoto-u.ac.jp) and as the last resource we used google.com. The obtained pictograms where vectorized to have a clean look of them maintaining their original representation.

2.4   Animation of Pictograms

For the first evaluation of this sample of pictograms, it is necessary to set our second hypothesis as:

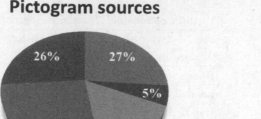

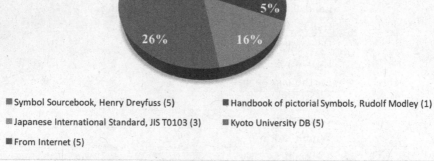

Fig. 2. Pictograms' sources

Hypothesis 2 (H2): Animated pictograms allow the user to have more understanding of the concept and meaning of intended to be transmited by the pictogram.

For the animation of the pictograms, a set of six defined animation patterns was created. Each pattern refers to the movements of the elements that are part of each pictogram. On Table 2 it is possible to observe the description and examples of each pattern.

The intention to limit to six these patterns, relies firstly on the interest in eliminate unnecessary movements inside the pictogram. With simple animations, it is possible to have a basic cause-consequence animations that will not distract the users in other than the main idea to be transmitted by the pictogram. Secondly, we have the intention to see if there is any relation between a well designed pictogram and the animation pattern. Into the examples observed, we can find the pictogram of Tsunami with an horizontal pattern. In this case, it is necessary to aware to the person that is observing the pictogram, the basic concept of a tsunami. Which is related to the approaching of big and strong waves into the land. In the case of this pictogram, we have three main elements that are the big wave, ground and the person that should escape to a higher land. This pictogram is being already used to aware of this possible situation. To add the animation it is necessary to set into the big wave the horizontal movement to make clear that the wave is approaching. Another case is in the pictogram used to represent drought. In this case, there are two elements, the sun and the ground. When the sun appears, the ground starts to present the effect of the lack of water, represented with the scratches that normally appears when this situation happens.

Table 2. Pictogram animation patterns

Pattern	Description
	Horizontal movement pattern of one or various elements from left to right.
	Transversal movement pattern of some elements from the upper part to the lower part followed by a left to right or the other way round.
	Rotation pattern movement of the element in a circle round an axis or centre.
	Undulatory pattern movement of some elements in the pictogram. Coming from the upper part to the lower part.
	Appearance pattern of elements change the visibility of the elements.
Complex patterns	In some cases the use of two of the previous mentioned movement patterns

In this case the animation pattern applied is appearance. It is applied to the two elements. First, the sun appears affecting the other element (which is the ground). This second element will change by the effect caused by the sun More examples can be found in Table 3.

3 Evaluation of Pictograms

3.1 Characteristics of the First Evaluation of Pictograms

For the first evaluation, we asked the help of 19 subjects to perform the test. 9 of them from different nationalities and 10 of them Japanese. We were looking for a comparison of the results of those that can be considered native speakers, and those that made the evaluation using English as their main language. Which is not their native language. A web application was used to perform the evaluation. After asking each user information such as language, age, nationality and educational background, the system started showing the pictograms. As observed in Fig. 3 the system shows the pictogram and ask directly to the user if the pictogram represent the concept. The user moves the slide in base of the degree of agreement Internally the slide will add points in base of each subject decision.

Subjects were separated in two groups. Each group will evaluate animated, and non animated pictograms. The difference is that while one group will evaluate one animated version of the pictogram, the other group will evaluate the non animated version of the same pictogram. This will allow us to compare results with and without the animation of each design. Time and user's score were saved for reference.

At the end of the evaluation, subjects were asked if they already knew or had seen the pictogram before this test.

Table 3. Examples of animation patterns

Pattern	Elements	Sequence
Horizontal movement pattern		
Transversal movement pattern		
Rotation pattern movement		
Undulatory pattern movement		
Appearance pattern		
Complex patterns		

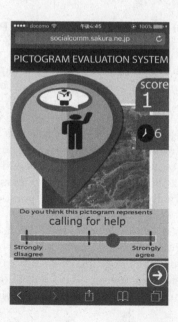

Fig. 3. Evaluation system main window

3.2   Results and Discussion

As mentioned previously, we had 19 participants in this first evaluation. The age of participants was between 20 to 39 years old. Our sample had a 55% of participants with age between 20 to 24 years old. Being this the biggest group, followed by 20% of participants with age between 30 to 34, 15% between 35 to 39 and 10% with 25 to 29 years old. Final results of the first evaluation can be observed on Table 4.

Into the final observations of the first evaluation, we can find that from the 19 pictograms that were evaluated, only 7 passed with high scores in both versions

Table 4. Results of first evaluation

Pictogram	Name	Pattern	Familiar	NA Score Eng	A Score Eng	NA Score Jap	A Score Jap	$P(T <= t)$ Eng	$P(T <= t)$ Jap	Comparisson	NA pass	A pass	NA Final Score	A Final Score
	Calling for help	Rotation	3	49.40	43.00	64.75	64.60	0.403105715	0.496527588	No dif.	No	No	56.22	53.80
	Fog	Horizontal	1	46.40	39.20	33.25	57.80	0.389446379	0.065837294	No dif.	No	No	40.45	48.5
	Food scarcity	Rotation and appearance	2	86.20	75.20	73.00	51.20	0.2073932	0.1970477	No dif.	Yes	No	80.33	63.20
	Lifting	Transversal	3	62.80	88.20	84.75	81.40	0.1178443	0.3881818	No dif	Yes	Yes	72.55	84.80
	Avalanche	Transversal	6	77.40	89.20	50.00	87.00	0.2628206	0.0122783	A higher	Yes	Yes	65.22	88.10
	House collapse	Appearance	1	90.80	90.00	57.00	70.60	0.475765	0.2525451	No dif.	Yes	Yes	75.78	80.30
	Landslide	Transversal	7	47.60	82.20	25.25	62.60	0.0519119	0.045286	A higher	Yes	Yes	37.67	72.40
	Hail	Transversal	1	70.60	74.60	72.25	42.20	0.4199571	0.0510193	NA slightly higher	Yes	No	71.33	46.00
	Epidemy	Rotation and appearance	2	74.60	28.20	37.75	24.40	0.0167525	0.1400281	NA higher	No	No	58.22	26.30
	Heat Wave	Horizontal	2	33.40	79.00	15.20	29.25	0.0206733	0.030963	A higher	No	No	24.30	56.89
	Bending and twisting	Rotation	1	24.20	24.20	43.40	51.75	0.5	0.3210017	No dif.	No	No	33.80	36.44
	Earthquake	Vibration and appearance	2	39.20	56.80	62.80	76.50	0.2478783	0.1785866	No dif.	No	Yes -	51.00	65.56
	Drought	Appearance	2	75.00	65.80	90.80	66.00	0.2897659	0.0808353	No dif.	Yes	Yes -	82.90	65.89
	Cold wave	Horizontal	2	54.60	51.60	82.00	42.50	0.4330555	0.0114658	NA slightly higher	Yes -	No	68.30	47.56
	Winter storm	Ondulatory	6	57.00	39.20	59.40	38.75	0.172937	0.1734407	No dif.	No	No	58.20	39.00
	Tsunami	Horizontal	5	94.00	98.80	75.40	66.80	0.195452	0.3227099	No dif.	Yes	Yes	84.70	69.66
	Tropical storm	Horizontal	3	93.60	58.60	54.00	84.50	0.0819696	0.0087033	No. dif.	Yes	Yes	73.80	70.11
	Storm	Transversal	8	42.40	38.00	34.20	66.00	0.429733	0.040072	No dif.	No	No	38.30	50.45
	Lost child	Rotation and appearance	4	95.40	54.40	97.40	85.75	0.0517043	0.0822639	NA slightly higher	Yes	Yes -	96.40	68.33

NA: Non animated A: Animated
Familiarity: Number of people that already knew the pictogram

animated and non animated. This is less than the half of the total sample. This means that our first hypothesis can be dismissed, because more than the 50% of the selected pictograms didn't comply with the minimum score requirements.

There were just two cases in which a significant difference between the results of the animated and non animated version can be found. Being the pictograms for avalanche with a result in the t-Test of 0.0347 in and landslide with a higher result of 0.00934 in the same test. These pictograms were the only examples in which the animated received a significant higher score. If we focus in our second hypothesis H2, we observe that 10 pictograms of 19 received higher score. This means just a little bit over the 50%. From those 10 animated pictograms, only 2 of them passed with high score. Which means that it still ambiguous the consideration of having an improvement in the understanding when we have an animated pictogram.

In the case of the comparison between the responses of the Japanese speakers and the English speakers, we can find that just in a few cases there are differences between the scores obtained. For example, in the case of the pictogram for tropical storm, for Japanese subjects the animated version represents better the meaning with a score of 84.50 and in the case of the English speaker subjects the non animated version received a high score of 93.60. Differences between both groups can be found in 14 pictograms of the sample. Which represent a big discrepancy between the preferences and understanding of pictogram's meaning. Resulting in just two pictograms with high scores for both groups which are Drought and Tsunami pictograms. In both cases the non animated pictogram received higher results.

As part of our initial conclusion of the first evaluation we can mention that:

1. If the pictogram is well designed, The need of an animation is low. However, animation may give some extra points for the pictogram's Translucency.
2. There are cases in which the lack of additional information or elements. Don't allow the user to understand the meaning. In some cases the subjects couldn't find any familiar figure in the pictogram. This means that each element should be well designed and it may be better to add more characteristics like color, size and an specific role in the situation that is intended to be represented in the pictogram.
3. In the case of the difference between the scores given by the native speaker (Japanese) and the English speakers. Depending on the case, there are differences in how they understand the concept of the pictogram. The only point to take into consideration for the design and the color used. Is that each element inside the pictogram should show basic forms that can be easy to recognize internationally.

After looking the results of this first evaluation, a redesign of the pictograms is necessary. After that a second evaluation should be conducted. Design should follow more specific patterns and guidelines, that can be considered after having the results from this evaluation. Even if the pictogram received high score, it was decided that it should be redesigned to have another sample with the same conditions. However, changes should be done based on the score. This means that if the score was high enough, the change should be minor.

4   Second Evaluation of Pictograms

4.1   Pictograms' Redesign

For the first evaluation, the selected pictograms kept the original design. However, based on the results obtained from the first evaluation, in most of the cases it was necessary to improve the design. Specially for those pictograms that didn't get enough score in any of their versions (animated and non animated).

The principal guidelines of design for the pictograms and the way they should be animated are:

1. Animation should change based on a cause-consequence movement in the pictogram: Applied into a main element showing a state change. The addition of some other movements of minor importance also can be applied. The order in which elements appear and change is important to show the concept behind the pictogram.
2. Alert and accentuation: To generate a focus in an specific part or element inside the pictogram.
3. Addition of color: The addition of color into the pictograms will make them to easily recognize each element into the pictogram. In the previous version pictograms were black and white maintaining their simplicity.

On Table 5 it is possible to observe the modifications made to get the new set of pictograms. For the redesign of the pictograms, previous design was used as the base for those cases in which the score was enough. In other cases, we added some new elements. Some elements were obtained from the search of keywords related to the concept of the pictogram in the internet. After looking some real images, elements that can complement the pictogram's conceptual idea were added into the design. If we take as an example the pictogram used to represent heat wave. In the first evaluation, this pictogram received bad scores. If we observe the main elements of the original pictogram, there are two main elements which are the wave and the heat particles. These elements move horizontally to represent the heat wave effect. However, this pictogram doesn't create any impact in other element. This mean that the wave only moves without affecting anything. In that case, the viewer don't see any change or effect caused by this wave. This pictogram doesn't gave the complete concept to be transmitted. For this case, we made a complete redesign with the same elements and then new element were added. This new element should experience an effect or change of it's initial state. When the heat wave starts to appear, the element (thermometer) will mark an increase in the temperature. This change fulfill the cause-consequence effect for the animation. On the other hand, we have the pictogram for landslide. In this case the pictogram had high scores in the first evaluation. For this case major changes are not required. However, to give the same changes to all the

Table 5. Comparission between new and old design

Previous	New	Description
		Calling for help: An emergency icon was added. In the previous design it was difficult to understand why the character was moving his hand.
		Earthquake: The original design received high score. However the lack of color made difficult the identification of each element. Another addition is the representation of vibration and the appearance of an fault in the ground as a consequence.
		Food Scarcity: The addition of new elements include the effect of hunger focusing on the human stomach that is empty.
		Winter Storm: There was lack of elements in the previous design. In this case we added the consequences of the winter storm. as the streets and houses start collecting snow.
		Avalanche: The previous pictogram's shapes were very simple. Also the addition of an alert to set the user focus on that side of the pictogram.
		House collapse: This pictogram had a high score in the previous evaluation. Only vibration effect icon and the alert icon was added.
		Landslide: The addition of color and the addition of an alert that appears in the point that should get the viewer's attention.
		Hail: The previous pictogram only included the cloud with the hail drops. There was lack of elements. For that case we added the house and a kick effect that appears.
		Storm: The previous representation had lack of information. In the redesign The thunder was added as in other representations of a storm.
		Liffting: The addition of color for the object that is being carried and the addition of an small accent that makes reference to the effort of doing that activity.
		Heat wave: Last design had very poor performance. Each element was changed. In this case the constant heat coming from the sun generate the consequence of the increase of the temperature.
		Bending and twisting: This pictogram needed a better animation. For that case the main element which is the Human should move according to the statement that we are representing. Appearance of the arrows and a green check alluding to the fulfillment of the action was also added.
		Cold wave: The elements run into the human and cause an effect in him. Alluding to the effects of a cold wave.
		Tsunami: In this case we added color and an alert icon to the person. Getting the viewer's attention in this part of the pictogram.
		Tropical storm: different colors were added to each element.
		Fog: In this case the majority of references of fog appeared using the car image. Representation of fog was also changed.
		Epidemic disease: This pictogram only showed one representation of a 'contagious'. On the new redesign , the addition of more groups as we found in the reference images was necessary. Also, the germ representation was added.
		Drought: Colors were added to this pictogram. Also the addition of one more element which is the trees drying up due to the bad conditions.
		Lost Child: In the case of this pictogram the addition of color was used to add more impact into the need of the child.

pictograms of this new sample, we added color and an alert mark. The intention for this is to give a clear message about the importance of being aware of an event like this. With this two examples and the other can be observed in the Table 5.

4.2   Characteristics

For the second evaluation, we had the help of 28 subjects to perform the test. In this test we wanted to have a similar sample as in the previous evaluation. In this case, 14 subjects from different nationalities and 14 subjects Japanese. Same web application was used to perform the evaluation. Subjects were separated into two groups. Each group will evaluate animated and non animated pictograms. The difference is that while one group will evaluate one animated version of the pictogram, the other group will evaluate the non animated version of the same pictogram. This will allow us to compare results with and without the animation of each pictogram. Time and user's score were saved for reference. In the case of this second evaluation, we didn't ask about the previous knowledge of the pictograms due to the redesign process made to the pictograms.

4.3   Results and Discussion

Results of the second evaluation were higher compared to those obtained in the first evaluation as we can observe on Table 6. As in the first evaluation, the total pictogram sample was of 19. 15 of these pictograms passed the test compared to 7 pictograms that passed during the first evaluation. From those 15, 8 of them received high scores and passed in both versions (Animated and non animated), in 4 cases only animated passed and in 3 cases only non animated version passed.

The four pictograms that didn't passed the test were calling for help, food scarcity, lifting and twisting & bending. The results obtained from Japanese and international subjects (subjects from different countries) are separated. We can find that the pictogram for food scarcity and twisting & bending in animated version score given by international subjects is just above the minimum score. There are other cases in which the pictogram passed the minimum requirement. In general due to the high score by international subjects, for example winter storm and storm pictogram received higher scores.

Following the T-test comparison between Animated and non animated pictograms:

1. 6 animated pictograms had remarkable result in t-Test. Calling for help (0.0159), house collapse (0.0013), landslide (0.00162), bending and twisting (0.01316), earthquake (0.00013) and tsunami (0.01097).
2. There is not a case in which the non animated received higher score in t-Test.
3. Other cases don't show any considerable difference between animated and non animated.

Findings after a comparison between the first and second evaluation resulted as shown in Table 7:

Table 6. Results of second evaluation

Pictogram	Name	Pattern	NA Score Eng	A Score Eng	NA Score Jap	A Score Jap	P(T <= t) Eng	P(T <= t) Jap	Comparisson	NA pass	A pass	NA Final Score	A Final Score
	Calling for help	Rotation and appearance	43.86	76.57	37.86	46.43	0.00747029	0.26032414	A higher	No	No	40.86	62.50
	Fog	Horizontal	68.71	86.71	75.85	64.71	0.09739635	0.21489132	No dif.	Yes	Yes	72.29	75.71
	Food scarcity	Appearance and vibration	46.14	65.14	47.14	36.86	0.11395431	0.16853199	No dif.	No	No	46.64	51.00
	Lifting	Transversal and appearance	49.29	52.43	17.71	54.71	0.41625347	0.00647024	A slightly higher	No	No	33.50	53.57
	Avalanche	Transversal and appearance	72.00	90.43	79.29	77.14	0.09693884	0.42835914	No dif.	Yes	Yes	75.64	83.79
	House collapse	Transversal and Appearance	55.57	91.29	71.00	85.43	0.00376911	0.1053367	A is higher	No	Yes	63.29	88.36
	Landslide	Transversal and appearance	59.00	89.29	52.29	83.43	0.01485709	0.03388672	A higher	No	Yes	55.64	86.36
	Hail	Transversal and appearance	76.14	76.00	71.57	51.86	0.49521393	0.10435888	No dif.	Yes	No	73.86	63.93
	Epidemy	Horizontal and appearance	57.29	61.14	76.29	51.00	0.4009192	0.04622331	NA higher	Yes	No	66.79	56.07
	Heat Wave	Transversal and appearance	71.14	85.57	73.00	91.43	0.15649577	0.07874677	A slightly higher	Yes	Yes	72.07	88.50
	Bending and twisting	Transversal	41.14	75.29	19.57	33.43	0.01882014	0.03694442	A higher	No	No	30.36	54.36
	Earthquake	Vibration and appearance	52.57	95.29	50.29	85.57	0.00229352	0.01759082	A higher	No	Yes	51.43	90.43
	Drought	Appearance	91.00	88.50	87.86	66.86	0.36869676	0.10487696	No dif.	Yes	Yes	89.43	77.68
	Cold wave	Transversal and vibration	79.14	83.00	64.00	76.29	0.31379128	0.18851738	No dif.	Yes	Yes	71.57	79.64
	Winter storm	Transversal and appearance	76.71	78.43	33.43	57.86	0.44136454	0.11663354	No dif.	No	Yes	55.07	68.14
	Tsunami	Horizontal	71.86	92.43	82.29	100	0.08173068	0.02541998	A higher	Yes	Yes	77.07	96.21
	Tropical storm	Horizontal	79.43	86.43	59.14	65.14	0.18813058	0.33609325	No. dif.	Yes	Yes	69.29	75.79
	Storm	Transversal and appearance	64.00	81.86	53.57	59.43	0.14037794	0.33687256	No dif.	No	Yes	58.79	70.64
	Lost child	Rotation and appearance	80.57	61.00	93.71	81.14	0.12077777	0.11958414	NA slightly higher	Yes	Yes	87.14	71.07

NA: Non animated   A: Animated

1. 12 pictograms had higher performance in this second evaluation compared to the first one. On the other hand, 2 cases presented higher results in the first evaluation. (Earthquake, winter storm, avalanche, landslides, hail, storm, heat wave, cold wave, tsunami, tropical storm, fog and drought).
2. In two cases the general score of the pictograms were higher in the fist evaluation. (Food scarcity and lifting).
3. In 1 case, the score of the previous evaluation were higher. (Lost Child).

According to the results obtained in both evaluations, we can say that our second hypothesis H2 can be accepted for most of the cases presented in the sample. Most of the problems are found in those pictograms that use any kind of human representation such as calling for help, bending and twisting. Which in both cases didn't passed any of the evaluations. Other pictograms with the human representation, received low scores and may require a more care in the animation and/or a better representation. Another important issue can be the need for additional context, that may lead the subjects to understand more the concept behind the pictogram.

Table 7. Comparison of both evaluations' results

Name	1st eval NA	1st eval A	2nd eval NA	2nd eval A	Best option
Calling for help	57.08	53.80	40.85	61.50	None
Earthquake	51.00	66.65	51.43	90.43	Second
Food scarcity	79.60	63.20	46.64	51.00	First
Winter storm	58.20	38.97	55.07	68.14	Second
Avalanche	63.70	88.10	75.64	83.78	Second
House collapse	73.90	80.30	63.28	88.36	Second, A higher
Landslide	36.42	72.40	55.64	86.36	Second
Hail	71.42	58.40	73.86	63.92	Second
Storm	38.30	52.00	58.78	70.64	Second
Lifting	73.77	84.80	33.50	53.57	First
Heat wave	24.30	54.12	72.07	88.50	Second
Bending and twisting	33.80	37.97	30.36	54.36	None
Cold wave	68.30	47.05	71.57	79.64	Second
Tsunami	84.70	82.80	77.07	96.21	Second
Tropical storm	73.80	71.55	69.29	75.79	Second
Fog	39.82	48.50	72.29	75.71	Second
Epidemic disease	56.17	26.30	66.78	56.07	Second, NA higher
Drought	82.90	65.90	89.43	77.68	Second
Lost child	96.40	70.08	87.14	71.07	Avg first higher

NA: Non animated A: Animated

5   Conclusion

In this paper we reviewed the results obtained from two evaluations that were conducted to pictograms that are intended to be used in a system created to be used in case of disaster. The main goal of our system is to present the information using pictograms instead of using language. Into the main reasons of this is to eliminate the language barrier that may be faced by people with different cultural and language background. For that reason we conducted the evaluation of two sets of 19 pictograms related to the disaster concepts.

After realizing the first evaluation we found out that the usage of previously designed pictograms don't warranty the success in the understanding of the pictograms' concept. Which was one of our hypothesis. After the poor performance of the first set of pictograms we decided to create a design guidelines focusing on three major points which are the cause-consequence change, alerts and accentuations and the addition of properties such as color. After the redesign, a second evaluation was conducted.

After the second evaluation we confirmed our second hypothesis related to the addition of animation to pictograms. Into the results obtained the majority of animated pictograms received higher scores compared to the non animated version of the same pictogram. In addition, most of the pictograms passed the test. Having only Two pictograms that didn't passed any of the tests. After observing the results, we found that this may be caused by the lack of elements and previous context. This can make difficult to understand those pictograms that in fact, have human representations as part of the elements. Also, better and more complex animation is required in these specific cases.

As part of the future work of this research starts with the usage of these pictograms in our system's user interface. After this addition, another test should be conducted. In which the usage of these graphical representations can be used directly in the application. It is necessary to measure the effectiveness of these pictograms in the application directly.

References

1. Ota, Y.: The societal role and design of pictograms as "Kansei Language" (perceptual language). In: Proceedings of 2011 International Conference on Biometrics and Kansei Engineering (ICBAKE), pp. 1–13 (2011)
2. Modley, R.: Pictographs today and tomorrow. Pub. Opin. Q. J. **2**(4), 659–664 (1938)
3. Neurath, M.: Isotype. J. Instr. Sci. **3**(2), 127–150 (1974)
4. Jansen, W.: Neurath, Arntz and ISOTYPE: the legacy in art, design and statistics. J. Des. Hist. **22**(3), 227–242 (2009)
5. Holmes, N.: Pictograms: a view from the drawing board or, what i have learned from Otto Neurath and Gerd Arntz (and Jazz). Inf. Des. J **10**(2), 133–143 (2001)
6. Hmeen-Anttila, K., Kemppainen, K., Enlund, H., Bush, J., Marja, A.: Do pictograms improve children's understanding of medicine leaflet information? Patient Educ. Couns. J. **55**(3), 371–378 (2004)
7. Shiojiri, M., Nakatani, Y., Yoshida, Y., Ino, Y., Yonezawa, T.: Automatic Generation of Animation with Multiple Pictograms Based on Physical Property of Verb, Human interface Systems Ronbun, p. 1528D (2014)
8. Shiojiri, M., Nakatani, Y., Yoshida, Y., Yonezawa, T.: Visual language communication system with multiple pictograms converted from weblog texts. In: IASDR 2013, pp. 1–12 (2013)

9. Boyd, D., Ellison, N.: Social network sites: definition, history, and scholarship. J. Comput.-Mediat. Commun. **13**(1), 210–230 (2007)
10. Sanghee, O., Soojung, K.: College students' use of social media for health in the USA and Korea. Inf. Res.: Int. Electron. J. **19**(4), 4 (2014)
11. Helsloot, I., Ruitenberg, A.: Citizen response to disasters: a survey of literature and some practical implications. J. Conting. Crisis Manag. **12**(3), 98 (2004)
12. Schmalzried, H., Fallon, L., Harper, E.: Assessing informational website communications during emergencies and disasters. Int. J. Nonprofit Volunt. Sect. Mark. **17**(3), 119–207 (2012)
13. Mok, G., Vaillancourt, R., Irwin, D., Wong, A., Zemek, R., Alqurashi, W.: Design and validation of pictograms in a pediatric anaphylaxis action plan. J. Pediatr. Allergy Immunol. **26**(3), 223–233 (2015)
14. Yovetich, W., Young, T.: The effects of representativeness and concreteness on the guessability of blissymbols. J. Augment. Altern. Commun. **4**(1), 35–39 (1988)
15. Roberts, N., Mohamed, Z., Wong, P., Johnson, M., Loh, L., Partridge, M.: The development and comprehensibility of a pictorial asthma action plan. J. Patient Educ. Couns. **74**(1), 12–18 (2009)
16. Bloomberg, K., Karlan, G., Lloyd, L.: The comparative translucency of initial lexical items represented in five graphic symbol systems and sets. J. Speech Lang. Hear. Res. **33**(4), 717–725 (1990)
17. King, S., McCaffrey, D., Bentley, J., Bouldin, A., Hallam, J., Wilkin, N.: The influence of symbols on the short-term recall of pharmacy-generated prescription medication information in a low health literate sample. J. Health Commun. **17**(3), 280–293 (2012)
18. Smith, K.: Environmental Hazard, pp. 5–30, Routledge, Abingdon (2013)
19. Dreyfuss, H.: Symbol Sourcebook: An Authoritative Guide to International Graphic Symbols. Wiley, Hoboken (1984)
20. Modley, R., Myers, W.: Handbook of Pictorial Symbols: 3,250 Examples from International Sources. Courier Corporation, North Chelmsford (1976)

The Gender Difference of Impression Evaluation of Visual Images Among Young People

Ayako Hashizume[1(✉)] and Masaaki Kurosu[2]

[1] Faculty of System Design, Tokyo Metropolitan University, Hachioji, Japan
hashiaya@tmu.ac.jp
[2] Faculty of Informatics, The Open University of Japan, Chiba, Japan
masaakikurosu@spa.nifty.com

Abstract. Kawaii is a Japanese word meaning cute or pretty. Authors classified this concept into three categories, i.e. the psycho-physical Kawaii, cultural Kawaii and generic Kawaii. Kawaii, especially the cultural Kawaii, could be regarded typical to the female in Japan. But the psycho-physical Kawaii and generic Kawaii may be shared by both of male and female. Authors conducted a questionnaire survey by showing 225 photographs to 89 university students including 54 male and 34 female students. Based on the statistical analysis of data, it was found that female students tend to evaluate the stimuli to be more Kawaii, beautiful and preferred than male students regarding the psycho-physical Kawaii and generic Kawaii. Further study is expected by conducting the comparative study among various cultural regions.

Keywords: Kawaii · Psycho-physical Kawaii · Cultural Kawaii · Generic Kawaii

1 Introduction

In western countries, it is said that the beauty is generally more important and valuable than cuteness or prettiness for girls and women, in general. Yomoda [1] wrote an episode in which he was warned not to use the word "cute" for a woman (except a small child). The female editor of a magazine told him that the use of "cute" for a woman may be regarded as a discrimination from the viewpoint of political correctness. In other words, cuteness is valuable only for children. But in Japan, girls and young women put more emphasis on "Kawaii" (cute or pretty) than beauty. The age that Japanese women start using the word beauty is after they have graduated the age of using Kawaii, roughly speaking after their 20s.

At least in Japan, Kawaii can be thought to be the young female culture. Historically, those who have been writing books or articles on Kawaii culture were mostly female and the consumers of Kawaii products and merchandises were almost all young females [2].

© Springer International Publishing AG 2017
M. Kurosu (Ed.): HCI 2017, Part II, LNCS 10272, pp. 664–677, 2017.
DOI: 10.1007/978-3-319-58077-7_51

Today, Marcus et al. [3] classified "Kawaii" in three ways as the psycho-physical Kawaii, cultural Kawaii and generic Kawaii. Psycho-physical Kawaii is gender free and is caused by such physical features as the small size, round shape and warm color. The concept of baby schema of Lorenz [4] is strongly related to the psycho-physical Kawaii. Cultural Kawaii is the Kawaii-ness found in the fashion of women in Japan. Such women loves themselves wearing Kawaii fashion and some men regards those women to be Kawaii. The use of generic Kawaii is more frequently found among girls and young women and among some boys and young men. In this case, the word Kawaii is generic and is frequently used in many situations by many people especially among young females for describing beauty, attractiveness, and appeal as well as cuteness and prettiness in many situations. Its connotation is vast and seems to be quite situation dependent.

Authors were interested in the gender difference of Kawaii concept, especially the generic Kawaii and psycho-physical Kawaii. Although men use the word Kawaii that belong to these categories, it is not clear if men are using the word with the same meaning with women.

2 Questionnaire Survey on "Kawaii" for University Students

In order to clarify if this tendency still exists in Japan today, we conducted a questionnaire among young people. The research was held as follows.

Informants were 89 university students (the average age was 20.07 years with a standard deviation (SD) of 1.06), including 54 male and 34 female students, all living in the metropolitan areas of Japan within a 30 km diameter. The research was conducted from October to December 2016. Informants were presented with 225 images that included photographs of paintings, female actors, cartoon characters, and other Kawaii related objects or people one by one and were asked the following questions (Q1-3). The 225 images that has been used for the questions was compiled in the Tables 1, 2, 3, 4 and 5 for protecting their copyrights or the like.

Q1: Have you ever heard of the object in the photo-graph before? (Yes/No)
Q2: On a scale of one to five how do you evaluate the photographic image?
     (1 for "Strongly disagree," 2 for "Disagree," 3 for "Neither agree nor disagree,"
     4 for "Agree," and 5 for "Strongly agree.") The ratings were asked in regards to
     the following aspects.
     2-1: Kawaii
     2-2: Beautiful
     2-3: Preference
Q3: How would you describe the image with words that you think will strongly match its content?

Table 1. The list of images (no. 1–45).

No.	Image
1	An ordinary Japanese girl
2	An ordinary Japanese woman
3	A female Japanese comedian (Kazuko Kurosawa)
4	A character (MiffY)
5	An ordinary Japanese girl
6	Fancy goods (multi-colored artificial nail chips)
7	An illustration (elephant painted on a picture scroll)
8	An animation character (Nagasawa-kun)
9	A dog (Maltese)
10	Ordinary Japanese girls (wearing Gothic Lolita fashion)
11	An illustration (strange animal with girla hum an face)
12	An American actress (Scarlett Johansson)
13	Yamanba girls
14	A 'Noh' mask
15	An animation character (Astro Boy)
16	A female Japanese comedian (Yui-P)
17	An illustration (adult duck)
18	An ordinary Japanese baby
19	An illustration (middle-aged man)
20	A French doll
21	Ordinary Japanese girls (wearing maid uniforms)
22	Sweets (Japanese-style confectionery)
23	A panda
24	A doll (child dressed in a Chinese style)
25	An illustration (puppy)
26	A Japanese doll (Ichimatsu ningyo)
27	Fancy goods (hair accessories)
28	Bubble wrap (Puti Puti)
29	A green caterpillar
30	The Bai-du logo
31	A female Japanese model
32	A work of art (sculpture)
33	A hedgehog
34	A character (Thomas and Friends)
35	A young female Japanese model
36	An illustration (anthropom orphized vegetable)
37	An ordinary Japanese girl (wearing maid uniform)
38	A cat (British Shorthair)
39	A comedic storyteller (Kikuoh Hayashiya, rakugo Performer)
40	A dog (Pug)
41	An illustration (goldfish painted on a picture scroll)
42	A character (Peter Rabbit)
43	An illustration (hanging rabbits)
44	A dog (Pekingese)
45	A baby girl model

Table 2. The list of images (no. 46–90).

No.	Image
46	A frog
47	A figure (spherical object)
48	An illustration (girl with wreath)
49	A British actress (Audrey Hepburn)
50	Sweets (jelly)
51	An illustration (pastel-colored sky)
52	An animation character (Pikachu)
53	A car (Subaru 360)
54	A Japanese columnist (Matsuko Deluxe)
55	A work of art (flowers with girla human face)
56	An illustration (girl wearing sailor uniform)
57	A baby boy model
58	A skull
59	An illustration (Sumo wrestler painted on a picture Scroll)
60	A girl's arm with corset piercing
61	An illustration (kids and rabbits)
62	A female Japanese model
63	An illustration (aliens)
64	A Canadian singer (Avril Lavigne)
65	A character (Hello Kitty)
66	A flower (red rose)
67	A cat (American Shorthair)
68	A koala
69	Many spiders
70	Scorpion
71	A flower (peony)
72	An abandoned baby doll
73	A model (wearing Gothic Lolita fashion)
74	A work of art (flower with girla human face)
75	A hairy caterpillar
76	A rabbit
77	A Japanese girl (striking a sexy pose)
78	An illustration (anthropomorphized wolf)
79	A little bird (Varied tit)
80	An ear pierced in 10 places
81	A young female Cosplayer
82	A Japanese doll (Ichimatsu ningyo with horror lighting)
83	A female Japanese comedian (Okarina)
84	An illustration (a girl drawn in pastel colors)
85	A figure (rectangular object)
86	A flying squirrel
87	A character (Godzilla)
88	A popart pattern
89	An illustration (Adam and Eve)
90	A character (Funassyi)

Table 3. The list of images (no. 91–135).

No.	Image
91	Ganguro girls
92	A character (Shrek)
93	A female Japanese comedian (Naomi Watanabe)
94	A Samurai figure
95	Matryoshka dolls
96	A car (Daihatsu Mira Gino)
97	A round-shaped buttocks
98	A character (Bai-du bear)
99	A picture (Diego Velazquez Infanta Margarita Teresa in a White DRESS)
100	A pop art pattern design (Keith Haring)
101	A split tongue
102	An ordinary Japanese girl (wearing her high school uniform)
103	An illustration (dogs painted on a picture scroll)
104	An ordinary Japanese girl (with Minnie Mouse bag)
105	A character (the original picture book of Winnie-the-Pooh)
106	Ordinary Japanese girls (wearing White Lolita fashions)
107	A small Chinese figure
108	An American actress (Marilyn Monroe)
109	Yamanba girl
110	A middle-aged man
111	Japanese wooden dolls (Kokeshi ningyo)
112	A lizard
113	An illustration (little girl and teddy bear giving off a creepy vibe)
114	Yamanba girls
115	A ghost (Oiwa-san of Yotsuya Kaidan)
116	Flowers (China pink)
117	A character (Kumamon)
118	The Bai-du logo
119	A Japanese doll (Ichimatsu ningyo)
120	Flowers (Cattleya)
121	A figure (diamond)
122	A snail
123	A Japanese actress (Mikako Tabe)
124	A baby boy with a rabbit
125	An illustration (girl strikng a sexy pose)
126	A female Japanese comedian (Kanako Yanagihara)
127	An illustration from the original Alice's Adventures in Wonderland
128	A female model with fair skin and hair
129	A large glacier
130	An illustration (scene of a banquet party painted on a picture scroll)
131	A character (Bai-du bear)
132	A middle-aged fat man
133	A picture (Leonardo da Vinci, Mona Lisa)
134	A young girl
135	A flower (cosmos)

Table 4. The list of images (no. 136–180).

No.	Image
136	A Japanese girl group (Perfume)
137	An old Japanese woman
138	A female model with fair skin and hair
139	Jellyfish
140	Breast feeding baby
141	Styled hair
142	Scene of a sunset
143	A female ghost with long hair
144	Tile art (flowers and house)
145	Little monsters
146	A character (Chinese black cats)
147	A Japanese actress (Setsuko Hara)
148	A dog (Pomeranian)
149	A character (Snoopy)
150	A naked Japanese woman
151	An illustration (excited birds)
152	People dancing in tight body suits (Zenshin taitsu)
153	A character (Gru and friends from Despicable Me)
154	A character (Scrat from Ice Age)
155	A Japanese actress (Norika Fujiwara)
156	An illustration (girl wearing cat ears and maid uniform)
157	A character (Baymax from Big Hero 6)
158	A character (Chinese red cats)
159	An illustration (adult dog)
160	A character (Garfield)
161	A Japanese idol group (Momoiro Clover Z)
162	A mascot character (Peko from Fujiya)
163	An illustration (cheerful face)
164	A character (sun motif)
165	A Japanese actress (Yui Aragaki)
166	A character (wearing Chinese dress)
167	A cat (Koyuki, Scottish Fold and American Shorthair)
168	A character (Shrek)
169	Bedspreads with Chinese red cat characters printed on them
170	A green and black caterpillar
171	A costume of a Chinese red cat character
172	A woman painted in old Chinese style
173	Fancy goods with aChinese red cat character design
174	A character (Bai-du bear)
175	A famous Japanese author from the past (Sei Shonagon)
176	A Japanese actress (Ryoko Yonekura)
177	A character (Mickey Mouse)
178	A sparrow
179	An illustration (girl wearing helmet and sword)
180	Sweets (chocolates covered with colored sugar)

Table 5. The list of images (no. 181–225).

No.	Image
181	A baby dog (Mame-shiba a small kind of Shiba Inu)
182	A spider (Mexican redknee)
183	Cactus shaped like a ball
184	Jellyfish
185	Sweets (cake with a Chinese red cat character on it)
186	Ganguro girl
187	A walus
188	A character (GeGeGe no Kitaro)
189	A Japanese playwright and novelist (Hisashi Inoue)
190	An illustration (duckling)
191	A female Japanese model
192	A ghost (Rokurokubi)
193	An illustration (girl wearing maid uniform)
194	An illustration (dogs painted on a picture scroll)
195	A horror doll with long hair
196	A female Japanese model
197	An illustration (animals with girla human face)
198	An illustration (skeleton)
199	Ganguro girls
200	Salmon roe
201	An illustration (boys wearing school uniforms)
202	An illustration (unicorn with colorful mane)
203	A character (Disney version of Alice's Adventures in Wonderland)
204	A French doll
205	An American actress (Scarlett Johansson)
206	A mascot character (Kewpie)
207	An illustration (girl who is sad)
208	A baby boy model
209	A character (white bird with fluffed out feathers)
210	Sweet (shortcake)
211	A character (Chinese kids)
212	A work of art (sculpture)
213	A figure (heart shape)
214	An illustration (anthropomorphized vegetables painted on a picture scroll)
215	An expectant mother
216	A fur seal
217	A female Japanese enka singer (Sachiko Kobayashi)
218	A newborn baby
219	Building illumination
220	An illustration (angels and hearts)
221	A big centipede
222	Owls
223	An illustration (girl wearing lab coat with pointer)
224	A character (Gudetama)
225	An illustration (anthropomorphized vegetables)

3 The Results of Questionnaire Survey on "Kawaii"

Tables show some of the results of the questionnaire. The results of Q1 were counted as 1 for yes and 0 for no. Three other columns of the table, "Kawaii", "Beautiful" and "Preference" is the average rating score on the 5-point scale. Scores larger than 3 means positive answers. The lowest row is the result of the t-test (p value) between male students and female students.

In the results of Q2, we found there are some differences in the feeling of images between young males and females (Tables 6, 7, 8, 9, 10, 11, 12, 13 and 14). Young female students made more positive evaluations than male on "Kawaii."

3.1 Characters (Tables 6 and 7)

Characters belong to the category of generic Kawaii. Table 6 shows the scores of simply designed characters such as Miffy (no. 4), Hello Kitty (no. 65) and Peko (a mascot character of Japanese confectionery Fujiya) (no. 162), that received the high evaluation on "Kawaii" by both young male and female.

Young female evaluated significantly higher than male in terms of "Kawaii" score at the level of 5% or 1% compared to male. Young female also evaluated significantly higher on "Preference" scores to the Hello Kitty at a level of 5% or 1% compared to male.

Table 6. Simply designed characters.

Q&A	A1	A2		
	Know	Kawaii	Beautiful	Preference
Image no. 4: a character (Miffy)				
Both	0.94	3.96	2.97	3.57
Male	0.93	**3.76**	3.02	3.38
Female	0.97	**4.26**	2.88	3.88
t-test	0.35	**0.05**	0.61	0.06
		*		
Image no. 65: a character (Hello Kitty)				
Both	0.93	3.74	2.78	3.18
Male	**0.89**	**3.44**	2.73	**2.82**
Female	**1.00**	**4.24**	2.85	**3.76**
t-test	**0.01**	**0.00**	0.64	**0.00**
	**	**		**
Image no. 162: a mascot character (Peko from Fujiya)				
Both	0.97	3.91	2.66	3.51
Male	0.90	**3.10**	3.00	3.00
Female	1.00	**4.24**	2.52	3.72
t-test	0.34	**0.03**	0.33	0.09
		*		

* p < 0.05, ** p < 0.01

Table 7. Many colored characters.

Q&A	A1	A2		
	Know	Kawaii	Beautiful	Preference
Image no. 42: a character (Peter Rabbit)				
Both	0.83	3.84	3.38	3.66
Male	**0.75**	**3.56**	3.24	**3.42**
Female	**0.97**	**4.29**	3.62	**4.06**
t-test	**0.00**	**0.00**	0.12	**0.01**
	**	**		**
Image no. 203: a character (Disney version of Alice's Adventures in Wonderland)				
Both	1.00	4.34	3.51	4.09
Male	1.00	3.80	3.60	3.50
Female	1.00	4.56	3.48	4.32
t-test	–	0.07	0.80	0.09

* $p < 0.05$, ** $p < 0.01$

Table 8. Geometrical shapes.

Q&A	A1	A2		
	Know	Kawaii	Beautiful	Preference
Image no. 47: a figure (spherical object)				
Both	0.60	2.19	3.17	2.70
Male	**0.47**	**2.42**	3.25	**2.91**
Female	**0.79**	**1.82**	3.03	**2.35**
t-test	**0.00**	**0.01**	0.43	**0.02**
	**	**		*
Image no. 85: a figure (rectangular object)				
Both	0.41	2.13	3.12	2.75
Male	0.35	2.31	3.16	**3.02**
Female	0.52	1.85	3.06	**2.32**
t-test	0.13	0.06	0.73	**0.01**
				**
Image no. 213: a figure (heart shape)				
Both	0.89	3.40	2.86	3.06
Male	0.80	3.40	3.00	3.10
Female	0.92	3.40	2.80	3.04
t-test	0.42	1.00	0.64	0.90

* $p < 0.05$, ** $p < 0.01$

Table 9. Sweets.

Q&A	A1	A2		
	Know	Kawaii	Beautiful	Preference
Image no. 22: sweets (Japanese-style confectionery)				
Both	0.74	3.30	3.90	3.76
Male	**0.63**	3.18	3.76	3.60
Female	**0.91**	3.50	4.12	4.03
t-test	**0.00**	0.24	0.20	0.12
	**			
Image no. 50: sweets (jelly)				
Both	0.76	3.02	3.33	3.36
Male	**0.65**	**2.80**	3.35	3.31
Female	**0.94**	**3.38**	3.29	3.44
t-test	**0.00**	**0.02**	0.85	0.60
	**	*		
Image no. 210: sweets (shortcake)				
Both	0.89	3.51	3.23	4.00
Male	0.70	**2.70**	2.90	3.40
Female	0.96	**3.84**	3.36	4.24
t-test	0.13	**0.01**	0.30	0.06
		**		

* p < 0.05, ** p < 0.01

Table 10. Small animals.

Q&A	A1	A2		
	Know	Kawaii	Beautiful	Preference
Image no. 38: a cat (British Shorthair)				
Both	0.74	3.30	3.90	3.76
Male	**0.63**	3.18	3.76	3.60
Female	**0.91**	3.50	4.12	4.03
t-test	**0.00**	0.24	0.20	0.12
	**			
Image no. 79: a little bird (Varied tit)				
Both	0.76	3.02	3.33	3.36
Male	**0.65**	**2.80**	3.35	3.31
Female	**0.94**	**3.38**	3.29	3.44
t-test	**0.00**	**0.02**	0.85	0.60
	**	*		
Image no.148: a dog (Pomeranian)				
Both	0.89	3.51	3.23	4.00
Male	0.70	**2.70**	2.90	3.40
Female	0.96	**3.84**	3.36	4.24
t-test	0.13	**0.01**	0.30	0.06
		**		

* p < 0.05, ** p < 0.01

Table 11. Female celebrities.1

Q&A	A1	A2		
	Know	Kawaii	Beautiful	Preference
Image no. 12: an American actor (Scarlett Johansson)				
Both	0.19	3.13	3.87	3.26
Male	0.22	3.20	3.78	3.33
Female	0.15	3.03	4.00	3.15
t-test	0.40	0.46	0.40	0.40
Image no.64: a Canadian singer (Avril Lavigne)				
Both	0.70	4.06	3.94	3.57
Male	**0.62**	4.00	3.98	3.71
Female	**0.82**	4.15	3.88	3.35
t-test	**0.03**	0.50	0.66	0.14
	**			
Image no. 165: a Japanese actor (Yui Aragaki)				
Both	0.89	4.34	4.14	4.17
Male	0.80	4.10	4.40	4.30
Female	0.92	4.44	4.04	4.12
t-test	0.42	0.29	0.30	0.62

* $p < 0.05$, ** $p < 0.01$

Table 12. Female celebrities.2

Q&A	A1	A2		
	Know	Kawaii	Beautiful	Preference
Image no. 49: a British actor (Aubrey Hepburn)				
Both	0.39	3.53	3.97	3.43
Male	**0.25**	**3.24**	**3.67**	**3.18**
Female	**0.62**	**4.00**	**4.44**	**3.82**
t-test	**0.00**	**0.00**	**0.00**	**0.00**
	**	**	**	**
Image no. 123: a Japanese actor (Mikako Tabe)				
Both	0.78	3.29	3.00	3.14
Male	**0.69**	**2.96**	2.87	**2.81**
Female	**0.91**	**3.82**	3.21	**3.65**
t-test	**0.01**	**0.00**	0.16	**0.00**
	**	**		**
Image no. 176: a Japanese actor (Ryoko Yonekura)				
Both	0.83	3.54	4.23	3.57
Male	0.80	3.30	**3.70**	3.40
Female	0.84	3.64	**4.44**	3.64
t-test	0.80	0.45	**0.04**	0.57
			*	

* $p < 0.05$, ** $p < 0.01$

Table 13. Female comedians

Q&A	A1	A2		
	Know	Kawaii	Beautiful	Preference
Image no. 3: a female Japanese comedian				
(Kazuko Kurosawa)				
Both	0.88	2.84	2.24	3.04
Male	0.85	**2.44**	2.27	**2.82**
Female	0.91	**3.50**	2.18	**3.41**
t-test	0.41	**0.00**	0.63	**0.03**
		**		**
Image no. 93: a female Japanese comedian				
(Naomi Watanabe)				
Both	0.89	2.88	2.61	3.13
Male	0.84	**2.35**	2.22	2.58
Female	0.97	**3.74**	3.24	4.03
t-test	0.02	**0.00**	0.00	0.00
		**		**
Image no. 126: a female Japanese comedian				
(Kanako Yanagihara)				
Both	0.90	3.16	2.52	3.05
Male	0.87	**2.82**	2.44	**2.69**
Female	0.94	**3.71**	2.65	**3.62**
t-test	0.27	**0.00**	0.34	**0.00**
		**		**

$* p < 0.05, ** p < 0.01$

Characters painted in many colors such as Peter Rabbit (no. 42) and Disney version of Alice's Adventures in Wonderland (no. 203). For Peter Rabbit, female students rated significantly higher than male students in terms of Kawaii, beautiful and preferred.

3.2 Geometrical Shapes (Table 8)

Figures such as spherical object (no. 42), rectangular object (no. 85) and heart shape (no. 213) belong to the psycho-physical Kawaii. Both male and female students rated them as beautiful. Regarding the scale on Kawaii, male students rated significantly higher for the spherical object than female students.

3.3 Sweets (Table 9)

Sweets belong to the generic Kawaii. But the small-sized Japanese confectionery has something related to the psycho-physical Kawaii because of its size. Sweets such as Japanese-style confectionery (no. 22), jelly (no. 50) and shortcake (no. 210) were preferred by both gender groups. But the jelly and shortcake were rated Kawaii significantly higher by female students. The jelly was rated beautiful by both of male and female students.

Table 14. General females

Q&A	A1	A2		
	Know	Kawaii	Beautiful	Preference
Image no. 2: an ordinary Japanese woman				
Both	0.13	2.80	2.97	2.63
Male	0.18	**3.07**	**3.18**	**3.04**
Female	0.06	**2.35**	**2.62**	**1.97**
t-test	0.07	**0.00**	**0.01**	**0.00**
		**	**	**
Image no. 37: an ordinary Japanese girl (wearing maid uniform)				
Both	0.20	2.44	2.15	2.16
Male	0.16	**2.67**	**2.44**	**2.44**
Female	0.26	**2.06**	**1.68**	**1.71**
t-test	0.28	**0.01**	**0.00**	**0.00**
		**	**	**
Image no. 81: a young female CosplayerImage				
Both	0.16	3.16	2.78	2.66
Male	0.15	**3.38**	**3.04**	**2.95**
Female	0.18	**2.79**	**2.35**	**2.21**
t-test	0.71	**0.04**	**0.01**	**0.00**
		*	**	**

* $p < 0.05$, ** $p < 0.01$

3.4 Small Animals (Table 10)

Small animals such as the bird, dog and cat are typical examples of baby schema of Lorenz, hence this category belongs to the psycho-physical Kawaii. Figures included Varied tit (no. 79), British Shorthair (no. 38) and Pomeranian (no. 148). Both gender students rated them as beautiful and preferred. But female students rated Viried tit and Pomeranian significantly higher than male regarding Kawaii.

3.5 Female Celebrities (Tables 11 and 12)

Female celebrities are singers and actors including Scarlett Johansson (no. 12), Avril Lavigne (no. 64), Yui Aragaki (no. 165), Audrey Hepburn (no. 49), Mikako Tabe (no. 123) and Ryoko Yonekura (no. 176). In this case, the category is the generic Kawaii.

For all 6 photographs, high scores were obtained for both scales of Kawaii and beautiful. In other words, actresses were regarded not just as beautiful but also as Kawaii in Japan. Another interesting result is that Audrey Hepburn was rated significantly more Kawaii and more beautiful by female students than male students.

3.6   Female Comedians (Table 13)

Female Japanese comedians such as Kazuko Kurosawa (no. 3), Naomi Watanabe (no. 93) and Kanako Yanagihara (no. 126) were used as stimuli. Their photographs will belong to generic Kawaii, if they were rated as Kawaii. Female students rated female comedians as Kawaii and preferred significantly higher than male students.

3.7   Pictures of General Japanese Females (Table 14)

Photographs of general Japanese females such as no. 2, no. 37 and no. 81 were rated Kawaii, beautiful and preferred by male students significantly higher than female students. The reason is unclear but chances are male students might have felt an affinity to general Japanese females because they were recognized as closer to male students.

4   Conclusion

These survey results show that young female students are using the word "Kawaii" as a similar meaning to positive feelings such as "like" or "love." It suggest the necessity for the future comparative study in different countries. The result of the comparative study may show us the difference of Kawaii-related concept between Japan and other countries.

References

1. Yomoda, I.: On Kawaii, Chikuma Shinsho, vol. 578. Chikuma-Shobo, Tokyo (2006). (in Japanese)
2. Yan, X.: Generation and transformation of 'Kawaii' concept in modern society. Hyogo University of Teacher Education, Graduate School of Education Master's thesis (#09141F) (2010). (in Japanese)
3. Marcus, A., Kurosu, M., Fu, X., Hashizume, A.: Cuteness Engineering. Springer, Heidelberg (2017)
4. Lorenz, K.: Die angeborenen Formen moeglicher Erfahrung. Z Tierpsychol. 5, 235–409 (1943)

Experimental Evaluation of Immersive Feeling in VR System with HMD

Yoshiki Koinuma[✉], Kazuki Miyamoto, and Michiko Ohkura

Shibaura Institute of Technology,
3-7-5, Toyosu, Koto-ku, Tokyo 135-8548, Japan
{AL13044, AL13102}@shibaura-it.ac.jp,
ohkura@sic.shibaura-it.ac.jp

Abstract. Virtual Reality (VR) had a banner year in 2016. VR has attracted a lot of media attention because many companies have launched Head Mounted Displays (HMDs) and other related products. As a result, the term "immersive feeling" has become more widely known. In this study, we evaluated immersive feeling using HMD. For that purpose, we created two types of content: one expected to generate high immersive feeling and another expected to generate low immersive feeling.

Keywords: VR · Immersive feeling · HMD

1 Introduction

Virtual Reality (VR) had a banner year in 2016 and has attracted a lot of media attention because many companies have launched Head Mounted Displays (HMDs) and other related products. [1]. As a result, the term "immersive feeling" has become more widely known. In previous studies, immersive feeling was evaluated using 2D or 3D displays [2, 3]. However, those displays can show only a frontal scene. On the other hand, HMD can provide a stereoscopic scene in all directions. Therefore, using HMD would give more a more immersive feeling than 2D or 3D displays. Thus, we planned to evaluate immersive feeling using HMD by creating VR content. We performed an impression survey of the term "immersive feeling," and performed factor analysis to create VR content and to determine question items for evaluation. We experimentally evaluated immersive feeling in VR systems using HMD with the two created pieces of content. The experimental result suggests a strong correlation between immersive feeling and a sense of excitement.

2 Impression Survey of Immersive Feeling

2.1 Method

The objective is to create VR content giving a high immersive feeling and VR content giving a low immersive feeling.

M. Kurosu (Ed.): HCI 2017, Part II, LNCS 10272, pp. 678–686, 2017.
DOI: 10.1007/978-3-319-58077-7_52

We created a questionnaire by referencing previous research [4] as follows.

1. Do you know the term "Virtual Reality (VR)"? (yes/no)
2. Do you know the term "Immersive feeling"? (yes/no)
3. If the answer to question 2) is "yes", go to question 3).
4. Which factors are necessary to give an immersive feeling?

We used a five-point Likert scale (−2 to +2) for this question. The following are the 12 pairs of adjectives used in this question:

- Dark - Bright
- Narrow - Wide
- Extraordinary - Ordinary
- Stressful - Relaxing
- Unease - Ease
- Natural - Artificial
- Planar - Stereoscopic
- Vague - Clear
- Static - Dynamic
- Boring - Exciting
- Complex - Simple
- Not thrilling – Thrilling

2.2 Results and Discussion

The impression survey on immersive feeling was conducted with 84 volunteers in their 20 s. Figure 1 shows results for questions 1 and 2. For question 1, 75 out of 84 (89%) answered yes. Therefore, it can be said that the term VR is generally recognized. For question 2, 35 out of 84 (42%) answered yes, which means that recognition of the term immersive feeling was much lower than that of VR.

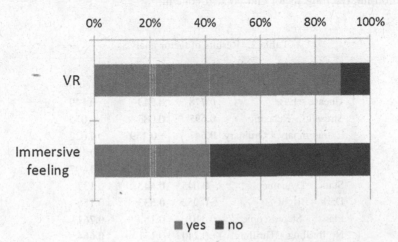

Fig. 1. Results of awareness of VR and immersive feeling

Table 1. Descriptive statistics of answers to question 3

Descriptive statistics

	N	Mean	d. Deviation	Variance
Dark – Bright	35	−0.34	0.968	0.938
Narrow – Wide	35	0.17	1.248	1.558
Extraordinary – Ordinary	35	−0.40	1.063	1.129
Stressful – Relaxing	35	0.57	1.170	1.370
Unease – Ease	35	0.20	1.079	1.165
Natural – Artificial	35	−0.46	1.039	1.079
Planar – Stereoscopic	35	1.66	0.482	0.232
Vague – Clear	35	1.31	0.832	0.692
Static - Dynamic	35	1.03	0.954	0.911
Boring - Exciting	35	1.09	0.853	0.728
Complex – Simple	35	0.63	1.140	1.299
No thrilling - Thrilling	35	1.03	0.822	0.676

Table 1 shows descriptive statistics of answers to question 3. We analyzed the results of question 3, and Table 2 presents the results of the factor analysis. Three factors were extracted from the analysis. The main components of these factors are as follows.

1. Ease, Relaxing, Ordinary, Natural
2. Artificial, Clear, Dynamic, Bright
3. Stereoscopic, Thrilling, Complex

Then, we named these factors "Relaxing", "Active" and "Exciting," respectively. Figure 2 shows ratios of answers for question 3 for each factor. As shown in Fig. 2, many volunteers answered that the Exciting factor was necessary. Therefore, we focused on the Exciting factor and created content.

Table 2. Results of factor analysis

Variable	Factor		
	Relaxing	Activeness	Exciting
Unease - Ease	**0.778**	0.243	−0.149
Stressful - Relaxing	**0.695**	0.083	−0.055
Extraordinary - Ordinary	**0.647**	−0.159	−0.022
Natural - Artificial	**−0.554**	**0.535**	−0.150
Vague - Clear	0.179	**0.751**	−0.097
Static - Dynamic	−0.045	**0.643**	0.137
Dark - Bright	−0.052	**0.533**	0.156
Planar - Stereoscopic	0.310	0.153	**0.761**
No thrilling - Thrilling	−0.240	0.131	**0.664**
Complex - Simple	0.178	0.048	**−0.499**

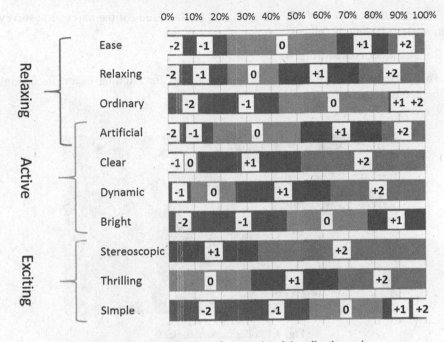

Fig. 2. Ratios of answers for question 3 in adjective pairs

3 Experimental Method

3.1 System and Content

The purpose of this experiment is to evaluate the degree of immersive feeling in the VR system with HMD.

Figure 3 shows our experimental system.

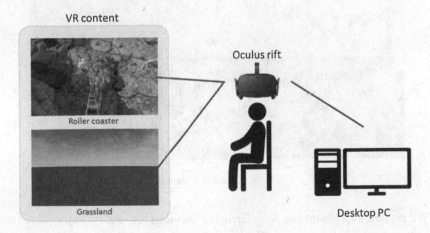

Fig. 3. Experimental system

We created two pieces of VR content based on the results of the impression survey of immersive feeling as follows.

- Roller coaster content (Fig. 4)

This is content that we expect to have high scores for Exciting factor. It contains falling and turning fast.

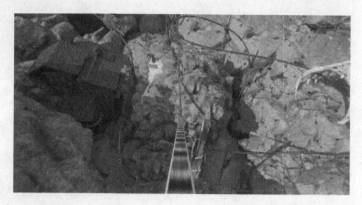

Fig. 4. Roller coaster content

- Grassland content (Fig. 5)

This is content that we expect to have low scores for Exciting factor. It contains only straight, flat forward motion.

Fig. 5. Grassland content

We created a questionnaire by referencing previous research [2, 5].

The questionnaire consists of questions related to VR content (Q1～Q6) and immersive feeling (Q7～Q17) as follows.

Q1. I was thrilled by the content.
Q2. I felt the content stereoscopically.
Q3. I felt the content to be simple.
Q4. I felt a response delay in the content.
Q5. I found the sound of the content strange.
Q6. I found the event in the content unnatural.
Q7. I found the content boring.
Q8. I enjoyed the content.
Q9. I was interested to know what might be happening around me.
Q10. I was able to concentrate on content experiences.
Q11. I felt detached from the outside world.
Q12. It felt like only a very short amount of time had passed.
Q13. I felt like I was going forward.
Q14. When I took off the HMD, I was confused.
Q15. I was interested in seeing how the game's events would progress.
Q16. I enjoyed the graphics and imagery of the game.
Q17. I was immersed in the content.

Evaluation was carried out using a five-point Likert scale (−2 to +2) and free description.

4   Experimental Results

4.1   Experimental

We performed an experiment with eight male participants in their 20 s. The experiment took about 40 min per participant. Each participant experienced the roller coaster content and grassland content, respectively. The order of experiencing content was counter-balanced. Figure 6 shows a scene of the experiment.

4.2   Experimental Results and Discussion

Based on the results of the questionnaire, we performed a difference test. Figures 7 and 8 show the averages for each question. There were significant differences between the two pieces of content in three items ("Q1～Q3") for Exciting factor and in eight items out of 11 for immersive feeling. As expected, the roller coaster content had higher scores for Exciting factor and immersive feeling than the grassland content. Table 3 shows the result of correlation analysis for questions related to exciting factor (Q1～Q3) and immersive feeling (Q7～Q17). There are strong correlations between Q1 and nine items out of 11 for immersive feeling (Q7～Q17). There were strong

Fig. 6. Experimental scene

correlations between Q3 and in six items out of 11 for immersive feeling (Q7~Q17). However, there is a strong correlation only between Q2 and (Q7~Q17) (Fig. 8) .

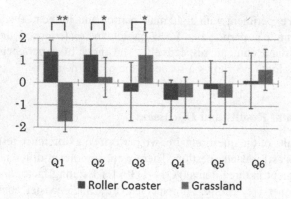

Fig. 7. Averages of questionnaire items related to VR

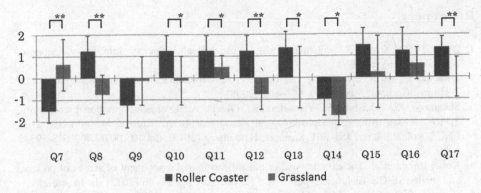

Fig. 8. Averages of questionnaire items related to immersive feeling

Table 3. Results of correlation analysis

Correlations			
	Q1	Q2	Q3
Q7	−.822**	−0.444	.670**
Q8	.821**	0.444	−.612*
Q9	−0.466	−0.404	.585*
Q10	.677**	0.388	−.530*
Q11	.531*	0.349	-0.205
Q12	.856**	0.405	−.524*
Q13	.550*	0.261	−0.428
Q14	.545*	0.349	−0.222
Q15	.524*	.636**	−.641**
Q16	0.333	−0.019	−0.029
Q17	.706**	0.335	−0.270

*. Correlation is significant at the
0.05 level (2-tailed).
**. Correlation is significant at the
0.01 level (2-tailed).

5   Conclusion and Future Work

We performed an impression survey for the term "immersive feeling," and performed
factor analysis to create VR content and to determine question items for evaluation. We
experimentally evaluated immersive feeling in VR systems using an HMD with two
pieces of content we created. The experimental results show that the immersive feelings
of the two pieces of content differed significantly, along with their impression of
"exciting feelings" for users. This result suggests a strong correlation between
immersive feeling and excitement. We also performed another experiment with measuring functional near-infrared spectroscopy (fNIRS). Analysis of the experimental
results including fNIRS data remains as future work.

References

1. 2016: The Year of VR? - Virtual Reality. Virtual Reality Society. http://www.vrs.org.uk/news/2016-the-year-of-vr
2. Jennetta, C., et al.: Measuring and defining the experience of immersion in games. Int. J. Human-Comput. Stud. **66**(9), 641–661 (2008)
3. Sakamoto, K., Sakashita, S., Yamashita, K., Okada, A.: Evaluating emotional state during 3DTV viewing using psychophysiological measurements. In: Kurosu, M. (ed.) HCI 2013. LNCS, vol. 8008, pp. 353–361. Springer, Heidelberg (2013). doi:10.1007/978-3-642-39342-6_39
4. Kohei Iimura et al: The experimental of quantification and assessment of senses of presence and reality, IEICE Technical report, vol. 112, no. 106, pp. 61–66 (2012) (In Japanese)
5. Witmer, B.G., Singer, M.J.: Measuring Presence in Virtual Environments: A Presence Questionnaire. Presence Teleoperators Virtual Environ. **7**(3), 225–240 (1998)

Relationship Between Worker Interruptibility and Work Transitions Detected by Smartphone

Kyohei Komuro, Yuichiro Fujimoto, and Kinya Fujita$^{(\boxtimes)}$

Graduate School, Tokyo University of Agriculture and Technology,
2-24-16 Nakacho, Koganei, Tokyo 184-8588, Japan
s166247q@st.go.tuat.ac.jp, y_fuji@cc.tuat.ac.jp,
kfujita@cc.tuat.ac.jp

Abstract. To avoid work fragmentation and the consequent decrease in intellectual productivity of office workers, control of interruptions based on estimated interruptibility is desired. While existing studies mainly focus on work on PCs, non-PC work is also performed in offices and is considered to affect the interruptibility of workers. In this study, we focused on the transitions between PC work and the use of smartphones or walking, which are likely interruptible moments. We developed an experimental system to detect the use of smartphones and walking and to collect users' subjective ratings of his/her interruptibility. As the result, it was revealed that the moments at the transitions to walking tend to more interruptible, whereas the transitions to or from smartphone use are not necessarily interruptible. Furthermore, it was also found that the transitions to smartphone use without an external trigger (self-transitions) are more interruptible moments than the transitions triggered by notifications.

Keywords: Interruptibility · Work transition · Smartphone · Office worker

1 Introduction

The proliferation of ICT devices and the Internet enables us to access information anytime and anywhere. Furthermore, a growing number of network services provide information to users without the users intentionally accessing them. Thus, business messages, private correspondence, news, and other miscellaneous information may automatically be delivered to both PCs at work and smartphones (SP) presumably for personal use. These network services facilitate smooth communication and let us access the latest information with almost no effort.

However, automatic delivery of information increases the risk of inappropriate interruptions, e.g., email delivery notifications while the user is concentrating on his/her work. Such interruptions potentially induce work fragmentation and lead to decreased intellectual productivity. Such interruptions should be reduced as much as possible [1, 2]; to this end, a number of studies on automatic estimation of worker interruptibility have been carried out.

© Springer International Publishing AG 2017
M. Kurosu (Ed.): HCI 2017, Part II, LNCS 10272, pp. 687–699, 2017.
DOI: 10.1007/978-3-319-58077-7_53

One such study was on interruptibility estimation based on PC operation [3]. The system developed in that study can easily be introduced to actual working environments because it does not require any additional hardware devices. However, the method has the disadvantage that interruptibility is mistakenly estimated as high when the user works without using a PC, e.g., even while discussing important issues with other workers.

One method of detecting a worker's non-PC activity is to use an SP, which has various sensors. Previous studies have developed methods to estimate interruptibility of SP users and to control the notification timing by using them [4, 5]. However, these studies focused only on the SP use; other activities such as PC work were out of their scope.

This study aims to improve the comprehensive accuracy of interruptibility estimation by expanding the applicable situation of the PC-based method by using SPs. As previous studies suggested that cognitive workload is lower at task switching moments [2, 6], it also appears to be low at transitions from PC work to other tasks and activities. Therefore, we analyzed the relationship between subjective interruptibility and work transitions detected by SPs to examine the effects of such transitions on interruptibility estimations.

2   Work Transitions in Offices

2.1   Target Work Transitions in Office

In today's offices, a large portion of the desk work is performed on PC; however, there are numerous other non-PC activities that are also performed, such as meetings, talking on the phone, paper work, use of SPs, and walking to other rooms. Even if actual office work is complex and consists of multiple subtasks, workers can only carry out one task at a time. Furthermore, it is known that one's cognitive workload is momentarily lowered at the breakpoints between subtasks [5]. Therefore, this study focused on the transitions from PC work to/from SP use or walking, because these transitions can be easily detected using a SP, and many workers carry SPs with them at work. Figure 1 represents the discrete state transition model of PC workers assumed in this study.

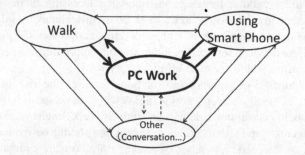

Fig. 1. Work transition model assumed in this study

Hereinafter, a transition from A to B is represented as "A to B" (e.g., PC to Walking, SP to PC) and a transition between A and B including both A to B and B to A is represented "A-B" (e.g. PC-SP, Walking-SP). Basically, interruptibility at transitions from PC to SP is expected to be high, because SP is mainly for private use, so that the use of an SP represents the worker's temporary disengagement from work. In addition, the PC to walking transition that represents leaving the desk also appears to be an interruptible moment. Thus, this study analyzes the interruptibility at the transitions between PC use, SP use, and walking.

2.2   Expected Correlation Between Transition and Interruptibility

In this study, we define the word "interruptibility" as the subjective degree to which a user can accept an interruption [3]. Generally speaking, work transitions are break-points between two tasks, so that the interruptibility at those times is expected to be high [2]. However, not all transitions are interruptible; for example, an "involuntary" transition to SPs would be triggered by an incoming e-mail notification during work. Thus, interruptibility will vary depending on the work that occurs after the transition.

The transition direction may also affect interruptibility between PC and SP use. Interruptibility at a PC to SP moment is considered to increase because it denotes a change in the operation target away from the PC, which is the main tool for work. On the other hand, interruptibility at a SP to PC moment may be lower because that moment is a time to restart work on the PC. Similarly, interruptibility at PC to walking transitions is presumed to be high because these are moments at which the PC work is suspended; in contrast, walk to PC transitions will be less interruptible because these are the times at which PC work starts.

In addition, interruptibility will vary with various factors even at the same type of transition. For instance, the interruptibility at the moment when a worker voluntarily uses a SP will be higher because such a "self-interruption" is basically controlled by the user; thus, he/she would naturally choose more desirable moments for themselves. On the other hand, PC to SP transitions caused by notifications appear to have lower interruptibility because notifications potentially happen even when the worker is focusing on the task at hand.

3   Experimental System

3.1   System Overview

We implemented the experimental system shown in Fig. 2 for collecting the interruptibility data at transitions as an Android application. This application software supports later versions than Android 4.1. It records the SP state in 0.5 s cycles by using Accessibility Service in the background. Recorded data are the screen state, notifications, SP operations, window state, and 3-axis acceleration.

The PC operations are recorded by another system running on 32bit Windows 7 in 0.5 s cycles. This system also runs in the background, so it does not disturb the

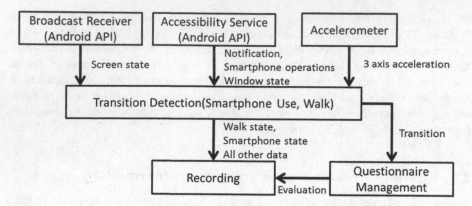

Fig. 2. Experimental system configuration for collecting data

participant. Recorded data are the number of keystrokes, clicks, wheel operations, and estimated interruptibility in three levels (calculated by Tanaka's method) [3].

We defined the transition from PC to SP as the start of SP use with PC operation activity within 1 min before the transition. We defined the PC to walking transition in a similar way. We also defined the returning transitions, from SP to PC and from walking to PC, by using the PC activity within 1 min after the end of SP use and walking detection. The threshold (1 min) was decided experimentally.

3.2   Management of Onscreen Questionnaire for Interruptibility Evaluation

When the system detects transitions such as to SP use, it automatically judges whether or not to display the questionnaire dialogue box for collecting the subjective interruptibility at the moment. The system notifies participants to answer the questionnaire at a stochastic timing, which is adjusted on the basis of the number of accumulated evaluations for each transition so that the number of evaluations for each transition is roughly equalized to a certain level.

If the participant responds to the notification and answers the questionnaire on the dialogue box, the system records the SP operations and the sensor data as well as the interruptibility level that the participant chose. It keeps at least a 7-min interval between notifications requiring the participant to answer the questionnaire; this is to reduce the influence of excessive notifications on subjective interruptibility. Figure 3 shows the questionnaire dialogue box for the interruptibility evaluation and additional items.

(1) Interruptibility
    Interruptibility when the notification was delivered (5 levels: Low: 1–High: 5). The participants were requested to score how willing he/she would be to engage in a 5-min conversation.

(2) Task
Actual task that the participant was engaged in at the moment of notification.
(3) Location
Location of the participant.
(4) Comment (free description)

We instructed the participants to tap the notification and answer the questionnaire on the dialogue-box immediately after the notification. We used the evaluations that were logged within 30 s of the notification because answers with longer delays are less reliable in terms of the interruptibility at a specific moment. In the cases in which there were no responses 30 s after the notification, the questionnaire was replaced with another dialogue box that asked for the reason he/she did not answer. If it was still not answered within 1 min, the notification was removed to avoid confusion.

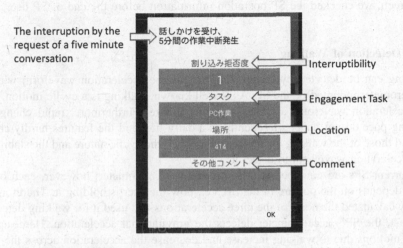

Fig. 3. Questionnaire dialogue box (Touch the notification, and this box pops up)

3.3 Detection of Smartphone Use

Table 1 shows the detection algorithm of SP use. The SP's screen is usually off to save power. Thus, the use of an SP can be detected from the SP screen state and the user operations. Here, the start of SP use was determined to be the time at which the screen turned on, and the end of SP use was determined to be the time at which the screen was manually turned off. After collecting the evaluations, we combined the PC operations data and the evaluations to distinguish the transitions related to PC use.

In order to determine the cause of a transition (by oneself or by notification), this system checks whether the notification was delivered within a threshold duration before the moment the screen turned on. We determined the threshold to be 30 s, which is the same as the threshold used in a previous study [7].

Furthermore, because SPs have an automatic screen-off function, which is not attributed to the user's operation, such automatic screen-off events should be

Table 1. Algorithm to detect the start and the end of SP use

Timing	Cause of use	Rules
Start	Oneself	Turn screen from off to on Absence of notification for the last 30 s
	Notification	Turn screen from off to on Existence of notification within last 30 s
End	Oneself	Turn screen from on to off manually Start of SP use was judged as self
	Notification	Turn screen from on to off manually Start of SP use was judged as notification

distinguished from manual screen-offs. To exclude the cases of automatic screen-off and analyze the interruptibility at the moment when the user intentionally turned off the SP screen, we checked the SP operation information before the end of SP use.

3.4 Detection of Walking

Walking can be detected by recognizing the unique acceleration waveform with the accelerometer mounted on the SP. As is well known, walking is a cyclic motion; thus, its acceleration waveform also has a cyclic feature. Furthermore, rapid changes in walking pace do not happen frequently in a daily life, and the features hardly change beyond those of the walking cycle. Hence, we used the cyclic nature and the stability of the acceleration waveform to detect it.

Current SPs are equipped with a three-axis accelerometer; however, each output value depends on the posture of the SP, i.e., how the user is holding it. Therefore, we simply calculated the norm of the three accelerations and used it for walking detection.

First, the SP's accelerometer detects the gravitational acceleration. Here, up and down motions due to walking increase and decrease the acceleration across the gravitational level in a cyclic fashion. Hence, the frequency of 9.8 m/s^2 crossings may be used as a cyclic feature. However, since the acceleration pattern while walking is not a simple sinusoidal waveform, the crossing frequency of the gravitational level is greater than the actual frequency due to steps. Therefore, we used the frequency when the acceleration norm passed across the range between 8.8 and 10.8 m/s^2, to reduce the effect of small accelerations and decelerations and detect the dominant cyclic motion due to steps, as shown in Table 2.

In addition, we used the autocorrelation value as another feature of periodicity because it represents the similarity of the two different regions of a waveform, i.e., strength of periodicity. The time-shift window was set between 0.5 to 1.5 s [8].

On the other hand, the acceleration waveform will not greatly change step by step while a person is steadily walking. Therefore, to include the stability of the waveform in the walking detection algorithm, we used the ratio of maximum and minimum acceleration values in the current and previous walking cycles. We also used the ratio of feature A in the current and previous walking cycle.

Table 2. Features and conditions for detecting the start and the end of walking

Features		Conditions	
		Start walking	End walking
A	Frequency when acceleration norm passed across the range between 8.8 and 10.8 m/s^2 in 1 s	2–11	Out of 2–14
B	Maximum autocorrelation value in 0.5 to 1.5 s shift windows	Equal or over 0.4	Less than 0.2
C	Ratio of maximum accelerations in the current and previous walking cycles	0.6–1.9	Out of 0.4–2.5
D	Ratio minimum accelerations in the current and the previous walking cycle	0.6–1.9	Out of 0.4–2.5
E	Ratio of feature A in the current and the previous walking cycle	0.5–2.0	Out of 0.3–3.0

Table 2 shows the rules for each feature to detect the start and end of walking. Equations 1 and 2 represent the final rules for detecting the start and the end of walking based on the features. Variables A_s to E_s and A_e to E_e are binary flags, which are set when the rule corresponding to each feature satisfies the condition for start or end of walking. Start of walking was determined as the time when all the features satisfied the conditions, while end of walking was detected when either of the features satisfied the conditions.

$$(\text{Start walking}) = A_s \wedge B_s \wedge_s C \wedge D_s \wedge E_s \tag{1}$$

$$(\text{End walking}) = A_e \vee B_e \vee C_e \vee D_e \vee E_e \tag{2}$$

As can be seen in the equations, the rules are asymmetrical. We also set different thresholds in the conditions for detecting the start and end of walking, as shown in Table 2. These processes give a hysteresis property to the state transition detection; thus, errors in the transitions between walking and not-walking statuses are reduced.

After collecting the evaluations, we distinguished the transitions related to PC use in a similar way as detecting the PC-SP transitions.

4 Collection and Analysis of Interruptibility at Work Transitions

4.1 Experimental Setup for Collecting Subjective Interruptibility

The participants were three graduate and four undergraduate students studying at the department of computer and information sciences at the Tokyo University of Agriculture and Technology. They mainly work on PCs every day, so we assumed that their work style was not much different from that of typical office workers [9]. Five participants were males, and two were females. Six participants (2 male graduate students and 3 male and 1 female undergraduate students) studied in the same room named A.

One graduate student (female) studied in another room named B, which is located approximately 10 m away from room A. All participants came and went from rooms A and B on a daily basis and used a meeting room located approximately 10 m away from room B once per week. We instructed the participants to install our experimental system described in Sect. 3 on their PCs and SPs and activate it while they were in the laboratory.

4.2 Results

The experimental system ran for 111 days and collected 577 evaluations in total from all the participants. In other words, each participant participated 15.9 days and evaluated their interruptibility 5.2 times per day one average. As mentioned in Sect. 3.2, the system controlled the probability of displaying the questionnaire dialogue box based on the already collected sample numbers in order to equalize the sample number for each transition. In addition, the probability of occurrence was naturally different for each of the transitions. Therefore, the collected sample numbers were fewer than the actual occurrences of transitions.

We further categorized the detected transitions based on the existence of PC operation activity. The transitions from/to PC, in which PC operation was detected within 1 min before or after the transition, numbered 221 out of 577. The number of the transitions between SP and walking was 24. The transitions related to activities other than PC use, walking or SP use numbered 189. Because our main interest was focused on the transitions related to PC work and the collected data for the transitions between SP use and walking were fewer in number, this study discusses only the PC-SP and PC-Walking transitions.

Relationship Between Transitions and Interruptibility. Figure 4 shows the average interruptibility at transitions related to PC work. A two-way ANOVA showed no significant difference in the transition direction, but interruptibility at transitions to/from walking were significantly higher than those at transitions to/from SP

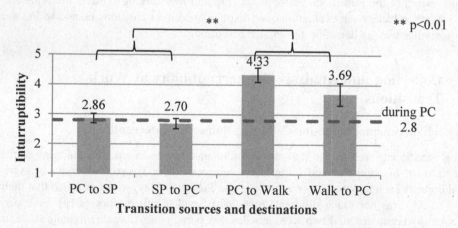

Fig. 4. Average interruptibilities at transition. Error bars represent standard errors.

(p < 0.01). According to the previous study focused on switching of application software [10], the average interruptibility is 2.8 during PC work and 3.2 at application switching moments. In comparison with those figures, the interruptibilities at the transitions to/from SP were not as high as we expected. On the other hand, the interruptibilities at the transitions to/from walking were obviously lower than at other transitions.

Interruptibility at SP Transitions Triggered by Oneself and by Notifications. Figure 5 shows the average interruptibilities at the transitions between PC and SP. They were divided into two groups: transitions triggered by the user (oneself) and those triggered by notifications. A two-way ANOVA showed no significant difference between interruptibilities for the two transition direction conditions, but interruptibility at transitions caused by notifications were significantly lower than in the case of transitions caused by oneself (p < 0.01). On the other hand, although interruptibilities at the transitions caused by oneself were higher compared with those caused by notifications, they were not much different from those during PC use (2.8 during PC use and 3.2 at application switching moments).

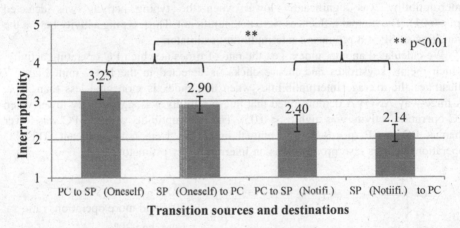

Fig. 5. Average interruptibilities at transition between using smartphones and PC work by self and notification (Notifi.). Error bars represent standard errors.

Relationship Between PC Operations and Interruptibility at SP Transitions. The interruptibility at transitions between PC and SP use was not as high as we initially expected. One of the reasons for the lower interruptibility appears to be the influence of the participants' working state before the transitions. For example, if workers were not concentrating on PC work before the transition, interruptibility would be high at PC to SP. Here, for further analysis, we targeted general PC operations such as typing and analyzed the relationship between those and interruptibility.

As an index for the engagement level of a worker engaged in PC work before a transition, we analyzed the effect of typing activity that was detected within 20 s before the transition. Figure 6 shows the averages of the interruptibilities when this index is

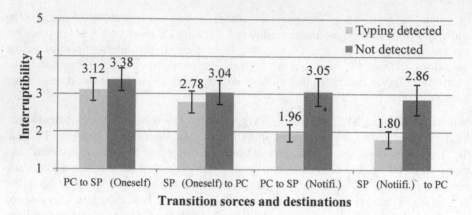

Fig. 6. Average interruptibility when typing within 20 s before transition is detected or not at transition. Error bars represent standard errors.

detected and when it is not detected. A three-way ANOVA showed that the average interruptibility was significantly lower when the typing activity was detected ($p < 0.01$). The mutual influences were not significant. Thus, typing activity before the transition to SP is a promising interruptibility estimator.

We calculated another index, i.e., the rate of times at which PC operating activity, which means keystrokes and mouse clicks, is detected in the last 2 min. Figure 7 illustrates the average interruptibilities when that index is more and less than 30%. A three-way ANOVA demonstrated that interruptibility was significantly lower when PC operation activity was high ($p < 0.05$). The interruptibility at SP to PC was lower than at PC to SP ($p < 0.1$). The mutual influences were not significant. This PC operation index is also promising as an interruptibility estimator.

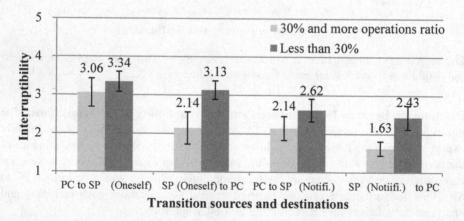

Fig. 7. Average interruptibility when operating rate in last 2 min is 30% and more or not at transition. Error bars represent standard errors.

5 Discussion

Although we expected that interruptibility at the transitions to/from SP use would be high, it was not necessarily high in either transition direction, as can be seen in Fig. 4. Thus, we further analyzed the relationship between PC operations before transitions to SP use and interruptibility. It revealed that interruptibility depends on the PC operation status as follows.

As shown in Fig. 6, in the cases that typing activity was detected within 20 s before the transition, the interruptibility was lower than in the cases without typing activity. The differences between average interruptibilities due to typing activity were 0.26 (PC to SP) and 0.26 (SP to PC) at self-transitions, and 1.09 (PC to SP) and 1.06 (SP to PC) at the transitions caused by notifications. These results suggest that the difference was greater in the transitions triggered by notifications than in self-transitions. The lower interruptibility could have been due to that the worker was interrupted, presumably by a notification, while he/she was engaged in the task at hand using a PC. Thus, detection of PC operation activity just before a transition may contribute to a better estimation. On the other hand, as shown in Fig. 6, that index appears not to be applicable to the self-transitions. A feasible explanation of the relatively higher interruptibility in self-transitions with typing activity is as follows; the task, which the worker was engaged in until just before the transition, had lasted for some time; then, the user voluntarily started to use SP. The results suggest that we need to distinguish the cases by using the PC operation activity index before the transitions to SP.

Figure 7 represents the relationship between another PC operation activity and the interruptibility. In the cases that PC operation activities, including both keystrokes and mouse-clicks, were detected more than 30% of time in the last 2 min before the transition, it turned out that interruptibility was lower. We assumed that this index roughly reflects the engagement of the worker in their task on the PC; thus, the interruptibility would be lower when the activity is higher. The result is consistent with our hypothesis. The differences in the average interruptibilities related to the PC operation rate were 0.28 (oneself) and 0.47 (notification) at PC to SP and 0.99 (oneself) and 0.80 (notification) at SP to PC. These results suggest that the engagement before a transition apparently affected SP to PC more than PC to SP (but the difference was not statistically significant). Mark et al. revealed that workers tend to compensate for the loss of time due to interruptions by working faster while experiencing more stress, more frustration, and time pressure and having to make more effort [11]. We might be able to make an inference that SP to PC included such compensation behaviors. Further analysis is needed.

In this study, we confirmed that several indices are potentially useful for the interruptibility estimation. At first, we expected that interruptibility at all the analyzed transitions would be high; however, this was only the case at walking transitions. Detection of walking could be used as a reliable index of interruptible moments. Interruptibility at SP transitions was not necessarily high, against our expectation. However, we found that the self-transitions to/from SP use are more interruptible moments than the transitions caused by notifications. Furthermore, it was shown that PC operation status before a transition affected interruptibility at transitions between

PC and SP. However, since the indices during PC use are not always effective for all transitions, we should further study the indices for each transition in the interruptibility estimation.

For a more accurate interruptibility estimation, we analyzed PC operations before transitions and confirmed the feasibility of detecting the worker's concentration on the task they were performing before the transition and reflect it in the interruptibility estimation. Similarly, we can expect that the detection of not only PC operation but also SP operation and walking states may improve the interruptibility estimation accuracy. For example, if the transition from SP to PC is detected after a long duration of SP use, such a transition may be a time to start a new task rather than one of returning to the original task before using the SP; thus, such moments would be more interruptible.

In the future, we should further explore the factors affecting interruptibility and develop an algorithm for accurate interruptibility estimation. Furthermore, the experimental results demonstrated that when people voluntarily use their own SP, they tend to interruptible. However, this might not be always the case if people use their SPs for business. To adapt the system to BYOD users, we will need to study ways to distinguish the purpose of the SP use.

6   Conclusion

We focused on the transitions between PC work, smartphone (SP) use, and walking and analyzed the relationship between interruptibility and these transitions. As a result, the following knowledge that might be useful for estimating the interruptibility of office workers was obtained.

(1) Interruptibility depends on the type of work that is done before and after a transition.
     Interruptibility at the transitions between PC work and walking is higher than at transitions between PC work and SP use.
(2) Interruptibility at PC work to SP use transitions is not always high.
(3) Interruptibility at transitions between PC work and SP use caused by notifications is lower than at self-transitions.
(4) The status of PC operations before a transition correlates with the interruptibility at the transition.

Our future work will include exploring new indices to detect high-interruptibility transitions and developing an estimation method based on the obtained indices.

Acknowledgements. This work was partly supported by funds from the Japan Society for the Promotion of Science (KAKENHI), funds for smart space technology toward a sustainable society from the Ministry of Education, Culture, Sports, Science and Technology, Japan, and funds from the National Institute of Information and Culture Technology.

References

1. Bailey, B.P., Joseph, A.K., John, V.C.: The effect of interruptions on task performance, annoyance, and anxiety in the user interface. In: Proceedings of the INTERACT, vol. 1, pp. 593–601 (2001)
2. Mark, G., Gonzalez, V.M., Harris, J.: No task left behind? Examining the nature of fragmented work. In: Proceedings of the SIGCHI Conference on Human Factors in Computing Systems, pp. 321–330. ACM, New York (2005)
3. Tanaka, T., Fukasawa, S., Takeuchi, K., Nonaka, M., Fujita, K.: Study of uninterruptibility estimation method for office worker during PC work. Inform. Process. Soc. Jpn. **53**(1), 126–137 (2012). (in Japanese)
4. Pielot, M., Oliveria, R., Kwak, H., Oliver, N.: Didn't you see my message? Predicting attentiveness to mobile instant messages. In: Proceedings of the CHI 2014, pp. 3319–3328 (2014)
5. Pejovic, V., Musolesi, M.: InterruptMe: designing intelligent prompting mechanisms for pervasive applications. In: Proceedings of the Ubicomp 2014, pp. 897–908 (2014)
6. Iqbal, S.T., Bailey, B.P.: Effects of intelligent notification management on users and their tasks. In: Proceedings of the SIGCHI, pp. 93–102 (2008)
7. Shirazi, A.S., Henza, N., Dingler, T., Pielot, M., Weber, D., Schmidt, A.: Large-scale assessment of mobile notifications. In: Proceedings of CHI 2014, pp. 3055–3064 (2014)
8. Brajdic, A., Harle, R.: Walk detection and step counting on unconstrained smartphones. In: Proceedings of the UbiComp 2013, pp. 225–234 (2014)
9. Skatova, A., Bedwell, B., Shipp, V., Huang, Y., Young, A., Rodden, T., Bertenshaw, E.: The role of ICT in office work breaks. In: Proceedings of the CHI 2016, pp. 3049–3060 (2016)
10. Tanaka, T., Fujita, K.: Study of user interruptibility estimation based on focused application switching. In: Proceedings of the CSCW, pp. 721–724 (2011)
11. Mark, G., Gudith, D., Klocke, U.: The cost of interrupted work: more speed and stress. In: Proceedings of the CHI 2008, pp. 107–110 (2008)

Derivation of Mobility Services Through the Usage-Centered Development Approach

Sigmund Schimanski[✉]

Faculty 6 – Electrical, Information and Media Engineering,
Chair of Automation/Computer Science,
Working Group: Human Factors Engineering,
University of Wuppertal, Rainer-Gruenter-Str. 21,
42119 Wuppertal, Germany
schimanski@uni-wuppertal.de

Abstract. Currently the digitization of processes often focuses on efficiency enhancement, productivity enhancement, individualization etc., i.e. on optimizing the min-max principle. Yet, there has been an economic paradigm shift in the last years. The complexity of the digitization makes the everyday use of technical systems, products or services considerably disadvantageous for users. Products do not fit into the users' familiar activity processes but rather stress them with additional secondary tasks.

By analysing the usage phases, it is possible to derive various service innovations according to the user requirements. In the course of this work, we identified a new approach for the structuring of development processes ("innovateurship") that will be evaluated and substantiated in further works. By establishing a normative development process in the fuzzy front end, we aim to optimise the efficiency of the development process.

Keywords: Usage centered development · Mobility services · Innovateur · Innovator · Innovateurship · Systems engineering · Perspective engineering · Requirements elicitation · SaaS · Platform · Software development · Transportation

1 Introduction

As a result of digitization, there are not only user requirements to be considered but also what the technical products require of the user. Thus, many solutions present an unappealing balance between expenses (e.g. transaction costs) and benefits. Additionally, companies partially pass on the development to the user because the concept expense is economically inefficient or difficult to assess due to need uncertainty – which prevents a rapid dissemination. This results in an enormous complexity and growing requirements in the early development stages (Verworn and Herstatt 2003). The usage-centred development approach (Schimanski 2016) identifies user requirements along the usage phases of a product (system, service, product), and serves as a tool for engineers in early development stages (Fig. 1). Engineers need this form of assistance to take mostly subject-specific, monodisciplinary requirements of the

© Springer International Publishing AG 2017
M. Kurosu (Ed.): HCI 2017, Part II, LNCS 10272, pp. 700–712, 2017.
DOI: 10.1007/978-3-319-58077-7_54

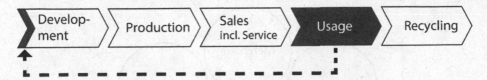

Fig. 1. Usage phases in the value chain (Schimanski 2016)

development (Schimanski 2013) into account, and to structure and reduce the conception phase.

2 Purpose

The self-developed focus on usage phases in the context of e-mobility was designed to create sustainable and complexity-reducing service solutions. The usage phases contain separate topics of technical system usage, which need to be considered for the conception of new system concepts. An open innovation survey is used to identify the beneficial potential for e-mobility services and to refine the usage-centred model. The aim is to offer developers a new tool for the reliable and repeatable identification of requirements and thus of beneficial potentials. The purpose is to open developers and engineers a new perspective for the development of usable and meaningful product solutions, since an internal and/or specialised point of view is often the only focus in development processes. Particularly in the early development phases, the so-called "Fuzzy Front End", the usage-centred development approach shall assist decision processes by providing usage-centred requirements in addition to technological possibilities.

Additionally, the results of the survey should provide further indications of the extent to which developers/engineers are able to use such an instrument, i.e. to what extent engineers are able to assess the results, and then use them for statements about relevance, feasibility or chances of success. Following the synthesis of the survey results, this matter was addressed in moderated focus group discussions with future engineers. This might offer new information on the requirements of engineering education in order to enable engineer students to act interdisciplinary and implementation-oriented.

3 Methodology

This investigation is based on the usage model according to Schimanski (2016), which has already provided results for further investigations within the context of mobility. The usage phases grounded in the usage model (Fig. 2) were used as representative items for the conveyed open innovation survey. They were primarily validated in a mobility context, and are grounded in the usage model. The usage phases are additionally used for an interdisciplinary scientific discourse in order to ensure a high degree of inter-subjectivity. The purpose of using the already validated items was to increase the reliability and repeatability of the qualitative empirical research.

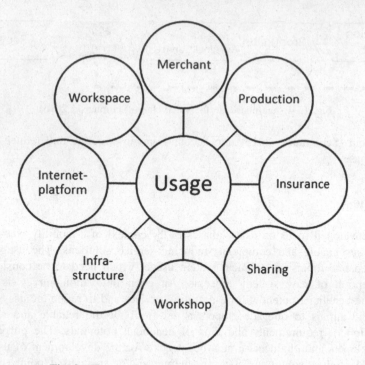

Fig. 2. Phases of the usage model (Schimanski 2016)

3.1 Objective

The objective of the open innovation survey is the collection of opinions, criticism and "innovative" (i.e. new) ideas with regards to mobility. By not using specific questions, the survey offers motorists as well as users of public transport the opportunity to freely express their thoughts and wishes on various keywords concerning topics such as individual transport, public transport and their interconnectivity. One focus is on integrating e-mobility into general transport. Text fields for free answers and only some basic guidelines are used in order to detect the aspects most relevant to the users. This survey method furthermore also encourages the participants to voice uncommon and innovative ideas without restrictions.

3.2 Structure of the Open Innovation Survey

The survey is broadly divided into four sections. The first section asks for demographic data and the used type of transport. Some are multiple-choice questions (e.g. "Please state your marital status"), others allow the statement of free answers (e.g. "In case you drive a car, which model is it").

The other three sections are structured in a similar fashion. They have a broad title in connection with various aspects/items and offer a large text field that the participants can use to write down their thoughts about the given combination. Additionally, there is a separate field for writing down ideas and thoughts that do not match the provided combinations. The three main titles are "Interconnected Mobility (Smart Mobility)", "Car Trade" and "Public Transport". There are also four concluding open questions about the connection between public transport and cycling.

3.3   Survey Participants

The online survey was conveyed over a period of two months. 32 participants between the age of 21 and 62 used all of the text fields to give sometimes quite extensive answers about their opinions and wishes. The participants were on average 34 years old with 31% of them being female. 88% owned a car with five of them being either an electric car or a hybrid.

3.4   Survey Evaluation

We used the statistic software IBM SPSS to evaluate the demographic data.

The analysis principles of problem-centred interviews and Grounded Theory (Witzel 2000) provided a guideline for an exact analysis of the open-ended comments. The objective of problem-centred interviews as well as of the open innovation survey is to record the subjective opinion of the participants. The interview guidelines as well as the survey questions work as an orientation guideline for the participants.

The aim of the Grounded Theory Method is the development of an empirically based theory, and was developed in the 1960s by Barney G. Glaser and Anselm L. Strauss as a qualitative analysis procedure (Truschkat et al. 2005). The Grounded Theory is a theory-generating method that does not determine steps for the operationalization in advance. Instead, its ex post evaluation is based on empirical frameworks, and follows a specified evaluation process. Thus, the results are not influenced by ex ante categorisations, which is crucial for an objective theoretical approach. Otherwise, the researchers could be accused of falsifying the results – or the method, the design of experiment, would be inconsistent and thus the result would be useless. "The grounded theory is a qualitative research method or methodology, which uses a systematic order or procedures to develop an inductively derived, grounded theory on a phenomenon" (Strauss and Corbin 1996, p. 8). The method is inductive and attempts to develop a theory by using methodical analysis. This procedure requires data that are mostly derived from interviews or observations. In this case the data are provided by the open innovation survey, which supports the procedure. The analysis consists of open coding, axial coding and selective coding.

The first step is the open coding. All relevant statements are divided into individual statements and assigned to a concept. The concepts are compared and categorised.

In a second step, the categories are axially coded – i.e. the categories are reasonably contextualised to show complete processes. This step is partially unnecessary for the evaluation of the open innovation survey, because the context is already provided by the three main titles of the subject sections. Nevertheless, it is necessary to examine whether there are further main topics desired or defined by the participants that the guideline did not take into account.

A third and final step, the selective coding, leads from the central categories to one or more basic statements that include all identified aspects.

The explorative procedure is in line with the aim of an unbiased, objective survey, and allows for the inclusion of new, innovative ideas.

3.5 Exploitation of the Survey Results

We presented the evaluation to a group of engineer students, who were asked to assess the results of the open innovation survey in various moderated sessions. The participants of this focus group are at least near the end of their bachelor's degree program (IT or electric engineering) with more than half of them being already with their master's degree programs. It was important that all participants had already absolved the majority of their studies in order to be at end of their education and just before entering the workplace. An additional criteria for selecting the students was their strong interest in research and development. The participants of this focus group will or are meant to already develop their first products in the coming years, or at least to support the development.

The reason for choosing this form of focus group was to implement a resource saving, "quick and easy" (Morgan 1997, p. 13) discourse procedure with fast and various results. As with the open innovation survey, a guideline is used for the focus group. The results of the open innovation survey provide the substantive guideline and were discussed consecutively within the group.

The evaluation of the results were limited to the group output (Schulz 2012, p. 17). It describes the various opinions and explanations given to the topics along the guideline. The evaluation considers only whether the participants came to results, and to what degree they match the previously made statements.

Group-specific processes and dynamic effects within the focus group are not investigated and thus not taken into account.

4 Results

The participants regarded the open innovation survey as a good opportunity to freely express their opinions about various broadly defined sections. The evaluation process allowed the detection of correlations and their categorisation into superordinate topics. These superordinate topics were sorted chronologically from the usage perspective and delimited accordingly. The results are presented in the following.

4.1 Interconnected Mobility

Individual mobility should be adjusted to the requirements of individual users, while public transport should be adjusted to the citizen's structure as well as the structural characteristics of the location. A paramount aspect is the request for a sensible connection of individual and public transport through Park & Ride parking, bike shelters and bicycle transport.

The form of interconnectivity depends mainly on the place of residence. Cities provide a great flexibility in public transport but charging facilities (garages, assigned parking spaces) for electric cars in residential areas are rare. The integration of electric vehicles into a smart-home-system is quite desired. Carsharing providers in residential areas are also generally missed.

The workplace should be easily reached by car and public transport alike. It also shouldn't be too far from the place of residence. Employers should support carpooling and carsharing. In the context of electric mobility, users expressed the desire for charging stations at the workplace and the support from employers in from of electric vehicle fleets or special leasing offers for employees.

A strongly criticised aspect is the charging infrastructure. There are too few charging stations in strategic locations, and charging times are considered to be too long. Prices were considered to be too high for electric vehicles as well as for combustion engines. The participants asked for a transparent price comparison system for petrol and charging stations, and furthermore for a financial support for environment-friendly electric mobility.

Payment systems for petrol and charging stations should be fast and standardized. Further important aspects in this context are data protection and optional payment methods without modern technology. There is also a general desire for a new information design that adjusts the route dynamically and in real time to traffic and current way of transport.

Type of mobility and interconnectivity should be adjusted to the individual user. While electric mobility is considered appropriate for every user group, some groups require certain adjustments – such as financial support for young users or adapted seat heights for senior citizens.

Generally, there is an expressed desire for a faster and easier interconnectivity between living and working spaces. Interconnectivity through Smart Mobility (apps, Smart Home) is considered appropriate if it allows better information and easier use of electric vehicles.

4.2   Car Trade

While some participants think that car dealers should focus on selling cars, others express the wish for something like a mobility dealer – someone who sells cars as well as electric vehicles, scooters, e-bikes and also packages in combination with public transport. The participants ask for fair offers and accommodation of individual customer requests. They also want honest and competent consultation. This consultation should not be mere sales talk and should also address more than one type of mobility.

Car rental should be fair, flexible and easy – including transparent rates as well as exact billing based on time, distance or consumption. Rental companies should provide various vehicles as well as additional features (e.g. child seats, trailers, bicycle racks).

All payment methods for purchase or rent should be available – yet high amounts of cash should be avoided. There should be various and clear financing options. One survey participant suggests to lower costs by making the own car available for rent.

The participants want unproblematic maintenance and repair services by the car dealer – including services for electric vehicles. Another request concerns a maintenance flat rate to avoid sudden high costs.

Insurance for electric vehicles should be cheaper and should also be included in rental prices. An advisable option is to offer full insurance package from one source.

The participants express various ideas with regards to full packages offered by car dealers – among them are combinations of car and public transport packages as well as flat rate for vehicle fleets (i.e. from van to bicycle). Overall, the participants can already imagine using their car in combination with other means of travel (public transport, bicycle) from the moment of purchase on.

4.3 Public Transport

In addition to convenient bus and train services – such as sale of beverages on busses/trains, umbrella rental, free Wi-Fi and comfortable, clean waiting areas – the participants desire uniform fares (for all provider of public transport) and options to plan complete routes. The coordination of departure times needs to be improved, especially since it is often problematic or impossible to change busses/trains directly due to delays. Furthermore, real-time information should be made available for smart phone as well as for clearly visible displays at each bus stop/station. Online tickets should be purchasable via smart phone and a uniform mobility-app should display travel information to-the-minute – including changes in stops, cancellations, delays etc. Train stations should provide carsharing, Park & Ride parking and secure bike shelters to support an interconnected mobility.

The participants generally consider public transport suitable for all user groups – as long as it is adjusted to certain circumstances: it requires accessibility, stops at frequent intervals, and a clear, efficient separation of passengers and luggage on long travels. Public transport should also support tourism with special tourist fares, package deals for hotels/organisers and information in all languages. The participants desire an extension of public transport to allow direct travel from one point to another without gaps.

4.4 Users Want Holistic Mobility Solutions

The survey results show a new requirement perspective on mobility that permeates cross-thematically: users want a preferably uniform solution for accessing mobility. However, that does not mean that they only want one "Google", "Facebook" or "Amazon", but they do desire one logic. The users want an interaction scheme within the diverse "many-to-many" mobility relationships. It is not important to them, whether the online presence they use belong to the railroad company, the city or to another mobility provider – the only thing that matters is that it works fast, uniformly, holistically, mobile and multimodal. Thus, users only demand the implementation of the opportunities that digitization and globalisation have made possible. But the users do not only want to adjust the digital world to their needs – they also want an adjustment of existing, real infrastructures to the digital world, e.g. regarding the usage and payment combination of individual and public transport. This also creates new business models and processes, e.g. "mobility flatrates". In the end it only matters that we arrive at our destination in a reasonable amount of time. Travel duration, availability, comfort and consistency define the transport fares. Nevertheless, users want thematically related, central platforms (PaaS and SaaS) that combine, summarize and structure solutions for their requirements in a suitable fashion.

4.5   Classification of the Results by Future Engineers

The above results of the open innovation survey were presented to the engineer student focus group. They were discussed in three of four meetings with an average of five participants, the moderator, a secretary and an additional observer. The fourth focus group meeting was not held, because the first three meetings already showed a clear pattern.

For the purpose of observing the students' assessments of the results, the moderator began each meeting with a short introduction, and then put the results up for discussion. It became obvious rather quickly that the assignment was very abstract, and that the students were only able to apply very few, if any, valuation criteria – with the exception of their own opinion on the results.

Thus, the moderator reacted shortly after starting the meeting, and began to create a real corporate situation. The moderator asked the participants to put themselves in the situation of an engineer working for the company's development department. Their task was to convince the management that their idea was beneficial, feasible, relevant and promising, and to name the necessary personal needed for the implementation along with their expertise. The main protagonists were exchanged for each result. The other group members supported, complemented and sporadically corrected the main protagonists. The staff present for the conduction detected a general, large uncertainty. The students didn't know how to deal with the abstract enquiry, and focused nearly exclusively on their own skills in the subsequent action example. The participants mainly named necessary staff members in their own field, regardless of the question. The electrical engineer believed that the implementation fell into his domain – so did the computer scientist and the information technologist.

In addition to their own skills, the students named marketing as a necessary element for the implementation of ideas. The investigators realised after two of four focus group meetings that the future engineers would not proceed differently. They students regarded the development process from an egocentric perspective and were incapable to differentiate even in a group with members of a variety of disciplines. The investigator held the third meeting without making adjustments, or changing the criteria for the assessment of the survey results. The reconfirmation convinced the investigators that further runs would not bring about any changes.

The result of the focus group is that the focus group came up with a similar approach for each question. It must be taken into account that the focus group members were only able to perform a form of "cognitive walkthrough" by the intervention of the moderator. Only the specific example of a potential future work situation enabled the students to assess the user-specific survey results.

The statements regarding relevance, feasibility and chances of success were only nearly exclusively made from a technical point of view. The statement that chances of success were the responsibility of the marketing and not the engineering department was made even several times. The investigators deliberately refrained from steering the conversations into a certain direction to avoid that the rapidly successive tasks would result in learning effects.

4.6 Practical Implications

According to this, the potentials of the results can not be exploited by inexperienced students about to enter the workplace. They can only appropriately assess the technical feasibility of wishes that are technically implementable. But in order to assess – or even help shaping – the increasingly complex systems of digitization and the related digital and hybrid value chains, it is necessary to further adjust the engineer education in the short or long term, and to pursue interdisciplinary approaches. Universities in particular – in addition to vocational education facilities – face the respective challenge that cannot resolve itself, and thus requires new interdisciplinary and constructivist learning concepts (Reich 2012) that request an independent/practical elaboration of knowledge.

If it is possible to teach engineers the procedure of modern business models and processes, and how to synthesize beneficial potentials and how to correlate all of them, the engineers are able to make their first own simple decisions already in early development stages and/or take requirements into account or reject them.

The skill to effectively and efficiently assess ideas right from the start is currently no component of teaching. Thus, there is currently no respective recommendation or methodology that allows to derive requirements for the development of products, systems or services reliably, objectively and reproducibly, and to asses them directly so that they can withstand the inclusion of economic aspects.

In contrast to invention (Schumpeter 1912) – which only includes the idea, the problem solution, i.e. the creation of something new – this identified but yet undefined skill and the related new type of engineer should proceed according to a specific procedure in order to objectively asses the invention in the fastest and most cost-efficient manner. On the other hand, this new type of engineer will not be responsible for the marketable implementation and commercial exploitation of the positively assessed and prototypically implemented invention. This type of engineer is thus not to be equated to the entrepreneur (Bull and Willard 1993), who is responsible for the external economical exploitation, nor to the intrapreneur (Antoncic and Hisrich 2003), who is responsible for the further internal development and optimization of the invention. Intrapreneurship is defined as "a spirit of entrepreneurship within the existing organization" (Hisrich and Peters 1995).

Inventors are rarely also subtypes – if so, it is usually a coincidence (Schumpeter 1912, pp. 122–24). From here on, this type of engineer between inventor and entrepreneur will be referred to as the "innovateur".

The assessment of ideas regarding various, mainly economical aspects also cannot be asked of the user. Like the specialists, the user is far too monodisciplinary – at least interdisciplinarity cannot be assumed. Also, the average user does not have the technical know-how, the state-of-the-art technology, competitive information or information about potential internal problems regarding the development. All participants of the research lacked different information, experiences or methods to give reliable statements on the identified, potential new solutions.

Thus, the developer is responsible for the assessment. The developer has to be able to understand the overall structure of the idea, and to view the development process from various perspectives. An "innovateur" should be able to consider the technical perspective as well as usage-centred and commercial perspective. It should always begin with the usage in order to consider the real user requirements objectively and to avoid any restrictions of the development process by applying other perspectives already at the beginning.

5 Conclusion

5.1 Derivation of Mobility Services

Mobility changes continuously. Its necessity and social relevance makes it a rapid and intensively changing field. The results of the open innovation survey provide information alterations the user desire for a practical everyday use of mobility.

Overall, users accept the complexity and variability of mobility. In the age of digitization, they wish for comprehensive mobility solutions, uniform payment terms as well as matured infrastructure, insurance and legal concepts. The participants demand new, clear and nationwide standardised regulations in various fields. In addition to regulations for autonomous driving and data security for car rental, the participants demand a minimum of charging stations in cities and the enforcement of parking prohibition at charging stations. Putting up charging stations and passing on electricity to others should be made easier. All in all, the participants strive for an interconnectivity of individual transport, including bicycles and public transport, in order to simplify the mobility and make travelling more practical. Mobility planning should include electric vehicles and new systems, such as carsharing.

The answers given by the users increasingly target new business models that transform or unify existing structures, and which support uniform multimodal platform solutions.

Geo-based service platforms with the frameworks mentioned by the users should continue to present a research focus for the research group Human Factors Engineering. In addition to new usage-centred route algorithms, the group investigates the usability of front and backend, booking modalities and payment terms of multimodal service systems as well as the inclusion of small providers. The currently initiated research contents target an intensive anaylsis of Big Data, Data Mining, and "Software as a Service" (SaaS). As a result, the groups analyses the effect of digital transformation on existing business models, and what kind of holistic structure is needed to make digital business models successful.

5.2   Development with Beneficial Potentials

Generating and evaluating usage-centred requirements in the context of mobility is not a problem. It also helped to acquire enlightening information and the identification of beneficial potentials for actors in that industry. The field-specific and nearly exclusively technical group output, shown in the course of the follow-up investigation about the assessment of the synthesized results of future engineers, identified a high demand. A gap exists between the invention, which is mainly awarded to the inventor, and the innovation that is independently or internally driven by the entrepreneur/intrapreneur. This gap can only be closed by the "innovateur" and their skills. Evaluating ideas – whether they were derived from a usage-centred or other perspective – according to market sensitive criteria requires the targeted teaching of interdisciplinary contents during the vocational education. Currently, the technical and economical perspective makes industrial engineering the best suitable study program for establishing a new focus in the short and medium term. Thus, it should strengthen the bridge between engineering and economics. A high level of understanding business models and processes are of crucial importance for developers in order to establish or reject ideas and requirements at an early stage.

The "Innovateurship Approach" (Fig. 3) shows the procedural gap between invention and innovation in form of a "blackbox". To develop innovations more

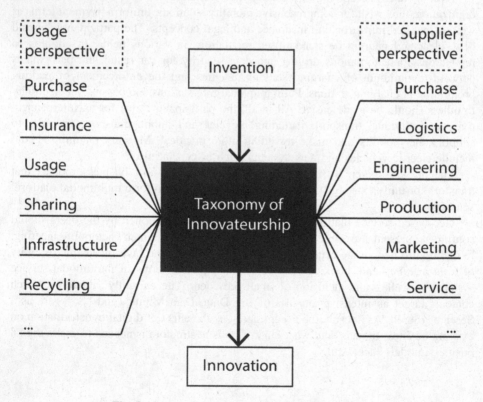

Fig. 3. Innovateurship approach (Schimanski 2017)

effectively and efficiently in the long term, engineers need a scheme that classifies ideas and proposals for solutions according to various criteria. It is presumed that the usage perspective and the provider perspective will influence the "blackbox".

Forthcoming investigations have to examine which further interdisciplinary skills/criteria are conductive to holistic and sustainable developments, and in which form. This allows to gradually decode and structure the "blackbox" and to make it available to engineers in form of a digital assistance system.

The results will gradually be integrated into the educational concept "Innovateur-ship" as a new focus in industrial engineering.

The long-term objective is to form a useful taxonomy for evaluating usage-centred requirements, and to strengthen it through a gradual, iterative, qualitative and quantitative empirical process, and to ground it into teaching.

References

Antoncic, B., Hisrich, R.D.: Clarifying the intrapreneurship concept. J. Small Bus. Enterp. Dev. **10**(1), 7–24 (2003)

Bull, I., Willard, G.E.: Towards a therory of entrepreneurship. J. Bus. Ventur. **8**(3), 183–195 (1993). Elsevier, Amsterdam, Netherlands

Hisrich, R.D., Peters, M.P.: Entrepreneurship: Starting, Developing, and Managing a New Enterprise, 4th edn. Irwin, Chicago (1998)

Morgan, D.L.: Focus Groups as Qualitative Research. Sage Publications, Thousand Oaks (1997)

Rasmussen, J.: Information Processing and Human-Machine Interaction. North-Holland, New York (1986)

Reich, K.: Konstruktivistische Didaktik: Das Lehr-und Studienbuch Mit Online-Methodenpool. Beltz, Weinheim (2012)

Schimanski, S.: Usage phases in the development of product systems exemplified by a route recommendation scheme for cyclists. In: Kurosu, M. (ed.) HCI 2016. LNCS, vol. 9733, pp. 331–342. Springer, Cham (2016). doi:10.1007/978-3-319-39513-5_31

Schimanski, S.: (2013) Production ergonomics – analysis methodology for human-system-integration in teamwork. In: Experimental Industrial Psychology IV: Human-Computer-Interaction, Proceedings of 16th EAWOP Congress – European Association of Work and Organizational Psychology, Münster

Schulz, M.: Quick and easy!? Fokusgruppen in der angewandten Sozialwissenschaft. In: Schulz, M., Mack, B., Renn, O. (eds.) Fokusgruppen in der Empirischen Sozialwissenschaft, pp. 9–22. VS Verlag für Sozialwissenschaften, Wiesbaden (2012)

Schumpeter, J.A.: Theorie der Wirtschaftlichen Entwicklung, Duncker & Homblot, Leipzig (1912)

Strauss, A., Corbin, J.: Grounded Theory: Grundlagen Qualitativer Sozialforschung. Beltz, Psychologie Verlags Union, Weinheim (1996)

Truschkat, I., Kaiser, M., Reinartz, V.: Forschen nach Rezept? Anregungen zum praktischen Umgang mit der Grounded Theory in Qualifikationsarbeiten. Forum: Qualitative. Soc. Res. **6** (2), 18 (2005). Art. 22. http://www.qualitative-research.net/index.php/fqs/article/view/470/1007

Verworn, B., Herstatt, C.: Prozessgestaltung der frühen Phasen. In: Herstatt, C., Verworn, B. (eds.) Management der Frühen Innovationsphasen, pp. 195–214. Gabler Verlag, Wiesbaden (2003)

Witzel, A.: The problem-centered interview. Forum: Qual. Soc. Res. **1**(1) (2000). http://www.qualitative-research.net/index.php/fqs/article/view/1132/2519

Agenda Planning - Design Guidelines for Holistic Mobility Planning

Tobias Wienken[✉], Heidi Krömker, and Sebastian Spundflasch

Ilmenau University of Technology, Ilmenau, Germany
{tobias.wienken,heidi.kroemker,
sebastian.spundflasch}@tu-ilmenau.de

Abstract. In view of new challenges, the boundaries of current travel planning systems are discussed and the need for holistic mobility planning becomes clear. The agenda planning approach frees passengers from the expensive single trip planning and leads to holistic planning based on the intentions behind mobility, such as daily appointments and to-dos of users. This research addresses a definition of agenda planning and describes its importance with respect to human-computer interaction as well as mobile passenger information systems. In detail, the article discusses the challenges for usability and user experience and furthermore presents a set of seven design guidelines that can support developers in developing mobile agenda planning applications.

Keywords: Agenda planning · Holistic mobility planning · User-centered design · Design guidelines

1 Introduction

Every day people travel 79 min and 39 km to deal with their daily affairs [1], for activities such as work, doctors' meetings, concerts, shopping, etc. Therefore, these activities are mostly combined with each other. Currently, in order to manage the mobility need for daily routine, passengers have to fall back on time-consuming manual trip planning, meaning they have to determine and calculate every single trip. In addition to mobility planning, passengers must also consult further sources of information to complete their affairs, e.g. opening hours of shops. These planning activities increase the workload for passengers additionally as well as the introduction of various means of transport for an intermodal journey, like carpooling and bike-sharing. In view of the emerging challenges, the boundaries of current travel planning systems will be discussed and the need for holistic mobility planning will become clear. As does the fact that passenger information systems have to be refined. The agenda planning approach combines mobility planning with personal daily routine planning. Passengers will be freed from single trip planning by automated features and can focus on reasons for mobility, such as appointments and to-dos.

Since the introduction of smartphones, practitioners and researchers have achieved a good understanding of the requirements in terms of usability and user experience in standard mobile passenger information applications. However, the agenda approach aims to integrate information about user activities and their environment as additional

© Springer International Publishing AG 2017
M. Kurosu (Ed.): HCI 2017, Part II, LNCS 10272, pp. 713–720, 2017.
DOI: 10.1007/978-3-319-58077-7_55

input for mobility planning. In doing so, context information can be leveraged to expand the planning process. These additional features create new challenges in developing user-centered mobility planning applications. Therefore this research discusses the implications of agenda planning for human-computer interaction.

2   Research Procedure

The research addresses a paradigm shift within the field of mobility planning and introduces the agenda planning approach. Within this paper, the authors define the agenda planning approach and describe its importance to human-computer interaction and mobile passenger information systems. In detail, the article discusses challenges for usability and user experience and furthermore presents a set of seven design guidelines that can support developers in producing mobile agenda planning applications.

The presented results were achieved in a research project funded by the German Federal Ministry for Economic Affairs and Energy (BMWi). The initial point for the entire development project was the future users of the agenda planning system. Based on a user-centered design process, a mobile agenda planning application was developed within several iterations. Finally, the prototype was tested by a field evaluation in the service area of South Lower Saxony transport association in Germany.

In total, 25 test persons took part in the evaluation. Within the test, each participant was faced with identical tasks. The tasks included the planning and execution of a complete agenda with the mobile application by using public transport. In order to gain comprehensive insights, a set of methods were used in the test: usability testing, user observations, retrospective thinking aloud and semi-structured interviews. The results presented in this paper refer to the summary and interpretation of collected data across all methods.

3   Agenda Planning Approach

As mentioned in the beginning, the traditional journey planning approach for public transport is limited by manual trip planning. The approach focusses only on a single connection instead of the holistic interplay, such as all trips on one day. Additionally, actual reasons for the need of mobility remain totally unregarded, like appointments and tasks. But from a user point of view, particularly this holistic interplay between mobility offerings and appointments as well as to-dos influences the mobility experience.

In order to address challenges of the approach, the agenda planning combines information of mobility planning and daily routine planning. In contrast to traditional trip planning, where users are entering data for every individual trip from A to B, users plan and enter only their appointments and to-dos within the agenda planning approach. In doing so the agenda planning system calculates and optimizes the route of a defined period as whole. Finally, the system provides users the daily routine with

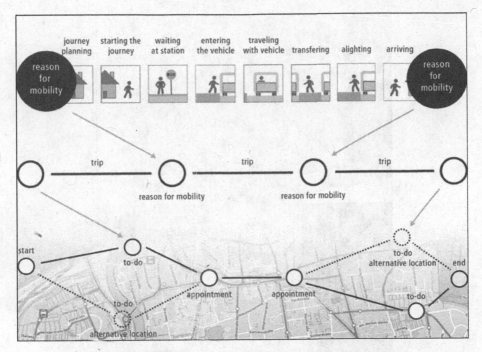

Fig. 1. Structure of agenda based on the journey chain (journey chain cf. [4])

their personal appointments, to-dos and all single trips at once, the so-called agenda. Based on the merging of mobility and daily routine planning, the approach can reduce the complexity and workload of the planning process by combining user tasks and using automation [2] (Fig. 1).

> *Agenda planning is defined as a holistic mobility planning approach that integrates the mobility into the daily routine planning. Passengers focus on planning their appointments and to-dos for the considered period and an optimal route along all appointments and to-dos is determined by the system.*

Structure of an Agenda

From a bottom up perspective, the agenda is based on the journey chain. This chain consists of journey stages through public transport, and presents the passengers activities with specific information needs assigned to corresponding locations [3]. In addition to the journey chain, an agenda includes the reasons behind the mobility need, such as a commuter wants to withdraw money for shopping or a tourist meets his friend in a restaurant. Moreover, the considered period is enlarged and contains several user activities and trips at once. The activities can be distinguished into appointments and to-dos. Based on different properties, the appointments form the basic structure of an agenda and the temporal as well as spatial flexible to-dos are used to optimize free time slots of the daily routine (cf. [2]) (Fig. 2).

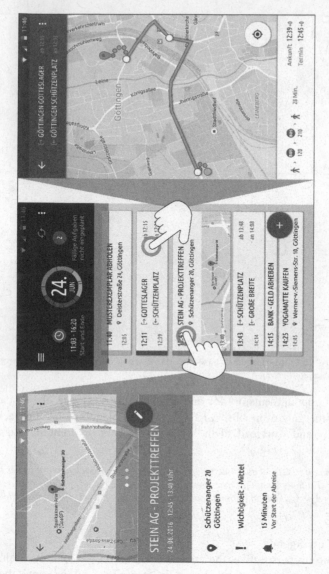

Fig. 2. Agenda planning application – implementation of the research project

4 Results

The presented results are based on iterative user tests during the mentioned research project and its final field evaluation. The objective was to investigate utility, usability and user experience when the passengers were using the mobile agenda planning application. Within the tests, positive and negative aspects were identified and then assessed regarding their impacts. This analysis was the basis for the subsequent classification. In this article, the categories are presented by the challenges for usability and user experience. In order to derive the insights from the empirical study, guidelines can be used as an appropriate method to communicate the recorded best practices to designers [5]. In the research project, the authors derived a set of design guidelines to address the issues regarding user interface and interaction design. The guidelines are oriented on the identified challenges for usability and user experience.

4.1   Challenges for Usability and User Experience

In contrast to a traditional trip planning system, an agenda also includes the information of a daily routine and so users must gather and process data of both disciplines at the same time. Additionally, users must deal with the increasing data volume on a limited display (**information overflow**). Besides data expansion, the combination introduces users to numerous variation possibilities. For example, after agenda calculation the user has to assess several different schedules, each with a unique sequence of to-dos and trips.

Agreeing with Dey and Häkkilä [6], the results show that a **lack of user control** occurs in automation on mobile devices, especially during the automated calculation of an agenda and the proactive execution of agenda re-organization. To visualize this phenomenon, the focus should be set on users with high knowledge of the location and mobility system. They partially tend to choose their favorite bus lines by themselves and want to intervene in the automated trip calculation. As shown in the example, the lack of user control is related to **imbalance of automated and user-initiated actions.**

Furthermore, **complexity of software** challenges the user. This occurs due to combination of both planning disciplines, what results in an increasing number of functionality. At the same time, a functional merger is required to implement the new mobility planning paradigm, forcing the users to create new planning routines. Based on these insights, the need of a framework for the planning process, suitable for the user's tasks and learning, becomes clear.

Several functionalities of an agenda planning application are based on the user's context. Context characterizes a user's situation focusing on persons, places or objects that are considered relevant during conducting an agenda (cf. [7]), such as a business partner who postpones an appointment and a delayed bus that causes a late arrival or supermarket with special opening hours. The user context is highly dynamic and difficult to understand completely for users. From the user's point of view, the **lack of context awareness** can lead to incomprehensible and unexpected system reactions.

Most passengers consider the extension of the mobility planning service as a plus point. But on the other hand the required integration of personal data causes uncertainty and distrust among users. For example, not only individually used connections become visible for system providers, but also the mobility behaviour of passengers over the entire day with all visited shops, bank branches and so on. Therefore user acceptance of an application is strongly related to the issues of **data privacy**.

4.2   Design Guidelines for Agenda Planning

Consider Agenda Planning Process
Agenda planning enable the integration of mobility into the daily routine planning and leads to a holistic planning process. Thereby users are faced with high complexity. They have to execute actions from various planning areas in certain sequence and must adapt their existing routines.

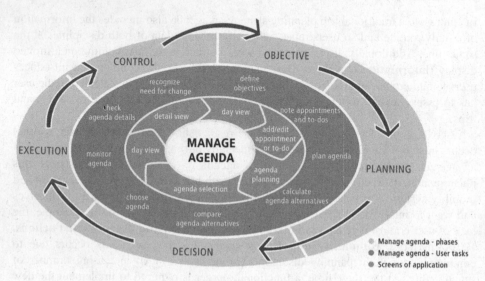

Fig. 3. Agenda planning process

► Allow users to perform the tasks according to the sequence and manner of their time planning behaviour (Fig. 3).

Present Information Tailored to User's Situation
Users are faced with a huge amount and high diversity of information based on the task combination of mobility and daily routine planning.

► Use timeline metaphor and various levels of detail to structure, reduce and focus on situated information needs of the users.

Provide Transparent Agenda Compositions
An agenda holistically controls the interplay of appointments, to-dos and trips. The agenda calculation is a complex optimization and often incomprehensible for users. Particularly, when the number of to-dos with temporal and spatial flexible properties increases.

► Explain optimization decisions done by the system within the agenda calculation in transparent and self-descriptive way. Users should understand the logic of the agenda compositions.

Balance Agenda Adaptations

Daily routines and mobility are constantly subjects to change, such as through postponements and delays in public transport. Based on these changes, an agenda has to adapt. However, every agenda adaptation interrupts the planned daily routine and leads to uncertainty and stress for the user.

► Avoid unnecessary short-term adaptations of the agenda.

Ensure Agenda Control

Based on the adaptive and automated system behavior, the user is faced with a lack of control. The desire to take control occurs when the system is executing erroneous actions, users want to correct a planned activity or just wishes to feel in control [6].

► Enable the user to easily take control of the planned appointments, to-dos and trips as well as of the agenda re-organization.

Offer Agenda Individualization

Users have usually a rough day's schedule and individual preferences in mind, e.g. at what time they want to complete the matters at the bank branch. These ideas vary from user to user and are based on their individual experiences and needs.

► To meet the users' expectations, offer possibilities to integrate individual preferences into the calculation of an agenda composition.

Consider User's Privacy

An agenda records the entire daily routine of a user, day after day. In this procedure, the system stores and processes a huge amount of personal data about the habits and preferences of the users.

► Allow users to configure the processing of personal data in order to ensure user's trust and acceptance.

5 Conclusion

Agenda planning enables the integration of mobility into the daily routine planning. The combined planning approach allows user to consider and plan their mobility needs as a whole. Thereby the passenger benefits from the holistic planning. For example, the planning effort for users will be reduced and user can better deal with unforeseeable incidents, like disturbances in bus traffic. From the user's perspective, the potentials of an agenda planning application becomes particularly visible, if the user is not familiar with the local conditions or has only limited knowledge about the mobility system.

Despite the active research in the field of human-computer interaction and mobility, holistic mobility planning approaches have hardly been investigated scientifically. More particularly, there exist numerous issues regarding the design for usability and user experience. Towards understanding of design space, in this research the authors have discussed the concept of agenda planning and pointed out a definition. Based on the research, the authors derived generic challenges for passengers during the usage of an agenda planning application on mobile phones. With those insights, a set of guidelines was developed to enable more useable and useful applications. Due the novelty of the field, the guidelines should increase the designer's awareness of the difficulties in developing agenda planning applications. Furthermore, the guidelines should also support the developers in order to take appropriate design decisions.

Acknowledgements. Part of this work was funded by the German Federal Ministry for Economic Affairs and Energy (BMWi) grant number 19P12013B within the DynAPSys project. The DynAPSys project developed an agenda planning system for individual task and mobility planning from "door to door".

References

1. Robert Follmer, R., Gruschwitz, D., Jesske, B., Quandt, S., Lenz, B., Nobis, C., Köhler, K., Mehlin, M.: Mobilität in Deutschland 2008. Ergebnisbericht. Struktur – Aufkommen – Emissionen – Trends. Technical report (2008)
2. Wienken, T., Mayas, C., Hörold, S., Krömker, H.: Model of mobility oriented agenda planning. In: Kurosu, M. (ed.) HCI 2014. LNCS, vol. 8512, pp. 537–544. Springer, Cham (2014). doi:10.1007/978-3-319-07227-2_51
3. Verband Deutscher Verkehrsunternehmen (VDV): Telematics in Public Transport in Germany. Alba Fachverlag, Düsseldorf (2001)
4. Hörold, S., Mayas, C., Krömker, H.: Analyzing varying environmental contexts in public transport. In: Kurosu, M. (ed.) HCI 2013. LNCS, vol. 8004, pp. 85–94. Springer, Heidelberg (2013). doi:10.1007/978-3-642-39232-0_10
5. Shneiderman, B., Plaisan, C.: Designing the User Interface: Strategies for Effective Human-Computer Interaction. Addison Wesley, Boston (2004)
6. Dey, A.K., Häkkilä, J.: Context-awareness and mobile devices. In: Mobile Computing: Concepts, Methodologies, Tools, and Applications, p. 14. IGI-Global, Hershey (2009). doi:10.4018/978-1-60566-054-7.ch238
7. Abowd, G.D., Dey, A.K., Brown, P.J., Davies, N., Smith, M., Steggles, P.: Towards a better understanding of context and context-awareness. In: Gellersen, H.-W. (ed.) HUC 1999. LNCS, vol. 1707, pp. 304–307. Springer, Heidelberg (1999). doi:10.1007/3-540-48157-5_29

Refining Supervisory Control Capability for Target User Populations

Robert E. Wray[⊠], Randolph Jones, Charles Newton,
and Ben Bachelor

Soar Technology, Inc., 3600 Green Court Suite 600, Ann Arbor, MI 48105, USA
{wray, rjones, charles.newton,
ben.bachelor}@soartech.com

Abstract. In designing and developing intelligent automation systems, there is often tension between the computational capabilities of the automated system and its usability and understandability. This paper presents a case study in which this tension was manifest and how we attempted to resolve it in a particular application. The application requires intelligent automation in distributed simulation for training. We describe an initial approach to such control, feedback we received from potential users, and a revision to the capability that eliminated some features but that was more acceptable to the user community. This case study may offer some observations and lessons applicable to other domains, especially in situations where penetration of a technology into everyday use is driven by informal user adoption criteria (transparency, trust, perceived usability) alongside formal functional requirements.

Keywords: Supervisory control · Simulation-based training · Requirements analysis and design · Interaction design

1 Introduction

Automation technologies are playing larger and more important roles in the lives of much of world's population. Aircraft largely fly themselves; soon automobiles may also be controlled in the main by automation. Industrial systems and processes are also becoming increasingly automated. Via networks, cloud-based data, and every-present controllers (like a smartphone), everyday tasks in the industrialized countries also are becoming more automated: computer assistants find information, schedule meetings and resolve conflicts, etc.

In designing and developing automation systems, there can be tension between the computational capabilities of an automated system and its usability and understandability by users [2, 3]. This tension is especially important for supervisory control applications, where a user sets conditions and preferences for the goals and performance of the automation and then the automation attempts to carry out its tasks, according to those conditions, which the user can adjust, override, or change during execution [4, 5]. In the examples introduced above, although the conditions for performance and the frequency of interaction differ, they all require the user's on-going

© Springer International Publishing AG 2017
M. Kurosu (Ed.): HCI 2017, Part II, LNCS 10272, pp. 721–731, 2017.
DOI: 10.1007/978-3-319-58077-7_56

interactions with the automation system to carry out tasks successfully, at least from the point of view of the user.

From a human-machine systems perspective, the automation system fulfills its purpose only to the extent it automates the execution of some task (flying the aircraft) and that it does so in the service of its users goal (e.g., staying within standard flight lanes, maintain a smooth flight while minimizing fuel use, etc.). In other words, the application of automation does not necessarily lead to increased task effectiveness. Users may both overly rely on automation and fail to use ("disuse") automation what it could support improved task performance [2]. Models and empirical studies provide useful design guidance [5–7] but finding a resolution to this tension for some new, specific application is seen as more art than science [8].

This paper presents a case study of a manifestation of this tension and how we attempted to resolve it in a particular application. The application requires supervisory control in distributed simulation for training. Below, we describe the problem that the automation was seeking to address and then introduce an initial approach, which we term *Dynamic Tailoring,* that addressed the functional requirements successfully. However, as we provided demonstrations and prototypes to potential users, we discovered that some of the functional requirements our analysis had identified were, in practice, less of a priority than the user's ability to customize, understand and trust the automated systems.

In response, we developed a significantly different capability that eliminated some features but that privileged usage requirements over some of the original functional requirements. This second capability, which we call the Scenario Director, was more acceptable to the user community and led to adoption, even though its ability to adapt scenarios is both less autonomous and less informed by learner state than the original Dynamic Tailoring prototype. The case study may offer some relevant observations and lessons applicable to other domains, especially in situations where penetration of the technology into everyday use is driven as much by informal user adoption criteria than formal functional requirements.

2 Dynamic Adaptation of Simulation Scenarios

Simulation offers a number of advantages over live training, especially for domains where repeated practice is expensive. When simulation-based training requires the presence of actors other than the trainee, simulated role-players (constructive entities, semi-automated forces, human behavior models, etc.) often are deployed to provide a reasonably realistic simulation of the interactive environments in which training occurs. These simulated role-players are typically designed to provide realistic but common/routine behavior within the context of a training simulation. For example, in tactical aviation training, a simulated "red" entity might present realistic tactics that a "blue" human pilot might expect to see in some real-world setting.

It is common, however, for a training simulation or exercise to require more of simulated role-players than typical or routine behaviors. Table 1, summarizing a more thorough analysis [9], lists situations where typical behaviors fall short of meeting the full spectrum of requirements. Typically, this gap leads to one of two outcomes:

Table 1. Scenario requirements not met by typical approaches to simulated role-players.

Requirement		Description
1	Narrative coherence	A trainee's decisions and actions in the scenario can result in a situation where the pre-defined goals of simulated role-players are no longer rational (e.g., positioning a tanker to refuel aircraft that have been inadvertently eliminated). A scenario should adapt to ensure that the future events within a scenario are consistent with past ones [10]
2	Target training goals	The trainee's behavior early in the training scenario can lead to a situation where a specific training opportunity designed for the training scenario cannot be satisfied by simulated role-players. A scenario should ensure that the trainee can undertake practice for specific training goals
3	Adapt to trainee skill and proficiency	A training scenario can be poorly matched to an individual trainee's current level of skill, potentially resulting in frustration (too hard) or boredom (too easy). Scenarios should attempt to meet (or slight exceed) each trainee's current level of capability (i.e., the "zone of proximal development" [11])
4	Conform to scenario and range constraints	In many cases, non-tactical behavioral constraints may be important for a scenario (e.g., rules for maintaining safety of flight in an LVC scenario). Scenarios should be able to enforce these constraints on participants, including simulated role-players

1. **Introduction of human intervention and control:** Human simulation operators are used to control and to direct the low-level behaviors of simulated role-players. This approach greatly increases the cost of simulation-based training, mitigating some of the advantage of using simulation rather than live training.
2. **Reduced training effectiveness:** In the absence of human control, training simulation may introduce unrealistic behavior (and potentially negative training) and may be inefficient (the resulting simulation does not provide the desired training opportunity). This approach also introduces additional costs at the systems level, manifest in either increased training (greater time on task) or reduced operational capability (trainees graduating with reduced average skill).

The requirements in Table 1 are requirements for a training scenario that is presented, rather than a requirement for any individual role-player in that scenario. We use the term *dynamic scenario adaptation* to refer to technical approaches for meeting such requirements. As summarized in [9], there are many architectural approaches and algorithms that could be used to realize dynamic scenario adaptation. In the next section, we introduce an initial approach that attempted to address all these requirements.

3 Trainee-Focused, Autonomous Scenario Adaptation

Having identified the requirements outlined in Table 1, we developed a prototype capability designed to address them. The high-level architectural approach is summarized in Fig. 1. This design pattern derives from the use of director agents in computer games [12, 13] and is here termed the *Director Architecture*. There are two primary components, a recognition component that identifies when and what change in the scenario is needed and then a direction and control component that interfaces to the simulation to modulate events. Because simulated role-players are such a critical component of these systems, the design pattern calls out the

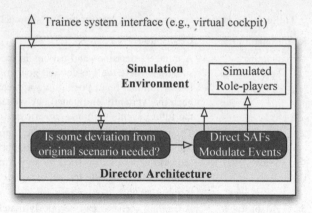

Fig. 1. The director architecture design pattern.

specific need in a functional system to control and to direct these role-players. The target result is a software capability that functionally acts similarly to the way an operator acts, taking control of a simulated role-player and over-riding its "native" behavior. One advantage of this approach, over different architectural approaches, is that it does not require significant changes to existing (and sometimes validated) libraries of behaviors of simulated role-players [9].

We had previously developed a software capability that instantiated this director design pattern with a particular focus on adaptation based on training need and trainee capability [14]. This *Dynamic Tailoring System* embeds a learner proficiency model to adapt and to customize scenario based on observer learner skill [15] and includes an explicit representation of a training scenario narrative [10] to enable adaptation for narrative coherence. Because training scenarios unfold in real time and instructors in many domains interact with students within the training context, the Dynamic Tailoring System is intended to be largely autonomous during scenario execution; instructors configure the system for the scenario and encode preferences for choices and then the system attempts to satisfy those preferences during scenario execution without requiring or relying on instructor control during execution.

We applied this capability to the tactical air training domain and showed it could be used to adapt realistic training scenarios to the requirements summarized in Table 1 [1]. Figure 2 illustrates the software implementation of the prototype. The Monitor and Pedagogical Manager components realize the recognition of when adaptation is needed and the Experience Manager undertakes actions in response to recognition, including both direct manipulations of events in the simulation as well as directing individual entities. The algorithms within these components depend on a number of data stores, most notably an assessment model (designed to determine how "correct" a trainee's actions are) and a proficiency model to track performance over time.

Given the potential complexity of the Fig. 2 system, it was designed to be configured and controlled by users via a series of high-level scenario-adaptation settings. For example, potential action choices of the Experience Manager could be labeled according to how directly helpful an action was, how simple or complex it was, and if

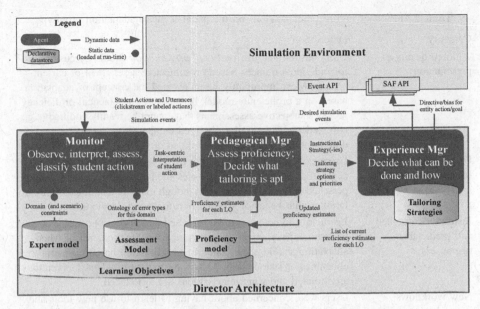

Fig. 2. Dynamic tailoring software design (adapted from [1]).

reflected a frequent/typical action or observation in the environment or an atypical/infrequent one. The motivation for this labeling was to enable the system to make choices according to an instructor's tailoring preferences without requiring an instructor to specify and to configure individual tailoring choices. In subsequent work in another domain, with different instructional goals and requirements, this approach was shown to enable instructors and other representative users to customize and configure a training scenario in about a day of effort [16].

4 Refining Requirements Based on User Feedback

In the tactical-air training domain, however, this approach, while functionally suffi-cient, introduced a number of concerns in the user community. Table 2 summarizes feedback we received as we demonstrated the Dynamic Tailoring prototype to potential users and simulation-system stakeholders. These comments suggest that potential users were concerned with both a lack of transparency [7] and usability [17]. Because we were not able to conduct formal and sustained user testing, it is not clear if greater familiarity would have resulted in the development of greater trust with experience, which is sometimes the case [18]. Generally, the users acknowledged that the scenario adaptation capability fulfilled a need but that the complexity of the solution introduced new requirements on users that would have made it difficult and rare to use (and meet the scenario adaptation need) in practice.

Most importantly, in this domain, a simulation operator is typically present during training to customize the training experience for the trainee, based on guidance from the instructor. Thus, to a significant extent, the limitation of the initial prototype was its

Table 2. Feedback and recommendations on the initial scenario-adaptation prototype

Category	Description
Tailored quality of presentation	Users desired that the *quality of presentation* should be customized for individual trainees based on subjective assessment of current actions. Most importantly, users resisted the concept of adaptation based on a proficiency model, because a pilot's tactical proficiency includes subjective assessments that cannot be readily codified (e.g., two students with similar observed competencies might receive different real-time interventions based on instructor judgment alone)
Direct behavioral responses	Users expressed a preference for direct specification of what behavioral responses should be presented in specific situations. They persisted in this preference even though many potential users are not familiar with behavior specification tools and development
Instructor-controlled and predictable responses	Instructors do not want to be surprised during the course of scenario execution. They expressed preference for direct control of when adaptation should occur, rather than adaptation based on narrative coherence or learner skill. They want to control when interventions are initiated and what interventions are introduced
New workflows	Users were concerned about having to learn to use new tools and develop new processes and workflows to support them. This concern was both related to having to codify information (such as proficiency) that is subjectively assessed in the current culture as well as the increased time to configure the components to enable an adaptive scenario

assumption that largely autonomous adaptation was needed for this domain. Instead, instructors desired adaptation to be driven by simulation operators and to focus on reducing their workload and enabling control of simulated role-players at a more abstract and task-focused level than they were able to accomplish with existing technology. For example, in a situation where the scenario requires that separate groups of aircraft maintain a desired distance from one another, the current level of control requires manually directing the heading and speed of aircraft to maintain the separation. Higher-level control might enable an operator to specify a minimum separation distance and require the intelligent automation to carry out how to satisfy this requirement as the scenario unfolds.

The feedback helped us understand that the existing training environments targeted for this technology were culturally and technically better suited for a supervisory control solution than an autonomous one.

5   Scenario-Focused Supervisory Control of Scenario Adaptation

Based on the feedback received for the initial prototype, we reviewed the initial requirements and reconsidered both the architectural approach (Fig. 1) and the detailed technical design (Fig. 2) for scenario adaptation. In reviewing the initial requirements, we recognized that all the requirements (i.e., narrative coherence, targeted training goals, proficiency-based adaptation, and conformance to exercise constraints) were less fixed/more fluid than the original approach assumed. For example, an instructor might adapt training goals themselves during a scenario (training goals within a scenario are not always fixed), change range constraints, decide whether some narrative-breaking, training-specific repair was worth the cost to the training experience in order to maintain it, and so forth.

Table 3 summarizes the new requirements, which are presented in roughly the order of priority that users identified in discussions and assessments with them. Rather than having the system make decisions to keep the scenario within bounds defined by the instructor, the basic functional requirement was to enable the system to adapt its presentation of the scenario to the instructor's goals and intents as the scenario was executing. Requirement #1 reflects this goal, which largely subsumes all of the functional requirements identified earlier in the effort (Table 1). The key insight was that adaptation based on the narrative, training goals, etc. is still desirable, but that adaptation should serve the instructor's intent, rather than static, pre-defined goals and constraints (such as the ability to meet training goals).

Requirement #2 specifies *how* scenario adaptation should be implemented to support users. Because the desired presentation quality can be fluid, there was shift from autonomous control to supervisory control, which allows simulations operators to

Table 3. Revised requirements for scenario adaptation (functional and usage requirements)

Requirement		Description
1	Improve scenario (presentation) quality	Scenario quality is a measure of how closely a scenario that trainees experience reflects the intent of the scenario designer/instructor. A solution must improve quality of presentations (training opportunities) within scenarios, given the instructor's assessment of what is needed to improve training experiences
2	Directable and controllable interventions	Supervisory control, rather than autonomous adaptation, is required. Simulation operators will anticipate undesirable deviations, interpret what should be done, and then activate control programs to intervene if/when undesirable deviations occur
3	Minimize workflow disruption	The simulation-training environment is already being used operationally with existing usage patterns, known technical skill requirements, etc. A solution should, to the extent other goals are met, minimize additional skill or operator-training requirements and not significantly change how models are produced and used today
4	Utilize existing simulated role-players	In addition to minimizing workflow disruptions, scenario adaptation should also employ, to the extent possible, existing simulated role-players, leveraging prior development investment and validation/acceptance of the models that implement the role-players

support more direct realization of instructor intent more easily than low-level control and more flexibly than pre-defined scenario-performance goals.

Requirements #3 and #4 further constrained the technical design space for a solution. Given users' familiarity with the existing simulation, the way it communicated the actions and status of simulated role-players, and the relative maturity of the implementations of those role-players (including validation of some behavior models), any technical solution needed to adopt, to the extent possible, familiar tools, workflows, and models.

Figure 3 illustrates the revised technical design for the scenario adaptation capability, the *Scenario Director*. Because preserving the existing models of role-players was important (Requirement #4), we preserved the Director Architecture design pattern (Fig. 1) but wholly re-implemented the scenario adaptation capability.

To satisfy requirements #1 and #2, we enabled users to specify small control programs (*directives*) that could be applied during a scenario to modulate or over-ride a simulated role-players' native program or to initiate events in the simulation. For example, an operator could specify that when a trainee reached some physical location in a scenario, opposing aircraft should be launched against it with specific instantiation parameters (location, initial heading, speed, altitude, etc.) based on the current situation (the trainee's position and some prior actions). These aircraft might then be modulated by other directives that dictated separation constraints from one another, altitude restrictions, and tactical maneuvers that the instructor desired to see presented to an individual trainee in this scenario.

The simulation operator can specify which directives should be available in a scenario via the Scenario Director user interface. When creating or configuring a scenario, the user can choose from a library of possible directives (directive templates), parameterize them for the scenario (e.g., create a specific altitude restriction for *eagle1* using the altitude restriction template), and then instantiate the directive, which makes

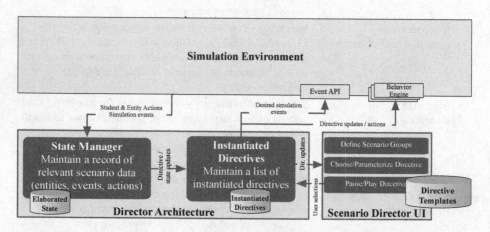

Fig. 3. Scenario Director (revised) software design.

it active in the scenario. Users can define groups (e.g., all aircraft in some region; all aircraft of a particular type or side, etc.). Then, when instantiating a directive, it can be instantiated for the every member of the group, which simplifies the application of directives for a scenario with many simulated role-players (e.g., all blue aircraft in the AO should use this altitude restriction). During run-time, to facilitate meeting instructor intent, individual (and group) directives can be paused or unpaused with a single operator action, enabling an operator to change the course of a scenario in a significant way with a few simple actions in the interface.

Users' are familiar with the technology used to implement simulated role-players in the operational simulation (Req. #3). We took advantage of this familiarity and adopted the behavior modeling language used for simulated role-players for the language of directives. This choice ensures that instructors and operators can specify exactly what interventions they wish to be available. For example, using the same authoring tool that is used for creating simulated role-players, they can also create a directive that encodes exactly what kind of intervention they prefer and the conditions for initiating it. Users add their new directives to the directive template library where other users can then adopt (and modify/customize) those directives.

Compared to the more dynamic and plan-based approach of the Dynamic Tailoring System, this approach to depending on pre-defined interventions is limiting. It requires a lower level of specification from the Scenario Director than the goal-based directability of Dynamic Tailoring, requiring the user to specify not just that an intervention is needed but also exactly what that intervention should be. Because the Scenario Director is limited to making changes to only exposed parameters, it range of direction is also limited. For example, if an aircraft's partner is not specified in one of the parameters in the scenario, then the Scenario Director cannot make dynamic changes to that pairing.

Overall, however, this approach has been advantageous. Because direct operator control of simulated role-players is already expected, most important parameters for control are already exposed, providing sufficient levers for direction. The challenge of codified interventions is offset by understandability and predictability. Because the Scenario Director adapts behavior using the same language and mechanisms that human operators use, operators both understand what the Scenario Director is doing and have an existing model for predicting what will happen when direction is initiated, including how to recover from surprises or errors if an intervention takes a scenario off-course non-productively.

The long-term impacts on performance have yet to be measured and initial assessments of trustworthiness and transparency are sometimes not correlated with long-term performance [18]. However, the user community has taken up the Scenario Director implementation of scenario adaptation. It has now met all milestones for transition to operational simulation. The software has been delivered to the simulation development team and is now incorporated in its development releases. This Scenario Director capability will be further refined and extended by the simulation-development team for a major version to be deployed in 2018.

6   Conclusion

This paper has presented a specific use case of the use of intelligent automation to support scenario adaptation for simulation-based training. We initially focused on functional requirements automatic run-time adaptation of scenarios, which was both consistent with prior requirements in other training domains and appeared apt for the fast-moving, high-workload tactical-air training environment. After initial prototyping and demonstrations to potential users, we identified additional constraints on solutions and usage requirements. These additional requirements led to a near-complete redesign and reimplementation of the scenario adaptation capability.

The new capability traded relatively simple and fast pre-scenario configuration and run-time autonomy for both greater pre-scenario configuration (including, possibly, the creation of a new control program/directive) and a more supervisory, rather than autonomous solution for run-time adaptation. Although users lost some capability in this change, they felt these losses were offset by the benefits of greater transparency (understanding what the system would do and when) and more flexible. Additionally, because the current environment of training delivery already includes personnel who can direct and control simulated role-players, the emphasis in the new solution was to attempt to make these staff more effective in delivering the training experience that the instructor desired, reducing workload and enabling more consistent training delivery. We expect that in training environments where staff is available and specific performance measures are not defined for individual training scenarios, an extensible, supervisory control approach to scenario adaptation is likely to be preferable to a more autonomous one that is standardized on the curriculum.

Acknowledgments. This work is supported by the Office of Naval Research project N00014-1-C-0170 Tactical Semi-Automated Forces for Live, Virtual, and Constructive Training (TACSAF). The views and conclusions contained in this document are those of the authors and should not be interpreted as representing the official policies, either expressed or implied, of the Department of Defense or Office of Naval Research. The U.S. Government is authorized to reproduce and distribute reprints for Government purposes notwithstanding any copyright notation hereon. We would like to thank collaborators and sponsors at NAWCTSD and ONR who have provided insights and operational perspectives in the development of the capabilities discussed herein: CDR Brent Olde, Ami Bolton, Melissa Walwanis, and Heather Priest.

References

1. Wray, R.E., Woods, A.: A cognitive systems approach to tailoring learner practice. In: Laird, J., Klenk, M. (eds.) Proceedings of the Second Advances in Cognitive Systems Conference, Baltimore, MD (2013)
2. Parasuraman, R., Riley, V.: Humans and automation: use, misuse, disuse, abuse. Hum. Factors **39**, 230–253 (1997)
3. Parasuraman, R., Wickens, C.D.: Humans: still vital after all these years of automation. Hum. Factors **50**, 511–520 (2008)

4. Sheridan, T.B.: Humans and Automation: System Design and Research Issues. Wiley, Hoboken (2002)
5. Parasuraman, R., Sheridan, T.B., Wickens, C.D.: A model of types and levels of human interaction with automation. IEEE Trans. Syst. Man, Cybern. - Part A Syst. Hum. **30**, 286–297 (2000)
6. Parasuraman, R.: Designing automation for human use: empirical studies and quantitative models. Ergonomics **43**, 931–951 (2000)
7. Lee, J.D., See, K.A.: Trust in automation: designing for appropriate reliance. Hum. Factors: J. Hum. Factors Ergon. Soc. **46**, 50–80 (2004)
8. Hoff, K.A., Bashir, M.: Trust in automation. Hum. Factors **57**, 407–434 (2014)
9. Wray, R.E., Priest, H., Walwanis, M.A., Kaste, K.: Requirements for future SAFs: beyond tactical realism. In: 2015 Interservice/Industry Training, Simulation, and Education Conference. NTSA (2015)
10. Wray, R.E., Folsom-Kovarik, J.T., Woods, A., Jones, R.M.: Motivating narrative representation for training cross-cultural interaction. In: Proceedings of the 6th International Conference on Applied Human Factors and Ergonomics (AHFE 2015) and the Affiliated Conferences, AHFE 2015. Springer, Las Vegas (2015)
11. Vygotsky, L.S.: Mind and Society: The Development of Higher Psychological Processes. Harvard University Press, Cambridge (1978)
12. Riedl, M.O., Stern, A., Dinini, R., Alderman, J.: Dynamic experience management in virtual worlds for entertainment, education, and training. Int. Trans. Syst. Sci. Appl. Spec. Issue Agent Based Syst. Hum. Learn. **4**, 23–42 (2008)
13. Magerko, B.: Evaluating preemptive story direction in the interactive drama architecture. J. Game Dev. **3**, 25–52 (2007)
14. Wray, R.E., Lane, H.C., Stensrud, B., Core, M., Hamel, L., Forbell, E.: Pedagogical experience manipulation for cultural learning. In: Workshop on Culturally-Aware Tutoring Systems at the AI in Education Conference Brighton, England (2009)
15. Folsom-Kovarik, J.T., Newton, C., Haley, J., Wray, R.E.: Modeling proficiency in a tailored, situated training environment. In: Behavior Representation in Modeling and Simulation (BRIMS) Conference, Washington, DC (2014)
16. Wray, R.E., Woods, A., Haley, J., Folsom-Kovarik, J.T.: Evaluating instructor configurability for adaptive training. In: Proceedings of the 7th International Conference on Applied Human Factors and Ergonomics (AHFE 2016) and the Affiliated Conferences. Springer, Orlando (2016)
17. Dillon, D.: Beyond usability: process, outcome and affect in human-computer interactions. Can. J. Libr. Inf. Sci. **26**, 57–69 (2002)
18. Schaefer, K.E., Chen, J.Y.C., Szalma, J.L., Hancock, P.A.: A meta-analysis of factors influencing the development of trust in automation: implications for understanding autonomy in future systems. Hum. Factors: J. Hum. Factors Ergon. Soc. **58**, 377–400 (2016)

User Requirement Analysis for Display User Experience in Smart Car

Hoon Sik Yoo[1] and Da Young Ju[2(✉)]

[1] Techno and Design Research Center, Yonsei University, Incheon, South Korea
yoohs@yonsei.ac.kr
[2] Yonsei Institute of Convergence Technology,
Yonsei University, Incheon, South Korea
dyju@yonsei.ac.kr

Abstract. The automotive display market has been expanding due to the combination of auto-mobiles and IT, and the role of displays comes to be more important by increasing demands for entertainment in a car in line with the development of self-driving car. The purpose of this study is to analyze the demand of the user regarding the location of display in smart car to improve user experience. For this study, the qualitative investigation through focus group interview was performed and based on this, the major issues related to the utilization of each location were deducted. In this study, the qualitative investigation is performed to analyze the motivation and needs of the user depending on the location of the display inside a vehicle. The FGI is performed as a qualitative investigation. This study is significant that the needs of the user regarding the location of the dis-play in smart car are deducted and future studies on appropriate utilization method of each location as well as contents are necessary.

Keywords: Smart car · Display position · User experience · User requirement · User-centered design

1 Research Background and Purpose

The automotive display market has been expanding due to the combination of auto-mobiles and IT, and the role of displays comes to be more important by increasing demands for entertainment in a car in line with the development of self-driving car. As the result of the development of self-driving cars, a car is not a mere means of transportation any more but becomes a moving living space, and thus displays mounted inside cars have been in the trend of being diversified, enlarged and with higher-definition (Fig. 1).

According to the report conducted by HIS, a market research company, it is expected that automotive display market will grow to 18.6 billion dollars by 2021. It is estimated that the scale will reach 115.14 million units and 161.7 million units in 2018 from 136.88 million units in 2016. The annual sales of automotive display in 2015 was about 9 billion dollars, and it is estimated the market will increase by approximately twice for the next 5 years. Also, the compound annual growth rate (CAGR) is expected

© Springer International Publishing AG 2017
M. Kurosu (Ed.): HCI 2017, Part II, LNCS 10272, pp. 732–741, 2017.
DOI: 10.1007/978-3-319-58077-7_57

Fig. 1. Bosch's integrated automotive display

to reach 11%. CID, HUD and Touch Screen, in the whole North American and European markets, are expected to show double growth rate in 2017 compared to in 2011 (Fig. 2).

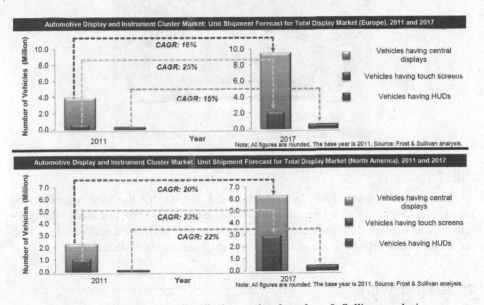

Fig. 2. Scale of automotive display market from frost & Sullivan analysis

Area of display for the purpose of system configuration and utilization within Smart Car is increasing. Volvo XC 90, released in 2014, minimized the buttons in control panel of the automobile and designed to perform most of the functions through touch display (Fig. 3).

Mercedes Benz F015, disclosed in CES 2015, has no internal buttons and is designed through NUI (Natural User Interface) technique using all necessary input with touch and gesture. Toyota Fun Vii Concept car proposed a concept of completely different experience by applying display to both internal and external part of vehicle (Fig. 4).

Fig. 3. Mercedes Benz F015's door display and dashboard

Fig. 4. Toyota fun Vii concept car image

The purpose of this study is to analyze the demand of the user regarding the location of display in smart car to improve user experience. For this study, the qualitative investigation through focus group interview was performed and based on this, the major issues related to the utilization of each location were deducted.

2 Related Work

Automotive displays can be subdivided into 5 types – Center Indicator Display (CID), Cluster, Rear Seat Entertainment (RSE), Head Up Display (HUD) and Room Mirror Display. Cluster and HUD provide major information on driving and CID and RSE, combined with navigation, mobile and audio system provide passengers with information on vehicle service and entertainment. Cluster, immediately providing drivers with essential information for driving such as running speed, RPM, engine temperature and fuel level, is also trending in mounting LCD and enlarging size of screens according to the recent increase in amount of information (Fig. 5).

BMW i3 is designed in a type which displays are installed on the cluster and CID. It is possible to remotely, through BMW i3 remote application, perform functions such as

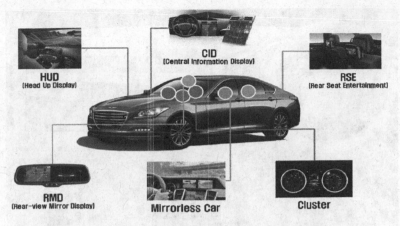

Fig. 5. KATECH's applied fields of automotive display

lock setting, HVAC setting, charging, sending address and parking-lot search. A gear shift lever is situated behind a wheel. Gears can be shifted by using a rotating knob which can be controlled to move back and forth. Convenient service is provided by BMW Connected Drive. Information on vehicle condition is automatically transmitted to BMW Communication Center and analyzed, and, if necessary, it provides service such as check reservation (Fig. 6).

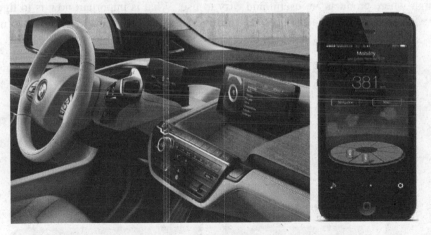

Fig. 6. Example of applying BMW's integrated display

New Interior Concept vehicle, Volvo unveiled at the Beijing Motor Show in 2016 is a good example of applying multi-display. For this concept car, it facilitates operational convenience by moving the touch screen panel, located at the existing center fascia, to the very front of the existing gear stick. This is the concept which reflects the situation of self-driving, and mode is converted to the self-driving mode in pressing the

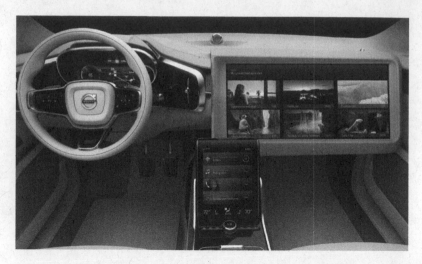

Fig. 7. Example of applying Volvo's integrated display

self-driving button at the hand part of the wheel for a few seconds. When it enters the self-driving mode, the driver's seat is tilted back. Also, the dashboard of the passenger seat is flipped and 25-inch display comes out (Fig. 7).

According to technology acceptance theory and Technology Acceptance Model, usefulness and ease of use are defined as the key factors that determine the willingness to use technology products. It means that the possibility for drivers to use such products is high where products are useful and easy to use. What is important now is to figure out what technology is most necessary to drivers and to design easier products to use.

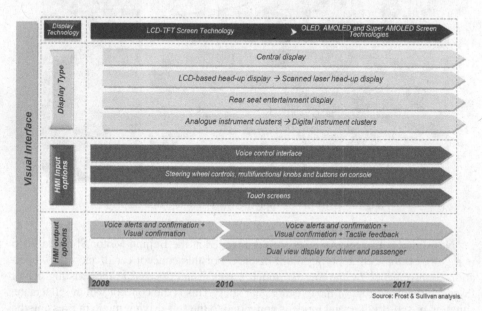

Fig. 8. Roadmap of automotive display and cluster technology from Frost & Sullivan analysis

However, to do this, there is still a lack of understanding on user's experience before designing the technology applied to cars and the interface. UX design is necessary in order to overcome this, which ensures driving safety and satisfies the user's needs from the user-oriented point of view. If such an environment is established, it is possible to increase the convenience of automotive environment of smart cars for drivers and passengers. To meet this need, this study collected users' qualitative opinions regarding a variety of displays (Fig. 8).

3 User Research

In this study, the qualitative investigation is performed to analyze the motivation and needs of the user depending on the location of the display inside a vehicle. The FGI is performed as a qualitative investigation and the profile of the participated drivers are shown in Table 1.

Table 1. Profile of Participants

Group	House wife	Worker in 20/30 s	Worker in 40/50 s	University/ graduate students	Foreign workers
# of people	6	3	4	6	5

Affinity diagrams is used to analyze the date. Affinity diagrams (KJ Method) is a data analysis methodology, suggested by Jiro Kawakita in 1960, and it is a useful method to categorize qualitatively collected opinions by major issue. The data collated by FGI are analyzed based on the four stages, which is generally applied by KJ Method. The process is as follow (Fig. 9).

The data gathered through FGI are classified into five types as autonomous navigation, display, space, navigation, and others. Each major result is summarized and arranged in the table below. For the qualitative user investigation, it can be identified that the user's demand toward side and ceiling display is low; low expectation on displays located on side may result from physical discomfort; low expectation on displays located on ceiling may result from lack of expectation due to lack of experience (Fig. 10) (Table 2).

Fig. 9. Participants groups

Fig. 10. Affinity diagrams results images

Table 2. Affinity diagrams results

Display	Space	Autonomous driving	Navigation	Minor opinions
① Front screen ② In front of driver's seat ③ Side window ④ Ceiling ⑤ Behind seats	① Interior ② Seats (Resting) ③ Seats (Communication)	① Autonomous driving usage situation ② Initiative deprivation ③ Autonomous driving reliability ④ Lack of reliability of autonomous driving ⑤ Accident prevention denial	① Information provided ② Information delivery method ③ Navigation location	① Future vehicle function ② Other comments

4   Results

(Tables 3, 4, 5, 6, and 7).

Table 3. Major opinion related to display

Classification	Major opinions
Front screen	Transparent HUD should be reflected on the front screen to the degree that it doesn't interfere with the driving
In front of driver's seat	If the voice can control most of it, the risk of accident may decrease even if the touch display installed in front of the driver's seat
	Front touch screen isn't preferred as it may be dangerous while driving
	Is expected to be inconvenient
	Risk of touch mistake and malfunction
Side window	Under the assumption that the seat can spin, the display on side window is preferable
	Without the movement of the seat, using side window display may hurt neck
Ceiling	Display from the ceiling is preferred so that it can be watched from the back seat
	Display on ceiling is preferred with contents such as time, weather, or other themes based on personal taste
Behind seats	Like that of the airplane, display behind the front seat is preferred

Table 4. Major opinions regarding vehicle space for the arrangement of display

Classification	Major opinions
Interior	Space to equip refrigerator and beer
Seats (Resting)	Completely flat seat
	Seat that can turn into a bed
	Sleep on bed, get massages, and watch TV in a car
Seats (Communication)	Can spin chair and a table is preferred
	Easier communication with the person next to by closer gap between seats
	Under the assumption that the seat can spin, the display on side window is preferable

Table 5. Major opinion related to autonomous driving

Classification	Major opinions
Autonomous driving usage situation	When I am sleepy, I want it to talk to me by me
	When I drank and when I'm tired, I use autonomous driving
	Only when I receive a call and when I'm tired, I use it for a while
	I only use it at low speed
	I only use it for short-haul driving
	It seems to be convenient for foreigners to use
Initiative deprivation	When I have to go at high speed, it is expected to be inconvenient if I have an automatic speed control system
	It would be more surprising if the car suddenly stopped when it was dangerous
	I do not think the car should suddenly slow down when I drive
	People who like to drive do not seem to like autonomous driving
Autonomous driving reliability (Accident prevention)	It is likely that traffic accidents will occur less frequently when one drives automatically
	It is possible to prevent an accident that a person may commit
	I hope the accident does not happen When driving at high speed
Lack of reliability of autonomous driving	Autonomous cars are incredible
	Because it is a machine, there may be a threat of malfunction, hacking, and so on
	I will use it when the safety is enhanced and proven
Accident prevention denial	It is good if all cars are self-driving, but it is not so good if not
	The driver must always be aware of the driving situation without driving

Table 6. Major opinion related to navigation

Classification	Major opinions
Information provided	It would be better if car speed information of the front and rear were recognized and displayed on the window
	I think it would be nice to have information on the surrounding sale and restaurants when driving
	GPS system like navigation should be available indoors as well as outdoors
Information delivery method	I hope the map from the navigation is similar to or the same as the actual road
	It's hard to catch the guidance like 'Turn left after 100 m'. I wish there was another way of guidance
	I hope that the information you see when you drive will become augmented reality
Navigation location	I'd like the navigation to be on the front, under the handle, on the dashboard, or on the clash

Table 7. Minor opinions

Classification	Major opinions
Future vehicle function	It would be nice if there was an automatic setting function for the driver to recognize the driver
	Automatically connect to phone when you get in the car
	I'd like to see it on a small screen in front without seeing a cell phone
	It would be nice if future cars could fly in the sky
	It would be nice if it changed automatically when changing music in the middle
	It would be nice if the color of the front panel changes
	It would be nice if the seat would automatically change shape to suit the road situation
Other comments	I hope the frame of the car is invisible and it is full glass
	In case of an accident, who should be responsible?
	The road will have to change a bit in order that an autonomous car is realized
	I think I can find information on the surrounding cars
	Price is important. It would be good if it was a standard car price

5 Conclusion and Future Work

As a result of qualitative investigation, the preferred location and issues regarding the display could be analyzed. It can be concluded that to utilize the display of back seat and ceiling, which weren't preferred, the appropriate provision of contents based on location and changes in internal structure of vehicle is necessary. This study is significant that the needs of the user regarding the location of the display in smart car are deducted and future studies on appropriate utilization method of each location as well as contents are necessary (Table 8).

Table 8. Comprehensive conclusions on 5 categories

Classification	Major opinions
Autonomous driving	It is expected that it will reduce traffic accidents by automatic driving
	The user should be self-driving in situations where he/she is in need, and the initiative should not be taken away by the car
	Because it is a machine, you must have confidence in security and safety
Space	I want to use it to communicate with others or use them as private spaces
Navigation	I want the information to pop up on the driver's windshield
	I want to see the information of nearby vehicles and surrounding buildings
	The information provided should be provided so that it does not interfere with my view
Display	Fear of malfunctions in the front display has been a major concern, but there is an expectation that this problem will be solved by speech recognition
	It is positive that there is a display elsewhere besides the driver
Other comments	I think that the functions provided will automatically recognize the user
	In addition to the functions, I'm interested in the surrounding environment, price, insurance, etc.

Acknowledgments. This research was supported by the MSIP (Ministry of Science, ICT and Future Planning), Korea, under the "ICT Consilience Creative Program" (IITP-R0346-16-1008) supervised by the IITP (Institute for Information & communications Technology Promotion).

References

1. Lee, J., Forlizzi, J., Hudson, S.E., Jun, S.: Use of the backseat driving technique in evaluation of a perceptually optimized in-car navigation display. J. Hum.-Comput. Interact. **31**, 128–138 (2015)
2. Jeon, M.: "i-passion": a concept car user interface case study from the perspective of user experience design. In: Proceedings of the Second International Conference on Automotive User Interfaces and Interactive Vehicular Applications, Pittsburgh, Pennsylvania, USA, 11–12 November 2010
3. Wittman, M., Kiss, M., Gugg, P., Steffen, A., Fink, M., Poppel, E., Kamiya, H.: Effects of display position of a visual in-vehicle task on simulated driving. Appl. Ergon. **32**(2), 187–199 (2006)
4. Tian, R., Li, L., Rajput, V.S., Witt, G.J., Duffy, V.G., Chen, Y.: Study on the display positions for the haptic rotary device-based integrated in-vehicle infotainment interface. Trans. Intell. Transp. Syst. **15**(3), 1234–1245 (2014)

Author Index

Printed in the United States
By Bookmasters